Left off at Pg 199

S0-AGM-081

human relations
STRATEGIES FOR SUCCESS

Lowell Lamberton

Leslie Minor

 Higher Education

Boston   Burr Ridge, IL   Dubuque, IA   New York   San Francisco   St. Louis
Bangkok   Bogotá   Caracas   Kuala Lumpur   Lisbon   London   Madrid   Mexico City
Milan   Montreal   New Delhi   Santiago   Seoul   Singapore   Sydney   Taipei   Toronto

Higher Education

HUMAN RELATIONS: STRATEGIES FOR SUCCESS

Published by McGraw-Hill, a business unit of The McGraw-Hill Companies, Inc., 1221 Avenue of the Americas, New York, NY 10020. Copyright © 2010 by The McGraw-Hill Companies, Inc. All rights reserved. Previous editions © 1995, 2002, and 2007. No part of this publication may be reproduced or distributed in any form or by any means, or stored in a database or retrieval system, without the prior written consent of The McGraw-Hill Companies, Inc., including, but not limited to, in any network or other electronic storage or transmission, or broadcast for distance learning.

Some ancillaries, including electronic and print components, may not be available to customers outside the United States.

This book is printed on acid-free paper.

1 2 3 4 5 6 7 8 9 0 CCI/CCI 0 9

ISBN   978-0-07-337704-9
MHID 0-07-337704-X

Vice president/Editor in chief: *Elizabeth Haefele*
Vice president/Director of marketing: *John E. Biernat*
Sponsoring editor: *Natalie J. Ruffatto*
Developmental editor: *Kristin Bradley*
Marketing manager: *Keari Green*
Lead media producer: *Damian Moshak*
Director, Editing/Design/Production: *Jess Ann Kosic*
Project manager: *Christine M. Demma*
Senior production supervisor: *Janean A. Utley*
Designer: *Marianna Kinigakis*
Senior photo research coordinator: *Jeremy Cheshareck*
Photo researcher: *Teri Stratford*
Media developmental editor: *William Mulford*
Media project manager: *Mark A. S. Dierker*
Cover design: *Jessica Lazar*
Interior design: *Marianna Kinigakis and Jessica Lazar*
Typeface: *10.5/13 New Aster*
Compositor: *Laserwords Private Limited*
Printer: *Courier Kendallville*
Cover credit: © iStockPhoto
Credits: The credits section for this book begins on page 587 and is considered an extension of the copyright page.

Library of Congress Cataloging-in-Publication Data

Lamberton, Lowell H.
    Human relations : strategies for success / Lowell Lamberton, Leslie Minor. — 4th ed.
        p. cm.
    Includes index.
    ISBN-13: 978-0-07-337704-9 (alk. paper)
    ISBN-10: 0-07-337704-X (alk. paper)
    1. Psychology, Industrial. 2. Personnel management. 3. Interpersonal relations. 4. Group relations training. I. Minor, Leslie. II. Title.
    HF5548.8.L24 2010
    158.7—dc22

                                                                2008047555

The Internet addresses listed in the text were accurate at the time of publication. The inclusion of a Web site does not indicate an endorsement by the authors or McGraw-Hill, and McGraw-Hill does not guarantee the accuracy of the information presented at these sites.

www.mhhe.com

Lowell Lamberton is a business professor with an extensive background in both writing and business. He has worked as an expert consultant to many businesses, especially in the area of human behavior, specializing in organizational behavior and management. He currently teaches management, human relations, and business communications classes at both Central Oregon Community College and Linfield College. He lives in Bend, Oregon, with his wife, Ruth, who is an artist.

He holds two degrees in English, one from Walla Walla College and the other from the University of Nebraska. He also holds an MBA and an advanced professional certificate (APC) in management from Suffolk University in Boston, Massachusetts.

Besides this textbook, he has also coauthored *Working with People: A Human Relations Guide* with Leslie Minor.

Leslie Minor is a social psychologist who completed a BA degree in psychology at the University of Washington in Seattle, and an MA and a PhD in Social Ecology from the University of California at Irvine. She taught sociology for two years as a Senior Visiting Fellow in Sociology at the National University of Singapore. She has now resumed her teaching career at Central Oregon Community College, along with adjunct appointments to the University of Oregon and Linfield College, since returning from Singapore. Currently she teaches sociology, psychology, and human relations courses, in both traditional and online formats. Leslie has three grown sons, Demitrius, Zamir, and Jawan.

authors

PREFACE »

Throughout our years of teaching and consulting in the fields of social science and organizational behavior, we have become increasingly aware of the need for a textbook that is down-to-earth, experience based, and grounded in sound research and theory. We believe strongly in the importance of understanding the relationship between self-esteem and human relations, and, by extension, the relationship between human relations skills and ongoing career success. On the other hand, we do not condone the approach of the "self-esteem peddlers" who encourage self-esteem building outside of a context of the real world. What realistic strategies and techniques can we teach our students to encourage their growth in human relations success, on and off the job site? How can students tap into the power that comes from working well in one-on-one situations, in groups, and in organizations large and small?

Human Relations: Strategies for Success attempts to provide answers to these questions and guidance in developing human relations skills that transfer from the classroom to the real world of work. Our commitment to the creation of a book that is at once interesting to read, motivating to study, and relevant to a wide variety of students has been the driving force behind *Human Relations: Strategies for Success*.

This text covers time-tested, research-based social science and management principles, as well as newer theories and philosophies of human relations drawn from management theory, group theory, personality theory, and relationship theory. More than ever, effective human relations skills are crucial to business success as organizations grow and compete in a global business environment. Employees must have the knowledge and skill to adapt to a workplace where change is as frequent as it is inevitable.

FEATURES OF THE FOURTH EDITION

This fourth edition features the following changes from previous editions:

- Updated Chapter 1, with the history of human relations reorganized, along with new material on generation differences among workers of the 21st century.

- Reorganization of Chapter 6, including the addition of Clayton Alderfer's ERG management theory to update and expand Maslow's hierarchy of needs theory.

- Elimination of a chapter dedicated to the study of transactional analysis, replaced by the new Chapter 10, on emotional intelligence. A more streamlined introduction to parts of transactional analysis is presented, while more detailed material is still available online for students and instructors who want to use it.

- A new section in Chapter 10 on anger management and one on defensiveness as an enhancement of the emotional intelligence material.

- A new section in Chapter 15, the customer service chapter, on the "internal customer" to acknowledge the widespread use of that concept in 21st-century human relations.

- A complete revision of Chapter 18, formerly dedicated to workplace health, has been revised to feature "Maintaining a Productive Workplace." The most important points of workplace health have been retained in that chapter. In the chapter we have also included material on procrastination, time management, and the relationship between morale and productivity.

- A further expanded Chapter 19, which includes material on career choice exploration, job search, and positive psychology.

- The beginnings of chapters are now introduced with solid learning objectives, which have been incorporated with what we formerly called "Chapter Concepts." This change further simplifies and clarifies the salient points of each chapter.

- Many new Web cases chosen for their lasting interest, value, and variety.

- Updated revisions of all other chapters, reflecting the changes that have affected human relations in the workplace since the last edition in 2007.

Human Relations Web Site. The fourth edition includes its own Web site, which features links to topics related to the contents of each chapter, additional information on all chapter topics, and enrichment activities for deeper learning.

Internet Exercises. Each chapter contains challenging Internet exercises that allow interactive learning related to the topics covered. Topic-related Web links, with suggestions for brief learning activities and exercises, are also included.

Strategies for Success. To highlight the connection between human relations theories and their real-world applications, this textbook contains a unique series of strategies that are integrated into all of the chapters. These strategies offer concrete guidance on how to use human relations skills to address situations that all people face.

Opening Vignettes. Each chapter opens with a short vignette to set the tone of the chapter. These vignettes use the narrative approach to make the chapter concepts more real to students at the outset, before they begin to absorb concepts and terms.

Key Terms. Important terms are highlighted within the text and called out in the margin. They are also listed at the end of each chapter and are defined in the glossary.

Review Questions and Critical Thinking Questions. Each chapter closes with thought-provoking questions. These questions call on students to go beyond simply reading the chapter, by asking them to consider its implications for their lives in the classroom and beyond. Many questions tap students' creativity and problem-solving abilities as they encourage students to think beyond the boundaries of the book.

Case Studies. Two realistic, job-based case studies (each with questions) are presented in every chapter. These classroom-tested case studies are drawn from familiar experiences in a wide variety of workplace settings. These cases allow students to resolve realistic human relations problems for which there is usually more than one viable solution. Each case study can be used as a springboard for classroom discussion and group problem-solving activities.

"Working It Out" Exercises. For most students, active participation is motivating, rewarding, and crucial to reinforcing learning. In a variety of classroom-tested Working It Out exercises, students are encouraged to build on their human relations skills as they role-play, interview each other, assess their own and each other's strengths and weaknesses, work on setting goals and developing strategies, practice giving and receiving feedback, and explore other applications of chapter topics.

Instructor's Resource Manual. This computerized teaching aid includes teaching suggestions for each chapter. It contains lecture outlines, answers and guidelines for all in-text questions, review questions, case study questions, and Working It Out exercises. Many additional in-class activities are also provided.

ACKNOWLEDGMENTS

Many people were involved in the writing and production of this book. We especially would like to thank Kristin Bradley, our developmental editor from McGraw-Hill Higher Education, for her help, kindness, and patience. Also, our project manager, Christine Demma, worked very hard with problems, many of them unforeseen. Natalie Ruffatto, our sponsoring editor, has also been hard at work behind the scenes. Thanks, Natalie. At home, too many students to mention have offered suggestions and help since the last edition.

We would also like to thank our colleagues and co-workers, friends, and family members for the help they have offered by presenting real-life situations involving human relations issues. This real-life material has been incorporated into opening vignettes and even into a few case studies. A special thanks goes out as well to our families who provided ongoing support and assistance: Lowell's wife, Ruth Lamberton; and Leslie's sons, Demitrius Zeigler, Zamir Zeigler, and Jawan Davis.

Solid previous editions have made this one possible. In the first edition, Betty Morgan, our adjunct editor, created the "Strategies" approach, for which we are extremely grateful. Heather Lamberton spent many hours doing research for nearly all of the chapters. Brian Dement contributed material for the Instructor's Manual and Test Bank. And without Carla Tishler, our first editor, we would never have completed the project. In the second edition, we were helped greatly by Cheryl Adams, adjunct editor for Glencoe/McGraw-Hill. Tammy Higham was invaluable in the creation of the third edition. Of course, the instructors and students who have used the textbook over the past decade have a special place in our hearts as well.

We would also like to thank the following people for their feedback and guidance as reviewers of this edition of the manuscript:

Rich S. Benard
Bryant & Stratton College

Charisse Cole
Utah Career College

Kathy Foley
Bryant & Stratton College

Kristie Kellis
Globe University

Janie MacDonald
Bryant & Stratton College

Judith Rozarie
Gibbs College

Maria Sofia
Bryant & Stratton College

Donna Slaughter
Bryant & Stratton College

Pat Sorcic
Bryant & Stratton College

Cheryl Sullivan
Bryant & Stratton College

BRIEF contents

contents

« part 4
Thriving in a Changing World

Chapter Sixteen

Chapter Seventeen

Chapter Eighteen

Chapter Nineteen

«« human relations and you

In Part One we'll explore the foundations of human relations skills. Specifically, we'll examine these questions: How does each one of us develop the necessary tools to work well together at home, in school, and on the job? What aspects of our personality contribute to our success at human relations? Are there strategies we can use to build human relations skills?

Chapters 1 through 6 define human relations, then look closely at the relationship between self-understanding and communication, test your ability to ask questions about personal and global values, and help you discover how to tap motivational strategies for yourself and others. These are important first steps to develop the human relations skills you need for success in personal life and in the world of work. »» »

HUMAN RELATIONS: A BACKGROUND

Human Relations in History: Life and death?

How important is it to understand others and get along with those at your workplace? Very! Compare the outcomes of the following two true stories as examples.

The Marquis de Mores was a French military officer who moved to the United States in the 1880s after military service in France. Famous in the American West as a rancher and gunslinger, he was arrested a few times for murder but was never convicted. Among his most famous conflicts, he is known for having challenged Theodore Roosevelt to a duel. The Marquis de Mores attempted to revolutionize the cattle and meatpacking industry by shipping beef long distances in refrigerated train cars. This business, and a stagecoach business, both failed; many say this was due at least in part to his poor treatment of business contacts and potential rivals. Returning to France and then sent to Southeast Asia for military service, he was a controversial figure for the rest of his life. He became famous for stirring hate in public speeches and for ongoing conflicts with well-known public figures. The Marquis was murdered in 1903 while on assignment to North Africa, under mysterious circumstances. An investigation concluded that enemies within his own French government were probably involved in planning his murder.

After studying this chapter, you will be able to:

1. Define human relations.

2. Explain the importance of human relations in business.

3. Discuss the challenges of human relations as these factors affect success in business.

4. Identify what is *not* human relations.

5. Describe the areas of emphasis for human relations in today's workplace.

6. Discuss a short history of the study of human relations.

STRATEGIES FOR SUCCESS

Strategy 1.1   Develop Mutual Respect

Strategy 1.2   Build Your Communication Skills

Few people remember his name today, but the town of Medora, North Dakota, still bears his wife's name.[1]

Now consider the story of another international businessman, Jim Thompson. Thompson was an American who had a distinguished career in the military before retiring to Thailand after World War II for a new career in design and manufacturing. Although trained as an architect, he revitalized the Thai economy with his remarkable success in the silk industry, starting a company in the 1940s that still bears his name. He gained the respect of his employees by allowing them to work from home on a flexible schedule, and helping them gain wealth by sharing part of the company's earnings with them. Thompson has been described as the most famous foreigner in Thailand, perhaps even Southeast Asia—and was so well known

in his adopted city that letters addressed simply to "Jim Thompson, Bangkok" would reach him with no problem. After 22 years in Thailand, he disappeared in 1967 while on vacation in neighboring Malaysia. His disappearance made international headlines. The mystery of his disappearance was never solved, and people today still search Southeast Asia to uncover the ending to his story. More than 40 years after his disappearance, Thompson's house in Bangkok remains a popular stop for visitors to Bangkok.[2]

THINK ABOUT IT

Think about how human relations affects most situations. Can you think of a circumstance in your own life that might have been improved by better human relations?

WHAT IS HUMAN RELATIONS?

Not all human relations decisions involve life-or-death outcomes, but they can have very serious impacts. The importance of human relations in our personal and work lives cannot be exaggerated. The skills that are necessary for good relations with others are the most important skills anyone can learn in life.

human relations
The skill or ability to work effectively through and with other people.

Human relations is the skill or ability to work effectively through and with other people. Human relations includes a desire to understand others, their needs and weaknesses, and their talents and abilities. For anyone in a workplace setting, human relations also involves an understanding of how people work together in groups, satisfying both individual needs and group objectives. If an organization is to succeed, the relationships among the people in that organization must be monitored and maintained.

In all aspects of life, you will deal with other people. No matter what you do for a living or how well you do it, your relationship with others is the key to your success or failure. Even when someone is otherwise only average at a job, good human relations skills can usually make that person seem better to others. Sadly, the opposite is also true: poor human relations skills can make an otherwise able person seem like a poor performer. A doctor who respects patients, a lawyer who listens carefully to clients, a manager who gets along well with others in the workplace—all of these people will most likely be thought of by others as successful.

THE IMPORTANCE OF HUMAN RELATIONS SKILLS

Other reasons for studying human relations include the following:

more about...

Internal customers can be defined as a department's employees, or as other departments within an organization.

1. *Human rights.* Today, managers and employees have a greater awareness of the rights of employees. This awareness calls for more skillful relations among employees, using tact, trust, and diplomacy with greater skill. The rights of all others involved in the dealings of an organization must be respected and protected as well. In today's workplace, the term *internal customer* is often used. This identifies a new attitude toward employees as the other customers in a company. Companies must also protect the human rights of traditional customers, managers, and even competitors.

2. *The global marketplace.* The United States seems to have fallen into disfavor in many countries—even countries we have long considered to be our friends. Often, when anti-American stories are told, they involve Americans using poor human relations skills when

doing business with other cultures. Improving interpersonal skills (the skills associated with getting along with others) can be a factor in fighting the widespread anti-Americanism that sometimes seems to be growing worldwide.[3]

3. *Emphasis on people as human resources.* Two decades ago, many forecasters predicted that by this time in history, strong computer skills would be the number one factor in the workplace. However, now, perhaps more that ever, managers and corporate planners are placing great emphasis on the human factor. The two sets of behaviors now considered the most important for new job applicants are communication skills and human relations abilities.[4] This trend will likely continue in the future.

4. *Renewed emphasis on working groups.* Today's employees tend to like working as teams and being involved in making decisions as a group. Helping groups work well together in such endeavors (as either a team member or leader) requires a great deal of human relations skill. Both managers and employees need to understand the dynamics of group interaction if such participation is to be effective.

5. *Increasing diversity in the workplace.* Few countries on earth contain the diversity of race, religion, and culture that exists in the United States. The number of foreign-born Americans in the United States in 1970 was estimated at 10 million, had grown to 28 million by the year 2000 (about 10 percent of the total population), and is projected to reach 38 million by the year 2020.[5] The United States gains an international migrant every 25 seconds.[6] Add to this reality the increase in the number of women in the workplace today compared with past years, and the number of employees staying in the workplace past typical retirement age. Experts predict that the number of older workers over the next several years will increase more than five times faster than the overall labor force, and that ethnic and racial diversity will continue to increase as well.[7] A deep understanding of the differences that diversity brings is one of the most important skills in human relations.

GROUP WORK IS A NECESSITY IN TODAY'S WORKFORCE

The ability to work well with others is a key component to personal and professional success. *Do you work well with others?*

Human Relations and You

The study of human relations can help you in several ways. Human relations skills can help you get a job, enjoy your work, be more productive at it, and stay there longer with better chances for advancement. An understanding of yourself and others can help you be happier and more productive in all areas of your life.

You, the Manager

A percentage of students who read this book will one day become managers. For a manager, no skill area is more important than human relations abilities. A manager with good human relations skills will retain employees longer, be more productive, and provide employees with an enjoyable environment. The most common reason for failure in the job of manager is faulty human relations skills.[8] Because interpersonal skills are so important, experts often suggest that new managers should put as much effort into studying people as they put into developing technical skills.[9]

You, the Entrepreneur

In the 21st century, an increasing number of today's business students are entering the exciting realm of entrepreneurship: owning their own businesses. When you are the owner and operator of a business, your people skills—or human relations—are the most important factors in your success. In an e-commerce business, though there is less face-to-face contact with customers and suppliers, the ability to work with people and to fulfill their needs remains extremely crucial to success.

In a larger sense, your knowledge of human relations helps the work you do—or the business you own—provide fulfillment. Famed Russian author Fyodor Dostoyevsky wrote, "If it were desired to reduce a man to nothingness, it would be necessary only to give his work a character of uselessness."[10] Many entrepreneurs become business owners to escape the feeling of uselessness associated with their former jobs. The entrepreneur is in the position of being able to control the human climate of the business he or she owns and operates.

more about...

An **entrepreneur** is someone who organizes and assumes the risks of beginning a business enterprise.

You, the Employee

Undeveloped interpersonal skills represent the single most important reason for failure at a job. This is especially true in the early days and weeks on a new assignment.[11] Making a good impression on your superiors, your peers, and all other co-workers will set you on a good track. Developing interpersonal skills is extremely important to the advancement of your career and will affect the ways in which your fellow employees, supervisors, and customers view your overall performance.

CURRENT CHALLENGES IN HUMAN RELATIONS

Today's Generation Y, the generation now just entering the job market, often finds good, family-wage jobs hard to come by and advancement very difficult. The problems faced by this group and by Generation X are often blamed on the "baby boomers," the middle-aged people who are mostly in management positions above them. Although a "generation gap" is nothing new in our history, this one affects human relations in the workplace directly and forcefully.[12] You will learn more about this topic in Chapter 16, when we study diversity in more depth.

Increased Competition in the Workplace

Competitiveness reaches into all areas—urban, suburban, and rural—and affects all businesses, large and small. Small businesses feel pressure to meet the standards of the foreign market and of the huge multinational companies that dominate the economy. When a chain retailer such as Wal-Mart moves into a small town, the competition felt by the local citizens is very real. The increasing number of people doing business on the Web has created a source of competition unlike anything else in human history.

Higher-paid family-wage jobs for all age groups are more competitive than before. Having a college degree is no longer a ticket to a meaningful career, as it was only a generation ago. This new reality causes a great deal of frustration for many people in the workplace, and many human relations problems result.

Another very important factor in competition is the current position of Asian countries, especially China, leading much of the world economy. During the past two decades, China developed economically at the rate of 9.7 percent annually.[13] Economic factors that have made this power position possible are lower labor costs, a nationwide desire to compete, and a government role that allows potent government help to businesses. Experts predict China, India, Japan, and other Asian nations will continue to be a major impact on world markets and will continue their growth and competition with the West.[14]

Dual-Career Families

Most families now need income from both adult members to survive comfortably. This has placed a strain on the family and its members—a strain that is felt in the workplace in several ways. First, additional financial pressures cause workplace stress. Second, the time needed for the everyday realities of child rearing—such as visits to the family doctor and transportation to and from school—create difficulties for everyone involved.

Single-Parent Families and Divorce

Two important factors have contributed to the existence of a higher number of single parents: a high divorce rate and an increase in the number of never-married parents. The parent—often the mother—must be the

more about...

Generation X is the generation of Americans born between 1965 and 1980, following the baby boomers who were born during the years 1946 to 1964.

Generation Y (also called the "Millennials") refers to Americans born after 1980, especially students who are now graduating from high school and either going to college or entering the job market.

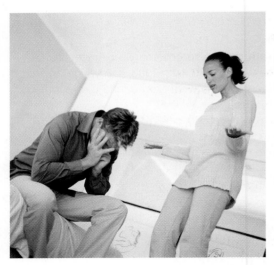

provider, taxi service, spiritual guide, and emotional support source. These many roles often result in frustration and stress in the workplace. This type of worker is truly overloaded.

A divorced person typically goes through a period of emotional recovery, during which many emotional issues can form. Such issues often negatively affect job performance and attitudes, harming relationships with co-workers, bosses, and fellow employees. The divorced parent often has *additional* barriers to success in the workplace. Besides the already heavy burdens of single parenthood that many of these workers have, they are often dealing with challenging issues of self-worth and self-esteem.

DIVORCE: A HEAVY IMPACT ON EMPLOYEES' LIVES

Many employees unintentionally bring depression, low productivity, and hostility to the workplace as a result of family breakups. *What can employers do to help employees in personal crises?*

Two Generations of Dependents

People are living longer now than ever before.[15] This rise in life expectancy, along with fewer high-income jobs for senior citizens, and cuts to pension funds and postretirement health insurance, means that many middle-age adults now find themselves helping to support their own children along with their aging parents and parents-in-law, all at the same time. These middle-aged adults who find themselves squeezed for time and finances are often referred to as the "sandwich generation" (with the elderly dependent parents as one piece of bread, and the dependent children as the other). The added responsibilities exist when parents or in-laws live with the adult children and their families, but also when elderly parents live alone or in retirement homes. The emotional impact affects all involved, including the dependent parent who usually would prefer self-sufficiency.

WHAT HUMAN RELATIONS IS *NOT*

Now that you know what human relations is, it's time to look at some characteristics it *does not* have. First, human relations is not a study in understanding human behavior in order to manipulate others. Good human relations means being real, positive, and honest. Practicing effective human relations means *being yourself at your very best*.

Second, learning better human relations skills is not a cure-all. Nor is it a quick fix for deep and ongoing personal problems. The skills you will learn in this book are skills to be built on, developed, and tried out whenever you can, as part of your own experience on the job and throughout your life.

Last, human relations is not just *common sense*. This argument is often used by people who think a skill like this is unnecessary. "Common sense," they say, "will carry you through." In the area of human relations, common sense (meaning ordinary good sense and judgment) is all too *un*common. The abuses of many workers on the job today, the misunderstandings that cost thousands of companies millions of dollars every year, the unhappiness of many workers with the jobs they have: all of these factors illustrate the need for human relations—even if much of it seems like simple common sense.

AREAS OF MAJOR EMPHASIS

In the broadest sense, the study of human relations has two goals: personal development and growth, and achievement of an organization's objectives. (See Figure 1.1.) All of the following areas of emphasis take both of those goals into consideration. You will notice that each of the areas is developed in the following chapters of this book. Most of them overlap, and some are dependent upon others. Those relationships will become clearer as you read further.

Self-Esteem

Self-esteem is your feeling of confidence and worth as a person. Psychological research has shown that lower self-esteem is related to a variety of mental health issues, including alcoholism, anxiety, and depression—all of which cause problems on the job. Higher self-esteem, on the other hand, improves attitudes, job morale, and overall quality of life. In the workplace, healthy self-esteem is the key to top performance and high-quality work—especially when the work directly affects other people.

Self-esteem is a buzzword in business circles today. Most Americans seem to have discovered this important part of themselves and its influence on every other factor in their lives. Self-esteem is at the core of most issues in human relations. Because it is so important, Chapter 2 is dedicated to that subject.

Personal development and growth

Satisfying the objectives of the organization

Self-esteem
Mutual respect
Self-awareness and self-disclosure

Communication Skills
Group dynamics
Motivation

figure 1.1

MAJOR GOALS AND EMPHASIS AREAS OF HUMAN RELATIONS

Which of these areas do you personally consider most important to effective human relations?

Mutual Respect

mutual respect

The positive consideration or regard that two people have for each other.

Notice that this isn't simply respect, but mutual respect. **Mutual respect,** the positive consideration or regard that two people have for each other, can exist only when your self-esteem is stable. If your self-esteem is too fragile, you will have little energy left for cultivating mutual respect. Also, without trust, mutual respect is meaningless. Many human relations specialists rate trust as the single most important element in human relations.[16] People at all levels of an organization need trust and mutual respect to perform at their best.

Self-Awareness and Self-Disclosure

These two concepts are interconnected. *Self-awareness* is the knowledge of how you are being perceived by others. *Self-disclosure* is the process of letting other people know what you are really thinking and feeling. Self-awareness allows individuals to know what in their own behavior is being perceived as real by other people; self-disclosure involves "being real" with others. In *The Seven Habits of Highly Effective People*, author Stephen Covey said, "Until we take how we see ourselves (and how we see others) into account, we will be unable to understand how others see and feel about themselves and their world."[17] Self-disclosure, on the other hand, reflects the positive side of human relations: By allowing others to see what feelings and thoughts you really have in a given instance, you can promote genuineness in the other person. A positive side effect is that your relationship with the other person is likely to become closer.

more about...

Stephen Covey, author of numerous books, is known globally for his emphasis on personal and professional integrity. He cofounded the Franklin Covey Company, which is the largest leadership development organization in the world.

Communication Skills

communication

The process of giving and receiving through listening and speaking, ideas, feelings, and information.

Communication is the process of sending ideas, thoughts, and feelings, and having them received in the way you intended.[18] The communication process is at the heart of all managerial functions, and it is directly related to success or failure at the managerial level. It is also a vital part of all personal interactions. When a human relations problem emerges, miscommunication is usually involved.

If you are to grow either as an individual or in groups, effective communication is essential.[19] Much of your success depends on your ability to express ideas and concepts precisely. Part of that ability is based on your listening level, which includes listening for feelings and emotions as well as for objective content.

Stephen Covey has lectured millions and conducted hundreds of interviews related to his self-improvement theories. A brief version of his philosophy can be found through **www.mhhe.com/lamberton4e.** Read the philosophy and write a brief summary.

Group Dynamics

Whenever two or more people form a relationship, there is, in effect, a group. Once a group is formed, it immediately requires understanding, planning, and organizational tactics appropriate to groups. Thus, understanding **group dynamics**—the ways in which groups operate—is a cornerstone in the study of human relations.[20]

As important as our individuality is, nearly everything that people value in life can be achieved only through groups.[21] For success, people learn how to make group processes more effective. In *The New Realities,* well-known management expert Peter Drucker said, "Management is about human beings. Its task is to make people capable of *joint performance,* to make their strengths effective and their weaknesses irrelevant."[22]

Knowledge of group dynamics includes understanding conflict management. Much of good human relations involves preventing negative conflict.

> **group dynamics**
> The set of interpersonal relationships within a group that determine how group members relate to one another and that influence task performance.

Peter Drucker (1909–2005), a management expert for over 60 years, is the author of several books that still carry the same strong impact as they did when they were published. His first influential work was the 1945 study *The Concept of a Corporation,* which compared his ideal of management with the management of General Motors.

more about...

Motivation

People often use the term *motivation* to describe the force that gets them to do their tasks. It is no longer enough to threaten punishment or even to reward a job well done. Motivation derives from the needs of an individual and of a group. It is also a major element in understanding human relations.

A BRIEF HISTORY OF HUMAN RELATIONS

One cannot fully appreciate the present state of human relations without at least a partial understanding of the past. The history of human relations is essential to a thorough understanding of its place in today's world.

Human relations has been important ever since human beings began to live together in groups. Of course, attitudes toward power—especially the sharing of power—have changed through the centuries. Most societies no longer tolerate slavery, nor do most cultures blindly follow leaders as they once did. Thus, the history of human relations problems can be viewed in different ways during different times.

The Early Years

Human relations began to be an issue as we know it today around the early to mid-1800s. Figure 1.2 gives a thumbnail view of major events in the field. The Knights of Labor, founded in 1869, was an organization much like the labor unions that came later. The founders of this group denounced the bad working conditions and unfair treatment in many workplaces of the time.[23] The labor union movement might never have started if human relations between managers and workers had been better, and if working conditions had been more tolerable. Anyone who is blindly antiunion needs to understand that negative management caused the movement of workers to organize into unions.

In early 19th-century England, a man named Robert Owen came up with the amazing idea that treating workers better would actually increase productivity and, thus, profits. Owen introduced many reforms in the industry of the time. For example, he stopped employing young children in his factory. He also encouraged his workforce to stay clean and sober. Although by today's standards these measures might seem quite basic, Owen was progressive for his time.[24]

Like Robert Owen, Andrew Ure (also from Great Britain) was interested in human relations in manufacturing companies. In 1835, Ure published a book called *The Philosophy of Manufacturers*. This book suggested that workers should have medical help, hot tea on a regular basis, good ventilation, and even sick leave—again, all ideas that were advanced for their time.[25]

Owen and Ure were definitely not typical. Both in Europe and in the United States, the first decades of the Industrial Revolution were full of abuses by bosses against workers, especially workers with few skills. Many of the immigrants to America during that time were forced to face inhumane working conditions.

Some of the better employers built "company towns." These were settlements, owned by the company, where workers would live in

more about...

Robert Owen (1771–1858) was a Welsh-born social reformer who influenced both English and American employers. His philosophy was known as Owenism and his followers, Owenites.

more about...

Andrew Ure (1778–1857) was, like many of his time, an avid enthusiast of the Industrial Revolution. He was the first person to write a detailed study of manufacturers and their management processes.
Max Weber (1864–1920), who was also a political economist, is best known for writing *The Protestant Ethic and the Spirit of Capitalism* (1904).

figure 1.2

Need to remember

A HUMAN RELATIONS TIMELINE

What are the major changes you see in human relations over the years?

1830	1870	1900	1920	1930	1940	1950	1960	1970–90s	2010
			World War I		*The Depression* *World War II*				
		Frederick Taylor							
		Elton Mayo							
		Frank & Lillian Gilbreth							
		Mary Parker Follett							
		Max Weber							
						Abraham Maslow			
							Doug McGregor		
							Eric Berne		
							Carl Rogers		
								W. Edwards Deming	
Robert Owen	Knights of Labor	Bureaucracy	Scientific management	Labor unions gaining power	End of WWII Birth of human relations	Hierarchy of needs	Theory X & Y Transactional analysis	Growth in classroom study of human relations	
Andrew Ure	Organized pre-labor union		Optimum shovel "One Best Way"						
"The Philosophy of Manufacturers"	Bad working conditions			Wagner Act 1935			Conflict management	Required courses in human relations	
Medical help	Unfair treatment								
Tea breaks				Hawthorne Studies: Informal organization Needs of workers			Group dynamics	Growth of Total Quality Management	
Ventilation									
Sick leave									

13

company housing, buy supplies at the company-owned store, and even send their children to a school owned by the firm. Though not popular today, this setup usually produced happier and more loyal workers, especially when the quality of the company town was considered high.

In Germany, a sociologist named Max Weber saw human relations problems as being caused by favoritism, nepotism (playing favorites with family members), and other unfair practices. In Weber's time, most European companies were managed like extended families. Employees were loyal to a single person, rather than to the company goals or mission statement. Weber came up with the bureaucratic organizations approach,[26] a system that was meant to be impersonal and rational. In Weber's model, called **bureaucracy,** each person had specific duties and responsibilities that were to be assigned on the basis of ability and talent only. Also, the work of the people in an organization was to be done in an orderly way, with only one supervisor to whom each worker must answer.[27] This approach reduced favoritism and many other unfair practices.

> **bureaucracy**
> A formal organization in which each person has specific duties and responsibilities and is assigned to only one supervisor.

Human Relations as a Science

Today the word *bureaucracy* often has a negative connotation. The word is often associated with government red tape and paperwork. Bureaucracy actually started out as a method of improving not only efficiency, but human relations as well.

Scientific Management

In the early years of the 20th century, Frederick Taylor and others began a movement called **scientific management.** Most people today who have heard of Taylor think of him as an industrial engineer who tried to find the "one best way" to do a job. He is often criticized as someone who cared more about production than about the needs of workers. However, Taylor is important to the history of human relations because he showed how crucial the human element is in the performance of any organization.[28]

> **scientific management**
> A system based upon scientific and engineering principles.

Like others in the scientific management movement, Taylor was concerned with increasing efficiency while getting as much work as possible out of employees. Taylor's approach contained two major features:

1. Managers should carefully select and train workers for specific tasks.

2. Managers should try to motivate workers to increase productivity. Careful hiring and in-depth training do not seem very earthshaking today, but Taylor was among the first to recognize the importance of both. Also, in Taylor's time, motivation was believed to be induced only through increased pay. Though shortsighted and a bit simplistic, his view of motivation at least focused attention on the issue. Increased pay was likely a larger incentive during Taylor's

time than it is today. Today's workers tend to value humane treatment and increased job satisfaction more than was the case a few generations ago.

One of Taylor's best-known victories was the invention of the *optimum shovel*. At an eastern steel mill, Taylor watched men shoveling coal for the large smelters. Using the same shovel, these men would also load cinders into waste containers. After carefully studying both processes, Taylor came up with two shovels: a much larger shovel for the light cinders and a smaller shovel for the coal. This shovel was exactly the right size and weight to allow the maximum work without the need for frequent rest periods. The productivity of the steel mill rose immediately, making Taylor and scientific management both very popular.[29]

Frank and Lillian Gilbreth

Living around the same time period as Taylor, Frank and Lillian Gilbreth were a married couple who were both industrial engineers—and scientific managers. The Gilbreths became especially well known for their research study of bricklayers. Frank Gilbreth identified 18 different motions that had been used by bricklayers, apparently for as long as people had been laying bricks. By inventing some laborsaving

> **more about...**
>
> **Frederick Winslow Taylor** (1856–1915) was also renowned as an inventor; the optimum shovel is perhaps his best-known invention. By experimenting with different materials, he was able to design shovels that would permit workers to shovel for the whole day.

> **more about...**
>
> **Frank Gilbreth** (1868–1924) and **Lillian Gilbreth** (1878–1972) were pioneers in time and motion study. Besides their early work refining the bricklaying process, they had a great impact on medicine by significantly reducing the amount of time patients had to spend on the surgical table. Thus, the Gilbreths were also responsible for saving many people's lives.
>
> ***Source:*** Daniel A. Wren, *The Evolution of Management Thought,* 2nd ed. (New York: Wiley, 1979), p. 171.

FRANK AND LILLIAN GILBRETH

The Gilbreths were instrumental in the evolution of human relations. *Do you see evidence of their efforts in your work life?*

When most of us hear the word "sweatshop," images likely come to mind of deplorable working conditions in American factories of 100+ years ago, or various Southeast Asian or Latin American factories of today. But sweatshops are found around the world even today, including in the United States. As recently as 1994, the U.S. Department of Labor reported results of a survey of garment factories in California, showing that more than half paid less than minimum wage and did not pay overtime. A whopping 93 percent did not maintain safe and healthy workplace conditions.

Source: U.S. Department of Labor, *Reinvention Success Story: Eradicating Sweatshops: Garment Industry Initiative,* Feb. 7, 1996. www.dol.gov/oasam/programs/rcindex/esa21.htm

devices and by changing the basic routine, the Gilbreths reduced those 18 motions to 5. The result was a system of bricklaying with more than double the productivity of the old system.

Lillian Gilbreth was especially interested in studying workers and their reactions to working under stressful conditions. She taught the importance of standard work days, relaxed and regular lunch breaks, and periodic rest periods. Her life's work helped influence Congress to pass child labor laws. The mother of twelve children, Lillian was among the first women in America to receive a Ph.D. in psychology. In her later life, she became known as "The First Lady of Management." She was an important early force in the human relations movement as well.[30]

Mary Parker Follett

In the early years of the 20th century, Mary Parker Follett became known for her lectures and writings on what we would now call human relations issues. Follett was a member of the upper classes—not someone with a work-related background. She lectured widely, however, and was quite influential.

Follett taught three concepts that were ahead of their time. First, she held that workers should be allowed to be involved in decisions affecting them. To her it was logical that the people closest to the action could make the best decisions. Second, she stressed that the workplace is dynamic—that is, constantly changing. Thus, inflexible, static rules are potentially harmful to maintaining a productive workforce. Finally, Mary Parker Follett believed that the main job of managers at all levels was to maintain positive relationships with workers. Happy workers with a sense of belonging, she said, would end up making more money for the

more about...

Mary Parker Follett (1868–1933) attended the college known today as Radcliffe. She studied philosophy and political science but became deeply interested in management. Always the advocate of humanizing the workplace, she stressed people over technology. One of her pieces of advice to engineers was "Don't hug your blueprints!"

Source: Henry Metcalf and Lyndall Urwick, eds., *Dynamic Administration: The Collected Papers of Mary Parker Follett,* New York: Harper & Row, 1940.

company and would remain at the same job for a longer time. These three concepts define Follett as a very important early pioneer of the human relations movement, and definitely ahead of her time.[31]

The Hawthorne Experiment

In the late 1920s, a group of scientific management scholars went to Hawthorne, Illinois, to study the effects of physical factors on workers and their productivity. Each time they would try an experiment, productivity would go up. However, when they reversed the experiment, productivity would still increase. The most popular of these experiments was with lighting. When the lights in this Western Electric assembly plant were brightened, productivity increased. However, when the lights were dimmed, productivity went up again.

> **Elton Mayo** (1880–1940) was born in Australia and didn't arrive in the United States until 1922. He was the driving force behind the Hawthorne studies and translations of his work appeared in German, Spanish, Italian, Japanese, and Arabic.

The experimenters were really confused. Why would workers work even harder under such poor conditions as very dim lighting? The problem confronting these scientific management scholars attracted the attention of Elton Mayo, a social psychologist from Harvard University. He traveled to Hawthorne and stayed. For nearly five years, from 1927 to 1932, he and his Harvard colleagues studied the **Hawthorne Experiment.**[32] Two important discoveries came from this five-year study. First, Mayo showed that the workers at Hawthorne performed better because someone was paying attention to them. This attention was more than they had been accustomed to receiving at work, and they responded with extra motivation. Second, Mayo found that the relationships that had formed naturally in the workplace made up what he called the **informal organization.** On days when a worker would not be as motivated as usual, the expectations of the group would make up the difference, and productivity would remain high.

> **Hawthorne Experiment**
> A five-year study conducted at the Western Electric plant in Hawthorne, Illinois, that showed—among other findings—that workers performed better when someone was paying attention to them.

Recent research studies have reported that the Hawthorne workers were very likely motivated by fear as well as by attention. Whether or not this new interpretation is true, the findings of Elton Mayo influenced decades of thought on the role of human relations on the job. Much of what has been written and practiced since Hawthorne has been influenced by what Mayo himself concluded—and although the findings have been reexamined, the original shape of those findings still influences people today.[33]

> **informal organization**
> The ever-changing set of relationships and interactions that are not formally put together; they form naturally in the workplace.

Human Relations and Management

Probably the most important improvement Elton Mayo brought about was to change the way management looked at workers. Rather than seeing workers

> **The Wagner Act,** also called the National Labor Relations Act, made it illegal for employers to use scare tactics or other techniques to prevent employees from forming or joining unions.

more about…

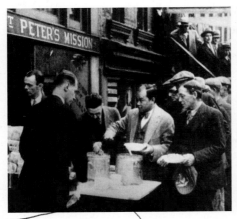

THE GREAT DEPRESSION: A HUMAN RELATIONS SETBACK

During the Great Depression, the great job shortage made many employers feel that they could "fire the problems and hire the solutions" by firing employees they disliked until they found ones who suited their needs. *Does this problem still exist today?*

more about...

Douglas McGregor (1906–1964) was a pioneer in industrial relations. His creation of Theory X and Theory Y allowed management to understand their influence on employee morale and productivity. Although McGregor was well respected in his lifetime, his peak popularity did not come until 1993, nearly 30 years after his death.

Theories X and Y

Theory X managers see workers as lacking ambition, disliking work, and wanting security above all else. Theory Y managers see workers as enjoying work, able to assume responsibility, and being creative.

mostly as people who need wages, managers now began to understand that the complex needs of workers include a unique combination of values, attitudes, and desires.

By the time Elton Mayo left Hawthorne, the Great Depression was several years old. Although the interest in human relations still existed, the stubborn fact was that a ruthless manager could mistreat workers now without much fear of losing them. After all, jobs were very hard to find.

During the Great Depression, labor unions began to gain power. Congress passed the Wagner Act in 1935, giving unions and union members more rights than they had enjoyed before. For example, businesses were now forced to negotiate contracts with union representatives.[34] Although this new union activity was good for workers, it did not necessarily mean that human relations issues were being emphasized. Many managers still had the attitude that one need only to "fire the problems and hire the solutions." Unions usually emphasized salary and benefits for workers rather than the more abstract issues of employee treatment and workplace morale.

By the time the Japanese bombed Pearl Harbor in 1941, the Depression was showing some signs of lifting. Once the country began gearing up for World War II, the workplace was affected drastically. With hundreds of thousands of young workers going overseas to fight, employers were forced to hire nearly anybody who would work. Sadly, human relations in the workplace always seems to be affected by the job market. The onset of World War II was no exception. Managers knew their employees would be very hard to replace, so treatment of workers temporarily improved. Cases of sexism, racism, and sexual harassment, however, were all too common.

Throughout the war, and in the years immediately following, many studies were being done on human relations factors. The noted psychologist Abraham Maslow devised a "hierarchy of needs," which teaches that people tend to satisfy their needs in a certain order; you will read more about this in Chapter 6. In 1960, psychologist Douglas McGregor wrote *The Human Side of Enterprise*, considered by some to be the most important book on human relations ever written.

McGregor introduced the concepts of **Theories X and Y.** These two theories are held by different types of managers, based on their ways of looking at workers. Theory X managers see workers as lacking ambition, disliking work, and wanting security above all else. Theory Y managers, on the other hand, see workers as happy to work, able to assume responsibility, and overall quite creative. These two theories—especially Theory Y—have influenced thinking in both management and human

Theory X and Theory Y are explained alongside McGregor's broader philosophy through **www.mhhe.com/lamberton4e.** Read the philosophies and write a comparison. Which theory do you prefer? Why?

relations since the year of their creation.[35] Theories X and Y will be discussed at length in Chapter 4.

Human Relations, History, and the Individual

The second half of the 20th century brought a great deal of attention to the study of the workplace from psychologists and other social scientists. In the early 1960s, Eric Berne had created his famous transactional analysis method of understanding interpersonal communication. Carl Rogers published his findings on the development of the personality, group dynamics, and conflict management. Some managers began experimenting with participative decision making and other human relations–based management.

By the late 1960s, an era had started that would affect human relations for years. A new emphasis was placed on the rights and needs of the individual person. For the first time, it was popular in this culture to "do your own thing." Perhaps even more important, other people were allowed to do their own thing as well. Also new was the revolutionary attitude toward success as having to do with people, rather than with money. Many of today's middle managers were so-called "hippies" then. Influence from that era has still not peaked.

By 1980, **Total Quality Management (TQM)** had been introduced in the United States as it had been three decades earlier in Japan. The man responsible for this new movement was an American named W. Edwards Deming. This important school of thought held that the *process* of whatever happens in an organization is more important than the *product*. Doing away with targets, "zero defects" programs, and slogans, the TQM people concentrated on the process—which inevitably includes people and relationships. The work that was pioneered by Elton Mayo and others became refocused with a process emphasis. People in organizations participated at work to an extent unimagined before. Working conditions had come to be seen as the most important single issue in many companies.[36]

By the late 1980s, Total Quality Management had changed industry both in America and abroad. From the mid-1990s to the present, the label TQM has been heard less frequently. However, the process of TQM survives under other names—sometimes simply "quality"—and

Total Quality Management (TQM)

An organizational philosophy that quality must be present in the product or service produced and in all support activities related to it.

The basic teachings of **W. Edwards Deming** (1900–1993) can be found through **www.mhhe.com/lamberton4e.** Write a paragraph explaining why you think TQM was effective.

remains an important part of many successful organizations. There must be quality in the process itself, as well as in the final product. Of course, TQM covers many other organizational issues besides human relations, but the positive effect of the quality movement on human relations promises to be lasting.

The 1970s through the 1990s saw a tremendous growth in the classroom study of human relations. Today, most college business and industrial education departments require courses in human relations. This trend reflects the growing awareness of the importance of understanding and working with others effectively. As an international economy develops, human relations takes on a broader significance.

STRATEGY FOR SUCCESS

1.1 Develop Mutual Respect

1. Develop your self-esteem.
2. Develop your self-awareness.
3. Develop trust.
4. Learn to self-disclose.
5. Cultivate mutual respect.

Although these are big tasks, they can be achieved by anyone with a clear understanding of human relations.

1. **Develop your self-esteem.** First, you must develop your self-esteem. Self-esteem can be encouraged or damaged very early in life, and some people who have self-esteem problems do not even realize it. However, no matter what your age or self-esteem level, you can always learn to like yourself more. Chapter 2 will cover self-esteem in great detail and provide tips on how you can build your own self-esteem.

2. **Develop your self-awareness.** Without self-awareness, you will find it hard to develop self-esteem or any of the other issues that are important to successful human relations. This is because you must know yourself before you can value yourself highly and express yourself honestly to others. You will learn more about how to develop self-awareness in Chapter 3.

3. **Develop trust.** Without adequate self-esteem, you will find it difficult to trust. With trust, however, you will find that your relationships will grow deep and meaningful, and that you will be able to tell other people what's in "your gut" without unnecessary fear.

4. **Learn to self-disclose.** As you develop trust, you will be able to disclose more about yourself. Self-disclosure and trust are areas that you can develop simultaneously: As you learn to self-disclose appropriately, you will develop deeper trust in your relationships. Chapter 3 will cover self-disclosure in greater detail.

5. **Cultivate mutual respect.** Developing trust will lead to mutual respect, as you forge relationships that are based on honesty. You will learn more about talking "from your gut," also called self-disclosure, in Chapter 3.

1.2 Build Your Communication Skills

1. Learn to communicate honestly.
2. Learn what effective communication is and how to develop this skill.
3. Know what you are communicating to others by increasing your self-awareness.
4. Know what you are communicating to others by your nonverbal signals.
5. Learn to deal effectively with conflict.

1. **Learn to communicate honestly.** When you communicate honestly by learning to say what you feel, by establishing trust, and by using effective and appropriate self-disclosure, your listeners will learn to respect and trust you more. Self-disclosure will be covered in Chapter 3.

2. **Learn what effective communication is and how to develop this skill.** Effective communication is communicating so that your listener receives the message you intended to send. When you use honesty and appropriate self-disclosure, and state your message in a clear way that shows high self-esteem, you will send your message more effectively.

3. **Know what you are communicating to others by increasing your self-awareness.** If you have low self-awareness, you may communicate so that your true meaning is unclear. By working on your self-awareness, you will improve your communication skill. Self-awareness is covered with self-disclosure in Chapter 3.

4. **Know what you are communicating to others by your nonverbal signals.** If you give nonverbal signals that are unintended, your message will be different than what you expect. This can lead to confusion and mistrust. Nonverbal communication is covered in Chapter 7.

5. **Learn to deal effectively with conflict.** Effective communication skill involves the ability to deal with conflict. Chapter 13 will show you how to deal with conflict to restore trust and mutual respect.

CHAPTER ONE SUMMARY

Chapter Summary by Learning Objectives

1. **Define human relations.** Whatever direction your life takes—whether you become a manager, an entrepreneur, or an employee—you will always have to deal with other people, and human relations skills will be essential. Human relations is the skill or ability to work effectively with and through other people.

2. **Explain the importance of human relations in business.** Human relations skills are especially important today for several reasons: greater awareness of human rights, current fluctuations in international markets, growing emphasis on the human resource in companies, current emphasis on teamwork, and increased diversity in the workplace.

3. **Discuss the challenges of human relations as these factors affect success in business.** Today's problems make workplace survival an even greater challenge. Increased workplace competition, the rise of the dual-career family, the divorce rate, and the problem of two generations of dependents: all of these factors increase personal stress and complicate the issues of human relations.

4. **Identify what is *not* human relations.** Skill in human relations does not mean being phony or manipulative; it is neither a quick fix nor a cure-all; and it is not just common sense. It is a skill area that is learnable, though growth continues for a lifetime.

5. **Describe the areas of emphasis for human relations in today's workplace.** The main areas of human relations are self-esteem, mutual respect, self-awareness and self-disclosure, communication skill, group dynamics, and motivation.

6. **Discuss a short history of the study of human relations.** Starting with the scientific managers in the early part of this century, and finding a focal point in the Hawthorne Experiment, the human relations movement began in the 1800s and spanned the entire 20th century. Names to remember include Robert Owen, Andrew Ure, Max Weber, Frederick Taylor, Frank and Lillian Gilbreth, Mary Parker Follett, W. Edwards Deming, and Elton Mayo. In 1960, Douglas McGregor wrote about Theory X and Theory Y managers, showing the latter as both more effective and more humane.

key terms

bureaucracy 14
communication 10
group dynamics 11
Hawthorne
  Experiment 17
human relations 4

informal
  organization 17
mutual respect 10
scientific
  management 14
Theories X and Y 18

Total Quality
  Management 19

review questions

1. In your own words, write a one- or two-sentence definition of human relations as you would have defined it before reading this chapter. Then, assuming your definition has changed a bit, write a new one.

2. Explain the importance of Elton Mayo and his work in the Hawthorne Studies to the history of human relations.

3. How can the development of human relations skills help you on the job as a manager? as an entrepreneur? as an employee?

4. Explain the role of W. Edwards Deming in the further development of human relations concepts during the past two decades.

5. List three reasons why human relations issues are more important today than ever before.

6. Why is self-esteem important to the development of human relation skills?

7. List the six "areas of emphasis" in the study of human relations and explain each one briefly.

8. Why did the human relations movement not make much progress during the Great Depression? Discuss the relevance that experience might have to today's workplace.

critical thinking questions

9. Explain the importance of the work of Frederick Taylor, and Frank and Lillian Gilbreth and the scientific management movement to the development of modern industry.

10. What are the problems of today's society that cause greater stress on the job, thus increasing the need for human relations skills? List and explain the importance of each.

COMMUNICATING WITH A SUPERVISOR

School-to-Work Connection: Interpersonal Skills, Thinking Skills, and Personal Qualities Skills

Situation: Doris Johnston is the president of Elko Manufacturing Company.

Workers are in short supply in the town where Elko is located. Doris noticed that the turnover rate has been extremely high in one department. The supervisor in this department, Janet Kent, has been having problems relating to her workers. Janet has become known as someone who abuses her power by intimidating her workers, and purposely conducting herself in a way that makes them constantly concerned that they will lose their jobs. Many workers never voice their complaints and simply find work elsewhere.

Doris has asked Janet six times during the past five months why the turnover is so high in her department. She also tells Janet that she has overheard workers complain about the way Janet treats them. Janet answers that the workers leave because they can't handle her demands and maintains that she is "tough, that's all, not unreasonable."

Procedure: Four volunteers should play Doris and Janet in two separate role plays. The first will present how Doris should not confront Janet with her concerns. Then, without class discussion, play the second role play, showing a better way that Doris can communicate her concerns with Janet. Finally, the class should discuss both role plays, sharing what they have learned from the process.

internet exercises

1. *Research and Evaluate*
   Several different organizations have identified the "Best Companies to Work For." Among the producers of such lists are *Fortune* magazine, the Society for Human Resource Management, and organizations in Canada and the United Kingdom. Using a search engine, find one of these lists. Choose any one of the listed companies and look it up on its own Web site to get more information. Then, write a short paragraph on the company, evaluating whether or not you would want to work there. Be sure to emphasize the human relations–related reasons for your conclusions.

2. *Compare and Contrast*
   The Singaporean Cultural Studies site can be found through **www.mhhe.com/lamberton4e.** Imagine that you have just learned that

your company is sending you on a one-year business trip to open and manage a branch office in Singapore. You have never traveled to Asia before, and you know little about the culture. Visit this page and write down the first five noticeable differences you observed between your culture and Singapore's. Then write a paragraph that answers these questions:

a. How could those differences create human relations issues?

b. How can effective human relations prevent or solve misunderstandings related to these differences?

3. *Self-Assess and Apply*

Lawrence K. Jones at North Carolina State University has posted an excellent set of online tools to help you with your career exploration. Visit this site and take the Career Key assessment through the course Web site at **www.mhhe.com/lamberton4e** or enter directly through **www.careerkey.org/english/index.html.** Report on the career that fits you best, according to this assessment.

The Side-Takers

Jody Gillam was facing some issues she would never have forecast when she started her women's fashion shop barely two years before. Her business had expanded to the point where she now employed nearly 20 people, most of them as full-time employees. Now, it seemed that she had four groups: two that were hardworking and dedicated and devoted totally to the needs of customers, and two that seemed to be out to destroy each other.

Today, Jody's floor manager, Mia, came to her with a great deal of urgency in her voice. "Jody, we've got to do something about the hostility level in this place. It's driving customers away and discouraging new ones from shopping here. I had a customer just yesterday tell me that she can 'feel the tension' whenever she walks in here."

Mia wasn't telling Jody anything she didn't already know. Jody even knew who the problem members of both groups were; the question was what to do about the issue. Two informal groups among the sales staff were sabotaging each other's work and insulting each other at every turn. Heather and LeeAnn were two strong personalities who disliked each other. Over the past few weeks, others in the store had gravitated to one or the other, forming a coalition of supporters on both sides. This created the tension felt even by the customers.

"One thing is for sure," Jody said softly. "This absolutely can't be allowed to go on."

"Well, we're together there," Mia replied. "The question is, where do we start?"

Case Study Questions

1. Which emphasis areas of human relations does this case mostly address?

2. What steps should Jody take to solve the conflict in her department?

3. Could Jody have done anything to prevent this problem from occurring in the first place? If so, what?

That "Stupid" Team of Mine

When Joaquin Salcedo received the phone call that he was hired, he could barely believe it was happening. "Frankly, I didn't expect even to be a finalist," he admitted to one of his friends.

Joaquin's new position was in the IT department of a midsized company. He went in feeling less than adequate for the position. Very soon, however, he began to discover just how much more qualified he was for job than he had thought. Nearly everyone else on his team, it seemed, was an "idiot." That was Joaquin's word, and he began using it more frequently as time went by.

Every day, Joaquin felt, his time was taken up answering questions that "anyone qualified to work here shouldn't have to ask." They were, indeed, often questions that would fall into the "everyone should know" category. However, there were other questions that Joaquin was uniquely qualified to answer; he was equally annoyed by both.

"These idiots are wasting my time—hours of it every day," Joaquin told his supervisor, Rick Jarwood. Rick replied, "Nevertheless, answering their questions is a part of your job. As the job description says, you are to clarify the plant computer systems to others in the company." "That part of the job I'm fine with," countered Joaquin. "It's the people on my own team I'm upset with. They are supposed to know something, aren't they?"

"Yes, but they need to be talked to with some respect, even when they don't know as much as they should," Rick added.

"Oh, I guess," Joaquin sniffed. Rick walked slowly back his office, unconvinced that he had gotten through to his new employee.

Rick's suspicions were confirmed when, during the next three weeks he began receiving an increasing number of complaints about Joaquin's performance. Not even one complaint mentioned anything about his technical knowledge or abilities—only about his interpersonal relations. Most of them accused Joaquin of being "arrogant" and "overbearing." It was a company employee, not one of his own team, who complained, "He called me a turkey and told me to 'figure it out yourself.'"

Another company employee produced an e-mail from Joaquin that said, "If you had a single brain cell, you wouldn't bother me with things like this."

Rick Jarwood sat at his desk one Monday morning, trying his best to decide what to do next. "I know I need to do something, but I'm not sure how to show Joaquin that he is destroying his own position. He needs to see the light, and right away."

Case Study Questions

1. How self-aware does Joaquin seem to be?
2. What advice would you give Rick Jarwood in dealing with Joaquin's human relations problems? Remember that his high level of expertise does make Joaquin potentially valuable in other ways, once the human relations issues can be addressed.
3. How could this situation have been *prevented*?

SELF-CONCEPT AND SELF-ESTEEM IN HUMAN RELATIONS

In the Workplace: First-day Jitters

SITUATION

Lena had been looking forward to a career in medical transcription ever since she learned about the health information technology field at her ninth-grade Careers Day. With her two-year degree completed and good recommendation letters from her instructors, she was hired after interviewing with just three transcription companies. Today was her first day of work, and she was excited as she set up to begin work at her computer station. But her excitement turned to nervousness and then panic as she realized she was not familiar with the software the new company used, and she couldn't remember any of the medical codes she had learned. "What made me think I could do this job?" she thought to herself. "All the other transcribers know what they're doing. I'll never catch on. I might as well quit right now before they realize what an idiot I am."

DISCOVERY

As time went on, Lena found a strategy that helped her combat these negative feelings and thoughts. Instead of thinking the worst

28

objectives

After studying this chapter, you will be able to:

1 Define self-concept.

2 Identify the four areas of the self-concept.

3 Describe the real and ideal selves.

4 Explain the importance of pleasing yourself and others.

5 Define self-esteem.

6 Discuss the relationship between self-esteem and work performance.

7 Distinguish among different types of self-esteem.

8 Explain the origins of your self-esteem.

« « STRATEGIES FOR SUCCESS

Strategy 2.1   Steps toward Achieving Higher Self-Esteem

Strategy 2.2   Steps toward Combating Low Self-Esteem

about fitting in and learning her job, she decided to think that she would be a good employee, and that her co-workers and supervisors would accept and appreciate her. She learned that other people accepted her opinion of herself—and that she was worthy of respect and friendliness from others. If her opinion of herself was bad, others would assume bad things about her. If it was good, they would see the good in her. This strategy improved her feelings of self-worth.

Lena discovered something else about the company and its employees: that many, if not all, of the employees also needed to boost their own feelings of self-worth. Lena began to pay attention to the things she said to her co-workers and supervisors, especially while she was still getting to know her way around.

She would ask herself, "Am I saying things in a way that will make this person like herself better, or am I making her feel threatened and resentful of me?" By the end of her first evaluation period, Lena had made many new friends and was feeling right at home in her new job.

THINK ABOUT IT

How can your opinion of yourself affect your self-esteem? How much does your self-esteem affect the ways that others react to you?

Think about former first lady Eleanor Roosevelt's famous quote, "No one can make you feel inferior without your consent." What does this mean? Do you agree or disagree?

Rosa yells at her co-worker Gail in front of everyone in the office for not filling up the paper tray in the printer. Several printer jobs are now backed up, and Rosa is going to have to wait for the document she is in a hurry to print. Afterward, Rosa feels bad about yelling at Gail. Her self-concept changes as she starts to think that she is an unprofessional and irritable employee. This makes her feel awkward around Gail and others in the office, which reduces her self-concept even more. This whole chain of events also threatens her self-esteem.

WHAT IS SELF-CONCEPT?

self-concept
The way you picture yourself to be.

Self-concept is the way you *conceive* of (or see) yourself; this view of yourself is the foundation of all your thoughts about yourself, including your self-esteem. Self-esteem is discussed in more detail later in this chapter. Most of what you do is controlled by your self-concept—the way you picture yourself to be. For example, you may say to yourself, "Other people are always asking me for help in their Internet searches. I must be pretty good at that." You have a good self-concept when it comes to this skill. This good self-concept then increases your opinion of yourself.

Your everyday actions also tend to affect your self-concept; in turn, your self-concept affects the things you do. When the things you do make you feel bad about yourself, and your self-concept is threatened or changed in a negative way, you wind up in a vicious cycle.

Once this cycle gets started, it is difficult to stop. You will need to take some definite action to break it, or your life and relationships with others simply won't be as fulfilling or successful as they could be. Once the cycle has begun, trying to analyze who started it—who is to blame—is nearly always pointless. Instead, you need to examine ways of stopping it, or at least minimizing the effects of the vicious cycle.

THE FOUR PARTS OF THE SELF-CONCEPT

The self-concept can be divided into four parts (as shown in Figure 2.1).[1]

In a perfect world, all four shapes in the self-concept diagram would be one single circle. However, the most realistic way of viewing the diagram is with the goal of pushing all four shapes together, knowing that they will probably never completely coincide—but may occasionally.

Ideal Self

ideal self
The way you would like to be or plan to become.

This is your vision of your future self. Everyone has some notion of what he or she would like to become. For some people, the image of the **ideal self** is sharp and clear; they know the changes they need in

All the while Danica is growing up, her parents tell her, "We expect you to become a dentist and join our dental practice. It's a family tradition." This statement tells Danica that she *must* plan her life around becoming a dentist. She feels obligated to excel in science classes while in school and to plan her classes around preparing for dental school. She can see that she doesn't have the interest and passion that her classmates have in these courses. She wonders what she is missing in other areas of study. But because she has accepted her parents' message of what her ideal self *should* be, this continues to motivate her and affect her self-concept and her self-esteem.

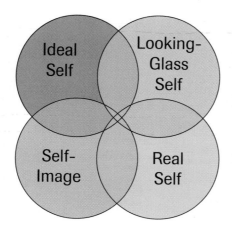

figure 2.1

THE FOUR PARTS OF THE SELF-CONCEPT

Self-concept can be divided into four parts. *How can you bring all four of these selves closer together?*

their lives and what they must do to make them happen. Many people, though, have a less clear picture of their ideal self, and still others have an unrealistic idea of what they want to become. One common mistake is to think that you have already reached your ideal, when actually you still have a long way to go. Another is to create an ideal self that is unrealistic and unattainable.

Some parents present their children with a picture of how the children must act to win approval. Such parents are said to hold *conditional positive regard* for their children. This idea will be discussed later in the chapter. Under those conditions, children may grow up either rejecting the parents' plans for them completely, becoming depressed and giving up, or falsely believing that they have already become their parents' ideal and do not have to go any further to find happiness.

Looking-Glass Self

The **looking-glass self** is the self that you *assume* others see when they look at you. It is also affected by your view of reality. Some people assume that others think well of them much more than is true, while many more tend to assume the opposite. For most people, the looking-glass self is much more negative than it deserves to be. Getting in touch with others' real feelings about you will also be covered in Chapter 3.

> **looking-glass self**
> The self you assume others see when they look at you.

Sarah, a college student, may think of herself as an A student in her ideal self. Then she gets her first graded exam back from her instructor, and the grade at the top of the paper is a D. This information about her real self is very different from her ideal self.[2] This difference results in a change in her self-concept and lowered self-esteem.

Self-Image

self-image
The way you honestly feel about yourself.

Your **self-image** is the way you truly feel about yourself. It can be *programmed* by your day-to-day behavior and by the things you say to yourself or others. If you say (even to yourself) that you are a loser, a bumbling idiot, or whatever other negative description you might use, your self-image will automatically memorize that message for future use. Fortunately, the opposite is also true: if you use positive words and phrases to describe yourself, those messages will also become a part of your memory, helping you to achieve your goals and increase your level of happiness.[3] You will learn more about this growth process later in this chapter.

Real Self

real self
The way you really are when nobody is around to approve or disapprove.

The **real self** is you as you really are, when nobody is around to approve or disapprove of your actions. Often this part of the self-concept is something that has to be discovered. Just as with the ideal self, what you think of yourself or what you present to others is not necessarily what is real; discovering your real self might take months, even years. This process, known as developing your *self-awareness*, is discussed in more detail in Chapter 3.

FOCUSING ON THE REAL AND IDEAL SELVES

Carl Rogers, a well-known psychologist, developed ideas about the self-concept in the mid to late 1900s that are still in use today. He said that your ideal self comes from the messages you receive from your parents and people around you about what you *should* be like.

The ideal self may be quite far apart from the real self, or the two may overlap to some extent. Rogers believed that people get little bits of information all the time about their real selves from their experiences in the world.

When the real self and ideal self are not very close, people feel bad about themselves. They can become depressed and unhappy and can have a lowered opinion of themselves. Rogers believed that in order to have a healthy self-concept, people need to work on making the ideal

Signs of High Self-Esteem

Clinical psychologist Thomas D. Yarnell has listed "15 Signs of High Self-Esteem." Go to **www.mhhe.com/lamberton4e** for a link to his Web site. Read through the signs on the Web site and make note of those signs that you believe are true for you. Which statement do you think may not be true for you? What will you do in order to raise your self-esteem in those particular areas? How will these changes affect your self-esteem?

and real selves much closer. This can be done by paying more attention to messages about one's real self, adjusting one's ideal self to fit the reality, and working up to a more realistic and attainable ideal.

PLEASING YOURSELF AND PLEASING OTHERS

Many people derive purpose from pleasing others. In American society, women often fall into this pattern of behavior even more than men. According to psychologist and author Mary Pipher, girls grow up in American culture surrounded by media messages that they are valued for their physical appearance, while their intelligence and other qualities are devalued. Girls then blame themselves for not being pretty enough, and their self-concept can be damaged in the process.[4]

Having a healthy self-concept means not allowing yourself to be a slave to other people's opinions. On the other hand, maybe you've known someone who honestly didn't care about what others thought of him or her. This individual was probably a bit hard to get used to. You may find it a bit uncomfortable to be around people who don't *need* anyone to like them, perhaps because most people would expect others to share their need for acceptance.

Balancing a need to nurture yourself with other people's needs to be accepted and liked is very important. When your self-concept is set and stable at a comfortable level, you will find that knowing and taking care of the "real you" will be quite possible without threatening others.[5]

WHAT IS SELF-ESTEEM?

Self-concept is closely tied to self-esteem; however, they don't mean exactly the same thing. Anyone in a situation such as Lena's in the opening vignette may discover two important concepts. First, many people don't feel as good about themselves as they should. Second, most individuals respond better to situations and to other people who help,

BALANCING YOUR NEEDS AND OTHERS' NEEDS

A crucial factor to a healthy self-concept and self-esteem is balancing your needs with others'. In a culture that values selflessness, and in jobs that require frequent caregiving, this can be a challenge. *What are ways to maintain healthy self-esteem while caring for others' needs?*

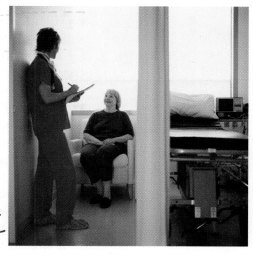

rather than hurt, the good feelings they have about themselves—feelings that people need to function well in business and in life. You may have had a similar experience in a new job or social situation. Everyone has probably felt this way at one time or another!

Have you ever met someone you just did not like, no matter how long you knew him or her? Most people have. If you were to look carefully, you would probably see one of two reasons for this dislike. Either you and the problem person had a real *personality clash* or that person simply *did not like himself or herself.* Disliking oneself is an indication of low self-esteem. **Self-esteem** can be defined as the extent to which an individual believes him- or herself to be capable, sufficient, and worthy.[6] It is the regard people hold for themselves as part of their self-concept.

Self-esteem is usually described as high or low. But the reality is that our self-esteem falls along a scale, from high to moderate to low. Higher self-esteem is healthy self-esteem. Because low self-esteem poses the biggest problem for human relations both in the workplace and in personal life, the rest of this chapter focuses on how to raise low self-esteem.

Liking and accepting yourself is one of the most important skills you can learn in life. All of the relationships you have with other people are affected by the way you see yourself, accept or reject yourself, and assume others feel about you. All of these factors combine to create your self-esteem.

Research shows that people with low self-esteem have more emotional problems than others do,[7] and that low self-esteem is widespread. When people compare themselves with others, they sometimes feel they don't *measure up.* You may feel this way at times, and you may think that you are the only one—but after asking others, you will find that this feeling of not measuring up is quite common.

You might wonder why some people brag about themselves. Most people who always need to tell about their accomplishments are actually **compensating** in some way for low self-esteem. Another form of compensating is when people focus on a single strength (such as good looks, mental ability, or athletic skills) to make up for their overall bad feelings about themselves. These feelings are also called **lower self-worth.** No matter how hard most people work at exercising those special abilities, many find that after months and years of trying, they still have lower self-worth.

In other words, these people are motivated by their own **lower self-esteem.** They excel in one or more areas of their lives in an unsuccessful attempt to overcome their low self-worth and find happiness. Wouldn't it feel better, though, to be motivated by something positive instead? People who have healthy feelings about themselves, or **higher self-esteem,** are more likely to succeed at their personal goals, career goals, and even more important, at *life.* They are not motivated by a need to compensate, but by a desire to see their dreams and goals achieved.

---

more about...

Compensating is a psychological defense mechanism people may use to reduce embarrassment, shame, anxiety, guilt, or other negative emotions that arise internally when facing unpleasant truths.

---

self-esteem
The regard in which an individual holds himself or herself.

compensating
The use of a strength to make up for a real or perceived weakness.

lower self-worth
Occurs when an individual believes himself or herself to have little value to offer the world.

lower self-esteem
Occurs when individuals are unable to see themselves as capable, sufficient, or worthy.

higher self-esteem
Occurs when people have healthy feelings about themselves and are therefore more likely to succeed in personal goals and career goals.

Raising Individual Self-Esteem

The La Belle Foundation is a self-described learning foundation to facilitate and implement the raising of individual self-esteem. Go to **www.mhhe.com/lamberton4e** to visit its Web site and link to three topics that interest you. Summarize any new information you learned from this foundation.

People with higher self-esteem believe in themselves and believe they can reach these goals. No matter what your occupational experiences are or how your career goals change, with a healthy self-esteem the experiences will be worthwhile and the changes usually successful.

SELF-ESTEEM AND WORK PERFORMANCE

Business success depends greatly on one's level of self-esteem. Both customers and employees quickly sense a businessperson's level of self-esteem. Positive self-esteem is often the key factor that separates success from failure. If you believe you are *good enough to succeed,* your chances of success are much stronger than they would be without such a belief.

Psychological research finds that people with lower self-esteem are more likely to experience anxiety, depression, irritability, aggression, feelings of resentment and alienation, unhappiness, insomnia, and other problems.[8] When people are experiencing these conditions, their work performance is bound to suffer. People with lower self-esteem also may feel awkward in social settings, including the workplace, and may feel self-conscious and vulnerable to rejection. Lower self-esteem is also associated with low job satisfaction and has even been linked to a higher likelihood of unemployment. People with lower self-esteem often work with little enthusiasm or commitment. In contrast, when an employee feels positive about his or her ability to compete and make a worthwhile contribution, work performance is usually higher.

A person with healthy self-esteem will be open and ready for new experiences. On the job, this readiness translates into usefulness and adaptability. When such people tackle problems, they tend to be more objective and constructive because they do not fear that their ideas will be rejected. Because employees with higher self-esteem like themselves, they can more readily accept their co-workers and take criticism from

SELF-ESTEEM AT WORK

Customers and co-workers can detect high or low self-esteem in employees. If your self-esteem is high, it will show in your body language, communication skills, and ability to handle setbacks and criticism. *How can you develop high self-esteem?*

Bob feels that he is not very intelligent, and he has a hard time keeping up with the new technology in his job and his daily life. This causes him to feel lower self-worth overall. At the same time, he just designed (on paper, without the help of a computer) and built a beautiful cedar deck for his home. He tells his wife, "You and the kids may be good on the computer, but I'm good at building things we need. I'll do the 'hands' stuff, and you can do the 'head' stuff." Bob feels high self-efficacy for his woodworking skills, even though he may feel lower self-worth overall.

others in their work team. All of these qualities make the person with healthy self-esteem a more valuable—and more satisfied—employee.

TYPES OF SELF-ESTEEM

self-efficacy

The confidence an individual has in his or her ability to deal with problems when they occur.

Currently, researchers describe two different types of self-esteem: (1) feelings, either positive or negative, about self-worth, and (2) confidence in the ability to deal with problems when they happen, often called **self-efficacy.** The first type has to do with how you feel about yourself when you are alone. The second type has to do with actions, problem solving, and the ability to succeed at particular tasks. Your self-esteem may be stronger in one of these areas than in others.

ORIGINS OF SELF-ESTEEM

more about...

Carl Rogers (1902–1987) revolutionized the way psychologists thought of therapy. He believed clients understood their own problems and experiences, and that the therapist's role was that of a consultant in assisting client treatment.

Where does your self-esteem come from? As with nearly all of the major influences in life, it starts to develop in early childhood from messages we receive from parents and others around us. According to well-known psychologist Carl Rogers, the sense of self is a guiding principle that structures the personality. Though inborn, the sense of self is shaped by many outside forces. In young children, self-esteem is just a reflection of the esteem that parents and others have for the child; it develops as children react to the ways that important people treat them. During childhood, parents are the most important people among those shaping self-esteem. Older children and adolescents are also influenced by teachers, coaches, friends, classmates, siblings, neighbors, and others who build up (or damage) their self-esteem.[9]

unconditional positive regard

The acceptance of individuals as worthy and valuable regardless of their behavior.

When your parents and other important people show you **unconditional positive regard,** or accept you no matter what your behavior may be at the moment, then you are likely to develop a healthy self-esteem. For example, a parent shows unconditional positive regard when he says, "Ashley, I want you to know that I love you and I'm proud of you, but the way you were teasing that little girl on the playground just now was not okay with me."

A four-year-old girl spends 20 minutes in the bathroom, using her mother's best makeup trying to make herself as beautiful as her mommy. When her mother discovers her, though, she is anything but happy. "Emmy, no! Why are you getting into my things?" she yells. "You're a bad girl!" When Emmy cries, she does so from fear of her mother's anger, and confusion at her mother's reaction to what she thought was a great idea.

When parents show children **conditional positive regard,** accepting their children only when they behave the way they want, then children may not develop a healthy self-esteem. Children may have a hard time understanding just what parents want from them, and they may end up believing that they are bad people who can't do anything right. They may be puzzled by the apparent double-talk that comes from their parents: parents react to behaviors that children think are good by labeling them either good or bad, which can be confusing to children. See Figure 2.2.

Parents frequently remind children that they aren't perfect and they aren't what they should be. With the best of intentions, they attempt to improve their children's behavior by comparing them with others. What happens is that these children find out that there are other children who do things better than they can, who in some way please adults more. From childhood onward, then, people learn to compare themselves with others and adapt their behavior around others' reactions to them—and react to the ways that all of this affects their self-esteem.

You may have had employers or supervisors who treated you with this same conditional positive regard: only treating you kindly or respectfully when you acted in the way that pleased them. They may have scolded you (even in front of others), or compared you disapprovingly with another, "better" employee.

This simple truth was first discovered by psychologist Alfred Adler, who like Rogers was another pioneer in the area of self and personality.

> **conditional positive regard**
> Acceptance of individuals as worthy only when they behave in a certain way.

figure 2.2

THE ORIGINS OF SELF-ESTEEM

Psychologist Carl Rogers believed that the self-esteem of a child depends on the acceptance of the parents. *How can a parent influence a child's self-esteem?*

37

Adler believed that the main motivation for everything people do, including efforts toward a successful career, is to get away from a deep childhood-based feeling that they are not as good as they should be—that they are not perfect. "In comparison with unattainable ideal perfection," he wrote, "the individual is continuously filled by an inferiority feeling and motivated by it."[10] Again, this is compensating for low self-worth by trying to succeed in other areas of life. An even more dramatic statement by Adler, who coined the term *inferiority complex,* is: "To be a human being means to feel oneself inferior."[11]

If Adler is even partly right, you can see just how important self-esteem must be to every part of life. While you read the rest of this book, keep in mind this important idea: *If you can improve in just one area—liking yourself better—you can improve in all other areas of human relations*. With a healthy self-concept and high self-esteem, you can become an effective manager of other people; in any area of life, you can become someone whom others listen to and respect. Most important, you can become a happy, contented person who is able to reduce harmful stress and solve problems.

more about...

Alfred Adler (1870–1937) developed theories about the inferiority complex and about compensation for feelings of deficiency compared with others. He also coined the term *lifestyle* (a style of life in which people strive to succeed in their strengths).

« « **STRATEGIES FOR SUCCESS**

2.1 Steps Toward Achieving Higher Self-Esteem

1. Learn to accept yourself.
2. Develop an internal locus of control.
3. Develop a winning skill.
4. Study confident people.
5. Read biographies of people you admire.
6. Make a list of your greatest talents.
7. Stop procrastinating.
8. Find a mentor.
9. Avoid surface analysis of yourself and others.
10. Use positive self-talk.
11. Don't forget the needs of others.

The following suggestions should be a great help in creating a better, healthier self-concept and higher self-esteem.

1. **Learn to accept yourself.** Don't feel that you have to be like someone else. Don't dwell on the past, but instead remember that the past does not equal the future. Avoid thinking that you should become your ideal self right now. That ideal is something to work toward for the future. Here, in the present, you are okay. Self-acceptance means learning to believe in your heart that you are valuable, and that your differences from others are more a plus than a minus. Differences are what make everyone so interesting!

2. **Develop an internal locus of control.** Julian Rotter, an influential psychologist, describes the **locus of control** as the perceived center of control over the events in people's lives. People with an **internal locus of control** feel that they are in control of events in their own lives and have more of a *take-charge* attitude. Rotter and others also believe that an internal locus of control is related to both higher self-esteem and better physical health.[12] On the other hand, people with an **external locus of control** feel that the world is happening to them, and that they have no control over the events in their lives.

To go back to the earlier example of Sarah, the student with a low exam score, if she has an *internal* locus of control, she might say, "I should have studied instead of watching videos all night with my roommates. Next time I'll do better." If she has an *external* locus of control, she might say, "Those questions were all too tricky. I can't help it if all the questions came from the chapters that I didn't understand. The instructor is probably just out to get me, anyway. I don't think she likes me."

3. **Develop a winning skill.** If you have a special hobby or interest, spend some time cultivating that skill. Developing these abilities puts focus on your positive qualities and takes focus away from the negative. This adds to your self-efficacy. Also, developing one area will teach you to focus on achievements, which is necessary for growth. And success in one area often "spills over" into other areas. Finally, you'll begin to feel more **self-respect**. Don't let a day go by without doing something that you can do very well.

4. **Study confident people.** Study those who seem to have strong self-esteem. Watch for things you could do to learn to like yourself better. Such behaviors might include ways of dealing with negative responses from other people, daily habits, or even ways of looking at others while talking. Remember Step 1. You do not need to be *just like* anyone else; in fact, losing your identity can destroy your self-esteem. However, you can learn skills from others that you can apply to your own life.

5. **Read biographies of people you admire,** or rent videos on the lives of successful people. You'll be amazed at how many self-esteem hints you can pick up from a good biography. While you are reading or watching, notice any misfortunes the successful person had to overcome—especially those that attacked his or her self-esteem. Try to put yourself in the situation and see yourself meeting the challenge.

While you are following the success stories of others, try not to get carried away in just admiring them. Start to think of healthy self-esteem as something that you already have. You *do* have it; it may just be out of focus, or you may be out of touch with it. See yourself when reading or watching biographies as discovering a lost treasure—your self-worth.[13]

6. **Make a list of your greatest talents.** If you draw a blank, ask someone close to you—a friend, family member, or significant other—to help you start

---

locus of control
The name given to the amount of control you feel you have over events that happen to you.

internal locus of control
Occurs in people who feel they are in control of the events in their own lives.

external locus of control
This occurs in people who feel they have no control of the events in their lives.

self-respect
Positive self-image with high self-esteem.

Julian Rotter (1916–) refined social learning theory to say that personality comes from an interaction of the individual with his or her environment. People develop internal or external explanations for control because of experiences.

more about...

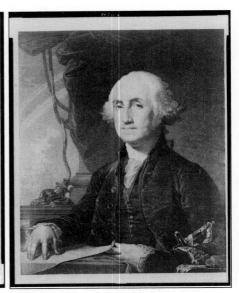

LOOK TO HISTORY

Eleanor Roosevelt, Martin Luther King Jr., and George Washington are three great examples of admirable people in history. *Whom do you admire that you would like to learn more about?*

PROCRASTINATION IS A TIME KILLER

Many people have the best of intentions, but putting off tasks is often an easy thing to do. *What strategies can you use to avoid the procrastination trap?*

the list. Others will often see your good points, talents, and abilities more clearly than you see them.

Once you have written the list, consider each talent as a section of your new self-concept. Put the talents you can develop with the least effort at the top of the list. Self-esteem is amazing in the way it reacts with emotions: the entire way you feel about yourself can improve or deteriorate based on little things. This step allows you to let these little things help rather than hurt you.

7. **Stop procrastinating.** If you honestly feel you never put things off too long, you can skip this section. Most people, though, tend to procrastinate, and procrastination can hurt self-esteem a great deal. When you are not working toward goals, this can easily bring your self-esteem even lower.

Some people think of procrastinators as lazy people. Actually, many very hard workers are terrible procrastinators. To overcome this common problem, identify the emotions that are blocking you from action. Although several emotions are often involved, the most important ones are fear and pain—or fear *of* pain—associated in some way with putting off the task. Once you realize that fear and avoidance of pain are involved, you can look more closely at the task and figure out what it is about it that seems painful or scary.

Getting tasks completed will give you a feeling of being "on top of things," which is very important to high self-esteem. If you've been meaning to do something about your procrastinating, don't put that off, too![14]

8. **Find a mentor.** A **mentor** is someone who will walk you through experiences that are new to you, but that he or she has already been through. True mentoring involves two people communicating well, one mostly teaching and the other mostly learning. If you find someone who will work with you in this way, you've discovered an excellent method of building self-esteem.

Mentors, though, are not always available. The next best person is a **role model.** A role model is someone you can look to for guidance by example, but who isn't necessarily actively interacting with you. Such a person can help you, although you are doing most or all of the work.

Remember that both role models and mentors are people who will help you be a better you. Once again, don't lose your identity in the process of adopting their habits. You need to find success on your own strengths.

9. **Avoid surface analysis of yourself and others.** Surface analysis means looking only at the apparent rather than underlying issues of life. Remember that people around you who seem controlled and even smug could be fighting back pure panic or depression. In his best-selling books *The Seven Habits of Highly Effective People* and *The 8th Habit,* author and psychologist Stephen Covey talks about the power of being able to see others, and yourself, in a new light—by finally understanding the underlying realities.[15]

10. **Use positive self-talk.** For generations, schoolchildren have used the proverb: "Sticks and stones may break my bones, but words can never hurt me." Teachers and parents have also taught this saying to children to help them overcome the bad feelings caused by name-calling and teasing. The sad truth, though, is that words *can* and *do* hurt, and they even cause permanent damage.

The flip side is that words are also powerful healers. The way you talk to others and to yourself about yourself can be a strong force for change in your life. **Positive self-talk** means telling your subconscious mind that you are a good person and doing fine.[16]

When using positive self-talk, don't use sentences like, "I want to be a great success." You might ask, why not? Doesn't that statement sound positive? Although it's much better than "I want to be a big failure," it can be improved in two ways. First, change "great success" to "great success at self-control," "great success at my retail sales job," "great success at bowling," or whatever specific goal you have. In other words, be specific rather than general. Second, use a present tense verb form. Say, "I am a successful bowler," or whatever you specifically want to improve. (See Figure 2.3.) Why does this work? Because of what psychologists call the **self-fulfilling prophecy,** also referred to as the *power of self-suggestion.* This means that when you believe something strongly enough, it becomes a reality: by your beliefs and the actions that follow, you fulfill the prophecy or expectation you hold about your future behavior.

Positive Self-Talk: Self-Esteem Affirmations

- I am effective because I have high self-esteem.
- I influence my own future by planning and taking action to meet my goals.
- I am a success at many things, such as: (insert your own list here).
- I share my strengths with others.
- I am responsible for my own choices.
- I accepts my feelings and manage them effectively.
- I overcome obstacles to meet my goals.
- I succeed because I am persistent.
- I can achieve goals I set for myself or decide when to revise them.
- I alone decide what success means to me.

---

mentor

A person who acts as a guide or teacher for another, leading that person through experiences.

role model

A person to whom an individual can look to for guidance by example, but who isn't necessarily actively interacting with the individual.

positive self-talk

A popular method of building self-esteem by thinking and speaking positively about yourself.

self-fulfilling prophecy

Tendency for a prediction to actually occur once it is believed; for example, a victim believes that prejudice against him or her is true, and then fulfills it.

figure 2.3

SELF-ESTEEM AFFIRMATIONS

Why is it important for affirmations to be as specific as possible?

Source: Adapted from Patricia A. Doherty, "Affirmations for Self-Esteem" 1998.

Whenever you have a success in your journey toward better self-esteem, take pride in your achievement. Reward yourself. Acknowledge your progress without fear of exaggerating it. If it was a big deal to you, then it was a big deal! No one else's judgment of your progress is more important than your own, but don't allow your current and past achievements to be enough. If you make that mistake, you'll stop trying to improve yourself, and the daily trying is what will make your self-esteem grow in the long run.[17]

Self-fulfilling prophecies can come from your beliefs about yourself, and also from your "buy-in" or taking as fact the beliefs that others hold about you. The self-fulfilling prophecy can also lead to both positive and negative outcomes. In a real study with schoolchildren, Robert Rosenthal and Lenore Jacobson conducted a research project with schoolchildren in which they told the children's teachers that some of the children were "late bloomers" who would increase their performance significantly over the year. The children were never told of these positive expectations their teachers had for them. Over the course of the year, these children, who had been selected at random from the classroom, did in fact blossom and soar in their performance. Their increased performance was due to the different treatment they received from their teachers, who expected the best from them.[18] Many adults also allow others' opinions of them to affect their behavior. The stronger or higher a person's self-esteem is, the weaker the effect other people's negative statements will have on his or her behavior.

11. **Don't forget the needs of others.** Competitiveness can keep people from allowing others to achieve the same things they are achieving. If you have this level of competitiveness, get rid of it. When you are a manager or in any other position of leadership, remember the awesome power you have—for both good and bad—over the person who works for you. (Don't go overboard, though, in giving in to others' needs.)

With all this discussion about boosting one's own self-esteem with positive self-talk, it may be a natural assumption that we can easily boost the self-esteem of others just by saying positive things to them. After researchers found a link between self-esteem and academic achievement in schoolchildren, schools all over the United States set up self-esteem programs, believing that boosting a child's self-esteem would also boost grades. But do admiring teachers and strings of gold stars really have this effect? Perhaps the high self-esteem arose *after* the high achievement; in other words, maybe successes lead to greater self-esteem, rather than high self-esteem leading to achievement.

So, should we say positive things to others in an attempt to help build their self-esteem? Many of the self-esteem-building programs asked teachers to give out any praise, even when children have not succeeded or put in much effort. These programs tend not to be very successful. Children can usually tell the difference between hollow praise, and genuine remarks for a job well done or effort put forward toward a difficult task. Genuine positive feedback *does* seem to have the effect of boosting self-esteem. Insincere praise, however, may backfire and result in children not trusting adults to tell the truth. Most teachers (and other experts) today would encourage giving authentic praise, that is, only when it is deserved, rather than lavishing undeserved praise at every opportunity.[19] Adults as well as children can usually tell the difference between insincere flattery and

Tools for Building Self-Esteem

The University of Illinois provides brochures and online information on topics related to self-esteem. Link to its Web site for topics such as assertiveness, positive thinking, self-confidence, and shyness at **www.mhhe.com/lamberton4e.** Choose a topic and write a summary paragraph.

sincere praise. So, if you're going to say positive things in an effort to help boost self-esteem, the bottom line is to mean what you say![20]

 2.2 Steps toward Combating Low Self-Esteem by Defeating the Pathological Critic

1. Find its purpose.
2. Talk back.
3. Make this pathological critic totally useless.
4. Forgive yourself.

Psychologist Eugene Sagan believes that most people have a negative inner voice that attacks and negatively judges their worth. He calls this voice the **pathological critic.** This critic came from the "shoulds" that parents and other adults give children while they are young. You listen to the critic because it helps shape your identity and, ironically, can make you feel somewhat better in the short run because it helps you run from the problems or challenges you are faced with: it allows you to blow off tension or avoid rejection. In the long run, though, the critic does a great deal of damage.[21]

The pathological critic knows that people have four basic needs. Nearly everyone needs to feel:

- secure and unafraid.
- effective and competent in the world.
- accepted by parents, family, and significant others.
- a sense of basic worth and "OK-ness" in specific situations.[22]

People with lower self-esteem tend to fulfill these needs in totally different ways than people with higher self-esteem, and they will use the pathological critic as a method of dealing with negative situations. Since this is an *easy way out,* relying on the critic can become a lifelong habit.

Knowing that this critic exists is the first step in toning it down. Really knowing the critic requires that you are skilled at recognizing when it invades your world. You should be especially aware of what sort of touchy situations bring it out of hiding.

1. **Find its purpose.** Obviously, this voice you keep hearing is trying to hurt you; that's its general purpose. In each case, try to see what the *specific* purpose is.

> **pathological critic**
> A negative inner voice that attacks people and judges their worth negatively.

Matthew McKay and Patrick Fanning, authors of the book *Self-Esteem,* give some examples of this, such as exaggerating bad feelings now as a way of avoiding worse feelings later (such as rejection or pain), or reducing tension by preparing you for the worst.[23]

2. **Talk back.** Talking back to a voice that comes from within yourself might sound a bit odd, but much self-esteem building involves just that type of strategy. It involves looking at the negative messages that have hurt your self-esteem and talking back to their senders—forcefully. Psychologist Albert Ellis, whom you will learn more about in later chapters, refers to this process as *confronting your irrational beliefs.*[24] You might find that talking out loud will work most effectively, but speaking these thoughts in your mind can also work well. The main idea is to prevent negative messages from harming your self-esteem.

   The success of the talking-back strategy will depend on the strength of your will in combating this enemy. One suggestion is to make a forceful statement, worded in a way to help you feel anger, which can make the critic stop sending messages: "This is ridiculous; now cut it out." "Not true!" "Stop it!" "Get off my back!" Use whatever works for you personally. If this first step doesn't stop the voice, try moving to positive affirmations, such as the ones suggested earlier in the chapter under "positive self-talk."

3. **Make this pathological critic totally useless.** You can do this by providing an avenue to fulfill all of the needs it is trying to fulfill for you. For example, the critic supposedly helps you block out a feeling of worthlessness by setting very high standards of perfection; but you end up feeling worse because you can never meet these standards. You can disarm the critic by separating your ideal self from your real self, thus becoming more realistic about what your goals really are and what they should be.

4. **Forgive yourself.** Once you have truly forgiven yourself for the fact that you are not perfect, you have taken perhaps the most important step toward healthy self-esteem. Remember that nobody else is perfect, either; why should you be the world's sole exception?

CHAPTER TWO SUMMARY

Chapter Summary by Learning Objectives

1. **Define self-concept.** Self-concept is the way you *conceive* of (or see) yourself; this view of yourself is the foundation of all your thoughts about yourself, including your self-esteem.

2. **Identify the four areas of the self-concept.** The self-concept is divided into four parts: the self-image, real self, looking-glass self, and ideal self. In a perfect world, all four would be one; in reality, people work to get the four together as much as possible.

3. **Describe the real and ideal selves.** The real self is you as you really are, when nobody is around to approve or disapprove of your actions. Often this part of the self-concept is something that has to

be discovered. The ideal self is your vision of your future self. When the real self and ideal self are not very close, people feel bad about themselves. They can become depressed and unhappy and can have a lowered opinion of themselves.

4. **Explain the importance of pleasing yourself and others.** Balancing a need to nurture yourself with other people's needs to be accepted and liked is very important. When your self-concept is set and stable at a comfortable level, you will find that knowing and taking care of the "real you" will be quite possible without threatening others.

5. **Define self-esteem.** Self-esteem can be defined as the extent to which an individual believes him- or herself to be capable, sufficient, and worthy. It is the regard people hold for themselves as part of their self-concept.

6. **Discuss the relationship between self-esteem and work performance.** In the workplace, high self-esteem usually separates success from failure. If you believe you are *capable enough to succeed,* your chances of success are much higher.

7. **Distinguish among different types of self-esteem.** The art of liking and accepting yourself is one of the most important things you can learn in life. Current self-esteem researchers have identified two types of self-esteem: self-worth—the value you place on yourself, and self-efficacy—your confidence in your own ability to deal with problems or tasks as they arise.

8. **Explain the origins of your self-esteem.** According to Carl Rogers, an inborn sense of self structures the personality from earliest childhood; this is affected by parents' unconditional or conditional positive regard. Alfred Adler said that everyone feels inferior to some degree, and people are motivated to do nearly all the things they do because of that common feeling.

key terms

compensating 34

conditional positive regard 37

external locus of control 39

higher self-esteem 34

ideal self 30

internal locus of control 39

locus of control 39

looking-glass self 31

lower self-esteem 34

lower self-worth 34

mentor 41

pathological critic 43

positive self-talk 41

real self 32

role model 41

self-concept 30

self-efficacy 36

self-esteem 34

self-fulfilling prophecy 41

self-image 32

self-respect 39

unconditional positive regard 36

1. What are the differences among self-concept, self-respect, and self-efficacy? Provide an example of each.

2. You are certain that your co-workers see you as a cranky, reclusive hermit. Actually, they think of you as a shy person who is quiet but nice to be around. How can this difference between self-concept and others' opinions exist side by side regarding the same person? Explain, using concepts from this chapter.

3. Imagine yourself back in the third grade. Your teacher is yelling at you for breaking the chalk while writing on the chalkboard: "Look at what you've done! You're such a bad student! Go back to your seat!" If you could explain the work of Carl Rogers to your teacher using this example, what would you say?

4. Do you ever find yourself compensating for a weakness you feel you have? For what behaviors are you compensating? Do you notice when other people compensate? Describe.

5. What specific skill or area of your self-concept needs work? Think of some examples of positive self-talk you could use to boost your self-esteem in this area.

6. Which would you rather have in your current job or profession, a mentor or a role model? Why? If you were mentoring a new employee in your field, what kinds of things would you say and do?

7. Two employees who are learning a new accounting system are talking about it. "It's no use," says the first. "Management is always dumping these new things on me that I can't learn." The second one replies, "We can learn this; it will just take a little practice. Come on, let's try it." According to Rotter, which employee has an *internal* locus of control, and which employee has an *external* locus of control? How will this likely affect each one's ability to learn the new system?

8. You are waiting for your appointment for an important job interview. A voice inside you shouts, "You're so stupid, lazy, and ugly! You'll never get this job!" Who is this voice? Why is it sending you these messages? What will you do to stop it?

9. Is an internal locus of control good to have in *all* situations? Can you think of a situation in which it would *not* be helpful to feel in complete control of your life? For example, when something truly terrible happens, such as a natural disaster or other tragedy, are you really in control of events? If you are not in control of events, what are you in control of in such a situation?

10. Some people say that when they were children, their parents lacked confidence in them and treated them with conditional (instead of unconditional) positive regard—and this treatment, rather than reducing their self-esteem, challenged them to work harder and succeed. Do you agree that such treatment, then, might be *good* instead of damaging to people's developing self-esteem? Explain.

11. As you might already be aware, some educators, politicians, and others in leadership positions have carried the self-esteem issue to extremes—far beyond what this chapter teaches. Some examples are removing any real competition from children so their self-esteem won't be threatened, praising people when they deserve anything but praise, and withholding discipline because any discipline might damage the child's fragile ego. Comment on this aspect of self-esteem awareness.

working it out 2.1

EXPLORING YOUR SELF-ESTEEM

School-to-Work Connection: Personal Qualities Skills
This scale was developed by Dr. Morris Rosenberg.
Instructions: Following is a list of statements dealing with your general feelings about yourself. Place a check mark under the answer with which you most agree.

	Strongly Agree	Agree	Disagree	Strongly Disagree
1. On the whole I am satisfied with myself.	X			
2. At times I think I am no good at all.		X		
3. I feel that I have a number of good qualities.	X			
4. I am able to do things as well as most other people.	X			
5. I feel I do not have much to be proud of.				X
6. I certainly feel useless at times.				X
7. I feel that I'm a person of worth, at least on an equal plane with others.	X			
8. I wish I could have more respect for myself.		X		
9. All in all, I am inclined to feel that I am a failure.				X
10. I take a positive attitude toward myself.	X			

To score these items, give yourself one point if you answered "Strongly Agree" or "Agree" for 1, 3, 4, 7, or 10. Give yourself one point if you answered "Disagree" or "Strongly Disagree" for 2, 5, 6, 8, or 9. Total your score. Ten indicates high self-esteem answers, while zero indicates low self-esteem answers.[25]

TESTING YOUR LOCUS OF CONTROL

School-to-Work Connection: Interpersonal Skills

Test whether your own locus of control is more internal or external by answering the following questions:

1. Do you believe that some people are just born lucky, while others are just born losers and there is nothing these people can do to change their lot in life? _____ yes __X__ no

2. Do you believe that skill and hard work are more important than luck? __X__ yes _____ no

3. Do you keep a good luck charm or have a good luck ritual? _____ yes __X__ no

4. When bad things happen to you, do you look for a cause and try to prevent the event from happening again? __X__ yes _____ no

5. Do you believe that good things happen to good people, while bad things happen to bad people? _____ yes __X__ no

6. Do you believe that if you try hard enough, things will turn out right? __X__ yes _____ no

7. Do you believe that fate determines what will happen, regardless of any planning for the future? _____ yes __X__ no

8. Do you believe that in the long run, people get the respect they deserve in the world? __X__ yes _____ no

9. Do you believe that no matter how hard you try, some things just never turn out right? __X__ yes _____ no

10. Do you believe that making a well-founded decision for the future is more important than believing in fate? __X__ yes _____ no

Scoring: If you answered yes to most odd-numbered questions and no to most even-numbered questions, you lean toward an external locus of control. If you answered no to most odd-numbered questions and yes to most even-numbered questions, you lean toward having an internal locus of control. Remember, though, that an internal/external locus of control cannot always be defined in black and white. Many people have a combination of these two that changes depending on the situation.

internet exercises

1. *Self-Assessment*

   The Self-Esteem Test lists questions related to self-esteem, with a scoring guide after you complete and submit the test. Go to **www.mhhe.com/lamberton4e** for the link to the Online Learning Center for this chapter. After opening the Internet site for the test (Queendom.com) open the link to "Attitudes & Lifestyle" tests. Take either the longer self-esteem test (79 questions) or the abridged test (10 questions). Once you have completed and scored your test, evaluate the aspects of your self-esteem. Ask yourself: What characteristics of my self-esteem can use some work? How can I work on these areas? Where might I look for help?

2. *Research and Write*

   What is resiliency, and how does it help build self-esteem? Link to the article "The Resiliency Route to Authentic Self-Esteem and Life Success" by Nan Henderson, found at **www.resiliency.com/htm/build.htm** and linked to the textbook Online Learning Center at **www.mhhe.com/lamberton4e**. Read the article and briefly summarize the main points. Then state your opinion: Do you agree with the author's views? According to the author, on what should you base praise, in order to build self-esteem? Does this view complement or contradict the information presented in the chapter? Explain.

3. *Research and Write*

   Low self-esteem is not just a problem with one's emotions; it has also been linked to brain health and activity over the long term. A study by researchers in Canada has found that people with low self-worth who were studied for 15 years suffered from greater memory loss and learning difficulties than people with higher self-esteem. These adults with low self-esteem actually experienced loss of brain size as well: their brains were up to a fifth smaller than those with higher self-esteem. The good news, according to scientist Dr. Sonia Lupien at McGill University in Montreal who found these effects, is that the effects of memory loss and difficulty with learning are reversible. Perform an Internet search for her research. Summarize her findings related to *reversing the effects* of low self-esteem on the brain and cognitive performance.[26]

4. *Self-Assess and Apply*

   Are you more of a green, a gold, a blue, or an orange? Take the "Follow Your True Colors" personality assessment, in use since 1979, to help you find a career that fits your personality style. Carolyn Kalil's Web site for this assessment is found through the course Web site at **www.mhhe.com/lamberton4e,** or link to it directly at **www.truecolorscareer.com/quiz.asp.** What did you learn about yourself?

Stage Fright

Julio Garcia was a young executive who had done very well with a business degree from a two-year college. Although he often felt overshadowed by his peers, Julio seemed to get along well unless he was asked to give an oral presentation. In the past couple of weeks, he had been asked—no, told—to give two 15-minute presentations.

As the day of torment approached, Julio found it increasingly difficult to sleep. When he finally did drop off to sleep, he woke up often, sometimes with his head pounding. During the wakeful times, he would imagine himself during the presentation, becoming tongue-tied and being forced to sit down because he couldn't go on. Then, the aftermath he pictured was even worse. He imagined the people he worked with laughing behind his back and ceasing to have any respect for him. In another of his often-repeated wide-awake nightmares, he did manage to get through the talk, but everyone thought it was simpleminded and boring. He could hear the voices of his colleagues as he walked through the halls at work. He had become the butt of their favorite jokes.

Finally, the day before the first presentation, Julio decided to see the company counselor. Although he felt ridiculous admitting what was happening to him, he realized that he needed to act or the worst would really happen. The counselor was really understanding. Julio found that just talking the problem out with her helped calm him down a bit. He was greatly relieved when she told him that dozens of people in the company had come to her with the same problem.

When Julio finally stood up speak, he did so with confidence. Although his presentation wasn't flawless, his hands didn't shake, and he kept the interest of the audience throughout the speech.. When Julio sat down, he felt a sense of newfound confidence. Somehow, he knew that however bad the public speaking experience might be in the future, it would never be even nearly as negative as it had been.

Case Study Questions

1. Let's say that you were Julio's counselor. What additional advice would you give him? Why?

2. Explain the role self-esteem played in this case.

3. If you get stage fright, what steps do you take to minimize its effects?

Jill, Self-Esteem, and the Job Search

Jill was unhappy with her job as a customer service representative for a company that did follow-up calls to customers of cars and other large consumer items. Many of her clients immediately assumed that she was a telemarketer as soon as they answered the phone. The negative reactions were getting her down. Worst of all, she had been letting the negativity affect her self-esteem.

As long as she could remember, Jill had wanted to do something creative in the field of marketing. She was especially interested in advertising. Although her friends would encourage her and express a belief in her abilities, Jill kept hearing from a part of herself that seemed to be telling her, "You can't do it. You don't have enough creative talent; your ideas are worthless. . ." and on and on.

Anita, one of Jill's best friends, was a successful advertising executive, working for a midsized company that specialized in magazine advertising. One day, Anita invited Jill to lunch supposedly to "talk about business." Anita had picked up on both Jill's ambitions and her self-doubt. "You know, Jill," she offered, "I've been concerned about that job of yours for quite a while. I see it taking you nowhere, when you have some real creative talents that a job like that just doesn't cultivate, in anyone."

"Well, what do you think about advertising for me? I'm a pretty fair artist, and I seem to have a sense of what appeals to customers; that's one thing I've learned from the dead-end job I have." Anita's answer was definite: "Jill, I think you'd be doing yourself and the rest of the world a disservice if you didn't get out there and at least give advertising a try."

Jill returned to work with a new perspective—and with some real optimism. Those persistent negative feelings were not so strong. That very week, she started searching for an opening in advertising. Within a month, she had landed a job with a local ad agency—and at a salary quite a bit higher than she had been getting. The most important change in Jill was her newfound motivation to succeed, no longer prevented by fear and low self-esteem.

Case Study Questions

1. Discuss the relationship of Anita's little "pep talk" and the self-fulfilling prophecy.

2. What was the source of the negative thoughts Jill had been fighting?

3. What steps does Jill need to take to make this new reality a permanent part of her life?

SELF-AWARENESS AND SELF-DISCLOSURE

In the Workplace: Campus Espresso

SITUATION

Jen and Laura were about to celebrate their fifth year in business. Their gourmet coffeehouse shop had become a very popular hangout for the undergraduate crowd in their small-college town. As the anniversary approached, it became more and more obvious to Jen that she and Laura, though

longtime friends, are seeing two different coffeeshops when they come to work each morning. Jen wants expansion. She is afraid that if Starbucks or another of the big chains were to come to town, Campus Espresso would be struggling to stay alive. Although Jen is dropping hints increasingly often, Laura just isn't "getting it."

LEARNING objectives

After studying this chapter, you will be able to:

1 | Define self-awareness.
2 | Explain how awareness-related barriers impact human relations.
3 | Use the Johari Window as a tool for self-understanding.
4 | Define self-disclosure.
5 | List the outcomes of failing to self-disclose.
6 | Understand the five major levels of communication as they relate to disclosure.
7 | Discuss the impact of making assumptions regarding other people.
8 | Explain the risk factor of disclosure.

STRATEGIES FOR SUCCESS

Strategy 3.1   Know When to Stop

Strategy 3.2   Pay Attention to Differences

Strategy 3.3   Facing Fear of Self-Disclosure

DISCOVERY

"Why don't you just tell her exactly what you feel—in detail?" Jen's boyfriend asked.

"What would that do?" Jen replied. "Laura already seems to understand my vision for this place. What she doesn't see is the *intensity* of how I feel. Why can't she see how much she is stressing me out?"

"Jen, you need to have a talk with her right away."

"Yes, I'll talk to her first thing tomorrow morning. I just don't understand why my dearest friend isn't responding to my feelings."

THINK ABOUT IT

Do you know anyone like Jen, who can't understand why others fail to read her feelings, or like Laura, who isn't receiving messages that other people are convinced they are sending?

self-awareness
self-awareness
The ability to see yourself realistically, without a great deal of difference between what you are and how you assume others see you.

self-disclosure
The ability to let another person know what is real about your thoughts, desires, and feelings.

WHAT IS SELF-AWARENESS?

The key issues between Jen and Laura are **self-awareness** and **self-disclosure**—two of the most important elements in human relations. Chapter 2 established the need that people have to be themselves. This means that people need to act in a way that is consistent with their true thoughts and feelings. Often, people refuse to reveal what is true and real about themselves, instead revealing only as much as feels comfortable. A goal of this chapter is to show how people can learn to be and to express their genuine selves.

The Scottish poet Robert Burns was sitting in church one Sunday morning in 1786. In Burns's era Sunday dress was very formal, and the lady in front of him was wearing an elaborate hat with so many plumes that Burns couldn't see the pulpit. Since the back of her head was all he could see, he started looking closely. Soon he noticed a louse crawling from beneath her hat. As Burns watched, the louse walked over a ribbon, across a bow, and onto one of the flowers that decorated the hat. He then wrote the poem "To a Louse" about the blindness this woman—and many others—have in their self-awareness. The poem (translated into American English from Scottish dialect) "To a Louse" ends like this: Oh, would some power the gift give us, To see ourselves as others see us. It would from many a blunder free us.

Chapter 2 introduced the *looking-glass self as* part of the self-concept. Quite simply, better self-awareness means roughly the same thing as *developing a better looking-glass self.* Without self-awareness, you will be unable to show your true self or expect others to do the same.

AWARENESS-RELATED BARRIERS TO EFFECTIVE HUMAN RELATIONS

Many people spend much of their lives building walls. In other words, they develop traits such as secrecy, dishonesty, or other defenses to prevent people from determining their true thoughts and motives. These people often believe that if these walls are not there, catastrophes such as rejection and loneliness will result. Also, once the walls are in place, the people who built them often forget they are there. They wonder why others often misunderstand them.[1]

Author Marie Lindquist quotes a friend: "I used to open my father's drawer and just stand there breathing. The drawer, to me, held all the smells of a grown man—after-shave, tobacco, chalky tablets for ulcers. A few years ago, I opened my own drawer and found all the same smells. Does that mean I'm grown-up at last? To the outside world, I guess I am. I have a house,

more about...

"**Self-awareness** involves knowing how your values, beliefs, assumptions, attitudes, and preferences affect your behavior."

—Robert E. Levasseur

Source: Robert E. Levasseur, "People Skills: Self-Awareness—A Critical Skill for MS/OR Professionals," *Interfaces* 21 (January/ February 1991), pp. 130–131.

Juanita's parents—especially her father—wanted badly for Juanita to become a medical doctor, preferably a pediatrician like her mother. Without knowing they were doing it, they gave nonverbal cues throughout childhood, letting her know how important their choice for her career was to be. Of course, they let her know in more direct ways as well. As is often the case, Juanita went along with her parents' wishes, excelling in science courses, and eventually entering medical school. The closer Juanita came to her goal, the more frustrated she became with her choices. Finally one day, she admitted to herself that she wanted to be a wildlife biologist, and that this field fascinated her vastly more than medicine did. When she finally entered that field and experienced the subsequent satisfaction, she became aware of the extent to which she had been allowing someone else to make her important life choices for her.

a family. I pay my bills and handle my responsibilities, but inside I don't feel finished at all."[2] Many people feel like the person in the story: their feeling of completion never arrives.

Do you know anyone like Juanita in the Real World Example above? Do you know people who are currently pursuing goals to impress others or to please parents? What could you say to people like Juanita that would increase their self-awareness?

THE JOHARI WINDOW

Have you ever said a key word or phrase that asked a disturbing question, or simply touched another person's sense of humor? Suddenly, you saw a frown, rolled eyes, or a chuckle—some reaction that showed a side of the other person that you had never seen before. Everyone has these different parts, or selves. If you are like most people, you are one person to your boss, another to your family, another to your close friends, and still another to strangers. Which one is the *real* you?[3]

Everyone shares four ways of relating to others: the open (or public) side, the blind side, the hidden side, and the unknown side. These are illustrated by the panes in the **Johari Window** (see Figures 3.1 and 3.2). These separate responses deal with two factors: people's understanding of themselves and the way they interact with others based on that level of understanding.[4] None of these panes will necessarily remain the same size for all of your relationships or interpersonal encounters.

Johari Window

A composite of four panes that shows you ways of relating to others: the open, blind, hidden, and unknown.

The Open Pane

This upper-left pane of the Johari Window contains information that you know about yourself and have no reason to hide from most people. This pane will become larger as a friendship develops. You will likely show more and more of yourself to the other person until the **open pane** begins to resemble the one in Figure 3.2. If you become friends with

open pane

The pane in the Johari Window that contains information that you know about yourself and that you have no reason to hide.

Self-Awareness and Social Awareness

Go to **www.self-creation.com/awareness.** On the "Overview" page, click on the other four titles one at a time: "Using Questions," "Question Tips," and "The Questions." Click first on **each title,** then on "social awareness," reading each short article carefully. (You may also access this Web site through **www.mhhe.com/lamberton4e.**)

Then, answer the following questions:

1. Has answering these questions to the best of your ability aided in your understanding of your own self-awareness issues—assuming you have any? Explain.

2. Of the following areas, in which one do you feel you did the *best* (wrote the most positive statements)? Which one is your worst? Why? (Social, Emotional, Significant Relationship, Spiritual/Ethical, Financial, Career)

figure 3.1

THE JOHARI WINDOW

This figure illustrates four ways people relate to one another. The Johari Window is divided into four "panes": the open pane, the blind pane, the hidden pane, and the unknown pane. It deals with both our understanding of ourselves and the way we interact with others. *Does everyone have all four of these "panes" of perception? Do you?*

Source: Joseph Luft, *Group Process: Introduction to Group Dynamics* (Palo Alto, CA: National Press, 1970).

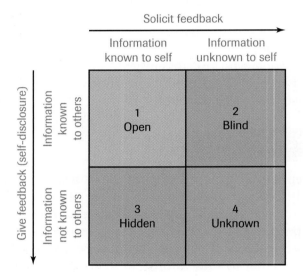

someone and she tells you her personal history and the way she views things, she is enlarging her open pane—at least in her relationship with you. The pane size increases with your desire to be known and understood.

Sometimes the act of showing more and more of your inner feelings can be done unwisely, as you will read later in this chapter. Usually, though, the more information that you mutually share with a friend, the more productively that relationship is likely to develop.

hidden pane

The pane in the Johari Window that contains information and feelings that you are hiding from other people.

The Hidden Pane

The **hidden pane** of the Johari Window contains information and feelings that you are aware of but hide from other people. People possess a great deal of private information, including information that they are

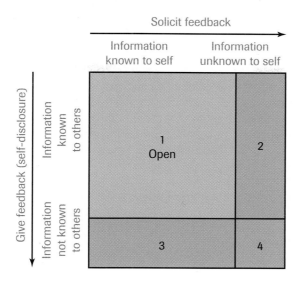

figure 3.2

THE JOHARI WINDOW AFTER ESTABLISHED RELATIONSHIP

The Johari Window allows for sharing personal information. *How does the open pane expand?*

Source: Joseph Luft, *Group Process: Introduction to Group Dynamics* (Palo Alto, CA: National Press, 1970).

ashamed of or afraid to share with others, such as things they regret or consider failures. If you are shy or secretive, your hidden pane might be quite large. As a close relationship develops and the open pane grows bigger, the hidden pane will become smaller. Increased trust in someone will help you decrease the size of the hidden pane. You will withhold fewer and fewer details about yourself.

The Blind Pane

This pane contains everything about you that other people can see but you can't. This pane can be disturbing to people who would rather not believe that others see personality traits that they don't see in themselves. Many people, like the woman in the Robert Burns poem, have blind spots they would be shocked to discover.

The **blind pane** can hide good qualities in people as well as bad traits. This pane can shrink if you heed another person's encouragement and allow yourself to look into your blind areas to a greater extent.

blind pane

The pane in the Johari Window that contains everything other people can see about you, but you can't see about yourself.

The Unknown Pane

If the blind pane can be frightening, the **unknown pane** is probably even more so because it deals with areas that nobody—yourself, your friends, or your family—can see. The unknown pane can include childhood memories that people block out for various reasons. In this pane, people also retain the unspoken attitudes and prejudices of their parents—feelings that they may have acted out but never actually said.[5] This pane contains all of the experiences, feelings, fantasies, and possibilities that people **repress.** It can be reduced in size by developing a close friendship.

unknown pane

The pane of the Johari Window that contains unknown talents, abilities, and attitudes, as well as forgotten and repressed experiences, emotions, and possibilities.

repress

To block off memories that may cause pain, embarrassment, or guilt.

John had never played a musical instrument until he entered college and became roommates with an accomplished guitarist. After hearing his roommate practice the guitar several times, John asked if he could play. His roommate was surprised at how easily John picked up the basic chords. He complimented John several times, which surprised John because he didn't think he played very well.

The next day John rented a guitar and bought a book of guitar chords at a music store. John made time every day to practice the guitar. After a few weeks, John discovered that he could play some of his favorite songs by ear. He went back to the music store and bought his own guitar and has played it for his own enjoyment ever since. The feedback from his roommate reduced the size of John's blind pane.

For the same reason, this can be an even more exciting pane than the blind pane. Information and emotions that are repressed often come out in dreams, fantasies, and even slips of the tongue. Once these desires or fears are recognized, the person can then open avenues of self-knowledge and make changes in his or her life.

Dreams and slips of the tongue are not the only ways to learn your underlying thoughts: The unknown pane can also be made smaller by a developing friendship. Feedback from the right person can trigger information that has been unexamined. The process can be painful, but it is usually rewarding if you communicate with friends who truly care about you. Sincere friendship is an important aid to self-awareness at any level.

SELF-DISCLOSURE IS A PART OF EVERY RELATIONSHIP

How much we choose to disclose influences the closeness of our relationships. *How does your disclosure differ depending on the people in your life?*

WHAT IS SELF-DISCLOSURE?

Self-disclosure is letting another person know your real thoughts, desires, and feelings. When people say that someone *is real* or *seems real* (or genuine, authentic, or legitimate), they are usually saying that the person is good at self-disclosure.

Self-disclosure allows people to know themselves and those around them better. Openness and honesty become especially important in the workplace. Since most people spend the majority of their days at work, they need to understand themselves and others so those hours are meaningful and productive.

Why do people pull back from letting others know what they are like? Very often, people justify withholding the truth for legitimate reasons. Perhaps you feel the need to get along with others and have them like you, or you avoid telling the truth to protect other people's feelings. If for these reasons you choose not

What Is Trust?

Go to **www.coping.org/growth/trust.htm.** (Or you may go to the link at **www
.mhhe.com/lamberton4e.**) Under "Contents," find "What Is Trust?" Go through the
entire exercise. Do you think that this type of trust-building can help your self-disclosure
level? If so, how? If not, why not?

to *overdisclose,* you might be correct. However,
in most cases, people withhold information in
order to:

- feel all-powerful.
- control the feelings of others.
- feel superior to those around them.
- believe that they are perfect.
- have everyone's approval.
- feel safe from people who might challenge
  them.
- deny that they have problems.
- avoid the fear that they aren't lovable.
- avoid feelings of inadequacy.[6]

Will reasons like these allow people to develop emotionally, become
happy, and work better with others? Probably not.

Other reasons behind avoiding disclosure stem
from childhood experiences. Many people learn
very early to shut away large parts of themselves
in the hidden pane. Were you ever shamed or
punished during childhood for showing pride,
anger, or some other emotion? You may have
been taught to hide strong emotions from others. If a young child's emotions or opinions are
silenced, those emotions can remain hidden for
the rest of that person's life.[7]

For years, psychologists have shown that
most people in this culture excessively tend to
adapt their behavior to the audience or listener
they are communicating with.[8] Americans have come nearly to glorify
the "nice person," that is, somebody who doesn't threaten the listener
and who makes others feel approved of and comfortable. However, what

---

more about...

Self-Disclosure

Psychologist Frederick Perls wrote that the
purpose of **self-disclosure** is to own one's
own feelings, claiming one's own secrets in a
way that allows people to be aware of them and
content in them.

Source: Fritz Perls, Ralph Hefferline, and Paul Goodman,
Gestalt Therapy (New York: Random House, 1988), p. 1120.

---

more about...

Reasons to Self-Disclose

"Secrets diminish self-respect; they foster
paranoia, and they make it impossible to
have honest and open communication."

Source: Karen Casey and Martha Vanceburg, *The
Promise of a New Day* (San Francisco: Harper & Row,
1985), p. 243.

A few years ago, Marisol found herself in a dilemma: she could enter a full-time MBA program at a high-ranking university or accept a job offer from a local respected company. Although she liked the idea of getting an MBA early in her career, she was unsure about giving up the security of the job offer. She knew that her family would criticize her if she did.

At the same time, she started having dreams of boredom and a feeling of imprisonment. Marisol then knew that her deepest fear—job unhappiness—was surfacing because of this dilemma. Finally, she entered the MBA program and graduated. In an ironic twist, she was offered a job at the same local company as before, supervising the position she was originally offered. Marisol had discovered traits in the unknown pane of her Johari Window.

price has been paid for this behavior preference? Should anyone avoid self-disclosure constantly just to appear "nice"?

OUTCOMES OF FAILING TO SELF-DISCLOSE

To understand why people should self-disclose, you can examine the *negative* things that can happen to you when you *don't*. Has a deep, dark secret ever gotten the better of you? You might have thought that the secret was causing you pain, but perhaps the pain was coming from the effort of holding it inside.

Some of the more common results of failing to self-disclose are shown in Figure 3.3. They include the following:[9]

1. *Loss of relationships with others.* When you withhold important parts of yourself, you untie the common thread that binds you to others, creating an "isolation booth" for yourself. When the basic human need to interrelate with others is gone, loneliness and isolation are often the result.

   When you share something about yourself, a relationship grows a little at a time. When there is little or no self-disclosure, the

figure 3.3

FOUR OUTCOMES OF FAILING TO SELF-DISCLOSE

Failing to self-disclose may result in the loss of relationships with others, the slowdown of personal growth, the waste of time and energy, and the loss of a sense of identity. *How can your identity be affected when you refuse to self-disclose?*

Source: Marie Lundquist, *Holding Back: Why We Hide the Truth About Ourselves* (New York: Harper & Row, 1988), pp. 27–33. Also see John Powell, *Why Am I Afraid to Tell You Who I Am?* (Allen, TX: Argus Communications, 1969), pp. 50–62.

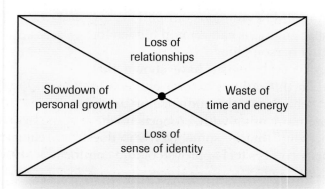

Tyrone's lack of self-disclosure created increasing problems as his relationships failed and friendships grew stale. Finally, his sister approached him at a family gathering and asked what was wrong. He brushed her off, but she persisted, and finally he admitted that he felt depressed about his ongoing problem with credit card debt. He felt embarrassed to admit it to his friends and girlfriends, all of whom were successful and perceived him as successful, too. In the end, he found it was easier to let relationships go rather than admit his problem to others.

As they talked and he disclosed more of his feelings, Tyrone realized that his habit of secrecy had made the problem worse because it allowed him to avoid dealing with it. On the other hand, after talking with his sister, he entered debt counseling and soon found that his debt problems, along with his self-esteem, quickly recovered.

relationships you develop are usually not deep ones. The result is an acquaintanceship rather than a friendship, a crush rather than a romance, or a superficial association rather than a deep and meaningful one. Judicious self-disclosure allows co-workers to understand each other better and promotes a smooth-running operation.

2. *The slowdown of personal growth*. One of the most positive by-products of self-disclosure is the personal growth it promotes. In contrast, failure to self-disclose prevents personal growth. You keep things from others not because self-disclosure poses problems for others, but because it poses problems for *you*.

3. *Waste of time and energy*. Have you ever noticed that it takes a lot of energy to create a false image? It requires constant self-awareness to ensure that you are maintaining the image. Many people waste time and energy that could be better spent on working, loving, or just having fun. Another related energy drain is the *fear* of being discovered. People are more willing than you may think to accept you for who you are.

4. *Loss of a sense of identity*. When you refuse to self-disclose, you're denying important parts of your personality. You are also keeping others from appreciating who you are. Since much of your self-knowledge comes through close, genuine contacts with others, your sense of identity can be threatened when that contact is either damaged or lost. Failure to self-disclose may hinder one's self-acceptance and assertiveness.

People who refuse to self-disclose at work can lose their sense of identity on the job and end up relying too heavily on family, friends, and outside organizations for social contact. People who rely too much on their workplace to make friends and plan social activities are in an opposite version of the same danger, since in effect they never leave the office. To retain a sense of who you are, strive to self-disclose and be real in all aspects of your life without overdisclosing.

India Times

Go to **www.mhhe.com/lamberton4e** for the link to the main page of the *India Times* and choose an article that interests you. Then write a paragraph answering: Was the approach and level of disclosure different from an American newspaper's? How? How was it similar?

LEVELS OF COMMUNICATION AS THEY RELATE TO DISCLOSURE

To enhance your self-awareness and self-disclosure skills, you need to better understand the levels of disclosure you use. Author John Powell identified five general levels of self-disclosure. These five levels of communication are helpful in understanding the amount of self-disclosure taking place. (See Figure 3.4.) The following list begins with the very lowest level of self-disclosure and concludes at the highest level.[10]

Level 5: Cliché Conversation

This is the level that most people rely upon during part of every day. **Cliché conversation** includes niceties, such as:

- "Nice morning, isn't it?"
- "How is your family?"
- "How's the weather up your way?"

cliché conversation
The level of communication with the least amount of self-disclosure, including niceties such as "Have a nice day."

figure 3.4

LEVELS OF SELF-DISCLOSURE

The five levels of communication are also the five levels of self-disclosure: what you communicate is what you disclose. These levels range from everyday cliché conversation to peak communication, which happens in times of great change, turmoil, or self-discovery. *On which level do you feel you are having "real" conversation and disclosure?*

Source: John Powell, *Why Am I Afraid to Tell You Who I Am?* (Allen, Tx: Argus Communications, 1969), pp. 50–62.

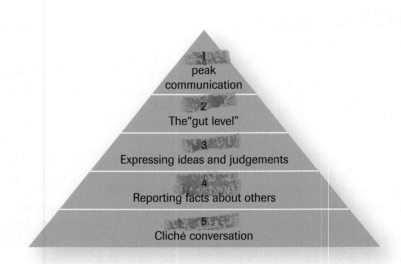

Tomás and Maryann had taken two classes together but never spoke. When they saw each other at the college bookstore they smiled at each other. They talked a little about the upcoming semester and the weather. It was an uneventful conversation, and after they parted they didn't think about it again.

The most common of these, repeated throughout the workday, is some variation of "How are you?" The primary purposes of such niceties are to acknowledge the other person's presence and, especially in the case of strangers, to present oneself as nonthreatening.

This is **nonconversation** in a real sense. It is dialogue said at a laundromat and at a supermarket checkout line. As speaker, you are called upon to disclose very little, and you ask little of the other person in return. Everyone remains emotionally safe. Nobody will challenge or threaten you, but then nobody receives any real rewards, either.

nonconversation
A way to describe the amount of actual conversation in cliché conversation.

Level 4: Reporting the Facts about Others

On this level, people move beyond clichés, although no real self-disclosure takes place yet. This level stays on a "what so-and-so has been doing" basis, excluding all personal comments that might reveal anything about the self, even in relation to the person being discussed. The only hint of self-disclosure comes from your choice of topic. Others can discern a little about you from what you choose to discuss.

ideas and judgments
Expressed through conscious thoughts, opinions, and theories in this level of communication.

Level 3: Expressing Ideas and Judgments

This level approaches honest expression because you reveal your conscious thoughts, opinions, and theories. When you express **ideas and judgments,** you take more risks, although undemanding ones: what you say on this level is filtered through some self-censorship, and you watch the other person carefully before you jump in. Unless you are willing to rise up to the next level, no real self-disclosure will take place here.

CLICHÉ CONVERSATIONS
Cliché conversations are a part of life. While they may not be rewarding, they are, oftentimes necessary. *Are there any benefits of cliché conversation?*

Level 2: Expressing Feelings and Emotions on the "Gut Level"

If you really want someone to understand who you are, you must tell the person what's in your "gut." Powell explains how you need to be honest about who you are when he says,

When Maryann saw that Tomás was in one of her fall classes, she sat by him. As they walked to their next class, they often talked about the instructor and eventually shared their opinions about other people whom they both knew, such as students from their class. They learned that they felt the same way about many issues.

They did not talk much about each other, but both could tell from their conversations that they held many of the same opinions about other people. This gave each of them clues about the other one's deeper beliefs.

"If I am a Republican or a Democrat by persuasion, I have a lot of company. If I am for or against space exploration, there will be others who support me in my conviction. But the feelings that lie under my ideas, judgments, and convictions are uniquely mine. . . . It is these feelings, on this level of communication, which I must share with you if I am to tell you who I really am."[11]

Your uniqueness, then, is what you communicate when you risk taking communication to the second level—**gut-level communication.** At this point you are beginning to apply genuine self-disclosure.

gut-level communication

Level of communication in which feelings are expressed honestly.

Level 1: Peak Communication

All deep and lasting relationships are based on complete openness and honest self-disclosure. Level 1 is based on the *peak experience* concept developed by Abraham Maslow, the first social scientist to study peak experiences. Maslow stated that the spiritual, emotional, and aesthetic high points in people's lives do not happen very often, but when they do, they create memories that help sustain them during ordinary nonpeak times.[12]

Powell translates this idea into communication. Like Maslow's peak experience, a **peak communication** experience does not occur very often. When it does, though, as Powell suggests, "The two persons will feel an almost perfect and mutual empathy."[13] The more often Level 1 self-disclosure takes place, the more you invite close relationships that can lead to enhanced opportunities for peak communication.

peak communication

Communication characterized by complete openness and honest self-disclosure. It happens rarely.

Nobody should expect peak communication to happen regularly. Such experiences can be triggered by unexpected events. For instance, a death in the family, winning the lottery, or experiencing an automobile accident could all create similar responses in

more about...

Abraham Maslow (1908–1970) was a founder of humanistic psychology in the 1960s, along with Carl Rogers and others. Their movement provided an alternative to the traditional beliefs of psychoanalysis which had been prominent in psychology up to that time.

Over the semester Maryann and Tomás began to study together at a local coffeehouse. It became a weekly ritual, and during that time they often stayed at the coffeehouse until it closed, talking about movies, books, and their families. At this point, they considered each other friends.

how you communicate with others. In cases like these, self-disclosure is often not a choice, but an automatic response. In other words, self-disclosure is essential to responding to a given situation and your feelings about it in a healthy way, and for regaining a sense of balance afterward.

A Key to Improved Human Relations–Level 2

If the first three of Powell's five levels represent less than real communication, and Level 1 of peak communication happens only rarely, then the only level left is Level 2. Making the gut level work for you is a key step in the process of learning to self-disclose. When people communicate on this level, human relationships grow, people understand themselves better, and conflict is reduced. In work environments, such benefits translate into greater efficiency and productivity throughout the organization.

The primary benefits include the following:

1. *Improving relationships.* The most important benefit to communicating on the gut level is that relationships often grow stronger. Powell believes that silence tends to promote involvement only in *fraudulent relationships,* which have little benefit for the individual or company.[14]

    With Level 2 communication, genuine emotions and viewpoints are shared, giving each person a stronger sense of identity. If you communicate your true thoughts and feelings, the things you have in common with others will become increasingly obvious. This can happen only when both sides are making an effort. Powell theorizes, "I will understand only as much of myself as I have been willing to communicate to another,"[15] because it is through self-disclosure that you are able to define your beliefs.

2. *Growing toward maturity.* When you are relating to others on a gut level, you may begin to notice patterns in the way you react that might reveal your weaknesses. Gut-level sharing can expose those

After knowing each other for a year, Maryann and Tomás began to see each other more frequently. They went camping together, talked about their futures, and shared their feelings.

reaction patterns, so that you can examine them—and, if necessary, change them. Perhaps your feelings get hurt too easily. You may conclude that you are taking matters too personally, or that you overreact to certain situations. You may get negative responses when offering your opinion. Perhaps your gut-level sharing is too confrontational. When a pattern like that becomes clear, you can (and probably will) change. You will never be able to explore your strengths and weaknesses unless you learn to communicate on a gut level.

3. *Bringing out the honesty of others.* The third advantage of gut-level disclosure is that it encourages openness and honesty in others. If you want someone to communicate more openly with you, try self-disclosing first. When you are bold enough to *break the ice*, the other person may be reassured and inspired to do the same.[16]

MAKING ASSUMPTIONS ABOUT OTHER PEOPLE

Another dimension of both self-awareness and self-disclosure is the way so many people operate on perceptions or hunches they have about each other. Consider this scenario. In a small company, Brandon meets Kathy, a worker in his own department. Brandon likes Kathy, but is unaware that she likes him, too. Kathy is also unaware that Brandon likes her. In fact, she is quite certain that he dislikes her, because he seems often to ignore her. However, Brandon ignores Kathy because he doesn't want her to think that he likes her romantically; he wants only to be her friend—at least for now. As you can see, the situation becomes more and more complicated simply because both people are operating on hunches, rather than on real information.

Psychologist R. D. Laing became well known for his work in this area of behavior. Laing says that assumptions or hunches we have about others keep us from operating in the real world. Here is an example that Laing often used:[17]

JANE AND JOE'S CONFLICT

Oftentimes, conflict results from a breakdown in communication. *Can you think of a time when this has been true in your life?*

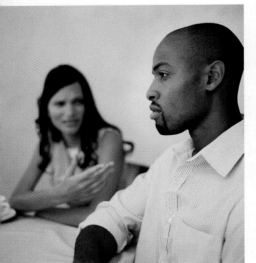

A few weeks before the holidays in his junior year, Tomás learned that his father had been killed in an auto accident. Devastated, he postponed his final exams and spent several days talking with Maryann about his father, his guilt over their arguments, and the genuine admiration for him that he never took the time to express. Such communication cannot be planned. In addition, it usually occurs only where self-disclosure already exists, such as that which developed between Tomás and Maryann as their friendship deepened.

Jane's Internal Conversation	Joe's Internal Conversation
She *thinks:* I'm really upset! She *says:* "I had an awful day!"	He *thinks:* Jane seems upset. He *says:* Sorry you had a bad day; let's have a nice evening.
She thinks: He doesn't understand; I'll tell him about everything that happened.	He thinks: She needs to forget about work. I'll get her mind off her work problems.
She thinks: Joe seems so unconcerned about my problems. She thinks: If Joe really cared about me, he would get upset about this, too. She thinks: He knows I'm really upset! She says: "Hey, why are you so uncaring!"	He thinks: I'll help her by staying calm and relaxed. He thinks: She's getting more upset. I'll try to stay *very* calm. He thinks: Hey, is Jane accusing me of hurting her? What's happening here?
She thinks: He knows that acting indifferent upsets me; he must want to hurt me. She thinks: No real friend would act so unconcerned; it just wouldn't happen. She says: "Joe, you're very mean. I really hate talking to you."	He thinks: I'm only trying to help! He says: "Why are you on my case?" He thinks: Man, she's really ticked off! What's wrong with her, anyway? He says: "Jane, you're neurotic! I give up."

Remember to clear up hunches both by working on your own self-awareness and self-disclosure and by encouraging self-disclosure from others. Though this example is not from the workplace, this same type of misunderstanding often takes place on the job, as well. Don't rely on your assumptions about others. Check them out.

Dealing with Fear

"Pushing through fear is less frightening than living with the underlying fear that comes from a feeling of helplessness."

Source: Susan Jeffers, *Feel the Fear and Do It Anyway,* New York: Ballantine, 1987, p. 30.

more about...

Self-Awareness Web Sites

Using a search engine, find a Web page that involves self-awareness. (You will have many to choose from, most of them free of charge.) Try "self-awareness disclosure" or "self-awareness research." Spend some time reading the articles you find. What common threads run through the material you have found? What else do you feel you need to know about self-disclosure after reading this material?

THE RISK FACTOR OF DISCLOSURE

As with virtually any worthwhile change in your life, choosing to self-disclose involves risks. Once you conclude that self-disclosure is productive behavior, you may run into another barrier: fear. Perhaps your fears include the following:[18]

- Losing control of a conversation or relationship.
- Becoming trapped or controlled by someone else.
- Facing something unpleasant within yourself.
- Losing self-respect.
- Appearing to be a loser to others.
- Being rejected or being belittled.

The first step in dealing with fear is *to look at exactly what you are afraid of.* If your fear is not on this list, you need to identify it and then decide how to respond to it.

In her book *Feel the Fear and Do It Anyway,* Dr. Susan Jeffers shows that eliminating your fears is not necessary for you to change your life. In a way, the title of her book says it all: everybody feels fear, although most fears are unfounded. You do not need to wait until your fears are gone to begin to improve yourself.

 STRATEGY FOR SUCCESS

3.1 Know When to Stop

1. Understand that self-disclosure can be difficult and awkward at first.

2. Be aware that you can overdisclose unintentionally.

When Adina went to her first job interview after graduation, she felt extremely nervous and was unable to relax. She attempted to make small talk as the interview began, but this backfired as she began blurting out inappropriate personal facts about her family, husband, and fears about not getting the job. She realized that she was embarrassing herself and tried to make a joke out of it by saying, "Well, this is my first interview," but then felt worse for admitting how inexperienced she was. She did not get the job, nor was she confident enough to go on another interview for almost a month. Adina found herself overdisclosing without having tried to do so.

3. Learn how to avoid overdisclosure, especially with strangers or in the workplace.

4. Learn how to self-disclose comfortably and appropriately.

Knowing the limits of your own self-disclosure is an important dimension of interpersonal experience. Use these four tips to help evaluate your own attempt at achieving appropriate and balanced self-disclosure.

1. **Understand that self-disclosure can be difficult and awkward at first.** Self-disclosure can be difficult and even uncomfortable, especially if you are not used to it. Prepare yourself and don't beat yourself up for feeling awkward.

2. **Be aware that you can overdisclose unintentionally.** Overdisclosing often happens when a person feels socially awkward and is trying to make conversation. Problems occur when someone goes too far in self-disclosing. Being aware of overdisclosure will help you avoid falling into this situation.

3. **Learn how to avoid overdisclosure, especially with strangers or in the workplace.**

4. **Learn how to self-disclose comfortably and appropriately.** Take self-disclosure one step at a time, at whatever speed is most comfortable for you. Most people will appreciate your efforts and respond to them.

3.2 Pay Attention to Differences

1. Know how much to disclose and how soon.

2. Remember: Different cultures, different disclosure.

3. Allow for the other person to take the lead.

4. Factor in gender, race, and social position.

5. Pay attention to the other person's level of openness.

The information on self-disclosure in this chapter will be helpful only if it can be applied wisely in different situations and in interaction with different types of people. These five tips will help you in dealing with the often complex differences that self-disclosure can present.

Lin Jin was the only female programmer at her dot-com company. Most of her male colleagues treated her like one of the guys, but some of the men at a higher level made her conspicuously aware of her lone status. It wasn't anything she could put her finger on, but more the way they looked at her and stood too close to her. Although no one ever made suggestive remarks, they brushed her clothes and skin more than was welcome. Her boss, Bruce, was one of the worst offenders: sometimes, Lin Jin caught him staring into her cubicle for no apparent reason.

It made Lin Jin uncomfortable and was starting to affect her job performance, but she didn't know how to handle it. She didn't feel she could file an official complaint because, after all, he hadn't actually *done* anything. So she decided to confront Bruce directly about his behavior. First, she tried to determine the worst case scenario: he could threaten to fire her, but she doubted it would hold up because she had a sterling work record.

Second, Lin Jin prepared herself for the worst possible outcome. Bruce could deny the truth and ignore her complaint or he could become angry and even more threatening. She carefully thought through how she might handle each of those situations. If he denied her complaint, she could put it in writing to his supervisor. If he flew off the handle, she'd remain calm no matter what. If he started sexually harassing her in earnest, then she'd file a legitimate complaint.

Third, Lin Jin carefully worked out a plan for the best time and place to approach him so she wouldn't be interrupted and he wouldn't feel cornered. She listed her complaints, citing specific instances so they were clear in her mind, and practiced exactly what to say and how she would phrase it, paying careful attention to keeping her voice steady and making eye contact. Finally, she reminded herself that even if she didn't achieve the desired results, she would feel better about herself for taking action than if she did nothing.

Feeling prepared and confident, Lin Jin approached Bruce. He was surprised and not only immediately backed down, but also apologized for his behavior.

1. **Know how much to disclose and how soon.** This often depends on many factors, including the specific circumstances and situation. People need to consider the other person's cultural, ethnic, religious, and even geographic background.

2. **Remember: Different cultures, different disclosure.** Always remember that people from different regions and countries respond differently because they approach self-disclosure with widely divergent expectations.

3. **Allow for the other person to take the lead.** Nevertheless, under all circumstances, you can minimize your uncertainty by allowing the other person to take the lead. By staying within the self-disclosure limits exhibited by the other person, you will be less likely to over- or underdisclose, especially when meeting someone for the first time.

4. **Factor in gender, race, and social position.** Other points that should be factored in include gender, race, and social position. Generally, people tend to disclose things to members of their own sex that they may withhold from the opposite sex. Also, different ethnic groups may hold varying attitudes toward self-disclosure, as do people from different regions of this country. Finally, socioeconomic position often influences how much disclosure is considered appropriate.

5. **Pay attention to the other person's level of openness.** Remain focused and interested in the other person with whom you are speaking. When you receive messages warning you that any self-disclosure would be unwelcome, you may want to avoid self-disclosure altogether, or you might try to ask nonthreatening questions. Be responsive and, above all, patient.

3.3 Facing Fear of Self-Disclosure

1. Start with the worst possible scenario.
2. Prepare yourself to accept the worst possible outcome.
3. Proceed with a plan.

Business success expert Dale Carnegie offers three suggestions for moving ahead even when fear is present. These suggestions can be applied to fears in any area of your life, not just to self-disclosure.[19]

1. **Start with the worst possible scenario.** This means imagining the very worst thing that could happen if you self-disclose. You'll find that often the worst thing that could happen is something you can live with. Then remind yourself that it will not happen unless everything goes wrong, which is unlikely.

2. **Prepare yourself to accept the worst possible outcome.** Be willing to accept the worst possible outcome. Consider whether you're feeling strong enough to survive the worst that could happen. Adopt the frame of mind that you are ready for whatever happens, and you will not let it get you down. Prepare yourself for the fact that anxiety might overtake you during some moments, but try not to let fear discourage you.

3. **Proceed with a plan.** Using the worst case scenario as a safety valve, map out a plan that you can realistically put into action. Remind yourself that the worst possible scenario most likely won't happen, plan to succeed, and don't let temporary setbacks discourage you. Allow your subconscious mind to absorb the plan by thinking about it as often as possible, then view it as a challenge—one you can meet.

Anticipate that not everyone may like what you have to say when you self-disclose. Be prepared for a variety of possible responses. Remind yourself that your reasons for self-disclosure are self-generated and prepare yourself for the fact that your honesty may invite honest reactions in return. If a relationship changes as a result of your self-disclosure, it may be time to reevaluate it. Any relationship based on reality and honesty can withstand more of the same.[20]

CHAPTER THREE SUMMARY

Chapter Summary by Learning Objectives

1. **Define self-awareness.** Self-awareness is the ability to see yourself realistically, without a great deal of difference between what you are and how you assume others see you. Better self-awareness means roughly the same thing as *developing a better looking-glass self.*

2. **Explain how awareness-related barriers impact communication.** Many people spend their lives unconsciously building walls around themselves to keep others from seeing them, but these walls also keep them from learning about themselves. The feeling of being complete may take years to achieve. As an individual, you need to grow, develop, and be open to change. To develop a meaningful life, you must learn more about yourself and those around you.

3. **Use the Johari Window as a tool for self-understanding.** Everyone has at least four areas of self-understanding. The Johari Window shows these with four *panes:* open, hidden, blind, and unknown. To understand what areas you need to develop within relationships, you need to examine all four panes.

4. **Define self-disclosure.** Self-disclosure is letting another person know your real thoughts, desires, and feelings.

5. **List the outcomes of failing to self-disclose.** Often, people shrink from letting others know what they think and feel. When individuals fail to disclose they risk losing relationships with others, slowing down personal growth, wasting time and energy, or losing their sense of identity.

6. **Understand the five major levels of communication.** Of the five levels of communication, which are also the five levels of self-disclosure, the highest level you can achieve most of the time is the gut level. The advantages of communicating on the gut level include improving relationships, growing toward maturity, and bringing out honesty in others.

7. **Discuss the impact of making assumptions regarding other people.** Assumptions or hunches we have about others keep us from operating in the real world. Working on your own self-awareness and self-disclosure and encouraging self-disclosure from others will help you avoid misunderstandings and conflict at work and in your personal life.

8. **Explain the risk factor of disclosure.** The final barrier in your path is fear. You can feel the fear but should go ahead anyway. Dale Carnegie offers three suggestions for pressing forward even when the fear is present: start with the worst possible scenario, prepare yourself to accept this worst possible outcome, and proceed with a plan.

key terms

blind pane 57	**Johari Window** 55	**self-disclosure** 54
cliché conversation 62	**nonconversation** 63	**unknown pane** 57
gut-level **communication** 64	**open pane** 55	
hidden pane 56	**peak communication** 64	
ideas and judgments 63	**repress** 57	
	self-awareness 54	

review questions

1. What does the term "self-awareness" mean to you after reading this chapter? Use an illustration from your own experience to clarify your definition.

2. Why do people often withhold from others their true selves—or parts of who they really are?

3. How can a lack of appropriate self-disclosure be a barrier to effective relations with others? Specifically, how can a failure to disclose affect your position in the workplace?

4. Briefly explain each of the four panes of the Johari Window. How can this model help you understand yourself better by understanding your relationships with others?

5. Think of an incident in your life when someone overdisclosed to you or someone else. How did the incident affect the relationship? What steps can you take to avoid overdisclosing?

6. How might self-disclosure help you in your relationship with your manager? with co-workers? Can you think of examples that illustrate either negative or positive effects of self-disclosure in the workplace?

7. Of John Powell's five levels of communication, what is the best one for everyday use? Explain why.

8. Discuss Dale Carnegie's three rules for reducing fear. Would any of them work for you when self-disclosure is the issue? Why or why not?

critical thinking questions

9. Have you ever experienced differences in people's level of self-disclosure based on where they live (in another country or a

region of your country, for example)? What did you observe, if anything?

10. Are you as self-aware as you would like to be? If not, what steps can you take to allow yourself to reach a higher level of self-awareness?

working it out 3.1

THE "OPENER SCALE" QUESTIONNAIRE

School-to-Work Connection: Personal Qualities Skills

Instructions: For each statement below, indicate your level of agreement or disagreement, using the following scale. Record your responses in the spaces on the left.

4 = I strongly agree

3 = I slightly agree

2 = I am uncertain

1 = I slightly disagree

0 = I strongly disagree

_____ 1. People frequently tell me about themselves.

_____ 2. I've been told that I'm a good listener.

_____ 3. I'm very accepting of others.

_____ 4. People trust me with their secrets.

_____ 5. I can easily get people to "open up."

_____ 6. People feel relaxed around me.

_____ 7. I enjoy listening to people.

_____ 8. I'm sympathetic to people's problems.

_____ 9. I encourage people to tell me how they're feeling.

_____ 10. I can keep people from talking about themselves.

This test measures your perception of your ability to get others to "open up" to you, their reactions to you, your desire to listen, and some of your other interpersonal skills.

To score, add up the numbers that you have recorded in the spaces on the left. The total is your score. In studies with this test, women tend to score a little higher because of society's higher tolerance of emotional expression in women. Here are average scores for others who have taken this test: High "opener" ability is 35–40 for women, 33–40 for men; this can indicate a higher level of honesty in communication, but it can also indicate a tendency to overdisclose. An intermediate score is 26–34 for women, 23–32 for men; this likely indicates people who do not jump into conversations *feet first*, but are comfortable with self-disclosure. A low score is 0–25 for women, 0–22 for men; this can indicate either a desire to self-disclose more selectively or an inability to do so.[21]

YOUR FEELINGS ABOUT SELF-DISCLOSURE

School-to-Work Connection: Personal Qualities Skills

Instructions: This exercise is designed to make you think about your self-disclosing behavior. Begin by finishing the following incomplete sentences. Go through the sentences fairly quickly; don't think about your responses too long. There are no right or wrong answers.

1. I dislike people who _____

2. Those who really know me _____

3. When I let someone know something I don't like about myself _____

4. When I'm in a group of strangers _____

5. I envy _____

6. I get hurt when _____

7. I daydream about _____

8. Few people know that I _____

9. One thing I really dislike about myself is _____

10. When I share my values with someone _____

Based on your responses to these incomplete sentences, do you feel that you engage in the right amount of self-disclosure? Too little? Too much? In general, what prevents you from engaging in self-disclosure? Are there particular topics on which you find it difficult to be self-disclosing? Do you receive much self-disclosure from others, or do people have difficulty opening up to you?[22] _____

_____

1. *Read and Write*

   Visit "Johari Window" at **www.mhhe.com/lamberton4e** and read the explanation and examples given. How did this help you develop a deeper understanding of the Johari Window? Read the "Parable of the Blind Men and the Elephant," which is linked to the second-to-last paragraph. Write a paragraph to answer these questions:

   a. What does this parable–poem tell you about people's ability to understand what they encounter?

   b. How does this relate to self-awareness, especially in relation to the blind pane?

2. *Self-Assessment*

   Take the online Anxiety Test or the Self-esteem Test at **www.mhhe. com/lamberton4e.** Answer the following questions:

   a. What did you learn about yourself from these two test? Does that knowledge increase your self-awareness? Explain.

   b. Based on what you have learned here, what changes, if any, do you plan to make in the ways in which you deal with others in the future?

3. *Self-Assess and Apply*

   How well can you identify your career interests and jobs that might interest you? Take the Career Focus 2000 Interest Inventory by James C. Gonyea to help you with some self-examination in these areas. Link to the site through the course Web page at **www.mhhe. com/lamberton4e,** or visit the site directly at **www.iccweb.com/ careerfocus/index.asp.** Report on your findings.

Anthony's Confrontation

Anthony Albertini was feeling frustrated with his job at a large suburban dry cleaning plant. The company ran on a set of standards known as *targets*. Anthony's target was always just a little higher than it seemed possible to achieve. During his morning break, his friend Stacey asked him what was wrong.

Anthony complained, "Mr. Youngberg just won't admit that my targets are always set too high. He has me down for 48 dozen garments a day. When I'm going full speed on a good day, I can maybe do 45 dozen, tops."

Stacey replied, "Well, why won't he lower the target? He must see that you're working as fast as you can! I think you really need to talk to him."

Anthony agreed to talk to his manager. "What's the real reason you won't take a look at the targets for my work station?" Anthony asked right away.

Youngberg seemed startled by the question. After a pause, he replied, "To be honest with you, Anthony, I don't like your attitude. Every time I say something, you seem to have something rude to say back. I just don't react well when someone treats me like that."

"Treats *you* like that?" Anthony was silent for a moment. "Mr. Youngberg," he said slowly, "I never meant to have a bad attitude. I've always thought that you were the one with the bad attitude. I was just reacting."

"Look," Youngberg replied, "I'm sorry if I made you feel defensive. We must have gotten started on the wrong foot."

"Well, I'm sorry that I made you feel that way."

"Anthony, I'll make you a deal. You show me a good attitude, and I'll lower the target for your workstation. Deal?" Anthony hesitated, then mumbled okay. "I'll need more enthusiasm than that," Youngberg countered.

This time, Anthony smiled as he answered, "Okay, I'll give it my best shot."

Case Study Questions

1. How did self-disclosure help the problem in this case?
2. Was Mr. Youngberg doing anything wrong? If so, what?
3. How could the problem of unfair targets have been avoided?

The Angry Computer Technician

Harry Cardwell worked at a large accounting firm as one of two IT supervisors. On Wednesday, he didn't feel well and decided to stay home. When he returned to work, he found that some of his equipment, including a new CD burner, was missing. He found that his friend Sam, the other IT supervisor, had borrowed them. "Why in the world did you take my equipment without asking?" Harry yelled at Sam.

Sam was surprised. "Harry, I can't believe you care. We've known each other forever. I mean, here they are—well, except for the CD burner. It doesn't seem to be reading the CDs I put in there."

"So now you've even ruined the new CD burner!" Harry fumed. "Don't ever touch my stuff again!"

Sam was really taken aback. During lunch, he approached Harry again. "I had no idea you'd be upset, but I guess I need to say I'm sorry. Look, I'll fix the CD burner myself after work tonight. I guess I just didn't know you felt that way about your stuff. I mean, you've bought me lunch a hundred times. I always thought you were a really generous guy."

Harry answered, "I *am* generous—too generous. I'm always helping other people. But you walk all over me and take advantage the minute my back is turned. I've had it!"

"Excuse me," Sam said, "but I never asked for your 'help.' Lots of times you *insisted* on buying me lunch, even when I offered to pay for yours."

Harry backed down. "Okay, okay, let's drop it. Just keep your hands off my equipment from now on."

Before Sam left, he concluded, "Look, Harry, I just wish you'd have let me know how you felt about your equipment. If you had, I guarantee I wouldn't have used it. Ever."

Case Study Questions

1. How self-aware is Harry? On what do you base your assessment?

2. How could self-disclosure have prevented this confrontation? How could it help now? Has it helped in some way already?

3. What else might you do if you were Sam?

ATTITUDES

In the Workplace: Name Plates and Negativity

SITUATION

Brianna was just leaving for lunch when she heard the news. Jay, the teller who worked beside her at the bank, was the one who told her about the nameplates. Brianna exploded: "Nameplates! They want us to have nameplates at our teller windows? Every customer who walks through the door will know my full name? What is this,

kindergarten? Why don't the customers wear nameplates, too? For crying out loud! Why doesn't everyone just walk around with a nameplate! Well, I've had it with all these stupid rules! I'm going to my union representative; this is going to be a fight! The bank can't get away with this! They've sent one too many stupid new changes down from their stupid bureaucrats at the top!"

LEARNING objectives

After studying this chapter, you will be able to:

1. Define an attitude.

2. Explain what makes up a good attitude.

3. Discuss what goes into changing an existing attitude.

4. Explain the importance of a positive attitude as it applies to optimal experiences.

5. Identify how "flow" factors into your everyday life.

6. Provide details regarding the link between positive attitudes and job satisfaction.

7. Understand the importance of positive attitudes as they apply to Theory X and Theory Y managers.

CHAPTER 4

STRATEGIES FOR SUCCESS

Strategy 4.1   Changing Pessimism to Optimism

Strategy 4.2   Building Positive Attitudes

DISCOVERY

Jay was shocked and disappointed at Brianna's reaction. "What's with all the negativity, Brianna? It's not that big of a deal! You get mad and overreact to every new change at work! Why don't you try a little positive attitude for a change? There's got to be a reason why we're getting nameplates. I'm sure it has something to do with improving customer relations. Hey, and while you're at it, why don't you try smiling at the customers sometime, and being more helpful? You'd have a better time at work if you did, and I bet you'd actually get those merit raises you are always dreaming about, and maybe even the promotion you were passed over for last year. Your attitude needs a little work!"

THINK ABOUT IT

Do you ever overreact to certain events or situations? What do you think are the reasons behind it?

WHAT IS AN ATTITUDE?

attitude
An evaluation of people, ideas, issues, situations, or objects.

An **attitude** is an evaluation of people, ideas, issues, situations, or objects. An attitude has three parts: thoughts, feelings, and actions. For example, you may have a negative attitude toward cats. You *think* that cats are too aggressive because they chase birds. Your *feeling* is dislike or disdain when you think of cats. Your *action* is to choose to get a dog instead of a cat for a pet. These three parts of an attitude are so intertwined that you probably do not even notice them as separate components. Your attitudes toward people are the result of the *beliefs* and *feelings* you have about yourself and about other people, and attitudes directly affect your *treatment* of both.

Attitudes range along a scale from positive to negative, and often don't change over time. Your attitudes have a lot to do with how you relate to others and to the world. Attitudes can make or break your relationships with others. Many people are unaware of how strongly their attitudes affect those around them.

Attitudes are usually tied in with self-esteem. People with low self-esteem will often show attitudes that are not based on the way things really are, but rather on their own feelings of inadequacy. An individual attitude might seem to have no direct connection to self-esteem, but the relationship will be there nonetheless. As with nearly all self-esteem problems, attitudes based on low self-esteem start in early childhood. If parents have attitudes based on low self-esteem, those attitudes are indirectly transmitted to their children. If parents treat their children with conditional positive regard, or if children feel rejected by their parents, the result is going to be feelings of low self-esteem carried into adulthood—and overall poor attitudes. Teachers, coaches, other family members, and classmates during childhood can cause the same damaging effects to self-esteem even when parents do treat their children with unconditional positive regard.

Attitudes are likely to be affected by self-esteem in several other ways. Low self-esteem is, after all, a negative attitude people have toward themselves. That basic beginning point will affect every other attitude people express, either consciously or accidentally. If you dislike yourself, everything you see will be colored with that feeling. As mentioned in Chapter 2, if you do not like yourself, you will also not be very well liked by those around you.

more about...

Work Attitudes

Regarding **work attitudes,** Martin Seligman advises, "How you handle adversity in the workplace tends to have much more impact on your career than how you handle the good stuff. The people who know how to overcome adversity are the ones who rise to the top of the organization."

Source: Heath Row, "Coping—Martin Seligman," *Fast Company*, December, 1998.

WHAT MAKES A GOOD ATTITUDE?

Happiness is an attitude—one that most people strive for. Many studies have shown that you can *choose* to have a happy or **positive attitude.** Whether or not you are happy has little to do with the traditional factors people usually connect with happiness. Happiness doesn't seem to have much to do with a person's age, gender, occupation, or wealth.[1]

> **positive attitude**
> A position resulting from healthy self-esteem, optimism, extraversion, and personal control.

What makes for a happy, positive attitude? Psychologist David Myers lists the following four characteristics that happy people *do* all seem to have in common:[2]

1. *Healthy self-esteem.* Start liking yourself more and you will be happier. Sounds simple, doesn't it? The point is that whatever works to increase your self-esteem—such as the strategies you've read in previous chapters—will be the same strategies that will improve your overall attitude of happiness.

2. *Optimism.* Happy people are hope filled. Several studies have shown that optimistic people are both happier and physically healthier than less optimistic people. Optimists are more likely to cope with their problems better than pessimists, and they are less likely to become ill.[3] They tend to try to find solutions to their problems; they rely on social support from others to help them through rough times; and they look for positives—the cloud's silver lining—in problem situations.[4] (See Figure 4.1.)

   By contrast, pessimists do not seem to cope with problems as well as optimists do. They tend to deny that problems exist, and they focus on their negative feelings instead of on solving their problems.[5] A lot of evidence suggests that pessimism is related to poor health. In one example, Harvard graduates who were rated the most pessimistic when interviewed in 1946 were also the least healthy people of those interviewed 34 years later. In another study, college students who were more pessimistic reported more symptoms of pain and illness over the course of a semester than optimistic students.[6] In a study of people who had coronary bypass surgery, pessimistic patients were in the hospital longer than optimists and took longer to get back to their normal activities than optimists.[7]

   The most dangerous kind of pessimism is hopelessness. Feeling hopeless leads to feeling helpless, which often results in giving up.

> ## A Positive Attitude
>
> Regarding **positive attitudes,** in a study at the National Institute on Aging, researchers found that regardless of changes in occupation, marital status, or location, people who were happy at the beginning of the study were also happy at the end, 10 years later.
>
> ***Source:*** David G. Myers, "The Secret of Happiness," *Psychology Today* 25 (July/August 1992), p. 38.

more about...

figure 4.1

HOW OPTIMISTIC ARE YOU?

Your level of optimism will indicate your ability to "bounce back" from obstacles, even catastrophes—and will increase your likelihood of success. *How optimistic are you?*

Test Your Optimism

Measuring optimism is one way to measure a person's likelihood of success, according to psychologists. How you handle setbacks is a good indicator of how well you will succeed in school, sports, and work. The test below shows you some examples of questions psychologists might ask to find out whether or not you are able to bounce back from a setback such as a poor grade or an unsuccessful sale.

For each of the following situations, pick the response that more closely matches your own, and rate your optimism. (a = 10 points; b = 20 points)

1. **Your credit card statement shows a $200 charge you did not make. What would you do?**
   A. Pay the bill and do nothing about it because you feel it would be a waste of time, and the credit card company wouldn't believe you anyway.
   B. Think they made an error, call the company to notify them of the mistake, and tell them that you won't be paying that portion of the bill.

2. **Your vacation week begins tomorrow, and you have a special trip planned, but you feel like you might be getting sick. What would you do?**
   A. Assume that your vacation is ruined, because this is just your luck. You call your travel agent and cancel the trip, forfeiting your airfare.
   B. Take some vitamins and get to bed early with the expectation that you will feel better in the morning.

3. **On your way to work, you get a flat tire. What would you do?**
   A. Panic while you're driving and barely miss hitting another car as you pull over to the curb, feeling sure that you will get in trouble at work for being late.
   B. Tell yourself to keep calm, slow down, pull over to the curb, and proceed to change your tire if you know how; or you look for the nearest phone to call for assistance. You tell yourself these things happen to everybody.

4. **Your home computer crashes, and you have a final paper due the very next morning. What would you do?**
   A. Kick your computer and then get depressed, knowing that your instructor will not understand and will probably give you an F.
   B. Call a friend to see if you can use his or her computer to finish your paper. If that isn't possible, you plan to ask your instructor for an extension of the deadline until you can use another computer at school, realizing that this situation was not your fault.

5. **You've just been interviewed for a job, and you have all the necessary skills the company requires. What do you expect will happen?**
   A. You are sure you won't get the job, because the interviewer didn't respond well to you when you fumbled while answering one of the questions.
   B. You believe you have a good chance of getting the job, because even though the interviewer doesn't know you well, you are qualified and you answered all the questions reasonably well.

What was your score? If it was 80–100 points, you are probably able to handle setbacks and rejections. People who see setbacks as permanent and pervasive are more pessimistic, more likely to feel helpless, and more likely to give up without resolving a problem.

Hopelessness can even be deadly: in one study, men in Finland who reported feeling moderately hopeless or very hopeless had a death rate two to three times higher than men who reported feeling little or no hopelessness.[8]

Imagine that you have just been told that your position at work is going to be eliminated. How do you feel? After the shock wears off, you probably feel angry and frustrated, but then what? You

INTERNET **exercise 4.1**

Develop Your Self-Esteem

The Web site address for The Positive Way can be found through **www.mhhe. com/lamberton4e.** Click on Self-Esteem Development, then take the Self-Esteem Questionnaire at the bottom of the page. What did you discover about your self-esteem?

may begin to feel depressed, hopeless, and helpless. While you are feeling this way, on what are you focused? Most likely, your focus is on yourself and your negative emotions, and not on what to do about losing your job. Your self-esteem may suffer as a result of your depression. You may internalize your negative feelings instead of looking for productive ways to find another job. It's not surprising that people with this negative focus on their feelings begin to have physical symptoms of illness and stress. Chapter 14 will examine stress and the body's reaction to stress in greater detail.

3. *Extraversion.* An *extravert* is an outgoing person—one whose behavior is directed outward toward others. As the famous psychiatrist Carl Jung said, behavior of extraverts is directed to the *objects in the external world.*[9] Notice, though, that this factor is also very directly related to one's level of self-esteem. People who feel comfortable in new situations and who feel certain that others will accept them are usually people with relatively high self-esteem. These people will most likely be relatively happy at work and in their personal lives.

4. *Personal control.* In Chapter 2, you learned about an *internal* and *external locus of control.* This is the idea that you believe either that *you* are responsible for your own situations and life events (internal locus of control); or that *other people, luck, chance, or fate* are in charge of the events in your life (external locus of control). A person with a positive attitude is more likely to have an internal locus of control. Happy people control their own destinies; they control their own futures. They plan and manage their time well. When someone else controls your choices, either large or small, your happiness will probably diminish.

Health psychologist Judith Rodin conducted research with nursing home residents on control and choices over many years. She found that those who were able to make their own choices about simple things, such as decorating their rooms with plants, were sick less often and actually lived longer than residents who had less control over their lives.[10]

extraversion

Characteristic of a happy attitude in which a person's behavior is directed outward, toward others.

personal control

The power people have over their destinies.

SATISFYING WORK EXPERIENCES

Satisfying work experiences largely depend on your self-esteem, optimism, extraversion, and sense of personal control. *How does your attitude positively affect your current job?*

Be Assertive!

People with an internal locus of control are in command of their own lives; they are assertive. This does not mean they are aggressive in a harmful way, but that they feel a sense of control over events in their lives. Are you in charge of your life, or do you let others make your decisions? Take the Assertiveness Test online at the Queendom Web site, found through **www.mhhe.com/lamberton4e** in the Chapter 4 research links (or go to **www.queendom.com/tests/minitests/assertiveness_abridged_access**.html**#h**). What does your score say about you? Bring your results to class.

more about...

Extrovert or Extravert?

Individuals wonder whether to use the spelling **extrovert** or **extravert.** Many people spell extrovert with an "o," but the "a" spelling was originally used by the renowned psychoanalyst Carl Jung, who coined both *extravert* and *introvert.* Because of this book's focus on his teachings, his spellings will be used.

HOW WELL DO YOU BOUNCE BACK?

People who "bounce back" quickly from setbacks tend to have internal, not external, locus of control. *Is your locus of control internal or external? How can you change an external locus of control?*

The characteristics of happy, positive people are helpful to know, but beyond just knowing about them, there are specific actions you can take to achieve a more positive attitude. Dr. David G. Myers says that by acting happy, you can actually help yourself become more happy. Does that sound too simple? When things happen to you, as they do every day—things over which you have no control—you *choose* how to react.

Many people are quick to blame the other person, the situation, or their own physical condition when things go wrong. People make the *choice* of the reactions they feel. Myers is simply suggesting that making the choice to act happy, and doing so on a regular basis, will go a long way to improving your overall attitude.[11]

CHANGING ATTITUDES

Most likely, at some time you will be in a position where you can (and should) work to change the attitude of a co-worker or employee. If you are in a management position, you might find yourself with an employee whose attitude must change "or else." You might be a member of a work group or a committee where the attitude of one or more members is getting in the way of productivity. However, changing a person's attitude is not always possible. At times, you will simply have to face the "or else."

Brianna, the angry employee in the opening story, was a tough case. She probably won't want to accept the advice her co-worker gave her. Luckily, not all employees are like Brianna. Often, people with attitudes like this need only to be shown how destructive their attitudes are; then a change

Mark was fresh out of college and in his first job as a computer repair technician. He noticed that some people at work were avoiding him. They were small things, like pretending not to hear him and not responding when he said hi, but it upset him. He spoke to Danelle, a co-worker. "Why wouldn't they like me?" Mark asked. "I help them out."

"Sometimes," Danelle began tactfully, "you make them feel kind of stupid."

"Oh!" said Mark smiling. "I just joke with them. They should see that."

"Well, I think it hurts their feelings. I'd suggest toning it down until you know the person better. Then they'll appreciate your sense of humor!"

Mark thought about what she said, and then his attitude underwent some subtle changes. He still had his enthusiasm and sense of humor, but the teasing part was gone. People grew warmer and friendlier to him, and he ended up happier than before.

takes place. The key is **feedback:** everyone needs feedback. Literally, feedback means "returning a part of the output . . . to the input."[12] Here, the person with the bad attitude is the input source; he or she needs some of that output returned, with comments.

When giving attitude-improving feedback, be sure to deal with facts rather than opinions, and descriptions rather than judgments. Instead of only asking Brianna, "Why don't you try a little positive attitude for a change?" her co-worker also described some ways she could improve (smile more, be helpful to customers). The co-worker could have gone even further and described specifically what these actions would do to improve customer relations and overall job attitude.

The giver of feedback should also try to strike a balance between negative and positive feedback. Some authorities on this subject suggest giving two positive messages for every negative one.[13] Searching out the good feedback to give on a two-to-one ratio just might be a good test of your own attitude.

> **feedback**
> Information given to people either on how well they are performing a task, or on how clearly they are being understood.

more about...

> **Happiness**
>
> The following is an apt quote about **happiness:**
>
> "The habit of being happy enables one to be freed, or largely freed, from the domination of outward conditions."
>
> —Robert Louis Stevenson
>
> **Source:** Maxwell Maltz, *Psycho-Cybernetics: A New Way to Get More Out of Life* (New York: Simon & Schuster, 1960), p. 92.

POSITIVE ATTITUDES AND OPTIMAL EXPERIENCES

"What makes you happy? Do you love what you do?" Psychologist Mihalyi Csikszentmihalyi (pronounced "me-high cheek-SENT-me-high") has spent more than 30 years asking these questions to people from all over the world. He has conducted more than 8,000 interviews and a quarter of a million questionnaires to ask people to describe the

"Gina," her co-worker Chris said one night, "you're great at your job, but you're overworking yourself again. You need to cut back. When you're tired, you make more mistakes and get more stressed out."

She sighed. "I know. I just feel like there's so much to do, and I'm not doing enough."

"There's *always* so much to do," he said. "Sometimes I have to pull myself away when I leave at 5:00. But you can change the way you look at your work and make time for yourself. I bet you'd be more productive in the long run, too."

She agreed, and after that her hours returned to normal.

activities that make them happy, and to describe how they feel when doing those activities.[14] He found similar answers whether he was talking with people in Thai and Cambodian mountain villages, Navajo towns in the United States, industrialized European cities, or South American peasant communities.

Whether people talked about gardening, playing tennis, mountain climbing, or performing surgery, they gave similar answers. They said they felt totally engaged and absorbed in the activity. Each step of the task seemed to flow into the next, and the task almost always challenged them and kept their full attention.

When people reached their goal, they felt a sense of mastery, but their real pleasure came from the process itself, rather than achieving the goal. Csikszentmihalyi calls these moments **optimal experience.** He refers to the process itself as **flow**, to describe the motion in which each step of the task seemed to flow effortlessly into the next.

Optimal experiences are intensely enjoyable, but very demanding. After examining many thousands of people's descriptions of flow, Csikszentmihalyi has found eight components that are usually found in a flow experience:

optimal experience

The pleasure in performing the process of an activity itself, rather than achieving the goal.

flow

The feeling of oneness with an activity that allows an individual to uniquely experience an event or activity by becoming totally engaged in the process; term was coined by Mihalyi Csikszentmihalyi.

1. *The activity requires a specific skill and is challenging.* The task is challenging enough to require your full attention, but it is not so difficult that it is impossible or makes you feel defeated.

2. *Attention is completely absorbed by the activity.* You stop being aware of distracting things going on around you, and you seem to become a part of the task itself. The task seems automatic and spontaneous.

3. *The activity has clear goals.* You are working toward a logical end point, and the direction is clear.

4. *Feedback is clear about how you are doing.* You may get feedback from yourself or someone else, or the task itself comes to its natural end.

5. *You are concentrating only on the task itself.* You become unaware of distractions around you.

6. *You achieve a sense of personal control.* You enjoy the feeling of being in charge of the activity, and you enjoy the control you feel over your actions.

7. *You lose a sense of self-awareness.* You are not thinking about yourself or how others are evaluating you. You are lost in the moment, with your attention focused on the activity and your goals.

8. *You lose your sense of time.* Hours can go by like minutes. You are surprised by how much time has passed. The opposite can also happen: you may sometimes feel a small span of time stretch out almost infinitely.

more about...

Mihalyi Csikszentmihalyi teaches at the Drucker School of Management at Claremont Graduate University in California. His interests "include the study of creativity, especially in art; socialization; the evolution of social and cultural systems; and the study of intrinsically rewarding behavior in work and play settings." His studies of finding happiness in one's work have changed the shape of psychology, and his theories have been adopted by many, including former U.S. president Bill Clinton and former U.K. prime minister Tony Blair.

"FLOW" IN OUR EVERYDAY LIVES

Csikszentmihalyi believes that everyone can incorporate optimal experiences into their everyday lives and learn to love their everyday professions. He believes that one key to personal happiness and life satisfaction is to take responsibility and find out for yourself what makes you feel flow in your work. As an example, many students working in the computer lab say that they are surprised by how much time has gone by while they are surfing the Internet looking for information for a class assignment. They get absorbed in the "flow" of the task.

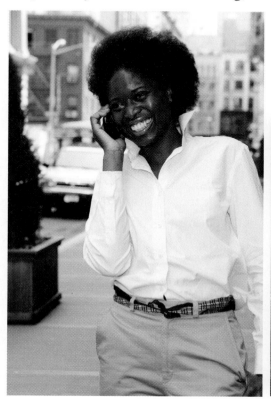

Do you believe that you can experience flow only when you are away from work, enjoying yourself in leisure time? Many people think that flow does not likely happen at work. However, this is not what Csikszentmihalyi found. He found that people are *more* likely to feel flow while at work. Therefore, people should stop buying into the conventional wisdom that work should be drudgery and that play should be fun, and learn to recognize and enjoy the parts of their jobs that make them feel alive—and feel flow!

YOU CAN FIND FLOW IN THE STRANGEST PLACES

Flow is one of those concepts that might be hard to define, but you know when you're feeling it. Flow and passion tend to go hand in hand. *What are some areas in your life that you feel flow?*

more about...

"**Optimal experience** is thus something that we make happen."

—Mihalyi Csikszentmihalyi

Csikszentmihalyi believes that everyone is entirely responsible for achieving these optimal experiences, and capable of making them happen. He also demonstrates that many of the things people do to try to make themselves happier are attempts to find the happiness that is already within if they would only look. Activities such as collecting material possessions, trying to turn back the clock by joining health clubs or getting plastic surgery, are examples of these attempts. They may work for a while, but he believes they will not bring permanent results. Csikszentmihalyi argues that you will be truly happy only when you take personal responsibility for finding out what gives you joy and meaning in life.

more about ...

Job Satisfaction

A study of human resource managers and employees cited in *The Wall Street Journal* showed that **job satisfaction** is more important to employees than any other factor, including pay level or job security.

Source: *The Wall Street Journal,* January 12, 1988, p. 1.

ATTITUDES AND JOB SATISFACTION

What do you find satisfying about your job? Since needs and desires vary from person to person, it is difficult to generalize about job satisfaction, but it is clear that a person's satisfaction with work is directly related to attitude. The degree of satisfaction any employee feels is based on the extent to which the job and benefits associated with it fulfill that employee's needs and desires.

Not very long ago, business experts assumed that if managers could provide good working conditions for employees, every other measure of the job would also be good. Experts are now becoming aware that the connections among job satisfaction and employee turnover, absenteeism,

figure 4.2

CHANGING ATTITUDES

Sometimes, you will note that a co-worker, employee, or supervisor needs to change his or her attitude in order to communicate better with the rest of your work team. By opening communication and giving constructive feedback, you can help others overcome difficult communication problems. *What are some ways that you can give constructive feedback?*

Working Conditions that Help Job Attitudes

1. Mentally challenging work with which the individual can cope successfully.
2. Personal interest in the work itself.
3. Work that is not too physically tiring.
4. Rewards for performance that are just, informative, and in line with the individual's personal ambitions.
5. Working conditions that are compatible with the individual's physical needs and help toward the accomplishment of his or her work goals.
6. High self-esteem on the part of the employee.
7. Agents in the workplace who help the employee to gain job values, such as interesting work, pay, and promotions; whose basic values are similar to his or her own; and who keep conflicts to a minimum.

and overall performance are not so simple. Recent studies showing connections among these factors have not been as conclusive as expected.[15]

We can draw two definite conclusions, though: First, when job satisfaction is very high, employees are less likely to be absent for unexcused reasons.[16] Second, job performance leads to job satisfaction, rather than vice versa. In other words, the successful performance of a series of tasks will often lead to feelings of satisfaction and well-being, which in turn will motivate the employee to complete other tasks that bring about an even higher level of satisfaction (see Figure 4.2). Thus, a manager needs to be in touch with the type of tasks—and rewards—that cause high satisfaction in employees.[17]

Recently, a number of research studies have focused on what is called **organization citizenship behavior.** This is really an attitude—an attitude of willingness to go above and beyond the behaviors that are generally associated with life in the workplace.[18] Here are some examples:

- Sally, an employee, finds several wads of wet paper towels in one of the hallways of her company. Fearing that someone might slip on the towels and suffer an injury, she removes the towels quietly and returns to work.

- José, a new employee, helps a fellow worker in another department with the translation of a document from Spanish to English.

- Sylvia, who is not an accountant but who did well in college accounting, helps a fellow employee understand how the new tax laws affect her department.

A detailed management study at Indiana University-Bloomington showed how critically important organizational citizenship behavior is to the productivity—in terms of both quantity and quality—of any organization or work group.[19] As teams become increasingly important in today's workplace, organization citizenship behavior is likely to be studied—and promoted more and more.

POSITIVE ATTITUDES AND MANAGERS: THEORY X AND THEORY Y

Psychologist Douglas McGregor coined the terms Theory X and Theory Y to show the two opposite types of managers in terms of their attitudes toward people. This management theory has made an important contribution to human relations, as we learned in Chapter 1. As with most attitudes, these two opposites are based on beliefs—in this case, managers' beliefs. McGregor called them assumptions. At the time he was writing (1960), he found that most managers held Theory X assumptions.

organization citizenship behavior

An attitude of willingness to go above and beyond the behaviors that are generally associated with life in the workplace.

SEEING ORGANIZATIONAL CITIZENSHIP CORPORATIONWIDE

While Starbucks may be a more well-known name in coffee and global responsibility, Green Mountain Coffee Roasters is even more highly regarded for fostering a sense of citizenship throughout their company. In both 2006 and 2007, the *Business Ethics Magazine* named them the most ethical company in America, due in large part to their employees. *What can you do to foster organizational citizenship within your own organization?*

Theory X managers believe the following:

1. Most people don't really want to work, don't enjoy working, and will avoid work when possible.

2. Because of this strong dislike of work, most people must be bribed, controlled, directed, or threatened with punishment to get them to put forth enough effort to achieve necessary goals.

3. Most people prefer to be directed, want to avoid responsibility, and want security above all else.[20]

Although a Theory X attitude is likely to be controlling and fear based, it can also be based on a misunderstanding of what motivates the majority of people in the 21st-century workplace. A Theory X manager might simply rely more on external rewards, such as pay raises or bonuses, to get his or her employees to perform. McGregor saw Theory X principles as necessary in certain work situations. When the work is repetitive and uninteresting, for example, it will often make sense to apply Theory X assumptions.[21]

If your attitude is mostly Theory X, you may need to take a closer look at the assumptions you make about people. If your attitude shows that you expect positive results from others, their performance is very likely to be better than when you express the opposite expectation.[22] You may remember this in Chapter 2 as the self-fulfilling prophecy.

A more positive attitude is the **Theory Y** attitude, which assumes that people are rewarded *by the work they do*. Specifically, Theory Y managers believe the following:

THEORY X AND THEORY Y MANAGERS REACT

Due to differing ideas about employees, a Theory X and a Theory Y manager will likely react to the same failure in opposing ways. *Would you prefer to have your supervisor subscribe to Theory X or Theory Y?*

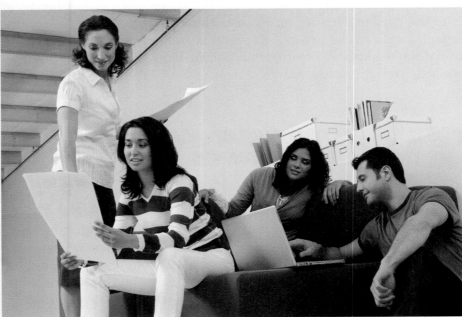

1. Putting forth physical and mental effort in work is as natural as play or rest. Depending on certain conditions (most of which can be controlled), work may be a source of satisfaction or a source of frustration. The choice is often the manager's.

2. Controlling employees' behavior and threatening them with punishment are not the only methods of getting employees to be productive. If people are committed to goals and objectives, they will direct themselves to make sure the essential tasks are completed.

3. The objectives of the organization can also be met by rewarding people with various forms of praise and recognition.

4. Most people can learn to accept and even seek responsibility.

5. Many, not few, people are creative and imaginative.

6. Under the conditions of modern organizations, the mental abilities of the average person are extremely underused.[23]

These six assumptions of Theory Y have called a great deal of attention to the influence of attitudes on the behavior of people in the workplace—especially the attitudes of managers.[24] (See Figures 4.3 and 4.4.) Attitudes also need to be flexible. A manager might oversee a boring, meaningless work situation where an attitude closer to Theory X is actually necessary. Most fast-food restaurants, for example, operate on Theory X assumptions, simply because of the nature of the work.

Three factors must be considered before implementing a Theory Y management attitude:

1. *The maturity level of the employees.* If the employees are not very mature, even interesting work and a supervisor with a positive attitude will probably not be enough to get them to perform without constant supervision and direction.

2. *The meaningfulness of the work.* If on the other hand the job is boring and repetitive, no amount of maturity will likely be enough for Theory Y assumptions to work.

figure 4.3

THEORIES X AND Y: THE BASIC DIFFERENCES

Theory X managers generally have a negative attitude toward employee motivation and creativity. On the other hand, Theory Y managers see employees as enjoying work, interested in taking responsibility, and largely creative. *What factors determine whether Theory X or Theory Y management is best for your company?*

Theory X	Theory Y
• Most people hate to work.	• Work is a natural activity.
• Most people have to be forced or bribed into working.	• People will find rewards in a job well done.
• Most people don't want responsibility.	• Most people like and seek responsibility.
• Most people want security above all else.	• Most people are creative and original.
• Threatening employees is often necessary.	• The mental abilities of most people are sadly underused.

figure 4.4

BEWARE

Just as Theory X is inappropriate for certain work environments, so is Theory Y. Theory Y will not work when employees are unmotivated, lazy, or unhappy with their jobs. *Can a Theory X manager succeed even when he or she knows that employees strongly dislike their jobs?*

Two common mistakes about Theory X and Y management styles are often made by students learning about them for the first time. First, Theory Y is not a cure-all that will motivate everyone magically or improve attitudes toward work. Just making positive assumptions about people won't necessarily make the assumptions true. Some people really do hate to work; some employees really are irresponsible and hopelessly unmotivated. Even with the best employees, some jobs are just too unrewarding for a manager to expect people to like them.

Second, Theory X management isn't all bad, just as Theory Y management isn't all good. One Theory X manager paid high wages, treated his workers well, and wined and dined them (often at his own expense). Never once, though, did he assume that his workers liked their jobs. This type of leader is often called a benevolent Theory X manager. Therefore, no generalized associations of good and evil should be made with either theory.

3. *The speed of the transition in management attitudes.* Employees with years of experience working under a boss with Theory X assumptions are going to be a challenge. If a manager tries to use Theory Y principles all at once, employees will often react as though the supervisor is a pushover.

STRATEGIES FOR SUCCESS

4.1 Changing Pessimism to Optimism

In his book *The Optimistic Child,* Dr. Martin Seligman describes a program for parents who want to change their children's pessimistic beliefs to optimistic ones.[25] He believes that by using this strategy, parents can reduce depression in their children and help them bounce back after facing problems. Using Seligman's strategy for changing pessimism to optimism in families, you can use a similar strategy to help yourself recover quickly from problem situations in the workplace.

Imagine a horrible situation that you are facing at work, one that you believe is a problem building up to a disaster. Go through the following steps to reduce the emotional impact this disaster will have on you:

1. Describe the situation.
2. What is the worst possible outcome of this situation, and is there anything you could do to prevent this outcome?
3. What is the best outcome that could occur in this situation, and is there anything you could do to make the best outcome occur?
4. What do you see as the most likely outcome, and what will you do to cope if the most likely outcome occurs?

Now try these steps yourself. Let's say that the Internet retail company you recently began working for is not doing well financially, and you have heard rumors that there will be massive layoffs. Going through these steps, you might come up with something similar to this:

1. "People are going to be laid off at work."

2. "The company is going under! They're going to call me into the human resources office and tell me I have 10 minutes to pack up my belongings and get out. There would be nothing I could do about that!"

3. "They're going to lay off other people and reorganize, giving me a big fat promotion. I'll keep working really hard so that they will keep me on."

4. "A lot of dot-com companies have financial problems, so there may be layoffs—including me. I'll get my résumé ready and *start looking at job announcements.*"

Seligman believes that if you stop and ask yourself questions such as these each time you find yourself feeling pessimistic, depressed, hopeless, and helpless, you can stop turning problems into catastrophes. When problems become just situations to handle and not catastrophes, you can figure out reasonable solutions to these problems instead of dwelling on them and failing to resolve them. In the process of getting rid of catastrophes, you become more optimistic and cope better with your problems.

An important point to remember is that using this strategy is not going to be second nature. It is something you will have to practice. Just like any new skill, it will become easier over time.[26]

4.2   Building Positive Attitudes

1. *As much as possible, be positive.*

2. *Don't get trapped in someone else's negative attitude.*

3. *Look for the good qualities in yourself, in others, and in your organization.*

4. *Don't let situations outside of you push you around.*

5. *Become goal oriented.*

How can you keep a positive attitude when you are tempted to be discouraged? What if the environment around you is negative? What about those days when all you have is problem after problem? Here are some suggestions that should help, whatever the situation.[27]

1. **As much as possible, be positive.** Try to see the good points about people even when they have many bad ones. Try to see and discuss the positive side of bad situations when possible. When problems come up, look for solutions rather than blame. If you've ever worked with someone who always had negative comments to make, you know how annoying such a person can be—and how contagious this negativity can be! Be the one with the positive attitude; be the optimist.

2. **Don't get trapped in someone else's negative attitude.** You might not be able to change the other person's negative attitude, but you can at least keep it from affecting you. When someone tries to pull you into a negative frame of mind, remind yourself, "This person has a problem. It's his problem, not mine." Listen carefully, actively, watching for nonverbal cues as well as verbal cues—but remember that there is a limit to what you can do for someone with a bad attitude. Beware of holding yourself responsible for the other person's problems. You don't need that burden.[28]

A POSITIVE ATTITUDE WILL TAKE YOU PLACES

A positive attitude can make all the difference in your career *and* your personal life. *What are some changes you can make to improve your attitude?*

3. **Look for the good qualities in yourself, in others, and in your organization.** You can choose which parts of another person's behavior, realities in your workplace, or tasks of your job to dwell on. Nobody can deny that many negative factors exist in life. However, people with positive attitudes select the good, try to change the bad when possible, and leave the rest alone.

4. **Don't let situations outside of you push you around.** Many people have bad attitudes because they feel helpless. This feeling of helplessness often comes from early childhood experiences.

   Psychologist Maxwell Maltz describes his response to a patient whose attitude was one of helplessness: "Have you ever been to a TV show and seen the master of ceremonies manipulate the audience? He brings out a sign that says 'applause' and everyone applauds. He brings out another that says 'laughter' and everyone laughs. They act like sheep—as if they were slaves, and meekly react as they are told to react. You are acting the same way. You are letting outward events and other people dictate to you how you should feel and how you should react."[29]

   This point is directly related to self-esteem. Those with higher self-esteem and an internal locus of control are less likely to be sheep.

5. **Become goal oriented.** Few factors can improve your attitude like goal orientation, which is having goals or definite accomplishments you are striving to achieve. It is a good idea to write down your goals with realistic timelines for achieving them. When setting personal goals, be sure to set them just beyond your present grasp, but not outside the realm of possibility. As goals are reached, set new ones.

CHAPTER FOUR SUMMARY

Chapter Summary by Learning Objectives

1. **Define an attitude.** An attitude is an evaluation of people, ideas, issues, situations, or objects. An attitude has three parts: thoughts, feelings, and actions. These three parts of an attitude are so intertwined that you probably do not even notice them as separate components.

2. **Explain what makes up a good attitude.** Many studies have shown that you can *choose* to have a happy, or positive, attitude. Four characteristics that happy people all seem to have in common are healthy self-esteem, optimism, extraversion, and personal control.

3. **Discuss what goes into changing an existing attitude.** People who have less than positive attitudes sometimes need only to be shown how destructive their attitudes are; then a change takes place. The key is feedback; everyone needs feedback.

4. **Explain the importance of a positive attitude as it applies to optimal experiences.** Attitudes are directly tied to self-esteem. Because they are important to self-esteem, they affect all facets of your life, including work performance. Everyone can increase personal happiness by finding out what activities lead to an optimal experience, or complete enjoyment of an activity. In an optimal experience, you flow effortlessly through the task. In other words, you feel flow.

5. **Identify how "flow" factors into your everyday life.** Csikszentmihalyi believes that everyone can incorporate optimal experiences into their everyday lives and learn to love their everyday professions. He believes that one key to personal happiness and life satisfaction is to take responsibility and find out for yourself what makes you feel flow in your work.

6. **Provide details regarding the link between positive attitudes and job satisfaction.** It is clear that a person's satisfaction with work is directly related to attitude. The degree of satisfaction any employee feels is based on the extent to which the job and benefits associated with it fulfill that employee's needs and desires. Job performance leads to job satisfaction, not the other way around. The successful performance of a series of tasks will often lead to feelings of satisfaction and well-being, which in turn will motivate the employee to complete other tasks that bring about an even higher level of satisfaction. Thus, a manager needs to be in touch with the type of tasks—and rewards—that cause high satisfaction in employees.

7. **Understand the importance of positive attitudes as they apply to Theory X and Theory Y managers.** Theory X and Theory Y managers hold attitudes toward employees: Theory X managers assume that employees hate work and try to avoid it, while Theory Y managers assume that people find work satisfying, and as natural an activity as play or rest. Managers' attitudes need to be flexible to ascertain whether a Theory X or a Theory Y management style is more appropriate in their work environment.

key terms

attitude 82   flow 88   personal control 85

extraversion 85   optimal experience 88   positive attitude 83

feedback 87   organizational citizenship behavior 91

review questions

1. How are attitudes related to self-esteem? How does a change in one affect the other?

2. Where do attitudes come from? When in people's lives do they develop?

3. How do positive attitudes affect the workplace? How can negative attitudes hurt the success of a business?

4. Explain the statement, "Happy people control their own destinies." Do you agree with it?

5. Can a person obtain a happy attitude just by desiring to do so, or do circumstances simply bring happiness into one's life by chance? Explain your answer.

6. What is meant by "flow"? Are there activities in your life in which you feel this optimal experience? Does your chosen career contain activities that will allow this experience? Explain.

7. Thinking about your present workplace, does it seem to be managed more with Theory X or Theory Y attitudes? What workplace factors caused you to answer as you did? Do you feel you respond better to a manager with Theory X or Theory Y attitudes? Explain.

8. Do your attitudes and your role in your company make you someone with *organizational citizenship behavior*? Do you function as a worker or manager, or as a citizen of your organization? Explain.

critical thinking questions

9. Bad things do happen to everyone at one time or another. Is it always possible to maintain a positive attitude? Is it always necessary? Can you think of examples in which maintaining a positive attitude (at least temporarily) is impossible and unnecessary? Include an example of something you can't change in the workplace, and in your personal life.

10. In a recent study on stress and coping, researchers found that people facing a terrible problem (e.g., taking care of a terminally ill family member) were better off if they could take a psychological "time-out" by allowing themselves to enjoy ordinary events. These were simple events such as admiring a beautiful sunset or pausing to think about a compliment they had received from someone else. They also took time to plan positive events, and to interpret neutral events in a positive way (e.g., by looking for the humor in a situation). Can you think of a time when you have done this yourself? Do you think this would be a useful strategy for you? Could you try this positive time-out the next time you face a long-term cause of stress, such as a difficult supervisor or co-worker?[30] Is there a downside to such a strategy?

11. Explain how job satisfaction or dissatisfaction can be directly linked to other (nonworkplace) attitudes.

working it out 4.1

DO YOU FLOW?

School-to-Work Connection: Interpersonal Skills

Stop reading for a few moments, close your eyes (but finish reading these instructions first!), and think about the activities that you do regularly, related to work, school, and your home life. Can you identify an activity among these that makes you feel "flow" in the way that Csikszentmihalyi defined it? Recall that this activity should:

1. require a specific and challenging skill.

2. completely absorb your attention.

3. contain clear goals.

4. contain clear feedback.

5. require you to concentrate only on the task itself.

6. give you a sense of personal control.

7. cause you to lose your sense of self-awareness.

8. cause you to lose your sense of time.

After you have thought about this activity with your eyes closed for a few moments, ask yourself: Have you identified an activity that fits? Maybe more than one such activity? Spend some time thinking about this activity and planning how you can incorporate it effectively into your life. You might find that you want to:

- change jobs or careers.
- change academic majors.
- get a new hobby.

Optimal experiences are worth the effort to build into your life!

working it out 4.2

ATTITUDES AND JOB OUTCOMES

School-to-Work Connection: Interpersonal Skills

How important are employees' general attitudes on the job when they are being considered for a promotion, or being hired? Role-play job attitudes in applicants interviewing for a job, and discuss the most likely outcomes in each situation. Each student acting as applicant should present similar credentials for the job. In the first role play, the student acting as job applicant should act somewhat bored and disinterested. In the second role play, the student acting as job applicant should act neutral, neither positive nor negative. In the third role play, the student acting as job applicant should act positive and enthusiastic about the job. Take note of how others respond to these different attitudes. Discuss your own, and others', emotions during these enacted interviews: Were you frustrated, relaxed, or some other emotion? Did the positive applicant seem the best for the job?

internet exercises

1. *Read and Review*

   Read an interview with Mihalyi Csikszentmihalyi linked through **www.mhhe.com/lamberton4e** or accessed directly at **http://tal-entdevelop.com/articles/Page8.html** and summarize what you have learned about the psychology of flow. Describe a situation using these ideas that you could utilize in your own life to improve a specific attitude or job performance that needs improvement.

2. *Self-Assessment*

   Go to **www.mhhe.com/lamberton4e** for the link to a Web site containing a resilience test. Check your score online. You will receive your score and an interpretation of the results. Did you learn anything about yourself?

3. *Compare and Contrast*

   Go to the Web site for the Conference Board linked through **www.mhhe.com/lamberton4e** and read the report on the study that finds curriculum and training programs are not keeping pace with current workforce attitudes. Are these conditions found at your own place of employment?

4. *Self-Assess and Apply*

   Go to **www.princetonreview.com/careers-after-college.aspx?uidbadge=%07.** You will find a list of topics called "Career Attitudes and Advice Index." Choose any article from the many there and write a three- to four-paragraph reaction to it. How was the article useful to your future (or current) job search?

Why Not "Y"?

Rikki Rowe had looked forward to her first job as a city planning intern for a long time—all during college. It took several months of sending out résumés, making endless phone calls, and smiling through interviews until she had almost given up, but then she landed a job with a consulting firm called Metro Planning in northern California. Rikki had been with Metro only six months when she started realizing that her initial enthusiasm was slowly draining away: Her attitude toward her job was changing for the worse.

"What's wrong with me?" she asked her co-worker Sergio. "I mean, I like what I do, we have a nice new building, the pay is good, the benefits are good—but I just don't look forward to coming to work every day. Maybe I need a new job. Sergio, am I crazy to feel this way?"

"I don't think it's you, Rikki. A lot of people are saying the same thing—that ever since Susan became a partner and took over the day-to-day management, things have changed. It's like she'd rather give us the stick than the carrot. You know that San Jose account? When we came in over budget, she blamed *me* right in front of the clients. I had nothing to do with that!"

"You're right! I've noticed that same kind of thing, too. She questions every one of the time reports I turn in. She acts like I'm lying to her, she always seems irritated, and she complains that we're all goofing off and working too slowly. I even heard her tell Mike last week that none of us seems to want to work very hard. Well, I'm not the one who's making my job miserable, it's Susan. So what do we do now?"

Case Study Questions

1. What type of management strategy does Susan seem to have that is affecting Rikki and Sergio in a negative way? What assumptions is Susan making about her employees?

2. Under what conditions, or for what types of employees, would Susan's management strategies perhaps be necessary?

3. If you were Rikki, what would you do to restore a positive attitude: confront Susan, say nothing to Susan and keep working at Metro, or look for a new job? What do you think the outcome of each of these choices would be?

Make Your Own Attitude

Candace Kaylor hated her job. "It's not the job I hate, exactly, it's the people I work with," she explained to her older sister Shelley over dinner one night. "They're so negative! Complain, complain, complain. They make me feel miserable, too! I go to work happy in the morning, and by noon I'm really depressed." She sighed deeply. "I wish everyone at work would quit making me feel so bad!"

Instead of sympathizing with her, Shelley just laughed. "What's so funny?" exclaimed Candace, indignantly. "Here I am trying to tell you about my problems, and you just laugh at me!"

"I'm sorry," Shelley said, suppressing a smile. "It's just that the way you said that, it made me remember back to when we were little kids. You'd always threaten to tell on me, saying 'I'm telling Mom you *made* me do this, or *made* me do that. . . .' And remember what I always said back to you? 'Nobody *makes* nobody do anything!' Well, guess what, sis, it's the same thing right now: your co-workers aren't the ones 'making' you miserable, *you* are making

yourself miserable! Sure, they have a negative attitude, but *you're* the one allowing yourself to be pulled down into it with them! Fix your attitude! And, by the way, Mom isn't going to get you out of this one, either!"

"Well, that's about the dumbest thing I've heard all day!" retorted Candace defensively, but the look on her face was more thoughtful than offended.

Case Study Questions

1. What is the basic problem at Candace's workplace?

2. Who really is responsible for Candace's attitudes: herself or her co-workers? What can she do to change to a more positive attitude?

3. If Candace continues to work at the same place without doing anything about her problem, what are some likely long-term outcomes?

PERSONAL AND ORGANIZATIONAL VALUES

In the Workplace: Vineeta's Values

SITUATION

Vineeta Sinha had always liked help-ing others, and she looked forward to a career working for a nonprofit agency. After she graduated, though, the jobs she interviewed for with a couple of nonprofit agencies just weren't paying as much as corporate jobs, and she had student loans to pay off. She took a job with an advertising agency that promised a fast track to promotions and an annual bonus based on merit. After only a few months, however, she realized she did not look forward to going to work anymore. It wasn't the workplace or the company itself that was a problem, and she liked all the others on her work team. There was just something about the nature of the work itself that bothered her.

objectives

After studying this chapter, you will be able to:

1   Define values.

2   Compare and contrast values and attitudes.

3   Explain the origins of your values.

4   Identify your personal values.

5   Define and explain value systems.

6   Discuss the role of integrity.

7   Identify strategies for coping with values conflicts.

8   Apply values in a global context.

STRATEGIES FOR SUCCESS

Strategy 5.1   Redefining Your Personal Values: The Rath Test

Strategy 5.2   Building a Character Ethic for Integrity

DISCOVERY

After a long weekend thinking about the goals and values she had held for such a long time—helping others, not manipulating people into buying products—she realized she just couldn't make a career at the advertising agency. The atmosphere seemed so competitive and uncaring compared with what she had thought she would be spending her life's work doing. On Monday morning after that weekend, she walked slowly and thoughtfully toward her supervisor's office to hand in her resignation.

THINK ABOUT IT

Have you found yourself in a situation in which your values clashed with those around you? How would you handle a situation like this?

WHAT ARE VALUES?

values

The worth or importance you attach to different factors in your life.

Values are the worth or importance you attach to different factors in your life. These factors are defined as any objects, activities, or frames of mind that you consider very important.[1] Nearly always, values come in a list of priorities we are not fully aware of most of the time. All of your values taken together are called a *value system,* the set of standards by which you have chosen to live. Values exist not only within individuals, but in organizations as well. A **corporate culture** is a system of shared values throughout any given company or other organization.

corporate culture

A system of shared values and assumptions throughout an organization.

Values are especially important to understanding human behavior. Conflicts between employees, as well as those between managers and employees, often are based on differences in values. When you seem to be at odds with another person, take a look at how your basic values differ. When you seem to be in conflict with your company, examine the company's value system against your own.

VALUES VERSUS ATTITUDES

more about...

Values may be *tangible* (something real in the physical sense, such as material goods) or *intangible* (something that is not real to the touch, but exists in connection to something else). For example, a wedding ring has a cash value (tangible), but it also signifies the value a person holds toward the commitment of marriage (intangible).

If you ask the average person what the difference is between attitudes and values, he or she might say that they are the same. They are not. Attitudes are often affected by values, and values conflicts with other people certainly involve attitude problems—but values are a deeper, and in some ways, more important part of everyone's lives and organizations.

WHERE VALUES COME FROM

Personal values are formed in early childhood and are affected strongly by the values of parents and the child's environment. The place and the time period of the first few years of most people's lives both have a great effect on the formation of values. Statistics expert Daniel Yankelovich believes that middle-class values give Americans a certain amount of self-esteem, a fairly clear idea of who they are, and especially a feeling that somehow their personal lives make a positive impact on the lives of others.

more about...

Values are also interpreted differently by people from different generations, religions, political systems, cultures, and ethnic groups. This is true when comparing cultures around the globe, but also in specific groups in the United States.

Yet, Yankelovich says that these values changed rapidly during the last century and are still changing. He shows that three value patterns related to work and home life have emerged since the early 1970s:

1. The nature of a person's paid job is now much more significant.
2. Leisure time is more valued, mostly because it has become a rare commodity.
3. Americans now insist much more strongly that jobs become less impersonal, and more human and humane.[2]

These three value areas have created more emphasis on individual freedom of choice, a movement away from rigid organizational and work systems, and a desire to live more closely with both nature and community.[3]

Since the Yankelovich study, human history has seen a shift toward the Internet that is profoundly changing the focus of people's values. Consumers are now demanding to be treated as equals to those who sell products and services. Many online companies actually allow customers to name their prices and thus to hold unprecedented power in the transaction process. In many other ways, widespread use of the Internet signals a change of even the most traditional values.

During the past few years, many nationally publicized scandals have grabbed our attention. Several corporations have been hurt greatly by allowing themselves to be involved in activities that show questionable values. The most serious of these incidents have even brought legal charges, such as those faced by some of the executives of Enron and Adelphia.

Another disturbing area of social values change has been in high school and college student cheating. *Who's Who Among American High School Students* recently published a survey that showed 80 percent of students featured in that publication admitted to having cheated at some point in their schooling. Nearly half the same students said that they didn't consider cheating to be "always wrong."[4]

In a book called *The Cheating Culture*, author David Callahan shows that American students are being taught "bottom-line economy" thinking. This mind-set makes it more likely than in the past that such students will carry their questionable behavior into the workplace after they have finished school. If they do, the workplace of the very near future is likely to feel the impact.[5] The material both in this chapter and in Chapter 17 (on ethics) will deal with ways of understanding your own values and the values of other people with whom you study and work.

Other historic periods have likewise affected the values of those who lived through them. If you know people who grew up during the Great Depression, you may have noticed that their values were probably affected a great deal by that experience. They knew poverty once, and they have never forgotten the values that experience taught them.

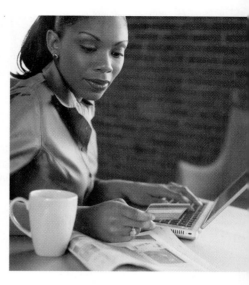

A BUYER'S MARKET

Since the beginning of online shopping, consumer values have shifted to an increasing demand for personalized service and more specialized products. *Do you feel that your needs are better met by online shopping than by traditional methods?*

Online Goods and Services

Using a search engine, search for sites of two or three companies that let you name your own price for goods and services. A good place to start is e-Bay. Write a paragraph to answer these questions:
What are the names of the companies?
Which of them is the most user-friendly?

What characteristics make it that way?
Why do you prefer or not prefer this method?
Do you prefer this method of buying things over traditional methods? That is, which do you value more in shopping: tradition or innovation?

more about...

The Great Depression (1929–1941), which was triggered by the Wall Street crash of 1929, resulted in millions of Americans losing their jobs, farms, and homes. It did not officially end until the United States entered World War II in December 1941.

Other important factors that help form values are religion, political views, parents, socioeconomic class, exposure to education, television, the Internet, and other mass media (see Figure 5.1). Often one generation may judge the values of another generation. Perhaps you have heard someone complain about the loud music teens play. This may be a generational complaint. At some point in one's growth, an individual must examine those values to see if they are really his or her own values.

Sometimes people might have certain values without real awareness of them. It might not occur to us to question those until they are challenged.

figure 5.1

SOCIAL FACTORS OF A GENERATION

Each generation has been affected by several social factors, which in turn help shape their values. *How do you see these differences in other generations?*

The Influence of Certain Factors as They Have Affected Values			
Areas of Change	**Pre-Baby Boomers (born 1920–45)**	**Baby Boomers (born 1946–64)**	**Gen. X, Y, and Beyond (born 1965–80s)**
Mass Media	Radio networks	Television	Internet
Comedians	Bob Hope	George Carlin	Jim Carrey, Chris Rock
Wars & Disasters	Depression World War II	Vietnam War	Iraqi War 9/11 terror attack
New Technologies	Radar Atomic power	Space technology	Digital technologies
Villains	Hitler, Stalin	Khrushchev Idi Amin	Saddam Hussein Osama bin Laden
Musical Choices	Jazz, Swing	Rock 'n' Roll Motown	Hip Hop, rap Alternative rock
Fears	Poverty Total warfare	Atomic warfare	Terrorism

You may know (or possibly be) someone who grew up in the 1960s, that period of rebellion against authority, fighting for rights for disadvantaged groups, and antiwar protests. Whatever else has happened to the members of that generation, most of them still have definite ideas about maintaining social justice, questioning people in authority, and "doing their own thing." Many of those who have become conservative and less antiestablishment will even admit that the strongly held values of the 60s affected their desire for a change in point of view. Influences on our values are difficult, if not impossible, to ignore.

Values can be placed in two categories. **Terminal values** (or end-point ideal values) are likely to maintain a high priority throughout your life. These will often be related to long-term goals that you want to accomplish during your lifetime. **Instrumental values** (or everyday action-directed attitudes), on the other hand, reflect the ways you prefer to behave. They are based on your actions and attitudes.[6] One could say that instrumental values help you reach your goals, while terminal values *are* those goals. (See Figure 5.2.)

terminal values
Values likely to maintain a high priority throughout your life.

instrumental values
Values that reflect the ways you prefer to behave.

Instrumental Values	Terminal Values
Ambition	A comfortable and prosperous life
Open-mindedness	An exciting, stimulating, and active life
Capability, effectiveness	A sense of accomplishment or lasting contribution
Cheerfulness	A world at peace, free of war and conflict
Cleanliness	A world of beauty, nature, and art
Courage	Equality, brotherhood, and equal opportunity
Forgiveness	Family security, taking care of loved ones
Helpfulness	Freedom, independence, and free choice
Honesty	Happiness and contentment
Imagination	Inner harmony and freedom from inner conflict
Independence	Mature love, sexual and spiritual intimacy
Intelligence	National security
Logic	An enjoyable life
Love and tenderness	Salvation and eternal life
Obedience, respect	Self-respect and high self-esteem
Politeness	Social respect and admiration
Responsibility	True friendship
Self-control	Wisdom in understanding life

figure 5.2

EXAMPLES OF TERMINAL AND INSTRUMENTAL VALUES

Instrumental values are those you use in your everyday life to achieve your terminal or end-point values; that is, values directly related to your long-term goals and dreams. *Can you think of an instrumental value of yours that is helping you achieve a terminal value?*

Source: Based on M. Rokeach, *The Nature of Human Values* (New York: Free Press, 1973), pp. 5–12.

Jill, a college student, was a politically active Republican. She campaigned for Republican candidates and expressed a great deal of enthusiasm for the Republican political party. One day a fellow student who was a Democrat asked her to explain why being a Republican was so valuable to her. The best answer Jill could come up with was that she loved her dad, and the GOP was his party. She had never examined the beliefs and practices of the Republican Party to decide whether it represented a political philosophy that she personally agreed with. One could say that her political beliefs were really based on someone else's values—not Jill's.

WHAT ARE YOUR VALUES?

Answering this question requires a very high level of honesty. Have you ever noticed that it is usually easier to be honest with other people than with yourself? Take a few minutes right now and test yourself. As soon as you've finished this paragraph, put the book aside and list at least 10 activities or principles that are very important in your life and most valuable to you. List them in any order, just as they pop into your mind. For example, the list could include family, success, improving the world, or religious beliefs.

When you have listed the 10 or more values, number them in their order of importance to you, with number one being the most important. Once you've finished numbering your values, ask the person or people who are most important in your life to make the same list—a list of what that person *thinks* are your top 10 values. Then compare the two lists, looking for differences and similarities. You should learn some very important things about what your top values really are, based on your attitudes and actions as opposed to how you see yourself.

> **more about...**
>
> **What are "American values"?**
>
> Does such a thing as American values really exist, or do we all hold individual values? Sociologist Robin Williams has identified 10 core values that are widely held among Americans. These include: (1) equal opportunity, (2) achievement and success, (3) material comfort, (4) activity and work, (5) practicality and efficiency, (6) progress, (7) science, (8) democracy and free enterprise, (9) freedom, and (10) status hierarchy in society.
>
> **Source:** John J. Macionis, *Society: The Basics,* 8th ed. (Upper Saddle River, NJ, Pearson Prentice-Hall, 2006).

value systems

Frameworks people use in developing beliefs about themselves, others, and how they should be treated.

Spranger's Six Value Systems

Theoretical, economic, aesthetic, social, political, and religious.

VALUE SYSTEMS

Early in the 20th century, Eduard Spranger defined six different types of people based on their types of **value systems,** or their frameworks for developing their own beliefs. See if you fit into any of **Spranger's Six Value Systems:**

1. *The theoretical person.* This individual seeks to discover truth. He or she observes happenings and thinks them through, trying whenever

possible to put ideas into a system. He or she avoids *judgments* about the beauty or usefulness of ideas.

2. *The economic person.* Personal needs, production, marketing, credit, and wealth are more important to this type of person than are social or artistic values. Things in life that are *useful* are the most important.

3. *The aesthetic person.* Beauty, form, and harmony are most important to this type of individual.

4. *The social person.* This person values and loves other people. Kindness and unselfishness are both very important values.

5. *The political animal.* This type is very power motivated. His or her values center on influence, fame, and power. These individuals do well in careers that involve the use of power and control.

6. *The religious person.* To this individual, the highest value is unity. He or she tries to understand the universe as a whole and relate to it meaningfully.[7]

Maybe you can't identify one single type as yours. Your value system could represent a combination of two or more. Most people have value systems that are complex mixtures of these factors.

Graves's Seven Value Levels

A more recent treatment of the subject of value systems comes from psychologist Clare Graves, who believed that people evolve through different levels *of psychological existence.* **Graves's Seven Value Levels** describe changing values at different points in life.

Level 1: Reaction Newborn babies just react. When they have a need, they cry to have it fulfilled. When a stimulus comes, they give an expected response. Very few people stay on this level past infancy.

Level 2: Tribalism Tribalism includes dealing with concerns about pain, shelter, and safety by giving in to the authority of a leader of some kind. In its purest form, tribalism can be seen in aboriginal cultures where ritual and strict social divisions are common.

Level 3: Egocentrism Egocentrism can be defined as rugged individualism taken to an extreme. This type of behavior says, "To heck with everybody else; *I'm* what matters." The egocentric person is aggressive, restless, impulsive, and not strongly inclined to follow the moral rules of society.

Level 4: Conformity Conformists are people who need clarity and straightforwardness; vagueness frustrates them. They have a hard time accepting

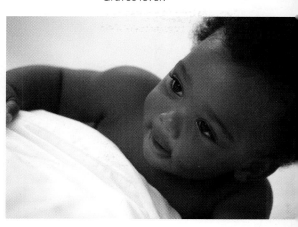

WE ALL START AT LEVEL 1
Since we all enter the world as babies, we begin life at the same level. *What can you do to change your Graves level?*

Graves's Seven Value Levels

Reaction, tribalism, egocentrism, conformity, achievement, social orientation, and existentialism.

other people's values but expect others to accept theirs. They are likely to join groups with strictly defined rules. Many people think of conformists as easygoing, but if their values are challenged, they can either sacrifice themselves or become violent. They like very specific job descriptions and have little patience with participative or free-rein managers, whom they see as *wishy-washy*.

Level 5: Achievement People at this level try to reach success by manipulating other people and situations to their advantage. They thrive on politics, competition, and independent business. They measure their success in terms of money and power and are likely to show off whatever status symbols they have.

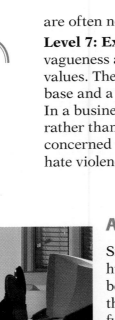

more about...

Clare W. Graves (1914–1986) believed that these levels are applied to people's work and overall health. His original research on "levels of existence" involved thousands of student volunteers over several years' time.

Level 6: Social orientation A member of this group is often called a *people person*. To a member of this level, getting along is more important than getting ahead. The approval of others who share their values is more important to them than either money or fame. The socially oriented are often thought of as *cop-outs* by people on Levels 4 and 5, and their values are often not well rewarded by the business world as a whole.

Level 7: Existentialism People at this level are able to accept vagueness and get along well with others who don't share their own values. They tend to be goal oriented, but their goals have a broader base and a longer time span than those goals of people at Level 5. In a business, they tend to be interested in overall, long-term profit, rather than short-term gains. Like people on Level 6, they are concerned with the dignity of their fellow human beings, and they hate violence.[8]

A RELAXED APPROACH

People at Graves's seventh level, existentialism, are comfortable with vagueness, do not feel a need to conform to others, and respect the dignity of those around them. *Which of Graves's seven levels best fits your personality?*

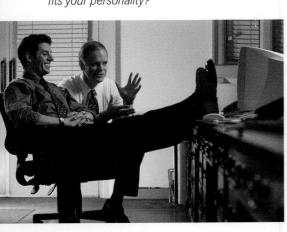

Another Way to See Value Systems

Since values are so very important to everything we do as humans, many different ways of systematizing values have been created over time. As many people have pointed out, these value systems all have one element in common: they fulfill basic psychological needs in the groups of people who created them. For example, if a person or a group values power, values that involve a need for power will develop. Likewise with materialism, security, conquest—whatever the value might be.

Here are some examples of systems of values that attract many people:

The Human Values Project

Go to this site through **www.mhhe.com/lamberton4e** to evaluate the project's goals and activities. Do you agree with the philosophy? How can you use a site like this to clarify your own values? Be prepared to discuss this philosophy in class.

Pragmatism. Someone who is a pragmatist sees the practicality and usefulness of an idea as more important than its ideal "truth." Pragmatists hold that "beliefs do not have to represent reality to be true." To oversimplify a bit, a pragmatist is more interested in what "works" than in what is considered "correct" by some other standard.[9]

Humanism. Humanists vary a great deal in the detail of their beliefs. However, people who regard themselves as humanistic generally believe in the worth and dignity of all humans. They see all people as unique individuals with something worthwhile to contribute. Since we all are part of the human condition, there is a worldwide morality that applies to all cultures. Divine issues are much less important that human ones.[10]

Idealism. Idealists believe that your own consciousness is the only thing that is possible to know. Thus, that which is ultimately valuable is only that which you hold in your own mind. Things beyond that reality are not real, and thus not valuable.[11] The more extreme forms of idealism teach that the material world as we know it doesn't exist, except in the minds of people. Of course, the term "idealism" is also used to designate any philosophy that is grounded in faith and principles.

> **pragmatism**
> The belief in the practicality of an action, rather than in strong belief in the idea behind that action.

> **humanism**
> A belief in the worth and dignity of all people.

> **idealism**
> The belief in the importance of ideas and thoughts. Also, it can be defined as a philosophy that is grounded in faith and high ideals.

THE ROLE OF INTEGRITY

> **integrity**
> Soundness of moral character, which involves living up to one's own beliefs and ideals.

Integrity can be defined as *soundness of moral character*. Others have defined integrity as living up to the principles you claim to believe in, putting values into action, *practicing what you preach* or *walking the talk*.[12] If you are living up to your own stated standards of professional conduct and appropriate behavior, you are said to have integrity.

Because of rapid changes in the world, realities everyone once took for granted are changing constantly. American society contains

Stephen Covey Interview

Read an interview with Stephen Covey posted on the ZenHabits Web site in which Covey discusses such topics as his daily routine, blogs, and personal beliefs and attitudes. Access the interview through **www.mhhe.com/lamberton4e (http://zenhabits.net/2008/02/exclusive-interview-stephen-covey-on-his-** **morning-routine-blogs-technology-gtd-and-the-secret/)**. Do Covey's responses seem to mirror the strategies of effective habits he has written about? How can you use an interview like this to think about and clarify your own values? Be prepared to discuss your responses in class.

---

numerous recent examples of *role models in the negative*—public figures whose values have shown a lack of integrity. Small wonder that the concept of integrity and what it means have been challenged by many. Lately, however, the word has received a new emphasis—especially as an element of trust. Noted management consultant Judith Bardwick says that without integrity, one can never achieve trust.[13] People with integrity, Bardwick says, must have clear convictions about their own values and their ability to see clearly the difference between right and wrong, between wisdom and foolishness. These qualities build the trust of those around you. A certain level of trust is necessary for a company to exist, but a lack of trust can destroy an organization.

In his popular book, *The Seven Habits of Highly Effective People*, Stephen Covey writes about important changes in human interactions that have taken place since the end of World War II. Since that time, Covey says, people have developed a focus on personality rather than on character. The most important element of success has become what Covey calls the **personality ethic.** This method of interacting with others places emphasis on being likable, making sure that you are received well, and maintaining a *positive mental attitude*. According to Covey, this personality approach has replaced what used to be the **character ethic,** which was based on principles, beliefs, and strong values rather than upon the use of various surface techniques. In the process, integrity has suffered.

If you are very skilled at the techniques of the personality ethic, you might seem to succeed, but the lack of reality—the *acting* rather than *being*—will catch up with you sooner or later. Covey says that the trust element will be damaged, because trust has to be based on reality, rather than on pretense, or only short-term success will be possible. In 2004, Covey followed his *Seven Habits* book with *The 8th Habit: From Effectiveness to Greatness*. This eighth habit is about finding your "voice," that is, your unique personal significance, while using the character

personality ethic

Emphasis is placed on being likable, making sure that you are received well, and maintaining a positive mental attitude.

character ethic

Emphasis is placed on principles, beliefs, and strong values rather than upon the use of various surface techniques.

ethic. In short, *The 8th Habit* is about you and your values—discovering what they are and how they are unique to you and to the contributions you can make to the lives of others. With your unique blend of talent, need, conscience, and passion, Covey says, you can uniquely impact the world.[14] For more on Covey go to **www.stevencovey.com/8thHabit/ learnmore.html**.

Values are the basis for both the purpose and the goals of any organization. Just as personal values are formed over a period of time, organizational values evolve as an organization develops a purpose and focus. They are usually formed and influenced by people (often managers) who seem to symbolize what the firm stands for.

Organizational values directly affect relationships within the organization. The importance people give to others within the organization is often based on shared values; the group uses these values to decide what qualities make someone worth knowing or worth working with. Similarly, the types of people who advance in the company will be determined by the values of both employees and managers.

In their pioneering best seller, *In Search of Excellence*, Tom Peters and Robert Waterman discuss the function of values in the companies they identify as excellent. The most important task, they say, is to *figure out your value system* and *decide what your company stands for*. A related question they suggest is: *What does your enterprise do that gives everyone the most pride?*[15] Answers to these questions will help you understand what those values are.

Dennis Bakke, author of the popular book *Joy at Work*, answers this question by showing that the workplace should be guided by values that are "meant to be ends in and of themselves." Winning—especially financially—is a second-order value, according to Bakke.[16] His highest four workplace values are integrity, fairness, social responsibility, and—above all—fun. This ultimate value of fun, or joy, gives people who work the freedom to use their abilities for the good of all, without the undue interference of supervisors.[17]

Whatever your organization's goals, you should assess your personal values and compare them with those of your company. Do they agree? If they don't, you may be unhappy with your organization because of this discrepancy. Are you ever frustrated in your attempt to find that kind of joy in your organization? Value conflicts could be the reason.

VALUES CONFLICTS

In the beginning of this chapter, Vineeta was deeply involved in a **values conflict.** This commonly happens when one set of values clashes with another, and a decision has to be made—sometimes very quickly. These conflicts happen quite often in most people's lives.

values conflict
Conflict that occurs when one set of values clashes with another, and a decision has to be made.

In a small midwestern college, four deans ran the institution's instructional wing. One was a Christian fundamentalist, one was Jewish, one agnostic, and the other a Zen Buddhist. People who saw this unusual assortment predicted chaos, but the period of time when they worked together was actually very productive, with little negative conflict. When asked how they managed to work so well together, they all gave similar answers. "We spent our energy on the goals of the college, a college we all love and want the best for; that gave us a unity that surpassed the values differences we might have had in other areas of life."

Interpersonal Values Conflicts

CONFLICTING VALUES HAPPEN EVERYWHERE

Even though our values are often shaped by our families, value conflicts can happen in any household. Conflicting values are not restricted to the workplace. *Would your handling of value conflicts differ depending on the environment?*

All people come from differing backgrounds, where they have learned various value systems. When they are thrown together in the workplace, they often must work with others whose values differ greatly from their own. A certain number of interpersonal values conflicts are nearly unavoidable. To deal with such potential problems, you are often called upon to look closely at your own values, trying whenever possible to understand and accept the values of others without compromising your personal integrity. Also, you will often find it necessary to discover common ground where you can agree with others on what is important to both the workplace and the goals that everyone needs to achieve.

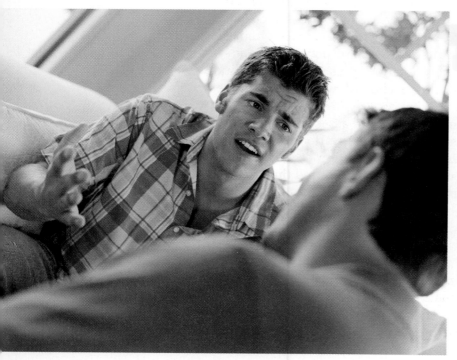

Personal versus Group Values

Values conflicts also often involve a clash between the individual and the group. Case Study 5.1 at the end of this chapter deals with such a situation, where the culture of the organization can work against an individual's values to the point of distress. If you are outnumbered this greatly, changing the group values is possible but very unlikely. When this happens, you usually must decide whether or not to stay in such a job.

As a salesperson in a car dealership, Halina found herself within a value system among the other salespeople that put a great emphasis on attending social gatherings, usually parties. She found that they always involved staying up until 2 or 3 A.M., even on weeknights. When she tried twice to excuse herself early, she was labeled a "party pooper." Since Halina valued both her health and her alertness, she finally decided she had to find another job, even though she was making very good money at auto sales. The value she placed on health—which included getting adequate sleep—outweighed the values of the group.

Internal Values Conflicts

Still another type of values conflict is one that is waged inside of you. People sometimes find themselves wanting two different outcomes that contradict each other. In some cases, you might want something that, if it is achieved, will eliminate the possibility of another outcome that is also very desirable. For example, a college student wants a new car and has the money to buy it; however, once the money is spent on the car, none will be left for tuition and expenses. In other cases, both outcomes could be had, but getting one would contradict the value of the other. Both types of conflict often result in **cognitive dissonance,** the emotional state that results from acting in ways that contradict one's beliefs or other actions.[18]

cognitive dissonance
The emotional state that results from acting in ways that contradict one's beliefs or other actions.

When the American forefathers proclaimed that "all men are created equal," many of them owned slaves. The cognitive dissonance between practice and values became increasingly stronger, until finally slavery was abolished. In a more personal example, Garth believes that cheating on his income tax is wrong; doing so violates some basic values he has in defining his own integrity. Yet every April, he finds himself *fudging* a little. This contradictory behavior causes cognitive dissonance in his own life. How can Garth take care of this internal conflict?

Most people have a certain amount of such dissonance in their behaviors. If the issues are small and create little compromise to people's values and attitudes, people usually live with the mild discomfort. However, if what is being compromised is an important value, people will usually take one of four possible actions.

Imagine that you are in a job in which you resent the management system. You have said that you hate all managers. Suddenly, a supervisor tells you she is being promoted and wants you to take her place. She has cleared the move with her superiors. It is now cognitive dissonance time!

What can you do? Here are the major choices you have, according to the cognitive dissonance theory:

Cognitive dissonance can also refer to the stress that is caused by holding two contradictory beliefs at the same time, such as when you like a friend for having certain traits but dislike him or her for having others.

more about...

117

INTERNAL VALUE CONFLICTS CAN HAPPEN TO ANYONE

Internal value conflicts are normal. Oftentimes, we find that we want conflicting things. *What are the best strategies for resolving internal value conflicts?*

1. *You can change your original beliefs about management.* "You know, I was probably overreacting a bit," you could say. "Managers are really important in any organization. I should have been more open-minded."

2. *You can use **denial**.* This can be defined as a failure to confront your problem. "I didn't really mean all of those things I said before. The things I said were so extreme, anybody could see I wasn't really serious."

3. *You can get into **self-justification**.* In other words, you can explain your behavior so that you feel it is correct, by saying something like, "Yes, managers are mostly oppressive jerks, but I can show everybody that you don't have to be a jerk to be an effective manager."

4. *You can change your own behavior.* You might say, "As a manager, I can treat people with respect and create a positive work environment."[19]

When you experience cognitive dissonance, you don't necessarily move toward trying to make actions consistent with values and beliefs. Instead, you might use any of these methods to make them appear more consistent and to lessen the stress caused by cognitive dissonance. All humans seem to need to justify their actions and make consistent sense out of their own contradictions. This process often happens instantly and without much deliberate thought—so it should not be surprising that it has been found to occur in four-year-old children, in patients with amnesia, and even in capuchin monkeys.[20]

denial
Failure to confront your problems.

self-justification
Explaining behavior so that you will feel it is correct.

VALUES IN AN INTERNATIONAL ECONOMY

As the world gets smaller, international differences in values need to be understood. Today's business world is now dealing with people from many different religions, political systems, cultural backgrounds, and ethnic groups. Many citizens of the United States tend to think that the U.S. value system is the only one in the world with anything going for it, but they need to understand that every other country has the same temptation—to think its own national and cultural values are the best. For example, the values system of America stresses "rugged individualism" and speaking out assertively. Traditional Asians, however, usually value the strength of the group over the strength of the individual. An American businessperson would be wise to understand such differences and adapt to them when necessary. Every year, more members of differing ethnic cultures join the American

more about...

Values from Another Culture's Eyes

People from other cultures will define your values by your behavior, so other areas of human relations, such as eye contact, tone of voice, and body language, will influence their interpretation of your values system.

When Jasper Arasco arrived in America from Panama, he was surprised that his manager asked for his advice in making several important decisions. Jasper's first reaction was to suspect that his manager was not very good at his job; in Panama, only someone very unsure of his or her job would take such an approach. After living in America for several months, Jasper began to understand that this was a style of management that he needed to become accustomed to. He realized that asking for advice was a way of sharing in decision making. However, when Jasper returned to a new job in Panama, he was forced to readjust.

workforce. In addition, a growing number of American companies are doing business abroad. Because of this, people of all cultures need to become increasingly sensitive to the values of others.

When you are dealing with people from other cultures, you will tend to find four major areas of difference in values—and in perception of the values of others.

1. *Views of power and authority.* In many emerging countries, the prevailing attitude is that what a manager says must be followed without question. The practices of power sharing and group decision making in the United States seem strange and unfamiliar to many people of other cultures. They follow the traditional values of the top-down organization and often must be urged to participate, even in decisions that affect them personally.

2. *Views of the individual versus the group.* Americans have been taught to value individualism and the individual effort. In many other countries, the group is seen as considerably more important than any of its individual members. In these cultures, taking individual credit for an accomplishment that the group did together would be considered extremely selfish and rude. The group is usually valued more highly than the individual. Our competitive culture encourages and rewards individual achievement. This can lead to a stronger focus on individual accomplishments rather than on group successes.

3. *Tolerance for uncertainty.* The history of the United States is a story of people who sailed here with little certainty of what lay ahead. Later, pioneers in covered wagons traveled to new territories. They had to have or develop the ability to live with the prospect of the unknown. Other cultures may view uncertainty as recklessness and lack of planning. To many

TOLERATING UNCERTAINTY

Different cultures have different ways of handling uncertainty. *What is your tolerance for uncertainty?*

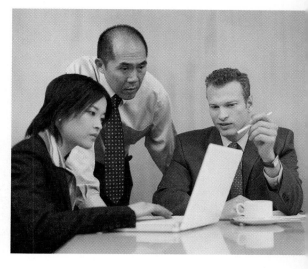

When Takara Nishi took a job in California after having worked in her native Japan, she was asked at a planning meeting if she would head a work team, since she had headed a successful one in Japan. Her reply was, "I have always worked well with my team; I would welcome an opportunity to do so again." Since her American managers expected her to "sell" herself more assertively, her response was misinterpreted as showing a lack of confidence. When a manager asked why she hadn't sounded more persuasive, she answered, "I didn't want the members of my team to think that I was taking too much credit. That would make it difficult for us to work together." In her culture, Takara had been taught that the group effort is much more important than any individual effort.

cultures, maximizing certainty is a value that should be respected by members of other cultures.

4. *The value of punctuality.* In the United States, people are often judged by their promptness and punctuality. Westerners, especially North Americans, often value people less when they are late for appointments. In many other cultures, time urgency is not a value at all. In fact, North Americans are often seen by others as impatient, judgmental, and overly stressed because of the time factor. When dealing with less time-focused cultures, North Americans need to relax and learn to behave in the others' time context. They especially need to examine the high value they place on time.

These differences can help you understand the values misunderstandings that North Americans might have with members of other cultures.

STRATEGIES FOR SUCCESS

5.1 Redefining Your Personal Values: The Rath Test

1. Did I choose this value freely, with no outside pressure?
2. Did I choose this value from several alternatives?
3. Did I consider the consequences of my choice?
4. Do I like and respect this value?
5. Will I defend this value publicly?
6. Will I base my behavior on this value?
7. Do I find this value persistent throughout my life?

One of the biggest problems with defining your values and who you really are is that most people have a tendency to lie to themselves. Your ideal self often wants to believe that the values you feel you *should* have are the ones you *do* have. One revealing question to ask yourself is "Do my values change depending on where I am and who I'm with?" If your answer is yes, are they really your values, or not?

A U.S. company opened a branch in Taiwan. Once they formed a management team, made up of both Americans and Taiwanese, the American top managers called a meeting to brainstorm ideas for entering markets with a new product. The Taiwanese members of the group found this method frustrating, especially when they suggested ideas that were added to, changed, or dismissed by the group. The problem came from differences between the two cultures in levels of uncertainty tolerance.

Louis Rath, a well-known expert on values, has put together the **Rath Test,** which you can use to find out if the values you think you have are the ones you truly have. Take any values you consider important in your life and ask these seven questions:

> **Rath Test**
>
> Finds out if the values you think you have are the ones you truly have.

1. **Did I choose this value freely, with no outside pressure?** Or did someone else—such as a parent, group, or religion—provide this value to you? The source of the value isn't the real issue; if it did originate somewhere else, did it later become your own value?

2. **Did I choose this value from several alternatives?** In other words, did you even notice that other values were possible, or did you just accept the value and look in no other direction?

3. **Did I consider the consequences of my choice?** Strong belief in a value is likely to have consequences in your life—not all of them positive. Did you take a good look at the cause-effect sequence of holding this value?

4. **Do I like and respect this value?** If a value really is your own, you will prize it, care for it, and be motivated by it.

5. **Will I defend this value publicly?** This may be the most important question in the Rath Test. If you value something others hate, will you defend that value in front of people who might dislike you because of such a stand?

6. **Will I base my behavior on this value?** It is one thing to say something is valuable to you, but will you make it a part of the way you act in everyday life?

7. **Do I find this value persistent throughout my life?** If it is really your value, you should be able to see it affecting all areas of your life throughout the years of your life. It should have a lasting, long-term effect on you.[21]

The values you have already written down in the earlier exercise can now be tested against these questions. This approach will help you separate the *real* values from the ones you *thought* were strong in your life.

5.2 Building a Character Ethic for Integrity

1. Focus
2. Respect

Bethany sells radio and television advertising. One of her customers is the Warm Springs Reservation in Oregon, a thriving reservation. Bethany soon found that she was dealing with a culture that has different attitudes toward time than she did. She has learned not to expect absolute punctuality from clients, because they view time and prioritize events in a different way from much of the rest of the American population. She has learned to be patient and tolerant and has done a large amount of successful business with the Native Americans. Bethany has also found that the Native Americans of Warm Springs make allowances for her culture as well.

3. Responsibility

4. Pride

5. Fairness and equity

6. Trust and being trusted

What steps can you take to develop your personality ethic and become more authentic as a human being? The following strategy should serve as a beginning point for your journey into building character.

1. **Focus.** Put the life you've lived so far into focus. Ask yourself, "What do I really want from life?" and then, "What kind of person do I need to become to make that goal become a reality?"

2. **Respect.** Do you respect yourself and, in turn, demand respect from others? Respect is a two-way street: don't ever abuse or mistreat others, and when possible, assume the best about them.

3. **Responsibility.** Be willing to accept responsibility for whatever you do, right or wrong. Make a practice of not placing blame. Work on the cure for problems, rather than placing blame for their existence.

4. **Pride.** Practice feeling good about yourself. Most important, remind yourself that you don't need the approval of others to feel good about yourself.

5. **Fairness and equity.** Believe in the rights of others and never violate those rights. Avoid double standards and treat all human beings as equals. Everyone should be treated with equal dignity and fairness.

6. **Trust and being trusted.** Never let someone down when that person trusts you. Also, allow others to know that you trust them by building a two-way trust relationship. Stand up for the beliefs you consider important, and don't act in any way that contradicts them.[22]

CHAPTER FIVE SUMMARY

Chapter Summary by Learning Objectives

1. **Define values.** Values are the worth or importance people attach to different factors in their lives. These factors are defined as any objects, activities, or frames of mind that you consider very

important. All of your values taken together are called a value system. A corporate culture is a system of shared values throughout any organization.

2. **Compare and contrast values and attitudes.** Attitudes are often affected by values, and values conflicts with other people certainly involve attitude problems—but values are a deeper, and in some ways, more important part of everyone's lives and organizations. Unlike attitudes, values come in a partially unconscious list of priorities.

3. **Explain the origins of your values.** Personal values are formed in early childhood and are affected strongly by the values of parents and the child's environment. The place and time period of the first few years of most people's lives have a great effect on the formation of values.

4. **Identify your personal values.** Everyone should evaluate his or her personal values both to see what they really are and to decide whether or not they are genuine.

5. **Define and explain value systems.** Value systems are frameworks people use in developing beliefs about themselves, others, and how they should be treated. Spranger's Six Value Systems can help you understand where your values and those of others fit into the general scheme of things. Graves' Seven Value Levels do the same thing in a more general way. Both perspectives can help you to understand the overall concept of value systems.

6. **Discuss the role of integrity.** Integrity, or soundness of moral character, is an important part of any value system. According to Stephen Covey, in the mid-20th century, people changed from maintaining a character ethic to a personality ethic, which has lessened the emphasis placed on integrity. You can take steps to improve personal integrity and return to the character ethic.

7. **Identify strategies for coping with values conflicts.** All people come from differing backgrounds, where they have learned various value systems. When they are thrown together in the workplace, they often must work with others whose values differ greatly from their own. When individuals experience cognitive dissonance (the emotional state that results from acting in ways that contradict one's beliefs or other actions), they don't necessarily move toward trying to make actions consistent with values and beliefs. Instead, they might use one of these strategies to lessen the stress caused by cognitive dissonance: changing their original beliefs, using denial, self-justifying, or changing their own behavior.

8. **Apply values in a global context.** In an international economy, everyone must deal with members of other cultures who may not share the same values. The chief values differences are: differing views of power and authority, of the individual versus the group, of tolerance for uncertainty, and of punctuality.

key terms

character ethic 114
cognitive dissonance 117
corporate culture 106
denial 118
Graves's Seven Value Levels 111
humanism 113

idealism 113
integrity 113
instrumental values 109
personality ethic 114
pragmatism 113
Rath Test 121
self-justification 118

Spranger's Six Value Systems 110
terminal values 109
values 106
values conflicts 115
value systems 110

review questions

1. How do values develop during the early part of people's lives?

2. What is the difference between terminal and instrumental values? Give examples of each.

3. How have values changed over the past several decades? Are the values of today's society the same as your personal values? If not, how do they differ?

4. How can you be sure that the values that you think you have are really your own?

5. What is the *personality ethic* as opposed to the *character ethic?* Which one affects your behavior more? Explain.

6. What is a values conflict? Have you ever been involved in a conflict that involved values differences? If so, what was the focus of the conflict? Interpersonal? You (or someone else) against the group? Internal?

7. Define *values system*. Do you have a values system that has influenced you in the formation of your individual application of values? Explain.

8. What is cognitive dissonance? How is an understanding of cognitive dissonance important to understanding your own values and how you act—or fail to act—on them?

critical thinking questions

9. How culturally determined are the values that you hold dear? What are the differences in how the four factors of values deal with other cultures?

10. Have you ever experienced cognitive dissonance in your own life? (More than likely, you have experienced it more than once.) How did you react? What strategies did you use to lessen the impact of the dissonance in your life?

working it out 5.1

VALUES AND YOUR CAREER CHOICE

School-to-Work Connection: Personal Qualities Skills

Your present values are very important to your future success in the career you choose.

In your search for the right career, which of the following value factors will you look for?

Check the appropriate *terminal* values:

_____ 1. Lifelong learning

_____ 2. Eliminating suffering and hunger

_____ 3. Achieving world peace

_____ 4. Raising a family

_____ 5. Variety of experience

_____ 6. Artistic expression

_____ 7. Achieving recognition

_____ 8. Security

_____ 9. Adventure and excitement

_____ 10. Serving God

_____ 11. Serving country

_____ 12. Other _____

Next, check the specific factors you will look for in the career you choose. The majority of these will be *instrumental* values for most people.

_____ 1. High salary

_____ 2. Great amount of freedom

_____ 3. Nice people to work with

_____ 4. Physical exercise on the job

_____ 5. Mental challenges

_____ 6. Opportunities for advancement

_____ 7. Fairness in the workplace (freedom from prejudice)

_____ 8. Ability to work without being around others

_____ 9. Ability to work in groups with others

_____ 10. Good vacation time

_____ 11. Flexible working hours

_____ 12. Freedom to plan your own job

_____ 13. Freedom to use leadership skills and abilities

_____ 14. Ability to be trained as you work

_____ 15. Freedom to work at home

_____ 16. Freedom to work outdoors

_____ 17. Other _____

Keep this list and refer to it in the future when job hunting. If you have already chosen a career, use this test to see how many of your values are affected by that choice. Consider the possible impacts on you in the long term if the organization's values conflict with your personal values.

internet exercise

1. *Research and Write*

   Go to **www.mhhe.com/lamberton4e** for the link to the Institute for the Study of Civic Values or link directly at **www.iscv.org.** Click into several of the subareas that you find there. Spend enough time reading and exploring to come to a conclusion about this organization. Write a brief essay of three or four paragraphs evaluating the organization and its potential impact on civic values. Take a position on the issues addressed here.

2. *Self-Assessment*

   Go to the Center for Rural Studies Web site through **www.mhhe. com/lamberton4e.** You can also link directly at **http://crs.uvm. edu/gopher/nerl/personal/growth/b.html.** Do the exercise called "Values Clarification." Partner up with someone who is *not* a close friend. Play this storyteller-scribe game to help establish your own (and perhaps your partner's) core values. Then write a brief essay about what you find.

3. *Self-Assess and Apply*

   How do your values affect the type of job you will find most satisfying? Take the self-surveys available through the course Web site at **www.mhhe.com/lamberton4e,** and linked directly at **www.test-ingroom.com/.** This page will link you to three tools to help you in values clarification and career exploration: *The Career Values Scale, The Career Interest Profiler,* and *The Personality Index.* What did you discover?

The New Claims Adjuster

When Cecelia started her job with Anchor Insurance, she felt quite gratified. After all, she had tried for years to enter a white-collar profession, and insurance had been her first choice. The claims office was always busy, and "emergencies," some real, some exaggerated, were the first order of business. She enjoyed the excitement and variety of the claims department.

Cecelia's section of the company was supportive, in that anyone who had a difficult claim would be helped by the others in the office. You were never alone, facing a difficult client. As a beginner, Cecelia found that supportive attitude to be really encouraging. The camaraderie was evident in other areas of work life at Anchor, too.

Before long, however, Cecelia started noticing that all of this group "togetherness" had other faces, not all of them to Cecelia's liking. For example, Friday evenings always seemed to be "get drunk night." Right after work, the whole claims department would meet at a local pub, "just to unwind," as one of her colleagues explained. Although Cecelia savored a screwdriver now and then, she definitely did not believe in excessive drinking. Besides, she would nearly always become ill if she drank more than one cocktail in an evening.

She tried to beg out of the Friday get-togethers. That approach worked for a Friday or two. However, the group pressure was so strong that bad jokes were told about anyone who was "antisocial" enough to miss the Friday parties regularly. After a few weeks, it became clear that Cecelia was being treated differently. When a truly difficult client who was filing a very suspicious claim came to Cecelia, she was left to solve the problem on her own. She was snubbed during lunch hour and found that others would stop talking when she came into a room.

"I've got to do something," she told Mike, her boyfriend. "Do you think it would work to go to the Friday bashes and just order Shirley Temples? Or do I need to start searching for another job?" "I don't know," answered Mike. "But I don't like seeing you this unhappy. You're right: you've got to do something."

Case Study Questions

1. Would you identify the conflict in this case as a values conflict? Why or why not?

2. Is it too late? Can Cecelia salvage the relationship she once had with her fellow workers? More importantly, *should* she? Why or why not?

3. What would you do if you were in Cecelia's place?

Honest Jane

Jane Johnston grew up with strong beliefs that her very religious family had taught her over the years. She placed a great deal of value on treating others fairly, on keeping her word, and on never being self-righteous. After graduating from high school, Jane decided to wait a year or two before going to college. She landed a job as a factory shipping clerk. However, that position didn't give her the kind of money she needed to save for college and to use for spending money, so she took a second job as a security guard at a large retail-chain warehouse.

Jane soon found that even with both jobs, she wasn't getting ahead. One night at the guard job, her co-worker Louis seemed to be acting strangely. Jane followed him as Louis walked his hourly round. Twice, she saw Louis grab something from the warehouse and put it under his coat. Back in the guard room, Jane watched as Louis took four objects out of his coat, then put them into his locker. Later, Jane checked the locker. She saw a stack of iPods and other assorted items that were obviously new and unopened.

After Louis returned to the room, Jane said quietly, "I saw what you have in your locker."

Louis replied, "So, Jane, what're you gonna do about it?"

"I don't know," replied Jane. "But, I'll admit I've been tempted myself. They leave the final inventory on the computer, where we could change anything if we wanted to."

"Yeah," smirked Louis. "We're the trusted law enforcers."

Jane replied, "I guess that's why I've never taken anything; they trust us."

"Well, I used to feel that way, too, but I don't anymore—as you can see. I've finally had it with their trust. So, what are you gonna do, tell on me?" asked Louis.

Case Study Questions

1. It seems clear at this point that Jane is not a thief. However, based on her values, what would you expect her to do at this point?

2. Do you think that Jane's value of "not being self-righteous" will keep her from telling management what she has seen? Who else is affected by this theft—for example, how are consumers affected if Jane stays silent, or if she tells management what she has seen?

3. Based on your own values, what would you do if you were Jane? Why?

MOTIVATION: INCREASING PRODUCTIVITY

In the Workplace: Motivated . . . or Not?

SITUATION

For months now, Antonio Garcia had been out of work. Although he did his best to remain optimistic, jobs were scarce in his region, and he had experienced some conflict with the supervisor at his most recent job, preventing him from getting a favorable letter of reference. Finally, he landed a job—and one that paid several dollars an hour more than he had made previously.

"Okay, it involves working outside in the cold weather, but just watch me laugh all the way to the bank. With that kind of money, who is gonna care? Not this guy." His family all remarked on how happy and motivated he was. "I've never seen you so jazzed about anything, Antonio," one of his closest friends remarked.

DISCOVERY

Only two months later, Antonio was telling a different kind of story. Not wanting to admit how grim his job really was, he told only a few of his closest friends how

objectives

After studying this chapter, you will be able to:

1   Define motivation.

2   Explain need-based theories of motivation.

3   Explain behavior-based theories of motivation.

4   Describe reinforcement theory and behavior modification.

5   Discuss the relationship between self-esteem and motivation.

STRATEGIES FOR SUCCESS

Strategy 6.1   Applying McClelland's Theory

Strategy 6.2   Changing Your Behavior

discouraged he had become. "I never thought I'd say this," he confided to his best friend one day, "but I'm not getting paid enough for the grief I have to put up with. My supervisor yells at me all the time, for no good reason. He shouts out unclear instructions on how to do a job and then loses his temper when I don't do what he thinks he told me to do. As soon as I can find another job, I'm out of here."

"I'd give anything to make that kind of money," his friend countered.

"You just don't get it," Antonio replied. "I'm finding out that it's really not about the money. If you had this job, you'd understand what I mean."

THINK ABOUT IT

Why did Antonio lose motivation so quickly? Why did money become less and less important to him as time went by?

WHAT IS MOTIVATION?

motivation

The force of the need or desire to act.

organizational climate

Emotional weather within an organization that reflects the norms and attitudes of the organization's culture and that affects worker morale, attitudes, stress levels, and communication.

morale

Overall mood of an individual or group, based on attitudes and satisfaction.

What motivates people? You are reading this textbook, which means you are probably taking a class in human relations. Why aren't you watching television right now, or doing whatever sport or activity you like best? You are obviously motivated to be studying. What motivates you? Is everyone motivated in the same way?

Questions like these have puzzled scholars and managers for many years. **Motivation** is the willingness to make an effort toward accomplishment. To be truly motivated means feeling a desire to do whatever task needs to be accomplished to reach a goal or purpose. Management expert Peter Drucker says, "The purpose of an organization is to enable common men [and women] to do uncommon things."[1] High motivation makes people want to do those uncommon things.

Organizational Climate and Morale

A large motivating factor on the job is the **organizational climate.** The climate within an organization can be compared with the physical climate outdoors, and it can also be described as warm or cold. Organizational climate affects the way employees feel and act because it is the emotional weather within an organization; it affects employee morale. **Morale** is the overall mood of a group of people and is based on employees' attitudes and feelings of satisfaction. Until a few years ago, many people made the false assumption that job morale has to be sacrificed for productivity to be high. Today it is generally agreed that climate and morale must work together for a company to function at its best. When the climate of a workplace is comfortable, morale is good, and high motivation levels are much more likely. Few factors can hurt productivity and job performance worse than low morale issues.

A good climate is much more than just people getting along well. An effective climate allows people to work to their full potential without becoming a threat to others. It encourages competent and rapid completion of tasks. It also allows employees to feel comfortable: employees in a positive and comfortable work climate can be themselves without feeling threatened.

Many methods can be used to improve the climate of an organization. Though managers are in the key position for making change, individual employees can also accomplish a great deal. They can listen to others carefully, step in and help with a task without complaints, and maintain a positive attitude. Often, employees also have opportunities to suggest changes. If you are an employee in a negative or uncomfortable climate, take a look at the situation and see what you can do. If you are a manager, start

MANAGERS AND ORGANIZATIONAL CLIMATE

The ability to listen to employee needs is a key component for the successful manager. *What are some other skills you can use to improve organizational climate?*

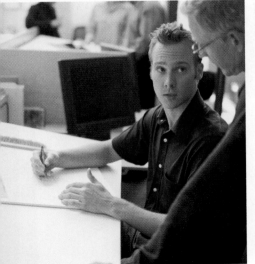

TeamBuildingInc.com

Visit **www.mhhe.com/lamberton4e** for a link to an information site on motivation from the Web site **TeamBuildingInc.com.** The site goes into great detail about motivation in a team atmosphere. Read it and think about how you can apply these ideas to a current or future work environment. Make a list of ideas to discuss in class. If you have time, follow one of the links to additional resources on this Web site. Summarize what you find.

with your own attitude. Then look to see where changes should be made in the physical environment, job assignments, and procedures. Institute an open-door policy, if such a thing is practical. Remember that organizational climate is directly related to motivation.

For some workers, motivation seems to work automatically: for most of us, it is not something we usually think about before beginning each task. These general theories of motivation are ways of looking at how motivation relates to people and their behavior. Please remember that these are only theories. No single theory completely explains human motivation. Why? Because social scientists still have much to discover about this complex topic (see Figure 6.1).

Recall that we studied Theories X and Y in Chapter 4—as attitudes that managers have toward workers. When the job, the employees, and the manager are right for Theory Y, motivation can be high. When Theory Y assumptions work, employees tend to stay with a company for longer periods of time. If you have to assume (either because of the work or because of the employees) that people will not be motivated by the work itself (Theory X), then other rewards should be used. These external motivators are called **extrinsic rewards,** as opposed to internal motivators, called **intrinsic rewards,** which employees get from the satisfaction of the job itself.

> This quote describes the importance of positive **organizational climates:** "Human relations that are not grounded in the satisfaction of good performance in work are actually poor human relations and result in a mean spirit."
>
> **Source:** Peter Drucker, *Management: Tasks, Responsibilities, Practices* (New York: Harper & Row, 1974), pp. 455–456.

more about...

extrinsic rewards
External factors intended to provide motivational incentives, including salary, bonuses, promotions, praise, or high grades in classes.

intrinsic rewards
In *expectancy theory,* the internal factors related to the value of work, including the amount of creativity allowed, the degree of responsibility, and the satisfaction of helping others.

Intrinsic and Extrinsic Rewards

For most people, there is one main reason to work: to make money. Economic need is the primary motivator toward work. Working allows you to pay your bills, collect benefits, and build financial security for your retirement—allowing you to work in the present without worrying

figure 6.1

MAJOR THEORIES OF MOTIVATION (AND THEIR CREATORS)

The main theories of motivation are listed here. As you learn about each theory, think about which one you feel is the most useful. *Which theory seems most accurate to you?*

ERG Theory
Clayton Alderfer

Need-Based Theories
Hierarchy of Needs: *Abraham Maslow*
McClelland's Needs: *David McClelland*
Two-Factor: *Frederick Herzberg*
Job Enrichment: *Hackman and Oldham*

Behavior-Based Theories
Expectancy: *Victor Vroom*
Reinforcement/Behavior Modification: *B.F. Skinner*

autonomy – Be on your own [handwritten annotation]

more about...

Dennis Bakke, a motivation author, says this about **motivation and workers:** "I am convinced that the next form of discrimination that needs to be overturned is the second-class treatment [of] working men and women."

Source: Dennis W. Bakke, *Joy at Work* (Seattle, WA: PVG, 2005), p. 121.

too much about the future. These are all extrinsic motivators. Working can also allow you to satisfy your intrinsic motives. (See Figure 6.2.)

Intrinsic rewards are the internal feelings of satisfaction you get from your job. These often provide more powerful motives than the extrinsic factors do. Researchers have found that professional women who are balancing the demands of work and families are more likely to quit their jobs for intrinsic reasons, such as feeling bored or unchallenged at work, than for extrinsic reasons like a lack of on-site day care or flexible hours.[2]

figure 6.2

TYPICAL INTRINSIC AND EXTRINSIC REWARDS

Intrinsic rewards come from within and motivate you to excel at your job. Extrinsic rewards come from outside sources, such as managers, co-workers, clients, and the company itself. *Which rewards do you feel are more valuable?*

Examples of Additional Intrinsic and Extrinsic Rewards

Intrinsic Rewards	Extrinsic Rewards
Increased responsibility	Performance bonuses
Opportunities for personal growth	Profit sharing programs
Ability to participate in decision making	Impressive titles
Variety of job activities	Pay raises
More job freedom	Preferred office furnishings and lunch hours
	Longer vacations

The general sense of satisfaction from a job is not the only intrinsic motivator. Other intrinsic rewards include:[3]

1. A work ethic

People with a strong work ethic believe that *not* working is somewhat immoral and lazy. The work ethic is a belief that in this society, people have a moral obligation to be productive and avoid being idle.

more about...

Intrinsic Motivators

Many people say they would continue to work even if they did not need the money, and many million-dollar lottery winners who quit their jobs say they felt aimless and dissatisfied afterward. (Wouldn't we all like to test that for ourselves!)

Source: H. R. Kaplan, *Lottery Winners* (New York: Harper & Row, 1978).

2. A sense of self-identity

Professional or occupational identity is so strong that it becomes a part of people's self-identity. Think of meeting a new person for the first time. You are likely to say, "I am a student," or "I am a salesperson," or "I am a store manager," instead of "I go to school," or "I work at a store," or "I manage a store." Many people tend to think of themselves as being a part of their occupations. Thus they are motivated to continue for fear of losing that identity.

3. A sense of self-fulfillment

Many people choose their jobs or occupations based on their interests and abilities. People can express their values, needs, and interests through work. This may seem obvious when thinking about artists or professional athletes, but people often find their jobs enriching because the jobs fit their interests or needs even in more ordinary occupations.

4. A sense of self-worth

Self-esteem is threatened when you fail at work but can greatly increase from success or recognition at work. A scientist whose experiment turns out well, a doctor who saves a life, or a freelance journalist whose story gets published—these people feel a great sense of self-worth from their accomplishments.

Life and Leadership

Visit **www.mhhe.com/lamberton4e** for the link to **http://danyettanajoli.blogspot.com/2007/08/leaders-who-blend-intrinsic-and.html** and read the blog entry, written by a motivation expert, on leaders
who blend intrinsic and extrinsic rewards. Summarize what you find: What does the author mean by leaders who "encourage the heart"? Do you agree with this philosophy?

5. The social value of work

People meet others and make social contacts at work. Many people say that their best friends are those they met at work. Work can take the form of a small community: you can meet friends, enemies, and perhaps mentors. For some people, the social contacts at work are a good reason to go to work. For others, social contacts at work are even more important: in this mobile society, they can substitute for family.

6. Social and community roles

Every community has an understanding of the roles that are filled by people in specific occupations. Communities need people to fill roles that make up the community's public identity: pharmacists, firefighters, police officers, librarians, day-care providers, and so on.

The way managers and employees see other people will affect both their own motivation and that of the people they influence.

NEED-BASED THEORIES OF MOTIVATION

Many psychologists agree that people are motivated by their *needs*. In the "scientific management" school of the early 20th century, the needs that money could satisfy were thought to be the main motivators. Today, inner needs are often just as important. Theorists' views differ about which needs are most important.

Abraham Maslow's Hierarchy of Needs

Psychologist Abraham Maslow believed that most people fulfill their needs in a certain order. Before you can bloom into your full potential, you must take these steps of **Maslow's hierarchy of needs** in the order that follows.[4] (See Figure 6.3.)

1. **Physiological needs** include necessities for life such as air, food, warmth, and water. These needs are often referred to as primary needs because they are necessary in order to stay alive. After these needs are met, you can move on.

2. **Safety and security needs** include physical safety from harm and the elements, as well as financial security. These are the next most important needs in the hierarchy. They include everything from having a danger-free and orderly way of life to buying health insurance. After meeting these needs, you can move on.

3. **Love and belongingness needs** include acceptance from family or friends. Everyone needs to feel love and affection, and these needs drive people to seek out others for meaningful relationships. Finding companionship and friendship are very important on this level. Then you can move on.

4. **Esteem needs** include recognition from peers and colleagues. The development of self-confidence and a healthy self-concept at this level builds self-esteem. At this level you experience some success and a feeling of having achieved something worthwhile. You begin to appreciate yourself. Then you can move on.

5. **Self-actualization** means reaching one's full potential. This is the highest level of the hierarchy. If you reach this level, you will have fulfilled your own inborn potential as a creative, unique person. Maslow believed that not all people would get to this level, but since people are all different, there are different areas in which they might feel self-actualized. Maslow himself made a list of suggestions to increase your self-actualization (see Figure 6.4).

Maslow's theory makes the following assumptions:

1. Needs that are not yet satisfied will motivate or influence a person's behavior.

2. When a need has been satisfied, it will no longer motivate the person's behavior.

3. Needs are arranged by order of importance.

4. A need in the hierarchy will not be a motivator until those below it are already satisfied.

According to this theory, a starving person might willingly give up the need for self-respect just to stay alive. However, once a person's basic needs have been met, that person is likely to look to higher needs.

Maslow's hierarchy of needs

Shows that people tend to satisfy their needs in a certain order: first, physiological needs, then safety and security, belongingness and love, esteem, and finally, self-actualization.

physiological needs

The most basic of Maslow's hierarchy of needs having to do with the satisfaction of physical needs, including food, water, air, and shelter.

safety and security needs

In Maslow's hierarchy and include physical safety from harm and the elements as well as financial security.

love and belongingness needs

Include complete acceptance from family and friends. The third level of Maslow's hierarchy.

esteem needs

In Maslow's hierarchy, self-esteem needs include recognition from peers and colleagues.

self-actualization

Highest level of Maslow's hierarchy of needs; occurs when one has fulfilled his or her potential.

figure 6.3

MASLOW'S HIERARCHY OF NEEDS

Maslow's theory states that people must satisfy basic needs before moving on to higher levels. *At which level do you see yourself right now? Do you see yourself in more than one level at once?*

Source: "Hierarchy of Needs" from *Motivation and Personality*, 3rd ed., by Abraham H. Maslow. Revised by Robert Frager, James Faiman, Cynthia McReynolds, and Ruth Cox. Copyright 1954. © 1987 by Harper & Row, Publishers, Inc. Copyright © 1970 by Abraham H. Maslow. Reprinted by permission of HarperCollins Publishers, Inc.

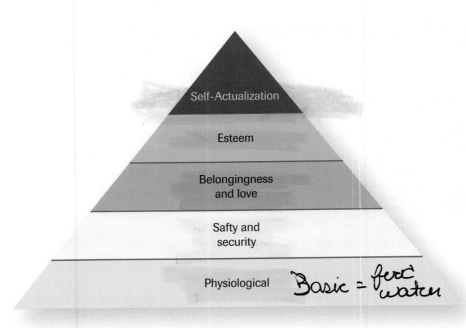

These higher needs will now motivate the individual to achieve the next level, and so on.

In its basics, Maslow's theory is quite simple. Applying it in order to affect the motivation of others and of yourself, though, is a bit more complicated. Maslow himself has pointed out that what *seems* to be motivating someone might not be what really is motivating that person at all.[5] He also pointed out that although the general needs in his hierarchy apply to people everywhere, people are motivated by factors that are motivating only to them as individuals, or only to people in a particular culture.

To complicate things, you might move around on the hierarchy ladder as you try to meet several needs at a time. You may go out of order, for example, if esteem needs and recognition from others are more important to you than the friendship and affection you would get from the love and belongingness needs. In addition, there are cognitive and aesthetic needs—that is, needs for learning and for beauty—that some people have in great amounts. Maslow agreed that these needs are very important for some people, but admitted that they didn't fit into his "hierarchy of needs" very well.

For managers, Maslow's main lesson on motivation is to notice the needs level of employees. When a manager is in touch with the employees' basic needs, he or she can be much more effective in getting employees to perform. For example, an employee might be at the level of esteem needs. The manager might make positive statements to build the employee's self-esteem; in turn, the employee will feel better about job performance and will work more effectively. In needs theory, people are more interested in the internal or intrinsic factors that make someone perform well.

☞ Experience life fully: Be alive and absorbed with what you are doing at the moment.

☞ Learn to trust your own judgment and feelings in making life choices, such as marriage and career.

☞ Be honest with yourself and take responsibility for what you do.

☞ Whenever possible, choose growth rather than safety or security.

☞ Recognize your defenses and illusions, then work to give them up.

☞ Even though peak experiences are temporary, keep the aspiration of these moments of self-actualization alive in your everyday thoughts and actions.

☞ Remember that self-actualization is a continual process; it is never fully achieved.

☞ Commit yourself to concerns and causes outside yourself, because self-actualization comes more as a byproduct of developing your fully capacities than by the self-focused pursuit of growth itself.

figure 6.4

HOW TO INCREASE YOUR SELF-ACTUALIZATION

Maslow offers several helpful suggestions for finding out what you want and how to get it. *What is holding you back in your progress toward self-actualization?*

Source: Abraham Maslow, *The Further Reaches of Human Nature* (New York: Viking Press, 1971).

According to management experts Richard Steers and Lyman Porter, Maslow's theory is useful when applied to organizational climate: "When the needs-hierarchy concept is applied to work organizations, the implication for managerial actions becomes obvious. Managers have the responsibility, according to this line of reasoning, to create a 'proper climate' in which employees can develop to their fullest potential."[6]

As mentioned earlier, organizational climate is an important motivational factor that should be considered when applying other theories as well as Maslow's.

Alderfer's ERG Theory

A scholar named Clayton Alderfer created a theory that is based on Maslow's hierarchy, but which in some ways improves on it. Instead of Maslow's five levels, **ERG theory** has only three areas: existence, relatedness, and growth.

1. *Existence needs* are the needs that have to do with making your way in life in a physical sense. Your physical well-being as a human is the issue.

2. *Relatedness needs* refer to what Maslow called "belongingness" needs and the part of esteem needs that are external, or socially fulfilling.

> **ERG Theory**
>
> A refinement of Maslow's hierarchy that includes only three needs areas: existence (mostly figure needs); relatedness (needs linked to relationships; and growth (internal esteem needs and self-actualization).

Applying Maslow's Hierarchy

Visit **www.mhhe.com/lamberton4e** for the link to **http://psychology.suite101.com/article.cfm/ fulfill_your_potential** and read the article on applying Maslow's theory to your own life. What characteristics of a self-actualized person (listed in the article) do you currently have? Reading over the suggestions for becoming self-actualized, do you identify areas of your life in which you could put those suggestions into use?

3. *Growth needs* are the more internal esteem needs that we all have, along with what Maslow called self-actualization.[7]

ERG theory presents three very important differences from Maslow's famous "hierarchy." All three should be noted when applying this theory.

First, unlike Maslow's theory that includes the same order of progression for all people, ERG theory teaches that the order in which you progress through the three stages can be different for different people. This makes the theory more flexible and more generally useful. Second, some people can even approach these needs steps simultaneously, in other words, some people might be progressing in all three need areas at the very same time.

frustration-regression principle

A principle that says that someone who fails to reach a higher need level will sometimes become frustrated and regress (go back) to a lower need level, and stay there for some time—perhaps forever.

Most important, ERG theory features the **frustration-regression principle.** According to this principle, someone who fails to reach a higher need level will sometimes become frustrated and regress (go back) to a lower need level, and stay there for some time—perhaps forever. For example, someone who has been attempting to fulfill growth needs might decide to settle for just making a living when frustrated in the attempt at career growth.

Both of these needs theories are useful in that they illustrate the importance of workers getting involved with such factors as participative decision making, increased worker freedom, and personalized work space. If you are a worker, they help you understand your own development; if you are a manager, they help you ask the correct questions about the needs level of the workers.[8]

manifest needs theory

Developed by David McClelland to show that all people have needs that motivate them in life and on the job. These three needs include power needs, affiliation needs, and achievement needs.

McClelland's Manifest Needs Theory

Like Maslow, David McClelland believed that all people have certain needs that motivate them both in life and on the job. Unlike some needs theories, McClelland's **manifest needs theory** isn't a hierarchy. McClelland, a Harvard University psychology professor, found through years of research that all people have three basic coexisting needs:

Growth and Frustration: Alderfer's ERG

Visit **www.mhhe.com/lamberton4e** for the link to **www.valuebasedmanagement.net/methods_ alderfer_erg_theory.html** and read the brief explanation of Alderfer's ERG theory. The author gives an example of how the frustration-regression principle may affect the workplace. Think of another specific example of how regression caused by frustration may impact employee productivity or morale.

power needs, the need to interact with others (which McClelland calls **affiliation needs**), and **achievement needs.** Every person has all three needs, but everyone has them in different amounts and combinations; nearly everyone will feel one need more strongly than the other two needs.[9]

Power Needs

When McClelland first started his research on motivation, he saw power as a basically negative force. Later he found that power, like the other two needs, can be either positive or negative, depending on how it is used. According to McClelland, a manager without a need for power will generally be less effective than one with a strong power need.[10] A person who has a strong need for power wants to control and influence other people. This person is also competitive and wants to win. This type of person also usually likes conflict—even confronting others and being confronted.

Affiliation Needs

Most people need to be with other people, to develop friendships and acquaintances. According to McClelland, some people have this need so strongly that it motivates them to go to work every day. These people often have an intense desire to be accepted and liked by other people. They usually like parties and other social activities, and they tend to join clubs and other groups. McClelland feels that someone with a strong affiliation need will generally *not* make the best manager.[11]

Achievement Needs

A person with a high need for achievement is usually very goal oriented, has a high energy level, and wants to take personal responsibility for achievements. This type of person tends to be attracted to careers such as sales and business ownership and likes to have some type of concrete feedback on how much he or she is

> **power needs**
> Desired by individuals who want to control and influence other people.

> **affiliation needs**
> Occur in people who want to be accepted and liked by others.

> **achievement needs**
> Occur in people who are goal oriented and take personal responsibility for achievements.

more about...

> **The Manifest Needs Theory**
> The **manifest needs theory** makes no judgment about whether any particular need is better or worse than others; instead, the focus is simply on which needs are the primary sources of motivation in people's lives.

achieving. If the work doesn't contain enough challenges, he or she will find a challenge elsewhere.[12]

More research has been done on the achievement need than the other two needs. High achievers have been found to differ from low achievers in several ways. People with a high need for achievement usually set goals that are moderately challenging. These goals are not so difficult that they are impossible, and not so easy that they do not present a challenge. Both high-risk and no-risk situations are seen as a waste of time. A businessperson with a high need for achievement would become successful taking a moderate risk that is more likely to pay off than a high risk that has little chance of success. McClelland believes that successful entrepreneurs are driven more by a high need for achievement than by the profit margin.

High achievers are more likely to credit their successes to their own hard work, ability, talent, and persistence. When they fail, they do not place blame on others, on bad luck, or on fate; they look to their own behavior for an explanation. On the other hand, people with low achievement needs seem to be motivated more by a fear of failure than an expectation of success. They set impossibly high goals or very low, simple goals. They blame their failures on their own lack of ability, on bad luck, or on fate.[13]

Although McClelland did not recommend developing one of these needs and ignoring the other two, recent researchers have found that a high or low need for achievement can become a consistent personality trait. This is generally good news for high achievers who more often excel in school and in their careers, but the news is less happy for low achievers. Low achievers in school are less likely to finish college, maintain a job, or stay married.[14]

According to McClelland, these three needs are not factors that people are simply born with. They are developed through life experiences. If, in later life, you wish to develop more in one of the three areas, you can make that happen. To McClelland, a need is like a muscle; with exercise, it will grow.

Herzberg's Two-Factor Theory

In his two-factor theory, psychologist Frederick Herzberg describes two forces that are often confused with each other. He calls them **hygienes** and **motivators.** *Hygienes* are factors connected with a job that make working there better. They are factors that workers don't want to go without. If someone were to take any of them away, workers would be unhappy—even to the point of quitting the job. However, even though people feel that way about them, hygienes—in themselves—do not motivate. They are not what get you up in the morning and out into traffic (see Figure 6.5).

---

more about...

Developing Your Motivational Needs
David McClelland says that a need is like a muscle; it will develop and grow when it is exercised.

---

hygienes (also called "dissatisfiers")

The qualities in the workplace that are outside the job itself (examples: company benefits, workplace policies, job security). When these factors are weak or missing, motivation will fall; however, when they are high, motivation will not be strong or long term.

---

motivators (also called "satisfiers")

The factors in Herzberg's theory that cause real, long-term motivation, usually containing *intrinsic* motivation factors (examples: interesting and challenging tasks, advancement, achievement, growth).

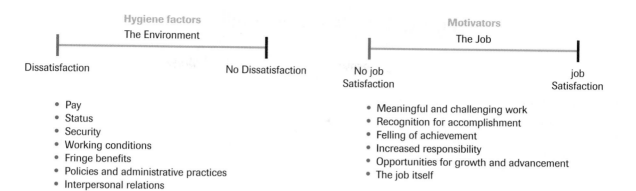

figure 6.5

HERZBERG'S TWO-FACTOR THEORY

Some examples of hygienes are piped-in music, attractive carpeting, a good health plan, or good relations with the supervisor. According to Herzberg, factors such as these will keep workers from becoming dissatisfied; for that reason they are also called **dissatisfiers.** But they *won't* be the factors that make you feel "pumped up" and ready to give the job your all—especially not over a long time period.

The factors on the job that really do motivate workers are called, appropriately, *motivators.* These are factors that are intrinsic—that is, they are found either within the work itself or within the worker. They include feelings of accomplishment, of worth, of a job well done, or of doing meaningful and interesting work. For example, if an experienced engineer is doing the work that any draftsperson could do, then the pay, the fringe benefits, humane treatment, and pleasant working conditions, although perhaps very real, will not be enough to motivate the engineer. He or she will simply not be getting a sense of meaning or accomplishment from the job. One can clearly see a relationship between the necessary motivators of Herzberg and the Theory Y philosophy of Douglas McGregor: both theories are based on a belief that employees find self-fulfillment in work and are motivated by it.

For motivation to take place, according to Herzberg, *both* the hygienes and the motivators must be used. First, the hygienes have to be in place; then the motivators can take over. If you have meaningful, fulfilling work, but the building where you work is damp and uncomfortable, the motivators won't be as strong as they otherwise would be. You might even quit, if you find a job with a more comfortable environment and an equal sense of accomplishment.

Hygienes include a person's desire to avoid unpleasant working conditions in both the physical and the psychological environment. For example, many businesses in the midst of downsizing have found that as morale becomes lower, even employees who were not going to be laid off sometimes decide to resign because the work environment has become too unpleasant.[15]

Job Enrichment as a Motivator

If your work isn't meaningful, what can be done to change the situation? You could find another position with a different set of tasks—maybe. If you are the manager, you could think about upgrading the job—that is, adding elements to the job that might make it more enjoyable, meaningful, and fulfilling. To Herzberg, this upgrading of the task, or **job enrichment,** is the only real way to motivate a previously unmotivated worker for any long period of time.

Herzberg says that if the job is not enrichable, that is, if management can't make it more interesting or rewarding, it should be eliminated or automated. The era of robotics and other technological developments have made the choice to automate jobs much more likely than even a decade ago. Thus, according to Herzberg, making jobs more challenging and fulfilling is the only appropriate approach to meaningful motivation. Herzberg also conducted international research that seems to support his claim that the two-factor theory of motivation is valid around the world.[16]

To enrich a job often means complete restructuring of the tasks related to the job, to make them more meaningful and fulfilling—giving the job more intrinsic motivators. Several factors are necessary for job enrichment to be effective. These are skill variety, task identity, task significance, autonomy, and feedback.[17] Figure 6.6 describes job enrichment in greater detail.

job enrichment
The upgrading of a job that makes it more interesting, meaningful, or rewarding and provides long-term motivation.

figure 6.6

HACKMAN–OLDHAM JOB ENRICHMENT MODEL

Source: J. Richard Hackman and Gerg R. Oldham, *Work Redesign* (p. 90); © 1980 by Addison-Wesley Publishing Company, Inc. Reprinted by permission of the publisher.

Skill Variety and Task Identity

If you work at a job where you have to use a number of different skills, you are much more likely to be motivated to work hard. You are also more likely to take pride in the job you do. Also, if you are able to start a job and see it through to its completion, the job will seem much more meaningful to you. If you have ever worked at a job on a factory assembly line or in any other situation that calls on only one skill, you probably know how important **skill variety** and **task identity** can be. Those who make midlife career changes often do so because they are looking for a job that is more meaningful to them.

Task Significance

Most people are motivated more by a job that seems to make a difference to other people or to the physical environment. If the work directly affects other peoples' work or lives, the job is said to contain **task significance.** Career choices such as the Peace Corps continue to be popular, even with low pay, because of this important quality. One former executive of a large company explained why he had voluntarily quit a high-salaried position. As he put it, "Every product they made could have been dumped into the ocean, and humanity would have been improved, not damaged." Although salary had motivated him for several years, the lack of task significance had reduced its motivational strength. Some people who start their own businesses do so because they feel that their own business will allow them to affect others more directly; it is a more task-significance environment.

Autonomy

Autonomy means the freedom to choose one's tasks and methods of work. When workers are given a great deal of autonomy, they feel ownership of the job and of the tasks it involves. They are more likely to feel responsible for—and motivated by—the success or failure of a project. Autonomy also involves time. When a worker is given a flexible schedule, with deadlines mostly self-imposed, both job satisfaction and motivation usually increase.

Feedback

When a job allows individuals to know how well they are performing, the job is enriched considerably. No matter how much autonomy a worker has, feedback is still essential. Knowing results of one's work can help someone who has some autonomy decide which tasks to emphasize. If a worker has performed poorly on a project, for example, he or she can take steps to improve performance the next time such a task is attempted.

By enriching jobs with these five elements, motivation can be increased greatly. The manager who is redesigning jobs should look carefully at the worker's talents, needs, abilities, and desires. All the job characteristics

skill variety
The opportunity and ability to use numerous different skills in one's position at work.

task identity
The worker's perception of the meaningfulness of a job, often based upon the worker's permission to start a job and see it through to completion.

task significance
A worker's perception that the task directly affects other people's work or lives.

autonomy
Independence, the ability to act and make decisions on one's own without undue interference from management.

David worked at an insurance company based in Laramie, Wyoming. For years he tried to get transferred to a larger metropolitan area. He loved big cities and was tired of the wide open spaces of Wyoming and nearby states. He was ready for a change. Finally, he landed a job in Los Angeles. He was happy with his new job and excited about living in a city with so much to offer. The first sales contest the Los Angeles company held offered the prize of a weeklong fishing trip to Colorado. Needless to say, David wasn't motivated to win. He never cared for fishing and he wasn't interested in leaving Los Angeles. Although both the expectancy and the instrumentality seemed to be in place, the valence was very low. A prize as simple as a family ticket to an amusement park or tickets to a concert would have involved a higher level of valence for this urban-loving salesperson.

listed will do little good if the match between the job and the worker is defective.[18] Job enrichment is essential. If your workplace is one where workers have a voice in major decisions, you don't need to be a manager to help design jobs that are enriched and are thus more motivating.

BEHAVIOR-BASED THEORIES OF MOTIVATION

Expectancy Theory

expectancy theory
Developed by Victor Vroom to explain human behavior in terms of people's goals, choices, and the expectation that goals will be reached.

Expectancy theory brings several ideas together, and different versions of it have become quite popular in the past few years. In the 1960s, Victor Vroom originally developed expectancy theory to explain human behavior in terms of people's goals and choices and the expectation that goals will be reached.[19] Its main concepts are expectancy, instrumentality, and valence.

expectancy
In *expectancy theory*, the likelihood that if a person tried, the result would be better performance.

Expectancy describes the likelihood that if a person tries to perform better, that will really be the result. For example, Carla can easily see that if she takes shorter breaks and works harder, a great deal more work will get done. Vroom would say that Carla thus has high expectancy.

instrumentality
The likelihood that something good (or bad) will come from an increase in effort.

Instrumentality refers to the likelihood that something good (or bad) will come from an increase in effort. If Carla can also see that her supervisor will reward her with a bonus when her output is greater, Vroom would say that her instrumentality is high. High instrumentality also implies trust in your company and its managers. Can you be confident that they will actually deliver on a promised reward?

valence
The value a person places on a reward.

Valence is the value a person places on a reward. Valence has a great deal to do with each person's values. A reward with no value to the worker will not be motivating.

In the late 1970s, expectancy theory was revised. In this new revision, Barry Staw showed that both intrinsic and extrinsic rewards are related to all three areas of this theory, but especially to valence. The value, or valence, of an expected outcome will be both intrinsic and extrinsic. When a manager is attempting to motivate an employee, both factors should be calculated. Intrinsic factors would include the amount of creativity allowed, the degree of responsibility, and the satisfaction of helping others. Rather than just putting together a reward system, a manager using this theory should look at these internal factors as well.[20]

Victor Vroom (1932–), a professor in the School of Management at Yale University, introduced expectancy theory in his book *Work and Motivation*. He has also written *Leadership and Decision Making* and *The New Leadership: Managing Participation in Organizations*.

more about...

REINFORCEMENT THEORY AND BEHAVIOR MODIFICATION

The ideas of reinforcement theory are becoming more and more popular in businesses today. Most of the ideas that this theory is based on come from the work of psychologist B. F. Skinner. **Reinforcement theory** explains human behavior in terms of the results—both good and bad—that have occurred under similar conditions in the past. When something good happens as the result of what you did, you are more likely to repeat that behavior. When you do something and there is no result, you will probably not do it again.[21] This process of changing behavior because of a reward, or a lack of reward, is called **behavior modification.**

This concept is not Skinner's alone: Some psychologists call it *stroking.* Just as infants need loving physical strokes, everyone needs encouraging emotional strokes. In the preceding example, Janie was getting strokes for her good performance. It has been said that *we get what we stroke,*[22] in other words, people get back what they reward others for. Management author Michael LeBoeuf calls this "the greatest management principle in the world."[23]

Skinner believed that you can help shape and mold people without making them feel that their freedom and dignity are threatened.[24] The method consists of positive reinforcement: reward the behavior that you like, and ignore the behavior that you don't like. Punishment can be very effective in changing someone's behavior, but this theory teaches that punishment has so many negative side effects that it will usually backfire on the manager. Positive reinforcement can be just as effective as negative reinforcement, and it has fewer unwanted side effects.

reinforcement theory
Explains human behavior in terms of repetition. Behavior that is rewarded enough times will be repeated, whereas behavior that repeatedly receives no reward will probably discontinue.

behavior modification
The process of changing behavior because of a reward or lack of a reward.

B. F. Skinner (1904–1990) was a behavioral psychologist who specialized in behavior modification. His ideas on positive reinforcement can be applied to reward and punishment systems within organizations.

more about...

Janie, a bicycle delivery person, is told every time she makes a fast and efficient delivery, "You're doing a great job; keep it up." The more often those words are spoken, the more high-quality work she performs. Then her boss leaves and is replaced by a manager who doesn't praise Janie when she does a good job. After a few weeks, Janie's performance is only average.

A manager trying to motivate employees should use sincere and frequent praise, letters of commendation, and other forms of recognition. To be effective, rewards must be given as soon as the desired behavior has happened. Even negative comments, if a manager must use them, can be reinforcing when carefully worded and told to an employee in a timely way.

Examples of effective **reinforcers** (or incentives) overlap considerably with examples of extrinsic rewards, since they are essentially the same thing. Examples include bonuses, awards, time off, praise, better office space, public posting of performance ratings, promotions, gifts or trips, and impressive titles.

reinforcers

Incentives such as awards, bonuses, promotions, gifts, and even compliments.

goal setting

Allows employees to set their own goals.

Goal Setting

To make reinforcers or incentives more effective, the employees involved should have the opportunity for **goal setting.** Telling people to *do their best* is not as effective in reaching higher performance levels as setting specific goals that are moderately difficult. Organizations can increase their employees' commitment to goals when they follow these four suggestions:

1. Have employees participate in the goal-setting process.
2. Make goals challenging but attainable, specific, and attractive.
   3. Provide feedback on how the employees are doing in meeting the goals.
   4. Reward employees for reaching their goals.[25]

THE POWER OF A COMPLIMENT

A sincere and specific compliment to an employee for a job well done can motivate him or her immensely. *How can positive reinforcement help motivate employees?*

Reinforcement, Values, and Self-Exteem

Self-esteem is basic to the success of a behavioral modification program of any kind. Much of what the reinforcer is doing is improving the feelings of value and worth that the employee has, or perhaps hasn't, felt before. If you are the reinforcer, be sure to make the praise and recognition sincere. Employees can see through shallow reinforcers that suggest, "I'm doing this because I'm supposed to, not because I care." Also, be sure to clearly identify what you are reinforcing. One supervisor would periodically tell each of his worker, "You're a heck of a guy." That type of praise is too general to be reinforcing. Soon the employees came to distrust the supervisor's sincerity because his comments did very little for their self-esteem, and the comments gave no information on which of the employees' behaviors were being praised—employees did not know what to continue doing or discontinue doing on the job.

Choosing the right type of reward is important, too. Just as valence is important in expectancy theory, reinforcement theory requires giving rewards that are valuable to the person getting them. As in some of the other theories, there must be a direct cause and effect between the reward and the action it is rewarding for that value to be effective.

Perhaps you have heard some of the criticisms of behavior modification: some people see it as unfeeling and inhumane because it manipulates people into doing what the reinforcer wants them to do; others see it as bribery. Even its loudest critics, though, have to agree that it is effective—even when other methods fail. And rather than seeing it as manipulation or bribery, we should consider it just for what it is: a reward or recognition for effort or a job well done.

MOTIVATION AND SELF-ESTEEM

As studies of motivational theories show, the desire to feel better about yourself is a main motivator in the workplace. In the same way, you are also motivated *not* to perform tasks that threaten your self-esteem. This attempt to maintain self-esteem on the job is important in understanding your motivation to do a task at all.

The role you play at work is probably a basic part of your self-concept. In other words, the way you feel about yourself on the job is a very important part of the way you feel about yourself overall. In Chapter 2 you learned about the importance of self-efficacy to self-esteem. Recall that self-efficacy is your feeling that you are competent enough to succeed in life.

Let's say that you are new on the job in a company where you know absolutely nobody. How likely are you to ask other people for help? The answer to that question will depend in large part on how high your self-esteem level is. When self-esteem is low, asking for help may make you feel dependent or stupid.

Self-Esteem and Job Performance

There are two more ways that self-esteem ties in with overall performance on the job. First, if the job calls for creativity in decision making, low self-esteem may keep an individual from making risky decisions. Mediocre decisions might be made instead of exciting and challenging ones. Second, a person with low self-esteem may perform at exactly the level where others expect performance to be, so as not to threaten others' values.[26] This is another side of the self-fulfilling prophecy that you studied earlier.

When your self-esteem is stable, you can throw yourself heartily into your work. When your self-esteem is healthy, you will be higher on Maslow's hierarchy—maybe even working on level five, self-actualization. You will feel good about asking for what you want, and you will find it easier to visualize the results that can come to a truly motivated person.[27] High self-esteem is the greatest motivator of all.

Perhaps now you can explain the lack of motivation in Antonio, whose story you read about at the beginning of this chapter. His self-esteem was threatened by the supervisor who wouldn't give him enough time or caring to communicate with him properly. Also, the extrinsic reward of money wasn't enough of a motivator to keep him on the job for a long time. McClelland, Maslow, and Alderfer might all say that Antonio's needs were not being fulfilled, though Maslow or Alderfer might point out that as soon as his basic or existence needs were met, Antonio was no longer motivated by the same needs. Skinner might say that the reinforcer was poorly chosen for the response that management wanted from Antonio. Vroom would say that pay, as a valence, was simply too weak.

All of these theories can be used to discover a different aspect of motivation. No single theory explains motivation completely, but all of them together can help you learn how to motivate yourself and those who work for you. If you can see the relationship of motivation to self-esteem, nearly any motivational problem can be better understood.

« « STRATEGIES FOR SUCCESS

6.1 Applying McClelland's Theory

1. Take a look at your needs.
2. Take a look at what you want in life.
3. Take a look at how the need areas apply in the workplace.

How can you apply McClelland's needs theory to daily life? First, take a look at your own needs profile. Usually, if you examine your daydreams, you will find a pattern that centers on one or two of the three need areas: power, achievement, or affiliation.

1. **Take a look at your needs.** Ask each other in class what you would do if you became instant billionaires. Some might say that they would buy a small island and rule over it (power needs); some might say that they would throw frequent parties (affiliation needs). Others might say that they would train themselves in some way to discover the cure for AIDS, cancer, or some other fatal disease; or to end world hunger or poverty (achievement needs). Obviously, endless answers are possible, but they usually reveal people's general needs areas.

2. **Take a look at what you want in life.** When you know what your needs profile is, take a look at your current job or the career you want. Does your career choice fit your needs? For example, if you are training to be a sales representative but are weak in the achievement need, it might be good either to take a new look at your goals or begin exercising the need area that fits better with your career choice.

3. **Take a look at how the need areas apply in the workplace.** If you are a manager, take a look at how the work you supervise fits the needs of each of the employees you supervise. For example, are you assigning heavy responsibilities to an employee with a very weak power or achievement need? Are you asking an employee with high affiliation needs to work alone? Sensitivity to employee needs can help everyone become more motivated. Higher motivation at work creates a better work environment for everyone, and this spills over into personal life motivation and satisfaction.

6.2 Changing Your Behavior

1. Change a behavior or bad habit.
2. Take small steps to reach your goal.
3. Find a small reward to motivate you.
4. Reward yourself to reinforce the desired behavior.

Is there a particular behavior you have, a bad habit perhaps, that you would like to change? Using Skinner's principles, you can set up a behavior modification program for yourself.

1. **Change a behavior or bad habit.** Think of a behavior that you would like to change. Let's say you don't like talking to people at work or in class, but you don't like your reputation as being standoffish, either, so you would like to become friendlier with your co-workers.

2. **Take small steps to reach your goal.** Using Skinner's idea of *shaping,* or taking small steps gradually toward the goal you are trying to reach, you can reward yourself along the way until you have completed your goal. Set up a series of small steps that you are willing to take, which can lead you toward your eventual goal.

3. **Find a small reward to motivate you.** Before you begin, figure out what small rewards you will give yourself for meeting these goals. What rewards would motivate you? A hot fudge sundae? Leaving the dirty dishes until tomorrow? Watching the playoff game on television after work? When you have chosen your small reward, you can begin your plan.

4. **Reward yourself to reinforce the desired behavior.** Let's say you plan to smile at two people the first day. You do so successfully. Now reward yourself! The second day, you smile at two new people in addition to the two from yesterday. Reward yourself. The third day, say, "Hi, how are you?" to one new person. Reward yourself again. See how easy this can be? (Just watch out for those extra calories from all those hot fudge sundaes! Maybe you can go jogging with your new friends from work to burn them off.)

CHAPTER SIX SUMMARY

Chapter Summary by Learning Objectives

1. **Define motivation.** Motivation is the willingness to move toward reaching a goal. Motivation can be intrinsic (internal) or extrinsic (external). Motivation can be kept high through an understanding of needs and behavior reinforcement.

2. **Explain need-based theories of motivation.** Of the theories based on needs, Maslow's is the earliest. The needs in his theory are based on a hierarchy. A need will not motivate behavior until the one just before it has been satisfied. McClelland's needs theory teaches that we all have needs for achievement, power, and affiliation, but in different amounts. Herzberg's two-factor theory shows the differences between hygienes (dissatisfiers) and motivators (satisfiers). Only the motivators make people look forward to going to work and keep them satisfied over the long term. The hygienes must exist, too, or workers will become dissatisfied, perhaps to the point of quitting. Herzberg teaches that job enrichment is the only constructive method a manager can use to motivate an otherwise unmotivated worker. To qualify as being enriched, a job must include skill variety, task identity, task significance, and feedback.

3. **Explain behavior-based theories of motivation.** Two behavior-based theories are expectancy theory and behavior modification. Vroom's expectancy theory brings several ideas together and shows three forces that affect the strength of motivation in any person: instrumentality, valence, and expectancy. All three of these areas must be strong. If even one is weak or nonexistent, motivational strength will lessen greatly.

4. **Describe reinforcement theory and behavior modification.** Skinner's reinforcement and behavior modification theory is technically a behavior-based theory of motivation, like Vroom's. However, Skinner's approach also involves the use of specific and sincere praise, as a form of reinforcement. Skinner's theory deals with the nature of rewards and their effect on continued performance of behaviors that can bring them about.

5. **Discuss the relationship between self-esteem and motivation.** When self-esteem is weak, motivation to work productively will often be affected negatively. Conversely, when self-esteem—especially self-efficacy—is strong, motivation is usually stronger.

key terms

affiliation needs 141

achievement needs 141

autonomy 145

behavior
  modification 147

ERG theory 139

esteem needs 137

expectancy 146

expectancy theory 146

extrinsic rewards 133

frustration-regression
  principle 140

goal setting 148

hygienes
  (dissatisfiers) 142

intrinsic rewards 133

instrumentality 146

job enrichment 144

love and belongingness
  needs 137

manifest needs
  theory 140

Maslow's hierarchy of
  needs 137

morale 132

motivation 132

motivators
  (satisfiers) 142

organizational
  climate 132

physiological needs 137

power needs 141

reinforcement
  theory 147

reinforcers 148

safely and security
  needs 137

self-actualization 137

skill variety 145

task identity 145

task significance 145

valence 146

review questions

1. Which of the motivation theories that you've just learned about best explains why Antonio Garcia's experience in the opening story ends the way it does? Why?

2. What can employees and managers do to improve an organizational climate? How is morale affected by the organizational climate?

3. What is a needs theory? Considering Maslow's hierarchy of needs, do you see yourself on this hierarchy? Where? What do you need in order to become self-actualized?

4. Which of the three needs in McClelland's manifest needs theory (power, affiliation, or achievement), motivates you the most? Give examples from your own life.

5. Do you identify the hygienes—or dissatisfiers—in Herzberg's chart as hygienes in your own motivation? If not, why not? Is money a motivator or a hygiene for you? Whatever your answer, do you think it has always been that way for you? Will it likely be that way later in your life?

6. Which motivates you more, intrinsic rewards or extrinsic rewards? When you imagine getting an "A" in your human relations class, are you more motivated by the tangible rewards of a higher GPA or by the self-satisfaction of a job well done? Explain.

7. Why does positive reinforcement seem to work? Can you think of examples in your life where positive reinforcement was used successfully? Unsuccessfully?

8. Overall, which motivation theory do you like best? Why?

critical thinking questions

9. Some people believe that trying to find a way to motivate others is somewhat unethical or manipulative. What are your views? Has there been a time when you have felt this was happening to you?

10. Alderfer's ERG theory proposes that when we feel frustrated by an inability to meet a need, we may regress to a lower-level need. If you are leading a work team, would it be important to have your team members motivated by growth rather than regression? Would you expect this difference in motivation to make a difference in their effort, morale, or overall efficiency? What could you do to reduce frustration that might lead to regression among team members?

working it out 6.1

WHAT CAREER MOTIVATES YOU?

School-to-Work Connection: Interpersonal Skills

In this exercise, you will be picking a career that interests you and doing research to find out more information about it. Think about what it is that motivated you to select it. Interview someone in the field. Summarize your findings using the following outline.

1. *The nature of the work.* What are the duties and responsibilities on a day-to-day basis?

2. *Working conditions.* Is the working environment pleasant or unpleasant, low-key or high-pressure?

3. *Job entry requirements.* What kind of education and training are required to break into this occupational area?

4. *Potential earnings.* What are the entry-level salaries, and how much can you hope to earn if you are successful in this field?

5. *Opportunities for advancement.* How do you move up in this field? Are there adequate opportunities for promotion and advancement?

6. *Intrinsic job satisfactions.* What can you gain in the way of personal satisfaction from this job?

7. *Future outlook.* How is supply and demand projected to shape up in the future for this occupational area?

Source: Wayne Weiten, Margaret Loyd, and Robin Lashley, *Psychology Applied to Modern Life,* 3rd ed. (Pacific Grove, CA: Brooks/ Cole Publishing, 1991, Copyright by Wadsworth, Inc.). Reprinted by permission of Brooks/ Cole Publishing Company.

working it out 6.2

IS EDUCATION A GOOD INVESTMENT? YES!

School-to-Work Connection: Information

Education pays in higher earnings and lower unemployment rates.

The federal government regularly analyzes statistics on education and employment. It is important to note that these are overall statistics, they will vary by region and will change as the national economy changes. Rather than seeing this chart as a guarantee of your future earnings, look for general trends in the relationship between education and income. Instructions: Compute the difference in weekly average salary you are likely to make after completing your current education activity (e.g., associate degree, bachelor's degree), with the average weekly salary for a high school graduate (or below, if you did not complete high school). Compute the difference in weekly salary over a year. How much does this add up to over 10 years? Now compare the average

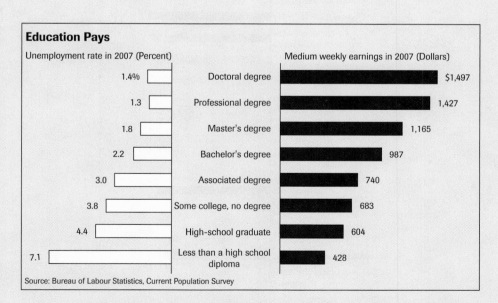

Education Pays

Unemployment rate in 2007 (Percent) | Medium weekly earnings in 2007 (Dollars)

Unemployment rate	Degree	Weekly earnings
1.4%	Doctoral degree	$1,497
1.3	Professional degree	1,427
1.8	Master's degree	1,165
2.2	Bachelor's degree	987
3.0	Associated degree	740
3.8	Some college, no degree	683
4.4	High-school graduate	604
7.1	Less than a high school diploma	428

Source: Bureau of Labour Statistics, Current Population Survey

Note: Data are 2007 annual averages for persons age 25 and over. Earnings are for full-time wage and salary workers.

Source: Bureau of Labor Statistics, Current Population Survey, www.bls.gov/emp/emptab7.htm.

unemployment rate for your current education activity with the unemployment rate for a high school graduate (or below, if you did not complete high school). What is the percent difference?

working it out 6.3

PUTTING IT ALL TOGETHER: INTEGRATING PART 1

School-to-Work Connection: Information and Thinking Skills
Think about what you have learned in Part One of this textbook. How would you explain why the particular jobs below are increasing in number of job openings? How does human relations play a part in each of these occupations? Do these particular occupations interest you?

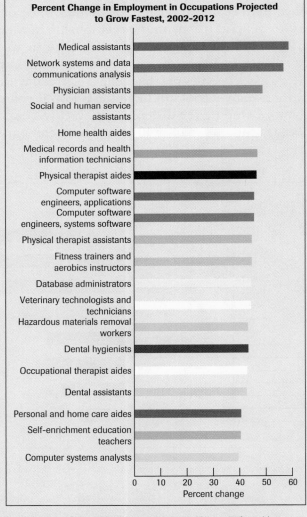

Percent Change in Employment in Occupations Projected to Grow Fastest, 2002–2012

Source: Occupational Outlook, U.S. Department of Labour (retrieved August 8, 2005) www.dol.gov.

1. *Read and Summarize*

   Go to **www.mhhe.com/lamberton4e** for the link to **www.sparkpeople.com/resource/motivation.asp.** Click on "Zig Ziglar—Goal Setter" for an audio clip of Mr. Ziglar, a well-known inspirational speaker and sales expert. The clip is about setting and achieving goals, an extremely important factor in motivation. Write at least three paragraphs summarizing and reacting to Zig Ziglar's message.

2. *Self-Assessment*

   Career Management International provides a fun and informative exercise to use in thinking about the type of job that would best fit your personality. This test, Kingdomality, uses a medieval theme to help you find out where you fit in the kingdom. Many students find this test both useful and fun. Go to **www.mhhe.com/lamberton4e** for the link to this test.

3. *Self-Assess and Apply*

   Have you considered a job with the federal government? The United States Office of Personnel Management maintains a Web site called "USA Jobs" at **www.usajobs.opm.gov.** Link to this site through **www.mhhe.com/lamberton4e.** Open the links to "Career Interest Guide" and take the short survey on *careers* best suited to your interests. Report your results. Now open the link to "Job Interest Matching" and investigate a particular *job* within the career you identified that may be a good fit for your interests. Report your results. Are they what you expected to find?

Dan the "Hobo"

Dan Trousdale is rapidly becoming known as "the hobo" in the insurance office where he works as an actuary. Although his appearance seemed average when he started nearly a year ago, everything in his life seems now to be getting, well, sloppier as time goes by. He often wears mismatched clothing, seems never to comb his hair, and maintains an office that many of his co-workers refer to as "ground zero."

Dalfour Insurance Company prides itself on its image of carefulness and orderliness in dealing with clients. Company advertising always shows well-groomed people with attractive, appealing offices. And, except for this one employee, the company has lived up to that image. Although Dan doesn't deal directly with more than two or three customers per day, he is always highly visible in the wing of the company where he works. Customers have made numerous comments about his appearance.

Jane Denton, Dan's supervisor, has decided that something has to be done with this image-destroying employee. However, she is at a loss as to how and where she should start. "How do you tell a very capable employee, 'You're a mess," she asked her manager, Tom Bell. Tom's answer surprised Jane a bit. "Trousdale needs some *motivation* to start caring more about his image and organizing himself," Tom suggested. "You're really effective at motivating your employees in other areas of their work life. What's so different about this one?" "I don't know, but I'm not sure anything I do or say will make a lot of difference, but, I'll have to try" was Jane's frustrated response.

Case Study Questions

1. Do you agree with Tom that this *is* a motivation issue? Why or why not?

2. Do you believe that the needs theories of Alderfer, Maslow, or McClelland would be useful here? If so, how?

3. Could Skinner's behavior modification approach be of any help in changing Tom's behavior? If so, what type of approach would be effective, and why?

Bonus Time at Fullerton's

Fullerton's Furniture Manufacturing was doing very well. As December approached, owner Jack Fullerton reflected on the successes of the past year. "I should give my employees something extra special," he mused. "Without them I wouldn't be showing six high figures in the black." Fullerton's employed only 60 people, but a mere four years earlier, a dozen workers had run the whole operation. Growth and success now seemed very real. Of course, the workers knew that, too.

"I know what I'll do!" Jack said to his wife that evening. "I'll give them a recreation room as an end-of-the-year surprise. That old storage shed isn't being used now that we have the new warehousing system. A small crew of carpenters would need only a couple of weeks to make it into a really comfortable rec room." "It sounds like a good idea," Jack's wife reflected. "But are you sure they would really like something like that?" "Are you kidding?" countered Jack. "I'll install a few Ping-Pong tables, some video games, and two or three pool tables that they won't have to pay to use. How could they not love it?"

At noon on the last day of the year, Fullerton called all of his employees out to the new rec room. With a brief but lively speech and an enthusiastic ribbon-cutting ceremony, Fullerton introduced his workers to their new gift . . . and waited for an enthusiastic response. Instead, the group ambled wordlessly through the new facility. Somebody mumbled, "If he has all this money, why didn't we get raises, instead of this?"

During the next week or two, a handful of workers came in to play pool during break. But they were chided by the others. Soon the recreation room became "off-limits" if a worker wanted respect from other team members. After a few months, Fullerton moved the equipment out and began using the building for overflow storage. Although he knew he had tried something that didn't work, he wasn't sure why.

Case Study Questions

1. How can you explain the strange reaction of the furniture factory workers to this well-meant gift from a thankful manager?

2. What steps should Jack Fullerton have taken before making the decision to build a recreation room?

3. What theories of motivation might have prevented this expensive incident? Would a review of McClelland's needs theory have helped? How about expectancy theory? Any others?

«« human relations in groups

7 Communication and Human Relations

8 People, Groups, and Their Leaders

9 Teams in Quality Organizations

10 Achieving Emotional Control

People spend a good deal of time interacting with others one-on-one and in groups. Every day brings a series of interactions, from the morning when you greet your family or roommates, during class or work time, until evening. Communication skills and relationship skills are key strengths for human relations.

Part Two takes a look at human relations in groups. Chapter 7 examines ways in which communication can be directed toward better understanding between sender and receiver. Chapter 8 considers communication in group settings. Chapter 9 examines how teams are formed in the workplace and types of leadership styles. In Chapter 10, we examine the concept of EQ (emotional intelligence) in terms of its role in interpersonal relationships. »» »»

COMMUNICATION AND HUMAN RELATIONS

In the Workplace: Megan's Big Jump to Conclusions

SITUATION

It was winter in Racine, Wisconsin, and everyone was trying hard to deal with the cold weather. General Manager Megan Knutson arrived at work a few minutes late. She had skidded off the road while driving to work, nearly causing a collision. After a cell phone call to the towing company, Megan was walking in the front of the store, badly shaken by the incident.

As she rushed in, Megan saw Juanita, one of her cashiers, having a confrontation with a male customer who seemed to be walking through the checkout line. "Get lost! Get out of here—now!" Juanita nearly shouted at the customer. "Okay, I've had it," Megan thought to herself. She motioned for Juanita to follow her to her office. Before even getting to the office, Megan had fired her distraught employee. "You're out of here, Juanita. We can't have our cashiers treating customers with that level of disrespect."

"But, but . . ." Juanita stammered.

LEARNING objectives

After studying this chapter, you will be able to:

1. Explain the crucial role of communication at work and what occurs when miscommunications happen.
2. Compare and contrast successful and unsuccessful listening skills.
3. Explain the importance of timing with regard to messages.
4. Examine the role of nonverbal communication.
5. Identify the functions of nonverbal communication.
6. Outline strategies for communication within an organization.
7. Explain the importance of intercultural communication in today's professional world.

STRATEGIES FOR SUCCESS

Strategy 7.1   Become a Better Listener

Strategy 7.2   Practice High-Context Communication

"Just get your things and move on out" was Megan's only response.

DISCOVERY

A few minutes after a distraught Juanita had stalked out of the store, Scott, Megan's assistant manager, walked up to Megan. "Uh, Meg, would you like to know what was really happening here a few minutes ago? Well, that guy," he pointed to the male customer, "bullied and crowded his way ahead of everyone else in Juanita's checkout line. He even tried to push that elderly woman over there out of his way so he could be served first. Juanita was only trying to restore some order by getting the man to leave. I had just reached for my cell to call the police when you got involved. The guy was totally out of control."

"Oh, good gosh!" Megan responded. "That's not what I thought I was seeing at all. I hope I can catch up with Juanita before she leaves the parking lot!"

THINK ABOUT IT

Have you ever misinterpreted something that you observed? Have you ever been misinterpreted? What were the results?

Your supervisor announces that she wants all employees who have questions about new computer equipment to come to her office without an appointment. However, when anyone asks a question, your supervisor fidgets and looks at her watch frequently. The supervisor has sent two messages: one of openness, another of irritation. She has made the false assumption that only the first message was communicated to you and your co-workers, when in fact both were very clear—and contradictory.

COMMUNICATION AND MISCOMMUNICATION

In the opening story, Megan *assumed* that she understood what she saw and heard. Making false assumptions about what is being communicated can be a crucial problem in miscommunication. (See Figure 7.1.)

False assumptions lie at the heart of many miscommunications. How many times have you noticed that people were sending you messages without being aware of it? Isn't it likely that you do the same?

As discussed in Chapter 1, communication can be defined as the giving and receiving of ideas, feelings, and information among people. Note the words *and receiving*. Communication includes listening as well as speaking. In fact, good listening skills are critical to success in work. This chapter examines the process of communicating both consciously and unconsciously, because everyone communicates in both ways every day. Why is this important at work? Without effective communication, no workplace can function properly. Miscommunication not only damages human relations and wastes time, but it also wastes billions of dollars a year in American industry.

The importance of communication in the business world cannot be overstated. The ability to communicate well on the job is often called the most important job skill for employees. Everything else about a specific

figure 7.1

FACTORS OF COMMUNICATION

Several factors go into communication. Major factors include attitudes and values, conscious and unconscious communication, and timing. *Who do you think plays a more important role in effective communication— the sender or the receiver?*

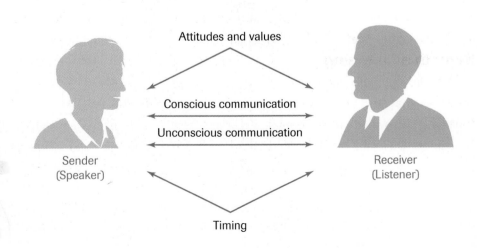

Evaluate Your Listening Skills

Go to **www.mhhe.com/lamberton4e** for the link to a Web site called "Listening Self-Assessment," where you can take a self-evaluation test. This will help you see how you would respond to special situations.

job can be taught. This means that being able to speak well and to listen well are probably the most important assets you—or anyone—can bring to a job.

LISTENING—AND HOW IT CAN FAIL

What do you really want when you communicate with someone else? You might need a question answered, or for someone to affirm that a job is being done correctly. Maybe you just want to be heard. This tremendous need to be listened to is crucial to human relations. Most people have a very strong need to have others hear them, understand them, and process the information they receive. This need is so strong that when listening is purposely withheld, the speaker's self-esteem can suffer.

Everyone needs to know they can be heard. You will probably be amazed at the results you can get once you become tuned in to other people and their needs. The need to be a good listener to others is often ignored by people who consider themselves good communicators. In *Harvard Business Review,* Ralph Nichols and Leonard Stevens wrote, "Immediately after the average person has listened to someone talk, he remembers only half of what he has heard—no matter how carefully he thought he was listening. . . . Two months after listening to a talk, the average listener will remember only about 25 percent of what was said."[1] Other recent studies have reached very similar conclusions.[2] What makes people miss so much of what they hear?

> **selective listening**
> The type of listening that happens when a listener deliberately chooses what he or she wants to pay attention to.

> **FAILURE TO COMMUNICATE**
> Actions on the part of the listener can contribute to miscommunication. What are some of the causes of poor listening?

Selective Listening

There are some legitimate reasons for poor listening. For instance, in modern society everyone is constantly bombarded with messages. No one could possibly give full attention to every message, so many people practice **selective listening,** which is when you deliberately choose what you want to hear. If you are in a personal environment with even more demands on your attention, the problem is greater. For example, picture a home with young children chattering and constantly trying to get attention; or a busy

Choon-Lan was explaining impatiently to Rick, for the umpteenth time, how to fill out the requisitions forms correctly. In the process, she was also scolding him for not paying better attention to her directions. Meanwhile, Rick seemed to be lost in space. "Are you listening to me?" she asked bluntly. "No," he replied, "to be honest, I was thinking of the next thing I was going to say to you to defend myself."

information overload

The type of listening that happens when a listener is overwhelmed with incoming information and has to decide which information will be processed and remembered; this is a common cause of poor listening skills.

office with several phones ringing, people talking, and keyboards clattering. In these circumstances, people often become selective listeners by default. The main cause of selective listening is **information overload.** You are overwhelmed with incoming information and have to decide which information will be processed and remembered. Information overload is just one cause of poor listening skills.

Many other reasons for poor listening come from bad communication habits. For example, when many people assume a subject will be too difficult for them to understand, they fail to listen. If they had listened, they may have seen how clear and understandable the subject was, or they could have narrowed down the difficulty with the subject.

The opposite often happens, too. A listener might reject a speaker because the message seems too basic and beneath the listener's level of knowledge. In either case, the message is lost.

more about...

The **"Ebbinghaus Curve of Forgetting,"** or the "Ebbinghaus Curve," developed by Herman Ebbinghaus (1850–1909), shows that we remember less than half of what we've heard after an hour, about a third after a day, and about one-fourth after a week.

Source: H. E. Ebbinghaus, *Memory: A Contribution to Experimental Psychology* (H. A. Ruger and C. E. Bussenius, Trans.) (New York: Dover, 1964). (From original work published 1885.)

When you are in a group, listening to a single speaker, you can easily allow your mind to wander. If you are attending a business meeting or conference, the success of the meeting can be destroyed by this habit. One reason for this tendency is that most humans have a capacity for listening at a speed that far exceeds the ability of the fastest speaker. You *could* listen and comprehend up to 500 words per minute; the average public speaker travels through a message at about 125 words per minute. How you spend that extra time and energy often determines your effectiveness as a listener.[3] If you can keep your focus on the speaker and use the free time to take notes or think about what is being said, you will hear more and remember more.

Tuning Out

prejudice

Prejudice in communication is the unwillingness to listen to members of groups the listener believes are inferior, such as other ethnic groups or women. It can also take more subtle forms.

Some people simply refuse to listen to co-workers or other people due to **prejudice;** they won't listen to people from different ethnic backgrounds or social classes, or from different parts of the world. Some people won't listen to teachers, or young people, or to old people; some don't think men are credible, some don't think women are credible. Prejudice can

Build Your Listening Skills

Go to **www.mhhe.com/lamberton4e** for a link to a highly informative site called "Build Your Listening Skills" that will give you tips on how to improve your listening skills. In what areas could you improve? Take notes for class discussion. Your instructor might ask you to write a short report on this site.

be more subtle than these examples, though. Sometimes a person looks unintelligent to the listener. Prejudice can also overlap with jealousy. Some people won't listen to a speaker who seems a little bit too perfect. People who want to improve listening skills should watch their personal listening habits because the process of doing business can be badly hampered by prejudice. Prejudice will be covered more fully in Chapter 16.

Red flag words and expressions are those that bring an immediate emotional response (usually negative) from the listener, generally because of strong beliefs on the subject. Some red flag words have implied meanings beyond their literal meaning. Words such as *communist* or *terrorist* might begin a flood of emotions that would prevent some people from hearing anything else for quite a while. The word *sex* might get similar results, although the emotions may be different.[4]

People do not hear what their co-workers really say for a variety of reasons. Listening expert Anthony Allesandra says that one major cause underlies most poor listening habits. From childhood, most people have been taught that talking requires energy, attention, and organization, but that listening is a passive, compliant behavior. Starting from kindergarten, children in Western society are taught to be assertive and to express themselves effectively. Until recently, though, little has been done to teach what Dr. Allesandra calls **active listening,** which is listening with greater concentration, less tolerance for distractions, and more feedback to the speaker.[5]

When you improve your listening skills, as you can learn to do from Strategy for Success 7.1 on page 179, you will find that you learn more from speakers than a poor listener does. You will also gain more speakers' respect as someone who understands their messages and cares enough to actively listen.

> **red flag words**
> Words that bring an immediate emotional response (usually negative) from the listener, generally because of strong beliefs on the subject.

> **active listening**
> Listening with greater concentration, less tolerance for distractions, and more feedback to the speaker.

THE TIMING OF MESSAGES

Many other factors can explain poor communication. Some are psychological, and others depend on the listening situation and circumstances. Timing can be a major factor when a message becomes distorted and misunderstood.

Toni, an executive, had just delivered a speech. She was still nervous and wanted to be sure that her talk was well received. Then her boss called her to his office to discuss a problem in their department, making no reference at all to the speech that Toni had just presented. To Toni, her boss's comments seemed off-the-wall and irrelevant. In the sense of relevance timing, they were.[6] This could create further miscommunication if she feels that he is avoiding the topic because he disliked something she said, or she had done a poor job in delivering the speech, or he thought the talk was not important enough to mention.

Emotional Timing

Emotional timing refers to the emotional readiness of the listener to hear a message. Sometimes a message gets to the receiver when the mood is inappropriate. "Time talks," wrote anthropologist Edward Hall in *The Silent Language*.[7] Have you ever received a phone call in the middle of the night? People who hear the phone ring at 2:00 A.M. may feel dread before picking up the phone. "The message must be urgent," they think, "otherwise the phone wouldn't ring at this hour."

The amount of time you take to return calls also communicates a message. For example, when a manager fails to answer a message until three days later, the employee who left the message may feel that the manager is either inefficient or is showing off power or status. This situation is not universal. As mentioned in Chapter 5, different cultures maintain different attitudes toward time. Americans sometimes forget this and make false assumptions when dealing with people from another culture.

TIMING IS EVERYTHING

Good communication depends on making sure that your audience is listening. How can you make sure that you are communicating your ideas to a receptive listener?

Situational Timing

Situational timing refers to the listener's situation when a message is received. Privacy is usually a key element. For example, most people wouldn't want to discuss intimate details of their lives in a crowded bus or subway. If two people are enjoying an emotional reunion, they will probably put off the more intimate parts of the meeting until they are alone. Often, communication that would be totally appropriate in one situation is out of place in another. Because of this, a listener usually can't fully hear the message unless the situation is appropriate.

Bad situational timing can also ruin an otherwise good business undertaking. For example, a crowded elevator would be a poor setting for introducing an important new idea to your boss. Your idea would require careful and focused listening that your boss would not be able to give in an elevator.

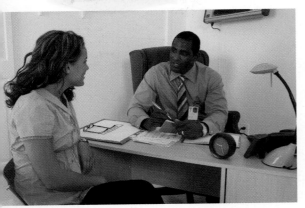

Supervisor: *Helen, I really believe you can complete the projects I've asked you to do, and your attitude is really good. But I need to start seeing your abilities and good attitudes translated into performance!*

Helen: *OK, sure. Thanks.*

Helen sees Jean a few minutes later, and this conversation takes place:

Jean: *How did your talk with the supervisor go?*

Helen: *Really pretty well. She said some really nice things about my abilities and attitude. I think she's pretty happy with me.*

Relevance Timing

Relevance timing is similar to situational timing. It simply means that communication should fit the other topics being discussed.

Filtering

When listeners engage in **filtering,** they may fail to receive messages correctly because they are *hearing only what they want to hear.*

Sometimes the listener wants something to be true so badly that he or she interprets the message to make it true.

The supervisor's message to Helen contained both negative and positive elements. However, the negative material is threatening to Helen's self-esteem, so she really heard only the good part. Helen had filtered the message to make it fit what she wanted to hear.

Filtering works both ways. It reflects what a person decides to *hear* and what he or she decides to *say.* In communicating to others, be sure that your filtering is appropriate and that you are not sharing too much or too little.

filtering
A method listeners use to *hear only what they want to hear,* which may result in failing to receive messages correctly.

more about...

COMMUNICATING WITHOUT WORDS

Nonverbal communication is also related to communication skills. Much of what people say is expressed by **nonverbals**—which are ways of communicating without speaking, such as gestures, body language, and facial expressions—rather than words. Next time you attend a class, look around the classroom to see if you can interpret the nonverbal communication around you. Notice the way your fellow students dress, the way they look at each other and the instructor, and the amount of interest they seem to have in the course. These factors send messages that can be read by nearly anyone around them.

Note that none of the nonverbal behaviors mentioned in Real World Example 7.5 could have been perceived with the interviewer's eyes. Yet they were still taking place, at least to the ear trained to hear and process

nonverbals
Ways of communicating without speaking, such as gestures, body language, and facial expressions.

Jerry was a salesperson who had been hired via a series of telephone interviews by a company a thousand miles away. After being hired, he was required to attend a session for new recruits at company headquarters. At that session, he met dozens of salespeople from all across the country who were similar in ability, age, and even in looks. The company had gotten the type of sales staff it wanted, although all of them had also been hired by telephone. During one of the sessions, Jerry asked how such a feat had been accomplished.

With a knowing grin, the company sales manager replied, "You'd be amazed at how many nonverbals you people gave us on the phone."

nonverbal signals. These signals can indicate degrees of self-confidence, maturity, fear, and many other key qualities by which to judge a person. Figure 7.2 shows some strong nonverbal and mixed verbal and nonverbal signals.

FUNCTIONS OF NONVERBAL MESSAGES

Albert Mehrabian, one of the first scholars to study nonverbal communication, describes three major functions of nonverbal messages. Basically, nonverbal messages reflect the *relationship* between speaker and listener. These three functions are as follows:

1. Showing the speaker's attitudes and emotions

The words you choose can say a great deal about the way you feel. However, nonverbal signals in this area tend to be both more powerful and more honest. If a speaker's nonverbal signals disagree with the words being said, which do you believe? Which *should* you believe? Both questions have the same answer: the nonverbal ones.

Beware of your feelings and emotions. Unless you are an actor, they will show themselves when you communicate with others. Much of what you communicate is done unconsciously. People often communicate feelings and opinions to others without any awareness they are doing so. Sometimes, people communicate feelings and opinions that they don't realize exist. The feelings are buried somewhere beneath the consciousness, but appear clearly in nonverbal signals.

When you communicate unconsciously, your *internal climate*—the way you feel within yourself—is likely to give you away. Self-esteem is the key to internal climate. If you

NONVERBAL COMMUNICATION

Nonverbal gestures, expressions, and other physical cues can cause miscommunication if they are not recognized by a speaker or listener. What might these people be communicating by using nonverbals?

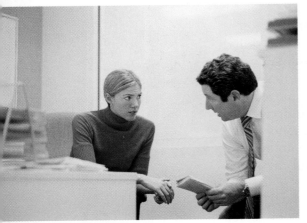

You are a manager. An employee comes into your office hanging his head, speaking in a soft voice, and shuffling his feet. These behaviors will tell you more about the message the employee is about to give you than the message itself. Your nonverbal reactions to such a speaker can also be important.

are feeling bad about yourself, it will show. If you are feeling good about yourself, that fact will show, too. If you have other issues on your mind, your lack of complete attention will most likely get in the way of real communication. Others will respond in a negative way to you when you project a negative attitude.

2. Clarifying messages

Imagine watching a movie that was filmed with a white sheet as the only background. This might cause the same kind of frustration as having verbal communication with no nonverbal *background*. Nonverbal communication allows you to understand and interpret meaning in context. **Context** is a point of reference, a place from which to begin.

Have you ever been forced to ask for directions in an unfamiliar city? If the person gives you just verbal signals, without nonverbals, you might feel slighted by the direction-giver. Also, you might be more likely to get the directions wrong. When a direction-giver points the way, along with the verbal explanations, the two-way communication will be better in many ways.

3. Showing the speaker's reactions to the listener

Watch someone walk down a hallway, greeting people along the way. You might be surprised at how many different ways there are of saying things as simple as "Hi" or "How are you?" Although the

context

A point of reference (or a place from which to begin) when communicating.

Nonverbal Signals	Mixed Signals Verbal & Nonverbal
gestures, arm movements	vocal pacing and pauses
eye contact, eye movements	loudness, vocal quality (timbre)
physical appearance, clothing	pitch of voice
space allowed between speaker and listener	silence
facial expression	confidence in use of vocabulary
touch	carefulness in listening

figure 7.2

NONVERBAL COMMUNICATION

Both nonverbal signals and mixed signals can tell you more about a speaker's message than the actual words. *What should you do when a speaker's verbal message does not match his or her nonverbal one?*

Left off w/ clairmont

intensity
The degree to which you show serious concentration or emotion; another dimension of nonverbal communication.

words are the same, variations in facial expression, tone and pitch of the voice, amount of time spent in the greeting, and eye contact are all likely to show at least some differences in emotional reaction. These differences include variations in acceptance, approval, and comfort level.

If you were to say, "Nice to meet you" to someone in a fairly neutral tone of voice, that statement could easily be taken as something casual. However, try shaking hands with the same person while saying, "Nice to meet you." The difference in intensity alone would be quite obvious. **Intensity,** the degree to which you show serious concentration or emotion, is another dimension of nonverbal communication.[8]

Over the years, many people have commented that the English language should have a least a dozen different words to express various types and intensities of love. For example, "I love chocolate" certainly means something totally different from "I love my mother." Because of gaps such as this in the English language, nonverbal expressions are often necessary to help communicate feelings more completely.

Nonverbal Messages about Self-Esteem

Nonverbal communication signals your *self-esteem level*. Does this mean you should try to act in ways that cover up low self-esteem? Indeed, when attempting to make a good first impression, such a tactic might be positive. Also, your own apparent dislike of yourself can trigger actions in other people that might actually threaten your self-esteem. In the end, though, there is no substitute for genuinely building up your self-esteem. When your self-esteem is high, it will be evident in your nonverbal behavior. You will be listened to more effectively, and the overall communication process will improve.

Gestures and Their Meanings

What about gestures—the movements you make with your arms, legs, hands, feet, and shoulders? By observing gestures, you can tell a great deal about how open or closed people are in their attitudes. Gestures also indicate the true leader of a group, and how open a person is to physical contact.[9] Another way of looking at gestures is to divide them into four categories. Every gesture you use falls into one of these four categories:

illustrators
Gestures that are used to clarify a point, such as pointing when giving directions.

- **Illustrators** are gestures people use to clarify a point they might be making. Pointing the way down the street when giving directions or pounding a fist to emphasize a point are illustrators.

- **Regulators** are used to control the flow of communication. When you raise your hand in class to get the instructor's attention, you are using a regulator. Perhaps you have seen someone point to someone else who hasn't been allowed to speak. With proper eye contact, the message is: "Please let this person say something." Regulators can also include raised eyebrows, head nods, or any other nonverbal indications that say, "Please let me (or this other person) into—or out of—this discussion."

- **Displays** are gestures that are used like nonverbal punctuation marks. These are gestures that show the emotions going on inside a person, and they effectively reveal just how strongly people mean what they say. Clenched fists displayed during a committee meeting would likely indicate emotional tension. Displays usually augment another type of nonverbal behavior, such as facial expressions and general body movements. If someone is saying, "Yes, that's a pretty good idea," yet the displays don't agree, the listener will likely not believe what the speaker is saying.

- **Emblems** are gestures used in a specific manner because they have a specific meaning, usually one understood by both sender and receiver. The peace sign used by war protesters in the 1960s would be one example. Another would be the "O" formed by the thumb and forefinger, which means (in American culture), "Everything is okay." Several obscene gestures would also fall into this category of emblems, as well. Remember, though, that emblems are culture-specific: An emblem we assume is universal can easily mean something quite different in another culture. This is especially important to remember when traveling and doing business in different parts of the world; many embarrassing blunders have occurred when travelers did not know the local meanings of nonverbal gestures.[10] In Figure 7.3, see if you can determine what the gestures indicate.

regulators

Gestures that are used to control the flow of communication; eye contact is a common type of regulator.

displays

Gestures that are used like nonverbal punctuation marks, such as pounding your fist on a table.

emblems

Gestures that are used in a specific manner because they have a specific meaning, usually one understood by both sender and receiver; the peace sign is an example of an emblem.

figure 7.3

WHAT DO THESE GESTURES MEAN?

Look at these gestures. *How would you interpret each gesture?*

Source: John Stewart and Carole Logan, *Together: Communicating Interpersonally* (New York: McGraw-Hill, 1993), p. 167.

Advice for Improving Communications Skills

Go to **www.mhhe.com/lamberton4e** for the link to find several recommendations for improving your ability to communicate effectively. Also, check out a few of the library links for further information. Write a paragraph summarizing what you learn.

Distance between Speakers

distancing

The distance of physical space that you maintain between other people and yourself.

Another area of nonverbal communication is called *proxemics*, or **distancing,** which can be defined as the distance of physical space that you maintain between other people and yourself. Most people carry around a *bubble of space,* or several bubbles. These are illustrated in Figure 7.4. The first bubble is reserved for intimate relationships, such as with mates, romantic partners, and children. It extends from physical contact out to 18 inches or so. The next, from about 18 inches out to 4 feet, is the area saved for close friends. The third bubble, from about 4 to 12 feet, is used

figure 7.4

THE ZONES OF DISTANCING

Everyone has different zones to communicate with different people in their lives. These four zones—intimate, personal, social, and public—can vary, depending on the person and the culture. *Which is the most common zone for you?*

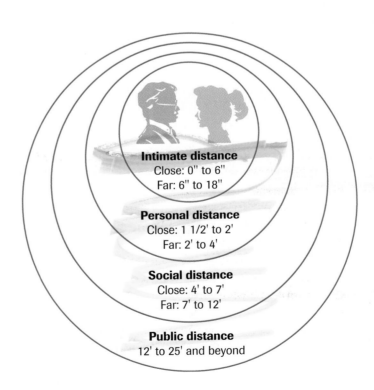

Intimate distance
Close: 0" to 6"
Far: 6" to 18"

Personal distance
Close: 1 1/2' to 2'
Far: 2' to 4'

Social distance
Close: 4' to 7'
Far: 7' to 12'

Public distance
12' to 25' and beyond

In a government community services agency, Mary was always coming into another department to make sure that the needy members in her own family and circle of friends were being provided for. In some cases, she even made requests of members in the other department, such as: "Make sure Debbie gets three boxes of apples." Needless to say, Mary was violating a basic rule of horizontal communication: Don't communicate orders in a department where you have no authority.

for communicating with business contacts and casual acquaintances. The last one, from 12 feet on out, is used for the general public.[11]

When any of the first three bubbles is violated, most people feel very uncomfortable. Even when Americans ride subways and crowded elevators every day of their lives, they usually never learn to like the daily violations of their personal space. Next time you are in a crowded public vehicle or elevator, notice your fellow passengers' facial expressions. On most of their faces you will see looks of resignation, or else they are showing an unemotional mask—which both show that they have accepted this invasion of their space as necessary, although they don't like it.

This distancing issue varies geographically. In some cultures, being very close to another person is much more acceptable than in the United States or in many European cultures. In most Arab countries, two businesspeople will typically stand about 18 inches from each other while talking. Most people in East Asian and Southeast Asian societies also feel more comfortable at close distances with strangers than most Americans do. As the world becomes more and more an international community, learning the norms of other societies is becoming increasingly important.

COMMUNICATING IN AN ORGANIZATION

Organizational communication has both formal and informal dimensions. In traditional organizations, most messages that need to be communicated must go through the chain of command. In other words, the flow of messages has to follow the organizational chart, both upward and downward. These are **vertical communication** channels. Also, the policies of most firms include formal methods of communicating in oral, electronic, and written form. These policies should be followed closely, because the formal dimension of organizational

organizational communication
The oral and written communication within an organization. It has both formal and informal dimensions and travels both vertically and horizontally.

vertical communication
Messages that are communicated according to an organization's chain of command by flowing both upward and downward.

Hooked Up to the Grapevine

By forming friendships with people on various formal levels of your firm, you can get an expanded version of the grapevine and you might be able to get a more accurate picture of what is really happening in your organization.

more about...

communication is important. If you went to your manager's boss, for example, to discuss something important, you could very likely be seen as *jumping rank* or going over your manager's head.[12]

Even in **horizontal communication,** which refers to messages between you and your equals in the formal organization, you should take care to communicate without causing problems for yourself and others in the company. In this type of communication, be sure that you are not intruding into someone else's area, and that you are not setting yourself up to be accused of causing trouble in someone else's department or division.

Grapevines

Probably even more important than a formal organization is the informal organization within it. When communication takes place in an informal context, the rules are less formal but still very real. Every company that has employees contains an informal organization. The informal organization is made up of friendships and friendly relationships that establish themselves naturally in any situation. You may have joined groups like this when you were in elementary school; the more exclusive ones were known informally as cliques. This can continue through high school and college right into the workplace. Informal groups are apparently something humans never outgrow.

The informal organization is made up of small groups based on particular interests, beliefs, and activities. These groups tend to communicate among themselves and with each other through a network known as the **grapevine.** The grapevine is not exactly the same thing as the **rumor mill,** which is a gossip network that produces mostly false information. When the informal organization communicates *incomplete* but somewhat accurate information, it is called the grapevine.[13]

You can learn a great deal by staying in touch with the grapevine. One of the most important characteristics of grapevines is that they are often selective: everyone doesn't always get all of the information, and everyone doesn't always get the same information. If you are a supervisor, the grapevine might leave you out of touch with information about your employees. If you are an employee, you might not hear what is happening in the world of the managers.

When companies have very poor formal lines of communication, the informal grapevine becomes even more important. Employees often complain that if it weren't for the grapevine, they would have no idea about what was happening. Grapevines are also usually slanted. Often, a grapevine will tend to be pro-employee, pro-manager, or in some other way biased, especially when other forms of communication are poor.[14] It is wise, then, to keep these biases in mind when listening to a grapevine; this will help you determine what to believe.

---

horizontal communication

Messages that are communicated between you and your equals in the formal organization.

grapevine

A network within the organization that communicates incomplete, but usually somewhat accurate information.

rumor mill

A gossip network that produces mostly false information.

COMMUNICATION IN INFORMAL NETWORKS

The rumor mill and grapevine are two types of networking you may find in a work environment. What can you learn by joining either network?

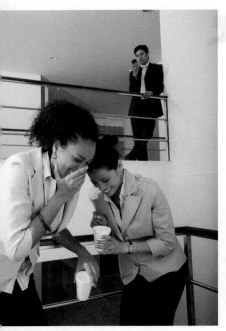

INTERNATIONAL AND INTERCULTURAL COMMUNICATION

Every year, more and more companies open overseas offices, and experts predict that the global economy will continue to expand. Multinational corporations now account for nearly half of the world's assets. Thus, the odds are very good that you will be working for one of these globe-trotting institutions sometime during your life.[15] With the entrance of China and India into the global economy in 2000 and their rising economic power since then, the size of the international market has grown remarkably.[16] Every year, there are more visitors to the United States from other countries.

Yet despite all of the changes, the average American is ill-equipped to communicate with people from other cultures. Did you know that pointing the sole of your shoe at someone in an Arab country or in India would be considered insulting? That in Chinese society it is all right to stare at people? Or that in several cultures, eating with the left hand is considered to be bad manners?[17]

Anthropologist Edward T. Hall has identified different cultures as being high context and low context (see Figure 7.5). In a **low-context culture,** a written agreement, such as a contract, can be taken at face value. In other words, one can assume that it means what it says and that it is in itself binding. Low-context cultures include German and Scandinavian cultures. North American business culture tends to lean heavily toward the low-context end of the scale.

In a **high-context culture,** on the other hand, the *social context* surrounding the writing is far more important than the writing itself. In a high-context culture, one must be very careful about cultural norms, nonverbal behaviors on both sides, and anything else involving the overall atmosphere of the communication. Notice in Figure 7.6 which countries have the highest- and lowest-context cultures. Do any of them surprise you?

Figures 7.5 and 7.7 show examples of communication problems that take place when high- and low-context cultures collide.[18] Obviously, the lower-context countries are not likely to cause trouble in communication when they are communicating only with each other.

more about...

Punctuality: A Global Issue

Many people from European and Asian countries value punctuality as much as, or even more than, people from in the United States. In Hong Kong and Tokyo, the trains are famous for always being on time, and people often show up early for appointments rather than risk being late.

low-context culture

A culture in which a written agreement, such as a contract, can be taken at face value.

high-context culture

A culture in which *social context* surrounding a written document is far more important than the document itself: One must be very careful about cultural norms, nonverbal behaviors on both sides, and anything else involving the overall atmosphere of the communication.

WORKING WITH HIGH-CONTEXT CULTURES

Americans who work with high-context cultures have to understand that success with their clients will depend on several factors other than the products or services being offered. *What makes a high-context culture different from a low-context one?*

figure 7.5

HIGH-AND LOW-CONTEXT CULTURE EXAMPLES

Cultural anthropologist Edward T. Hall illustrates how high- and low-context cultures are different, as well as their reasons for being this way. *Is the United States a low-context culture or a high-context culture? Why?*

Source: Edward T. Hall, "How Cultures Collide," *Psychology Today* 10 (July 1976), pp. 66-74.

These excerpts are from "How Cultures Collide," an article by Edward T. Hall:

"In some cultures, messages are explicit; the words carry most of the information. In other cultures, such as China or Japan or the Arab cultures, less information is contained in the verbal part of the message, since more is in the context. That's why American businessmen often complain that their Japanese counterparts never get to the point. The Japanese wouldn't dream of spelling the whole thing out. To do so would be a put-down; it's like doing your thinking for you."

"Several years ago I was traveling in Crete and wanted to visit the ruins at Knossos. My traveling companion, who was from low-context, fast-moving New York, took charge of the arrangements. He bargained with a taxi driver, agreed on a price, and a deal was made. We would take his taxi. Without warning, just as we were entering the cab, he stopped, got out and asked another driver if he would take us for less money. Since the other driver was willing, my friend said, "Let's go." The first taxi driver felt he had been cheated. We had made a verbal agreement, and it had been violated. But my friend, from a low-context opportunistic culture, felt no moral obligation at all. He had saved the equivalent of 75¢. I can still see the shocked and horrified look on the face of the first driver."

figure 7.6

HIGH- TO LOW-CONTEXT CULTURES

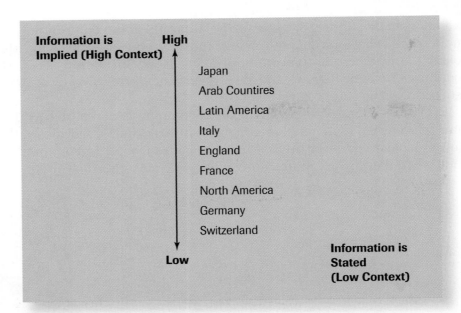

Information is Implied (High Context)   High

Japan
Arab Countires
Latin America
Italy
England
France
North America
Germany
Switzerland

Low   Information is Stated (Low Context)

International Communication Traps—Some Examples

In **Japan**, the practice of giving small gifts is nearly an obligation in most business situations. In **China**, on the other hand, gift-giving to an individual in a business situation is strictly forbidden.

In the **United States**, "tabling" an agenda item means putting it off until later. In **England**, "tabling" means "putting it on the table" right now and discussing it immediately.

In most of **Latin America**, no offense is taken when someone is late for an appointment. In fact, tardiness is somewhat the norm. In **Sweden**, to-the-minute promptness is expected.

In **Mexico**, it is courteous to ask about the spouse and family of a customer. In **Saudi Arabia**, you should never ask about such things.

figure 7.7

INTERNATIONAL COMMUNICATION TRAPS

Every culture is different. What is okay in Mexico may be considered rude in Saudi Arabia. When traveling or working abroad, it might be best to prepare oneself beforehand, by learning about the country's norms and customs. If that is not possible, then one should still enter open-mindedly, without expectations that norms and behaviors are the same everywhere. *Is there any other rule for doing business in differing cultures?*

Source: Lennie Copeland, "Training Americans to Do Business Overseas," *Training,* (July 1983), p. 12.

《 《 STRATEGIES FOR SUCCESS

7.1   Become a Better Listener

1. Stop talking.
2. Get rid of distractions.
3. Try to enter into the speaker's reality.
4. Use pauses for reflecting.
5. Listen for main ideas.
6. Give feedback.
7. Listen for feelings as well as for facts.
8. Encourage others to talk.

What can you do to become an active listener? You can change your listening habits, but as with all habits, these changes take time and effort.

1. **Stop talking.** If you are talking, time and opportunity to talk are being taken away from the other person or people. In many ways, this is the most important rule. Remember that most humans have a strong need to be heard—to be listened to.

2. **Get rid of distractions.** Distractions can be external (such as noise and movements near you), or internal (such as your thoughts and emotions). Move closer to the speaker, change your physical position so that you face the speaker directly, and put any nagging personal problems out of your mind. All of these steps will help eliminate distractions.

3. **Try to enter into the speaker's reality.** Even before beginning to listen, prepare yourself to enter the world of the speaker. If the conversation is one-on-one, while you are listening *try to make your own needs temporarily less important than those of the other person.* Understand that the other person has very real needs. With a public speaker, listen and watch for clues about the world of the speaker.

4. **Use pauses for reflecting.** When a speaker pauses, use the time to make associations in your mind with other things he or she has said. Think of your own past experiences in order to see relationships among the ideas being offered. In all cases, avoid the temptation to let your mind wander.

5. **Listen for main ideas.** When listening to a public speaker, jot down key words and phrases. Try as early as possible to see the outline headings the speaker is using. When talking one-on-one, make sure you understand each point made by the speaker. In many cases, this involves asking questions to make certain you have understood.

6. **Give feedback.** Many people mistakenly think of feedback only as communication in a one-on-one situation. Eye contact and facial expressions are also examples of feedback. When talking with another person, you should respond with "I" statements. This way, it is clear that you are expressing your feelings, not placing blame. Rather than saying, "Your ideas on this project are hard to understand," say something like, "I feel that an important step has been left out. Why don't you examine the marketing plan before you proceed?" or "I'm having trouble understanding your point here; could you explain to me again?

7. **Listen for feelings as well as for facts.** Watch for nonverbal messages that communicate how the speaker *feels* about the subject. Eye and body movements, vocal tone, and posture are examples. By listening for feelings, you will also become more aware of your own feelings about what you're hearing.

8. **Encourage others to talk.** Encouraging others to explain their ideas in more detail can make you more responsible for what you say yourself. In a public speaking situation, this means allowing others to be involved when the speaker calls for questions and listening carefully to both sides.

Notice how many of these eight steps involve self-esteem. If you feel good about yourself, implementing all eight of these strategies will be easier and more effective. People who like themselves tend to be better listeners. This is because they are less likely to need attention and can listen to others without an excessive need to be heard.

7.2 Practice High-Context Communication

1. Recognize that people in high-context cultures need to know how to put you into context, to help them understand you better.

2. Speak slowly and clearly.

3. Sprinkle your conversation with at least a few words and expressions from your listener's native language—but only if you are sure what they mean, and how to pronounce them.

4. Be careful about your nonverbal signals.

---

more about…

Active Listening

Empathy is when you attempt to feel another person's feelings, attitudes, or thoughts. It can play an important role in effective active listening.

Workbook on Communication

To find a useful electronic workbook on better communication, go to **www.mhhe .com/lamberton4e** for a link to a site called "Self-Evaluation: Do You Listen?" Under General Communications, click on "The Seven Challenges." Do the work asked for in at least one of those seven challenges. Write a paragraph or two on what you learn.

5. Here are some additional hints that you can use with businesspeople from high-context cultures:

1. **Recognize that people in high-context cultures need to know how to put *you* into context, to help them understand you better.** They need to know not only about you, but also about the company or organization that you represent. Without that knowledge, any agreement could be meaningless.

2. **Speak slowly and clearly.** Stay away from jargon, slang, clichés, and too many idioms. When nonnative speakers learn English, they often learn a textbook version of the language. Expressions such as, "Let's get all of our ducks in a row" will likely be lost on them. Since Americans use a great deal of informal language, expressions like this slip out even when you are careful.

3. **Sprinkle your conversation with at least a few words and expressions from your listener's native language—but only if you are sure what they mean, and how to pronounce them.** In nearly all language groups, it is considered to be good manners to learn some of the other person's language. Such an attempt shows the listener that you care and are interested enough to do a little learning. Of course, you must be sure you understand the meaning before using such phrases, and be careful not to mispronounce the words and phrases—at least not beyond recognition.

4. **Be careful about your nonverbal signals.** If you are communicating through a translator and the listeners are listening to you for periods of time without understanding, your listeners are even more likely than usual to pick up on gestures, tone of voice, and all of the other nonverbals.[19]

These rules should help greatly in high-context situations. Most of these, though, would be good to follow when dealing with companies from any other cultures. Even when context is low, thoughtfulness always pays off.

CHAPTER SEVEN SUMMARY

Chapter Summary by Learning Objectives

1. **Explain the crucial role of communication at work and what occurs when miscommunications happen.** Communication takes place even when speakers and listeners do not realize that it is happening. When people communicate unconsciously, feelings are projected outward. If you are feeling bad about yourself, that emotion will show. When miscommunication happens, the results include bad decisions, damaged feelings, and loss of productivity,

2. **Compare and contrast successful and unsuccessful listening skills.** Listening skills are important for anyone who wants to communicate effectively. Reasons for poor listening include selective listening, information overload, perceived difficulty of the subject, prejudice, daydreaming, red flag words, and the misunderstanding of listening as a passive position. Good listening is related to self-esteem. It is also a matter of priorities. People who like themselves and understand the importance of good listening tend to be better listeners.

3. **Explain the importance of timing with regard to messages.** Messages need not only to be carefully planned in terms of content, but in terms of timing. A message that would otherwise be clear and well received can be destroyed when it is delivered at a bad time. The areas of possible timing mistakes include emotional, situational, and relevance timing.

4. **Examine the role of nonverbal communication.** Without nonverbal communication, effective exchange of ideas and thoughts is more difficult. Gestures are an important part of the communication process. They include illustrators, regulators, displays, and emblems. Proxemics, or the study of distancing, states that people carry around several bubbles of space. When any of the first three bubbles is violated, the violated person feels uncomfortable.

5. **Identify the functions of nonverbal communication.** Nonverbal messages exhibit attitudes and emotions, help clarify the verbal message, and show something about the emotional reactions of speaker and listener.

6. **Outline strategies for communication within an organization.** In any organization, communication has both formal and informal dimensions. Everyone who works in an organization also needs to understand the different requirements of vertical and horizontal communication channels. Within the informal organization, the grapevine is the informal channel of information. It includes information that is largely accurate, but incomplete. When the information is distorted, the channel is called the rumor mill.

7. **Explain the importance of intercultural communication in today's professional world.** International and intercultural communication become more important as the world becomes smaller. One can see international cultures as either high-context or low-context. Doing effective business with other cultures requires some knowledge of context expectations.

key terms

active listening 167
context 171
displays 173
distancing 174
emblems 173
filtering 169
grapevine 176
high-context culture 177

horizontal
   communication 176
illustrators 172
information
   overload 166
intensity 172
low-context culture 177
nonverbals 169

organizational
   communication 175
prejudice 166
red flag words 167
regulators 173
rumor mill 176
selective listening 165
vertical
   communication 175

review questions

1. What is communication? In your definition, use an illustration from your own life.

2. Explain why your internal climate is so important to communicating effectively. Explain the importance of self-esteem to the communication process.

3. Are you usually an active listener? If not, do you know anyone who is? What qualities set an active listener apart from other people?

4. Think of people you have been around who are poor listeners. Do they all have certain qualities in common? If so, what are they?

5. How does nonverbal communication help people understand each other? How can nonverbal cues be negative, especially in the workplace?

6. What are the main differences between communication in the formal organization and in the informal organization? What cautions should you use in each area?

7. What is meant by filtering? Do you ever find yourself filtering a message being sent to you? How can one reduce the filtering of messages in the workplace?

8. What are the major differences between a high-context culture and a low-context culture? What steps could you take to prevent misunderstandings when dealing with a culture that is opposite in context from your own?

critical thinking questions

9. Do a brief self-evaluation. Ask yourself, "How effective am I at communicating with people from cultures that are higher-context or lower-context than my own?" Have you ever been guilty of ignoring such differences? Most of us have been. If so, what were you doing that could be done more effectively?

10. Think of an incident in your life when someone you were listening to was sending nonverbal messages that seemed to contradict the verbal message. Perhaps it was a public speaker or someone on television. What was your reaction to the mixed message?

working it out 7.1

GRAPEVINE OR RUMOR MILL?

School-to-Work Connection: Information Skills
This exercise graphically illustrates how quickly distortions of facts can take place, even when they are communicated in a controlled environment.

This exercise requires seven volunteers from the class. Six of the volunteers must leave the classroom, taking their places in the hallway. The other volunteer will remain in the classroom. The instructor will choose a very short story that contains several characters and a bit of action. The instructor first reads the story to the entire class, including the first volunteer. When the reading is finished, the second volunteer will be allowed to enter the room.

Volunteer number one will then retell the story he or she has just been read, without any coaching from either the instructor or the rest of the class. Then, one by one, each volunteer will be ushered into the room to hear the story retold by the last person who heard it. When volunteer number seven has heard the story, he or she must retell it to the rest of the class. Finally, the instructor will ask the seventh volunteer to read aloud the story in its original form, for the benefit of the volunteers who have gotten only distorted versions of it.

Although degrees of distortion will vary from class to class, you will readily see how messages become muddled, sometimes to ridiculous extremes. If most of the facts are correct, but the story is incomplete, the class has created a grapevine example. A rumor mill example that includes gross distortions is much more likely.

Note: This exercise has also been done successfully with a photograph or drawing that contains many different elements and/or people to remember. The picture should be shown on a screen or copies should be distributed to all class members—except six of the seven participants. Let the first participant have one minute to observe the picture; follow the same procedure as for the story.

working it out 7. 2

THE IMPORTANCE OF FEEDBACK

School-to-Work Connection: Information Skills
This exercise illustrates the importance of two-way communication that includes feedback from all communicators.

A volunteer from the class will study a geometrical figure provided by the authors of this textbook to the instructor. (The other class members will not be allowed to see the figure.) Then, with the student's back to the class, he or she will describe the figure exactly enough so that each class member can reconstruct it on a piece of notebook paper. Fifteen minutes will be allowed for this portion of the exercise. During this phase, only the volunteer will be allowed to speak. No questions are allowed, except for one request to repeat each instruction. The volunteer is not allowed to explain any single descriptive instruction more than twice, and the second time is allowed only if requested by a class member.

The same volunteer will face the class and will describe the geometric figure, while classmates start over with another sheet of notebook paper. This time, the members of the class are allowed to ask questions. They may ask any question that will help clarify an accurate drawing of the figure. After 15 minutes, compare the results from the two phases. You will very likely see a vast improvement in the second part of the exercise. This is probably because the person who gave the instructions was able to provide helpful nonverbal clues while facing the class. Did the first exercise—with the student facing away—cause any frustration or confusion? If so, give specific examples. Perhaps the more complex instructions left a lot of people unsure the first time, but were somehow easier to comprehend the second time.

To the instructor: The geometrical pattern can be found in your *Instructor's Resource CD.*

1. *Nonverbal Communication*
   Read through the free online tutorial on nonverbal communication presented by "GetAhead" linked through **www.mhhe.com/lamberton4e** or found at **www.getahead-direct.com/gwnonver.htm.** What new information did you find most interesting? Practice using these suggestions in your next interview or presentation.

2. *Listening Skills*
   Take the self-administered test posted by L. A. Harbor College found on the Web site at **www.lahc.cc.ca.us/tutortraining/listtest.html** to rate your listening skills. If you mark it honestly, it should help you assess how good a listener you are. Were you surprised by your results?

3. *Careers Tracking*
   Embark on an adventure in career exploration with Career Voyages, a Web site created by the U.S. Department of Labor. Link to their site through **www.mhhe.com/lamberton4e** or find them online at **www.careervoyages.gov/index.cfm.** Begin your journey by selecting the link for *students, career changers, career advisers,* or *parents.* Find out what industries are growing, how you can be trained and qualify for a job, and how you can help pay for your education along the way. What did you discover about yourself and your future in your career voyage? Explain.

The Mysterious Strangers

When Jan Wood came to work on Monday morning, she noticed a group of people she had never seen before at the insurance company where she was a claims supervisor. "Who are those people?" she asked one of her co-workers. Nobody seemed to know. The presence of these strangers seemed especially suspicious because they were often seen talking quietly among themselves. They would stop talking as Jan, or anyone, walked past them.

For a week, rumors spread throughout the building. Since Jan was a supervisor, her crew found it hard to believe that she didn't know what was really happening. The more questions her employees asked her, the more frustrated she became. Although Jan approached her own manager, Ron Morris, several times, she was met only with vague answers.

Finally, on Friday morning, she caught Morris alone and demanded a straight answer. "I'm looking like a fool here, Ron," Jan complained. "Now, come on; as a supervisor I really need something to tell my workers. It's gotten so they spend more time talking about the mysterious visitors than they spend working on claims." "Okay, Jan," Ron replied. "The top brass have hired a management consulting firm. Mostly, they're just looking at cost cutting. It wasn't supposed to be a big deal." "Does the cost cutting involve cutting people's jobs, by any chance?" was Jan's automatic response. "No," said Ron.

"In fact, we've kept quiet about this because we were afraid a panic might start on that very issue." "Well the panic has started anyway, and I think it's time to get everyone calmed down," said Jan, shaking her head.

The next morning, Jan Wood held a briefing with all of her workers in which she explained what Ron Morris had told her. Most of her 10 employees were still skeptical. They found it hard to understand why they hadn't been told the truth from the start if, in fact, there was nothing to fear. Top management had still not sent even a brief memo to all the employees telling them that no positions were being cut. After three more weeks, Jan's two best claims workers left for other companies. Three others told her that they are looking for work elsewhere.

Case Study Questions

1. How could the company have handled this situation differently? What principles of effective communication have been broken in this case?

2. If you were Jan Wood, what would be your next step? Why?

3. If the company decides to explain the situation, what form of communication should they use? Meetings, memos, personal letters? Why?

Un-Gorgeous George

George had been working for the same company, a local television cable installation business, for 11 years. During that time, he had completed an apprenticeship program and had made it through the required entry-level training programs. He had also applied for promotions four times—and had been passed over each time. George simply could not understand why he was not getting promoted. He worked hard, was never late to work, and often helped others after his own assignments were finished. He thought of himself as competent and deserving of promotions, and he wanted more than anything to move into a supervisory office position.

What George didn't know was that behind his back his co-workers called him "Gorgeous George"—but not because he was so good-looking. His nickname came from the way he presented himself, which was the opposite of gorgeous. George dressed more like he was getting ready to work in the yard than to work in an office. He also seldom made eye contact during conversations. He had a tendency to mumble, and he usually looked down at the ground while talking or interacting with others. He seldom smiled, and usually did not speak to people in the office unless they spoke to him first. His friend at work, David, offered to help him with practice interviews to increase his prospects for promotions, but George was uncomfortable with the offer and declined.

Case Study Questions

1. How are George's nonverbal behaviors contradicting the message he is trying to get across about wanting to be promoted? What is each message channel saying, and which will you most likely believe?

2. How do others likely respond to his nonverbal behaviors? How would *you* respond?

3. David may be able to convince George to do the practice interviews if he can convince George to listen to him. How might he work with George to help his active listening skills?

PEOPLE, GROUPS, AND THEIR LEADERS

In the Workplace: A Collision with Group Norms

SITUATION

Earl was a college student working in a small tree nursery to help pay his tuition. His job was "budding," a grafting process to encourage the growth of high-quality fruit trees. Just a few days into the new job, Earl discovered that he could finish nearly twice as many trees per hour just by trying a little harder and by using some shortcuts that seemed to occur to him occasionally.

DISCOVERY

After a week, one of the other workers, Jenny, cornered Earl behind an outbuilding. "What's the deal with you?" she asked in a harsh tone. "It looks like you've been trying to show the rest of us up! Are you trying to get us regular grunts fired so you can look good? Well, it's not going to work, so back off. We're watching you." With that, she walked away. "Well," thought Earl to himself. "I never figured on

LEARNING objectives

After studying this chapter, you will be able to:

1. Explain why people join groups.
2. Define a group.
3. Discuss formal groups and how they develop.
4. Explain the importance of status and conformity within groups.
5. Discuss informal groups.
6. Examine barriers to group effectiveness.
7. Define leadership.
8. Compare and contrast leadership styles.

STRATEGIES FOR SUCCESS

Strategy 8.1   Watching for Hidden Agendas

Strategy 8.2   Strengthening Your Leadership Power

getting trouble for trying to be more efficient. This is a crazy place."

Following some reflection, though, Earl decided to stand up for himself. He found Jenny in the tree yard the next day and told her, "I've thought about what you said. I'm really not trying to make anybody look bad. And in no way do I want the rest of you to get in trouble. But this is how I do my job, and if I do any less, I don't feel good about myself."

Jenny didn't bring the issue up again. Later Earl learned that some of the other workers were actually on his side. He started to make friends with more of them, and the pressure eased a great deal.

THINK ABOUT IT

Can you think of a time when you worked with a negative work group? How would you handle a situation like Earl's?

CHAPTER

8

WHY DO PEOPLE JOIN GROUPS?

If you're like most people, you started joining groups when you were in elementary school, or even earlier. As you progressed through junior high and high school, membership in groups probably became increasingly important. Most of these groups fell into two categories: formal and informal.

formal group

A group that is usually governed by the formal structure of the organization.

informal group

A group that tends to form around common interests, habits, and personality traits.

A **formal group** is one that is usually governed by the formal structure of the organization. In school, formal groups included athletic teams, the band or chorus, or the student government. In the workplace it might be the planning team, the junior sales force, or an ad hoc committee. In these groups, members don't necessarily have the final say about whether or not they can be members. In contrast, the **informal group** just happens. As Elton Mayo found in the Hawthorne studies, informal groups tend to form around common interests and habits, as well as personality traits (see Chapter 1). Informal organization can be defined as the ever-changing relationships and interactions that can be found within an organization, but they are not formally put together by anyone.

People join groups to fulfill needs that can't be fulfilled when acting alone. Those needs and their fulfillment fit the following categories:

- *Affiliation.* Everyone has a basic need to be with other people and relate to them. Although some people seem to need it more strongly than others, all people have the need to belong. For example, Jean eats lunch every day with two friends at work simply because she prefers it to eating alone.

- *Attraction.* Normal humans tend to be attracted to people who are like them, or who are the way they would like to become. People are drawn to others who have attitudes, values, personalities, and economic positions similar to their own. In short, they like to be around people who are attractive by these standards. For example, in a college cafeteria that employed 20 students, informal groups formed on the basis of how attractive students were to each other, rather than on the basis of job type or even proximity (working near each other).

- *Activities.* You may often become a member of a group because the group is involved in interesting activities. For instance, you might belong to the student newspaper staff because you are interested in journalism, or you might have a group of work friends who all like to share activities such as skiing, swimming or card-playing.

- *Assistance.* Sometimes people join groups because of the help or assistance the group can give them in some area of their lives. Joining a labor union would be a good example for one's work life. Joining a wholesale food co-operative or a health club would be an example of joining a group for personal assistance.

- *Proximity.* People often form groups just because they tend to form close ties with people they see frequently, such as the people they work with, attend classes with, eat with, and so on.[1] For example, Josh was close to the four men he worked with in the claims department of an insurance office. When he moved up three floors to a different department, he rarely saw any of them, because he had a new group, with closer proximity, with whom he spent his time.

WHAT MAKES A GROUP?

All groups have certain qualities in common. A **group** is defined as two or more people who:

- interact with other members on either an individual or network basis.
- share common goals.
- are governed by unspoken or formal rules or norms as a system of attitudes and behavior.
- maintain stable role relationships.
- form subgroups through various networks of attraction and rejection.[2]

A closer examination describes each of the preceding characteristics.

Interaction

Some definitions of groups state that each member of the group interacts with every other member. However, studies have shown that you might be a member of a group in which you hardly ever talk to some members, but you still work together as a network, with a leader (or leaders) tying activities together. In an informal group, personal interaction with each member is much more likely. This is partly because informal groups are often smaller than those whose size and membership are controlled by people outside of the group.

Shared Goals

In a two-person informal group, the only shared goal might be good conversation and friendship. Larger informal groups might have fun as their goal, and large formal groups may have only one major goal in common. An unconscious goal that is always present, though, is

group

Two or more people who interact, share common goals, have unspoken or formal rules or norms, maintain stable role relationships, and form subgroups.

GROUPS IN THE WORKPLACE

Groups help people to work more effectively and find satisfaction through interaction. *What are some of the ways that groups form in the workplace?*

fulfilling the need to belong. If any group, formal or informal, has opposing goals within itself, the group will not be effective.

Unspoken or Formal Rules and Norms

If any group is going to work effectively, it has to maintain some basic rules upon which it has agreed. In Earl and Jenny's story at the beginning of the chapter, the rules were tied in directly with the norms. A **norm** is a standard of behavior that is expected of group members. One group norm said, "Working hard is bad." The related rule was, "Don't work too hard or the group will be unhappy with you." Smaller groups often have unspoken rules that aren't brought up until someone breaks one of them. Such unspoken rules usually evolve from shared values or norms.

> **norm**
> A standard of behavior expected of group members.

Larger and more formal groups usually require more rigid norms, although informal norms also exist, even in the largest groups. The effectiveness of a group depends on each member's understanding and following of the rules of behavior. The Roman Catholic Church has been used as an example of a remarkably effective organization because "they have an explicit and widely debated hierarchy of sins, with a matching hierarchy of punishments."[3] An effective group also needs ways of *enforcing* its rules and norms, as well as methods for a member to rejoin the group after an offense has been corrected.[4]

Stable Role Relationships

Even in a two-person group, one member will usually be considered the stronger one, the source of emotional support, whereas the other will be the problem solver.[5] When groups form in classrooms for special class projects, a leader will often emerge within just a few minutes. The same thing often happens in groups such as juries and work teams. In groups that work together for days, weeks, or longer, leaders will nearly always become identifiable by others, if not by themselves. The leader is not the only member with an identifiable role. Others soon become recognized for individual contributions they can give to the group. Examples include team problem solvers, accountants, and soothers of hurt feelings.

Subgroups

When a large group cannot meet growing group needs, a subgroup will often form. Subgroups usually continue to interact with the larger group while maintaining an identity of their own. In informal groups, the subgroup sometimes forms because of the growth of the larger group. Throughout the informal organization, a network of attraction and rejection is constantly changing the formation, growth, and segmentation of groups.

FORMAL GROUPS AND THEIR DEVELOPMENT

When a group forms, it has a number of issues to resolve before it can really start to work. There are usually four distinct stages of the development of any group, and all four of these focus on two behaviors of the group: **task activity** and **group process.** Task activity is the assignment of tasks to get a job done. Group process is the way group members deal with each other while working on a task.[6] If you analyze any formal group you have been in, you'll see both of these factors at work. If you have been assigned small-group activities in a classroom, you may have been graded on both the quality of the task and the group process.

> **task activity**
> The assignment of tasks to get a job done.

> **group process**
> The way group members deal with one another while working on a task.

1. Forming

The first stage, taken when the group is new, is also called *orientation.* During this phase, members take a close look at their task, adjust themselves in terms of what behaviors are expected of them, and begin accepting one another.

2. Redefining

At this point, group members reexamine the task as a group problem. The group also tries to define itself in relation to solving this problem. Members will usually reveal different levels of enthusiasm. The greater the differences in this enthusiasm, the stronger will be the internal conflict during this stage of group development.

3. Coordinating

This stage often lasts the longest. Here the group starts collecting information and translating it into group objectives. Discussion about issues from the redefining stage brings feelings out into the open in this stage, and more conflicts take place here than in any other stage. This conflict can be so strong that it destroys the group.

4. Formalizing

This is the point where the group works smoothly in its roles and can accomplish its objectives. New roles are assigned as needed. Group members have accepted the role of both the group and their role in the group. The group is now at a point where it can perform meaningfully, and where it is much more likely to last.[7] Be sure to read Real World Example 8.1 for a step-by-step example of this process.

Assertiveness is expressing thoughts, feelings, and beliefs in a direct, honest, and appropriate way, while respecting everyone involved. Assertive people are always working toward a win-win situation.

more about...

Chris Mendez was one of about 40 young workers hired to staff a new lake resort in New Mexico. During the first week, everyone was involved in training. Meetings were followed by role-play exercises and other practice drills on how to treat the guests. By the time the resort opened for business, quite a few groups had formed. Workers had established who among them made them feel comfortable, shared their interests, and so on; but the new company was structured in such a way that many formal groups had to work together to achieve the goals set by the company and the supervisors, who were the group leaders.

After the second week in business, Chris's group consisted of six employees. This group, which was in charge of organized recreational activities at the resort, had encountered dozens of problems that hadn't been included in the formal training. Examples included how to deal with expired credit cards, how to deal with customers who found damaged recreational equipment, and—most important—how to deal with drunk and disorderly guests.

The group realized it would have to meet quite often to identify problems, refocus on the issues and goals, and communicate their findings to the top manager.

Chris's group began to meet and redefine its goals. This redefinition included returning to the question, "Why are we here?" Many of the activities were proving to be either unpopular with guests or too complicated to manage in the way the group had planned. For example, horseback trail rides turned out to be difficult to schedule and manage. To complicate matters, two group members resented that the activities they managed were the least popular. The conflict became so intense that Juan, the supervisor, had to become a conflict manager.

At the end of three months, Chris's group had established its methods of operation; its function, which included some marketing; and its relationships with one another and the company. In the process, two members had quit and were replaced by two very enthusiastic activities people who fit in well with the rest of the group.

When you are a member of a newly formed group, keep these four stages in mind. When conflicts begin, consider them to be normal parts of the group development process. Don't allow them to hurt your self-esteem or reduce the group's effectiveness. Remember that member assertiveness plays an important role in allowing the group to form and evolve realistically.

STATUS AND CONFORMITY IN GROUPS

status

The rank an individual holds within a group.

As groups form, members begin to develop respect for one another. Rarely, however, is everybody in a group respected equally. Thus, status in the group becomes increasingly important. **Status** is the rank an individual holds within a group. It comes from a variety of different sources, some based on formal factors and others on informal ones. Formal position in the company is one source of status. Other sources are factors such as interpersonal skills, personal charm or charisma, educational level, physical appearance, and persuasive ability. Many other bases for status can be added, depending on the values shared by the group. For example, Mickey once worked at a company where most of the employees played team sports together. As a result, most of the groups placed a high value on athletic ability. The highest-status members were the best athletes, because athletic talent gave an individual higher status. In a group with different norms, these athletes might have held positions of less status.

Status has a great deal of effect on the total performance of the group. Group members with high status will usually have a heavy impact on the group morale, and thus on its output. An important related factor is degree of *status acceptance*. If you have lower status in a group than you feel you deserve, then your own morale, and in turn, the group's morale, will be badly affected. Even the opposite—giving people more status than they deserve or feel they deserve—can cause problems such as resentment from other group members, or guilt feelings in the person with higher status than is deserved. People with healthy self-esteem may be more content with the status level the group has given them and may attain higher status than those who have trouble liking themselves.

When group norms have been established and status issues have been sorted out, conformity becomes an issue. **Conformity** is acting in coordination and agreement with one's group. One reason members of groups conform is to avoid pressure or rejection by the rest of the group. Other goals may include a desire to meet the group's shared objectives or to be rewarded for their work. For a group to function effectively, a certain amount of conformity is necessary. If you've ever seen a group in which everyone wants to be heard, but nobody wants to listen, you know how much a little conformity can help.[8] You may have heard the expression "it's like herding cats" used to refer to the difficulty of getting people in a particular group to conform to group norms and act as a unified group. This expression reminds us how difficult it can be to coordinate group tasks when no one conforms.

Conformity also has an ugly side. Too much of it can kill creativity and discourage people from saying what is really on their minds. One example is the problem called **groupthink,** which is a type of mistaken thinking that results from groups "getting along too well." Picture a group in which members like and respect one another but have fairly low collective self-esteem. Add some stress and time pressure, and you have bad decisions based on the self-created illusion that "everybody else wanted it that way." Another deception that can come out of groupthink is the illusion that the group is good and moral. "We're the good guys; who has a right to oppose us?" We will come back to groupthink again.

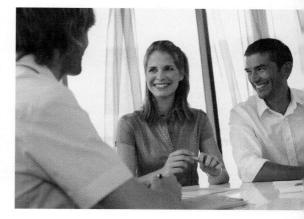

GROUP PROCESS IN ACTION

Groups need to solve internal and external conflicts. *How did Chris's group identify problems?*

conformity

Behaving in a way that meets a specified standard, in coordination with a group.

groupthink

A problematic type of thinking that results from group members who are overly willing to agree with one another because of time pressure, stress, and low collective self-esteem.

Status symbols are possessions or affiliations that reflect the owner's wealth and social standing. Expensive cars and homes, country club memberships, and certain types of clothing are typical examples. However, in groups with norms that disapprove of wealth and numerous possessions, owning *less* can actually be a status symbol. In such a group, driving an old car could, for example, provide a concrete symbol of a member's true value as a person.

more about...

Informal Group Dynamics

Go to **www.mhhe.com/lamberton4e** for the link to a Web site with useful information on informal group dynamics in leadership, communicating in groups, and the importance of group norms. First, read the brief article called "Informal Group Norms or Values." Then, at the bottom, click on "Change Informal Group Norms." Write a brief essay on how informal group norms can be changed, along with pitfalls in the process.

INFORMAL GROUPS

In the opening story, Earl found out how powerful an informal group can be. In addition, Jenny may not have realized the role she was actually playing—and the effect it had had on others before Earl came along. In an informal group, nobody specifically organizes the members, and leaders will rarely, if ever, have formal titles. In fact, leaders will often deny their roles when someone asks about it.

Someone once asked a member of a college student committee, "Are you the chairperson?"

"Are you kidding?" the student scoffed, "I'm just filling in because nobody else has the guts." Yet all five of the other members acknowledged that she was *definitely* the leader. Informal group leaders usually become leaders in one of two ways. One way is by appointing themselves. The group might have a "leadership vacuum" that makes it possible for the first person who shows any initiative to be followed immediately. Otherwise, the group chooses the leader by consensus. The person who most closely fits the norms of the group is usually chosen as leader. This process often takes place without anyone in the group being consciously aware that it is happening.

Although informal groups are as different from each other as the people who form them, all such groups within organizations have some basic qualities in common:

- *They fulfill the needs of members.* People join informal groups to satisfy needs—anything from a need for friendship to a desire to get ahead in an organization. Humans require being with others. Thus, the need to belong is in many ways the most urgent need that group membership fulfills.

- *They are usually necessary to an organization.* Far from being a negative factor, informal groups can be very helpful to the overall operation of a company or other organization. Any manager who

At the Citrus Time bottling company, nine line workers were expected to clean up spills and broken glass at their workstations before leaving. This usually took around an hour for each employee. The employees had formed an informal work group that interacted off the job, drinking together at a nearby bar. They decided that each day only two of them would stay late, work very rapidly to clean everyone's areas, and punch the time clocks for both themselves and the other seven when they had finished. They found that nobody in management seemed to notice the extra half-hour that it took for two of them to do the job of seven people. When their supervisor discovered the system, he felt that the workers were undermining orders from management and wanted to fire all of them. His manager disagreed. What is your opinion?

tries to break up an informal group should consider the effects of such an action. One exception is any group that is subversive and serves to tear down the larger organization. A theft ring would be an obvious example.

- *They are always changing.* Because there is little or no formal control over informal groups, they are likely to change as people and relationships change. When members join and drop out, the overall values and attitudes of the group usually change. Static, unchanging groups seldom stay together very long.

- *They are not affected by formal boundaries.* Informal group members in the same group can be from higher or lower positions in an organization. They can involve people in other divisions, as well as people who aren't even working for the company.

Any business with more than two or three employees will contain informal groups. Although informal groups can sometimes work against the good of the firm, they usually do much more good than harm. A group of workers involved in an embezzlement scheme would obviously have a negative effect, and the group would have to be broken up and probably prosecuted. However, extremes like this are unusual. Most often, informal groups deserve respect.

BARRIERS TO GROUP EFFECTIVENESS

Nearly everyone who has worked for an organization has seen ineffective groups. One reason has already been mentioned—groupthink. Groupthink is defined by Irving Janis in his book *Victims of Groupthink* as "A mode of thinking . . . when the members' striving for unanimity overrides their motivation to realistically appraise courses of action." In other words, instead of evaluating other courses of action, the group gets to 100 percent agreement as soon as possible. Three different types of bad decisions come out of groupthink: those that result from believing too much in the great worth and status of the group, those that lead to closed-mindedness, and those that have to do with too much pressure for conformity. By definition, according to Janis, groupthink always results in a bad decision. Examples of bad decisions in the business world attributed to groupthink include the Enron collapse (2001), the WorldCom bankruptcy (2002), and bank collapses such as Washington Mutual (2008). The first two company failures alone resulted in the largest corporate financial disasters in the United States up to that time and led to changes in corporate laws.[9] Figure 8.1 lists suggestions to help avoid letting groupthink happen to you.[10]

GROUPS AND GROUPTHINK

Groupthink can block groups from working effectively by limiting constructive disagreement. *What steps can you take to try to prevent groupthink?*

Solutions to Group Effectiveness Barriers

Many other problems can come out of group interaction, such as excessive conflict among members, lack of creativity, one-member domination, and resistance to change. Three steps will help improve group effectiveness:

1. *Changing ineffective norms.* Making a group more effective can be done most efficiently by changing its norms. Since most groups haven't ever discussed their norms, examining norms is the first step. The group leader must get the group to agree on the purpose for the group's existence, the role each member can play in achieving that purpose, and why a specific norm needs to be changed.[11] One year a university student committee spent most of the fall semester trying to establish just why they existed and what they were supposed to be doing. Once they decided that changing the quality of on-campus entertainment was their reason for existing, they became very effective at producing student dances, concerts, and barbecues. Once this self-definition was in place, the group's norms changed in a way that matched the new, better-defined mission.

more about...

Irving Janis, who coined the term groupthink, is also known for writing *Groupthink: Psychological Studies of Policy Decision,* as well as *Decision Making; A Psychological Analysis of Conflict, Choice, and Commitment.*

2. *Identifying problems.* Try to identify problems the group is facing so that members can discuss ways to solve them. Is one person dominating the discussion? Are some group members in conflict? Are members resisting change and new ideas? Once the specific problem is identified, group members or the group leader can create a solution to address the specific problem. The solution should be designed so that it uses the full potential of each group member.[12] New job assignments given to members may make them feel they are contributing in a more useful way to the project, using their individual talents and abilities in the process. In one case, an organizational

Ways to Reduce Groupthink

Dr. Irving Janis suggests the following eight actions to reduce the possibility that groupthink will take place.

1. **Assign critics.** The leader of a decision group should assign all group participants to be critical evaluators of what will take place in the group. Reasonable objections and doubts should be encouraged.

2. **Leaders act impartial.** At the beginning of group deliberations, the leader should take an impartial role, free of biasing comments. This allows participative freedom in the exploration of several alternatives.

3. **Set up subgroups.** Groups should routinely establish several decision-making subgroups under separate leaders to look at some of the same issues and problems. Although this may seem to be a duplication of efforts, if done correctly it increases the breath of data generated.

4. **Consider alternatives.** During group consideration of alternatives, members should be divided into smaller subgroups again with separate leaders. The result may be different perspectives that will be reviewed when the larger group reassembles, and this will ensure that all known issues are handled with equal consideration.

5. **Consult with outsiders.** Each group member should periodically discuss the group's progress with trusted associates outside the group, then report back their input.

6. **Invite experts.** One or more outside experts who are not core group members should be invited individually to group meetings and encouraged to challenge the views of the group.

7. **Assign devil's advocates.** At every meeting devoted to considering alternatives, at least one member should be assigned the role of "devil's advocate." This person comes up with all the reasons why alternatives may not work.

8. **Consider the competition.** Whenever a competing organization is at the center of the problem, a significant amount of time should be given to the analysis of the rival's signals and intentions.

figure 8.1

AVOIDING GROUPTHINK

Dr. Janis suggests different ways in which groups can avoid conformity. *What are some of the ways in which groupthink can be reduced?*

Source: Irving L. Janis, *Groupthink,* 2nd ed. (New York: Houghton-Mifflin Company, 1982).

development committee at a large urban church found endless frustration in trying to accomplish anything. They finally realized that they could not identify the problems they needed to solve as a group. Every meeting was a waste of time until they finally identified the problems and then went after the solutions.

The student government team at a small community college was made up of seven students, all of whom wanted to be student body president. The group was torn because everyone wanted to be a leader, and no one wanted to work as equals on a team. Not until most of the members either graduated or quit was the group replenished with a more balanced composition. Then the group could identify and pursue its goals.

3. *Improving the composition of the group.* Some groups are ineffective because their composition is poor. For example, they may have members whose abilities, interests, or personalities clash. They may have members who do not have the right mix of expertise to solve a problem they are assigned. The group itself may be too large or too small for the task. In these cases, group leaders should try to change the group's composition, if possible, to make it more effective. The leader should look for a balance of skills and knowledge to allow the group to be effective. Whenever a group's composition is changed, it will go through the group process stages described earlier. The group will improve, but this growth toward improvement won't happen without some "growing pains." The leader must be ready to help in the readjustment that will be necessary when group composition changes.[13]

more about...

Passive Aggression

Sometimes a member with a hidden agenda will show unusual stubbornness or resentment toward a group goal. He or she will not openly criticize it, but will do indirect things to sabotage it because it does not match his or her agenda. This kind of behavior is called *passive aggression*.

hidden agendas

Secret wishes, hopes, desires, and assumptions hidden from the group. People often try to accomplish hidden agendas while pretending to care about the group goals.

Hidden Agendas

Have you ever been in a group where nothing seemed to be getting done? Perhaps you looked around to figure out why. **Hidden agendas** may have been part of the problem. Hidden agendas are individual members' secret wishes, hopes, desires, and assumptions that they don't want to share with the group, although they will work hard to accomplish them without being discovered. Often, people try to get these agendas accomplished even as they pretend to care more about the goals of the group. They might also try to persuade the group to make its agenda fit their own.[14]

When group leaders and members can identify and confront hidden agendas, the strength and integrity of the group increase.

Kerry joins committees and attends their meetings for only one reason: She wants to get to be known by the people on each committee so she will have political power in the managers' association to which she belongs. Her hidden agenda is to network and look good to others, and she doesn't truly care about any of the groups' goals.

LEADERSHIP: WHAT IT IS AND WHAT IT REQUIRES

Without effective leadership, groups function poorly or not at all. **Leadership** is usually defined as the ability to influence people toward the attainment of goals.[15] Effective leadership, an extremely important factor in the study of human behavior, is also one of the most talked about but least understood human relations topics. (See Figure 8.2.)

leadership
The ability to influence others to work toward the goals of an organization.

Leadership versus Management

In his popular books on leadership, management expert Warren Bennis makes a strong distinction between a manager and a leader. According to Bennis, good managers *do things right,* whereas effective leaders *do the right things.*[16] In other words, managers follow the rules and go through the motions, while leaders have the real power in an organization. The manager who is also a leader is the most effective of managers.

A great deal of controversy surrounds the issue of what exactly makes a leader effective. Some argue that leaders are simply born with *traits* that make them effective. Others argue that leaders have mastered different sets of *skills* that nearly anyone can develop. This latter school of thought encourages leadership training as a realistic method

figure 8.2

LEADERSHIP STYLES

Leaders may interact with others differently depending on their leadership styles. *Which style of leader would you prefer?*

Test Your Assertiveness

Are you more conforming, or more assertive? Take the Assertiveness Test located at the Queendom Web site at **www.queendom.com/tests/minitests/assertiveness_abridged_access.html#h** and linked through **www.mhhe.com/lamberton4e.** It takes about five minutes (a longer version is also available). What does your score say about your level of assertiveness? Are you surprised, or not?

of becoming an effective leader. Still others emphasize the *situation* in which a leader finds himself or herself. They show how leaders who were unquestionably effective in one situation were much less effective in another, dissimilar situation. Which position do you agree with?

LEADERSHIP STYLES

One popular method of understanding leadership is to examine the four common styles used by most leaders. These styles are based mostly on the extent to which the leader includes others in the process of making decisions. They are usually called autocratic, consultative, participative, and free-rein.

Autocratic Leaders

autocratic leaders
Leaders who make all the decisions and use authority and material rewards to motivate followers.

Autocratic leaders make it very clear that they are in charge. The power and authority autocratic leaders have from their position in the organization are important to them because they use it freely, not expecting it to be questioned. Followers usually have little or no freedom to disagree or to disobey. Although this style sounds arrogant and dehumanizing, autocratic leaders are often neither. Many simply operate in a reality where the leader is unquestioned.

In some cases, the autocratic leader operates as a benevolent dictator. The message this style sends to followers is: "As long as you do things the way I tell you to do them, I will do whatever I can to make your life positive." Also implied, however, is: "If you don't do things my way, I am also capable of making your life miserable." In many ways, the benevolence is a weapon used to enforce obedience, especially when the negative consequences of disobedience are clear

more about...

Warren Bennis was chairman of the Organization Studies Department at MIT and was former president of the University of Cincinnati. He has also taught at Harvard and Boston Universities. Two of his books have won the McKinsey Award for "Best Book on Management."

and well understood. If you have worked for this type of leader, you will clearly recognize this pattern.

Consultative Leaders

Consultative leaders will often spend a great deal of time and energy getting information from followers about what decisions should be made for the good of the organization. This behavior sets the consultative leader apart from the autocratic. However, when the actual decision is to be made, the consultative leader makes it alone, usually accepting responsibility for the decision regardless of how much input on that decision has been provided by others. In some ways, the consultative leader is an autocratic leader who is a better listener.

Consultative leaders are also more likely to delegate authority. They are comfortable assigning certain tasks to subordinates. When you read about the autocratic leader, you might have thought that style seems like the military. Actually, especially in today's armed forces, the typical military leader is just as likely to be consultative. One reason is that delegation is essential to military effectiveness. In World War II, Adolf Hitler's autocratic leadership style, compounded by his hesitation to delegate, was one major factor in his defeat. In the same war, Dwight D. Eisenhower was a consultative leader who made decisions only after carefully listening to his advisers—and to the enemy.

LEADERSHIP
The success of a group depends on its having a capable leader. *What are the differences between a manager and a leader?*

Participative Leaders

Participative leaders have both high concern for people and an equally high concern for getting the job done.[17] This type of leadership invites subordinates to share power with the leader. This style is very popular in organizations that use teams and team building. Although a participative leader encourages others to help make decisions, he or she can and will act decisively, even when not receiving the amount or quality of participation asked for. The effective participative leader is not willing to sacrifice the goals of the organization to the harmony of the group. Instead, he or she will hold company needs equally with group morale, placing great emphasis on both factors.[18]

Free-Rein Leaders

Free-rein leaders often have subordinates who don't complain about the leadership; however, these leaders are not really leading at all in any strict sense. This approach is often called *laissez-faire leadership*. Laissez-faire is a French term that means "allow them to work at will"; in other words, let them do as they please in a "hands-off" leadership style. This type of leader usually acts as a representative for the group, while allowing them to plan, control, and complete their tasks as they wish.

consultative leaders
Leaders who tend to delegate authority and confer with others in making decisions.

participative leaders
Leaders who encourage the group to work together toward shared goals.

free-rein leaders
Leaders who set performance standards, then allow followers to work creatively to meet the standards.

Dr. Leo Haines was a college president who would openly tell the members of the faculty and staff that he would "give them the world" if they would implement his policies without complaint. Everyone who worked at the college knew that if you openly disagreed with or disobeyed Dr. Haines, you would be placed on his "blacklist." Some faculty members who disagreed with him often actually found themselves without jobs. Dr. Haines was an example of a benevolent dictator.

The free-rein leader requires a certain kind of follower for any type of success. This follower must be self-directed and motivated to act without intervention. He or she must also have a clear vision of what is necessary to get a job done. When they are effective, free-rein leaders usually allow expectations to be adequately communicated to the followers. Department chairpersons at many colleges and universities are free-rein leaders. They can afford to be, because they are leading departments made up of professionals who largely perform on their own.

Which of these four styles of leadership is best? That will depend on two variables. First, the *situation* will often determine the most effective style. As mentioned, high-ranking military personnel will usually expect a consultative style, whereas musicians in large orchestras will more likely expect the autocratic approach. Whenever very quick and important decisions are a part of everyday life, the autocratic method is useful. College and university professors, on the other hand, will often expect either a free-rein approach (since they expect to be treated as professionals) or the participative style.

The second variable focuses on the *personality and skill level* of the leader. Many managers seem unable to use more than one type of leadership style. This often has to do with the flexibility of the leader. Thus, even when the situation calls for a different style, the leader will "default" to the style he or she is accustomed to, sometimes with negative results.

Leaders and the Use of Power and Authority

The effectiveness of a leader also depends greatly on the leader's attitude toward power. **Power** can be defined as the ability of one person to influence another. This is not to be confused with **authority,** which is

---

more about...

Laissez-faire also refers to a system of government in which industries and other economic influences are controlled very little.

---

power
The ability of one person to influence another.

authority
The vested power to influence or command within an organization.

One of the cofounders of Compaq Computers Corporation, Rod Canion, served as CEO for the first decade of the company's history (1982–1991). He and the other two cofounders, Jim Harris and Bill Murto, built their ideas from an investment of $1,000 each and ideas written out on a pie store placemat, into a record-breaking business success story. During Canion's term as CEO, the company became one of the fastest-growing companies in U.S. history. His success was based on a participative leadership model. When the company needed to make important decisions, he was only one voice in what the founders called "consensus management." He believed that the best time for a CEO's input is early in the decision process. In his experience, "that way, people don't think of it as getting my stamp of approval; they think of it as getting my contribution."[19]

the power vested in a specific position within an organization.[20] Some leaders have authority, but little or no power. Other people—sometimes not even designated leaders—have power despite having very little authority.

Sources of Power

The way followers respond to power largely determines its effectiveness. Followers have three choices: *commitment, compliance,* or *resistance.* If either of the first two choices is made, the leader's power is likely to produce effectiveness. With resistance, however, the leader's power is often undermined. How the leader's power is received often depends on where the power comes from.[21] Three power sources are based at least in part on the position of the person using them. Therefore, they are often seen as different forms of position power. They are as follows:

- **Legitimate power.** This source of power is very similar to authority. It is based on the position the person holds in the organization. This type of power is effective only when followers believe in the structure that produces this power, and hence in the legitimacy of the leader's position.

- **Reward power.** This type of power comes from the user's ability to control or influence others with something of value to them. Rewards can be as simple as praise and recognition, money, or a promotion. The reward must be obtainable, and the potential receiver of the reward must believe in the other person's ability to bestow it. Reward power interacts with legitimate

legitimate power

Power based on the position a person holds in an organization that is effective only when followers believe in the structure that produces this power.

DIFFERENT WAYS TO LEAD

There are several different leadership styles. *What are some of the factors that determine the success of a particular style?*

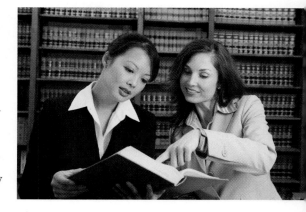

reward power

Power that comes from the user's ability to control or influence others with something of value to them.

coercive power

Power that depends on the threat of possible punishment.

networking power

Power that is attained by gaining contacts and knowing the right people.

expert power

Power that comes from a person's knowledge or skill in areas that are critical to the success of the firm.

charismatic power

Power that is based on the attractiveness a person has to others.

power, when the ability to reward depends on the use of legitimate power.

- **Coercive power.** Just as reward power depends on promises of future rewards, coercive power depends on the threat of possible punishments. Coercive power is commonly used to enforce policies and regulations. When a leader has a great ability to intimidate followers, this type of power is often used. Usually, working for or with someone who uses coercive power is not a pleasant experience.

    By contrast, some types of power have their sources in the personalities of those who use them; they are often referred to as types of personal power.

- **Networking power.** This source of power is sometimes also called "connection power." It is attained by "knowing the right people." You have probably heard the expression "It's not what you know; it's who you know." By gaining contacts that will help you influence whoever you are dealing with, you can use this power source in many different situations. Often, other people's perception that you have that connection or network of connections is just as powerful as the fact itself. For example, if you are seen as being a close friend of a vice president in your company (when you are actually just a family acquaintance), your perceived power could be as high as if you really were close to the vice president.

- **Expert power.** Expert power comes from a person's knowledge or skill in areas that are critical to the success of the firm. The employee or manager with expert power has a power source that can often be amazingly strong.

- **Charismatic power.** This power source is based on the attractiveness a person has to others. To produce genuine power, though, the user of charismatic power must also be respected and have characteristics that others admire. Someone with a great deal of charismatic power can often compel others to do favors simply on the basis of positive personal response. Much recent study has been devoted to charismatic leaders and their effects on followers and organizations.[22]

STRENGTHENING YOUR NETWORK POWER

This source of power comes from gaining contacts. *Can networking help you strengthen other areas of power?*

One woman quit her job as a systems analyst at a small manufacturing company because of sexism, expressed as much lower pay than her male co-workers received. After frantically searching for a replacement, they hired her back as a systems consultant. Now, the company was forced to pay her nearly three times what she had been paid before she quit. They had underestimated the strength of this woman's expert power.

« « STRATEGIES FOR SUCCESS

8.1 Watching for Hidden Agendas

1. Be aware of strong emotions in other members.
2. Note contradictions between verbal and nonverbal signals.
3. Pay attention to themes that keep coming up, perhaps disguised, even after the formal topic has been changed.
4. Recognize agenda conflicts that involve a group member's self-esteem.

The key to eliminating hidden agendas from your behavior in groups is self-knowledge. Before you join a group, ask yourself, "Am I too focused on what I personally want from this meeting? Do I know what I expect, and do I know how to keep personal needs from blocking my judgment?"

A tougher problem is dealing with the agendas of other group members. As the group leader, you have the power to prevent people's agendas from hurting the group. Even as a member, you can help by watching your behaviors and those of other group members. Important signals include the following.

1. **Be aware of strong emotions in other members.** A hidden agenda will often go beyond the immediate problem. What are those emotions based on, and how appropriate are they? Are they based on a prejudice against the group's real agenda? On fear? On jealousy? On a desire to intimidate other members?

2. **Note contradictions between verbal and nonverbal signals.** Group members may show hidden agendas through gestures, eye contact (or lack of it), head nods, and other body movements.

3. **Pay attention to themes that keep coming up, perhaps disguised, even after the formal topic has been changed.** If it's a deeply personal agenda, it could become an underlying issue in any discussion.

4. **Recognize agenda conflicts that involve a group member's self-esteem.** Often, these are the easiest to spot. Self-esteem issues are behind all or part of nearly any agenda issue in a group. The issue is often personal self-esteem versus the esteem of the group as a whole.

8.2 Strengthening Your Leadership Power

1. Strengthen your legitimate power.
2. Strengthen your reward power.
3. Strengthen your coercive power.
4. Strengthen your networking power.
5. Strengthen your expert power.
6. Strengthen your charismatic power.

Once you have learned where power originates, you can examine your own power base to discover which types of power you are most likely to use. Remember that you need not be a manager or be in any other authority position to use these power sources more effectively. Also, some of these behaviors might be outside your comfort zone. Such is the price of power. You can use the following strategies to strengthen whatever combination of power sources is best for you.

1. **Strengthen your legitimate power.** The beginning point for this is somewhat obvious: You simply need to place yourself within the organization in a formal position that will give you a legitimate power base from which to operate. Remember, though, that you can have other kinds of power and be extremely effective even without legitimate power.

2. **Strengthen your reward power.** Begin by finding out what people value the most, then discover which of those things you have access to and use them as rewards. Even the informal organization can be used in this context. For example, even if you are not a manager, perhaps you have some clout in your own informal work group. Since reward power is a type of position power, your position in either the formal or informal structure will be very important to your ability to use rewards successfully. Including others in the activities of the group might be a form of reward. Most important, you must be perceived as being able to provide the rewards that others value.

3. **Strengthen your coercive power.** When you use coercive power with legitimate power, you can officially hire, fire, promote, and discipline workers. However, you can also strengthen your position without possessing legitimate power by being consistent and disciplined in your approach to tasks and other people. Your example as a dedicated and focused individual will go a long way toward giving you the respect that coercive power requires.

4. **Strengthen your networking power.** The best method is to broaden your network of friends and acquaintances. When you do, you will gain a certain amount of expert power as well, for knowing key people will nearly always give you information that others don't have. You should also get publicity for yourself and your department. Don't allow your accomplishments to go unnoticed, especially by the people who will be interested and impressed.[23]

5. **Strengthen your expert power.** Become more of an expert. Don't hesitate to take all of the training courses and workshops the company provides. Don't rule out night school at a local college. In some organizations,

attaining another degree might be helpful, since part of expert power is being *perceived* as an expert. Whenever possible, become involved in complex tasks and avoid routine, repetitive jobs that will neither broaden your knowledge nor gain you recognition.

6. **Strengthen your charismatic power.** To increase this area of power, stand up for others and help them when they really need help. (Don't force your help on others; that practice can backfire.) Be genuine. Form close bonds with others, remembering that respect is still a key issue in charismatic power. You must be liked *and* respected. In particular, gain your manager's confidence. Let your boss know that you are interested not only in your own success but also in his or hers, as well as the success of the entire operation.

While working to build a base of power for yourself, don't let your ethics get out of focus. Many of these strategies can be abused very easily, especially when you are acting as an insincere opportunist. Above all, remain sincere. Ask yourself why you want power to begin with and what you plan to do once you have achieved it. Don't compromise your core values. Remaining with little or no power would be better than violating the values you believe in.

CHAPTER EIGHT SUMMARY

Chapter Summary by Learning Objectives

1. **Explain why people join groups.** Some needs can be fulfilled only by group membership. People become group members because of a need to belong (affiliation), to be with attractive people (attraction), and to interact with those who are physically near to them (proximity).

2. **Define a group.** A group is two or more people who interact with one another, who share common goals, who are governed by norms, who maintain stable role relationships. Many groups form subgroups.

3. **Discuss formal groups and how they develop.** Usually, four distinct stages of development are involved, all of which focus on both group process and task activities. They are forming, redefining, co-ordinating, and formalizing.

4. **Explain the importance of status and conformity within groups.** Status is the rank a group member holds, and conformity means behaving in a way that meets a specific standard, in co-ordination with the group. These concepts are both very important to an understanding of how groups operate. For example, understanding that too much conformity can lead to groupthink is important to preventing such problems.

5. **Discuss informal groups.** Informal groups are formed without design or planning. They usually form around common habits, traits, or activities. Informal groups have these basic qualities in common: they fulfill the needs of members, they are usually necessary, they are always changing, and they are not affected by formal boundaries.

6. **Examine barriers to group effectiveness.** Two major enemies of group effectiveness are groupthink and hidden agendas. Removing barriers to group effectiveness includes identifying the specific problems facing the group, changing group norms, and—when possible—changing the composition of the group.

7. **Define leadership.** Leadership is the ability to influence people toward the attainment of goals. To be effective, leaders must be flexible. Leadership and management are not the same concepts. Leadership always involves the use of power, which comes from six possible sources: legitimate power (similar to authority), reward power, coercive power, networking power, expert power, and charismatic power.

8. **Compare and contrast leadership styles.** Different leaders follow different leadership styles which involve different approaches to the use of power. Most leaders fall into one of the following style categories: (1) autocratic, (2) consultative, (3) participative, (4) free-rein.

key terms

1. Think of groups you have joined, both formally and informally. What were the benefits you expected to receive upon joining? Were those expectations fulfilled?

2. Recall a group to which you have belonged and identify the major norms the group followed. What were the penalties for breaking from a group norm?

3. How did the same groups assign status in the group? What status symbols, if any, were important? Why?

4. The informal organization is said to help in getting work done. How does it help? How can either a manager or a worker make it help?

5. Do groups always develop following the four steps listed in this chapter? Can you think of exceptional situations that would force groups to speed up these steps or even skip some of them?

6. Do you ever watch for signs that others in a group have hidden agendas? If so, what are the signs? What can you do to confirm or disconfirm your suspicions?

7. Recall a leader whose direction you once followed. Do you recognize that leader's style as autocratic, consultative, participative, or free-rein? Provide examples of behaviors that showed that style. Explain whether you liked or disliked this style of leadership.

8. Can you imagine the same leader using more than one of the styles of leadership mentioned in question 7? Would this improve his or her abilities as a leader? How can flexibility influence a leader? Are there any drawbacks to flexibility?

9. Which of the leadership styles is yours or would most likely be yours? Why did you choose this particular style? Does your profession of choice match with this style? How does this leadership style reflect your personality?

10. Which of the six sources of power do you consider to be the strongest in most cases? Which of them would you be most likely to develop and use? Why? Which of the six sources of power do you consider the least important? Why?

GROUP COHESIVENESS

School-to-Work Connection: Thinking Skills, Personal Qualities Skills, Information Skills, Interpersonal Skills, and Systems Skills

"NASA: Survival on the Moon" is a famous exercise by Dr. Jay Hall that demonstrates the effectiveness of group interaction. Following is a list of 15 survival-related items. On your own, rank them from highest (what you need to survive on the moon) to lowest (what you want or need the least). At this time you will not be sharing your list with your group. Place number "1" by the most important item, number "2" by the second most important, and so on through number "15," the least important.

_____ Matches, 1 box

_____ Food concentrates

_____ Nylon rope, 50 feet

_____ Parachute silk

_____ Portable heating unit, solar-powered

_____ Pistols, two .45-caliber

_____ Dehydrated milk, 1 case

_____ Oxygen, two 100-pound tanks

_____ Stellar map (of the moon's constellation)

_____ Life raft, self-inflating

_____ Magnetic compass

_____ Water, 5 gallons

_____ Signal flares

_____ First-aid kit (w/injection needles)

_____ FM receiver–transmitter, solar-powered

- Form into groups of four to six. Each member should have his or her own list of survival-related items completed.

- Each group should arrive at a consensus on each rank. Don't use a democratic vote or try to change someone's vote. Consensus means that each team member must at least agree somewhat with each conclusion, so the final decision will be unanimous.

- Next, the instructor will provide the numbers that go into the "Survey Score" section. The "Survey Score" section is in the *Instructor's Resource Manual.* These rankings are the result of an official survey of astronauts' opinions.

- Subtract the difference between the rankings in the individuals core column and the survey score column, and add up the total at the bottom. Ignore plus and minus; what you are measuring is the degree of difference in either direction.
- Next, subtract the difference between the group score column and the survey score.
- Add up this total at the bottom.

Answer the following questions:

1. Did any individual have a total higher than the team? If so, either the group was not working as efficiently as it could have, or the individual member was not being sufficiently assertive with his or her knowledge.

2. Also, describe the group processes of each group.

   a. Did any of the groups function without a leader? If so, how did they make decisions?

   b. If the group had a leader, what style of leadership did the leader use?

   c. Were there any disagreements? If so, how were they resolved?

Reprinted with permission from Teleometrics International. All rights reserved.

working it out 8.2

QUALITY OF WORK LIFE

School-to-Work Connection: Thinking Skills, Personal Qualities Skills, Information Skills, Interpersonal Skills, and Systems Skills

You have probably belonged to many small groups throughout your life. Some have likely been effective, some ineffective. Some have lasted briefly, some perhaps for years.

You most likely had leaders in these groups. Some leaders may have been effective; others may have been ineffective.

Examine your memories carefully. List the groups that were the most effective. Then write as much detail as possible about each one. You will then do the same thing for an ineffective leader and group.

- What was the effective leader like?
- What were the interests or duties that brought the group together?
- What seemed to keep the group from falling apart?
- Can you find a common thread that unites the positive group experiences?

Now use another sheet of paper and do the same type of analysis for truly ineffective groups you have belonged to.

- What was the ineffective leader like?
- What interests brought the group together?
- Why were they not strong enough to hold the group together and make it effective?
- Can you identify common elements that might have made them fail?

If you have completed this exercise carefully and thoughtfully, you should be able to draw some meaningful conclusions about what makes groups succeed and fail. Conclude this assignment by writing two brief paragraphs. The first paragraph should describe what makes a successful group. The second paragraph should describe what makes a group ineffective.

internet exercises

1. *Self-Assessment*
   Access "Awesome Library" through **www.mhhe.com/lamberton4e** or directly at **www.awesomelibrary.org.** Click on "College Students," then on "Leaders." Next, click on "Leadership in Business." Now, take the "Leadership Style Quiz." Write a brief essay about your performance on this quiz. How does your leadership score fit with the leadership styles described in this chapter?

2. *Apply*
   Locate an online encyclopedia or dictionary such as **www. answers.com** and search the term *groupthink*. How does this source define groupthink, and what events does this source use to illustrate the concept? Write a short paragraph illustrating famous historic examples of groupthink that fit with the definition given.

3. *Careers Tracking*
   What occupations would make good use of your skill sets? Find out at America's Career InfoNet, a Web-based component of the "Career OneStop" sponsored by the federal government, through **www.mhhe.com/lamberton4e** or link to **www.careeronestop. org/SKILLS/SkillCenterHome.asp.** Open the link to "Assess Your Skills" and then "Identify Your Skills Using the Skills Profiler." What does the Skills Profiler say about you? Does this fit with your career interests as you've identified them through career interest tests? If you are obtaining a certificate rather than a degree, link to the information in "Assess Your Skills" on certificates and certifying agencies (open the "More" link to find these). What did you discover?

Mariko's Promotion

Part of Mariko Koide's promotion in the advertising firm where she worked was a transfer to another division of the company. The promotion seemed like a totally positive experience for her, and she was very happy—at least initially. Her first day in the new division was one of handshaking, smiles, and welcoming comments. Things looked really positive.

However, after a few weeks had passed, it became apparent to Mariko that this division had a different "feeling" to it. In her old office, her fellow employees had spent a great deal of time on what they called "idea creation." Some nights, when ideas were a bit slow in coming, everyone would work two or three hours late. Throughout the process, everyone had seemed positive and upbeat and not at all resentful of the long sessions.

The new division was not like that at all. It seemed that a great deal of conflict was always afoot. One worker was always complaining about what a "jerk" someone else was. Overtime sessions, when they rarely happened, were resented and typically resulted in dozens of oral and written complaints. The walls of the ladies room had insulting caricatures of managers on the walls, with equally insulting comments written below them.

Also, all of the employees seemed to be heavily involved in outside activities that had nothing to do with company business, or even with the talents needed to work there. The very idea of working late *voluntarily* was laughable.

Mariko began wondering whether she should have accepted the promotion. Instead of being excited and happy, she began finding it difficult to get up in the morning and drive to work. "I wonder if I could get back to the other division," she found herself thinking one day. She began planning a strategy that would allow her to do just that.

Case Study Questions

1. If you knew Mariko as a friend, what would you advise her to do at this point?

2. Is Mario helpless in her new position? If you don't think so, suggest some courses of action she could take.

3. Evaluate Mariko's situation in terms of norms and status.

Through the Ranks

Daura had been promoted through the ranks of her company to her present supervisory position in management. The president of the company recently asked her to create another administrative position, one that would report directly to Daura, to be filled internally. The president was aware that a lot of recent conflict between administration and nonadministrative staff members had led to low morale and high employee turnover, and she had decided one way to reduce this was to create the new position to bridge the gap between these two employee groups. Seven people applied for the newly created position, and Daura sent each of them an e-mail saying that she would be interviewing only the top two or three candidates.

Soon, grumbling among applicants and other employees interested in the process began to be heard, based mainly on the decision to interview only a few candidates. Since interviews for seven applicants could be managed pretty easily, and employee morale was already low, they reasoned, *all* applicants deserved at least a "courtesy interview." Before the final candidates were announced, Daura's administrative assistant approached her and asked her if it would be possible to schedule interviews for all seven candidates as a way to reduce growing resentment among employees.

Daura's response was straight to the point as she snapped: "If they don't like the process, they can quit. They'd better be happy I even agreed to go along with the decision to open this position. I'm in charge here, and none of you had better forget it. Anyone who wants to stand up to me on this had better do it now, so I know who the troublemakers are and I can make sure they don't get promoted."

Case Study Questions

1. What leadership style does Daura seem to be using?

2. What are Daura's sources of power? Are these the most appropriate ones she should be using in this situation?

3. If you were Daura's manager, would you try to change behaviors in her leadership methods? Which ones? Why?

TEAMS IN QUALITY ORGANIZATIONS

In the Workplace: To Team or Not?

SITUATION

When Pete's company was bought out two years ago, an entire new management structure was put into place. At the time, the new management had given existing employees the option of either continuing to work on projects by themselves, as they had always done, or joining permanent work teams. Pete chose to continue to work alone. He just didn't see the value in wasting time talking to other people about getting something done. Why not just do it himself and get finished a lot faster?

Besides, what if he didn't like the team member he was assigned to work with? Then he would be miserable, he thought, caught in a bad situation.

DISCOVERY

But today as he looked around the office, he wondered if he'd made the right choice.

After studying this chapter, you will be able to:

1 Identify the history, foundations, and major points of the quality movement and the ISO 9000 movement.
2 Explain how to build a team.
3 Compare and contrast the models of decision making in teams.
4 List ways to determine the organizational climate of the workplace.
5 Distinguish among different types of corporate culture.
6 Describe the value in the "new" corporate culture, and its link to self-esteem.
7 Explain the importance of fairness in a work environment.

9 CHAPTER «

« « **STRATEGIES FOR SUCCESS**

Strategy 9.1   Building a Successful Team

Strategy 9.2   Changing Your Workplace Climate

Strategy 9.3   Creating Fairness in the Workplace

He was stuck on how to finish a project and he didn't know who to ask: the others in his original office staff had all joined work teams. Amy and her team were brainstorming ideas and coming up with a lot more creative possibilities than Pete could have thought of alone. Jasmine and her team were deciding how to divide up the project tasks; they would have it done in no time. Now, the idea of a team seemed to Pete both more efficient and more pleasant. As he struggled with the project, he wondered if it was too late to reconsider the teamwork idea.

THINK ABOUT IT

Can you think of a time when you worked alone on a work or school project, when a team approach would have been more successful?

QUALITY ORGANIZATIONS AND WORK TEAMS

Current management practices in the United States and elsewhere often call for work teams in organizations. Management decisions, such as the decision to assign work to individuals or to teams, greatly affect the organizational structure and the corporate culture.

The Quality Movement

As you read in the first chapter, W. Edwards Deming and the **Total Quality Management (TQM)** movement had a huge international impact on management philosophy and style, with the **quality movement** that changed business practices beginning about 60 years ago. This has influenced decisions and practices even today. In the United States, this impact was especially great in the 1980s through the mid-1990s.

In creating TQM, Deming created 14 points he believed would produce a quality organization (see Figure 9.1). All 14 points must be in place for this style to be successful. Although working in teams is not explicit in these points, the focus on *process* in the workplace lends itself to team and group work.

Deming's TQM requires that quality must be present in the goods and services produced by an organization. Both the process and the product must be evaluated for quality.[1] Changing to this management style requires sweeping changes that can take years and can drastically change corporate culture.[2] The two most important areas of emphasis are **empowerment** and **rewards.**

Empowerment in this management style usually means forming people into groups to solve problems and complete tasks. It also means giving them power to put decisions into place. Rewards for employees usually mean profit sharing or paid bonuses. Since higher quality means higher pay for employees, this incentive increases productivity and creativity.

The quality movement arose with TQM in Japan after World War II during that country's postwar rebuilding. Managers in the United States had rejected these ideas, but seeing how successful they were in Japan, businesses in the United States widely adopted them beginning in 1980. Although the use of TQM declined in the mid-1990s, many organizations still use it. Other organizations call their management styles by a different name, but the ideas often come from TQM. These ideas for quality organizations include the following:

- Do not accept poor quality in workmanship, products, and service.
- Measure efficiency and quality in all phases of production, not just in postproduction.

quality movement

A business development that was established in Japan in the 1940s and spread to the United States in the 1980s, and that emphasizes the highest standards in the process of production as well as in the final product.

empowerment

A TQM strategy that involves forming people into groups to solve problems and complete tasks.

rewards

In TQM, benefits for employees, including profit sharing or paid bonuses.

more about...

To learn more about changes and current practices in the **quality movement** in the United States, visit the American Society for Quality at **www.asq.org**. Many other countries have similar organizations, illustrating the global impact of the quality movement.

Deming's 14 Points on the Path to Quality Organizations

1. Establish constancy of purpose.
2. Constantly improve every system.
3. Eliminate financial goals and quotas.
4. Drive out fear.
5. Institute leadership.
6. Stop awarding business solely on the basis of price.
7. Break down barriers between departments.
8. Institute training on the job.
9. Eliminate annual ratings.
10. Promote education and self-improvement.
11. Abandon slogans.
12. Cease dependence on mass inspection.
13. Adopt the new philosophy of quality in its entirety.
14. Structure management to accomplish this transformation.

figure 9.1

THE DEMING PLAN

These basic guidelines can help most companies improve their processes, and by doing so, improve their overall products and services. *Which of these guidelines seems most important?*

Source: Mary Walton, *The Deming Management Method* (New York: Putnam, 1986), pp. 55–86.

- Use suppliers with high-quality goods, rather than shopping around for lower prices.
- Train and retrain employees to improve quality, rather than relying on slogans.
- Encourage employees to feel that they are part of the organization, and allow them to report poor quality conditions.
- Train managers to find, measure, and eliminate sources of mediocre quality.[3]

Deming and Total Quality

In 1951, Japan established the highly esteemed Deming Prize in honor of **W. Edwards Deming,** creator of TQM. This prize is given annually to organizations that excel in quality management, with a focus on quality control, quality assurance, and quality improvement.

more about...

Quality organizations create loyalty and commitment among employees. This also increases their self-confidence and self-esteem.[4] When comparing a quality organization management style with the more traditional style of management—that is, constant surveillance of employees and analysis of product quality only after production—it is easy to see why management and employees alike prefer a well-managed quality organization environment.

Notice that the quality movement requires changing company philosophy and probably organizational climate as well. These changes will most likely change corporate culture. Many of the points have an impact on human relations in the workplace. You can probably tell that an organization with the history of a successful quality management style would most likely be a positive place to work, with a warm organizational climate and built-in solutions to many human relations problems.

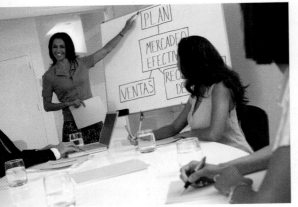

FOURTEEN POINTS FOR QUALITY

Deming emphasized the importance of process over product, and a key way to improve process is through effective training. *How would you improve training at the job where you currently work, or at the workplace of someone you know?*

ISO 9000

A management philosophy that seeks to put into place formalized standards throughout businesses and industries by providing evaluation and certification for compliance with standards of quality.

ISO 9000

During World War II, munitions factories in England were having problems with bombs going off in the factories. The British government began requiring that factories be inspected for quality control. As part of the process, each company was required to write up explanations of the procedures they used in production, and then to follow those procedures. This standardized the process of production by creating a set of clear directions on how the work was to be done.

In 1947, the International Organization for Standardization (ISO) was created. Over the first two decades since its creation, the use of ISO standards and certification spread to all types of manufacturing and technology. Countries outside the United Kingdom began using these standards or developing similar systems. From a dramatic and specific set of events in a bomb factory, **ISO 9000** has grown to include thousands of companies in about 100 countries today. Most companies doing business in the European Economic Community are now required to file ISO 9000 certification. For more information on the history, compliance standards, current memberships, and other topics related to ISO 9000, visit the Web site for the International Organization for Standardization at www.iso.org.

The standards required by ISO 9000 to increase quality in organizations are not specific to any one type of business; all businesses can use them. They are different from the quality movement in that the focus is not on a conscious examination of the company's processes, but instead on explaining procedures in the organization and on keeping careful records of how things get done. Although these two systems designed to promote quality organizations are very different, the basic ideas surrounding ISO 9000 guidelines have been influenced by the quality movement.

In short, ISO standards ask organizations: "Tell me what you do (describe the business process). Show me where it says that (reference the procedure manuals). Prove that that is what happened (exhibit evidence in documented records)."[5] Outside auditors and internal staff members then examine the documents to decide whether or not the organization should be granted ISO 9000 certification. In the process, auditors who examine these documents also make judgments about what is effective or ineffective in the company's processes.

As with other quality movement management structures, ISO 9000 certification does not require the formation of work teams. But as with other quality management styles, once managers begin to examine the work processes in place, they often begin to move toward setting up teams in the workplace.

TEAM BUILDING

A fairly recent use of groups and committees in the organization is known as **team building.** Through conscious effort, a manager can build a team of employees who will function as a unit and achieve group goals. Such a group is known as a **work team.** In building a work team, many of the qualities of informal groups that have already been discussed are created by the team leader. If you think such a process sounds difficult, you are correct. Team building is a process that requires effort from everyone involved and usually takes quite a bit of time.

Why, then, are many organizations willing to put the necessary time and effort into building work teams? They do so for many good reasons, but from the position of management, the best reason is the "bottom line." Teams save companies money by reducing the need for middle management, increasing productivity, doing work that individuals or normal work groups can't do, and making better use of resources.[6] And in a global workplace, people located in different parts of the world may need to "team up" to get a product through production and onto store shelves.

Some employees, like Pete in our opening vignette, are not sold on the idea of work teams; they may even be downright hostile. They may see working in teams as a challenge to their individual expertise or abilities. Making good use of individuals' talents in the best possible combination, however, is exactly what effective teams do. Some employees may not want to do things in a "new" way; others think teamwork causes a duplication of effort or a waste of time. But none of these fears are borne out by research on effective work teams.

Work teams actually allow individuals to have more say in their jobs, because they can discuss ideas with peers rather than just following instructions from a supervisor. Job satisfaction is then improved. When job satisfaction is improved, morale, self-esteem, and productivity rise. Most people who work in teams say they would not want to go back to the "old" way of doing business. Work team members may soon work with more enthusiasm and creativity, miss fewer work days, anticipate and solve problems more easily, pay better attention to customers, and meet deadlines better. All of these results improve the company's bottom line while producing a higher-quality workplace atmosphere for employees.

Another important reason for work teams is the creation of **team spirit.** As in an athletic team, a work team succeeds only when members seek success for the whole team, rather than seeking individual success. Employees who belong to a successful team will be more loyal, will have better attitudes, and will be more productive.

In the more traditional approach to management, companies are run in a traditional management style—often with no pretense about groups and work teams. The traditional manager is more like the dictatorial captain of a ship than the player-captain of a basketball or football team.

team building
The process of creating and encouraging a group of employees to work together toward achieving group goals and increased productivity.

work team
A group of employees with shared goals who join forces on a work project.

team spirit
The energy and shared commitment that result from shared teamwork.

Groups that Work

Go to **www.mhhe.com/lamberton4e** for the link to read an article about groups at work. Ask yourself, "Can all of these ideas apply to my current (or most recent) work team? If so, how? If not, why?" Be prepared to discuss your answers in class.

If you want a team-building approach to work in your company, several guidelines should help. First, good intentions are not enough. A formal training program should be used, preferably with a leader who has had some experience with team building elsewhere. People who have spent most of their work lives dealing with tasks individually will likely need training to learn new skills and habits.

If you are a manager, you may need to learn to let go. Team building involves delegating responsibilities to the group—responsibilities that were once only the manager's business. Such delegation often makes managers feel threatened by a loss of authority. The new management role they must learn is more like a coach or captain of a sports team. Whatever the manager says or does, the responsibility to get the job done still ends up with the group. (See Figure 9.2.)

Implementation

When a team-building consultant starts working to create a work group, he or she will ask the following questions:

1. What do you want from this team? What can your membership in this group do for you personally? What do you want it to do for you personally?
2. What do you have to give to this team?

These questions will often be asked in writing. From the answers, the team builder can learn a great deal about the needs and concerns of the people who will make up the team. The answers to these questions will determine the complexity of the task of building the team. Suppose, for example, that several people responded to question 1, "I want the team to leave me alone and let me do my work." This might have been the answer given by Pete in the opening vignette. Those members would require some selling on the idea of team building before any real progress could be made.

Forming, Storming, Norming, and Performing

Bruce Tuckman created a model of team development in 1965 while working at the Naval Medical Research Institute at Bethesda, Maryland. It is, arguably, still the most widely used model of team development. He named the four stages of group development *forming, storming, norming,* and *performing* (so you see why this is sometimes called "The 'Orming Model").

- **Forming** The team mission is finalized, and the members agree generally on team behavior, leadership, and governance. This is usually a peaceful and nonconfrontational time for team members.

- **Storming** Group members begin to get down to business, and conflicts arise. Team members share ideas and develop action plans, and conflicts over the value of those ideas, and over turf, are likely to arise at this time. Team leaders need to be especially sensitive to these possible conflicts, and exert control to quash them.

- **Norming** The team is really getting down to business. Informal roles and formal assignments are taken on. While some roles (for example, information gatherer, peacekeeper, writer/reporter) will emerge naturally, others will be assigned by the team leader.

- **Performing** The team hums along and completes its work.

    Dr. Tuckman added a fifth stage, 10 years after developing his model. It is:

- **Unforming (adjourning)** In this stage, the team evaluates its work, recognizes what it has accomplished, and ends its membership. Team members may feel a sense of loss because of the ending of the team identity.

The descriptions of these stages may sound similar to the four-stage description of group formation we discussed in Chapter 8. Although they are similar, these stages are more relevant to the formation of work teams.

Business consultants Florence Stone and Randi Sachs caution organization leaders not to develop teams in situations where individual work would be more effective in meeting the organization's objectives. They also encourage managers to take advantage of existing technology when appropriate and available (for example, a conference call or e-meeting instead of a group meeting), and to take the time to identify the right mix of people, with the necessary qualities, for each team.

figure 9.2

AN ALTERNATIVE PROCESS

In this process, the team is formed and the task determined; work is assigned and everyone knows his or her role. *What factors need to be in place for effective teamwork?*

Source: Florence M. Stone and Randi T. Sachs, *The High-Value Manager: Developing the Core Competencies Your Organization Demands* (New York: American Management Association, 1995). See also: Beth Cole, "When You're in Charge: Tips for Leading Teams," Teambuilding.com (retrieved July 15, 2005), www.teambuildinginc.com/article_kiwanis.htm. For a complete list of Dr. Tuckman's work, visit his Web site at www.coe.ohio-state.edu/btuckman/ (retrieved July 2005).

Trust

Building trust is one of the first steps in creating a team. Without trust, there can be no team building. Imagine a basketball team whose members didn't trust one another enough to pass the ball. Whoever had the ball would only dribble and shoot. The idea of such a team winning even one game is unthinkable. Often, a great deal of group interaction must take place for a beginning level of trust to develop. Whatever method of trust building is used, it must get members' feelings out in the open. When two members have a trust problem that involves only each other, they need to work on the problem outside of the group.

Goals

Finally, the team needs to review and agree upon goals, both individually and collectively. Establishing and refining goals can be aided by using two questions: "What do you want the team to accomplish, and what can you give?" Goals must be clear and attainable, and they must be considered important by all members of the team.[7]

DECISION MAKING IN TEAMS

It may seem that if a group of people is working as a team, then the entire team will have equal say in making decisions. That is not always the case. Managers or team leaders must figure out which decision-making model will work best for each situation or for each team. The model chosen will be based on such things as time pressure for a decision, how important the quality of the decision is, how important it is that the group accepts the decision, the manager's expertise and philosophy of managing, and the group's composition and potential for conflict.[8]

Having chosen a decision-making model based on the preceding considerations, decisions will be made using one of the following options:

1. *Minority.* As few as one person (autocratic) or perhaps a few group members (partial group) make the final decision. This is the fastest way to reach a decision. However, there will be low commitment from nonparticipants.

2. *Majority.* More than half of the team decides (partial group). This is also a quick way to reach a decision, but there is often low commitment from those on the team whose decision is "lost" in the decision-making process.

3. *Unanimous.* All team members agree on the decision (whole group). This option produces high commitment from the group with fast implementation, but the group may have overlooked other options. In the worst case, groupthink may be the result. (See Chapter 8.)

4. *Consensus.* All group members agree to carry out the decision, even if they don't agree with the decision made (whole group). This option has the advantage of high commitment; but of all these models, it takes the most time, patience, and the best facilitation skills.[9]

TRUST AND TEAM BUILDING

Trust among team members is essential for a team to be successful. *What are some of the consequences of lack of trust among team members?*

Group Skills

Go to **www.mhhe.com/lamberton4e** for the link to a site with information on groups. Decide which skills your current work (or study) group needs to develop. Then click on one of the links and gather the information. Let this be the first step in an action plan to improve your group's performance and potential. *Note:* Look beyond the many products this site is trying to sell; search out the team-building material.

ORGANIZATIONAL CLIMATE: THE WEATHER OF THE WORKPLACE

The interaction of groups within the workplace aids in the formation of **organizational climate,** a term introduced in Chapter 6. Climate in the workplace has some qualities in common with climate in the context of weather. Climate can change rapidly, without warning. A manager with a negative attitude can change a positive climate to a stressful one just by walking into the room. Climate in the workplace can be influenced by environmental factors, such as the color of the room, the noise level, and the way people dress. It also involves the attitudes, stress levels, and communication of the people in the organization.

Major Qualities of Organizational Climate

The way people see things as individuals, their interactions, and the way an organization is put together produce the climate that all perceive with similar eyes. *Perception* is a very important part of organizational climate, as are *structure* and *interaction*.[10]

1. Organizational climate involves the way members of an organization see it in terms of trust, recognition, freedom to create, fairness, and independence.

2. Organizational climate is produced by the way members relate to one another.

3. Organizational climate reflects the norms and attitudes of the organization's culture.

4. Organizational climate influences and helps to shape the behavior of individuals.

5. Organizational climate is a basis for understanding any situation in the organization.[11]

The large hospital where Kim works is old and noisy. Everyone who works there wears the same type of uniform. The walls are painted standard pale green, and the floors are covered with a dreary gray vinyl flooring. The institution's employee policies have not been changed in decades. It is no wonder than Kim finds the hospital to be an oppressive and stressful place to work. Patients have the same reactions. There are no carpets or plants in the waiting room, and the attitudes of the employees are stiff and cold, just like the hospital.

more about...

Organizational Climate

The manager or person in charge is a major force in creating **organizational climate.** Climates produced by the manager can be autocratic (thunderstorms), participative (sunshine), consultative (clearing off), and free-rein (partly or mostly cloudy).

A manager has a heavy responsibility to lead the organization in a way that will produce a good, or positive, organizational climate.[12] Everyone in the workplace can affect the climate, but the manager's position allows more influence than managers themselves often realize.

Maintaining a Climate

What is a good climate? The best organizational climate is one that allows the most productivity over the longest period of time. That type of climate will almost always include qualities such as high trust levels, a reasonable level of freedom, high standards of fairness, and fair recognition for the work of each person. The best way to communicate these qualities is to set a conscious example. Many managers just give lip service to these ideas but treat their employees without freedom, trust, recognition, and fairness.

What can such a manager do to change the company's climate to one that is more pleasant? Such a manager would need to trust employees enough to give them the freedom to make good choices. This manager would need to recognize the tasks that they complete successfully, and to be fair. A good place to begin is just basic politeness. This conveys respect. The manager could also thank individual employees for work done well. These small efforts go a long way toward making an organizational climate more pleasant.

A WARM ORGANIZATIONAL CLIMATE

Several physical and psychological factors make up a warm, or relaxed and inviting, organizational climate. *What do you look for in an organization's climate?*

CORPORATE CULTURE: SHARED VALUES

How does corporate culture differ from organizational climate? Some writers make little distinction between the two. When corporate culture is discussed in this

A Federal Express office was located in a remote area of Colorado. It was much like all the others in that it had a firm commitment to reliable customer service. One day the Federal Express driver headed across the Rockies to deliver his very last package. Without warning, a blizzard hit the area with full force. The driver tried to forge ahead but just couldn't see the road. He was forced to turn back.

Back at the office, he called the customer and received permission to fax the contents of the package. Soon the storm had downed the phone lines, and he could not use the fax machine. So the supervisor took over. With package in hand, he went to the airport where he rented a helicopter. Although it cost Federal Express over $3,000, the package was delivered on time.[13]

book, though, the discussion is referring to the collection of values and assumptions a group of people share. Climate, as defined here, reflects the norms and attitudes of the organization's culture. That is the basic tie-in between the two concepts.

Corporate culture is the network of shared values. Values are more deep-seated than attitudes. As mentioned in Chapter 5, values also tend to involve a rank order. In other words, the very nature of values places them naturally in a list of varying importance. The values of an organization will set a pattern for its activities, opinions, and actions.[14] Cultures can be good, bad, or mixed. The trend today is to build a strong, positive culture that motivates employees to work harder, to feel greater loyalty, and to stay with the company and remain productive.

Corporate cultures are also described as strong or weak. A *strong* corporate culture is one in which employees feel a strong connection to the organization's values. In a *weak* corporate culture, employees do not feel such a connection to the company, so they may not "do the right thing" on their own. In such organizations, leaders control employees more often through formal procedures and more heavy-handed bureaucracy.[15] But watch out for groupthink in a *very* strong corporate culture: Employees who never question the leadership and have an almost evangelical view of the company's leaders may fall victim to groupthink (see Chapter 8).

Any culture, be it corporate, national, or familial, is preserved and defined by *oral history* or **culture stories.**[16] Is the Federal Express story in Real World Example 9.2 above true? Writer Paul Hellman says he asked the company and they replied, "Nothing like that ever happened."[17] However, the story is "true" in the sense that it illustrates and helps to define the culture of Federal Express.

> **Culture stories** are miniature myths. The culture of an organization can be understood more fully by listening to these stories and finding common themes in them.

more about...

> **culture stories**
> Stories that illustrate the values of the people who make an organization work.

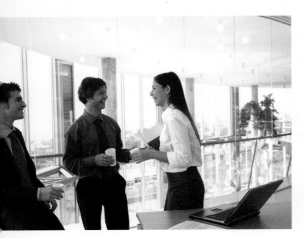

CORPORATE CULTURE

The network of shared values in a workplace, similar to its organizational climate, is an important element to consider. What are some ways to learn about the values of a firm, if they are not clearly stated?

Fact or Fiction?

Before you rush to judgment, keep in mind that many of the stories related at your authors' family reunions are not factually "true," either. (The grandfather of one of your authors is featured in a book about the greatest liars in the history of his region.) In some family stories, the plot line remains the same, but the people involved have changed. In other stories, the characters remain the same but the facts have been modified or greatly exaggerated. The factual truth of culture stories is less important than the symbolic truth. On a corporate level, Federal Express, IBM, and National Cash Register Corporation (NCR) are just a few of the companies that have hundreds of these culture stories. Some of them actually have the powerful qualities of myth and legend.[18]

Every organization has a culture. Sometimes it is difficult to see, especially if you look at it from the outside. Some cultures are loyal to management; some are loyal to the union. Some are very close-knit, with a great number of culture stories or myths inspiring loyalty and enthusiasm. Others lack the togetherness and team spirit enjoyed by the stronger cultures.

In addition to culture stories, leaders transmit organizational culture in many other ways. The way they react to crises at work, divide up limited resources, train and coach employees, even recruit and select employees—all of these actions tell employees what is important to the person in charge. Employees also look at the design and layout of the physical work space, the leadership structure of the organization, its systems and policies, rites and rituals, and reinforcement for employee behavior, in order to see what is valued. In a well-run organization, these will all be consistent with the company's formally stated mission and philosophy or paradigms—which in itself is a public summary of its culture and values.[19]

ESSENTIALS OF CORPORATE CULTURE

The following elements that make up corporate culture overlap with, interact with, and affect one another.

Paradigms: A company's paradigm is the set of beliefs it operates under. What is the organization about? What is its mission? What are its values?

Control Systems: How is the company controlled? Are there rulebooks, handbooks, and procedures manuals? Who makes the decisions?

Organizational Structures: Who reports to whom? What does the status hierarchy look like? How does work flow through the company?

The National Cash Register Company, founded in 1884, is still functioning today as NCR, a global technology corporation. In August 1945, S. C. Allyn, now a retired chairman of the board for NCR, was one of the first Allied civilians to enter Germany at the end of World War II.

"He had gone to find out what had happened to an NCR factory built just before the war but promptly confiscated by the German military command and put to work on the war effort. . . . Through bricks, cement, and old timbers, Allyn came upon two NCR employees whom he hadn't seen for six years. Their clothes were torn and their faces grimy and blackened by smoke, but they were busy clearing out the rubble. As he came closer, one of the men looked up and said, 'We knew you'd come!' Allyn joined them in their work and together the three men began cleaning out the debris and rebuilding the factory from the devastation of war. The company had even survived a world war.

A few days later, as the clearing continued, Allyn and his coworkers were startled as an American tank rumbled up to the site. A grinning GI was at the helm. 'Hi', he said, 'I'm NCR, Omaha. Did you guys make your quota this month?' Allyn and the GI embraced each other. The war may have devastated everything around them, but NCR's hard-driving, sales-oriented culture was still intact."[20]

Power Structure: Who holds the power? On what is it based? How widespread is this power? Is individualism allowed?

Symbols: What logos or designs symbolize the company itself? Within the company, what symbols of power are used (reserved parking spaces, executive restroom, and so on)?

Rituals and Routines: What committees are maintained because they have become routine and institutionalized? Are meetings held out of habit, or are they necessary?

Stories and Myths: What messages are conveyed about people, events, or objects? What do these stories say about what is valued within the organization?[21]

TYPES OF CORPORATE CULTURE

Professors Robert Poupart and Brian Hobbs, of the University of Quebec, have developed descriptions of five types of corporate culture (see Figure 9.3). Although the company where you work or hope to work might not fit neatly into one of these categories, they are useful in understanding general directions that company cultures tend to take.[22]

Father-founder   Bureaucratic   Participative   Professional   Managerial-entrepreneurial

figure 9.3

THE FIVE TYPES OF CORPORATE CULTURE

Each type of corporate culture has its own benefits and drawbacks. Some are better suited for certain types of businesses than others. *If you were to start your own business, which type of corporate culture would you foster?*

Source: Terrence E. Deal and Allen A. Kennedy, *Corporate Cultures* (pp. 3–4), © 1982 by Addison-Wesley Publishing, Inc. Reprinted by permission of the publisher.

Father–Founder Culture

This kind of company was usually founded by the person who runs it. In the father-founder culture, only one person has to act when something needs doing. This is a very *centralized* organization, with power at the top. The father-founder or mother-founder wants things to be flexible and adaptable. Often the reason this type of person started a business was to get away from the bureaucracy, or the "red tape" of other companies. This one person solves conflicts, runs the business personally, and tends to filter all information through the main office.

Bureaucratic Culture

Language in this type of culture includes terms like "cost efficiency" and "following procedures." Order, predictability, and avoidance of the whims of any individual are all important values. In this type of culture, any information you get is likely to be in a formal memo or meeting. All of the power in the company is based on what is "legal and rational."

Participative Culture

This type of culture evolved from the 1960s and 1970s with that era's emphasis on small groups working together. In this culture, the values are based on judgments about how well people work together, how well they get along, and how committed each member is to the goals and objectives of the whole organization. Participative culture will be discussed in more detail later in this chapter.

Professional Culture

In this type of culture, the shared values center on expertise and the development of skills and knowledge. Because members of the professional culture respect the power of the intellect, they tend to dislike hierarchy. Usually, this type of culture is quite territorial. Professionals tend to be specialists in certain areas of knowledge. Boundaries are created between these areas, and keeping those boundaries in place becomes, in itself, a kind of value.

Managerial–Entrepreneurial Culture

In their best-selling book *In Search of Excellence,* Thomas Peters and Robert Waterman write about this type of culture. The member of this culture is an adventurer. Customer satisfaction is an extremely important shared value, as is productivity. Power is important. In this culture, power is associated with success with clients and customers, and with providing service, quality, and dependability. Formal divisions of labor are done away with, or overlooked, and replaced with the pattern of what Peters and Waterman call "thriving on chaos." The champion, the doer, makes his or her own position in the organization.[23]

THE "NEW" CORPORATE CULTURE: THE IMPORTANCE OF SELF-ESTEEM

These days, many companies are working on changing their culture in order to make it more humane, more closely knit, and above all, more profitable and productive. The so-called new corporate culture is made up of a set of new assumptions about how people should be treated. It doesn't necessarily fit into any of the five categories just discussed, but it shares good qualities with several of them. Much of this new thinking is based on a deeper understanding of the importance of employee self-esteem on the job. This is moving well beyond the early findings of Elton Mayo, discussed in Chapter 1, which influenced decades of thought on the role of human relations and have since been re-examined.

Here are some of the commonly accepted qualities that a new corporate culture should have. All of them are directly related to human relations and self-esteem issues.[24]

1. Instead of bullying or shouting, or otherwise being autocratic, a manager should avoid making an employee feel intimidated or overly uncomfortable. The reason for this is simple: Although the autocratic approach will get obedience, it will not inspire the dedication that is needed in a strong organizational culture.

2. Among the shared values of the culture, *fairness* is very high. To avoid the feeling of inequality and injustice, managers should work very hard on a fairness agenda. Managers need to respond to the same behavior by different people in a consistently equal and just manner.

3. An emerging element of the new culture is *participative management*. The idea of allowing everyone to be a part of the decision-making process is not brand-new; Douglas McGregor wrote about the idea as early as 1960.[25] A participative culture is open and unthreatening. It allows everyone to give input when decisions that affect the whole group are made. The manager acts like the captain of an athletic team, and everyone feels free to discuss issues openly.[26]

4. The new corporate culture allows for the *self-esteem development* of all members of the organization. Management experts have shown that few factors in the workplace are more damaging than those that decrease or threaten people's self-esteem. Membership in a

BENEFITS OF PARTICIPATIVE MANAGEMENT

Participative management helps empower employees by letting them take part in the decision-making process. *How does participative management help employees feel wanted and respected at their jobs?*

closely knit group helps. *Stroking* or giving positive reinforcement (giving encouragement and sincere praise) is another self-esteem booster. Individual goal attainment is another.

5. The new corporate culture is goal-oriented. Individual goals and group goals are combined to produce a sense of direction and purpose that, ideally, is the most important of the culture's set of shared values.

THE IMPORTANCE OF FAIRNESS

A strong corporate culture must contain a sense of justice, equality, and lack of emotionalism in its treatment of people. Figure 9.4 is part of a questionnaire that has been used to study the fairness level of an organization.

Trust in the workplace is the main tool for employees' confidence in management. It also works the other way. Anyone who has been a manager knows the importance of trust. One's actions provide a record of trustworthiness. Building trust can be difficult, especially where there has been a record of unfairness or other untrustworthy behavior.

Consistency means remaining predictable and fair. There is nothing worse than a culture that is inconsistent and unpredictable. Stability is threatened when there are apparent contradictions in the behaviors of people whom others are depending on, especially managers. High stress levels come with lack of stability.

Truthfulness is one of the most obvious necessities for fairness. Yet the temptation can be great to tell "white lies," withhold information, and tell people what they want to hear.

Integrity is a way of describing the extent to which managers and others are truly willing to put the shared values and expectations of a culture into action. It also means maintaining an ethical code. An ethical code of some kind is basic to all cultures. Ethical codes will be examined in greater detail in Chapter 17.

Expectations, as used here, refer to those that come from management. Through their expectations, managers allow the employees to know exactly what is expected of them both individually and in groups.

Equity means treating everyone with the same rules. If a culture has both consistency and equity, all are treated the same under all conditions.

Influence means allowing each member of the organization to have a stake in a wide range of activities, including goal setting, problem solving, and helping to make changes. This aspect of fairness overlaps

more about...

Fairness

"In all people, without exception, there lives some instinct for truth, some attraction toward justice."

—Former U.S. President Franklin D. Roosevelt

Measuring the Fairness Level of an Organization

Check which sentences apply to you. Does your selection reveal what kind of climate you have at work?

Trust
- ❏ My manager follows through on and carries out promises.
- ❏ My manager often hides his or her true feelings from others.

Consistency
- ❏ My manager tells the same story no matter who is asking.
- ❏ My manager acts inconsistently.

Truthfulness
- ❏ My manager sometimes tells white lies to help others.
- ❏ My manager does not change facts in order to look better.

Integrity
- ❏ My manager keeps his or her word when he or she has made an agreement to do something.
- ❏ My manager is concerned more with watching out for himself or herself than with helping others.

Expectations
- ❏ My manager has clear ideas about expectations of employees.
- ❏ My manager makes sure employees know what is expected of them.

Equity
- ❏ It is obvious by my manager's actions that he or she has definite favorites among employees.
- ❏ My manager takes a person's work contributions into account when giving praise recognition.

Influence
- ❏ My manager makes sure that those who have a "stake" also have a "say."
- ❏ When an employee is capable of dealing with a job independently, my manager delegates appropriately.

Justice
- ❏ My manager administers rewards and discipline that fit the situation.
- ❏ My manager does not give rewards that are out of proportion or inappropriate.

Respect
- ❏ My manager shows with actions that he or she really cares about employees.
- ❏ My manager recognizes the strengths and contributions of employees.

Overall Fairness
- ❏ My manager is fair in how he or she treats employees.
- ❏ My manager always deals with employees equally.

figure 9.4

MEASURING FAIRNESS

Factors such as trust, consistency, and honesty—among many others—shape the overall fairness of an organization, and in turn shape that organization's climate. *Which factor do you consider most important?*

Source: Marshall Sashkin and Richard L. Williams, "Does Fairness Make A Difference?" *Organizational Dynamics,* Autumn 1990, pp. 56–71. Reprinted by permission of the publisher from *Organizational Dynamics,* Autumn 1990. American Management Association, New York. All rights reserved.

HONORING THE PSYCHOLOGICAL CONTRACT

Managers must be careful to honor their psychological contracts with employees, giving them what they have both promised and implied. *What happens when the psychological contract is broken?*

psychological contract

An agreement that is not written or spoken but is understood between people.

with respect. Each person's opinion is received with respect and is discussed carefully before being accepted or rejected.

Justice means that the reward must fit the achievement; the punishment must fit the crime. The two extremes in violation of this quality are overkill (strict zero tolerance, while looking for infractions to punish) and "looking the other way" by ignoring the situation when an infraction occurs.

Respect, or a deep sense of high regard for people, is the basis of all fairness. When you believe that others truly value you, you tend to consider their actions fair. Nonverbal signals, such as looking away or walking away while the other person is talking, often show lack of respect for others.

Overall fairness means much more than simply treating people nicely. Fairness is a central issue in the **psychological contract** between managers and subordinates. This contract is not a piece of paper; it is a sometimes unconscious, usually unspoken, agreement between two people to behave in certain ways toward each other.[27]

Psychological contracts are a part of all cultures. Although they may not be written down or discussed, they are understood between people. When fairness is implied by managers, employees expect such behaviors from them. Without fairness, the employee usually feels betrayed.

A healthy organization will not violate employees' psychological contracts, but will have a pleasant organizational climate, regardless of the type of corporate culture.

more about...

Fairness and the Psychological Contract

The violation of a **psychological contract** is the most obvious and painful violation of the principles of fairness.

Source: Marshall Sashkin, "Does Fairness Make a Difference?" *Organizational Dynamics,* Autumn 1990, pp. 56–71.

« « STRATEGIES FOR SUCCESS

9.1   Building a Successful Team

1. Train the team.
2. Manage the team as a team.
3. Delegate authority specifically.
4. Be a clarifier.
5. Be a communicator.

As is any new method of dealing with people, team building is full of possible areas of error. These possible errors should be examined carefully by anyone attempting team building before the first implementation step is attempted. Each of the following steps will help avoid common pitfalls in the team-building process.

George began work for a company with a reputation for allowing all employees to help make decisions. After two weeks on the job, he found that two major decisions had been made without him. His psychological contract with the company was broken. He felt betrayed and left out.

1. **Train the team.** An untrained team might be an informal group; it may be several other things, but it is not a work team. By definition, a work team must be aware of the steps that are to be taken, and the members must be sold on the idea of team building. Often a would-be "team" will feel victimized by management unless each member receives training and understands the role he or she is expected to play.

2. **Manage the team as a team.** The manager has to allow the group to be managed as a team. Any traditional manager will be tempted to continue many of the management functions on an individual basis. Some managers may not be able to break the habit of calling each team member into their office privately to discuss major group problems that arise. They will need to work harder at using athletic coaching as their model, addressing the group as a whole.

3. **Delegate authority specifically.** The team leader needs to make it very clear what parts of the management responsibilities are to be taken over by the group and which are to be retained. The team builder often makes the mistake of thinking that since the team is in place, the leader needs only to sit back and watch.

4. **Be a clarifier.** A major role of the team leader is to clarify the nature of a task and the implementation of the solution. A particular manager, thinking he or she is a team leader, will tell the team to "work out the details" of plans and goals. The team leader needs to be a detail person, allowing the group to work together but coordinating those efforts through careful monitoring.

5. **Be a communicator.** Whether you are the team leader or a member, you need to listen, write, and speak carefully. Of the three skills, listening is the most important.

To appreciate the usefulness of a successful work team, one needs only to examine a company that has made the concept work. Morale is high, turnover is less, and productivity is higher.

9.2 Changing Your Workplace Climate

1. Check your own example.
2. Listen to your colleagues.
3. Notice physical details.
4. Get rid of ambiguity.
5. Make people feel respected and important.

Climate can be changed more readily than many think. It changes regularly without an organized effort, sometimes for the better, often for the worse. Here are several guidelines for building a positive, productive, and warm organizational climate.

1. **Check your own example.** How do you react to pressure? How well do you keep promises? How easy are you to approach? Do you ever give people the feeling that their needs are unimportant to you? Do you use positive or negative comments to improve work?

2. **Listen to your colleagues.** Are they unhappy? Do they feel overworked and unappreciated? What are they saying "between the lines" (or behind your back)? Are people's talents and abilities used to the best advantage for both themselves and the organization?

3. **Notice physical details.** Is there anything in the environmental makeup of the organization that causes a stressful or unpleasant climate? Examples of this include poor phone service, bad decor, high noise level, crowded quarters, and so on. These details might not seem very important, but they can be a big part of why a workplace has a negative, or cold, climate.

4. **Get rid of ambiguity.** Usually, people work better when tasks are specific, roles are definite, and scheduling is exact. There are a few people who thrive on ambiguity, but most employees do not.

5. **Make people feel respected and important.** Self-esteem has a great deal to do with organizational climate. Anything that injures the self-esteem of either a group or an individual is damaging to the climate. Many managers today say, "People are our most important assets." Making such a statement is one thing. Practicing it as a work philosophy is another.[28]

9.3   Creating Fairness in the Workplace

1. Maintain trust at work.
2. Create consistency at work.
3. Expect truthfulness at work.
4. Maintain integrity from yourself and employees.
5. Create expectations for employees.
6. Treat everyone with the same rules.
7. Allow employees to have influence in decisions.
8. Administer appropriate rewards and discipline.
9. Show respect at work.
10. Create a corporate culture of overall fairness.

Employee morale and trust will only exist if there is a sense of fairness in corporate culture. Every employee deserves to be treated in a way that is just. Each of the factors of measuring fairness reveals the overall fairness of an organization. Remember these as important qualities to strive for in corporate culture. The following qualities are useful to everyone, but especially to managers.

1. **Maintain trust at work.** An employee's confidence in management is built on trust. A manager may have encountered untrustworthy behavior in prior experiences with employees. However, this should in no way prevent future expectations of trust in other employees.

2. **Create consistency at work.** A culture that is not consistent is an unstable culture. A manager needs to watch for contradictions in behaviors of people. A lack of stability can increase stress levels.

3. **Expect truthfulness at work.** Avoid telling "white lies," and only telling people what they want to hear. Truthfulness is necessary in a work environment that values fairness.

4. **Maintain integrity from yourself and employees.** Keep an ethical code of conduct. Have clear expectations and shared values in your corporate culture. Managers have integrity when they follow the shared values and expectations of their corporate culture.

5. **Create expectations for employees.** Managers need to have clear and appropriate expectations for their employees. A positive corporate environment depends on individuals and groups understanding these expectations.

6. **Treat everyone with the same rules.** A manager who has a culture that has consistency and equity will allow employees to work under similar conditions.

7. **Allow employees to have influence in decisions.** Each person's opinion needs to be heard before being accepted or rejected. A person who has control over activities such as goal setting and problem solving will feel that he or she is respected and treated fairly.

8. **Administer appropriate rewards and discipline.** A manager must reward an employee's achievement or reprimand an employee's poor behavior in a just way. Two extremes in punishing employees are overkill and "looking the other way."

9. **Show respect at work.** Be aware of nonverbal signals, or other signs of disrespect for others. Respect and value for people are directly related to fairness.

10. **Create a corporate culture of overall fairness.** The psychological contract is not something spoken, but rather the way two people treat each other. The message implied by a manager needs to be followed through, or else the employee might feel betrayed.

CHAPTER NINE SUMMARY

Chapter Summary by Learning Objectives

1. **Identify the history, foundations, and major points of the quality movement and the ISO 9000 movement.** Total Quality Management (TQM) is a reorganization movement that began in Japan after World War II and spread to the United States. It is associated with W. Edwards Deming and his 14 points in quality organizations. Teams are an integral part of TQM, and their use has grown in every area of organization. The ISO and its standards for certification were begun during World War II. Quality organization standards such as these are used widely both nationally and internationally.

2. **Explain how to build a team.** A manager can build a team of employees who will function as a unit and achieve group goals. Team building is a process that requires effort from everyone involved and usually takes quite a bit of time.

3. **Compare and contrast the models of decision making in teams.** Managers or team leaders must figure out which decision-making model will work best for each situation or for each team: majority, minority, unanimous, or consensus.

4. **List ways to determine the organizational climate of the workplace.** Climate can be influenced by environmental factors, such as the color of the room, the noise level, the way people dress, and the attitudes and communication of people in the organization.

5. **Distinguish among different types of corporate culture.** Corporate culture refers to the organization's shared beliefs and values. It affects the organizational climate. Five types of corporate culture are father-founder, bureaucratic, professional, participative, and managerial-entrepreneurial.

6. **Describe the value in the "new" corporate culture, and its link to self-esteem.** The new corporate culture focuses on making the workplace more human and humane by building self-esteem, trust, and fairness into the organizational culture.

7. **Explain the importance of fairness in a work environment.** Justice, equality, and lack of emotionalism are important elements that make up the fairness level of an organization. The psychological contract involves the transfer of confidence among managers and employees.

key terms

culture stories 231	**psychological contract** 238	**team building** 225
empowerment 222	**quality movement** 222	**team spirit** 225
ISO 9000 224	**rewards** 222	**work team** 225

review questions

1. Think of an ideal version, in your opinion, of a perfect organizational climate. What characteristics would be included?

2. Fairness is an important quality of a positive, or warm, organizational climate and culture. What qualities are necessary for a perception of fairness to exist throughout an organization?

3. Explain the "new corporate culture." In your opinion, would this type of culture lead toward success for America as an international competitor? Why or why not?

4. At a national conference attended by one of your authors, a facilitator introduced a workshop topic as "How to Work in Teams, and Other Raising-Morale Crap." The audience's reaction was one of surprise at the speaker's negativity toward the announced topic. Based on information from this chapter, what type of corporate culture would you guess this facilitator worked in? How well does it fit with the "new" corporate culture?

5. Think about each of the types of corporate culture described in this chapter: father-founder, bureaucratic, participative, professional, and managerial-entrepreneurial. Which type would you prefer to work in? If you had your own company, which type of culture would you create?

6. What are the advantages of working in teams rather than individually? What are the advantages of developing a team spirit? Do you feel a team spirit where you work (or where you would like to work, in the ideal)?

7. Look over Deming's 14 points for quality. In your opinion, which three would be the easiest to implement? Why? Which three would be the most difficult to implement? Why?

8. Imagine yourself as (a) a ship captain, and (b) a football team captain. What are the advantages and disadvantages of each? Considering these advantages and disadvantages, why do you suppose that the team captain, rather than the ship captain, is a more popular analogy for management styles today in the United States?

critical thinking questions

9. One of the standards of quality organizations is empowerment, or giving employees decision-making power in their work-related problems and goals. After reading this chapter, do you think this is a good idea? Why or why not? Is it possible to give employees too much power? Is there a downside to giving employees power? In your ideal work setting, how much power would you have?

10. Is a corporate culture necessary? That is, can we all just go to work and get our tasks done in an organization that does not have a shared culture? How important is it for an organization to have a shared corporate culture? Why is this such a common—practically universal—phenomenon? Think about an organization that has no corporate culture: What would that be like? Would people get as much accomplished?

HOW IS THE "WEATHER" IN YOUR ORGANIZATIONAL CLIMATE?

School-to-Work Connection: Resource Skills, System Skills, and Interpersonal Skills Organizations have a pleasant or unpleasant climate, whether it is stated or not, whether it is admitted or not. The corporate culture that may be captured in a company's mission statement can sometimes give you clues about the organizational climate. Even though an organization may formally state its climate goals, and these are then agreed upon by an organization as a whole, the intended organizational climate may be interpreted in different ways by different members of the organization.

In this exercise, think about three different offices you have visited within the same organization (your own workplace, or somewhere else), or think about three different professors' offices at the college you are attending. What differences do you note in pleasantness or unpleasantness of the organizational climate?

Consider these factors in your descriptions of each of the three offices:

1. How is the furniture arranged? Does the desk act as a barrier between the office occupant's chair and the visitor's chair? (Are there even any chairs for visitors?)

2. Is the office stark or inviting? Are there personal effects in the office, such as plants, pictures of family members, or artwork?

3. Is the office cluttered and disorganized, or neatly arranged?

4. How is your interaction with the office occupant: Does he or she make eye contact, or avoid it? Does the person do other tasks while talking with you—take phone calls, look at his or her watch while talking—or give you full attention? Does the person smile and act inviting, or frown and act annoyed to see you?

Compare your evaluations of the three offices and discuss your findings in a small group of classmates. What does this exercise tell you about how you will set up, or modify, your own office?

ROLE-PLAY

School-to-Work Connection: Interpersonal Skills
Procedure: Break the class into groups of five or fewer. One person will be the team leader, and the others will be the team members. The team

leader will read the following script while the team members respond where they think appropriate, correcting the team leader on his or her misunderstood concepts of work teams.

Scenario: You are working in a company that has just now enthusiastically embraced the idea of work teams. Your former supervisor, now "Team Leader," hasn't been to the team leader training yet, but really likes the idea of working as a team. The team leader delivers the following pep talk on teamwork one Monday morning.

As you listen, decide what your response will be whenever you think your team leader is saying the wrong thing. Try not to interrupt the team leader as he or she speaks.

"Hey, Group! Team of mine! Good morning! Wow, we're all together again after a great weekend! Hey, how about that Blazers–Lakers game? So, this morning we're going to start working as a team, just like those Lakers. You all know what to do, you know your parts, so get out there and play ball! I'm going to be calling each one of you into my office, one at a time, to talk about this team thing. Now, when I call you in, bring in a pad and pencil, because I'm going to be giving you all the team directions. Don't worry about thinking up stuff to say or making any decisions, I've got it all figured out how this is going to run. In the meantime, if you need me, I'll be in my office; but try to make an appointment, because I'll be doing my regular administrative stuff. Okay? Then here we go, team! *Go team, go!*"

When the team leader is finished with the pep talk you may do the following:

1. Ask any questions you have about the pep talk.

2. (Gently!) Correct his or her misconceptions about working as a team.

internet exercises

1. *Read and Summarize*

   In this chapter, you learned about the importance of team building in the workplace. You also learned about the importance of the manager as coach. What does it mean to be a coach? Business coaching has become a career in itself over the past few years. Is this something you could see yourself doing? Enter "business coach" or "manager coach business" into your search engine. Your search will likely return many thousands of hits. Find and compare five sites that offer advice and training on business coaching; then answer the following questions.

   a. Do the sites' authors seem to mean the same things when they describe business coaching?

   b. Do these management experts contradict one another in their advice?

   c. After comparing some Web sites, would you consider a career in business coaching?

   d. What advice will you put into practice now, after reading through this information?

2. *Self-Assessment*

Effective teams have team spirit. This spirit, or lack of it, is evidenced by the team's mood or climate. How is the atmosphere within *your* work team? Access the Center for Coaching and Mentoring Web site through **www.mhhe.com/lamberton4e** or directly at **http://coachingandmentoring.com/Quiz/teamspirit.html,** and take the quiz entitled "How's Your Team's Spirit?" Interpret your score. What can you, and will you, change about your team's spirit? Summarize your ideas.

3. *Career Tracking*

Explore your career interests with excellent and informative videos you can download and watch online in brief, realistic footage. Link to the videos created by America's Career InfoNet, a component of the One Stop Career Centers (CareerOneStop) program of the federal government, through **www.mhhe.com/lamberton4e** or **www .acinet.org/acinet/videos.asp?id=27,&nodeid=27.** The "Cluster and Career Videos" show and talk about the types of work people do in more than 400 different careers for the 16 clusters recognized by the Department of Education. The "Industry Videos" provide information on specific industries such as insurance or health services. The "Work Option Videos" explain nontraditional work and work settings such as apprenticeships and on-the-job training. The "Ability Videos" describe types of work suitable to specific skill sets such as verbal, memory, or physical strength. Many of the videos are available in Spanish. To watch them, you may need to download a video player such as Windows Media, RealPlayer, or QuickTime.

Introducing Quality Management

Tom Pine had just been elected sheriff of the small county in Idaho where he'd been living for the past 10 years. He was elated! He had worked hard to get to this point in his career. Part of his preparation for this job had been to get a four-year college degree in law enforcement.

Tom had taken management and human relations courses that discussed Deming's contributions to management philosophy, including the quality movement. He found the quality management approach fascinating, and he couldn't wait to put it into effect in his new role.

There was just one stumbling block: his staff. They liked the old sheriff and his more traditional style of management, which basically consisted of ignoring their performance day to day on the job and just tallying up monthly arrest rates, arrest cases gone to trial or settled out of court, and citizen complaints.

When Seth, a police officer, came in to talk to Tom about his management changes, he was speaking for most of the rest of the staff. "Why do you have to see the *process*? Why don't you just look at the *product*? We get our job done; we get the 'bad guys' off the street. We feel like you're breathing down our necks. We don't have *that* many citizen complaints, anyway!"

Tom knew that quality movement practices would not work if they were *forced* on the staff, but could only work if the staff "bought into" them. "Seth, think about this: You know how high the reputation of agencies in the tri-county area is? Well, they use the management style, and didn't you say your brother-in-law was on the police force there, and he's really happy?"

"Well, okay then, Tom, let's do this new approach," sighed Seth. "But it might have to grow on us." Tom just smiled. He knew it would.

Case Study Questions

1. What does Seth mean by asking Tom to just consider the product and not the process? How does this relate to quality organizations?

2. Does this type of organization technically "fit" with the standard view of teams and quality organizations? Is Tom right when he describes the products and the clients involved?

3. What differences do you think will occur in this small law enforcement agency with the implementation of a new management style? Explain your answer.

The Reorganization Meeting

President Sergio Montoya called the meeting to order and announced that this was to be the first of a series of meetings on restructuring. "You mean 'on messing things up,'" muttered Ralph Hanes from the back row. "Everybody knows that we've just merged with Allycon Electronics. It's only a matter of time until we start being forced to do everything their way. Just wait and see. They're Chinese-owned, and everything will have to be done their way."

Montoya was obviously trying hard to influence employees like Ralph; it was apparent that many shared his attitude. "We'll be organizing teams throughout the company," Sergio announced. "Although we have used the team approach only on a limited scale, the new company will be totally made up of teams. If you work here, you'll be a team member."

"Oh, great," Ralph intoned. "We're going to be subjects whether we like the king or not!"

"Take it easy, Ralph," his friend Tony said. "It's probably not going to be like that at all.

Anyway, most other companies are based on teams nowadays; we're actually late getting started with it here."

"Well, I don't like the sound of it," Ralph complained.

"Just hang in there; you'll see I'm right," was Tony's reply.

Case Study Questions

1. Based on what you've learned in this chapter, how likely is it that the new team approach will actually be bad for the newly merged company?

2. What are some steps the company can take to win over employees like Ralph Hanes?

3. What type of corporate culture does it sound like Sergio Montoya is trying to instill in the new company? What can you guess about the intended organizational climate?

ACHIEVING EMOTIONAL CONTROL

In the Workplace: Two Different Styles

SITUATION

Diana and Carson are both on the technical support staff at a midsized biotech company. To their co-workers, they look like opposites. Both have more than adequate technical skills to get the job done; however, Diana tends to talk to customers using computer jargon. She typically talks very rapidly and uses long sentences and big words. She often seems impatient with clients, and some have reported that she seems to be "trying to make us feel and look stupid."

Carson, on the other hand, puts a great deal of energy into making sure that he understands what the clients' needs are. Then, he carefully translates the information he needs to give the customers or employees in language they can understand. Sometimes, Carson has to ask Diana technical questions, since she knows more about current software than he does, though he is learning fast.

One day, a very important client told their immediate supervisor, "Either get that Diana

After studying this chapter, you will be able to:

1	Identify the eight forms of intelligence.
2	Explain the significance of emotional intelligence and how it compares with earlier theories of measuring intelligence.
3	Describe how to apply emotional intelligence.
4	List ways to deal with anger.
5	Compare and contrast assertiveness, aggressiveness, and anger.
6	Give examples of defensive behaviors and how they affect the workplace.
7	Distinguish among the various scripts that influence our actions.
8	Explain why people "play games" in the workplace, and how to deal with games.

STRATEGIES FOR SUCCESS

Strategy 10.1   Stopping Games before They Start

---

person out of here, or I'll be taking my business elsewhere." Unwilling to fire a very knowledgeable employee because of what one customer said, the company assigned Carson to their account with strict instructions for Diana to avoid even talking with anyone from that company.

DISCOVERY

Diana was furious. "I know vastly more about what's going on than Carson does. Why should I be shoved into the back corner whenever they want help?"

"It's not how much you know that is in question here," explained her supervisor. "It's the way you interact with clients when you're talking about the hardware and software. They just don't seem to like your approach."

THINK ABOUT IT

What is the real problem here? Can you explain why a more experienced and knowledgeable employee might be replaced by one with less knowledge? Think about other ways to be considered intelligent than knowing more facts, as explained in this chapter.

THE EIGHT FORMS OF INTELLIGENCE

intelligence

Traditionally seen as reasoning ability, as measured by standardized tests.

For many years, people assumed that **intelligence** was a one-dimensional concept of just reasoning ability, measured by standardized tests. For example, an intelligent person could either make it through college or fail, based on the ability to perform well on college exams. Those who made it through college and graduated were thought to be smart; those who failed were not. Lately there is more agreement among experts that intelligence comes in many forms.

eight intelligences

Eight separate areas in which people put their perceptiveness and abilities to work.

Researchers, such as psychologist Howard Gardner, have discovered that there is more than one way to be *smart*. Instead of asking, "How smart are you?" Gardner would ask, *"How* are you smart?" He is referring to the **eight intelligences**—eight separate areas in which people put their perceptiveness to work. (See Figure 10.1.) Examine your talents and abilities, to see which of these intelligence categories best describes you: language (the ability to put thoughts into words and to understand words), math and logic, music, spatial reasoning, movement, interpersonal intelligence, intrapersonal intelligence, and/or naturalist intelligence.[1]

figure 10.1

THE EIGHT DIMENSIONS OF INTELLIGENCE

These different types of intelligence are reflected in various talents and skills. You will know your areas of intelligence by the areas in which you excel. *In what areas of intelligence are you strongest?*

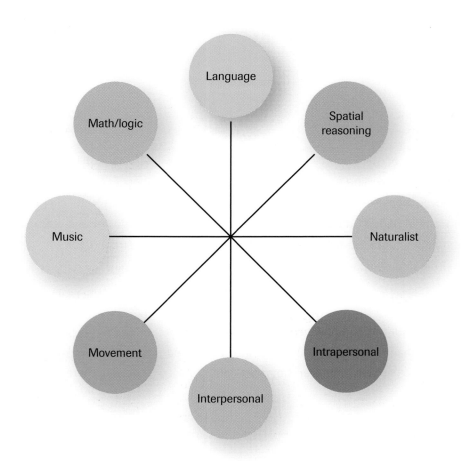

Language

People who have verbal intelligence are gifted writers, poets, songwriters, and speakers. If you love language and are fascinated by its meanings, expressions, and rhythms, your intelligence falls into this area. Standardized intelligence tests usually tap into this intelligence in questions on verbal comprehension and vocabulary. Mark Twain is one of America's most celebrated authors. Alice Walker, who won the Pulitzer Prize for fiction in 1983, is another; and so is Toni Morrison, the Nobel Prize winner for literature in 1993. All three writers provide good examples of intelligence in language.

Math and Logic

Scientists and mathematicians find pleasure in using the logical, reasoning parts of the brain. If you enjoy puzzles of logic or brain teasers, you are strong in this type of intelligence. Most of the standardized intelligence tests measure math and logic ability levels. Albert Einstein is a good example of someone who understood the world through his strength in math and logic.

Music

Most people whose intelligence falls into this category have a relationship with sounds. As children, they may have tried to produce new combinations of sounds on their own. As adults, they may become professional musicians. If you can play, write, or read music with ease and enjoyment, you have this strength. Ludwig van Beethoven, who continued to write music even after he lost his hearing, provides an example of musical intelligence. Your favorite musician or musical group is another example.

Spatial Reasoning

A person who excels in this area has a knack for seeing how elements fit together in space. This type of intelligence can be expressed by building things, or by something as simple as perfecting the art of flying a hand glider. If you can picture how items will look if they are rearranged, you have this strength. Spatial reasoning is physical and mechanical, and less tied to ideas and concepts. Michelangelo's understanding of spatial elements in his sculptures provides an example

more about...

Ninth Intelligence

In his 1999 book *Intelligence Reframed: Multiple Intelligences for the 21st Century* (published by Basic Books, New York, NY), Howard Gardner talked about the possibility of a ninth intelligence, called "existential intelligence." It is the capacity or sensitivity to wonder about deep spiritual questions such as why we are here, why we die, and the meaning of life. In July 2004, he posted a "FAQ" sheet on his Web site (**www.howardgardner.com/index.html**) saying that he still was not convinced that this is a separate ninth intelligence, but he is working on the idea.

more about...

Ludwig van Beethoven (1770–1827), a German composer, was already deaf when he conducted his Ninth Symphony. He had to be turned around to see the ecstatic reaction of the audience.

of spatial intelligence. Frank Lloyd Wright's architecture is another example of this strength in his architecture and designs.

Movement

Most people probably haven't thought of physical movement as a part of intelligence because it is not part of the traditional definition, but the ability to use your body or parts of your body to solve problems is a type of intelligence (also known as kinesthetic intelligence). Athletes and dancers are examples of people who excel in this area. Michael Jordan and Tiger Woods, recognized as two of the best athletes in the country, provide examples of kinesthetic intelligence; so does Mikhail Baryshnikov, the great Russian dancer. Another person with kinesthetic intelligence is Olympic athlete Michael Phelps, who won eight medals in swimming at the 2008 Olympics in Beijing, China, breaking seven world records in the process, and giving him the status of Olympian with the highest number of gold medals ever won at one Olympics game.

Interpersonal Intelligence

This area of intelligence deals with one's ability to understand and deal with the world of people. It is an essential skill in all aspects of life and is particularly important in business. You may find a person with interpersonal intelligence in a position of power and leadership, respected by others. If you have a special skill in communicating with others, or if many people have told you that you are a born leader, then you have this strength. Eleanor Roosevelt exhibited this strength in her ability to communicate with all types of people. Nelson Mandela is known throughout the world as a leader who understands others and can speak for them.

Intrapersonal Intelligence

Intrapersonal intelligence means knowledge of yourself. The person with this type of intelligence is *introspective,* or able to examine his or her own life and experiences. A person with a large amount of this type of intelligence knows his or her own strengths, weaknesses, desires, and fears—and can act on that knowledge realistically. Aristotle, who advised that you should *know thyself,* understood the importance of the introspective process known as intrapersonal intelligence. Sigmund Freud devoted his career to helping people understand themselves. Both Aristotle and Freud illustrate intrapersonal intelligence.

Naturalist Intelligence

The person who is high in this type of intelligence has an understanding of nature and natural processes. This person becomes a

TYPES OF INTELLIGENCE

Recent research suggests that there is more than one way to measure intelligence. *Where do your strengths and skills lie? To which intelligences do they relate most closely?*

part of the rhythms and cycles of nature. If you are happiest when you are outdoors and have a natural understanding of the natural world, you have this strength. Jane Goodall, famous for her work with chimpanzees in central Africa, provides an example of this type of intelligence. Another example is Dian Fossey, who studied gorillas in Rwanda; the book and movie *Gorillas in the Mist* tells her story.

> **Aristotle** (384–322 b.c.) is one of the Western world's most influential philosophers. His writings emphasized logic, concrete facts, and deduction.
>
> *more about…*

If you are a manager, watch for the type of intelligence each of your employees exhibits and learn to use their abilities to the fullest capacity. Such knowledge can help you to significantly raise the level of an organization's creative output.

EMOTIONAL INTELLIGENCE

Another, more recent approach to intelligence is the concept of **emotional intelligence**, also referred to as EI. How often have you observed the life of someone with a very high IQ (a score on an intelligence test) who seems to make mistake after major lifetime mistake? Or have you noticed how often people with high IQs fail to translate their strong ability to learn into other areas of their lives? For a very long time, we had been taught that our traditional idea of intelligence, measured by how well one does on an IQ test, is the most accurate predictor of success. Daniel Goleman, a prominent writer and scholar, has exploded that opinion, showing instead that *emotional* intelligence is a much better predictor of success in nearly every area of life, not always including academic success. He says, "At best, IQ contributes about 20 percent to the factors that determine life success. . . ."[2]

> **emotional intelligence (EI)**
> The ability to see and control your own emotions and to understand the emotional states of other people.

> **Jane Goodall** (1938–), a British naturalist, studied chimpanzee behavior at Gombe Stream Game Reserve in Tanzania for over 20 years. Today she is a leading animal rights activist.
>
> *more about…*

Goleman explains emotional intelligence by pointing out that we all have "two minds." First, we have the **rational mind,** which is aware of reality and which allows us to ponder and reflect. The **emotional mind** is another way of knowing. It is powerful, impulsive, and sometimes illogical. As he puts it, "each feeling has its own repertoire of thought, reactions, and even memories."[3] Several dozen definitions of EI have been expressed. In its simplest terms, however, emotional intelligence is *the ability to see and control your own emotions and to understand the emotional state of other people.*[4]

> **rational mind**
> An awareness of reality, which allows you to ponder and reflect.

> **emotional mind**
> A powerful, impulsive, sometimes illogical awareness; an ability to perceive emotions.

Daniel Goleman teaches also that **emotional competence** is an extremely important factor in understanding EI. Emotional competence can be defined as "a learned capability based on emotional intelligence that results in outstanding performance at work."[5] In other words, it is the application of EI use in the workplace.

> **emotional competence**
> A learned capability based on emotional intelligence; results in outstanding performance at work.

In his book *Successful Intelligence,* Robert Sternberg tells an apparently true story about two students named Penn and Matt. Penn was very brilliant and creative. The problem was that he was very much aware of his own abilities and acted the part of an incredibly arrogant person. So, in spite of his brilliance, Penn tended to offend people everywhere he went. Of course, he looked fantastic on paper. When he graduated, he had a great number of offers for job interviews. When the interviewing was over, though, Penn ended up with only one real job offer, and it was with a second-rate company.

Matt, on the other hand, wasn't as brilliant academically as Penn. However, his social presence was very positive. People who worked with him really liked him. Matt ended up with seven solid job offers and went on to be successful in his field. Matt had emotional intelligence; Penn didn't.[6]

personal competence
The ability to be self-aware, motivated, and self-regulated.

social competence
Empathy for others combined with sensitivity and effective social skills.

According to Goleman, there are two types of emotional competence: **personal competence** and **social competence.**[7] These are the ways in which we manage ourselves. If you have effective personal competence, you are self-aware (see Chapter 3), motivated, (see Chapter 6), and self-regulated. Being self-regulated means being trustworthy, conscientious, and self-controlled. It also means that you are adaptable and innovative. A worker who constantly procrastinates and who seems unmotivated likely is lacking in the personal competence area.

The socially competent person has empathy for others and has effective social skills. His or her empathy includes a genuine desire to understand other people and to be sensitive to political and social differences of others.

Recent studies have isolated four different areas of emotional intelligence. These are called "clusters," because they each contain a set of related EI skills.

1. *Self-awareness.* This is the ability to understand the way you are "coming off" to other people. In Chapter 3, *healthy* self-awareness was defined as "the ability to see yourself realistically, without a great deal of difference between what you are and how you assume others see you."

   If you have healthy self-awareness you will be able to make decisions that others might describe as "intuitive," when actually you can make such decisions safely because you understand the reactions of other people toward you. A self-aware person will know when he or she is seen as underrating or overrating another person. In other words, such a person will have a clearer view of what other people are really about.

2. *Social awareness.* When you have social awareness as it is defined by the founders of EI, you have a set of skills that allows you to understand the politics of your own workplace. You can discern different

attitudes from different people toward themselves, the work they are engaged in, and each other. You can also interpret nonverbal communication effectively. You are in tune with facial expressions and body language that disclose the real feelings and political positions of others.

3. *Self-management.* One of the most important parts of self-management is what we commonly call self-control. It is the ability to hold yourself in check and not overreact when something bothers you. A self-managed person will seldom, if ever, lose his or her temper or get involved in shouting matches with other people. Coming to work with a bad mood from home is another behavior less likely to happen with someone who has this group of skills mastered. Finally, well self-managed people will not allow frustration to get the best of them.

4. *Relationship management.* Someone with effective relationship management skills will be able to settle conflicts and disagreements between groups and between people. This set of EI skills enables the individual to communicate effectively and to build meaningful interpersonal relationships both with individuals and with groups. They can be depended on to settle disputes within a team or other group and have the ability to stay focused on the relevant issues, rather than on the other peripheral things that might be involved.

EMOTIONAL INTELLIGENCE

Social awareness and sensitivity to the emotions of others are just as important for success as your knowledge and abilities. *How do the emotional mind and rational mind function together? Can a lack of emotional intelligence sabotage a person with other types of intelligence?*

LEARNING TO APPLY EMOTIONAL INTELLIGENCE

How can someone with a lower level of emotional intelligence grow and develop into someone with a higher EI? The experts tell us that emotional intelligence *can* be learned. One can learn, for example, to trade one set of reflexes with another.[8] According to several studies, not only can EI be learned, it can improve over time, often as a lifelong learning process. In one study of business college graduates, continued improvement could be seen as long as seven years after the initial training had taken place.[9]

Motivation expert Richard Boyatzis says that the most common mistake made by people wanting to improve their EI is thinking that knowing more about the issue will make a person's skills better.[10] The trick is learning to *apply* and *use* that knowledge in a practical, real way, rather than just learning about it. Here are a few practical approaches that nearly anyone can take:

1. *Review what you know about self-awareness.* Revisit Chapter 3 of this book, recalling all of the skills one needs to be more self-aware.

Next, ask yourself each time you interact with someone whether or not you are tuning in to the manner in which you are coming off during the process. Perhaps you understand what you feel. However, the important issue is *how well does the other person seem to be picking up on those feelings?* Are you hiding them, either purposely or accidentally?

2. *Carefully watch others whose social competence seems to be high, who have social awareness skills that you don't have but would like to attain.* For example, observe someone who is better at empathy than you are. (Empathy is the ability to identify with the needs and feelings of others.) Watch the person as he or she listens to others; observe the facial expressions used to communicate careful listening; listen carefully to the words used to ask about feelings and needs.[11]

3. *Work actively on improving your self-management skills.* Self-management is an important part of EI. It includes emotional self-control, adaptability, and optimism, along with other related qualities. Try spending a few extra seconds deciding how you will react whenever something threatening or challenging comes from another person. Those few seconds can make a tremendous difference in how well you self-manage.

4. *Develop relationship management skills.* This is a set of skills identified by Giles and Boyatzis that involves the skills needed to work successfully in groups or teams.[12] Look at others who operate well in the arena of relationships with others. Watch them carefully as they take care of conflicts between people, as they use things people have in common to take care of their differences, as they use humor as a human relations tool.

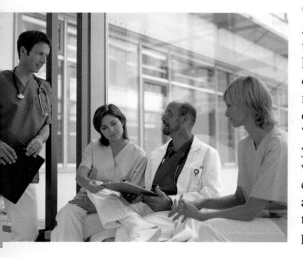

IMPROVING YOUR EMOTIONAL INTELLIGENCE

To increase your emotional intelligence, you should take the time to apply the knowledge and perceptions you gain through awareness of yourself and others. *What are some opportunities to improve your EI at your current job, or at the workplace of someone you know?*

DEALING WITH ANGER

Anger is one of the most potentially harmful of all emotions. One of the most important parts of emotional intelligence is the ability to deal with this important area of our personality. Many psychologists say that anger comes more from how we process events than the nature of the events themselves. Anger becomes what it is because of "trigger thoughts" about the things that happen around you. These trigger thoughts usually come to the surface when at least one of two things has happened: (1) You are convinced that other people are to blame for deliberately and unnecessarily causing you trouble or (2) you interpret the behavior of other people as breaking the rules of appropriate behavior.[13]

In his first book on EI, Goleman writes about his early teenage years. "Once when I was about 13, in an angry fit, I walked out of the house, vowing I would never return. It was a beautiful summer day, and I walked far along lovely lanes, till gradually the stillness and beauty calmed and soothed me; and after some hours I returned home repentant and almost melted. Since then, when I'm angry, I do this if I can, and find it the best cure."[14]

Anger produces three basic results that are negative and damaging:[15]

1. *Anger blinds you in several ways.* First, it blinds the individual to other ways of seeing reality. For example, if someone misses a deadline, it is tempting to see the guilty person as irresponsible and uncaring and to be blinded to any other interpretation of the guilty person's behavior. Second, anger blinds the individual to his or her responsibility for what has happened. The fact that someone missed that deadline could possibly be even partly your fault. Third, anger can blind one to other, less painful ways of dealing with the problem.

2. *Left unchecked, anger will grow.* This is how many wars start. Anger is discussed, pondered, and rediscussed to the point where the anger turns to aggression, and, almost unavoidably, to armed conflict.

3. *Anger is often based on fear of some type.* Many types of anger stem from fear. Fear causes apprehension, which in turn causes new layers of pain. Then the pain increases, damaging the people on both sides of the conflict.

Five Steps for Dealing with Anger

Here are some simple steps that should help anyone who is dealing with the control of anger:

1. *Examine your anger to find the inner causes.* Instead of focusing on the other person or persons as "the wrongdoers," focus on what it was that triggered your anger in a given situation.

2. *Learn to recognize your own "flashpoints."* At first, this might seem identical with step 1. This self-examination, though, needs to be ongoing and must examine what it is that usually arouses your anger. These flashpoints might include fatigue, excessive stress, even factors such as excessive alcohol intake.

3. *Examine specifically what damage your anger has caused.* Examples would be damage to relationships, retaliation from others, or health issues.

4. *Work on developing and using conflict management skills.* For example, work on being assertive, rather than passive or aggressive. (See definitions further in this chapter.)

5. *Get in touch with what types of things help calm you down.* Instead of berating others or lashing out, think about what constructive steps you can take—steps that specifically work for you.[16]

ASSERTIVENESS, AGGRESSIVENESS, AND ANGER

assertiveness

Standing up for your rights without threatening the self-esteem of the other person.

aggressiveness

Hurting others and putting them on the defensive.

Lately, there has been a great deal of emphasis on assertiveness training. **Assertiveness** means standing up for your rights without threatening the self-esteem of the other person. **Aggressiveness** involves hurting others and putting them on the defensive. A working knowledge of these differences can help you avoid the excesses of aggressiveness while maintaining assertiveness.

Assertiveness is based on your rights *and* the rights of others, and it is important to use when you sense that someone is trying to take advantage of you. When your equal rights as a human being are threatened, you might be tempted to be either passive or aggressive. Both of these extremes will damage you and your relationship with the other person. By remaining sensitive to the attitudes of the other person, and giving yourself time to react assertively, you can improve both your self-esteem and your human relations skills.

DEFENSIVE BEHAVIORS

defensiveness

The inappropriate reaction to another's behavior as though it was an attack.

Have you ever felt you were under attack from someone only to discover later that you weren't? When another person is actually physically or emotionally attacking you, reacting to protect or defend yourself might be quite appropriate. However, when the attack is only imagined, not real, such behavior is not only inappropriate, but also often destructive. At its best, it is a waste of time. This is what we mean by **defensiveness:** the inappropriate reaction to another's behavior as though it were an attack.

Defensiveness also can be seen as your body's method of keeping you from being unduly uncomfortable. It usually comes from two sources: low self-esteem and fear.[17] When people really like themselves and feel comfortable with their own value, avoiding defensiveness is much easier than it is for an individual with low self-esteem. Most of us become defensive from time to time. After all, most of us struggle with self-esteem issues, and many people deal daily with different kinds of fears.

Try to remember the most recent time you yelled or snapped at another person. What happened? What were the basic assumptions you were acting on? What did you say, and with what tone of voice? Was something involved in the encounter causing a fear response inside of you?

We all react defensively in different ways, depending on our own personalities, emotional positions, and fear sources. Here is a brief list of the most common defensive reactions used in the workplace:

Counterattack. When you feel under attack, the automatic response is often simply to turn the situation around by going into the attack mode ourselves. This is known as counterattack. When this happens, you will also be provoking the other person himself or herself to become defensive. When that happens, as it often does, this usually starts a vicious cycle that can continue for a very long time. For example, someone Keith is working with asks, "Why did you decide to approach the project this way?" Perceiving a personal attack, Keith shouts, "If you have some kind of problem with my approach, you can just stuff it!" The "attack" has been counterattacked.

Passive-aggressive behavior. The person who uses a passive-aggressive approach seems to be shutting down. Someone not watching closely would not necessarily see the anger or frustration behind the calm behavior. However, by acting in that way, this person will usually be expressing an understated rage. Again, this variety of defensiveness can cause even more negative behavior from both sides. In this case, Keith just stares into space for a while, then says, "Well, okay, if you don't like it, I'm sure I can do something to improve it. It might take a while. I hope you can wait," and so on. What Keith is *really* thinking is just as negative as it was in the counterattack example.

Pointless explanations. This defensive behavior seems to stem from a belief that the other person has been on the attack only because that person "doesn't understand." Thus, seemingly endless and pointless explanations result, frustrating everyone involved. If he were in this mode, Keith would say, "Well, let me show you what I was thinking when I decided to go this direction. You see, I was thinking not only about product integrity, but also about market acceptance, so I . . ." (You don't want to hear the rest of his explanation; it's boring and—most important—pointless.)

Creating a distraction. This defensive behavior is sometimes called using a "red herring," because it introduces a point or fact that is irrelevant to the issue at hand. Red herring was once used by people opposing fox hunting, to confuse the nostrils of the hunting dogs. In a similar manner, the person who uses this defense brings up something totally unrelated simply to distract attention from the real issue or issues. For example, "Last Thursday at 3 P.M.—no, it was more like 4 P.M., just before closing time—you told me that that I needed to be involved with this project."

Ending the defensive cycle is actually not difficult for the person who is paying close attention to what others are saying. Defensiveness is like putting on heavy armor, armor that keeps you from functioning as you would normally. Only by shedding that armor, making yourself vulnerable, will you encourage the other person to do the same. Then, once the armor is off the backs of both people—or more, if it's a group issue—those involved can talk normally and in a more detached and constructive manner.

At some point, one of the people involved in the defensiveness chain needs to stop and challenge the assumptions he or she is using. Assume, for example, that you are *not* under attack and that you are not being threatened personally. Acting on that new set of assumptions can change the situation radically.

Here are some steps one can take in reducing defensiveness and its destructive effects in the workplace:

1. *Back off and cool down.* Give yourself a bit of time to get refocused and let yourself get a renewed perspective. Often just a few minutes makes a great deal of difference.

2. *Use "I statements."* Rather than saying, "You always go out of your way to mess up my schedule with your rescheduling policies," try, "When someone changes my schedule without consulting me, I feel like I'm being treated like a thing instead of as a person." It is unlikely that the other person will come back with, "No, you don't feel that way!"

3. *Avoid absolutes.* Two of the most damaging absolute words are *always* and *never.* What if the employee in the preceding situation said, "You *never* consult me about scheduling decisions; you *always* change my schedule without warning." That type of wording is very likely to produce defensiveness in the other person. Also, remember that it takes only one exception to prove "always" or "never" statements to be wrong. If the supervisor could point to even one time when she consulted the employee about the schedule, a new issue would have come up, to cause still more defensiveness.

4. *Make positive assumptions about the other person or persons involved.* We all have faults. However, when you choose to zero in on the positive trait and behaviors rather than the faults, defensiveness becomes less likely—from both sides.

5. *Learn to separate your work from who you are.* When someone criticizes your work performance, do you take that as an attack on you personally? If so, you might be making the mistake of thinking of your job as what you are, rather than as what you do. This is especially important to remember when you are doing creative work,

Ian's supervisor phones him just as he rolls out of bed in the morning. "Ian, I need you to meet a customer downtown and have breakfast with him. His new proposal could mean a lot to us. I was going to go, but I'm swamped. The boss's voice sounds like a parent speaking to a child ("please be a good boy and do as I say"). Meeting with clients (especially before work) is not on Ian's job description, and the boss knows it. Besides, if anyone is "swamped," it's Ian. Ian wants to say, "Get off my back; just because you schedule your time so poorly you have to go to work at seven, don't come to me to bail you out!" This would have been aggressive. Instead, Ian chooses an assertive stance: "Mr. Tolbey, I have clients scheduled back-to-back all day." A passive Ian would have said "OK, Mr. Tolbey, tell me where to meet the client."

work that came from your mind. Just remember that, although it came from your mind, it's not a part of your mind—or of your being. When someone questions your method of doing a part of a task, that person is not necessarily attacking you.

SCRIPTS

Part of a school of psychology known as "transactional analysis," the concept of scripts has been used to explain some important facts about our behavior as humans. Much of what we do and say in our daily lives is based on scripts that most people heard repeatedly as children. A psychological **script** is very much like a movie or theater script. Like the ones in show business, your scripts have a cast of characters, dialogue, acts, scenes, themes, and plots—but you didn't write them yourself. Instead, they came from parents, other family members, friends, adult role models, the media, teachers—in short, from nearly all human influences during your first years of childhood.[18] You use these same lines (or variations on them) every time you interact with others, including at work.

> **script**
>
> In relationship transactions, a psychological script like a movie or theater script, with characters, dialogue, and so on, that most people heard as children; used in transactional analysis.

Although you are also the casting director, you don't necessarily cast yourself into good roles. You could be the villain as easily as the hero of the script. People usually choose their favorite scripted parts during the casting process. Some people who learn to understand scripts get rid of the old ones and write new ones. Most people, though, have some scripts they would be better off without. The information here can help you understand your scripts better, and hopefully can help you throw off those you don't want.

Whenever Fred attended a meeting in the government agency where he worked, he would sit at the table looking at the other people and reflecting on how much more confident they seemed than he felt. Although he had many years of experience at his job and a good education, he still felt inferior. When asked to speak, he would often stumble over his words, even though he knew what he was talking about. Fred seems to be stuck in a negative script about his own life.

Scripts can be divided into four basic categories:

- *Cultural scripts* say that Alaskans are tough, Americans are free and rich, and New Englanders are traditional and intelligent.
- *Family scripts* say that the Smiths are honest, the Johnsons are medical people, and the Kennedys enter politics.
- *Religious scripts* are sometimes the strongest: Catholics don't believe in abortion, Jews don't work on Saturday, and Protestants believe in hard work.
- *Gender scripts* tell you how members of your gender should behave: Men don't cry, women cook and clean houses, and men should be able to fix cars.[19]

game

An encounter between two people that produces a "payoff" for the one who starts the game, at the expense of the other player.

REWRITING SCRIPTS

If you feel that scripts in your life do not allow you to appreciate life fully, you can rewrite them to help turn yourself into a happier person. *How can you rewrite your own scripts?*

GAMES PEOPLE PLAY

Like scripts, the concept of "games" comes from transactional analysis. A **game** can be defined as an encounter between two people that produces a "payoff" for the one who starts the game—at the expense of the other player. Negative game playing can hurt positive relationships. Usually, there is something sneaky or deceitful behind the message or action of the game starter. This definition also implies that both players are playing, willingly or not. The two characteristics that all games have in common are that they include: (1) at least one insincere statement per game, and (2) a payoff of some kind to at least one of the players.[20]

Games are usually emotion-based activities that allow one person to feel "one up" on someone else, or—in some cases—"one down." Although they sometimes seem to help one person gain something of value, games usually don't really help any of the players. Instead, they cause damage

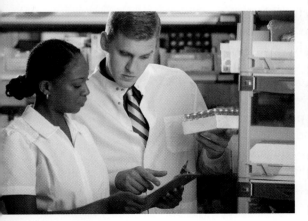

Secretary: Stacy, the fax machine is out of toner, and five people are waiting to use it.
Receptionist: Well, why don't you just put in a new cartridge?.
Secretary: I would, but I really don't know how.
Receptionist: Well, why don't you call the service rep?
Secretary: That's a good idea, but he's expensive, and he takes so long to get here!

Receptionist: Well, why don't you ask the maintenance staff to help you?
Secretary: I would, but they're too busy right now. I already asked them for help.
Receptionist: (frustrated) Well, why don't you blow it out your ear!

to the organization in wasted time, lowered morale, and decreased output. Some games are worse than others, especially in terms of intensity. **First-degree games** are usually quite harmless, whereas a **third-degree game** can result in physical injury. **Second-degree games** flirt with being harmful and often cause anger.[21]

Let's look at some examples of commonly played workplace games. All of the possible games won't fit into this chapter, because there are so many of them.

"Why Don't You . . . Yes, But"

Have you ever been at a committee meeting where the leader asked for constructive suggestions, but never really considered any of them? Have you ever had an instructor who asked students for input on how a class should be run, just to go ahead and do what he or she had planned from the start? The payoff for "Why don't you . . . yes, but" is that the person (acting like a sympathetic parent or adult) reassures both her- or himself and the other individual: "Nobody's going to tell me what to do." It is also sometimes a way that game players can get others to take over their responsibilities for them.

Blemish

Blemish is a true trivia game. This game is a petty time waster. The payoff to the player is a temporary boost to his or her ego. Detail-oriented people who feel that they aren't good at much else sometimes thrive on this game.

> **first-, second-, and third-degree games**
>
> In transactional analysis, categories of games based on intensity of play. First-degree games are relatively harmless; second-degree games are moderately harmful; third-degree games are extremely damaging.

> **Office Politics**
>
> By understanding defensiveness and game playing, you will be able to answer many puzzling questions about office politics: who does it, what their true motives are, and how you can end its negative effects (at least in relation to yourself).

more about...

Anthony, a restaurant manager, spends most of his time checking inventory and other cost-related matters. He looks carefully for any contradictions in his employees' reports. When he finds one, he has discovered "proof" of the worthlessness of either whole projects or otherwise very good employees.[22]

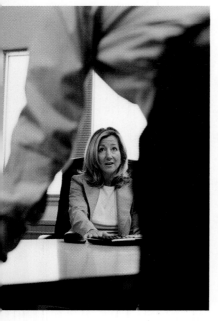

PLAYING GAMES IN THE OFFICE

Games in the workplace produce "payoffs" for a few, but ultimately hurt everyone involved and cause damage to the organization itself. *What can you do to prevent or avoid games in the workplace?*

Wooden Leg

This game is also known as "My Excuses Are Better Than Yours." Excuses are the focus here. Time, illness, and childhood poverty all are useful as excuses for whatever might go wrong. Real reasons for things going wrong exist in many situations, but this game makes an art out of creating excuses. In the end, excuses take the place of a job well done.

Harried (or Harried Executive)

This game is played by someone who uses being "too busy" as an excuse not to interact with others. The reasons for this type of payoff are fairly complex. People might have a variety of reasons for not wanting to get close to others. Nearly always, though, the reason is related to low self-esteem. This may also be why they want to be seen as working harder than others.

Now I've Got You

This is a game in which one person tries to trap the other in a mistake, a lie, or some other type of negative situation. If the player is successful in trapping the victim, he or she will usually feel justified in harming the person—firing someone, taking back a raise that was offered, or simply insulting the victim.[23]

These aren't all of the game categories that exist. The entire experience known as *office politics* can be seen as a large game that contains many combinations of these and other games. If you learn these basic categories well, your knowledge of them should help you identify other games people might attempt to play with you. Most important, you can learn to *stop* playing games, and to stop allowing other people to play them in the workplace. Game playing prevents employees from enjoying open, honest relationships with others, and it wastes company time and money.

Manager: "What's the matter, John? You're way behind on contacting those companies we were talking about for potential convention business."

Sales executive: "Well, Mr. Ripley, you know how tough it is to make contact with these firms. Monday is out because they're catching up with the weekend accumulation, and you can't call early in the morning because they're trying to wind up the previous day's business."[24]

STRATEGIES FOR SUCCESS

10.1 Stopping Games before They Start

1. Work on your self-esteem.
2. Try to remain rational, regardless of the other person's state of mind.
3. Try to get the other person to be rational and honest.
4. Give positive feedback to other people.
5. De-emphasize the weaknesses of others.

The best way to become aware of games and of the people who play them is to watch for conversations and events that happen repeatedly. People who are major game players tend to play new episodes of the same game over and over again.

You can stop a game at any time by simply refusing to play. Remember that games are made up of messages with double meanings. Just as in any conversation, you can decide whether or not you will play along with something as negative as most games are. Here are some tips on stopping games before you get hooked into them:

1. **Work on your self-esteem.** Low self-esteem is the single most important reason why people both play games and get stuck playing the games of others. You can also get other people to play fewer games by doing and saying things that help *their* self-esteem.

2. **Try to remain rational, regardless of the other person's state of mind.** Notice that games are not usually played by people who are trying to be fair and honest. One way to stay fair and honest is by asking *how* questions, rather than *why* ones. Of course, you probably aren't going to succeed in preventing games every time.

3. **Try to get the other person to be rational and honest.** Do everything you can to lead the would-be game player to be reasonable. When the game player starts talking as a selfish child or an attacking critic, say something like, "Explain that point a bit further; what do you mean by (whatever was said)?"

Three co-workers come by Brad's office and invite him to go out to a new French café for lunch. Brad protests, "I'm just too busy to get away," until they leave him alone. He does this again the next two times they ask, and finally they stop asking. The truth is that he wants to avoid the friendship of his fellow workers. His low self-esteem warns him that nobody will like him in a social setting.

4. **Give positive feedback to other people.** A great deal of game playing is based on negatives. Getting rid of those negatives is a good method of also getting rid of games.

5. **De-emphasize the weaknesses of others.** All people have weaknesses. By spending more time and energy noticing people's positive points, you can avoid the desire for payoffs—the unhealthy desire that urges people to play games in the first place.

Create a climate at work where people see game playing for what it is: a waste of time. We often play games because we are bored. We can all do a lot to reduce boredom on the job, through job rotation, job enlargement, and job enrichment, for example. Most important, people should be allowed to work up to their full potential, so they can get a sense of fulfillment from their work.

CHAPTER TEN SUMMARY

Chapter Summary by Learning Objectives

1. **Identify the eight forms of intelligence.** The eight forms of intelligence refer to intelligence in the following areas: language, spatial reasoning, naturalism, intrapersonal issues, interpersonal issues, movement, music, and math/logic, These replace the old one-dimensional view of IQ.

2. **Explain the significance of emotional intelligence and how it compares with earlier theories of measuring intelligence.** Emotional intelligence is the ability to see and control one's own emotions and to understand the emotional states of other people. Earlier theories measured ability to comprehend, memorize, and analyze facts only.

3. **Describe how to apply emotional intelligence.** Recent studies have shown that emotional intelligence can be learned. Here are the basic steps towards application: (1) Review what you know about self-awareness. (2) Carefully watch others whose social competence seems to be high, who have social awareness skills that you don't

U.S.A. Transactional Analysis Association

Go to **www.mhhe.com/lamberton4e** for a link to read about the games people play. Write down which game you play most often—or watch other people play. Then write which one you find yourself playing most often. What are the key differences between what you want to do and what you end up doing??

have, but would like to attain. (3) Work actively on improving your self-management skills. (4) Develop relationship management skills.

4. **List ways to deal with anger.** These are the steps in dealing with the most destructive human emotion: (1) Examine your anger to find the inner causes. (2) Learn to recognize your own "flashpoints." At first, this step might seem identical with #1. However, it refers to the specific areas that trigger anger in you. (3) Examine the damage caused by your anger. (4) Learn to develop and use conflict management skills. (5) Get in touch with the types of things that calm you down.

5. **Compare and contrast assertiveness, aggressiveness, and anger.** Assertiveness means standing up for your rights without threatening the other people who are involved. Aggressiveness, on the other hand, involves hurting other people and putting them on the defensive. Though it can be channeled constructively, anger is usually a negative emotion that damages relationships and productivity in organizations.

6. **Give examples of defensive behaviors and how they affect the workplace.** Defensiveness is the reaction to someone else's behavior as though it were an attack. Defensiveness often brings out further defensiveness and can cause tremendous trouble in any workplace.

7. **Distinguish among the various scripts that influence our actions.** A psychological script is like a movie or theatre script, with characters, dialogue, and so on. Cultural scripts, family scripts, religious scripts, and gender scripts often determine our behavior.

8. **Explain why people "play games" in the workplace, and how to deal with games.** Games are nearly always played with some type of "payoff" in mind. The payoff is the main reason most games are played. This payoff might be feeling temporarily better about oneself, showing the faults of the other person, or the ability to make excuses for our own failures and weaknesses. Most games are destructive and time-wasting.

Boss: (noticing that a letter is still in the secretary's word processor, unprinted): "Did you finish that letter I gave you this morning?
Secretary: "Er, uh, yes I did."
Boss: "Oh, really? Then what is this? Have you *ever* done anything right?"

key terms

assertiveness 260
aggressiveness 260
defensive behavior/
    defensiveness 260
eight intelligences 252
emotional
    competence 255

emotional intelligence
    (EI) 255
emotional mind 255
first-, second-,
    and third-degree
    games 265
game 264

intelligence 252
personal
    competence 256
rational mind 255
script 263
social competence 256

review questions

1. Briefly explain each of the "eight intelligences." How are these categories more helpful in understanding the whole idea of intelligence, specially as it impacts the workplace?

2. What is emotional intelligence? How does this concept relate to the "eight intelligences"? Explain the relationship among intrapersonal, interpersonal, and emotional intelligence.

3. Briefly explore each of the four general areas ("clusters") of emotional intelligence. Show how each area can be encouraged to develop.

4. Explain why anger can be so damaging. What are the three major effects of anger?

5. What are the five steps for dealing with anger? Which of the five seems the most effective for you personally? Why?

6. Briefly explain the process of defensiveness. List at least two of the four most popular defensive reactions. Have you seen (or used) any of these in your own life?

7. What are the steps one can take to reduce defensiveness? Which of the five seems the most important to you?

8. What specific steps can you take when you suspect that you are dealing with a game player? What steps can you take to prevent yourself from initiating games?

9. How can a knowledge of emotional intelligence improve human relations in business situations? How can it help you understand more about your interactions with others?

10. Think of a conflict situation you were in recently. Define the terms assertiveness and aggressiveness. Then answer these questions:

    a. What role did aggressiveness or assertiveness play in the conflict?

    b. Were you aggressive, assertive, or passive?

    c. Did the situation work out the way you expected?

    d. Would you act differently if you had to do it again?

working it out 10.1

NEW WAYS TO RESPOND

School-to-Work Connection: Interpersonal Skills

Think of an emotionally intelligent response to the following workplace statements:

1. Boss: "What's the matter, can't you ever do anything right?"

   Response: _____

2. Customer: "Is there anyone in your company who has one living brain cell?"

   Response: _____

3. Husband: "Why do you always have to be running off to work functions and church activities? Did it ever occur to you that you have a family to care for?"

   Response: _____

4. Customer: "I got this part for my washing machine here yesterday and it doesn't fit. I've about had it with your incompetence. Give me my money back and make it snappy!"

   Response: _____

5. Employee: "Gee, I can't seem to figure out how to get this new computer program to work. I've never been too good with electronic stuff. Will you please help me? I'm really frustrated."

   Response: _____

ANALYZING CONVERSATIONS

School-to-Work Connection: Defensiveness

Rewrite each of the following situations in a way that will eliminate defensive behaviors and use the concepts of emotional intelligence.

1. **Manager:** (calm tone of voice) "Please get these reports out by the end of the day."

   Employee: "Why are you always criticizing me? What's the matter—don't I always get my reports done on time?"

   _____

   _____

2. **Employee:** (calm, matter-of-fact tone of voice) "My schedule is really tight. Could you give me a hand with this mass mailing?"

   Manager: (soft, reassuring tone of voice) "Sure, I'll get Jean to help you. Looks like you've got a big job there, all right."

   _____

   _____

3. **Employee:** "My schedule is really tight. Could you give me a hand with this mass mailing?" (Meaning: "I don't have the confidence to do this by myself.")

   Manager: "Sure, I'll get Jean to help you. Looks like you've got a big job there, all right." (Meaning: "I can never depend on you to finish a job by yourself; you're hopeless.")

   _____

   _____

4. **Customer:** (harsh, critical tone) "I've been standing at this counter for 20 minutes, and you've waited on four people who came in after I did! What gives with you guys? Are you all blind and deaf, or just rude?"

   Sales Clerk: "Look, lady, you can yell at somebody else. I'm doing the best I can. If you don't like it, get lost!"

   _____

   _____

5. **Customer:** (harsh, critical tone) "I've been standing at this counter for 20 minutes, and you've waited on four people who came in after

I did! What gives with you guys? Are you all blind and deaf, or just rude?"

Sales Clerk: "I'm very sorry, madam. Sometimes it just gets crazy around here. Now, tell me what you need so we can take care of you quickly; heaven knows, you've been waiting long enough." (calm, subdued tone of voice)

_____

_____

working it out 10.3

WHAT JOBS ARE DECLINING? TOP 20 OCCUPATIONS IN THE U.S. WITH THE LARGEST JOB DECLINE, 2002–2012 (NUMBERS IN THOUSANDS OF JOBS)

School-to-Work Connection: Information and Thinking Skills

Occupation	EMPLOYMENT		CHANGE	
	2002 (Actual)	2012 (Projected)	Number Decline	Percent Decline
Farmers and ranchers	1,158	920	−238	−21
Sewing machine operators	315	216	−99	−31
Word processors and typists	241	148	−93	−39
Stock clerks and order fillers	1,628	1,560	−68	−4
Secretaries, except legal, medical, and executive	1,975	1,918	−57	−3
Electrical and electronic equipment assemblers	281	230	−51	−18
Computer operators (not analysis or programmers)	182	151	−30	−17
Telephone operators	50	22	−28	−56
Postal service mail sorters, processors, and processing machine operators	253	226	−26	−10
Loan interviewers and clerks	170	146	−24	−14
Data entry keyers (keypunch operators)	392	371	−21	−5
Telemarketers	428	406	−21	−5

(*Continue on next page*)

	EMPLOYMENT		CHANGE	
Textile knitting and weaving machine setters, operators, and tenders	53	33	−20	−39
Textile winding, twisting, and drawing out machine setters, operators, and tenders	66	46	−20	−30
Team assemblers	1,174	1,155	−19	−2
Order clerks	330	311	−19	−6
Door-to-door sales workers, news and street vendors, and related workers	155	137	−18	−12
Travel agents	118	102	−16	−14
Brokerage clerks	78	67	−11	−15
Eligibility Interviewers, government programs	80	74	−5	−7

Source: U.S. Department of Labor, Bureau of Labor Statistics (retrieved August 2005) ftp://ftp.bts.gov/pub/special.requests/ep/Ind-occ.matrix/mirtabs.txt.

Instructions: Look over the table on pages 273 and 274 and think about why some of these jobs are declining and what these declines mean for your future. Will any of these specific job shortages hit your state or local area especially hard? Explain. Relate these declines to some of the material discussed in this section of the textbook: For example, which jobs are declining due to the economic growth in other countries? Explain. Which jobs are declining due to worldwide technological advances? Give examples. Which jobs are declining due to changes in our population and the workforce? What patterns do you notice in the types of jobs that are in decline?

internet exercises

1. *Read and Write*
   Enter the Web site for "Queendom, The Land of Tests" linked through **www.mhhe.com/lamberton4e.** Take the emotional intelligence test. Then share your performance on the test with your instructor by writing a brief summary of what the test taught you. Be as specific as possible.

2. *Compare and Contrast*
   Find out more about workplace game playing by accessing the "Of Frogs and Princes" Web site linked through **www.mhhe.com/lamberton4e.** Find at least three types of games not mentioned in

this chapter and respond to your view of how important each one is in understanding the workplace and how to work there.

3. *Read and Write*

No matter where you are in your career path—seasoned workforce veteran or first-time job seeker—you can find information on jobs through the federal government's "USA Jobs" Web site created by the Office of Personnel Management at **www.usajobs.opm.gov** or linked through **www.mhhe.com/lamberton4e.** If you are a student seeking a job, open their "StudentJobs.gov" link from their home page. Identify a job opening located in the city or town where you attend classes or in a particular career area of interest you may have. Report on your findings. If you have lots of job experience, you may find the link from the home page to "Career Interests Center" and then a link to "Specific Job Exploration" to be more useful. Research a specific job category in your area of interest and report back on minimum qualifications and job descriptions.

4. *Compare and Contrast*

How does your state rate? Find out what the typical wages are for occupations in your state. Open the Web site for the U.S. Department of Labor (from the Occupational Employment Statistics at the Bureau of Labor Statistics), linked through **www.mhhe.com/lamberton4e** (or find it at **www.dol.gov**). Click on your state, then link to the occupation of your choice. What are the average hourly and annual earnings for the occupation you selected?

Missing the Glory at Morning Glory

Siti Abdullah's new job at Morning Glory Day-care Center placed her in charge of a crew of 12 day-care providers in a large suburban day-care center. All of her new employees were people who had owned and operated children's day-care services out of their homes. Nearly all of them were burned out from the loneliness and frustration of running a stressful home-based business. They were happy to be part of something bigger, and for most of them, the pay was as good as or better than what they had been used to.

Siti's major stressor was the owner, Marie Estrada. Marie chose to show up at the business only an hour per day at most, and when she was there, she was constantly criticizing Siti. To Siti, everything she said seemed to be patronizing. "You must stop pandering to the parents' every whim," Marie told Siti on one exceptionally stressful day.

"Why don't you try running this place some time and see how you like it!" Siti replied.

"I *do* run it. You just work for me, and don't you ever forget that!" was Marie's immediate comeback.

"I'm sorry," Siti replied. "These kids have just gotten to me today." However, secretly, she was thinking. "I want this job, and I have to deal with this miserable excuse for a person only an hour a day."

A year passed with no improvement. As long as she had to deal with the owner less than an hour each day, Siti succeeded in shaking off the frustration and going on with a job she otherwise enjoyed.

Then in early June, Marie's youngest child graduated. She was now an empty-nester. The one hour she worked changed to four, then to nearly the entire workday. This was too much for Siti. Two months later, Siti gave her two-week notice and decided to open a day-care center of her own.

Case Study Questions

1. Could Siti have kept this situation from ending the way it ended?

2. Briefly analyze this situation using what you have learned about emotional intelligence.

3. What would you have done in Siti Abdullah's place? Why?

The Never-Ending Game

Walter Langley, marketing vice president of Comfort Furniture, Inc., was holding his weekly meeting. Langley began the meeting with the same plea he had been using for the past three months: "You all know that we are in a downward sales spiral. Something has to be done. Now, I hope you have some creative suggestions that will turn this trend around."

At that point, people offered their suggestions.

John Bettermore: "We could get production to start using that new synthetic padding for our living room furniture line. We could sell our line for at least 15 percent less; we'd be more price-competitive."

Langley: "That's a good suggestion, but that new synthetic doesn't have a track record. We'll be worse off because of quality complaints from our customers."

Allen Avery: "We've been getting stung in the South, especially in Mississippi and Georgia. Why don't we just eliminate those states and concentrate on the Midwest, where our business is more dependable?"

Langley: "Yes, but that's giving up. If we ever try to penetrate the southern states again, we'd just be that much further behind."

Shirley Keener: "One of our biggest problems is that we can't produce enough of the one product line that's in great demand: our dining room furniture. What if we put another shift in that plant at least until we catch up with the demand?"

Langley: "Well, I've thought of that, but do you have any idea what the union will do to us if we try something like that?"

This sort of dialogue continued until two hours had passed. Then Langley said, "Well, thank you for your time and effort. Please think carefully and come back next Monday morning with some better ideas."

Case Study Questions

1. Walter Langley is playing a repetitive game here. What is it called, and what are its payoffs?

2. What can Langley's team do to end this game? Be specific.

3. Specifically, what would you do if you were in one of Langley's time-wasting meetings?

«« building your human relations skills

In Parts One and Two, you learned about some theories and practices in the field of human relations. In Parts Three and Four, you will examine applied human relations in the business world.

There is an old saying—the more things change, the more they stay the same. Chapter 11 offers strategies for finding constants within change and dealing with the effects on personal and organizational levels. Chapter 12 presents human relations skills that tap your creativity and encourage creativity in others. Chapter 13 gives tools to anticipate and avoid conflicts, and to resolve those that are inevitable. Chapter 14 covers stress and how to recognize, cope, and channel it. Finally, Chapter 15 looks at customer service, a key growth area for all organizations. »» »»

INDIVIDUAL AND ORGANIZATIONAL CHANGE

In the Workplace: Too Much Change

SITUATION

Rain was falling as Brandy walked out of her building at Ashland Industries where she was a customer service representative. The rain definitely matched her mood. "Too many things have been happening at once to me," she muttered to herself. "How can I even stay in focus, let alone deal with customers and all of their problems?"

During the past three months, Brandy's marriage had failed, she had changed jobs because of her need to relocate, and her mother had just called a week before to say that her father was seriously ill. "The only

After studying this chapter, you will be able to:

1. Discuss why change is a fact of life in the 21st century.
2. List the seven major life changes.
3. Describe the seven stages of personal change.
4. Compare and contrast models of organizational change.
5. Give reasons for why employees resist change.
6. Explain the Japanese approach to change in the business world.
7. Discuss organizational development.

11 CHAPTER

STRATEGIES FOR SUCCESS

---

things that have stayed the same are my goals. I'm still really interested in the insurance field, and I know that I want a business degree," she reflected as she walked to her car.

DISCOVERY

"I guess my best bet is to stay focused on the things I know I want for myself while I get used to all these big changes in the best way I can," she resolved.

THINK ABOUT IT

Does Brandy seem to be responding to her major life changes in a positive way? What are some signs that help you form your answer? Would you respond the same way?

CHANGE AS A FACT OF LIFE

Change is a reality we all live with. Swift, radical changes such as the ones Brandy was going through can be overwhelming. In this chapter, you will look at two different types of change. First, you will take a look at the kind of emotional personal changes that Brandy has experienced. Second, you will examine the type of necessary, planned changes that an organization must go through. This chapter also examines how both types of change affect the workplace.

Since the beginning of the Industrial Revolution, change has become a way of life in Western civilization. Centuries ago, it was very likely that you would spend your entire life in the same social class or occupational group. Whatever was meaningful to one generation would remain so in the next. The changes that did take place were usually so gradual that one hardly noticed them.

By the 20th century, the pace of change in all areas of life had picked up greatly, and today it is still increasing. In the past, progress was expressed in terms of *bigger* and *more*. In today's realities, the world has more than ever: more people, more gadgets and electronic devices, more information—and more problems. The industrial world is now learning to emphasize the quality factor in change. Increasingly, people are asking whether a given change is always better. If this trend continues, the future will bring better realities, rather than just more and different ones.[1]

When changes affect your personal life or the lives of those around you, some very specific coping plans are essential. *Coping* means being able to deal with change and its effects without allowing them to injure you emotionally. Significant changes happen to everyone. The first step is to realize that intense change is a part of being a human in today's changing world.

THE SEVEN MAJOR LIFE CHANGES

Holmes–Rahe Readjustment Scale

A tool that measures the relative impact of many kinds of changes, which are rated from 100 to 0 on the basis of their intensity and the adjustment problems they can create.

Severe change can create tremendous stress and is usually accompanied by a great sense of loss. This type of change usually involves something coming to an end—perhaps a marriage, your friendships in a town you had to leave, or a job that was extremely important to you. But stress-causing events aren't always negative; they could also include marriage (the end of life as a single person), promotion (loss of a lower position which was well within your comfort zone, the challenge of new responsibilities), or relocation (loss of familiar surroundings, time and effort needed to learn about the new location).

Figure 11.1 presents the **Holmes–Rahe Readjustment Scale.** This scale lists many kinds of changes, which are rated from 100 to 0 on the

Life Events	Score	Life Events	Score
Death of spouse	100	Trouble with in-laws	29
Divorce	73	Outstanding personal achievement	28
Marital separation from mate	65	Spouse beginning or ceasing to work outside the home	26
Detention in jail, other institution	63	Beginning or ceasing formal schooling	26
Death of a close family member	63	Major change in living conditions	25
Major personal injury or illness	53	Revision of personal habits (dress, manners, associations, etc.)	24
Marriage	50	Trouble with boss	23
Fired from work	47	Major change in working hours or conditions	20
Marital reconciliation	45	Change in residence	20
Retirement	45	Change to a new school	20
Major change in the health or behavior of a family member	44	Major change in usual type and/or amount of recreation	19
Pregnancy	40	Major change in church activities (a lot more or less than usual)	19
Sexual difficulties	39	Major change in social activities (clubs, dancing, movies, visiting)	18
Gaining a new family member (e.g., through birth, adoption, adult moving in, etc.)	39	Taking out a mortgage or loan for a lesser purchase (e.g., for a car, TV, freezer, etc.)	17
Major business readjustment (e.g., merger, reorganization, bankruptcy)	39	Major change in sleeping habits	16
Major change in financial status	38	Major change in the number of family get-togethers	15
Death of close friend	37	Major change in eating habits	15
Change to different line of work	36	Vacation	13
Major change in the number of arguments with spouse	35	Christmas or major holiday season	12
Taking out a mortgage or loan for a major purchase	31	Minor violations of the law (e.g., traffic tickets, etc.)	11
Foreclosure on a mortgage or loan	30	Total	___
Major change in responsibilities at work	29		
Son or daughter leaving home (e.g., marriage, attending college)	29		

Scoring

Less than 150 life change units	30 percent chance of developing a stress-related illness
150–299 life change units	50 percent chance of illness
Over 300 life change units	80 percent chance of illness

figure 11.1

THE HOLMES–RAHE READJUSTMENT SCALE

Read through this scale, and take it as a self-test. Look for events that have happened either to you or to someone close to you. What does your score show?

Source: Adapted from T.H. Holmes and R.H. Rahe, "The Social Readjustment Rating Scale," *Journal of Psychosomatic Research* (Pergamon Press, Ltd., 1967), pp. 217–218.

more about...

Changes and Stress

"From a stress standpoint, you're better off making a choice and having it turn out to be the wrong choice than to have the choice made for you, even if it's right."

—Psychologist Eric Margenau

Source: Quoted in Sharon Faelten et al., *Take Control of Your Life: A Complete Guide to Stress Relief* (Emmaus, PA: Rodale Press, 1988), p. 119.

seven major life changes

Loss, separation, relocation, a change in relationship, a change in direction, a change in health, and personal growth.

MAJOR LIFE CHANGES

Everyone is likely to experience all seven major life changes at least once during their lives. *Which of these changes have happened to you, and how have you managed the stress that came with them?*

basis of their intensity and the adjustment problems they can create. Go through the scale as a self-test. You might find more stress-producing changes in your life than you knew.[2]

The most important dramatic changes in a person's life can be placed in seven categories:

- Loss
- Separation
- Relocation
- A change in relationship
- A change in direction
- A change in health
- Personal growth[3]

Notice that not all of these changes are negative. In fact, some—such as personal growth—are almost completely positive. Often the effects of change are both positive and negative, and yet the impacts are similar.

These **seven major life changes** have basic characteristics in common:

- **They happen to everyone.** Although they don't happen *regularly* to everyone, they are all bound to happen at least a few times throughout one's lifetime. They are simply part of being alive. A change in direction, for example, can come in many different forms—a career change, a change of religion, or a change in values brought about by a near tragedy.

- **Many of them seem to happen without your control.** Changes that are beyond your control (or seem to be) are likely to be more stressful and difficult to deal with than those you can affect. People try their best to hold on to things they can control—factors in their lives about which they feel some certainty—but change often comes to them anyway.

- **Each one of these changes has its own ripple effect.** Significant changes create other changes that go far beyond the original change. Sometimes the most severe trouble comes from the side effects of the major change. For example, a divorce can affect your relationships with your friends, your job, and your extended family.

- **People feel the results of change before, during, and after the event.** You've probably heard someone say that worrying about an event is worse than the event itself. With these seven change areas, that is certainly often the case.

THE SEVEN STAGES OF PERSONAL CHANGE

Humans process major transitions through basic, recognizable steps. Figure 11.2 shows a diagram of the **seven stages of personal change** that make up the process of healthy reaction to such change. An emotionally healthy person takes each of these steps in order.

Suffering through personal losses is never abnormal, nor is admitting your suffering a sign of weakness or inability. The truth is that *failing* to go through each of these steps is often detrimental. If you skip one, you will likely have to return to it at some time.

1. Emotional Standstill

The first reaction someone usually has to the news of a sudden death, for example, is to come to an emotional standstill. "Oh no!" they say. "How did it happen? When?" In shock there is a gap between rational thinking and emotions.[4] In his famous self-help book *Transitions,* William Bridges points out that the **beginning** of the personal change process nearly always involves an **ending.** Admittedly, that sounds ironic. In other words, something that was once an integral part of your life is no longer there.[5] For example, many people think of moving to a new city as stressful because of all the new, strange realities one has to face and learn. Actually, the greatest stress comes from *what you no longer have,* that is, from the losses you have suffered. This would include your old circle of friends, that familiar grocery store, the family physician you'd grown used to, and dozens of other lost connections.

seven stages of personal change
Emotional standstill, denial, anger, helplessness, bottoming out, experimenting, and completion.

beginnings
The *last* of three general steps in the acceptance of personal loss. This is where "experimenting" and "completion" take place.

endings
The *first* of three general steps in the acceptance of personal loss. This is where "emotional standstill," "denial," and "anger" take place.

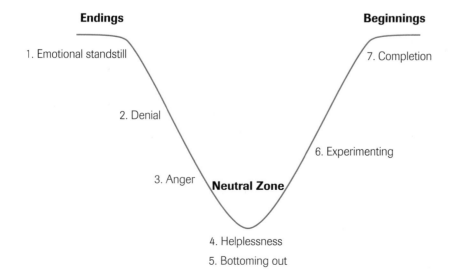

Endings   **Beginnings**

1. Emotional standstill

7. Completion

2. Denial

6. Experimenting

3. Anger   **Neutral Zone**

4. Helplessness

5. Bottoming out

figure 11.2

SEVEN STAGES OF PERSONAL CHANGE

These stages can apply to any serious change in a person's life. It is generally agreed that you will adapt to the change with greater speed and ease if you can take each step in the order in which they appear. *How can you ensure that you moved through each stage with awareness and ease?*

The mother of a large family died unexpectedly. All eight members of the family—except one—reacted openly, showing the emotions they felt in various ways. However, one of the adult sons in the family remained unemotional, not showing any feelings except the surface statements of sorrow. The other family members were quick to say, "I'm worried about Sui-Toon. He's not letting any feelings out. When they finally come out, he's going to have a rough time." None of them are psychologists, but they were right. They acknowledged that all human beings need to go through certain steps in dealing with a personal loss—steps that cannot and should not be avoided. Even though people may have a delayed or mild reaction to such a loss, they will have to process such a change in some way. Several months later, Sui-Toon broke down and spent several weeks in severe depression.

Even when an event is expected, as in the case of a death after a terminal illness, a separation that ends in divorce, or an expected job loss, an element of shock exists. The reality of the event produces a different mental state, no matter how much advance notice is available.

2. **Denial**

Although many peoples' *minds* can accept a major change, they often continue to deny it emotionally. This denial can take many different forms. If the loss is a death, bereaved people might not allow themselves to believe the loved one is really gone. In a divorce, it might be the false hope that the marriage will survive. With denial, the mind is keeping the sufferer from accepting reality fully and completely. Ideally, this denial period will be over in a few weeks or months. The longer the period lasts, the longer it will take to move through the healing process.[6]

3. **Anger**

Some form of anger usually replaces the emotional vacuum left by denial. The anger felt at this time usually contains a feeling of helplessness—of being a victim who was unable to prevent the change. Most psychologists advise that this anger should be expressed in a way that will not harm others. This is the point where support groups can be helpful: having other people who will listen and empathize with you can help you defuse your anger.

4. **Helplessness**

At this step in the process, the individual is trying but still failing to move forward. In Figure 11.2, the individual is shown as having entered the **neutral zone,** what William Bridges calls "a gap in the continuity of existence." This is a temporary state of loss that Bridges says "must be endured."[7] The person is still suffering and now is

neutral zone

The *second* of three general steps in the acceptance of personal loss. The neutral zone is the area where "helplessness" and "bottoming out" take place.

Years ago, when ex-Beatle Paul McCartney was sought out by the British press on the day after the death of his first wife, Linda, he told them that he was sorry, but that he just wasn't ready to make any statements. His was a typical reaction: shock had blanked out other emotions for the time being. He was going through an emotional standstill.

afraid to bottom out into the helpless condition of total despair. The individual will usually make one of two mistakes. Either the suffering person might try to share too much emotion with other people, or will retreat into isolation. Both extremes are negative. The first one is a quick way to lose friends, and the second is self-destructive.[8] To move through this stage effectively, the individual must be constantly aware of the reality of others—that most friends cannot, and should not, enter into another person's sorrow. The others in the person's life should be treated only to small doses of shared grief.

> ### more about...
>
> **Sharing Your Grief**
>
> Not sure how much is too much? The best thing to do is to talk about it: ask your friends and loved ones to honestly tell you their comfort levels. It is also good to ask yourself, "How much will this really benefit me?"

5. **Bottoming out**

   At this bottom point, for the first time since the event, it becomes possible to let go of the emotional burden. Sometimes a person recognizes this turning point by a peaceful feeling that comes upon awakening one morning. More often, the step is gradual. Bottoming out means releasing the thoughts, tensions, memories, and emotions that force you to hold on to the past. At this point, you are allowing the life-completing processes to take their course. The shock, denial, and anger are becoming memories.[9]

6. **Experimenting**

   Once a person bottoms out, the recovery can begin. Normal curiosities and desires come back and new experiences become evident. Notice that Figure 11.2 shows a movement upward—toward healing. If the event was a divorce or death of a spouse, this is the stage where it might become possible to date again. If it was a job loss, your experimentation could be with tasks and opportunities that probably weren't previously considered. Emotions left over for other people and other projects are not all being consumed by your recovery.

   One thing to remember, though, is that people are sometimes forced into another job out of financial necessity, before they are

When Laurie learned that the dot-com company she worked for was downsizing, she refused to believe she would be affected. It was the perfect job with a great salary. When she found out she was one of the many employees who lost their jobs, she became angry. "How could they do this to us?" she said crying as she packed her things. She went home, closed her door, and was unable to do anything that day. The next few days were difficult for Laurie. With the help of some close friends, she found out about some possible jobs. With the support of friends and family, Laurie was able to get through a difficult time in her life.

emotionally ready to adapt. In these cases, the bottoming out and experimenting must be done in different contexts.

regression

Slipping backward to an earlier stage of growth; it can be either temporary or permanent.

7. Completion

Some people call this step *rebirth*. Although that term might sound excessively dramatic, it is somewhat accurate. The cycle is complete. This is not to say that the past won't reemerge, nor does it mean there won't be fallback days. That sort of occasional **regression** is also normal. Now there is a new perspective. You have entered the area of beginnings. You can start anew. Far from being blocked out, the event has become a part of active memory that can be thought about without undue pain.

However, *regression* often takes place, even in the best of mending cycles. Although your progress has been normal and healthy, you still will likely have bad days now and then—days when it seems the change happened only yesterday. The important thing to know about regressions is that it is normal and human and is nothing to be disturbed about.

THE POWER OF DENIAL

Although denial is a normal stage in the change process, dwelling in it for too long will prevent you from adapting to a situation as it really is. *When have you felt yourself dealing with a problem through denial?*

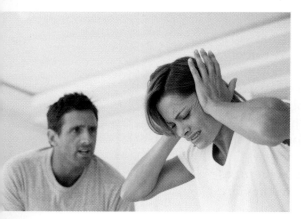

One danger with the seven-step recovery diagram is that people might be tempted to think they should passively let these steps happen to them. The process is a natural process, but sufferers still need to maintain control of their destinies. Going through the steps does require some effort, but millions of people who have never heard of these steps come through them successfully. Knowing what the steps are can help you see that your emotional recovery is both important and normal. It can also help you understand what is happening to you, so that you can evaluate your progress.

Personal change can affect your self-esteem. In fact, any change that affects something or someone close to you

Emotions and Personal Change

Go to **http://ianrpubs.unl.edu/family/nf382 .htm** or link to the article through **www.mhhe .com/lamberton4e.** Under "Adulthood and Aging," find the article on "Understanding Grief and Death" (G1803). What new perspectives does this article shed on the material thus far in this chapter? Write two or three paragraphs reacting to the contents of the article.

is likely to upset your self-concept, which is your view of who you are. (See Chapter 2.) Healing is the process of returning to a point where you know who you are and feel good about yourself once again. Figure 11.3 contains specific advice on how to do this.[10]

Helmstetter's Six Steps for Dealing With Change

In his book *You Can Excel in Times of Change,* Shad Helmstetter lists what he calls Six Steps for Dealing With Change. His application is broader than the major changes you just read about. Rather than dealing with only the large-scale changes, he is writing about all changes that directly affect people's lives.

1. **Recognize and understand the change.** Be sure you can identify the change.
2. **Make the decision to accept or reject the change.** When you include changes over which you might have some control, this is an important decision. When you have no control over it, it's still good to think in terms of acceptance. The seven-step change process you just learned involves accepting the change and allowing it to become a useful part of your life.
3. **Choose the attitude you are going to have toward the change.** People often make the mistake of seeing themselves as victims, unable to form their own attitudes when outside forces affect them. Remember that the choice of what attitude you are going to have is yours and yours alone.
4. **Choose the style that you are going to use to deal with the change.** Some examples of choices are giving in, partnering with someone else, passively or actively resisting, retreating, and actively accepting.
5. **Choose the action that you are going to take *every day*.** A way of dealing with change is to live one day at a time. Each day needs a new plan. Make sure that each day represents a renewed effort.
6. **Review the steps and evaluate your progress daily.** The best way to make that renewed effort is to do a daily progress check. With some idea of where you're headed, your progress can be both faster and more effective.

figure 11.3

DEALING WITH CHANGE

These six steps can help you move through the seven stages and also through any minor, everyday changes you encounter, such as finding a different place to shop after your favorite store goes out of business. *How does this six-step list help you adjust to any change?*

Source: Based on Shad Helmstetter, *You Can Excel in Times of Change* (New York: Simon & Schuster, 1991), pp. 145–180.

MODELS OF ORGANIZATIONAL CHANGE

organizational change

Change that a group of people must learn to accept and implement.

Organizational change is change that a group of people must learn to accept and implement. For a manager, this type of planned change is a real challenge. If not managed correctly, the whole situation could blow up. For an employee, the process requires a sense of flexibility, team spirit, and—often—adventure.

Change is a necessary part of doing business, yet members of an organization can get so comfortable with the *status quo* (the way things already are) that it becomes easy to ignore warning signs that something has to change. Not long ago, the most urgent change issue for most companies was getting online and building and maintaining an accessible Web site. Companies needed to be available online to be competitive both with traditional businesses already online and with the companies who were exclusively doing online business. Despite the obvious pressure for change, some companies found many excuses to avoid taking the necessary steps. Some organizations still held out, but many went out of business. Most of the ones who procrastinated found that when they did finally change, the competition was far ahead of them, especially in many areas related to Web sales and marketing.

One common mistake is that many companies have spent too much money on traditional strategies, instead of changing their style to adopt newer and more creative approaches. Also, many have a hard time adjusting to customer service standards for the Internet, which are more demanding because the customer has many more shopping choices than before. Companies that ignore these necessary changes will probably find themselves failures at e-business.

There are several ways to view and understand organizational change. Next, we look at the Lewin change model, force field analysis, and logical incrementalism.

more about...

E-Business and Change

Perhaps the *only* constant factor in e-business is change, and to thrive in it you must have a high tolerance for uncertainty. How do you feel this fits (or doesn't fit) into American cultural norms?

The Lewin Change Model

Once an organization has established the need to change, management must come up with a method. A good beginning point is to examine a *change model*, which outlines the steps one must take to change an organization effectively.

One of the most popular workplace change models is the **Lewin change model.** Kurt Lewin saw three different levels where any change has to happen. First, the *individuals* who work for a company must be convinced that a change is essential, then guided to the necessary

Lewin change model

A workplace change model with three steps: unfreezing the status quo, making changes, then refreezing to the previous work mode.

attitudes and behaviors. Second, the *systems* of an organization need to be changed. Systems include work design, information systems, and compensation plans. Third, the *organizational climate* must be adjusted. Essential climate change areas include methods of conflict management and the decision-making processes.[11](See Figure 11.4.)

The Lewin change model contains three steps: unfreezing the status quo, moving to a new condition, and refreezing to create a new status quo.[12]

1. *Unfreezing.* In any group change process, people's habits, attitudes, and positions usually have to change to adjust. Sometimes, even personnel must change. On the individual level, this unfreezing could involve promoting employees or letting them go, preparing them for change, or convincing them of the need for the change. On the structural level, redesigning the organization could be the focus of the change effort. On the climate level, the company could create a new open-door policy or begin a data-based feedback system showing how employees are reacting to the proposed changes.[13] In the unfreezing process, *fear* in some form is nearly always one of the major obstacles.

2. *Moving to another condition.* This is the step where the actual changes are made. On the individual level, people should be developing the new skills that are required for the change. On the structural level, you would probably see changes in actual organizational relationships, reward systems, or reporting relationships. On the climate level, there should be more openness and trust, with fewer conflicts.[14]

3. *Refreezing.* Kurt Lewin referred to this final step as being "relatively secure" against change. The refreezing might involve new hiring policies, so that employees hired after the change would be more accepting of the new system. During this stage, the company must ensure that the new behaviors actually become new norms or standards on the job.

Refreezing in the Rapids?

Management expert Peter Vaill has shown that although the Lewin model worked well in slower times, it is much less useful in today's "white water rapids" business climate.

Source: Peter B. Vaill, *Learning as a Way of Being: Strategies for Survival in a World of Permanent White Water* (San Francisco, CA: Jossey-Bass, 1996.)

more about...

figure 11.4

THE LEWIN CHANGE MODEL

This change model shows that to make change, the status quo must first be "unfrozen." After that, you can make change and then, in some cases, refreeze back to your original working environment. *What is your chief criticism of the Lewin change model?*

Source: Based on Jurt Lewin, "Group Decisions and Social Change," in G.E. Swanson, T.M. Newcomb, and E.I. Hartley (eds.), *Readings in Social Psychology* (New York: Holt, Rinehart & Winston, 1952), pp. 459–473.

TECHNOLOGY AND THE RATE OF CHANGE

In e-business, traditional companies have had to learn fast what works and what does not. Traditions are often ignored because there are newer, faster, and more efficient ways to do business on the Internet. In this environment you must be ready and willing to accept almost constant change. *How tolerant toward change are you? What are some ways you could increase your tolerance of change?*

force field analysis

A model in which the status quo is like a battlefield being fought for by two armies: the driving forces and the restraining forces.

Current Criticism

Since the mid-1990s an increasing number of people in the fields of management and organizational behavior have begun to see flaws in this model. The most important criticism has been that refreezing is not a realistic concept in today's business world. The 21st century faces a growing number of change situations, where taking the time to refreeze would simply hinder progress. In the areas of high technology, this scenario seems to be especially accurate. Moreover, nearly every area in today's business world is touched at least indirectly by ever-changing technology. The refreezing step is unrealistic when environmental and technological changes are everyday realities.

The Lewin change model is still useful, however, given this one qualification. In today's world, one must be realistic about the fact that changes take place so rapidly that people don't have the luxury they once had of refreezing, even for a short time, because they may fall behind.[15]

Force Field Analysis

Another approach to change that was developed by Lewin is the concept of **force field analysis** (illustrated in Figure 11.5). According to this model, the status quo is like a battlefield being fought for by two armies: the driving forces and the restraining forces. The driving forces are trying to take over and change the status quo, and the restraining forces are trying to defend it.[16]

In today's world, staying with the status quo is not realistic. As just mentioned, today's world moves too rapidly for that. However, the driving forces generally face the opposition of the restrainers. Much like a real battle, the task is either to build up the driving forces or to decrease the restraining forces in order to win. If driving and restraining forces are equal in strength, no change will take place—only frustration on both sides; and the status quo remains unchanged.

The driving forces can be strengthened in several ways. If resistance takes place, more driving forces must be added. Another method is to improve the quality of the driving forces. Diminishing the restraining forces involves persuasion by showing the benefits of change—in short, eliminating the many factors that keep change from happening.

Force field analysis is positive in three ways. First, it gets the changers to *plan* for the change. Second, it allows those who are organizing the change to take a close look at the forces likely to restrain them and put together a strategy to overcome that restraint. Third, analyzing the restraining forces before a conflict starts can often keep the conflict from beginning at all.[17]

Force Field Analysis

Read Accel Team's discussion of force field analysis at **www.mhhe.com/lamberton4e.** Write a paragraph to explain how you believe this change model applies to today's workplace. Like the Lewin change model, do you think this one needs updating? Why, or why not?

Logical Incrementalism

Another useful model is **logical incrementalism.** This model acknowledges that bringing about changes in a large organization is usually time-consuming and complicated. Many forces, both inside and outside the firm, can put pressure on those who are involved in the planned change. Management professor James Brian Quinn studied many large organizations involved in important changes and devised a system to address those forces.

Like the Lewin model, logical incrementalism can address change at the individual or corporate levels. This approach starts on a general level, then moves slowly into the more specific needs for change.[18]

The five stages of logical incrementalism are:

1. *General concern.* A vague feeling or awareness of a threat or opportunity.
2. *Broadcasting a general concern or idea without details.* The new idea is tried out on others in general terms, with details to be filled in later. This procedure is often described as the *trial balloon.*
3. *Development of a formal plan for change.* The new idea is outlined both in terms of its nature, and of the method of making it happen.

> **logical incrementalism**
> A model that uses a five-step process to implement planned change in a large organization.

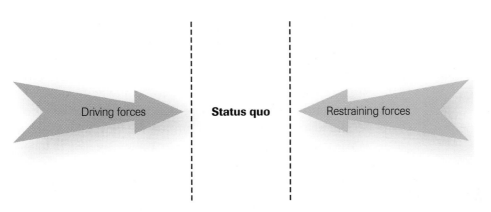

figure 11.5

FORCE FIELD ANALYSIS

This change model compares change with a battlefield, in which some forces attempt to bring change and others attempt to stop it. *What are the positive effects of this change model? How could you use it in planning?*

4. *Using an opportunity or crisis to begin the change plan.* Something important that gets everyone's attention, such as a crisis that the change plan can solve, can be used to get the ball rolling.

5. *Ongoing adaptation of the plan.* Many managers see logical incrementalism as an accurate description of how change occurs in most successful companies. Thus, the model shows a natural process as it should happen. Critics of logical incrementalism see it as generally ineffective; indeed, when the change plan is poorly defined, the process does fail. Logical incrementalism is most successful when used to bring a well-designed plan into general acceptance.[19]

WHY EMPLOYEES RESIST CHANGE

The major problem with getting organizational change to take place is nearly always the same: human opposition. People resist change for a number of different reasons. For one thing, the status quo is often just too comfortable. Employees ask, "Why should I get out of my comfort zone and try something new?" This is because they are more secure in knowing exactly what they are going to do each day.

Among the other reasons people resist change are:

- *Hearing only what they want or expect to hear.* All humans create a world based on their unique perception of reality. Once that world is built, it resists change. People often choose how they see and hear data, and they ignore information that challenges the stability of their world. If an employee's perception of reality is threatened by any introduction of change, that employee might hear and see the arguments for change in a negative way.

- *Fear of the unknown.* As is often perceived in the study of human relations, fear is everywhere. What people do or refuse to do is often influenced by fear, but people would never admit this. "Me, afraid? No, I just can't see why we need a change right now." Fear of the unknown does overwhelm some people—and often becomes a major barrier to organization-wide change.

  - *Fear of loss.* Many people dislike the thought of a major change at work because they feel insecure in their jobs. Back in the 20th century when computerization was new, rumor mills everywhere were issuing stories about people losing their jobs to computers. Few such stories were true. Another common fear involving loss is loss of status. "Maybe I won't be able to learn to operate a computer, and I'll be given a lesser job" could have been the cry of a frightened person during that era.

RESISTING CHANGE

Employees resist change for several reasons, most of which are based on fear and denial. *How have you seen change resisted in an organization, and what happened?*

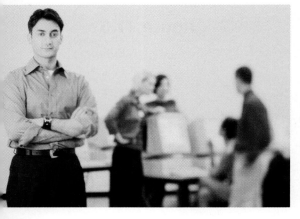

Before Kathleen started college, she had no real sense of what college life would be like. She tried, but she couldn't paint a mental picture of a typical college day and put herself into it. It was frightening because she did not know what to expect. Obviously, though, the fear didn't overwhelm her, because she went on to college—and found that most of the changes she encountered were pleasant ones.

- *Resentment of the change agent.* The person responsible for an organizational change effort is known as a **change agent.** Sometimes, change is resisted because of feelings of hostility or distrust toward the change agent. To counteract this, an effective change agent must build good relations and credibility with people who will be affected by the change. If the change agent is not effective, the change will usually fail.[20]

change agent
The person responsible for an organizational change effort.

- *Belief that the change is wrong.* Many people resist change simply because they are not convinced that the change will work. It is very hard to buy into a change that appears to be doomed. Resistance can also come from resentment or distrust of the *method* that was used to make the change happen. If a company fires several good employees to make a structural change that will save money and guarantee other jobs, other employees may still distrust the company and fear for their own jobs, even if the change does make the promised improvements. This problem can be prevented by encouraging all employees to be involved in the change process in one way or another.

Unfounded Fears

Two decades ago, rumor mills everywhere said that people would lose their jobs to computers. Few of these stories turned out to be true. In fact, computers have created jobs for the people who design, build, program, sell, install, and fix them. They have also enabled people to create thousands of new businesses on the Internet.

more about...

- *Rebellion against the speed of change.* Many change efforts fail because the pace of change is inappropriate either to the situation or the mood of the people. When change takes place too rapidly, without proper initiation or training, employees may rebel.

The other extreme is bringing the change about too slowly. When the pace of change is so sluggish that employees sometimes question whether any real change is going to happen, attitudes again are affected negatively.

You can probably think of other reasons why people resist change. Figure 11.6 lists 25 common excuses. Most are related to either fear or insecurity. Those are the two common denominators that seem to unite people who resist organizational change.

Renata, a word processing supervisor at a large accounting firm, changed all of the computers over a weekend without warning the employees. "They know how to use computers," she thought. "They'll get used to it; they should be happy to have new equipment." She left manuals on everyone's desk in case they had questions.

The employees arrived on Monday morning to find new computer systems. Their reactions were different from what Renata expected. Many of them were not comfortable with computers in general, so any new system seemed foreign and frightening. Renata had to spend the whole morning calming them down. She then had to find somebody in tech support to give everyone lessons on how to use the new computer systems.

THE JAPANESE APPROACH

Despite ups and downs in recent years, Japanese businesses have succeeded impressively, especially in manufacturing. They also seem to be remarkably adaptive to change. Employees are typically involved in

figure 11.6

RESISTING CHANGE

Throughout an organization, people will think of excuses, many similar to those on this list, for resisting change. They may believe in these excuses very strongly and may spend a lot of effort trying to prevent change from occurring. *What can you do when you encounter resistance to change?*

Excuses for Resisting Change

- We don't have time to do it.
- We've tried something like this before, and it didn't work.
- It's impossible; it just won't work.
- It would have worked years ago, but not now.
- You can't teach an old dog new tricks.
- Let's spend some more time thinking about it.
- It's a good idea; it just won't fit this company.
- It's unrealistic; reality will kill it.
- It's not on my job description.
- We're already too busy to start something new.
- Let's appoint a committee to look at it.
- We're too far along to change now.
- The company is doing fine already; who needs it?
- The union just won't go for it.
- Top management won't accept it.
- I like the job the way it is.
- We don't have the technology to make it work.
- Write a report on it, and I'll take a look.
- It will cause conflict in the company.
- It will upset our stockholders.
- Our competitors will jump right on it.
- If it fails, we'll lose our jobs.
- Why haven't our competitors already tried it?
- The results just aren't clear to me.
- Too many changes have been made already.

Sudha, the director of marketing at the same accounting firm as Renata, saw what happened in Renata's department and decided to make her next departmental change very slowly. She changed over to Web marketing by training her staff of 20, one at a time, in detailed training periods that lasted two weeks each. By the time she had nearly finished, nearly a year later, her employees were ready to revolt. "Web marketing changes every day," they complained. "The people in the early training missed the stuff you covered in later training, and the people who weren't trained until the end felt like they were in the dark and being cheated."

change decisions, and most managers communicate change well. (See Figure 11.7.) The following are some specific characteristics of the Japanese approach to change:

1. Japanese managers are generally not hesitant to get the employees directly involved with the change process from the very beginning.

THE JAPANESE APPROACH

Japanese success in manufacturing can be attributed to many factors, but in particular to the way that many Japanese organizations adapt to change. *How is the Japanese approach different from approaches you have witnessed?*

Source: Robert R. Rehder, "Japanese Transplants: A New Model for Detroit," *Business Horizons* (January–February 1988), pp. 52–61.

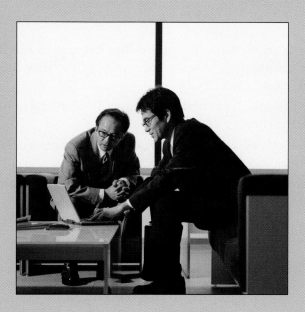

figure 11.7

WELCOME TO CHANGE

Japanese organizational culture encourages change and fosters healthy change in its companies through employee involvement, communication, and intensive research into the problem at hand. *Could your current organization (or the one for which you worked most recently) benefit from this approach?*

From question-and-answer sessions, Japanese managers discover the fears and misgivings of the employee concerning the change, and they receive suggested solutions, many of which are actually used.

2. Before a change takes place, Japanese managers may spend hours studying the problem, examining each possible solution, and analyzing the possible results from any action they might take.

3. Japanese companies typically have few layers of management, which reduces red tape and the traps of bureaucracy. It also encourages communication to take place in all areas of the firm.

4. If a problem comes up in the change process, most Japanese companies don't blame the employees. Instead, they blame the process, the system, or the management.[21]

ORGANIZATIONAL DEVELOPMENT

organizational development (OD)

A planned, companywide, systematic method of achieving change in an organization.

Organizational development (OD) is a planned, companywide, systematic method of achieving change in an organization. It requires the participation and support of top management. Usually the change agent is an outside consultant who specializes in planned change. This person is called an **OD change agent.** This agent's job is to use **OD interventions,** which are training tools that teach members of the organization how they can solve the problems they are facing.

OD change agent

A company's formal change agent, often an outside consultant who specializes in planned change.

OD change agents base their procedures on specific ideals concerning organizations. These specific ideals usually involve the following values:[22]

OD interventions

Training tools that teach members of the organization how to solve the problems they face.

1. *Participative operations.* The more that employees are involved with a change effort, the stronger their commitment will be to putting that change into effect.

2. *Equality.* Effective organizations must de-emphasize hierarchy and heavy-handed authority.

3. *Respect for others.* Since people are mostly responsible and conscientious, they should be treated accordingly.

4. *Confrontation.* Problems are to be confronted and dealt with immediately, never swept under the carpet.

5. *Trust and mutual support.* A climate of openness and trust is the most productive in any organization.

Nearly all of the emphasis of organizational development is on changes affecting people and their relationships. Thus, the importance of OD to human relations is obvious. Today OD is often used as a tool for **empowerment.** Empowered employees feel that they are in control of their own contributions to the firm. OD interventions can serve another purpose— to help make employees more comfortable and accepting of the new position that empowerment gives them.

more about...

OD Interventions

OD interventions include team building, sensitivity training, role playing, and survey feedback. Members of the organization are involved in the implementation process.

《 《 **STRATEGIES FOR SUCCESS**

11.1   Managing Personal Change in the Workplace

1. Become aware of it.
2. Talk about the change.
3. Maintain the organizational ideal.

When personal changes take place, they are nearly always both unavoidable and energy-consuming. These steps can be helpful in such situations, both to managers and to fellow workers.

1. **Become aware of it.** Don't distance yourself from all issues that seem personal. Major life changes are never *just* personal because they nearly always affect the workplace in many ways.

2. **Talk about the change.** By doing this, you allow the affected person to talk about it. People can often bear large emotional burdens if they just have an opportunity to talk about their situation and their feelings.

3. **Maintain the organizational ideal.** Recognize that although this person is in a special part of his or her life, and needs careful handling, the tasks of the organization still must be done. Work with the present limitations of the person, yet insist that goals be achieved. You are not doing anyone a favor by allowing the workplace to be a temporary vacation spot.[23]

11.2   Breaking Down the Resistance to Change in Your Organization

1. Create a climate where change is acceptable.
2. Involve everyone in the change effort.

Resistance to change is often caused by poor communication, resulting in a hazy understanding of the purpose and consequences of the change. Given the potential for resistance, what steps can be taken to overcome antichange forces? One approach is to be honest and open. The manager can communicate to employees the entire situation with all of its implications. Usually in a situation that calls for change, the alternative—remaining the same—will produce negative consequences. Employees should know specifically what those consequences will be, and how their positions will be affected.

1. **Create a climate where change is acceptable.** The manager's responsibility is to create a work environment that allows employees to be comfortable with change. This includes educating employees and communicating with them on an ongoing basis. If managers maintain a rigid, inflexible attitude toward new ideas, they create climates that discourage change-oriented thinking. A manager who communicates with employees only when a change is coming misses the power that regular communication brings.

2. **Involve everyone in the change effort.** People who have been involved with the creation of a change will find that change is very difficult to resist. Even when employees don't have the expertise to make technical decisions connected to a change effort, they usually can be involved somewhere in the process. Sometimes top management orders a change, and the supervisor must announce it to employees. Some participation is better than none at all. One note of caution: employees should be told how their input is going to be handled. If their advice will be considered but they will not actually have a vote, this should be clearly stated. Failure to make that point clear can result in very low morale.

CHAPTER ELEVEN SUMMARY

Chapter Summary by Learning Objectives

1. **Discuss why change is a fact of life in the 21st century.** Since the beginning of the Industrial Revolution, changes have come with increasing speed. When we think about change in today's world, we often think about changing technologies. That is the area of the most obvious change. However, social change is also a common part of 21st century life. Despite all of the changes, individuals and groups at work often fight against change when it is introduced.

2. **List the seven major life changes.** The seven major life changes are loss, separation, relocation, a change in relationship, a change in direction, a change in health, and personal growth. These are not all negative, but all have important impacts on people's lives.

3. **Describe the seven stages of personal change.** The normal person requires a process of adjustment to cope realistically with dramatic changes. The process involves emotional standstill, denial, anger, helplessness, bottoming out, experimenting, and completion.

4. **Compare and contrast models of organizational change.** Several models can be used for the process of group change management. They are the Lewin change model, force field analysis, and logical incrementalism. The Lewin change model has been strongly challenged recently because the refreezing step is often unrealistic in today's

high-tech environment. All three change models describe the forces of change and deal with human opposition to the change effort.

5. **Explain some reasons why employees resist change.** One important reason for employee resistance of change is fear of loss. Also, workers often resent the change agent, or actually believe that the change is wrong. Another reason is resistance to the speed of the change (either too fast or too slow).

6. **Explain the Japanese approach to change in the business world.** Japanese managers get employees directly involved in the change effort. Before the change, managers in Japan spend long hours studying the problem, analyzing possible results from different possible cures. Also, Japanese companies, with their fewer layers of management, are able to make change decisions with little "red tape." Perhaps most importantly the Japanese tend to blame the system for problems, rather than blaming workers.

7. **Discuss organizational development.** Organizational development is a planned, company-wide, systematic method of change achievement in an organization. It involves employees in implementing humanizing changes that are based on workplace equality and participation.

key terms

beginning 285

change agent 295

ending 285

force field analysis 292

Holmes–Rahe Readjustment Scale 282

Lewin change model 290

logical incrementalism 293

neutral zone 286

OD change agent 298

OD interventions 298

organizational change 290

organizational development (OD) 298

regression 288

seven major life changes 284

seven stages of personal change 285

1. Many major changes are listed in the Holmes–Rahe Readjustment Scale. What characteristics do they all have in common? Explain. What factors would you add or otherwise change in this scale?

2. Explain the seven steps of personal change management. Why are they all essential?

3. Imagine yourself as a manager with an employee who is going through a painful divorce that is affecting his or her quality of job performance. How could the material in this chapter be helpful to you?

4. Do you agree with the critics of the Lewin change model who say that it is no longer relevant—especially refreezing? Why or why not?

5. Briefly explain how force field analysis can be helpful to someone attempting change in an organization.

6. Someone once said that recognizing the need for change is the most difficult step in the change process. Why would that be true? Explain.

7. Explain the concepts behind logical incrementalism. Make sure to discuss the different steps that organizations go through based on James Brian Quinn's research of meaningful changes within organizations. Do you find this model helpful? Why or why not? Do you think it would ever be helpful in managing change in a smaller company? Why or why not?

8. What is organizational development? How is it used in a company that wants change? On what types of change does it usually focus?

9. How has change impacted your own life? When you reflect on your past, which changes were positive? Which changes were negative? Did changes that you originally thought would be negative turn out to be positive? In general, do you see change as mostly a positive or negative force? Explain why.

10. Identify organizations you have seen or heard about that resisted change. Why did they resist change? What consequences did such companies suffer, if any?

TURBULENT WORLD TOLERANCE TEST

School-to-Work Connection: Information Skills

Purpose: To discover your own level of tolerance for life in an ever-changing reality.

Procedure: Listed next are some statements a 37-year-old manager made about his job at a large, successful corporation. If your job had these characteristics, how would you react to them? After each statement there are five letters, *a* to *e*. Circle the letter that *best* describes how you think you would react according to the following scale:

a. I would enjoy this *very much;* it is completely acceptable.

b. This would be enjoyable and acceptable most of the time.

c. I'd have no reaction to this feature one way or the other, or it would be equally enjoyable and unpleasant.

d. This feature would be somewhat unpleasant for me.

e. This feature would be *very* unpleasant for me.

1. I regularly spend 30 to 40 percent of my time in meetings.

   a   b   c   d   e

2. A year and a half ago, my job did not exist, and I have been essentially inventing it as I go along.

   a   b   c   d   e

3. The responsibilities I either assume or am assigned consistently exceed the authority I actually have for discharging them.

   a   b   c   d   e

4. At any given moment in my job, I have an average of about a dozen phone calls to be returned.

   a   b   c   d   e

5. There seems to be very little relation in my job between the quality of my performance and my actual pay and fringe benefits.

   a   b   c   d   e

6. About two weeks a year of formal management training is needed in my job just to stay current.

   a   b   c   d   e

7. Because we have very effective equal employment opportunity in my company and because it is thoroughly multinational, my job consistently brings me into close working contact at a professional

level with people of both sexes and of many races, ethnic groups, and nationalities.

a   *b*   *c*   *d*   *e*

8. There is no objective way to measure my effectiveness.

a   *b*   *c*   *d*   *e*

9. I report to three different bosses for different aspects of my job, and each has an equal say in my performance appraisal.

a   *b*   *c*   *d*   *e*

10. On average, about a third of my time is spent dealing with unexpected emergencies that force all scheduled work to be postponed.

a   *b*   *c*   *d*   *e*

11. When I need to have a meeting of the people who report to me, it takes my secretary most of a day to find a time when we are all available. Even then, I have yet to hold a meeting when everyone is present for the entire time.

a   *b*   *c*   *d*   *e*

12. The college degree I earned in preparation for this type of work is now obsolete, and I should probably go back and get another degree.

a   *b*   *c*   *d*   *e*

13. My job requires that I absorb 100–200 pages per week of technical materials.

a   *b*   *c*   *d*   *e*

14. I am out of town overnight at least one night per week.

a   *b*   *c*   *d*   *e*

15. My department is so interdependent with several other departments in the company that all distinctions about which departments are responsible for which task are quite arbitrary.

a   *b*   *c*   *d*   *e*

16. I will probably get a promotion in about a year to a job in another division that has most of these same characteristics.

a   *b*   *c*   *d*   *e*

17. During the period of my employment here, either the entire company or the division I worked in has been reorganized every year or so.

a   *b*   *c*   *d*   *e*

18. Although there are several possible promotions I can see ahead of me, I have no real career path in an objective sense.

a   *b*   *c*   *d*   *e*

19. Although there are several possible promotions I can see ahead of me, I think I have no realistic chance of getting to the top levels of the company.

    a   *b*   *c*   *d*   *e*

20. Although I have many ideas about how to make things work better, I have no direct influence on either the business policies or the personnel policies that govern my division.

    a   *b*   *c*   *d*   *e*

21. My company has recently created an *assessment center* where I and all other managers will be required to go through an extensive battery of psychological tests to assess our potential.

    a   *b*   *c*   *d*   *e*

22. My company is a defendant in an antitrust suit, and if the case comes to trial, I will probably have to testify about some decisions that were made a few years ago.

    a   *b*   *c*   *d*   *e*

23. Advanced computer and other electronic office technology is continually being introduced into my division, necessitating constant learning on my part.

    a   *b*   *c*   *d*   *e*

24. The computer I have in my office can be monitored by my bosses' offices without my knowledge.

    a   *b*   *c*   *d*   *e*

Scoring: Score 4 points for each *a,* 3 for each *b,* 2 for each *c,* 1 for each *d,* and 0 for each *e.* Compute the total, divide by 24, and round off to one decimal place.

Although the results are not intended to be more than suggestive, the higher your score, the more comfortable you seem to be with change in today's world. The test's author suggests analyzing scores as if they were grade-point averages. In this way, a 4.0 average is an A, and so forth.

Using replies from nearly 500 MBA students and young managers, the range of scores was found to be narrow—between 1.0 and 2.2. The average score was between 1.5 and 1.6—equivalent to a D/C grade. If these scores can be generalized to apply to the work population, clearly people are not very tolerant of the kind of changes that come with a turbulent environment.

Source: Peter B. Vaill, *Managing as a Performing Art: New Ideas for a World of Chaotic Change* (San Francisco: Jossey-Bass, 1989), Exhibit 1, pp. 8–9. Copyright 1989 by Jossey-Bass, Inc., Publishers. Code 8913. Used with permission.

1. *Read and Write*

   Find out about Kurt Lewin's change model. The Web site address can be found through **www.mhhe.com/lamberton4e.** Write a brief paragraph to answer each of these questions:

   a. Do you feel that this theory is outdated; if so, how?

   b. How does this theory still work in today's business world?

   c. Did you learn anything that you consider useful?

2. *Personal Life Changes*

   Go to **www.eoslifework.co.uk/transmgt1.htm** or link to the article through the Web site at **www.mhhe.com/lamberton4e.** You will access the Eos Life-Work Centre. Choose one of the seven categories and click on the one that interests you most. If you can't decide, try "Personal Life Changes." Write a brief summary of the material you have found there.

3. *Self-Assess and Apply*

   Go through the steps in the "Job Search 101 Tutorial" published on the Web by Quintessential Careers. Link to their Web page through **www.mhhe.com/lamberton4e** or go directly to **www.quintcareers. com/job_search/plan.html.** The steps in this tutorial provide advice in helping you determine what type of job you want, based on where you want to live, what type of company you want to work for, and so on. After going through the tutorial, summarize what you found. Look at the list of "Career Tutorials" for others that you may find useful.

The Web Page Fiasco

Carole Monroe is the marketing vice president for Sharpco, a small company that designs and markets business forms. Every year her firm holds a client council conference. More than an hour of the morning meeting involves all Sharpco employees leaving the room while an independent management consultant listens to candid suggestions from clients for improving Sharpco's operations. For the past three years, most of the criticisms have been aimed at technology, specifically at how Sharpco is not keeping pace.

A year ago, clients complained that Sharpco had an inadequate Web site. "I'd really like to be able to use the Web to order," one major client suggested. This year's conference featured the same complaints, but voiced even more loudly. Carole said to her assistant Eldon Brown after the meeting, "I can't figure out why Doug and Marge are dragging their feet on expanding the Web page. They've got to know that these customers are right; all of our competitors can order from Web pages. We'll get trounced if we don't act fast."

"As the senior partners in this company, Doug and Marge have the most to lose if they don't get going," said Eldon. "What do you think the real problem is on this issue?"

"I'll tell you what I think," answered Carole. "They're both frightened. For some reason, this Web page ordering thing scares them silly."

"Well, then," replied Eldon, "it's our job to do whatever we can to find out the exact fear and help get rid of it. Our future as a company depends on it."

"I totally agree," Carole answered. "Let's work to resolve this problem."

Case Study Questions

1. Do you agree that fear is likely the main issue here? If not, what other factors might be involved?

2. Assume for a moment that fear is at least a major issue here. What can Carole and Eldon do, as marketing specialists, to attack the fear that seems to be delaying progress to a danger point?

3. Briefly evaluate the client council conference as a device for change suggestions from major clients. Would such an approach work in other types of organizations?

The Family Tragedy

It was midafternoon on a busy Friday when everyone in the company learned that Carlos Garcia had been seriously injured in an auto accident. Juanita, Carlos's partner in life, was a popular agent at Javca Insurance. Carlos himself was a former employee of Javca and was himself very well known and loved by many in the company. The weekend was to be a long one: doctors immediately placed Carlos in intensive care, and his condition remained critical. Javca employees swarmed through the hospital, encouraging family members, hoping for the best, and praying in the small chapel near the intensive care unit.

Early on Sunday morning, Carlos lost the fight. With only 24 hours to get back into a working frame of mind, the Javca employees struggled to make up some badly missed sleep. Needless to say, the situation wasn't exactly business as usual when Monday morning came. Nobody seemed to be working up to speed, and the company was uncharacteristically quiet. Customers who walked unknowingly into the service office inevitably asked what was wrong.

Days passed, then weeks. Soon the surface behavior of the employees seemed to return to normal, but more than ever the focus was still on Juanita. She had seemed numb at first, but now her behavior seemed confusing. Some days she acted nonchalantly, denying that she was having a tough time—then she would suddenly show a burst of anger. Few of her coworkers understood exactly why she was acting this way.

Devi Ramasamy, the CEO, decided to bring in a grief counselor. When she described the situation to the counselor, he said, "It sounds to me like everybody at Javca needs this, not just Juanita."

Case Study Questions

1. How could an understanding of the seven steps of personal change help everyone at Javca?

2. Explain the grief counselor's statement, "It sounds like everybody at Javca needs this, not just Juanita."

3. There are some obvious disadvantages to the company in keeping Juanita at work at this time. What are some advantages of having her remain on the job during her healing process?

CREATIVITY AND HUMAN RELATIONS

In the Workplace: More Than Two Ways

SITUATION

The community college business club held its first annual flea market in the fall. Despite hard work and much planning, the results were turning out to be disappointing. It was an indoor event, but customers wanted to be outdoors on what turned out to be a beautiful autumn day. Also, a similar event was being held nearby—out in the open.

Around lunchtime, the club members met to decide how to salvage the day. One member suggested giving the participants back their table space rental money and taking only 10 percent of their sales, rather than both, as contracted. Someone else suggested the opposite: just keep their rental money, but don't ask for a percentage. Then members took sides on those two approaches and argued. After 20 minutes, the members with the louder voices and greater persuasive ability won. The club then announced to each of the participants that they wouldn't be asked to pay the percentage.

310

LEARNING objectives

After studying this chapter, you will be able to:

1. Explain the importance of creativity.
2. Define creativity.
3. Discuss the relationship between perception and creativity.
4. List the steps in the creative process.
5. Describe creativity in the workplace.
6. Compare and contrast creative methods for groups.
7. Give examples of ways to solve problems creatively.

STRATEGIES FOR SUCCESS

Strategy 12.1   Increase Your Creativity

Strategy 12.2   Roger von Oech's "Ten Mental Locks"

Strategy 12.3   Use SCAMPER to Solve Problems

DISCOVERY

When the club adviser, a management instructor, returned from lunch and heard about the decision, she was irate. "What happened to creative problem solving?" she asked. "You've made the old mistake of choosing from two alternatives, while ignoring other creative possibilities." Earlier, the adviser had polled the participants. Only 12 of the 40 had been seriously unhappy with the sales they had made. "With a little creativity, you could have come up with a solution to make everyone happy and still realize a nice profit. I hope you've all learned a lesson from this," she exclaimed. The club later estimated that they had lost over $700 just from one bad, noncreative decision.

THINK ABOUT IT

What could the members of the business club have done to improve their creative process? What would you have suggested if you had been a club member in this situation?

THE CREATIVITY CONNECTION

creativity

The ability to produce ideas or problems to solutions that are unique, appropriate, and valuable.

You may be wondering what a chapter on creativity is doing in a human relations textbook. At first the connection might indeed seem vague. However, you will see in this chapter how much **creativity**—the ability to produce ideas, or solutions to problems, that are unique, appropriate, and valuable—has to do with self-esteem and, in turn, your relationships with other people. Creativity is your ability to come up with original and effective solutions. Simply put, it is thinking up new and useful ideas.[1] Business factors such as the number and quality of products created are affected strongly by the creativity of the people in an organization.

The importance of creativity cannot be overstated. International competition is forcing American businesses to take a new look at how American creativity compares with that of other nations. U.S. companies are emphasizing creativity to an extent that hasn't been seen since the late 1950s. When the Russians launched Sputnik, the first satellite, in 1957, Americans feared that the Russians were going to win the space race. As a result, nationwide campaigns began for better scholarship and creativity. Now, Americans are trying to increase creativity for a different reason: international business competition. Many companies and some countries have started taking the creativity issue seriously. Hewlett-Packard has established what they call a "solution factory" that uses creativity to solve an amazing 99.6 percent of the problems customers bring them.[2] In the past several years, companies from China have shown an increasing ability to find creative methods of entering new parts of the global marketplace.[3]

Creativity is something that no one completely understands. You can usually tell the difference between what is creative and what isn't, but can you really put your finger on what causes creativity? To truly understand creativity, you need to understand yourself.

more about...

Creativity and the Future

". . . concepts such as artificial intelligence and neural networking could put us in the position of being intellectual inferiors by the year 2021. . . . Many of us will live to see [that] happen. But we shouldn't panic. In the meantime, what John C. Lilley called the 'human biocomputer' will remain the only mechanism on earth that can think creatively and develop new and original ideas—which means that we get to determine the future and the role that technology will play."

Source: Nick Souter, *Breakthrough Thinking: Brainstorming for Inspiration and Ideas* (New York: Sterling Publishing, 2007), p. 8.

WHAT IS CREATIVITY?

A good place to start in defining creativity is to decide what creativity *is not*. Research has shown that creativity has little to do with personality type, with the materials used in creating, with the products produced, or with a particular environment. In other words, people can be creative whether they are outgoing or shy, naive or sophisticated, impulsive or steady as a rock. They can also be creative whether they are involved in

Creativity Exercises

Go to a creativity Web site or link from **www.mhhe .com/lamberton4e** or access the site directly at **www. cre8ng.com/newsletter/news23.shtml.** You will find a huge list of creativity exercises at this site. Choose the one that seems to be the most interesting and useful to you and respond in whatever manner requested. Hand both the exercise exactly as it was written and the results to your instructor.

painting, writing, architecture, mathematics, teaching, or child rearing. They can be creative in the city or the country, in poverty or in wealth.[4]

So what *is* creativity? Psychologist Mihalyi Csikszentmihalyi, whom you first read about in Chapter 4, describes creative people as having flexibility and fluency in ideas, with the ability to know a good idea from a bad one.[5]

Csikszentmihalyi also makes a distinction between creativity with a big "C" and with a small "c." The large "C" type sees creativity as a new concept or item that is accepted and valued by society and really is produced to fulfill that role—not just dreamed about. The small "c" variety is related more to one's personal experience. It directly affects the individual's life, making it more energized, interesting, and stimulating. The small "c" makes life more fun, but it doesn't make you successful or famous.[6] In this chapter, we will be examining both of these areas.

Because people often use the word *genius* when talking about extremely creative people, many make the mistake of linking creativity with traditional intelligence. You have probably heard stories about creative people, such as Thomas Edison and Albert Einstein, who did badly in school. Actually, **intuition,** which is direct perception or insight, has been shown to be much more important to creativity than scholastic ability. "You don't have to have a high IQ to be intuitive," said the late Frank Barren, a psychologist at the University of California at Santa Cruz who studied creativity for the last half century. "Intuition depends less on reasoning and verbal comprehension [the main devices used to measure IQ] than it does on feelings and metaphor."[7]

> **intuition**
> Direct perception or insight.

How are traditional intelligence and creativity linked? How close to being a genius do you have to be in order to be creative? These questions were asked by Lewis Terman in 1921. Terman was a pioneer in the study of intelligence, intelligence testing, and creativity. Terman followed more than 1,500 academic geniuses throughout their lives and found that they usually excelled in their careers, were socially and personally well adjusted, and were physically healthier than others. They were not, however, likely to be more creative than other people. By 1959, after almost 40 years, not one of them had produced highly creative works or been awarded Pulitzer or Nobel Prizes.[8]

Since Terman's pioneering research many other psychologists have reported similar findings. Creative people are usually average or above average in intelligence, but being a genius (in the way that traditional intelligence is measured) does not automatically make someone creative. Review Chapter 10 for a more complete treatment of the different types of intelligence.

Csikszentmihalyi says that although creative people tend to be smart, they are often also naive. To be truly creative a person has to be able to engage in what Csikszentmihalyi calls "divergent thinking." Just learning the facts and rules—even learning them very well—is not enough. A creative person will be able to challenge those facts and rules, or nothing new is likely to be created.[9]

PERCEPTION AND CREATIVITY

Most of the researchers who have studied creativity agree that creative people are somehow able to get away from the ordinary, everyday way of seeing things. In his book *The Act of Creation,* Arthur Koestler describes all of the major scientific inventions of the past and shows the creative processes that produced them. Koestler says that *habit* is the stumbling block to creativity. How many people throughout history never tried to invent the airplane because they were in the habit of believing that humans cannot fly?[10] Even Galileo, the great pioneer astronomer, fell into this trap. He saw comets through his telescope, but refused to accept them because he was used to believing that all heavenly bodies must move in a circle. Those that didn't move in circles, he decided incorrectly, were optical illusions.

collective habits of thought

Ways of thinking that occur when groups have their own beliefs about *what* should be done and *how* it should be done.

perception

The way in which a person views the world.

Likewise, groups of people (such as companies, committees, and universities) are often unable to move beyond habits of thinking.[11] Groups often have their own beliefs about *what* should be done and *how* it should be done; these are called **collective habits of thought.** Both individuals and groups need to get past the old, established ways of seeing things if they are going to increase their creativity.

Perception is the way in which a person views the world. When you are sitting in a classroom with 25 other students and your instructor, in a sense, there are 27 different instructors teaching the class. This is because everything that each person sees is filtered through his or her own perceptions. Each person in the room *perceives* the instructor in a slightly different way.

more about...

Imagination

"Imagination is more important than knowledge."

—Albert Einstein

Being able to look at the world from different angles makes a great difference in how creatively you deal with the world and solve problems.

When Albert Einstein was 14 years old, he asked an interesting question: "What would the world look like," he asked, "if I rode on a beam of light?" As an adult, he finally answered the question, and that answer became the principle of relativity.[12] Einstein was like many others labeled as *creative geniuses:* he started out with a unique perception and built an answer. It's easy to see why he achieved as much as he did.[13]

Consider Einstein's question: "What would the world look like if I rode on a beam of light?" Research has shown that highly creative people aren't afraid to ask what might seem to be silly or childish questions. They might ask questions such as: "Why do rivers rarely run north?" or "Why don't spiders get tangled up in their own webs?" The curiosity everyone has as a child is an essential part of the creative process. Most major discoveries would not have been made without curiosity. Whatever you can do to retain or regain some of that childlike curiosity will help you produce more creative ideas.

Abraham Maslow, who is best known for his hierarchy of needs theory (Chapter 6) has also talked about highly creative people. In his words, "They tend to be called childish by their more compulsive colleagues, irresponsible, wild, crazy." His opinion has elements of truth. "It should be stressed," he went on, "that in the early stages of creativeness, you've got to be a bum or a Bohemian or an eccentric."[14] By this remark, Maslow means that by remaining in and being unduly influenced by conventional society, any thinking is likely to become conventional and noncreative. The lesson for businesspeople is to learn to look beyond the conventional business world for ideas.

No matter how you score on the perception test in Figure 12.1, be aware that your perceptions are just that—*your* perceptions. Other peoples' perceptions also have their own life and reality. Both are open to be challenged, reexamined, and reevaluated.

Sometimes people's perceptions are blocked or distorted by rules that they think they need to follow. Often, they are rules that actually don't exist. The **nine-dot puzzle** is often used as an example of people's respect for such rules. Participants are told to connect nine dots using only four straight lines, without lifting the pen or pencil from the paper.

nine-dot puzzle

A puzzle that is used to show people's respect for rules that don't exist. Participants are asked to connect nine dots using only four straight lines, without lifting the pen off the paper. Most fail because they feel the need to stay "inside the box" formed by the nine dots.

CURIOSITY AS CREATIVITY

Sometimes your ability to solve problems creatively is limited by your fear of being childish. However, using the "childish" freedom of curiosity is an important way of increasing your creativity. *What kinds of questions can you ask—and answer—by being curious and thinking creatively?*

figure 12.1

PERCEPTIONS

Take this quiz and evaluate how typically creative or ordinary your responses are. Remember, though, that this short quiz cannot give any final answers about your creativity. *In what areas do you want to be more creative?*

Source: Based on Sugato Lahiry, "A Blueprint for Perception Training," reprinted from *Training and Development* (August 1991), pp. 21–25. Copyright August 1991, the American Society for Training and Development. Reprinted with permission. All rights reserved.

Your Perceptions: Creative or "Ordinary"?

What is your perception of reality? Here are a few statements about perception. Read each one, then decide whether it is true or false.

_____ **1.** A fact is a fact. There can be no difference of views on something that is a fact.

_____ **2.** If two people view the same event differently, it is only logical to conclude that one of them is right and the other one is wrong.

_____ **3.** Your perceptions of people and events are almost always colored by your attitudes, values, and beliefs.

_____ **4.** Intelligent people do not ascribe meanings to things and events, they take them as they are.

_____ **5.** People usually see what they want to see.

_____ **6.** In perceiving people, events, and objects, people have a natural tendency to leave out certain aspects that don't square with their views.

_____ **7.** Besides a person's qualities and mannerisms, there are other factors that can influence the way you see that person.

_____ **8.** If you are careful, you can always trust your eyes and ears to give you a true picture of the world around you.

_____ **9.** You view the world around you through your own colored glasses.

_____ **10.** Differences in views about people, objects, and events usually result from different levels of intelligence.

How did you do? If you got more than two wrong, you need to take a closer look at perception.

1. F, **2.** F, **3.** T, **4.** F, **5.** T, **6.** T, **7.** T, **8.** F, **9.** T, **10.** F

Try it. Can you do it? An amazing number of people won't come up with the solution because they are afraid that by going outside of the "square" that is formed by the nine dots, they are breaking a taboo or a rule of some kind. Even some people who solve the puzzle will ask, "Is this cheating?"

As James Adams from Stanford University explains it, all people who live in civilization have developed an unconscious but very strong respect for squares and rectangles. These are shapes that don't occur in nature. Because of this irrational but very real "hang-up," most people are stumped by the puzzle.[15] You can find solutions to the puzzle at the end of this chapter on page 340.

Additional characteristics of creative people include:

1. *Expert knowledge.* It is difficult to be creative about things that you don't know much about. Creative people generally come up with new ideas and solutions to problems in their own, or related, areas of

expertise. The process of becoming an expert in any field is a good beginning point for creativity because it takes practice and hard work to become an expert at anything. On the other hand, you do not have to be a top expert in your field to be creative in it.

2. *Openness to new experiences.* Creative people are typically less rigid and more flexible than most other people. Rather than being closed-minded or inhibited, they are curious and questioning. Later in this chapter, this idea of being in the *open mode* (open to new ideas) will be explored again.

3. *Independent spirit.* Creative people are usually independent thinkers who prefer to do things their own way. They don't mind working alone, and they are not easily swayed by others' opinions. They are usually seen as nonconformists, which is not surprising since conforming hampers creativity.

4. *Internal motivation.* Creative people are usually motivated by intrinsic motivators. As you learned in Chapter 6, **intrinsic (or internal) motivators** are those that motivate a person from within, such as the joy and excitement of the discovery process. These move people more than **extrinsic (or external) motivators,** which are motivators that come from outside sources, such as money and fame. These ideas will be discussed again later in this chapter.

5. *Persistence.* Creativity requires patience, hard work, and the ability to persevere. Many ideas fail when turned into action, but persisting with new ideas and solutions allows the creative person to eventually succeed.[16]

intrinsic motivators
Factors that motivate a person from within, such as the joy and excitement of the discovery process.

extrinsic motivators
Those motivators that come from outside sources, such as money and fame.

British comedian John Cleese gives an example of the rewards that come from looking for the second right answer. He emphasizes the ways in which creativity and persistence allow for a quality finished product. "I was always intrigued that one of my Monty Python colleagues, who seemed more talented than I was, did not produce scripts as original as mine. I watched for some time and then began to see why. If he were faced with a problem and fairly soon saw the solution, he was inclined to take it, even though the solution was not very original. Whereas if I were in the same situation, although I was sorely tempted to take the easy way out, and finish by 5 P.M., I just couldn't! I'd sit there with the problem for another hour and a quarter, and by sticking it out, almost always come up with something more original. It was that simple. My work was almost always more creative than his because I was prepared to stick with the problem longer."[17] Thus, hard work and dedication play a role in creativity, as well.

A couple of decades ago, a young mother went toy shopping for her two-year-old daughter. To her dismay, all she could find were poorly made plastic toys, not the durable long-lasting ones like those her daughter played with at her day-care center. Although she had no business

Fingertip Creativity

Developed by Southwell Enterprises, "Fingertip Creativity" contains dozens of examples of creative solutions to business problems, marketing ideas, and operational concepts. Go to **www.privateclubexclusive.com/fingertip_ creativity.htm** directly, or go to **www.mhhe.com/** **lamberton4e** for a link to this site and read any three of the selections. Answer these questions in a brief paragraph: What did you find out from this site? Do you think the solutions tie in with the creativity process described in this chapter? Why, or why not?

experience, the woman borrowed $5,000 from her grandmother to start her own company. The woman was Lane Nemeth, and the toy company was Discovery Toys, a company that now makes over $70 million in gross sales every year. Ms. Nemeth saw a need that probably thousands of parents had already seen; her important contribution to the creative process was *putting the solution of that need into action*.[18]

In other words, creativity doesn't do anyone much good if ideas aren't followed through with action. As Thomas Edison once said, "Creativity is 1 percent inspiration and 99 percent perspiration." He was right. Without putting your ideas into action, creativity is meaningless.

INSIDE THE CREATIVE PROCESS

> **creative process**
>
> The way in which creativity helps you develop ideas and solve problems.

Even though there is much about creativity that we don't really understand, we can trace the *process* of creativity as it happens in most people. The idea of the **creative process**—the way in which creativity helps you develop ideas and solve problems—has been around since the 1920s. At that time, Graham Wallas described four basic steps or stages in this process.[19] This model is still in use today by psychologists to describe the process of creativity. Whether we intend to do so or not, most of us follow some fairly consistent steps whenever we create anything.[20]

Step One: Perception and Preparation

As mentioned earlier, *perception* is the beginning point for creativity. The first part of dealing with a creativity issue is making sure you are perceiving the problem accurately. As mentioned earlier, perception is simply one's way of seeing the world. As you are beginning the creative process, then, make sure that your way of seeing the one particular part of the world you are dealing with is useful and real. When Thomas Edison began the creative process of inventing the light bulb, he must have had a perception of bright light coming from electricity. Because he had seen many lightning storms, he had something useful and real in his perception of the power of electricity.

Another point to remember is that your perception of reality might well be aimed at something that already exists. Your idea might be to adapt, change, or update a concept that is already created. Edison once gave this bit of advice to his colleagues: ". . .keep on the lookout for novel and interesting ideas that others have used successfully. Your idea has to be original only in its adaptation to the problem you're currently working on."[21]

Step Two: Incubation

The metaphor of a bird sitting on a nest of eggs, waiting for the baby birds to hatch, is fitting. An "unhatched" idea has come into your perception, and now, something fairly dramatic has to happen, or the creation of the new concept won't take place. The process might take minutes or hours, but it also could take months or even years.

In some creative processes, this step will involve research and experimentation. Depending on the nature of the creation, it could also involve simply turning the ideas over and over in one's mind until the breakthrough finally takes place. In his invention of the light bulb, Thomas Edison's incubation included thousands of experiments with different metal alloys to use as a filament.

Step Three: Inspiration

This third step can also be called "illumination." Whatever we choose to call it, it is the stage where the creator yells, "Aha!" "Eureka!" or "That's it!" It is the moment when the incubation and all of the struggling finally come together, transforming the developing creativity into a solid, real concept. This magic moment doesn't always happen on anyone's schedule. In fact, it can readily happen at less than convenient times—such as in the middle of the night. However, when it does happen, the person it happens to usually feels rewarded and positive about the next step. Wallas called this step the *happy idea(s)*.[22]

Step Four: Verification

Although unlike the other three, this step is quite important for most of us. This is the step where the newly created concept, product, or service is proven to be worthwhile. Now you can transform the new solution to your problem into useful action, and verify your solution.[23]

If it's the writing of a book, this is where its publication pays off, whether financially, intellectually, or both. If it's a functioning mechanism of some kind, this is where the test takes place as to whether or not it really "works." This is the point when the Wright brothers test flew their airplane and found that it did, indeed, get airborne.

Whatever you are creating, these four steps will be covered in some way.

EXPERIMENTATION

The second step in the creative process is incubation, which often includes experimentation. *When have you experimented in order to creatively solve a problem?*

ILLUMINATION

The third, and probably most satisfying, step in the creative process is illumination. This is where your mind has processed all of the information it has received, then offers you solutions. Illumination can be summed up by the famous phrase, "Eureka! I've found it!" How do you recognize when you've reached illumination?

Let the problem *sit* while you process the relevant information, turning it over in your mind. Some of this incubating will take place outside your conscious awareness; this explains why many people think that creative problem solving occurs in a flash of insight.

CREATIVITY IN THE WORKPLACE

Recently the American Management Association asked 500 heads of large corporations, "What must one do to survive in the 21st century?" By far the most popular answer was "Be more creative and innovative." Here is the sad part: A mere 6 percent of the managers interviewed thought that their companies were doing a good job of being creative.[24]

Most workplaces ignore or even discourage creativity. Few external rewards are offered for it in most companies. Little time is allowed for it, although creativity can increase internal rewards. Managers are often notorious creativity killers. Many managers have a vocabulary of *killer phrases* that are designed to stop creative thoughts before they start. Some common ones are: "It's not in the budget," "Top management won't go for it," "We could never sell it to the stockholders," and "We tried that last year." Others are like the reasons people resist change discussed in Chapter 11. Managers need to realize that employees' ideas are often better than those coming out of boardrooms, and that discouraging creative ideas damages workplace morale.

An effective manager encourages creativity among employees by creating a climate of deferred judgment. Not all ideas will be useful, but all should be listened to before any judgments about them are made. The manager may use a formal method for receiving suggestions, with all employees knowing the procedure. Many companies are beginning to use reward systems to encourage employees to make creative suggestions that save company money.

For a creative spirit to emerge from a company or a department, the environment must encourage enthusiasm and commitment from the employee. Work must be made rewarding, challenging, and fulfilling for a creative atmosphere to exist. Some of the ideas on increasing employee motivation also apply in increasing employee creativity. If a company shows that the employee's opinions are respected and valued, it will logically follow that the employee's creative solutions to problems will be valued as well. Figure 12.2 illustrates the interrelatedness of these conditions with creativity.

There are many stories about scientists who worked alone in laboratories. Poets such as Emily Dickinson wrote in isolation with few readers. For most people, however, creativity has a social aspect. One could ask how many songs John Lennon would have written if he had not been discovered with the Beatles. How many inventions would Thomas Edison

The Summit Creative Awards

This Web site will introduce you to awards given each year to the most creative companies. Learn about these companies by linking to the Summit Web site through **www.mhhe.com/lamberton4e** or directly through **www.summitawards.com/awards.html.** Open the link for "Award Winners." After reading the brief profiles of each of this year's winners, answer this question: What common elements do these companies seem to have in common (besides the obvious one that they are all creative)? Which of these companies would you most want to work for? Why?

have completed if absolutely everything he did had been rejected? To what extent does the quality and quantity of your creative output depend on the opinions of others? The way any creative effort is received does make a difference. The received group or audience ultimately determines the value of the creative work and whether it is to have a large impact.

Managing Corporate Creativity

In their book *Corporate Creativity,* Alan Robinson and Sam Stem introduce six elements that, when implemented, will lead organizations to higher levels of creativity. These elements include:

1. **Alignment**   This is the degree to which all employees' interests and actions are lined up in support of the organization's key goals. Creative organizations are strongly aligned. Misalignments interfere with creativity.

2. **Self-initiated activity**   Organizations that allow employees to explore their interests unleash a natural desire to be creative. Intrinsic motivation will spur this activity.

3. **Unofficial activity**   In order to increase creativity, organizations must allow employees time for unofficial activity. Official, planned activities seldom result in creativity.

4. **Serendipity**   This element involves *a fortunate accident that meets with keenness of insight.* Organizations that encourage tinkering and experimentation promote serendipity.

5. **Diverse stimuli**   This element relates to new or unexpected experiences that stimulate creative thinking. All employees in an organization, not just those involved directly in research and development, should have such experiences.

6. **Within-company communication**   Creative ideas can lurch along and become lost in official channels, especially in large organizations. Regardless of size, if communication channels in an organization are open, creative ideas can flow well enough to arrive where they will be heard.

figure 12.2

CORPORATE CREATIVITY

Corporations can nurture creativity in a way that improves productivity and morale. Ways to do this include offering diverse stimuli and allowing employees time for unofficial activities. *How can your workplace benefit from increased creativity?*

Source: Alan G. Robinson and Sam Stern, *Corporate Creativity: How Innovation and Improvement Actually Happen* (San Francisco, CA: Barrett-Koehler Publishers, Inc., 1997).

Classroom experiments have shown that positive reinforcement improves both the quality of creative work and the number of projects attempted. If college students are complimented on a project, with a brief, "That's really good—keep it up," the difference in creative output is remarkable, even when the students for the experiment are chosen totally at random. The opposite is also true. Creativity is often discouraged when it is not positively reinforced. When your creative output is rejected, you tend to take the rejection personally. Negative responses can affect self-esteem, and lowered self-esteem results in less effort and lower quality of work.

CREATIVE METHODS FOR GROUPS

In today's workplace, creative problem solving is increasingly done in group settings. Whatever an individual can produce creatively, a group may be able to produce more effectively. Groups can produce more ideas in shorter time periods if the creative process is structured carefully. Approach any process of group creativity carefully; it must contain just enough structure to be effective and must allow sufficient freedom to remain creative.

Brainstorming

brainstorming

A type of spontaneous group discussion to help find multiple solutions for problems.

In 1934 a sales manager named Alex Osborne devised a method of sparking creativity in a group situation. He called his idea **brainstorming,** which is a type of spontaneous group discussion to help find multiple solutions for problems. The process starts with a small group of people; groups of five to eight work best. With a leader in front to record their ideas, they begin by addressing a problem. In this first session, nothing is allowed except free-flowing ideas. Everyone is encouraged to speak in phrases rather than in sentences, to *hitchhike* on the ideas of others, and to be as wild and crazy as they can be within the social context. No one is allowed to criticize anyone else's ideas. Statements such as "Get serious!" or "That's stupid!" are forbidden.

When this first session is over, the second session begins. In this part of the brainstorming process, the adult part of everybody's personality takes over. The group examines the ideas that have come up, noticing whether any of them duplicate each other. The group can then prioritize the ideas, agreeing together which is the most important, second, and so on. (These rules are shown in the following list.) When a group brainstorms, following these rules correctly, an amazing number of high-quality ideas is produced in a fairly short period of time. Note that brainstorming works best for the solving of simple, well-defined problems, although it can be used in nearly any context. Although a lot of shallow, even useless ideas are suggested, there are usually gems among the dust.[25]

Innovation and Creativity

Visit Omega 23's "Innovation and Creativity—A Starting Point" by going to **www.mhhe.com/lamberton4e** for the link to the Web site. This page provides "continuing monologues and dialogues regarding innovation in the hope of stimulating thought, creativity, and thinking about thinking." Write a paragraph to answer these questions: What anecdote did you find entertaining? Which recommended books caught your eye? Why?

First Session

1. Participants speak in phrases.
2. Hitchhiking on others' ideas is encouraged.
3. Criticism is forbidden.
4. Silliness is encouraged.
5. Climate is relaxed.
6. All ideas are recorded.
7. A large quantity of ideas is encouraged.

Second Session

1. Return to rational mode.
2. All ideas are analyzed and prioritized.
3. Idea duplications are eliminated.
4. Ideas are ranked in order of importance.
5. Everyone gives evaluative input, just as all gave creative input in Session One.

After the second session before putting new ideas into place, the leader may ask some employees to take on the task of researching the new ideas. Finally, after the new ideas are put into place, the group may need to make adjustments or "tweak" the new process depending on follow-up examinations of the results of these new ideas or new processes.

The Nominal Group Method

The **nominal group method** of group creativity is designed to provide a structure that encourages individual creativity within a group framework. The reason this method is called nominal is because the

> **nominal group method**
> An exercise that encourages creativity within a group framework by allowing everyone to offer ideas individually.

members are actually a group in name only. The group is basically a tool for voting. Usually, nominal grouping involves six steps:

1. Each employee puts his or her ideas down in writing.
2. The leader lists all of the ideas up on a board or chart where everyone can see them.
3. The leader leads a discussion to clarify the ideas and add new ones.
4. Each group member rates the ideas and votes; the voting eliminates other ideas at this point.
5. After the vote, there is a brief discussion of the voting results. The purpose is to clarify points, not to persuade anyone.
6. The group casts a final vote to select the proposal or proposals that will be used.

The nominal group method can be especially effective when used with people who are shy, unsure of themselves, or simply not used to being assertive in public. The ideas are anonymous; nobody in the group should know who wrote what, unless the writers give themselves away in the discussion.

CREATIVE PROBLEM SOLVING

As with brainstorming, it is important when solving problems creatively to reward—rather than ridicule—any ideas put forward. In considering how to stimulate ideas, however, rewards are not everything. Even more influential than positive reinforcement from outside is the reward that comes from inside. In study after study, in the field of psychology and in the business world, whether through experiments or case studies, creativity is found to flourish with intrinsic motivation. Dr. Teresa Amabile finds that intrinsic motivation is more powerful than extrinsic motivation in encouraging creativity, regardless of whether you are talking about rats, children, or scientists. In her explanation, she uses the example of a rat going through a maze to get to the cheese reward (see Real World Example 12.2).

When companies do reward creativity, they often focus more on extrinsic than on intrinsic rewards. W. Edwards Deming explains that this does not work because intrinsic rewards, which can result from allowing creativity, drive employee self-esteem.

more about...

Teresa Amabile

Teresa Amabile has been doing research on creativity and intrinsic motivation for 30 years. Her main focus is increasing creativity and motivation in work settings. She began a career as a chemist, then earned a Ph.D. in psychology from Stanford University. She is currently a professor in business administration at Harvard Business School and heads their entrepreneurship program. She is also a consultant for businesses and government agencies on team creativity and leadership.

"If you [the rat] are extrinsically motivated, your primary motive is to achieve the extrinsic goal. . . . You have to earn the reward, or win the competition, or get the promotion, or please those who are watching you. You are so single-minded about the goal that you don't take the time to think much about the maze itself. Since you're only interested in getting out as quickly as possible, you will likely take only the most obvious, well-traveled route.

By contrast, if you are intrinsically motivated, you enjoy being in the maze. You enjoy playing in it, nosing around, trying out different pathways, exploring, thinking things through before blindly plunging ahead. You're not really concentrating on anything else but how much you enjoy the problem itself, how much you like the challenge and the intrigue."[26]

As time goes on, group creativity will likely become increasingly important. Creative problem solving—especially in teams and other groups, face-to-face or online—is a useful skill all employees will need to develop. Since creative problem solving is one of the hot topics of today's workplace, new ideas for group creativity will continue to be invented. All new techniques will try to inspire creativity in those who have not considered themselves creative before. New problem-solving strategies will all have one thing in common: All of them will be attempts to extract the greatest number of quality ideas from a group of people in a short time.

Intrinsic Motivators

"Some extrinsic motivation helps to build self-esteem. But total submission to external motivation leads to destruction of the individual. Extrinsic motivation in the extreme crushes intrinsic motivation."

—W. Edwards Deming, creator of Total Quality Management

Source: W. Edwards Deming, *The New Economics* (Cambridge, MA: MIT Center for Advanced Engineering Study, 1994), pp. 108–109.

more about...

STRATEGIES FOR SUCCESS

12.1 Increase Your Creativity

1. Get into the open mode.
2. Think of yourself as a creative person.
3. Learn to see problems as opportunities.
4. Look for more than one or two solutions to a problem.
5. Learn to play the violin.
6. Turn your ideas into action.
7. Don't be afraid to break some rules.
8. Don't be afraid to make mistakes.
9. Spend time with creative people.
10. Capture creative ideas when they happen.

When Alexander Fleming had the thought that led to the discovery of penicillin, he must have been in the open mode. The previous day, he had arranged a number of [laboratory] dishes so that the cultures would grow in them. On the day in question, he glanced at the dishes and discovered that on one of them no culture had appeared. Now, if he'd been in the closed mode, he would have been so focused upon his need for dishes with cultures grown in them, that when he saw that one dish was of no use for that purpose, he would have simply thrown it away. It was useless to him. . . . But, thank goodness, he was in an open mode. He became curious about why the culture had not grown in this particular dish, and that curiosity led him to penicillin. In the closed mode, an uncultured dish is an irrelevance; in the open mode, it's a clue.[27]

The question, "How can I become more creative?" has no easy answer. However, you can learn some basic steps. Only you know what specific barriers keep you from reaching your own creative potential.

1. **Get into the open mode.** In the daily routine of work, most people are in a *closed mode.* When most people are working, they feel pressured because they keep thinking about how much they have to do. This everyday mode contains a certain amount of anxiety, not much humor, a lot of stress, and a definite element of fear—but it doesn't contain creativity. The **open mode,** on the other hand, is relaxed, expansive, and less purposeful. Operating in the open mode often involves giving yourself sufficient time. Although you are likely to meet many people who claim that they do their most creative work under time pressure, the truth is that most people produce better when they have given themselves enough time to relax and reflect. In it, people tend to let things come as they may, act more thoughtful, and smile and laugh more often. You can have fun in the open mode!

    Playful is a word that British comedian John Cleese uses when discussing the open mode. In Real World Example 12.3, he tells the story of Alexander Fleming, who discovered penicillin.[28]

    This does not mean that you should stay in the open mode permanently. Important parts of your life require that you stay in the closed mode just so that you can concentrate on a noncreative task. As mentioned, asking childlike questions is important; answering those questions, though, may involve—and even require—the closed mode.

2. **Think of yourself as a creative person.** One of the biggest stumbling blocks to creativity is the belief that you somehow aren't good enough to create anything worthwhile. Many people carry around a self-image that includes statements like "Oh, I couldn't come up with a new idea if my life depended on it; I'm just not a creative person." This kind of self-image, with its accompanying low self-esteem, causes a person to put creative people on a pedestal.

    The key to this step is **self-perception**, which is what and how you believe yourself to be. Research has shown that people who produce more

open mode

A state of mind where you are relaxed, expansive, less purposeful, and more fun than in the everyday closed mode.

self-perception

What and how you believe yourself to be.

To file away important documents at work, Jody has more fun filing them in a unique and playful system that she invented, but no one else can find the files when they need them. It is more productive in the long run for everyone at Jody's company if she files them appropriately and carefully, paying attention while performing this task. In this case, the closed mode works better.

creative output are different in one major way from those who create less: the more creative people *believe that they are creative*. The others have serious doubts, and this directly hurts their performance. Believe in yourself creatively, and you will have accomplished an important step. Don't let self-doubt reduce your self-esteem and your creativity![29]

3. **Learn to see problems as opportunities.** Once you put yourself into an open mode and see yourself as creative, you'll need to get a mind-set that doesn't see problems as anything to get depressed about.

4. **Look for more than one or two solutions to a problem.** A major stumbling block with traditional methods of learning is that people are taught to look for *the one right answer.* Instead of casting about for the many right answers and numerous ways to view a problem, they tend to go after the one surefire answer that will please the teacher or the boss and make them feel they have succeeded. If you think there is only one right answer, you behave accordingly, and stop looking once you have found an answer that works—even if it isn't a perfect fit.[30]

People settle for the one right answer out of a tendency to grab the first idea that comes to mind. They are more likely to make this error when they feel pressured, frustrated, or afraid they aren't going to succeed in solving the problem. That first idea might be good, but how do you know it's the best? Again, taking some extra time might be the only way to proceed.

Another common mistake in decision making is called the **either/or fallacy,** which sees only one of two extremes as a possible solution without really looking at the great number of compromises and other creative choices that might exist in between. This was the mistake made by members of the community college business club in the opening story at the beginning of this chapter. When you are in the closed mode, you are much more likely to fall for this mistake.

To get beyond this trap, learn to look for the **second right answer**, the third, the fourth, and so on. In other words, get rid of the stumbling block that prevents most people from looking for more than one answer. Think of an idea as a letter in the alphabet. Everything ever written in English was written with the same 26 letters, yet the relationship of those letters to other ones forms words and ideas in a limitless number of possibilities. Get in the habit of finding at least three right answers for each problem you encounter. Chances are that once you discover three, you won't stop there.

either/or fallacy

When you see only one of two extremes as a possible solution, while ignoring the endless number of creative choices that might exist between the extremes.

second right answer

Refers to a method of decision making in which people get rid of the stumbling block that prevents them from looking for more than one solution.

Nolan Bushnell, the inventor of the video game, is a good example of just how easy creativity can be. He says that he noticed that people like to watch television and that they also enjoy playing games. He just put the two ideas together.[31]

more about...

The Second Right Answer

"Nothing is more dangerous than an idea when it is the only one you have."

—Emile Chartier, French philosopher

Source: Eugene Raudsepp, "Overcoming Barriers to Effective Problem Solving," *Supervision* 52 (February 1991), pp. 14–16.

Many people feel a need to be able to make decisions rapidly. After all, such a reputation is certainly better than one of being wishy-washy. If you are truly decisive, great. If you're not, don't fake it. Instead, examine the alternatives. Try to get at least a few possible solutions before going on to finish solving a problem. Use combinations of ideas other people have thought of, bringing them together for your own creative result. Of course, even in the world of business, one will sometimes encounter a problem that truly has only one right answer. In such a case, methods of discovery still need to be varied, rather than limited.

5. **Learn to play the violin.** Management expert Peter Drucker was once asked how one can become a better manager. "Learn to play the violin" was his reply. He didn't literally mean that learning to play the violin was a solution. His point was that anything that gets people outside of their regular context would force them out of their comfort zone and into different ways of thinking. You are more likely to be creative when you are outside of your comfort zone.[32] As an added bonus, you may get to be really good at the violin, or at golf, or at wind surfing—and your self-esteem will grow. That is a bonus that improves your performance in all areas of your life.

6. **Turn your ideas into action.** How many ideas have you thought of, then dismissed, only to find later that someone else who thought of the same idea had put it into action? You may have thought, "That was *my* idea!" Painful, isn't it?

   Creativity doesn't do anyone much good if its products aren't followed through into action. What if all of Robert Frost's poems or Michelangelo's artwork or Marie Curie's scientific breakthroughs had simply remained unexecuted ideas?

7. **Don't be afraid to break some rules.** Whatever the task at hand, most people feel compelled to follow the rules. Many of those rules aren't rules or laws at all, only customs—customs that everyone has been afraid to change. This does not mean that you should break the law or break a rule that will get you fired. Instead, it is a suggestion that you break away from outdated or pointless customs and think creatively. Remember the lesson of the nine-dot puzzle!

   Sometimes rules outlive their usefulness, but people continue to follow them anyway.

Roger von Oech, creativity guru of California's Silicon Valley, writes, "I like to run, and I have three or four runs that I'll take depending on how far I want to go. . . . As a rule, the run ends about two blocks from our house, because two years ago, when I started this route, there was a big, friendly golden retriever living at the house where I stopped. His name was Aslan. After my run, I would take some time to pet him and cool down. So stopping at Aslan's house became the rule for having a nice ending to a fun run.

"But things have changed. His owner moved away a year ago, and took Aslan with her. Nevertheless, whenever I take this route, I still stop at the same place—even though Aslan no longer lives there. There are probably more pleasurable places to end my run, but because I am following an obsolete rule, I haven't looked for them."[33]

Von Oech calls this problem with rules the **Aslan phenomenon:**

- People make rules based on reasons that make a lot of sense.
- They follow those rules.
- Time passes and situations change.

The original reasons for generating these rules may no longer exist, but the rules are still in place and people continue to follow them.

> **Aslan phenomenon**
>
> A circumstance that exists when people make rules, then follow them even after the situations to which they originally applied no longer exist.

8. **Don't be afraid to make mistakes.** Most people have two selves: the safekeeping self and the spontaneous self. The safekeeping self keeps you clothed, fed, and out of trouble. The spontaneous self allows you the freedom and fun of doing things without structure and detailed planning. Childhood training warns people not to be too spontaneous or too messy, not to *color outside the lines,* and (most important) not to make fools of themselves. Actually, making mistakes is one of the most effective ways of learning, and being a bit foolish is part of being human. The president of a successful, fast-growing computer company tells his employees, "We're innovators. We're doing things nobody has ever done before. Therefore, we are going to be making mistakes. My advice to you: Make your mistakes, but make them in a hurry."[34]

9. **Spend time with creative people.** Creativity researcher and Harvard professor Teresa Amabile finds that creative people spark creativity in others. Whether the setting is formal or informal, being around others who *think outside the box* helps you to do so, too.[35]

10. **Capture creative ideas when they happen.** Change your routine and do things a little differently. Pay attention to your thought processes and feelings, and when inspiration hits, be ready: have a notebook, sketch pad, tape recorder, or other device ready to capture new ideas as they occur. Creativity has a way of not happening at convenient times![36]

12.2 Roger von Oech's "Ten Mental Locks"

1. Look for the one right answer.
2. That is not logical.
3. Follow the rules.

Several years ago Steve completely thought out the idea for what is now called multi-level marketing, but he didn't put it to use. Three years later the founders of Amway, Inc. put the same idea (which they certainly didn't get from him) into action. Amway is now a billion-dollar corporation, and Steve was left with the regret that he didn't act on his idea sooner.

4. Be practical.

5. Play is frivolous.

6. That isn't my area.

7. Don't be foolish.

8. Avoid ambiguity.

9. To err is wrong.

10. I'm not creative.

ten "mental locks"
Rules or beliefs that keep people from being as creative as they otherwise could be.

According to creativity guru Roger von Oech, **ten "mental locks"** keep people from being as creative as they otherwise could be. Read them over and see how many of them might apply to your life and to your attempts to be more creative.

1. **Look for the one right answer.** When you start out with the assumption that there is only one right answer to a given problem, you have just limited yourself to a very narrow set of possibilities. Von Oech quotes French philosopher Emile Chartier: "Nothing is more dangerous than an idea when it is the only one we have." So, learn to look for the second "right answer," and the third, and so on.

2. **That is not logical.** Although logic certainly has an important place in life, one who spends too much time and energy trying to view everything as logical at all times is likely to miss out on the use of intuition—"one of the mind's softest and most valuable creations." Von Oech makes the distinction between "soft" and "hard" parts of reality. Logic is a valuable tool for the "practical phase" of the creative process.

3. **Follow the rules.** If you don't challenge the rules, but just follow them blindly, you will likely either fall prey to the Aslan phenomenon (see Real World Example 12.6), or you will get locked into a single approach without seeing other possibilities. Thus you're back to the "one right answer" rut.

4. **Be practical.** Von Oech says we all have an "artist" and a "judge" within us. Both of them are important to the creative process. Most of us have to challenge our judge with "what if" questions.

5. **Play is frivolous.** "Necessity may be the mother of invention, but play is certainly the father" (Roger von Oech). Play is, in fact, not frivolous, but actually essential to the act of creation. "Playing" with a problem is often the best way to solve it. Children are more creative than adults, and ability to play is one of the reasons.

Bill Browerman, an athletic coach at the University of Oregon, noticed that his track athletes were having great difficulty with sore feet and blisters. After examining the shoes his runners were wearing, he decided that he could make a better shoe that would work with nature rather than against it. Using the most lightweight and tough materials he could find, he made a shoe that improved both cushion and traction. Browerman went on to form Nike, which is now a billion-dollar company.[37] He saw the problem as a challenge, and he was able to meet that challenge in a remarkable way.

6. **That isn't my area.** Specialization can be a real enemy of creativity. How often could someone who specializes in one area learn to apply a principle or process that is peculiar to another area? So often in companies, someone will say, "Oh, that's an advertising problem," or "That's a customer service problem," when a bit of overlapping between departments was exactly what was necessary.

7. **Don't be foolish.** This statement is mostly about conformity, especially about the human desire not to "stick out" and look weird or different to others. Occasionally, try letting yourself look stupid. Also, learning to laugh at oneself is a helpful exercise. New ideas often look stupid to others.

8. **Avoid ambiguity.** The reason most of us actually follow this lock is because ambiguity can hamper communication with others—because we need to be specific when we communicate. However, in the creative process, being too specific can prevent the flow of new ideas.

9. **To err is wrong.** Actually, success can have a negative side. If too many things we try succeed, an anticreative smugness can stifle creativity. Think of a huge error you made some time in your life. Did something good come out of it in the long run? If not, is there something you could have done to make something positive come from it?

10. **I'm not creative.** This statement usually develops into a self-fulfilling prophecy. We need to let our own creative style develop and to allow ourselves to let go and be creative. Often, people need to give themselves permission to be creative.

Source: Roger von Oech, *A Whack on the Side of the Head: How You Can Be More Creative* (New York: Business Plus, 2008).

12.3 Use SCAMPER to Solve Problems

Have you ever found yourself stuck—unable to think of a creative solution to a problem? When the "creativity block" hits you, try Bob Eberle's **SCAMPER**[38] strategy to release your creative mind. Eberle is author of several teacher resource books on increasing creativity in the classroom. Think of a current problem or issue you are having at school, work, or home; or a problem facing your campus, student body, or local community. Once you have identified the issue or topic you

> **SCAMPER**
>
> A strategy, created by Bob Eberle, to release your creative mind.

Dr. Spencer Silver, a scientist for the 3M technology corporation, invented an adhesive in 1968 that was considered a failure for the purpose he wanted. Nearly 10 years later, Dr. Art Fry, another 3M scientist, had an idea for Silver's "failed" adhesive: to keep his bookmark from falling out of his church hymnal. From this simple idea the Post-it note was created, now used internationally and one of 3M's more popular office products.[39]

want to work on, apply Eberle's SCAMPER strategy to the problem. To do this, ask yourself "To come up with a creative solution, what might I . . .":

Substitute? Is there a person, place, or object that might work better?

Combine? Are there ideas, goals, or purposes that could be combined?

Adapt? Are there parts of the plan or the process I can reshape or fit to this issue?

Modify? How and what can I alter, revise, enlarge, or shrink to resolve this issue?

Put to another use? What can I put to different or new uses to resolve the problem?

Eliminate? What can be omitted, simplified, or removed?

Rearrange? Can I change the order of events, the plan itself, or the desired outcome?

What new solutions did you come up with?

CHAPTER TWELVE SUMMARY

Chapter Summary by Learning Objectives

1. **Explain the importance of creativity.** Business factors, such as the number and quality of good products created, are affected strongly by the creativity of the people in an organization. Although positive reinforcement can increase people's willingness to try out new ideas and to be creative, creativity is more likely increased by intrinsic motivation. Competitiveness depends on creativity as does success at business or nearly anything else.

2. **Define creativity.** Creativity is the ability to produce ideas, or solutions to problems that are unique, appropriate, and valuable. It has to do with self-esteem and, in turn, with relationships with others. In a nutshell, creativity is thinking up original and useful ideas.

3. **Discuss the relationship between perception and creativity.** Whatever model of creativity one uses, perception is nearly always the first step. Perception is one's unique way of seeing the world. If problem solving is the issue, perception also means perceiving the problem correctly.

4. **List the steps in the creative process.** The process begins with perception and preparation, and is followed by incubation, inspiration, and verification. Whatever one is creating, these steps will be covered in some way.

5. **Describe creativity in the workplace.** The typical workplace of today is not set up to handle creative ideas. More often than not, creativity is stifled by companies of all sizes. The challenge is to transform the workplace into a place where creativity is encouraged and rewarded.

6. **Compare and contrast creative methods for groups.** The major methods of creativity in groups are brainstorming and the nominal group method. Both use techniques to stimulate original thought and to discourage negativity and low self-esteem.

7. **Give examples of ways to solve problems creatively.** Get into the "open mode." Also, learn to think of yourself as a creative person and to see problems as opportunities. Learning to look for more than one possible solution to a problem will also help. In addition, try to avoid creativity traps, such as the either/or fallacy. "Learn to play the violin," which is a figurative way of saying that one must be willing to go beyond the company 's job description. Turn your ideas into action, and don't be afraid to break some rules or to make some mistakes. Spend time with creative people, and capture creative ideas when they happen.

Creativity in Groups

key terms

Aslan phenomenon 329
brainstorming 322
collective habits of thought 314
creative process 318
creativity 312
either/or fallacy 327

extrinsic motivator 317
intrinsic motivators 317
intuition 313
nine-dot puzzle 315
perception 314
nominal group method 323

open mode 326
SCAMPER 331
self-perception 326
second right answer 327
ten "mental locks" 330

review questions

1. Is creativity the same as intelligence? How are they related? In what ways are they different?

2. Explain the differences among the four steps of the creative process described by Wallas, using examples from your own experience of a problem you have solved.

3. Why do workplaces so often lack creativity? What steps can managers take to increase the quality and quantity of their employees' creative output?

4. What does it mean to be in the open mode? What does this feel like? How can the open mode allow for greater creativity?

5. Explain the difference between brainstorming and the nominal group method. How can both help produce more creative group results?

6. How many right answers are there to any one problem? What is meant by the *second right answer*? How many right answers should you look for in solving a problem before deciding on a solution to implement?

7. How does the phrase *playing the violin* relate to an increase in creativity? What skill or talent would you like to explore? How would a new skill increase your creativity?

8. Which better promotes creativity: positive reinforcement or intrinsic motivation? Explain.

critical thinking questions

9. Do you think creative geniuses are more likely *born* or *made?* Do you think you could become more creative if you were to work at it?

10. Which type of talent do you think has greater worth to society, creativity or academic intelligence? Why? Do you think one of these is more important than the other?

working it out 12.1

HOW CREATIVE ARE YOU?

School-to-Work Connection: Interpersonal Skills
Instructions: Have you ever wondered how creative you are? Here is a simple quiz you can take to find out. The results may give you some indication as to your CQ—your creativity quotient. Circle the letter that corresponds with your feelings.

1. Planning your activity for the day:

   a. appeals to you   b. cramps your style

2. Do you get ideas just before you fall asleep?

   a. frequently   b. seldom, if at all

3. Do you often spend more time on puzzles, riddles, or trick questions than the average person?

   a. yes   b. no

4. Do you sometimes worry about the success of your efforts?

   a. yes   b. no

5. Do you like to engage in activities in which you might influence others?

   a. yes   b. no

6. Are you basically happy?

   a. yes   b. no

7. Do you like to daydream at work, as well as at home?

   a. yes   b. no

8. Do you enjoy remembering trivia?

   a. yes   b. no

9. Do you worry about getting behind in your work?

   a. yes   b. no

10. Which would you rather be considered?

   a. sensible   b. resourceful

The answers below are for those who are highly creative:

Answers: 1 = b, 2 = a, 3 = a, 4 = a, 5 = b, 6 = a, 7 = a, 8 = b, 9 = b, 10 = b.

The more of these answers you gave, the more you are inclined to be creative. Five of the high creativity answers is average. However, if you only had three of them, this does not mean that you are not creative. And remember one of the most important points of this chapter: creativity is a skill that can be increased—it's not a matter of "either you have it or you don't."

Source: Jack Halloran, *Applied Human Relations: An Organizational Approach Activity Guide* (Englewood Cliffs, NJ: Prentice Hall, 1978, pp. 84–85).

working it out 12.2

CREATIVE BRAINSTORMING

School-to-Work Connection: Interpersonal Skills
This exercise is designed to stimulate creativity in groups. Each pair of words should suggest a third idea in which the elements of both are combined. How many new ideas can groups of four or five people create

from each pair of words? Write your new ideas on the line. Don't worry about how many *great* ideas you come up with. The important point is to come up with a great *many* ideas. Be original.

Remember to use the same rules that are used in brainstorming:

1. Speak in phrases, not sentences.

2. Be spontaneous.

3. Add ideas to other people's phrases.

4. Avoid negative comments.

5. Say things like "That's a great idea."

6. Have fun, and make silly comments; it may encourage other ideas.

1. bird, chair

_____

2. shoe, trumpet

_____

3. sweater, horse

_____

4. crocodile, store

_____

5. carrot, cart

_____

6. monkey, music

_____

1. *Creativity Games*

   Go to the Hipbone Games page at **http://home.earthlink.net/~hipbone/** and linked through the course Web page at **www.mhhe.com/lamberton4e.** You will be given 10 choices as to "where you can go from here." Search until you find a game that in your opinion will stimulate your own creativity. After playing the game, write a brief review of the game, explaining what it did for your creativity and how.

2. *Read and Evaluate*

   Go to the Innovation Tools online page linked through the course Web page at **www.mhhe.com/lamberton4e** or directly accessible at **www.innovationtools.com** for a site that offers a large number of articles on innovation and creativity—some recent, some archived from the past. Choose two of these articles; then write a brief essay showing their relationship to the material in this chapter.

3. *Research and Report*

   Do you know about the hidden job market? Find out how you can apply for jobs that are not advertised through the usual means, by visiting Job Star through the course Web site at **www.mhhe.com/lamberton4e** or by going directly to **http://jobstar.org/.** Summarize what you discovered about creative methods of job searching in the hidden job market.

Inland's Widget Woes

Garth Peters was alarmed. He managed the production line for Inland Widgets, a manufacturing company specializing in making small mechanical devices used in hand-held television remote controls. Because of one very small typing error, he now had one very large problem. Instead of the 10,000 widgets that should have been produced for one of his customers this month, his crew had produced 100,000! Now he had to come up with an immediate plan to market the remaining 90,000 widgets. His job was on the line, and he knew it.

As Garth sat thinking in his office late one night, he turned the situation over and over in his mind. "We could try to sell them to our customer's competitors, even though we agreed not to do that. We could hold them in storage and hope another order comes through. We could lay off all 51 employees in the plant until this thing blows over . . . or we could . . . I don't know!"

Just then, Garth's assistant manager, Lynn Sen, walked in. "Lynn," Garth said hopefully,

"I need some new ideas. This company needs as many new ideas as possible for getting these extra widgets off the plant floor if we're going to survive. I sure hope you're feeling creative."

"That's ironic," countered Sen, "I just came in here to see if *you* had gotten any brainstorms."

Case Study Questions

1. Imagine you are Garth or Lynn, and come up with 20 new possible uses for these widgets.

2. How should Garth and Lynn use the talents of their 51 employees in solving this problem?

3. Explain how Garth and Lynn could use first the nominal group method, and then brainstorming, to come up with ideas for marketing the widgets. Which would work better in this case? Why?

Smarts, Luck, or Skill?

Carlos Mendez sat slumped at his desk, unhappily staring into a blank computer screen. The cursor seemed to blink accusingly at him, "Write something! Get busy!" but he just couldn't seem to get started on his piece of the city planning proposal, due later that afternoon. His co-worker, Debi Desmond, walked by his office waving a greeting, stopped, backed up, and walked into his office. "What's wrong, Carlos? You don't look like the usual happy camper I see in this office!"

"I just can't do this job, Debi. I'm not smart enough to come up with something creative and original for every different project, week after week after week. I can't do it any more!"

"Wait a minute! What are you saying? You think that smart and creative are the same thing? No way! You don't have to be *smart,* you just have to be *lucky!* Creative ideas pop into people's heads out of nowhere! Right, Susie?"

They both turned to the vice president, Susan McKee, who had just walked into Carlos's office. "Actually, you're both wrong. I was just coming to check on that proposal, Carlos, and I'm glad I did. You both need to hear this: creativity is a *skill* that can be practiced and improved on. It's not luck, and it doesn't take a genius. It's a strategy you both would benefit from." She then said thoughtfully, "You know, maybe we should schedule a full office meeting to talk about this creativity thing. We all seem to be in a little slump lately."

Case Study Questions

1. Who's right about the definition of creativity: Carlos, Debi, or Susan? Is there more than one right answer to this question?

2. Suppose you are Susan. What kinds of information would you bring to a meeting on creativity?

3. Do you see a link between Carlos's creativity slump and his self-esteem? Explain.

SOLUTIONS TO THE "NINE-DOT" PUZZLE

(This is the "standard" solution):

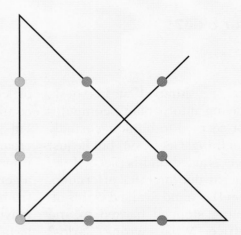

The solution below also works if you don't go through the middle of each dot. Also, it uses only 3 straight lines:

Creative people have come up with several other possible solutions. One is with the edge of a long crayon, connecting all dots using only *one* line!

CONFLICT MANAGEMENT

In the Workplace: Bringing Home the Conflict

SITUATION

"I just don't know what I'm going to do," Jeanne said to her husband. "I'm always needing information from the production department. I mean, in marketing we have to know about new products before we can get an angle on them, right? But some of those people in production. . . . It's like they don't want to

give out any information, or maybe they think we wouldn't understand it. Today we started on a product we haven't seen yet, and Phillippe in production told me I should talk to research and development. Then, I heard that R&D said, 'Oh, those marketing guys. They always want to come by and talk, but we can't get any work done if we keep stopping to talk

After studying this chapter, you will be able to:

1. Identify the types of conflict.
2. List sources of conflict.
3. Define conflict analysis.
4. Give examples of potential solutions to a conflict.
5. Compare and contrast styles of conflict management.
6. Explain how to deal with special conflict cases.

STRATEGIES FOR SUCCESS

Strategy 13.1   Negotiate Win-Win Solutions

Strategy 13.2   Make Collaboration Work

Strategy 13.3   Stop Conflicts Before They Start

---

to them.' I feel like my whole department is being stalled by a bunch of people who don't understand how important marketing is. They need to realize that without marketing, the whole company would fold."

"Well," Jeanne's husband replied, "at least you're not having any issues with your clients."

DISCOVERY

"I'll tell you something," Jeanne replied. "I expect to have to take more effort making appointments with clients, compromising and avoiding conflict with them.

After all, they are our customers. But from people in my own company—well, that's just too much. We need to find a way for all the departments to work together better."

THINK ABOUT IT

Does Jeanne contribute to her unfavorable work conditions in any way? What can Jeanne do to improve the situation at work? What can her organization do as a whole?

TYPES OF CONFLICT

Wherever there are people, there is conflict. Jeanne's frustration with the people in her own company is quite typical. The results of conflict can range from minor inconveniences to major losses, even company failures. In American business, the workplace contains a greater amount of conflict today than in the past, mainly because of the movement of the United States from an industrial economy to a service-dominated economy. In a service economy, work tasks depend much more on successful interactions between people. The service sector of the U.S. economy now accounts for more than 70 percent of all jobs. Everywhere, business leaders are striving to increase the productivity of services. Since conflict nearly always damages productivity, the U.S. workplace is in need of both workers and managers who can deal with conflict in a realistic and helpful way.[1]

Several common aspects are involved in all types of conflict:

- Conflict must be perceived by all people involved in it, because whether or not there is a conflict is often a matter of perception.
- Nearly all definitions of conflict involve opposition or incompatibility.
- Some type of interaction is going on, or all parties would be avoiding conflict.[2]

conflict

A process that begins when one person sees that another person has damaged—or is about to damage—something that the other person cares about.

For the purposes of this chapter, **conflict** will be defined as a process that begins when one person sees that another person has damaged— or is about to damage—something that the other person cares about.[3] Someone might perceive that damage is a possible outcome, and that perception itself can begin a conflict. The damage or perception of attempted damage does not have to involve a physical object; it can mean threat or damage to ideas, values, or goals.

Conflict is usually seen as a negative factor in the workplace. However, it can be both beneficial and constructive when approached correctly. One way to classify conflicts is by seeing them as either **functional** or **dysfunctional,** that is, either constructive or destructive. For example, when a group of employees meets to make a decision that affects all of them, some conflict can be good because too much harmony and agreement can result in a poor decision (groupthink). When people focus more on getting along well than on coming up with creative solutions in decision making, they may not generate as many ideas as they would have otherwise. However, if the same group generates so much conflict that fighting and polarization result, that decision could also be faulty. A manager should try whenever possible to change a dysfunctional (destructive) conflict into a functional (constructive) one.

functional conflict

Constructive conflict.

dysfunctional conflict

Destructive conflict.

Another way to classify conflict is by the participants in the conflict. **Inner conflict** is conflict within an individual. It might involve values, loyalties, or priorities. Suppose that your manager wants you to

inner conflict

Conflict within an individual; it might involve values, loyalties, or priorities.

Jim works at a service organization. His purpose for working is to help people, and he puts in a lot of time and effort in doing so. Robin sits at the desk next to him and is someone Jim perceives to be a time waster—someone who doesn't hold his values. Values, personalities, and loyalties could all be involved in the conflict that may occur between Jim and Robin.

do something, but your co-workers will call you a "fink" or informant if you do. Or suppose that you have two job offers, both with attractive qualities that pull you in opposite directions.

A **person-versus-person conflict** involves two people who are at odds over personality differences, values conflicts, loyalties, or any number of issues. When only two people are involved in a conflict, the focus tends to be personal on both sides (see Real World Example 13.1).

Intergroup conflict takes place when already-formed groups have conflicts with each other. When this type of conflict takes place, the conflict often becomes widespread. War is an extreme example of intergroup conflict.

Intragroup conflict occurs when a conflict arises among group members, and they choose sides and split off into factions within the existing group (see Real World Example 13.2). Sometimes intragroup conflict evolves from person-versus-person conflict because people take sides with the two opposing individuals.

Person-versus-group conflict occurs most often when a member of a group breaks its rules, or norms. It also can involve someone who never was a member of the group, but who opposes it (see Real World Example 13.3).

SOURCES OF CONFLICT

The preceding four types of conflict describe in general terms *who* is involved in each type, but not *how* conflict starts. No two disagreements are alike; each one starts at a different point over different issues. If you know what type of conflict you are involved in, that knowledge can help you discover how best to resolve it.[4] Figure 13.1 shows the sources of conflict and their potential solutions.

Content Conflict

When disagreements stem from a **content conflict,** they tend to focus on disagreements over what a statement or concept means. The only real issue is whether or not an idea is right. The rightness of an idea usually

person-versus-person conflict
Conflict that involves two people who are at odds over personality differences, values conflicts, loyalties, or any number of issues.

intergroup conflict
Takes place when already-formed groups have conflicts with each other.

intragroup conflict
Conflict arising when members of an existing group split off and choose sides.

person-versus-group conflict
Conflict that occurs most often when a member of a group breaks its rules, or norms.

content conflict
Conflict that tends to focus on disagreements over what a statement or concept means.

Several medieval monks were having a heated discussion about how many teeth a horse has. After the discussion had gone on for nearly an hour, a young monk offered to go out to the post where his horse was tied and count the horse's teeth. He was promptly scolded and called a troublemaker. Because the young monk wanted to solve the debate, he indirectly showed the others that their arguing was pointless—and they were angry.

> **values conflict**
>
> Conflict that occurs when one set of values clashes with another, and a decision has to be made.

CONFLICT ON THE JOB

Conflict comes in more ways than many people imagine. Like Jeanne at the beginning of the chapter, you may expect conflict from certain aspects of your job—such as dealing with customers. However, conflict among employees, or between levels of employees, can also be very destructive. *What conflict do you feel is most common in organizations?*

focuses on one of two factors: existence or meaning. For example, if the argument is about whether or not there is a Loch Ness monster, the disagreement is over existence.

If the conflict is over existence, it helps to have some way of verifying whether or not something is real. The Loch Ness monster is real to a few people, so the conflict over its existence still abounds—as it does over the conspiracy theories of President Kennedy's death, the existence of UFOs, and many other issues that are difficult to prove or disprove to everyone's satisfaction. However, when a book or other factual source can settle the dispute, arguing is pointless. Many existence issues are more like the number of a horse's teeth. Both sides should wait until proof is available.

More commonly, content conflicts are over meaning and interpretation. If the argument is about whether or not the task you were just assigned is included in the vague wording of your job description, you have probably moved into a disagreement over meaning. You might find a copy of your job description and discover that it contains wording so ambiguous that your present task may or may not be appropriate to it, according to different interpretations. Even the interpretation of certain laws by different attorneys would fall in the category of content conflicts over meaning, as Americans witnessed in the very close presidential election of 2000.

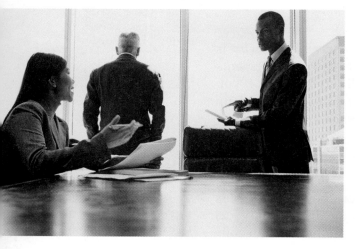

Values Conflict

A **values conflict** usually goes very deep. For example, a Democrat and a Republican would likely disagree on many issues related to politics. In the workplace, managers may have deep disagreements with each other over management practices. These disagreements may be rooted in their values and the basic beliefs they hold about people and how they should be treated.

Values conflicts can be solved, rather than avoided. The solution is that many people need to develop a greater tolerance of values differences. By listening carefully and communicating your

The six mechanics from Nello's Paint & Body Shop had a tradition of shooting pool together at a local bar every Friday evening. After this continued for over a year, one of the six quit the body shop and was replaced by Raffi, a non-pool player. Many conflicts resulted from Raffi's unintentional breaking of this group norm.

values cautiously, you can often create a sense of trust and mutual respect for differences. You will find that if you think carefully about your own values, examining them regularly, you will feel less threatened by someone with values unlike your own. Often that security becomes contagious!

Negotiation-of-Selves Conflicts

This type of conflict erupts over differences in self-definition. Individuals generally define who they are based on their own self-concepts. Many people see themselves as less worthy than they really are.

figure 13.1

SOURCES OF CONFLICT

These are the four basic sources of conflict. *Which of these sources do you feel is easiest to confront and resolve?*

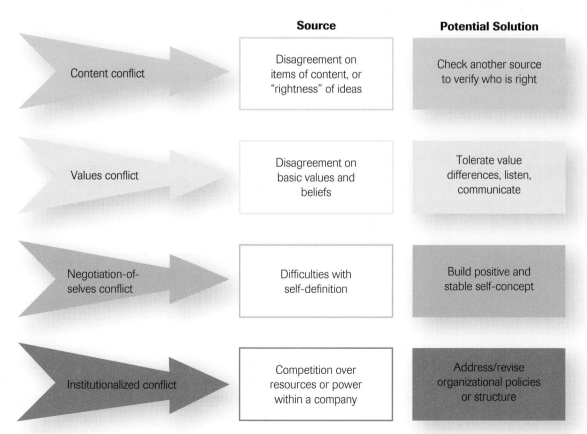

	Source	Potential Solution
Content conflict	Disagreement on items of content, or "rightness" of ideas	Check another source to verify who is right
Values conflict	Disagreement on basic values and beliefs	Tolerate value differences, listen, communicate
Negotiation-of-selves conflict	Difficulties with self-definition	Build positive and stable self-concept
Institutionalized conflict	Competition over resources or power within a company	Address/revise organizational policies or structure

A state government agency was planning its annual budget when factions formed behind two leaders who were both perceived as powerful and who disliked each other. The conflict continued until members of the majority "winning" side were running the agency and in charge of the funds. The opposing members gradually quit and found other jobs.

more about...

Values Conflicts

Often, many people exaggerate the number of **values conflicts** they have. A conflict may seem to be over values but is actually over the other person's perception of you and your perception of yourself, with neither side identifying the real issue.

negotiation-of-selves conflict

Conflict that is involved in the process of defining yourself to others and responding to their implied definitions of themselves.

Employees are likely to see themselves differently than the manager sees them; children see themselves differently than their parents see them, and so on.

Many interpersonal conflicts are based on a **negotiation-of-selves conflict.** Part of being human is being constantly involved in the process of defining yourself to others and responding to their implied definitions of themselves. Most of this activity goes on unnoticed. A rude bank loan officer will hardly say, "Well, I'm responding this way to you because I feel that I'm superior to you." Even the nonverbal cues in such a case might not deliver the correct message, because people try to play the roles that society has constructed.

Consider the following real-world negotiations-of-selves conflicts.

- **Employee:** Why is it always my job to take messages? I'm not good at things like that. I get messages wrong and mess up a lot.

  Boss: I ask you to take messages because you are, in fact, very good at it.

- **Mother:** What on earth are you thinking, coming home at this ungodly hour? You're not old enough to be trusted out this late.

  Daughter: I'm only two years younger than you were when you met Dad. Lighten up. I can take care of myself.

- **Employee 1:** What do you think of this report? I'd really like some input on it.

  Employee 2: Don't look to me for approval. I'm not your boss.

All three of the preceding brief exchanges in the Real World Examples mentioned in the previous paragraph have something in common. They express conflicts that originate from the speakers' self-concept and self-definition. Conflicts such as these can focus on power or authority (as the first two do), on personality traits (as all of them do), or on questions of duty and obligation.

Institutionalized Conflict

Institutionalized conflict occurs when a conflict factor is built into the structure or the policies of the organization. Some organizations encourage conflict, just by the way they are structured.

institutionalized conflict

Conflict that occurs when a conflict factor is built into the structure of the organization.

CONFLICT ANALYSIS

Anyone wishing to manage a conflict should begin by looking closely at what is really happening. When strong emotions are involved, people are often tempted to jump to conclusions before examining the interests of both sides and their own interests as well.[5] Instead of making that common mistake, try focusing on these questions instead:

- **Who is involved?** How many people are taking part in this conflict? How well do they understand the basic issues? Are any of them repeatedly involved in conflicts, or is this a unique situation? By knowing these details, a leader can do a better job of designing a conflict management process that addresses everyone's interests.

- **What is at stake?** Do all or both sides in the dispute agree about what is really at stake? If duties and responsibilities are at stake, does everyone agree on exactly what those issues are? If money is involved, is everyone talking about the same amount? Does the issue center on assigning blame for misconduct, or could the issue be expressed as a desire to define proper conduct for the future? Without this step, the entire issue can become blurred.

- **How important is time?** Does this dispute have to be settled right away? Does one side benefit from stalling? A conflict manager should consider if the time factor will cool tempers on both sides, or if the passage of time will simply aggravate the issue.

- **What are the tie-ins with other issues?** What relationship does this dispute have with other disputes between the individuals or groups involved? What working relationships will likely be affected by the outcome of the conflict?

After these questions are answered (and assuming you decide that the issue is worth resolving), a solution can be negotiated.

POTENTIAL SOLUTIONS

Generally speaking, there are three possible solutions to a conflict: win-lose, lose-lose, and win-win. The first two tend to produce a negative, side-taking mentality and are not likely to solve the problem permanently. Yet sometimes, because of time constraints and the other side's unwillingness to work toward a win-win solution, you may be forced to use win-lose or lose-lose tactics.

Win-Lose

win-lose strategy
A strategy that allows one side of a conflict to win at the expense of the other.

The **win-lose strategy** allows one side of a conflict to win at the expense of the other.[6] It works as a quick-fix conflict solution that sometimes must be chosen when a win-win approach isn't feasible. One win-lose approach is the *democratic vote*. Democracy sounds like a wonderful approach to conflict resolution, and it is in a political system. Unlike a political system, though, most organizations don't contain a series of checks and balances, political rallies, or campaigning. In these situations, the majority vote will leave a minority of unhappy people without any real recourse. These are the people who are likely to bring the problem back, perhaps in another form.

Another win-lose approach is the *arbitrary approach* (arbitration). With this method, the conflict manager decides which side is right and which is wrong, then considers the issue to be resolved. Like the democratic vote, this approach produces a situation in which the losers tend to have hard feelings against both the winning side and the conflict manager. A skillful conflict manager or arbitrator can soften the effect of the arbitrary approach by using persuasive explanations. Usually, however, the gains from win-lose are short-term ones only, and problems will continue.

more about...

Win-Lose

The American legal system takes a **win-lose strategy** (also called an *adversarial system*). What are the benefits of this? The drawbacks? Is there a better approach for certain situations?

Lose-Lose

lose-lose strategy
A strategy in which everyone gives up something and the focus is on compromise.

In the **lose-lose strategy,** everyone gives up something. The main approach in lose-lose is compromise—compromise in the sense that nobody gets what they want, but everyone can live with the decision. Like win-lose, this method usually fails to solve the underlying causes of the conflict. *Unlike* win-lose, the lose-lose strategy produces unhappy people on both sides of the issue. In the lose-lose strategy, the arbitrator gives little attention to tracing the development of the conflict; thus, the solutions are mostly short term.[7]

Win-Win

win-win strategy
A strategy that leads to a solution in which both sides feel that they have come out on top.

A **win-win strategy** is one in which both sides feel they have come out on top. One might ask how both sides in a conflict could end up feeling like winners. The reason is that most conflicts stem from multiple sources and reasons. Because of this complexity, win-win can be accomplished. The key to the success of the win-win strategy is to satisfy as many of each side's needs as possible.[8] People in conflict almost always have more than one reason for being involved in the dispute, and they tend to attach different priorities to each of those reasons. They will, as a rule, be satisfied with less than the entire package if they feel their main goals are achieved. (See Strategy for Success 13.1.)

STYLES OF CONFLICT MANAGEMENT

Everyone has his or her own style of managing conflicts, usually divided into five common approaches, discussed in the following list (also see Figure 13.2). The style you use will have a tremendous impact on the outcome of a conflict and will determine whether it has negative or positive consequences (see Figure 13.3 for an effective conflict resolution strategy). Before you read any further, take the Conflict Management Style survey at the end of this chapter in Working It Out 13.1 to find out what your preferred style of conflict management is.

1. A **competitor** is the most likely to try a win-lose approach to conflict resolution, especially if he or she is personally involved in the conflict. The ideals of teamwork are foreign to competitors, and they rarely move to a win-win solution. If the conflict manager (who should be neutral) is a competitor, he or she might use the lose-lose style to resolve the issue. In this role, competitors are afraid of the disruption that could result from other people's conflict, so they work rapidly and energetically to eliminate the potential disruption.

2. An **avoider** would rather not be around conflict at all. Remaining neutral is very important to an avoider. When the avoider is a manager, he or she will often mistakenly assume that if a conflict involves only other people, it should be left only to them. However, if any conflict is causing even the slightest morale problem at work, *it is the manager's business.* Some avoiders will say positive things about the conflict if someone else should bring it up; others will pretend that nothing significant has happened. In either situation, though, the avoider often feels great internal stress.

3. A **compromiser** uses his or her skills to blend differences of both sides together and form a workable alternative. Although allowing the issue some real urgency, compromisers tend to see *agreement* as more important than the issue itself. A compromiser generally doesn't feel as much of a need to rush to a solution as a competitor does. If you

competitor
Someone who is most likely to try a win-lose approach to conflict resolution, especially if he or she is personally involved in the conflict.

avoider
Someone who would rather not be around conflict at all and values neutrality highly.

compromiser
Someone who uses his or her skills to blend differences and form a workable alternative.

WINNING ON BOTH SIDES

With win-win situations, companies and individuals grow. Conflicts are resolved with higher morale than before, and communication stays open. *How can people bring more win-win situations to their work environments?*

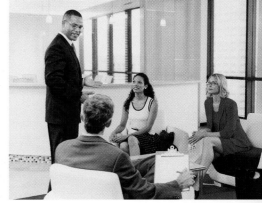

Williams Home and Auto Insurance has five departments, all bidding for a portion of a limited company budget. Whatever one department gains, the other four see as a loss. In the end, it's very possible that none of the five will be completely content with the outcome. Conflict thus seems to be built into the way the company allocates funds.

are a compromiser, watch for the tendency to settle for a lose-lose compromise. Push instead for a win-win solution, following all the steps in that process, so that both sides will feel their main goals have been achieved.

accommodator

Someone who wants to avoid conflict by engaging in positive thinking.

4. An **accommodator** might tell both parties involved in the conflict, "Don't worry; be happy!" Accommodators want to avoid conflict by positive thinking. They tell people to "count their blessings" or "look on the bright side." Keeping the manager happy is also a top priority. The downside to this is that people involved in the conflict may feel they are not being taken seriously, and the accommodator may not be able (or willing) to get others to fully express their reasons for being angry, which may be counterproductive.

figure 13.2

THE THOMAS–KILMAN CONFLICT MODEL

These are the five styles of conflict management. Each has a different level of assertiveness and cooperation. *With which style do you identify?*

Win-Lose Style	Problem-Solving Style
Competitor	**Collaborator**
Confrontational, assertive, and aggressive. Must win at any cost.	Needs of both parties are legitimate and important. High respect for mutual support. Assertive and cooperative.
Compromiser	
Compromising Style	
Important all parties achieve basic goals and maintain good relationships. Aggressive but cooperative.	
Avoider	**Accommodator**
Avoidance Style	**Accommodating Style**
Nonconfrontational. Ignores or passes over issues. Denies issues are a problem.	Agreeable, nonassertive behavior. Cooperative even at the expense of personal goals.

figure 13.3

CONFLICT RESOLUTION METHODS

Qualities of an Effective Conflict Resolution Method

An effective strategy for conflict resolution:

1. Clarifies interests
   - by encouraging both sides to examine the real best interests of their positions.
   - by aiding both sides in exploring what interests they have in common.
   - by communicating each side's interests to the other without unduly exposing anyone to manipulation.

2. Builds a good working relationship
   - by giving *both* sides the chance to deal effectively with their differences.
   - by fostering the type of relationship both sides would have wanted if it weren't for the dispute.
   - by making it easier for both sides to deal with each other next time.

3. Generates good opinions
   - by spurring both parties to brainstorm many options before evaluating them and choosing which one to use.
   - by encouraging both sides to come up with creative solutions that benefit everyone.

4. Is seen by both sides as legitimate
   - by not causing one side to give up more power than the other.
   - by not being seen as going against public interest.
   - by instilling in both sides a sense that the solution will be fair and equitable.

5. Improves communication
   - by encouraging the questioning and testing of underlying assumptions.
   - by aiding the understanding and discussion of differing perceptions of reality.
   - by establishing effective two-way communication between decision makers.

6. Leads to wise commitments
   - by enabling both sides to devise commitments that are realistic, useful, and not likely to lead to future confrontations.
   - by positioning both sides with recourse if the agreement breaks down or is not honored.

A good method for resolving conflict results in better overall morale, communication, and commitments. *Can you think of other qualities of an effective conflict resolution method?*

Source: Reprinted from "How to Design a Conflict Management Procedure That Fits Your Dispute," by Danny Ertel, *Sloan Management Review 22* (Summer 1991), p. 32, by permission of the publisher. Copyright 1991 by the Sloan Management Association. All rights reserved.

5. The **collaborator** brings both sides together for discussion. The collaborative approach is not only the most likely to bring about a win-win solution, but is actually necessary for it. The collaborator opens communication channels and learns about what issues each party feels are most important. Collaboration requires more skill

collaborator
Someone who brings both sides together for discussion toward a win-win solution.

Before leaving for vacation, Jennifer wrote a memo that gave an unclear duty assignment to her department, which caused her employees to quarrel over who should be doing what. When Jennifer's supervisor saw a conflict developing in the workplace, she took a minute to look into it and read the memo. She then decided whether the conflict was being encouraged by the structure or policies of the organization. As it turned out, behavior like Jennifer's was typical for their company, where managers often wrote vague and sometimes confusing memos. In this case, the company's written communication was a structural factor that was not functioning well and thus was causing conflict.

low conformers

Individuals who think independently, solve problems creatively, and often cause some conflict in the process.

DIFFERENT STYLES OF MANAGING CONFLICT

People have many different styles of managing conflict. They include the competitor, the avoider, the compromiser, the accommodator, and the collaborator. *Why might the collaborator require the most skill and diplomacy of all the styles of managing conflict?*

than the other styles of conflict management. For example, it is fairly simple to use the competitive method and force your will on others—so it is easy to see why many conflict managers fall back into that style or one of the simpler methods.

DEALING WITH SPECIAL CONFLICT CASES

Other conflict issues are caused by the specific behaviors of those identified as *problem people*. Such people are those who for one reason or another aren't living up to the expectations of an organization. Some are involved with alcohol or drug abuse. Others are simply people who don't like to do things the way other people do them.

Low Conformers

High conformers are usually easy to work with. They like to fit in, work well in teams, and are generally friendly toward policies and group norms. **Low conformers** are just the opposite: They think independently, solve problems creatively, and often cause some conflict in the process. Working with and managing this type of personality requires a special capacity for patience and good will.[9]

Here are some suggestions that will make working with low conformers less problematic:[10]

- Learn to tolerate their honesty. Low conformers are usually straightforward, using less tact and diplomacy than you might be used to.
- Accept the low conformer's firm method of self-expression without labeling it as stubbornness or disloyalty.
- Support low conformers when others are overly critical.

Maclaren Auto Mall often places salespeople in a higher-status position than the mechanics who work on the cars and must be highly skilled to perform their jobs. Mechanics often see salespeople as unskilled employees who get to dress in nice clothes and often get better pay. Companies like Maclaren are workplaces where conflict is always waiting to happen.

- Accept their independence, and don't be offended if they don't ask for advice.
- Resist the urge to force them to conform.
- Give relevant positive reinforcement even when they don't seem to need it.

You won't be able to change the low conformer any more than you're likely to change the high conformer. Both personality types are important to an organization, one balancing the other.

Envious People

Envy is wanting what another person has, to the extent of feeling ill will toward the person who has it. Envious co-workers cause conflict that can be damaging to morale and productivity and can spread through a department or division like a virus.

The following are several suggestions for dealing with an envious person at work. Some will be more appropriate for you than others, depending on whether you are a manager or an employee. Some may seem to contradict each other, but just remember that they are simply strategies to try. If one doesn't work, go on to the next.

1. **Avoid destructive conflict with the envious person.** If you keep that goal in mind, your actions will be more focused and purposeful.

2. **Confront the envious co-worker.** Some envious people are dealt with best by calling them on their envy, openly and honestly. Once you have called the play, the game usually changes. Because of your approach, you are now perceived as having the power advantage. The envious co-worker will back away and choose someone else as a target (hopefully not another co-worker). One warning: *A vengeful, envious person* often will work even harder behind your back after a confrontation.

3. **Avoid excessive contact with the envious person.** Say hello and good-bye, but avoid making prolonged eye contact or starting a conversation. If the other person wants to chat, politely cut the conversation

Conflict Management Exercise

Go to **www.mhhe.com/lamberton4e** and link to the PharmaOnline page on "Unifying Corporate Mismatches." Summarize what you learned in this article in terms of how it relates to conflict management.

short. Politeness is very important, for you must avoid making the person feel snubbed. Have short conversations; then, move on.

4. **Discuss the problem with your manager.** This meeting should be a perception check. You're just checking to see if your boss perceives the same attitude that you perceive. Don't turn the discussion into a gripe session; remember that you are trying to avoid open conflict.

5. **Build up the envious person's self-esteem.** People often are envious because of low self-worth. Even when other methods fail, this one often reduces the intensity of the envious behavior.

Whatever course of action you decide to use, don't play into the other person's game: Don't descend to subtle insults and backstabbing. If you wait long enough, the problem will usually pass, and the envy will eventually burn itself out.[11]

Whiners and Complainers

How would you deal with Helen in Real World Example 13.10 on page 360 if you were her co-worker? What if you were her boss?

One can readily find people in the workplace who are never happy and who discuss their problems constantly. Whether you are their manager or co-worker, these steps can help you deal with this common source of conflict:

1. **Listen, but not too much.** Whiners and complainers are good at taking advantage of sympathetic listeners. Although you should give honest, relevant complaints an ear when they involve you, learn to pull a rambling gripe session together by asking, "What is your point?" or "What are you going to do to solve this?"

2. **Do frequent reality checks.** You might be able to call the bluff of the chronic whiner by saying something like, "OK, tell me exactly what the problem is and what you want me to do about it." By forcing the complainer to focus on the purpose for the gripe session, and by stressing the limits of your own power to change things, you can often reduce the complaining.

Avoiding Conflict

Link to the course Web page at **www.mhhe.com/lamberton4e** and open the link to the article "Cultural Diversity: Think Twice Before Offering Advice." Summarize what you learned, and how it can be applied across many situations.

3. **Challenge the word *unfair*.** *Unfair* is one of the commonest words used by whiners and complainers. With them, the word often means "I'm not getting what I want." By demanding specific examples of unfairness, and by demanding facts rather than implications or innuendoes, you can force the whiners to focus on what they are really saying.

4. **Be a team leader or player.** As a manager, you can promote a spirit of teamwork and camaraderie in the workplace. You can stress the possibility of transfer for people who aren't team players. As a team member, you can be the kind of team player who won't tolerate the whiners.

> **Complainers and Whiners**
>
> This combination is a conflict waiting to start. Learn to recognize the legitimate complaint when you hear it, but don't tolerate this type of chronic behavior. It is counterproductive and causes negative conflict.

more about...

Passive, Unresponsive People

Unresponsive people are sometimes the most difficult people to work with because on the surface they often seem agreeable and even easygoing. These personality types react to any confrontation or potential conflict by shutting down.

How can you be sure you are dealing with a passive person? Not all quiet people are passive. Some people don't speak up until they are absolutely sure they have something relevant to say; others are very good at screening out irrelevant material and thus seem somewhat unresponsive.[12] Passive people are different: when you most need a response, they will disappoint you.

Passive people have a variety of different reasons for their behavior. Some people use their absence of response as a way of intimidating—a method of calculated aggression. Others remain quiet because they are afraid of sounding foolish. Still others keep quiet to escape responsibility. Words give a concrete reality to thoughts and

> **Passives** are often angry people who express their anger silently and indirectly.

more about...

Janel was a low conformer. She used her own shorthand in memos (which everyone in the office had to learn), turned in her work on her own schedule (which made other people wait), and maneuvered her 9-to-5 job into a flextime schedule nobody else had (which made many people envious). Working with her was often chaotic. Since Janel was very productive and pleasant otherwise, she was able to survive in the company.

feelings. When you speak inner thoughts, you are admitting you have them—a frightening admission for some people. The safer course is to hide them from both others and yourself.[13]

How would you have handled Janel if you had been her manager?

Once you are convinced that it is a passive person you are dealing with, you can take some positive steps to get meaningful feedback from this type of difficult person:[14]

1. **Ask open-ended questions.** Don't ask passive people any question that can be answered with a *yes* or *no,* or even with a brief phrase. Develop questions that encourage them to open up. Some examples are: "How do you react to that?" "What thoughts on this subject occur to you right now?" or "What would you do if . . . ?"

2. **Develop and use a friendly, silent gaze.** After asking an open-ended question, look directly at the silent person with a quizzical, expectant expression on your face. This expression should not be unduly threatening, but it should urge a hesitant person to talk. If you are to use this technique successfully, you must be willing to maintain the gaze *beyond the limits of your own comfort.* Sometimes, this technique won't work. If it doesn't, move quickly to another method.

3. **Don't fill the space.** A supportive person often is tempted to make enough small talk to fill the uncomfortable empty pauses. If you rescue passive people, you will have enabled them to remain passive.

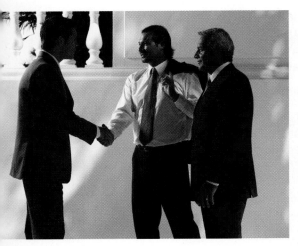

4. **Make statements to help break the tension.** Call attention to what has been going on. Make a statement such as "I expected you to say something, Ignatio, and you're not. What does that mean?" Then return to the friendly, silent gaze. You might also ask, "Can you talk about what you're thinking?" or "What's on your mind right now?"

5. **Set time limits.** Plan in advance how much time you plan to spend dealing with the passive silent person. Tell the person what the time limit is. Often, a great deal will be said in the last few minutes by the silent person who knows that time is short.

Josh was an employee who would begin sulking whenever a co-worker was given a job assignment that he wanted. Sometimes he seemed to want jobs that others had despite the duties involved. Josh simply was not happy with himself, and his self-esteem problems led him to believe that the jobs others had must be better simply because he hadn't gotten them. Some self-esteem boosting helped, but Josh continued to cause conflict through his excessive envy.

Other types of difficult people produce conflict in the workplace. Dealing with all of them requires patience, good listening skills, and time. Whenever a conflict with a difficult person begins, you must become aware as soon as possible that a difficult person is involved; then plan your strategy accordingly. Once the problem is identified, work toward a solution, attempting to get a commitment from the difficult person.

Because of the nature of difficult people, most of them will never completely stop being difficult. Deal with their difficulties on an event-by-event basis, realizing the limitations of any conflict management procedure.

《 《 STRATEGIES FOR SUCCESS

13.1 Negotiate Win-Win Solutions

1. Get emotions under control.
2. Agree on ground rules.
3. Clarify all positions.
4. Explore multiple needs and issues.
5. Develop alternatives.
6. Choose solutions that are win-win.

The conflict manager should look for underlying reasons, interests, and needs. Once these areas are identified, the leader should get each side to list them in order of importance. The rest of the negotiation process is a series of exchanges, with one side giving up one issue in order to gain another from the other side. At this point in the process, a creative negotiator can bring off concession bargaining moves that would not occur to a less creative mind. **Concession bargaining** is the process of getting each side in a conflict to willingly make concessions in exchange for concessions (compromises) made by the opposing side.

> **concession bargaining**
> The process of getting each side in a conflict to willingly make concessions in exchange for concessions made by the opposing side.

Of course, this process isn't as easy as it sounds. The conflict manager must take the group through a series of steps, following some important guidelines, before the win-win method can work.

1. **Get emotions under control.** If emotions are strong on one or both sides, a conflict manager must put most of the creative effort into calming people down. Leaders should be especially careful that their own emotions

Helen was a factory employee who spent virtually all of her free time complaining about her job, personal life, co-workers, or manager. Her favorite word seemed to be "unfair." Everyone was unfair. The job was unfair, especially the pay, and—of course—her manager. Not only did Helen cause daily misery for herself, but she made others around her miserable as well.[15]

more about...

Concession bargaining is used frequently by union bargaining teams to negotiate flexible issues, such as salaries, benefits, and employee rights.

are not involved with either side. A good beginning might be "Look, I know you're angry, but if we're going to resolve this, we need to put our feelings aside and try to work on some alternatives. Would you be willing to do that?"[16] The final question is crucial. Press for a commitment to solving the problem, rather than placing the blame.

People handle their anger in different ways, and the anger itself can become a source of conflict. One side's anger will often feed the anger of the other side until the situation seems hopeless. Both sides may think that the other is not acting in good faith. When you are sitting down to reach a solution, that distrust must be dispelled. Anger *must* be expressed or the other person will not be able to understand the focus of your emotions—yet expressing that anger too strongly (such as with personal insults) can block further communication. If nothing else works, the leader should try getting both sides to explain why they are angry. The focus then becomes the *reasons* behind the feelings, rather than the feelings alone.

2. **Agree on ground rules.** Once the anger has been dealt with, the conflict manager should establish ground rules. He or she should explain that the rules are meant to keep the process running smoothly, not to force either side to conform. To emphasize this, when establishing ground rules, the conflict manager should encourage both sides to suggest rules. The earlier in the process you can get participation, the better. Some of the basic rules could include:[17]

   - Agree to listen as carefully as possible, without interrupting.
   - Agree to control anger, even if someone disagrees with your position.
   - Agree to treat each other with the respect you would like to receive.
   - Agree on the amount of time you will devote to achieving a solution.
   - Resist the urge to force the participants to conform.

   Once ground rules have been established, they can be used as calming and disciplinary devices if the discussion threatens to get out of control. By reminding each side of the rules they agreed to, the leader has a better chance of retaining control.

3. **Clarify all positions.** When emotions are dealt with and the ground rules are set, it is time to get all of the issues, facts, and opinions out for close

An auto dealer who had been forced to reduce his accounting staff heard constant complaints from the head bookkeeper about working with fewer people. He finally asked, "If you can't manage the job with two fewer people, can you recommend someone who can?" The complaining stopped abruptly.

examination. When both sides have seen what the problems are from the other's perspective, they can move toward an understanding that makes both feel like winners. Both sides will still push for whatever they want most, but they will also be listening to the needs of the other side.

Allow both sides equal time for self-expression. If either one is dominating the discussion, the conflict manager should call for more input from the opposition. Some people become suddenly silent during this phase and need to be encouraged to participate. Stay in the *objective mode* as consistently as possible. Everyone involved should take care not to form value judgments.

4. **Explore multiple needs and issues.** Begin this phase by allowing both sides to explain why they chose their position rather than the other one. Then find multiple interests in the issue and look for the ones that both sides share.

5. **Develop alternatives.** Based on the needs and issues you have uncovered, list each possible alternative to be examined carefully later. This can be done much like a brainstorming session: don't allow any value judgments or editorial comments by either side, and strive for *quantity* of ideas, rather than *quality* at this point.

6. **Choose solutions that are win-win.** Explain carefully what a win-win solution is: one that gives something of perceived value to both sides. Then go through each alternative, asking how it can be seen as a win-win solution. Usually a list of acceptable solutions will evolve by consensus. When that fails to happen, the conflict manager must make the decisions alone, asking for a consensus of the solutions he or she selects.

For these six steps to work as a conflict management model, several requirements must be met. First, everyone involved in the conflict must be willing to go through the steps, desiring a long-term solution rather than merely fighting to win. Second, all must be willing to take the *time* required to carry out the process to its conclusion; the win-win strategy is often abandoned for lack of time. Third, the conflict manager must be flexible, sensitive, patient, and calm under fire.[18]

> **more about...**
>
> **The Objective Mode**
>
> The **objective mode** means being "computer-like," not unduly swayed by feelings or emotions. It is calm and does not let emotions interfere with objective decisions.

Renardo, an elderly man, would always shrug and mutter, "Sure, why not?" whenever he was asked to do anything. He showed anger in subtle ways nearly all the time. One reason he was angry was because he had found himself working for a manager who was 20 years younger than he was. The age difference made him feel inferior. His manager found that by asking for his advice, even sometimes when the advice wasn't really needed, the passive anger was reduced.

13.2 Make Collaboration Work

1. Identify the problem.
2. Generate a solution.
3. Identify an action plan.
4. Put the action plan to work.

People in collaboration approach conflict resolution as a problem-solving process. This process should include four phases:

1. **Identify the problem.** Make sure that you are dealing with the real issue, not a result of a deeper problem. Otherwise, even a solution that seems to be win-win will be dealing with symptoms, rather than problems.
2. **Generate a solution.** A group can take this step in many different ways, from group discussion to written questionnaires. This method should involve everyone who is directly affected by the conflict.
3. **Identify an action plan.** If possible, get input from both sides in the creation of this plan. Then get an agreement from both sides to follow it.
4. **Put the action plan to work.** Don't forget to follow up on the results. The follow-up is important in preventing future destructive conflict.

13.3 Stop Conflicts Before They Start

1. Turn the people around you into winners.
2. Work together on common goals.
3. Communicate, communicate, communicate.

The best way to handle negative conflict is by preventing it. Of course, no workplace is totally without negative conflict, but both managers and employees can take steps to prevent many conflicts and soften their impact when they happen.

1. **Turn the people around you into winners.** When people feel they are winners, they are less likely to start harmful conflicts. Self-esteem is a key element in conflict management. Often conflicts are really about self-esteem being undermined. Whatever you can do as either a manager or an employee to bolster the self-esteem of others is likely to prevent harmful conflict. Also, whenever possible, allow for others to be successful at the tasks they perform.

2. **Work together on common goals.** When a workplace is dedicated to common goals, there is usually little room for harmful conflict. Many times, the goals of the company aren't clearly defined, and employees grope in a fog, working more on their own goals and agendas than on the united purpose of the group. If you are a manager, help your staff recognize that the common goal they share is more important than personal status.[19]

3. **Communicate, communicate, communicate.** Listen carefully for hints of discontent. When you need to say something, find the right time and place; then say it clearly but tactfully.

CHAPTER THIRTEEN SUMMARY

Chapter Summary by Learning Objectives

1. **Identify the types of conflict.** Although conflict is always present in the workplace, it isn't always negative. Conflict can be seen as either functional or dysfunctional. When classified by the actors in the conflict five types can be found: inner conflict, person-against-person conflict, intragroup conflict, intergroup conflict, and person-against-group conflict.

2. **List sources of conflict.** Conflict usually springs from one of four sources: content conflict, values conflict, negotiations-of-selves conflict, and institutionalized conflict.

3. **Define conflict analysis.** Analyzing the situation is the first step toward resolving a conflict. Ask such questions as: *Who is involved? What is at stake? How important is time?* and *What are the tie-ins with other issues?* Conflict prevention often involves asking these questions early on.

4. **Give examples of potential solutions to a conflict.** The best solution is nearly always win-win, the solution that makes everyone who is involved feel like a winner. Although they usually don't give permanent solutions to conflicts, win-lose and lose-lose can be used as well.

5. **Compare and contrast styles of conflict management.** The Thomas-Kilman Model shows five different types of conflict management styles for use as strategies in conflict resolution: competitor, avoider, compromiser, accommodator, and collaborator. The best one is collaborator, because it can solve most conflicts when allowed enough time and energy.

6. **Explain how to deal with special conflict cases.** Problem people produce a different type of conflict. Learning to deal with major problem personality types can be helpful in conflict management. Different strategies must be used for low conformers, envious people, whiners and complainers, and passive people.

key terms

accommodator 352

avoider 351

collaborator 353

competitor 351

compromiser 351

concession
   bargaining 359

conflict 344

content conflict 345

dysfunctional
   conflict 344

functional conflict 344

inner conflict 344

institutionalized
   conflict 349

intragroup conflict 345

intergroup conflict 345

lose-lose strategy 350

low conformers 354

negotiation-of-selves
   conflict 348

person-versus-group
   conflict 345

person-versus-person
   conflict 345

values conflict 346

win-lose strategy 350

win-win strategy 350

review questions

1. What are the major causes of conflict in the workplace?

2. What are the four major sources of conflict within organizations? Explain each one, using an example.

3. Explain the Thomas–Kilman Conflict Model. What does this model show as the best method of conflict resolution?

4. Is conflict always negative? If so, what are some effective ways of preventing destructive conflict in the workplace?

5. You are trying to negotiate a workplace conflict through to a win-win solution. What steps would you follow? What pitfalls would you need to avoid?

6. What is negotiation-of-selves conflict, and why is this source of conflict probably the most important in the workplace?

7. What should you do when a person who constantly complains confronts you? Why should you avoid being indifferent or ignoring the person? How would reality checks and being a team leader help?

8. How can a manager or employee tell if he or she is dealing with a passive person? What is the best way to deal with a passive, silent person who is determined not to communicate?

9. Try to remember a conflict you have had with someone recently. What were the sources of the conflict? Was the conflict ever resolved? If so, how? Would you resolve it differently if you could replay the event?

10. Have you ever tried to work or study with a difficult person, such as a whiner or envious person? How did you relate to that individual, if at all? Have you ever confronted an envious person? If so, what happened?

working it out 13.1

YOUR CONFLICT MANAGEMENT STYLE

School-to-Work Connection: Interpersonal Skills

This exercise will help you discover the strategies you use, or would be likely to use, in a conflict situation. In the space next to each statement, write "5" if the statement applies often, "3" if the statement applies sometimes, and "1" if it never applies. (This test will not be accurate unless you strive to be completely honest with yourself in answering.) When I differ with someone:

_____ 1. I explore our differences, neither backing down nor forcing my own view.

_____ 2. I disagree openly, then invite some more discussion about our differences.

_____ 3. I look for a mutually satisfactory solution.

_____ 4. Rather than let the other person make a decision without my input, I make sure I am heard and also that I hear the other person out.

_____ 5. I agree to a middle ground rather than look for a completely satisfying solution.

_____ 6. I will admit that I am half-wrong, rather than discuss our differences.

_____ 7. I have a reputation for meeting the other person halfway.

_____ 8. I expect to be able to get out about half of what I really want to say.

_____ 9. I will give in totally rather than try to change the other person's opinion.

_____ 10. I avoid any controversial aspects of an issue.

_____ 11. I agree early on, rather than arguing about a point.

_____ 12. I give in when the other person becomes emotional about an issue.

_____ 13. I try to win the other person over to my side.

_____ 14. I work to come out victorious, no matter what.

_____ 15. I never back away from a good argument.

_____ 16. I would rather win than end up compromising.

To score your responses, add your total score for each of the following sets of statements:

Set A: Statements 1–4 _____

Set B: Statements 5–8 _____

Set C: Statements 9–12 _____

Set D: Statements 13–16 _____

A score of 17 or more on any set is considered high. Scores of 12 to 16 are moderately high. Scores of 8 to 11 are moderately low. Scores of 7 or less are considered low.

Each set represents a different strategy for conflict management:

Set A: Collaboration (I win; you win.)

Set B: Compromise (Both win some; both lose some.)

Set C: Accommodation (I lose; you win.)

Set D: Competition (I win; you lose.)

internet exercises

1. *Read and Write*

   Go to **www.managementhelp.org/intrpsn/conflict.htm,** or go to the link at **www.mhhe.com/lamberton4e** to read "Addressing Interpersonal Conflict." Think about an interpersonal conflict you have recently experienced. Write a brief paragraph to answer these questions:

   a. How could the issues discussed in this essay have helped you bring the conflict to a more satisfying conclusion?

   b. How could the issues you read have helped you avoid conflict altogether?

2. *Read and Write*

   Visit Susan Kramer's Web site on spiritual growth and harmony with others at **www.susankramer.com/DifficultPeople.html#3** or enter **www.mhhe.com/lamberton4e.** This is an article with four sections. Read all four sections; then write a brief essay showing what you learned from this colorful little Web site. In your essay, please include answers to the following questions:

a. What conflict seems to be the most common in the workplaces you have encountered?

b. How could information in this article help with such conflicts?

c. What—if anything—would you add to the instructions in this article?

3. *Summarize and Report*

What are the best companies to work for? We don't usually know how companies handle conflict from within, but other factors can make companies more or less attractive to employees. Think about what is important to you in looking for employment. What makes a company best? What are specific companies really like? Are there specific companies you are interested in and would like to know more about? Research companies at **http://jobstar.org/hidden/ coinfo.cfm** or link through the course Web site at **www.mhhe. com/lamberton4e.** Summarize and report your findings.

The Wrenches and the Suits

José Ortega now had a job he'd always wanted—selling new cars in a large, well-known dealership. His manager was generous with commissions and didn't ride his sales staff the way his other bosses had. José was selling more than his quota of cars each week, and he got along well with the rest of the sales staff.

Soon, though, José began to notice that this dealership was split into two factions. Some employees called them the suits and the wrenches. The sales staff and accounting department were the working suits, and the service department and body shop employees were the wrenches. Several times a week, José would have to deal with the service department. Nearly every time, he would be insulted or otherwise mistreated. "I'm a gentleman," José told one of his co-workers, "but I come closer to telling them off every time they're rude."

One Monday morning José walked up to the service desk and asked Juanita, the assistant service manager, for a special appointment for a customer who was very upset about a defective muffler. "Who does he think he is, anyway?" asked Juanita. "We're booked full all day."

José wasn't in the mood for Juanita's defiance. "I work here just like you do! But unlike you, I try to keep my customers happy. It's the customer who's important here, not me. Now give me an appointment some time today or tomorrow, or I'll make you wish you had!"

"What's that, a threat? What are you going to do, fire me?"

"Just do it!" José shouted as he walked back toward his office. After a couple of minutes at his desk, he got up and walked slowly into his supervisor's office.

"Barry," he began, "there's a problem in this company that we really need to talk about."

Case Study Questions

1. What are the sources of the conflict in this case? Explain.

2. Is Barry, the sales manager, the right person to be the conflict manager in this situation? Why or why not?

3. What would you do if you were José? What will happen if Barry chooses to do nothing? Can José and his fellow salespeople do anything to effect a change? If so, what?

The Rush Order

Hans was a salesperson at Enco, Inc. One morning he approached Norma, the production manager. "Hey, Norma," he said. "I just got an order for 150 units. I had to promise speedy delivery to get the order."

Norma asked, "Well, how speedy did you promise them?" Hans said he promised two-day delivery. Norma replied, "Hans, you know we have to have at least two shifts to even get the production finished, without figuring in shipping time."

"What are you saying?" Hans exploded. "That you won't even try? Well, Mr. Carlson will override your stubbornness. I'll just go see him."

Later that day, a rather sheepish Hans again approached Norma with a different tone. "Hi, Norma. So, what did you tell Mr. Carlson? He's never said 'no' to one of my rush orders before."

"I didn't say anything to him. Mr. Carlson could see that our present orders are at least as important as your 'urgent' one."

"Look, Norma, I guess I was scared about losing an order. Can you see where I was coming from?"

Norma said, "I understand your position. But you are the one who got yourself in this predicament. Using impossible delivery schedules as a major selling point is not wise."

"You're right," Hans agreed. "About an hour ago, I called the customer, and you know what? They'll go for three days if we ship two-day mail service."

Norma stayed firm. "Tell you what, Hans. You talk to Mr. Carlson about budgeting the extra money for overnight delivery. If he goes for that, I'll see to it the order gets out in three days."

"When Carlson finds out we'll lose a big client unless we ship overnight, I know he'll go for it. I really owe you one."

"No, you don't 'owe me one.' Just please lay off the rush orders. You're good enough at sales to not let this happen."

Case Study Questions

1. What are the sources of conflict in this case?

2. Is the solution a win-win? Explain.

3. If Hans should come up with another situation like this one, what would you do if you were Norma? If you were Mr. Carlson?

STRESS AND STRESS MANAGEMENT

In the Workplace: What's Wrong with Me?

SITUATION

Stephanie Williams is a lower-level supervisor at a county agency. At first she enjoyed her job, but lately she just can't seem to concentrate at work. She has also been having trouble sleeping, has lost her appetite, and resumed smoking. To top it off, she seems to be getting every cold and flu that goes around the office.

At home, things have not been easy financially since her divorce last year. Her three children are pretty easygoing kids, but over the summer Stephanie missed two weeks of work when her daughter had chicken pox, and several more days this fall when her son fell off the playground equipment at school and broke his arm. Now she has used up all her vacation time and sick leave, and she has even had to take some unpaid leave days. Meanwhile, her ex-husband has fallen behind in his child support payments, and she is feeling overwhelmed.

Stephanie's supervisor, Donna Clark, has called her in several times in the past month to talk about Stephanie's performance. She has told Stephanie that

LEARNING objectives

After studying this chapter, you will be able to:

1. Identify the main causes of stress.
2. Give examples of external and internal sources of stress.
3. Compare and contrast type A and type B personality behaviors.
4. Describe the physical effects of stress.
5. Explain the cost of stress in the workplace.

STRATEGIES FOR SUCCESS

Strategy 14.1 Discard Irrational Beliefs

Strategy 14.2 Change Your Behaviors to Reduce Stress

Strategy 14.3 Take Care of Yourself

the office is getting complaints from clients about poor service in the office, and she wants to know why Stephanie is not handling routine things in her usual efficient manner.

Over lunch, Stephanie tells her friend and co-worker Lakeesha Jones, "I just don't know what's the matter with me. I can't seem to get anything done, I lose my train of thought all the time, I don't feel well half the time, I'm always tired, and I keep snapping at the kids for no reason. Am I going crazy? What's wrong with me?"

DISCOVERY

Lakeesha answers, "I don't know what your problem is, but you'd better snap out of it or you're going to lose your job. I heard that Donna has been looking over files in personnel, and you know what that means! Somebody is going to get the ax!"

"Oh, no!" Stephanie wailed. "Lakeesha, I just *can't* lose my job! What am I going to do?"

THINK ABOUT IT

What seems to be wrong with Stephanie? What kinds of actions could Stephanie take on her own to help herself? If you were Lakeesha, what would you identify as Stephanie's problem? What would you suggest Stephanie do to help her situation? Have you had friends or co-workers in similar situations, or have you yourself experienced them? How were they resolved?

CAUSES OF STRESS

Which of these two situations do you believe would be more stressful?

- During the past year, you were fired or laid off from your job, and a close friend died.
- During the past year, you got married, added a healthy baby to your family, received a big promotion at work, and moved into a new and bigger house.

The answer may surprise you: stress researchers would say that the second situation is more stressful. This is because the more major life changes you are experiencing, the more stress you are likely to feel. This reasoning will be explored in more detail in this chapter. First, though, is an explanation of what is meant by *stress* and *stressors*.

According to psychologists, **stress** can be defined as *the nonspecific response of the body to any demand made on it.*[1] In other words, any reaction or response your body makes to a new situation is stress. Ongoing situations that seem to be too much for us to handle will also cause stress. The *reaction* is both emotional and physical. Hans Selye, a Canadian physiologist who researched stress and its effects for 50 years, believed that human bodies are nearly always in some kind of stress. He maintained that some stress is necessary for life, and he distinguished between two kinds of stress. The first is **eustress,** or good stress—the kind of pleasant, desirable stress you might feel when playing tennis or attending a party. The second is **distress,** or bad stress—the kind of stress you might feel during an illness or when going through a divorce.[2] Even though there are positive effects of stress, and some kinds of stressful events are pleasurable, this discussion of stress will actually refer to *distress,* which fits the everyday definition of stress.

Stress is your *body's reaction* to a new situation, or an ongoing situation that seems overwhelming. A **stressor** is the situation or event itself that caused your body to react. Stress can be caused by major life changes and everyday hassles, as well as many other sources. Stressors can be caused by internal factors, such as a negative or suspicious thinking style, or the kind of worry about ongoing life problems that Stephanie was experiencing in our opening vignette. Stressors can also come from external sources, such as "red tape" or bureaucracy at work or school that is outside your control.

stress

Any reaction or response made by the body to a new situation.

eustress

Positive stress, the kind felt when playing tennis or attending a party.

distress

Negative stress, the kind felt during an illness or when going through a divorce.

stressor

A situation or an event that causes the body to react (causes stress).

major life changes

Changes in your life, such as divorce, that increase daily hassles, leaving you stressed and worn out.

daily hassles

The daily annoyances, such as getting stuck in traffic or misplacing your keys, that can cause stress in your life.

Life Changes and Daily Hassles

Any change can be stressful, especially **major life changes.** However, according to some stress researchers, the **daily hassles** that everyone experiences can be very stressful as well, possibly even more so because they happen more frequently and seem to pile up on top of one another.[3]

One day you might be rushing out the door for work and you spill coffee on yourself. You set your keys down, run and change your clothes, only to forget where you put your keys. You finally find them, but by now you are late for work. You drive too fast, get pulled over, and receive a speeding ticket. You make it to work and find there is no place left to park. You finally find a space, grab your belongings from the car and run for the office, but in your haste you drop a set of important papers into a nearby mud puddle—and your workday has not even started yet!

Major life changes and daily hassles can go hand in hand— especially when major life changes *cause* daily hassles.

Imagine that you have just gotten a divorce. This is a major life change that can lead to many daily hassles you may not have had before. You may have to move, set up a new day-care arrangement, take over a larger share of the housework or yardwork, open a new bank account, find a new grocery store, explain your situation repeatedly to friends or acquaintances, and so on. These daily hassles can leave you feeling stressed and worn out.

Even if your stress is due to a pleasant change, such as starting college, daily hassles can occur. You may be very excited to begin your new adventure in college, but the little hassles such as finding the bookstore, figuring out which books to buy, finding the library, filling out forms for your library card, getting your picture taken for your student identification card, applying for your student computer account, and filling out forms for your campus parking sticker can leave you feeling drained and stressed— and you haven't even found your classrooms or started classes yet!

MANY SOURCES OF STRESS

Stress can be caused by many different factors: both positive and negative major life changes, as well as smaller everyday problems. *Do you have different ways of dealing with different kinds of stress, whether in the workplace or in your personal life?*

Chronic Stressors

Chronic stressors are inescapable, day-to-day situations or conditions that cause stress. They are more stressful than daily hassles, but not as stressful as a major life change. Things like poverty, ongoing abuse, and long-term health problems are examples of chronic stressors. Being discriminated against because of issues such as race or ethnicity, gender, age, or religion is also a chronic stressor.

In the past few years, researchers have focused attention on the chronic stress of being a member of a minority group. Even when there is no outright evidence of racism, simply being the only member (or one of the only members) of a particular race in a variety of settings such as work or school can cause stress.[4] Diversity issues will be discussed in more detail in Chapter 16.

> **chronic stressors**
> Inescapable, day-to-day situations or conditions that cause stress.

SOURCES OF STRESS

In addition to studying major life changes, daily hassles, and chronic stress, psychologists studying causes of stress have identified specific internal and external sources of it in people's lives.

Stressed Out

Go to **www.mhhe.com/lamberton4e** to find information that is useful for everyone. Find methods that you find valuable for coping with stress. Practice using the suggested deep relaxation techniques for reducing stress. Then write a brief paragraph about what you have learned.

external stressors

Stressors that include anything from outside sources that causes you pain or discomfort.

frustration

The feeling people get when goals they are trying to attain are blocked.

External Stressors

According to psychologists, **external stressors** can include anything and everything from outside sources that causes you pain or discomfort, frustration, or conflict.[5]

1. *Pain or discomfort.* Chronic or even temporary pain can make you feel stressed and lower your job performance. Think of the last time you had a bad toothache or headache and how much that interfered with your concentration. Discomfort (even something as minor as the workroom being too hot or too cold) can have a negative effect on you as well.

2. *Frustration.* The feeling you get when a goal you are trying to attain is blocked defines **frustration.** For example, you might feel frustrated when a co-worker takes credit for your creative ideas.

3. *Inner conflict.* Chapter 13 introduced you to several ways of thinking about conflict. In this chapter, we will examine one of those in more detail, as a source of stress: **inner conflict.** Inner conflict is the kind of pressure you feel when you are forced to make a choice. Even though you feel it internally, it is considered an external stressor because the *source* of this conflict comes from outside. This type of conflict is the feeling you get when you are torn in two or more directions.

   We all experience several kinds of inner conflict. These include approach-approach, approach-avoid, and avoid-avoid conflict.

more about...

Hans Selye (1907–1982) was a Canadian doctor and medical educator who pioneered research on different types of stress. He began his studies on stress in 1926, during his second year in medical school. He cofounded the Canadian Institute of Stress in 1979, still active today offering training programs and consultations for workplaces and individuals, and reporting findings on stress research. You can visit the Institute's Web site at **www.stresscanada.org/.**

inner conflict

The pressure you feel when you are forced to make a choice.

External	Internal
Bureaucracy, deadlines	Suspicious outlook, overanalyzing
Financial problems	Negative thinking and negative self-talk
Unemployment	Chronic worry, dread, depression
Poor health	Poor social skills
Relationship issues	Shy or unassertive personality
School pressures	Aggressive or bossy personality
Problems in the workplace	Hostile, impatient, time-urgent
Loss (grief, bereavement)	Overly competitive, perfectionist
Daily hassles	Calm outside, agitated inside
Unexpected bad news	Poor time management
Organizational rules, policies, red tape	Poor lifestyle choices (lack of sleep,
Physical environment (heat, noise, etc.)	smoking, overeating, etc.)
Behavior of others (rude, bossy, etc.)	Self-critical, take things personally
Major life changes	Unrealistic expectations, all-or-nothing thinking, rigid thinking

EXTERNAL AND INTERNAL SOURCES OF STRESS (EXAMPLES)

Sources: "What Are the Sources of Stress?" Woodbridge Hospital, Singapore; Institute of Mental Health Online (retrieved June 1, 2008), www.imh.com.sg/patient_education/overcm_stress.htm. See also The Stress Clinic, TheStressClinic.com, www.thestressclinic.com/ (retrieved June 1, 2008).

The first of these, approach-approach, is the feeling of conflict you get when torn between two desirable goals. For example, you may really like your job and enjoy your co-workers, but when offered a promotion, you are also excited about the prospect of making more money. You want to stay in your current job and not move away from your friends, but you also want the promotion that would give you more money. You can't have both at the same time.

An approach-avoid conflict occurs when you are drawn toward and away from something at the same time. For example, you may really want that promotion, but it would mean transferring to another state, and you are reluctant to pull up stakes and start over again somewhere else.

more about...

Job Stress in the United States

A survey done in 2007 by the American Psychological Association on work-related stress in the United States found that more than half of people answering the survey said they had left a job or thought about leaving because of stress. More than half (55%) also said that stress on the job made them less productive at work. One-third of them reported they are living with extreme stress, and the most commonly listed source of stress—for 74 percent of respondents—was work. This percentage was up from 59 percent just a year earlier.

Source: *New York Times,* www.nytimes.com/2008/03/23/jobs/23mgmt.html (retrieved May 28, 2008).

DAILY HASSLES

When daily hassles start to pile up, especially early in the day, they can have a strong effect on you. Even though the stress is short term, it can be as intense as some types of long-term stress. *How do you deal with those days when nothing seems to go right?*

An avoid-avoid conflict occurs when you are torn between two *un*desirable options. For example, you may not get along with your supervisor and you may dread going to work each day, but at the same time you hate the idea of pounding the pavement looking for a new job.

Internal Stressors

According to psychologists, **internal stressors** can include your own perceptions or interpretations of a stressor, as well as personality factors.[6]

Every person has a different perception of the same situation or stressor. A major problem to one person may be an exciting challenge to another. Let's take the example of a common event in the business world since the 1980s: downsizing. Two middle managers who are laid off may see their situations quite differently: One sees the layoff as a chance for a new start in another work situation, whereas the other sees it as a terrible personal and professional disaster. What makes each of them perceive the same events differently? Two basic internal factors are their cognitive appraisal of each situation, and their individual personality factors.

1. *Cognitive appraisal.* Cognitive appraisal can be thought of as your "thinking evaluation" of an event or a situation. In the process of making a **cognitive appraisal,** you unconsciously ask yourself two questions. The first one is: *Is this stressor harmful to me in any way?* If the answer to that question is yes, then you also ask yourself: *Do I have the resources (time, energy, and so on) to handle this stressor?* If the answer to that question is no, then you feel stress. These questions and responses are processed in a fraction of a second, usually faster than you are aware.

Cognitive appraisal varies not only from person to person, but from day to day with the same person or the same situation. What makes you spend some mornings in rush-hour traffic cursing and shaking your fist at other drivers, while you spend other mornings during the same traffic-filled commute singing along with the radio, smiling at other drivers? Part of the answer lies in the number of daily hassles you experience: The more stressors you encounter, the more annoyed you feel at new stressors and the more difficulty you have adapting to them. Sometimes you may feel a particular situation is potentially harmful; at other times you may not. Sometimes you *do* feel you have the energy (a resource) to handle a particular situation, but at other times you just *don't* have the energy.

more about...

Climate Stressors

At one college, uncomfortable classrooms and office temperatures were two of the most common complaints listed by staff members and students alike, beating such stressors as tuition hikes and staff layoffs.

internal stressors

Your perceptions of stressors, which may vary depending on personality.

cognitive appraisal

The thinking evaluation of an event or situation that varies from person to person and, for an individual person, from day to day.

Another part of the answer to why cognitive appraisal varies so much lies in the individual internal factors that make each person unique. Here is a closer look at another specific type of internal factor, the irrational belief system.

2. *The unnecessary stress of irrational beliefs.* Albert Ellis, a well-known psychologist, believes that one of the internal causes of stress (i.e., stress that you put on yourself) is an **irrational belief system.**[7] These irrational beliefs include such things as believing that everyone must like you, or that you must never make mistakes. At worst, some people **catastrophize,** or turn an irrational belief into an imagined catastrophe. For example, let's say that in Zena's weekly department meeting, her co-worker made a remark that sounded innocent enough, but which made her look very industrious, while it made Zena look a little incompetent: "I noticed that Zena wasn't able to finish the accounts receivable forms in time to ship out yesterday, so I went ahead and finished those up last night. You can thank me by buying me lunch, Zena!" Other people in the meeting just smile or chuckle, but Zena is thinking, "I will never make a good impression with these people. I am never going to get ahead in this company. I'll probably just get demoted for the rest of my life. And I can't work anywhere else, because no one here will give me a good recommendation. They'll probably turn my friends and family against me too, somehow. Why can't I ever do anything right?" Zena turned one event into a catastrophe with her irrational beliefs.

According to Ellis, it can be understandable to believe things should turn out better than they actually do. However, it is irrational to *expect* that they will, and irrational to believe that you cannot survive unless they do. Ellis feels that not just stressors themselves, but also people's *beliefs* about stressors, are sources of stress. Using an example in which your supervisor asks you to redo some work, take a closer look at Ellis's ABC approach to stress in Figure 14.1. In this idea, the A stands for an *activating event*—in this case, being asked to do the work over again. The B stands for your *belief* about the activating event—in this case, the irrational beliefs that arise from having to redo the work. The C stands for the *consequences* of the eventual outcome caused by the activating event and your beliefs about it—in this case, the anxiety and misery you feel, and the behavior resulting from those feelings.

Irrational beliefs, then, can lead to catastrophizing an event—a stressor—or blowing it out of proportion. This makes you less able to cope with it, which in turn makes you less able to solve the problem and adds more stress. Thus, the biggest culprit in your emotional stress and anxiety, according to Ellis, is the B (or belief) part of the ABC. It is not the event itself that is responsible for your emotional response; it is your belief about it. Unfortunately, irrational beliefs

DEALING WITH EXTERNAL STRESSORS

Stress can be caused by external factors that are both ordinary and out of your control, ranging from an uncomfortable environment to frustration and conflict. *How do you manage the stress caused by factors beyond your control?*

irrational belief system

A way of thinking that causes internal stress by substituting a realistic belief with one that is destructive, illogical, and largely false.

catastrophize

To expand an irrational belief into an imagined disaster.

figure 14.1

ELLIS'S ABC APPROACH TO STRESS

This ABC formula illustrates how stress develops inside of people. An *activating event* triggers people to form a *belief* about it, which in turn shapes the *consequences. How much can your beliefs affect the outcome of stressful situations?*

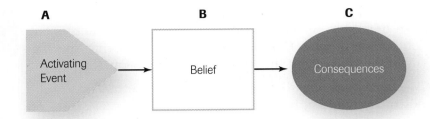

can become a vicious cycle and repeat themselves endlessly as negative emotions turn into negative behaviors. (See Figure 14.2.) Using the earlier example of the remarks made in the department meeting,

figure 14.2

IRRATIONAL BELIEFS AND STRESS

Irrational beliefs can cripple people facing stress because they make them fear outcomes that do not actually exist. Most of these irrational beliefs take situations to extremes—even though that can create more problems and stress. *What are your irrational beliefs, and what do they do to your stress level?*

Ten Irrational Beliefs

Although everyone has irrational beliefs, according to Ellis, each person has a different set of them. Ten of the most common ones can be summarized as follows. As you read this list, ask yourself (honestly!) how many of them you believe or have you believed.

Irrational belief #1: I must have love or approval from all of the people who are important to me.

Irrational belief #2: I must prove myself to be thoroughly competent, adequate, and achieving at something important.

Irrational belief #3: When people act obnoxiously or unfairly, they should be blamed for being bad, rotten, or wicked individuals.

Irrational belief #4: When I am seriously frustrated, treated unfairly, or rejected, I must view the situation as awful, terrible, horrible, and catastrophic.

Irrational belief #5: Emotional misery comes from external pressures and I have little ability to control or change my feelings.

Irrational belief #6: If something seems dangerous or fearsome, I must preoccupy myself with it and make myself anxious about it.

Irrational belief #7: It is better to avoid facing my difficulties and responsibilities than it is to use self-discipline to obtain rewarding things.

Irrational belief #8: My past experiences remain all-important. Since something once strongly influenced my life, it has to keep determining my feelings and behavior today.

Irrational belief #9: It is awful and horrible if I do not find good solutions to life's grim realities.

Irrational belief #10: I can achieve maximum happiness by inertia or inaction or by passively and uncommitedly "enjoying myself."

A working mother was having a rough morning, full of hassles and feeling overwhelmed. Rushing to finish breakfast with her son, she spilled her coffee on her black sweater. Her young son said to her, "Mommy, you should always wear black clothes, because then no one can see the coffee you spill on yourself and you don't have to change your clothes." Children have a way of putting stressors into perspective!

more about…

we can see that Zena's irrational beliefs can lead to depression and anxiety, and these lead to low motivation and low energy, which can make her less likely to finish other projects in the future. This just repeats the cycle until she says, "I was right; I can't do this job at all. What's the point of even trying?" And the eventual outcome is that she quits trying.

Is there any hope for reducing the stress of irrational beliefs? Yes, according to Ellis. You can try to reduce the stress of irrational beliefs by changing them yourself, using his principles of "rational-emotive therapy" to improve your own belief system and replace irrational beliefs with more rational ones. In a nutshell, this means changing the B of the ABC. Strategy for Success 14.1 explains this in more detail.

Survivor Guilt

Research on the *survivors* of mass layoffs and downsizing (i.e., those who kept their jobs) has found that these employees often suffer more stress effects than the *victims* of layoffs. Survivors have reported feeling more stress, less control on the job, lower job satisfaction, and "survivor guilt," along with poorer health and quality of life than victims of layoffs who later found jobs. Survivors also missed work more often and reported more drug use.[8]

TYPE A AND TYPE B PERSONALITY BEHAVIOR

So far in this discussion of the internal stressors, you have examined cognitive appraisal and irrational belief systems. Turn your attention now to the third type of internal stressor, personality factors—also known as **type A and type B personalities.**

This personality theory has become so popular that most people are already familiar with it. According to this theory, people can be categorized into either of these two personality types on the basis of their behaviors and personality styles. Type A people are seen as impatient, hostile perfectionists with a sense of time urgency.

The danger of being like Marco in Real World Example 14.2 on page 380 is that type A people seem more likely to have cardiovascular problems such as heart attacks and strokes. Type B people, on the other hand, are more flexible, more relaxed, better able to delegate work, and

type A and type B personalities

Two standard personality-related behaviors. Type A personalities are characterized by impatience, hostility, perfectionism, and a sense of time urgency. Type B personalities are characterized by flexibility, the ability to relax and delegate work, and a minimal sense of time urgency.

Marco has a type A personality. He walks and eats quickly and combines two or more tasks to save time. He finishes other people's sentences for them, finishes other people's work if he feels they are too slow, and feels guilty when he is not busy. He also becomes extremely irritated when having to wait for anything such as a dentist appointment or a meeting.

HOLDING ON TO SELF-DEFEATING BELIEFS

An important step in getting rid of irrational beliefs is to dispute, or argue against, beliefs that sabotage your ability to stay calm in stressful situations. Think about your beliefs; if any are self-defeating, eliminate them. *How can you get rid of self-defeating beliefs?*

less time-urgent.[9] Two bits of folk wisdom are sometimes heard about type A and type B people in the workplace. The first is that top-level executives are likely to be type Bs, with type A assistants frantically running around doing their work for them. This is because type Bs can delegate responsibility, whereas type As are such perfectionists that they have to do all the work themselves and will never get to the top because of this. The second thing heard about types A and B is that the road to becoming a CEO is paved with the dead bodies of type As (presumably dead from heart attacks), with type Bs stepping over the bodies on their way to the top.

Although the type A and type B personality idea has been very popular in recent years, psychologists now say it may not be as useful as originally thought. People are not so simply categorized. They may act like a type A one day and a type B the next, or with some issues they act like one type and with other issues the other type. In addition, they may act like one type on the outside but feel completely different inside. The best point to learn from the type A/type B personality theory and stress debate is that it is most important for people to examine their *behaviors*. The truth seems to be that the behaviors of constant anger (sometimes called *toxic hostility*) and, to a lesser extent, time urgency (sometimes called *hurry sickness*) probably have worse health effects than does an overall personality type.[10]

If you recognized yourself in the risky type A behavior profile above, relax! These behaviors are just habits; they don't have to be permanent. Later in this chapter you will examine ways to change behavior, or cope with stress in a healthy way. If your behaviors are more relaxed than hostile, don't gloat! Too much of a good thing is a problem, as well: People who are overly relaxed, to the point of having depressive personalities, also have an increased risk of disease.

To find out if you fit into a type A or a type B personality behavior profile, take the test at the end of the chapter (see Working It Out 14.1). Remember, these are just *behaviors*, which can be changed. Behaviors are not some unchangeable aspect of personality that has been set in stone.

You may know someone with a different kind of personality than type A or type B, someone who just seems be a *survivor*. This type of person, in spite of stressors and problems that seem impossible to overcome, manages just fine. Why are some people in stressful situations able to come out smiling, while others fail? Suzanne Kobasa and others in the past decade have been studying what they call the **hardy personality,** or resilient personality.[11]

Regardless of the situation, these people seem to have three things in common—the "three Cs" of a hardy personality: challenge, commitment, and control. Where others see terrible problems to overcome, they see *challenges* to meet. People with a hardy personality also have a sense of *commitment*. It doesn't matter to what; it could be to their jobs, education, a religion, a political cause, to raising their children, or to a healthier lifestyle for themselves. They just feel a sense of purpose or a mission in life. Finally, they feel that they are in *control* of their lives and in charge of what happens to them, instead of seeing themselves as passive beings with no say in the course of their own lives. This is the idea of the "internal locus of control" introduced in Chapter 2.

THE PHYSICAL EFFECTS OF STRESS

You can see that stress can have more than just emotional and psychological effects. It can also have serious, even life-threatening, physical effects. To reduce the harmful effects of stress, you need to understand how this process works.

How Our Bodies Adapt to Stress

In his book *The Stress of Life*, Hans Selye developed and tested a theory about what stress does to people physically. He called it the *general adaptation syndrome*, or GAS. According to this theory, when you are first confronted with a stressor, your body responds with an activation of the sympathetic nervous system. This has come to be known as the *fight-or-flight response*. During the fight-or-flight response, your body quickly (in a matter of seconds) gets ready to confront or to escape the stressor by specific physical and chemical reactions. These include increased heart rate, blood pressure, respiration, stomach acid, tensed muscles, and a sudden release of adrenaline. When the fight-or-flight response is activated, according to Selye, you have entered the first stage of GAS, the *alarm stage*.[12]

LEARNING FROM THE OTHER SIDE

Neither a type A nor a type B personality is free from stress. They both deal with stress in different ways, with benefits and risks to each method. *Why is it important to learn from the opposite type if you classify yourself according to this personality theory? What can you learn by observing others who act differently under stress than you do?*

hardy personality
A resilient personality type, characterized by the ability to meet challenges, a sense of commitment, and a feeling of being in control of life.

Time Urgency

In the final words of Queen Elizabeth I (1533–1603), "All my possessions for a moment of time."

more about...

Resources on Stress

This "Stress Virtual Library" offers resources on identifying and handling almost any type of stress. Go to **www.mhhe.com/lamberton4e** for the link to this site. Compare the solutions given for different types of stress and write a brief summary including what you believe to be the best solution.

Once the alarm is sounded, you enter the second stage of GAS, the *stage of adaptation*. You adapt to the stressor and can usually return to normal. As you try to restore lost energy and repair any damage done to your body, your sympathetic nervous system is still activated, but not at the high level it was during the alarm stage. As you successfully cope with the stressor, you activate your parasympathetic nervous system. Heart rate, blood pressure, respiration, and muscles then relax. Most of the time, people at this stage are able to cope with the stressor and soon return to normal.

In some cases, though, you are not able to adapt to a stressor and can end up using up (or exhausting) all of your physical resources. You then enter the third stage of GAS, the *stage of exhaustion*. During this stage, the parasympathetic nervous system is still activated, so you appear relaxed, but the stressor is still present. In this stage, you are unable to cope with the prolonged stressor, and you can become vulnerable to other stressors.

As the school term nears an end, for example, stress increases so that during final exams week many students are using up all their stored energy and physical resources. By the end of the term, students have completely used up their energy and resources, and they enter the stage of exhaustion. Then, instead of enjoying the break between terms, they may wind up catching a cold or the flu, or becoming accident-prone. The same thing can happen at work when employees exhaust themselves trying to get everything finished and out of the way before they go on vacation. Instead of enjoying their vacation time, they get sick!

Selye would say these students and employees have succumbed to a *disease of adaptation*. In the

---

more about...

Taking Charge

An anonymous quote says, "Yesterday is a canceled check, tomorrow is a promissory note, today is ready cash: Use it!"

---

more about...

Stressors . . . or Situations?

As one woman said during her treatment for cancer, "Stop feeling sorry for me! I'm not *dying* of cancer, I'm just *living with* cancer!" This rethinking of her diagnosis, she says, helped her fight the disease and eventually recover.

most extreme cases, people exposed to pro-longed stress may even die. You may know of a case where an elderly friend or relative fell and broke a hip (because balance declines and bones get more brittle with age), entered the hospital for treatment of the broken hip, and died soon thereafter of pneumonia or heart failure. According to Selye's theory of GAS, if the stress of healing the broken hip was pro-longed, then the patient entered the stage of exhaustion and fell victim to a disease of adap-tation (pneumonia or heart failure).

According to Selye, extreme responses to stress may have been essential in early times when people were facing attacks by wild animals. Today, however, these reactions are harmful if they persist. Think about the physical symptoms present during the fight-or-flight response. What happens in the long run, say, when you are stuck in traffic every day during your commute to work and your heart rate, blood pres-sure, respiration rate, and stomach acids increase? The muscle ten-sion in your neck, head, and back that appeared because the traffic (a stressor) triggered the alarm stage may, over time, turn into a headache, stiff neck, or backache. The increased heart rate may eventually turn into cardiovascular disease. The increase in blood pressure may turn into hypertension, eventually resulting in a stroke or heart attack. The increase in stomach acid may turn into heartburn, indigestion, or ulcers.

Remember that in Selye's theory, eustress and distress both pro-duce the physical and chemical changes of the fight-or-flight response because your body cannot tell the difference between the two. Imagine a friend telling you, for example, that he wasn't able to sleep, had no appetite, felt dizzy and lightheaded, and couldn't concentrate. Without any more information, would you guess that he was coming down with the flu or falling in love? Events that you interpret as good or bad can produce the same physical reactions. They are both stressors because they make demands on your body to adapt or to change. As you have learned, it is adapting to change that is stressful.

Although Selye's original book is more than 50 years old, its theories are supported even more today by the work of health psychologists and medical researchers who study long-term effects of stress and the relationship of stress to the immune system.

In a "meta-analysis" (a study of studies) made public in 2004, researchers examined the results of almost 300 studies that took place over a 40-year span (1960–2000)

Adding Fuel to the Fire

Researchers found that one reason people with type A behaviors are more susceptible to coronary artery disease is that they are also more likely to smoke and to eat high-cholesterol foods. Reducing stress and learning to relax may reduce the "need" to smoke, which then reduces the risk of heart disease.

Source: From *The Harvard Heart Letter,* President and Fellows of Harvard College, January 1992 p. 104.

more about...

INCREASE HEALTH BY DECREASING STRESS

By paying attention to factors such as nutrition, exercise, and proper sleep, you can avoid the debilitating long-term effects of most types of stress. *What do you do to strengthen your body against stress?*

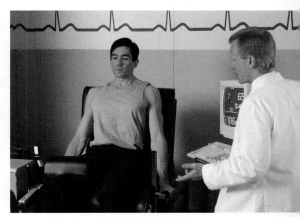

and included almost 20,000 people. What they found supported Selye's ideas about the GAS's stages of alarm, resistance, and exhaustion. In the short term, stress gets the immune system "revved up" and ready to fight the stressor. In the long term, though, chronic stress wears down the immune system, and immunity begins to break down. This long-term wear and tear makes the immune system much less able to fight new stressors as they come along, or handle continuing stressors. Not surprisingly, these researchers also found that people who were at risk—for example, who were elderly or already ill—had the worst outcomes. This research reminds us of the importance of keeping stressors in check, and finding ways to manage the possible damage of long-term, chronic stress.[13]

Stress and the Immune System

The immune system serves three basic functions. Briefly, these include:

1. Recognizing foreign cells and attacking them.
2. Developing antibodies to recognize foreign invaders in the future.
3. Sending white blood cells and other helper cells to the location of an injury or infection to speed healing.

Just by having chronic stress, you can actually weaken your immune system and fall victim to an illness that you would normally fight off with ease.

Medical research is finding evidence that even serious chronic illnesses such as cancer are linked to stress as well. Because your immune system is weakened by stress, anything from the common cold to an uncommon cancer is more likely to invade when you are under stress for long periods of time. Other stress-related illnesses can include asthma, ulcers, colitis, skin disorders such as eczema or hives, allergies, strokes, and heart attacks. Medical research suggests that the effects of stress can strike back as long as 20 years later. Men who were highly anxious in middle age, studies show, are much more likely 20 years later to have high blood pressure than men who had a calmer outlook on life.[14]

You can probably recognize the fight-or-flight feelings of immediate stressors, but how can you know when you are overstressed? Take the stress self-test at the end of this chapter to find out how much stress you are under. How can you recognize excessive stress in other people? Researchers have found that people under stress may act restless, impatient, competitive, and pressured. They may have had recent changes in work or personal lives that would help explain the excessive stress.[15] (See Figure 14.3 for ways managers can reduce workplace stress.)

exercise 14.3

Stress at Work

NIOSH (The National Institute for Occupational Safety and Health) is a federal government agency of the Centers for Disease Control and Prevention, in the Department of Health and Human Services. NIOSH is in charge of conducting research and making recommendations on work-related injury and illness prevention. This includes research on stress. Go to their Web site and download and watch the video "Working with Stress" at **www.cdc.gov/niosh/video/stressdvd1002 .html,** or read through any of their articles related to causes of stress and recommendations to reduce it, at **www.cdc.gov/niosh/topics/stress/.** Write a paragraph identifying your own work-related stress issues described by NIOSH. These Web sites are also linked through the course Web site at **www.mhhe .com/lamberton4e.**

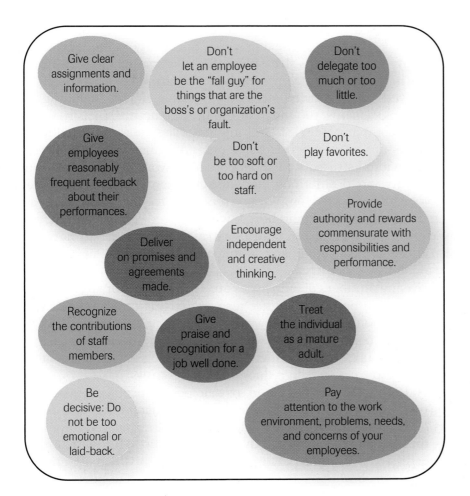

figure 14.3

REDUCING CORPORATE STRESS

Managers can do a lot to reduce stress in their work environments. The key elements are clear, positive communication and "leading by example" by handling stressful situations with calmness and fairness. *What can your current (or most recent) manager do to reduce stress at his or her workplace?*

Source: Sigmund Ginsburg, "Reducing the Stress You Cause Others," *Support Management* 35 (December 1990), p. 5. See also: Christina Maslach and Michael P. Leiter, "Take This Job and Love It," *Psychology Today,* September/ October 1999.

THE COST OF STRESS IN THE WORKPLACE

In this chapter we have focused on the effects of stress at the individual level. However, there are enormous costs to business and to society because of stress, as well. According to the American Institute of Stress, stress-related problems cost the American economy more than $300 billion every year![16] These costs are an estimate based on lower productivity due to stress, lost days of work, worker's compensation claims, health insurance and health-care costs, stress management programs, and lawsuits that are a result of stress-related illness or injuries.

Employees increasingly report stress-related headaches, back pain, exhaustion, anxiety, anger, insomnia, and digestive upsets from their jobs. Close to 90 percent of visits to the doctor are for stress-related symptoms. Up to 80 percent of industrial accidents are blamed on stress. In a survey of employees' stress-related symptoms, most employees reported feeling at least three symptoms. About one-fifth of those surveyed had missed work because of stress, and one-third had thought about quitting as a way of relieving stress. Specific conditions on the job that employees reported as stressful included crowding, noise, air pollution, poor lighting, and uncomfortable temperatures.

Employees also reported stress from management, including having no say in decisions, too much or too little structure, racism, sexism, frustrating company policies, and low pay. They also reported stressful relationships with supervisors, peers, and other staff members, as well as individual stressors, such as boredom, work overload, too much responsibility, no promotions, and disagreements with management. Psychologically stressed employees reported feeling depressed, anxious, frustrated, fatigued, and bored, with lowered self-esteem. Stressed employees were more likely than nonstressed employees to have accidents on the job, eat or smoke too much, have outbursts of anger, and abuse alcohol or other drugs.[17]

Increasing numbers of employees are seeking help for stress through employee programs, and they are also increasing stress-related workers' compensation claims and lawsuits. There is no reason to think that stress and the costs of dealing with stress are going to decrease any time soon. It is up to the organizations to research and implement programs and resources to help reduce workplace stress.

Considering the physical and psychological problems associated with stress, it is not hard to imagine that stress also affects self-esteem. Stress makes you feel overwhelmed, unable to do what you have to do. Stress makes people less productive and less successful, which lowers self-esteem. These become part of a vicious cycle in which effectiveness and self-esteem both sink lower. Stress can also make people turn to poor coping substitutions such as substance abuse. Being caught in a web of substance abuse can lower self-esteem still further. Therefore, stress impacts all areas of people's lives: physical health, mental health, social life, and job performance. Learning to change the things you can change to reduce stress in your life is certainly worth the time and effort! (See Figure 14.4 for ways to alleviate the stress that leads to **job burnout.**)

job burnout

Physical and emotional exhaustion resulting from long-term stress or frustration in one's workplace.

Beating Burnout

Employee stress can lead to **job burnout.** Employees who feel insecure, misunderstood, frustrated, overloaded, overwhelmed, undervalued, and alienated often do the bare minimum at work or leave their jobs. Burnout is bad for employees and employers alike. Can job burnout be beaten? Experts Christina Maslach and Michael P. Leiter have interviewed thousands of people about job burnout. They list six key areas for employee happiness and reduced job burnout.

1. **Workload** must be manageable. Employees who feel that they have too much work to do in too little time with too few resources feel burned out. When workload is manageable, employees can meet demands and seek out new challenges.

2. Employees need a sense of **control.** Rigid office policies or chaos in the work environment can prevent employees from finishing work and feeling productive. Employees who are allowed to make decisions, solve problems, and determine the outcomes of their projects are more productive.

3. Employees must have an opportunity for **rewards.** Low pay, little praise, and no recognition leave employees feeling undervalued, unhappy, and resentful. When the work seems valuable to others, employees take pride in their work and work harder at tasks.

4. A feeling of **community** buoys employees. Conflict or tension among co-workers leaves everyone feeling angry, anxious, suspicious, and fearful. Being physically or socially isolated also leaves employees without a sense of community. Being able to share ideas, praise, and humor with co-workers leads to greater cohesiveness, respect, support, and team spirit.

5. Trusting the workplace to be **fair** keeps employees loyal. When some employees feel they do the lion's share of the work while others get the praise, a feeling of fairness is lost. Favoritism isn't fair. Employees are left feeling distrustful, cynical, and disloyal. Respect and justice, along with mutual respect between co-workers, form the basis for fairness in the workplace.

6. Shared **values** promote ethical behavior. Employees who don't share the company's values may do something unethical, or may do something that clashes with their personal values. This leads to employees feeling bad about themselves and their work. Meaningful work that doesn't cause a clash between the organizational norms and personal principles is more satisfying to employees.

figure 14.4

AVOIDING JOB BURNOUT

Managers can beat burnout in themselves and their employees by adhering to these simple principles. *Which of these principles seems most important to you?*

Source: Christina Maslach and Michael P. Leiter, "Take This Job and Love it," *Psychology Today,* September/October 1999. See also: Michael P. Leiter, and Christina Maslach, *Banishing Burnout: Six Strategies for Improving Your Relationship With Work* (San Francisco, CA: Jossey-Bass, 2005).

« « **STRATEGIES FOR SUCCESS**

14.1 Discard Irrational Beliefs

1. Evaluate the consequences of the belief.
2. Identify your belief system.
3. Dispute the self-defeating belief.
4. Practice effective ways of thinking.

Since one of the internal sources of stress is an irrational belief system, to reduce stress you must change your irrational beliefs by replacing them with rational beliefs. Whenever you start thinking along the lines of "I've failed the midterm exam! I'm going to flunk this class and get kicked out of school!" you must stop that irrational thought. Replace it with something more rational, such as "I've failed the midterm exam. If I get a tutor and spend more time studying, I can do better on the next exam and still pass the class."

Albert Ellis believes that for any irrational belief, you can follow these four steps to replace it with a more rational belief:

1. **Evaluate the consequences of the belief.** (Part C of the ABC) Negative emotions as a result of a stressor may seem to be natural, but they aren't inevitable. Ask yourself if these reactions are helping you live effectively, and helping you solve your problems.

2. **Identify your belief system.** (Part B of the ABC) Ask yourself why you are feeling the specific emotions aroused by the irrational belief. Ellis believes that by examining the irrational belief, you can figure out what is causing the negative consequences (negative emotions).

3. **Dispute the self-defeating belief.** After you have identified an irrational belief, you can argue against it.

4. **Practice effective ways of thinking.** Continue to examine your reactions to activating events. Try substituting more real beliefs and imagining more successful outcomes.

14.2 Change Your Behaviors to Reduce Stress

1. Take charge of your life.
2. Use humor.
3. Compare yourself with others.
4. Take advantage of stress.
5. Learn to live with unavoidable stress.

Remember that one of the internal sources of stress is your personality style or behavior. Changing your personality involves both cognitive (thought-related) and behavioral strategies. You may assume that you cannot change your personality, but you can change your behaviors to more healthy and less stress-producing ones. Learn to recognize and monitor the toxic hostility behaviors and the hurry sickness, which cause you more stress. Use the following strategies to reduce these behaviors:

1. **Take charge of your life.** Think of the three Cs of the hardy personality—challenge, commitment, and control. Tell yourself to think positive thoughts—that the stressor you are facing is a challenge, not a problem, that you are in

Sun Microsystems, a major computer company in California, encourages humor on the job, even to the extreme of financing elaborate practical jokes played on executives by employees. These have included building a life-size replica of the vice president's office in the bottom of a shark tank, and floating the cofounder's Ferrari in the middle of a fish pond. According to company officials, humor at work increases productivity, makes employees feel more like team members, and boosts morale, in addition to relieving stress at work.

control of your own life. Take charge! Confront stressors when you can in a thoughtful and assertive way. Stay committed to your goal instead of giving up. Remind yourself.

2. **Use humor.** Learn to see the humor in situations, and increase the amount of humor in your life. An increase of humor reduces stress, because you physically can't feel both at the same time. Humor also makes you feel better, distracts you temporarily from the stressor, and lets you relax.

3. **Compare yourself with others.** Another cognitive strategy is social comparison. By comparing yourself with others who are in a similar situation but worse off, you may feel better about your situation. This does not mean you should listen to the horror stories that well-meaning friends or co-workers delight in telling! You will cope better when you hear encouraging stories about people in situations like yours.[18]

4. **Take advantage of stress.** Pay attention to your stress levels and learn what your optimal level is in order to be productive. Remember, with too little stress or challenge, you may become bored, unmotivated, and unproductive. With too much stress, you will be overwhelmed. Find out how much is right for you.

5. **Learn to live with unavoidable stress.** Finally, as a cognitive strategy for coping with stress, learn to live with the stressors you cannot avoid. This does not mean giving in to stress; it means accepting the fact that some stressors are unavoidable. Learn to think about these stressors in different ways than before.

14.3 Take Care of Yourself

1. Use relaxation techniques.
2. Increase your fitness: exercise, eat well, and reduce/quit smoking and drinking.
3. Make time for rest and leisure.
4. Get social support.
5. Try to reduce stress in the workplace.
6. Manage your time.
7. Stop procrastinating!

Kodak, the well-known camera company, added a "humor room" to its plant in New York. The room, stocked with comedy videotapes and toys, successfully relieves stress, according to management. People also used humor to deal with the stress of layoffs due to downsizing and outsourcing.

According to stress research, some amount of stress is inevitable and even good for you (it keeps you motivated and alive!), so you don't want to eliminate all stress. Your goal should be to reduce or minimize the negative effects of stress by coping with or managing stress.

1. **Use relaxation techniques.** In addition to changing your thoughts, you can use specific relaxation strategies as a way of reducing or managing stress. Since relaxing and feeling stress are not physically compatible, you can't do both at the same time. Forcing yourself to relax means you are getting rid of stress (at least temporarily!). Some simple relaxation techniques include deep breathing, progressive relaxation, meditation, and biofeedback.

   To use *progressive relaxation,* you would close your eyes and imagine your entire body becoming relaxed, slowly, one muscle group at a time. *Meditation* is a relaxation technique that teaches you to focus outward, becoming aware of sensory input around you; or inward, becoming more self-aware.

   Biofeedback requires the use of a machine that gives you information (feedback) about specific biological (bio) processes. By learning to recognize what a change in heart rate and skin temperature feel like, you can actually learn to control such processes as heart rate, respiration, skin temperature, and perspiration. Many people have successfully used biofeedback to treat such stress-related illnesses as asthma, migraine headaches, epilepsy, and high blood pressure, as well as to control other physical processes that were once thought to be out of their control.[19]

2. **Increase your fitness: Exercise, eat well, and reduce/quit smoking and drinking.** Relaxation is one behavioral strategy used to manage stress and increase wellness. Another strategy is to increase general overall fitness. The more physically fit you are, the less negative the effects of stress will be, and the stronger your immune system will be to fight stress-related illnesses. Stay healthy by eating a nutritionally sound diet that is low in fats and sugars and high in fibers. Follow an exercise plan. If you are overweight, lose weight. If you smoke or drink alcohol a great deal, cut down or stop. Avoid long exposure to the sun or to harmful chemicals. If your workplace is excessively noisy, ask for earplugs and use them.

C. W. Metcalf, a business consultant and entrepreneur, makes his living by teaching ways of adding humor to the workplace. He says that he has more requests than he can handle because companies across the country are beginning to recognize the value of humor. Metcalf set up workshops for Owens-Corning Fiberglass during its downsizing that were successful in preventing possible problems such as sabotage, threats to management, and suicide attempts.[20] Visit his Web site at **www.cwmetcalf.com** or link to it through **www.mhhe.com/lamberton4e.**

3. **Make time for rest and leisure.** Getting enough sleep at regular times and building leisure activities into your schedule will help you manage stress better. You need sleep to stay healthy. You may be thinking, "I can't add leisure activities to my schedule! I have too much to do already!" If so, you are just the person this suggestion is aimed at. Stop and think about the stress that your behaviors are creating for yourself.

4. **Get social support.** Friends, family, or even a support group can help in relieving stress. Examples of social support may include things such as receiving a tuna casserole when you are sick or personal loans when you are low on cash. It also includes emotional support, such as sympathy and understanding, when you are unhappy or stressed. But remember: Whatever your support network gives you, you will probably be asked to return at some time when others are stressed. Be clear on whether some family members or friends cause more stress than they relieve.

5. **Try to reduce stress in the workplace.** Organizations can help reduce stressors in the workplace, too. One source of stress that employees often mention is rigid work schedules that don't allow for family obligations or emergencies. Companies are increasingly offering flextime, job sharing, telecommuting, and compressed workweeks. Scheduling that allows employees to meet their needs means less absenteeism and higher productivity. Helping employees cope with stress on the job means lower turnover rates, more commitment and loyalty from employees, higher productivity, and better relationships with co-workers.[21]

   Nationwide, companies are offering services to reduce workplace stress. Services range from counseling (e.g., psychological, nutritional, weight control, and substance abuse counseling) to onsite health and fitness centers and day-care facilities. What, you might ask, does day care have to do with workplace stress? Businesses are realizing that stress at home spills over into stress at work (and vice versa), so the best way to combat workplace stress is to reduce overall stress.

   Many companies take this subject seriously enough to catch the attention of outside agencies: Johnson & Johnson, for example, has won several awards for their employee health programs. If you are looking for resources to help your company get started in reducing stress in the workplace, the NIOSH Web site is a good place to begin **(www.cdc.gov/niosh).**

6. **Manage your time.** One of the easiest and most productive ways to combat stress behaviorally is to learn to manage time better. This will help you know what to expect and how to feel some control over your schedule and your life. Time management can be a problem when you waste time (underutilization), or schedule too many things into one time slot (overload).

   Whether your problem is overload or underutilization, you can take specific steps to learn to manage your time better. Start by making a list of all the regular activities you carry out in a day for work, school, family activities, and even leisure time. Make another list of upcoming events and deadlines. Put together a master time schedule with daily activities as well as dates to remember, filling in each time block with activities scheduled. Keep a daily time plan (an index card will fit neatly into a pocket), but also a monthly calendar for those upcoming events. Plan ahead, but set realistic timetables for getting work done. Allow an extra cushion of time for emergencies or unforeseen events. Reward yourself along the way (but not until *after* you have completed your work!) with activities you like, such as talking to friends, going out to eat, watching television, and so on. Modify the schedule until it is workable. Then stick to it!

7. **Stop procrastinating!** *Procrastination,* or putting things off until later, allows you to avoid things you don't really want to do. Procrastination ultimately increases your stress level! To reduce procrastination, make a specific plan about what you need to do, break large tasks into small chunks, reward yourself for work done along the way, and give yourself credit for a job well done.[22] Reread the material on procrastination in Chapter 2.

Everyone will have different approaches that work, as well as different types and levels of stress; therefore, you will want to choose what applies to you to suit your needs. Perhaps you plan too much work in too short a time frame. Then, to make matters worse, you procrastinate and fail to meet all of your deadlines. At the same time, your fitness level is high, and you have a large social support network. In a case like this, you would probably want to focus on preceding steps 6 and 7. You probably would not need to focus on steps 2 and 4. You might also want to incorporate the remaining steps in your life to increase overall well-being.

CHAPTER FOURTEEN SUMMARY

Chapter Summary by Learning Objectives

1. **Identify the main causes of stress.** Stress is a part of everyone's life. Stress is the body's reaction to a stressor, which can be caused by life changes and daily hassles; by chronic stressors; by external circumstances; or by internal cognitions, belief systems, and personality-related behaviors.

2. **Give examples of external and internal sources of stress.** External stressors can include anything from outside sources that cause pain, discomfort, frustration, or conflict. Examples are deadlines, poor health, work or school pressures, or financial problems. Internal stressors can include your own reactions of a stressor, as well as personality factors. They include irrational beliefs, poor social skills unrealistic expectations, and poor time management, just to name a few.

3. **Compare and contrast type A and type B personality behaviors.** Type A and type B personalities are two standard personality related behaviors. Type A behaviors include impatience, excessive time-consciousness and perfectionism. Type B behaviors include a more relaxed and flexible outlook, with less focus on time and deadlines.

4. **Describe the physical effects of stress.** Stress occurs in three stages as your body sounds the alarm that a stressor is occurring, tries to cope with the stressor, and if coping fails, exhausts its resources and becomes vulnerable to illness due to a weakened immune system.

5. **Explain the cost of stress in the workplace.** Stress-related problems cost the American economy more than $300 million per year. These costs include lost work, insurance claims and costs, stress management programs, and stress-related lawsuits.

key terms

catastrophize 377
chronic stressors 373
cognitive appraisal 376
daily hassles 372
distress 372
eustress 372
external stressors 374

frustration 374
hardy personality 381
inner conflict 374
internal stressors 376
irrational belief system 377
job burnout 387

major life changes 372
stress 372
stressor 372
type A and type B personalities 379

review questions

1. What is meant by stress and stressors? Identify two sources of eustress, and two sources of distress, in your own life.

2. How are major life changes different from daily hassles? How can a major life change lead to daily hassles? Discuss examples of these in your own life.

3. Suppose that you were really looking forward to going to work one day, but when you left for work you realized your tire was flat. Your stress level increased. Discuss how this situation leads to internal and/or external sources of stress.

4. Are there any chronic stressors in your own life, or the life of someone you know? Describe the stressor, and possible coping strategies.

5. Do you hold any of the irrational beliefs described by Ellis? How do they affect your perception of events?

6. According to Ellis, what is catastrophizing? Do you ever find yourself catastrophizing? In what situations? How can you minimize it?

7. What is the difference between meditation and biofeedback? How can each be used to reduce stress? What other specific suggestions for coping with stress can you incorporate into your own life?

8. Suppose you are driving to work one day on your usual route past the City Zoo, when a giant grizzly bear escapes, runs out of the entrance, growling and roaring, and heads straight for your car. Describe the physical and chemical changes that you would experience, according to the general adaptation syndrome (GAS).

critical thinking questions

9. A life without stress seems like a pleasant and desirable goal. Do you agree with Selye that stress is necessary in order to motivate you and keep you alive? Why or why not? What do you think would happen if you didn't have any stress in your life?

10. Some people say that since everyone is going to die anyway, it would be better to enjoy life without worrying about diet, exercise, and other behaviors that may prolong life while reducing the enjoyment of life. Why do you think these people feel this way? What do you think?

working it out 14.1

TYPE A OR TYPE B PERSONALITY BEHAVIORS

School-to-Work Connection: Personal Qualities Skills
Are you more like a type A or B? Complete the questionnaire by checking "yes" if the behavior pattern is typical of you and "no" if it is not. At a glance, more "no" responses suggest the type B behavior pattern.

Do You	Yes	No
1. Strongly accent keywords in your everyday speech?	_____	_____
2. Eat and walk quickly?	_____	_____
3. Believe that children should be taught to be competitive?	_____	_____
4. Feel restless when watching a slow worker?	_____	_____
5. Hurry other people to get on with what they're saying?	_____	_____
6. Find it highly frustrating to be stuck in traffic or to wait for a seat at a restaurant?	_____	_____
7. Continue to think about your own problems and business even when listening to someone else?	_____	_____
8. Try to eat and read, or drive and jot down notes at the same time?	_____	_____
9. Catch up on your work during vacation?	_____	_____
10. Bring conversations around to topics of concern to you?	_____	_____
11. Feel guilty when you spend time just relaxing?	_____	_____
12. Feel that you're so wrapped up in your work that you no longer notice office decorations or scenery when you commute?	_____	_____
13. Find yourself concerned with getting more things, rather than developing your creativity or social concerns?	_____	_____
14. Try to schedule more and more activities into less and less time?	_____	_____
15. Always appear for appointments on time?	_____	_____
16. Clench or pound your fists, or use other gestures to emphasize your views?	_____	_____
17. Credit your accomplishments to your ability to work rapidly?	_____	_____
18. Feel that things must be done now and quickly?	_____	_____
19. Constantly try to find more efficient ways to get things done?	_____	_____
20. Insist on winning at games, rather than just having fun?	_____	_____

21. Interrupt others often? _____ _____

22. Feel irritated when others are late? _____ _____

23. Leave the table immediately after eating? _____ _____

24. Feel rushed? _____ _____

25. Feel dissatisfied with your current level of performance? _____ _____

Count up your "yes" checkmarks. "Yes" responses suggest the type A behavior pattern, which includes a sense of time urgency and constant struggle.

Source: Spencer Rathus, *Psychology* (Fort Worth, TX: Harcourt, Brace, Jovanovich, 1993). Reprinted by permission of the publisher.

working it out 14.2

STRESS SELF-TEST

School-to-Work Connection: Personal Qualities Skills

How much stress are you under? To measure the degree of stress you suffer, take this stress test. Circle the appropriate number for each question and tally your total score. A score of 12 or lower indicates a low degree of personal stress reactions; between 13 and 24 reflects a moderate degree; higher than 24 indicates that you're experiencing a high degree of stress. Although your score might not altogether surprise you, it would be wise to consult your doctor to determine whether you have a health problem that requires medical attention, one that might be contributing to your stress level and your ability to withstand it.

How Often Do You Suffer From	Never	Hardly Ever	Sometimes	Often
1. Aches in back, head, or neck	0	1	2	3
2. Too many issues on your mind at once	0	1	2	3
3. Chest pains	0	1	2	3
4. Low interest in physical intimacy	0	1	2	3
5. An urge to drink a lot of alcohol	0	1	2	3
6. Feelings of anxiety and being uptight	0	1	2	3
7. Difficulty falling or staying asleep	0	1	2	3
8. A feeling of depression	0	1	2	3
9. A feeling of being overwhelmed	0	1	2	3
10. An inability to think clearly	0	1	2	3

Source: "Vital Signs," *Sales and Marketing Management,* November 1992, p. 93. Reprinted with permission of *Sales and Marketing Management.*

1. *Read and Write*

   Enter the home page for the American Institute of Stress at **www.stress.org/.** Link (at the bottom of the page) to "Mementos— Reminiscences of Hans Selye, and the Birth of Stress" and read through the history of this topic of research. You can also use the link from **www.mhhe.com/lamberton4e.**

   a. One of the interesting facts presented is that in the Chinese language, the characters for "stress" are a combination of "danger" and "opportunity." How does this differ from your perception of stress?

   b. Differentiate "stress" from "strain" as explained in the article. Do you think defining this topic differently would have made a difference in its history of research or application?

2. *Self-Assess and Apply*

   There are many available Internet resources to help you learn about and deal with stress. Go to the Web site from LearnThat.com related to stress at **www.Learnthat.com/courses/lifestyle/stress/ index.shtml,** or you can use the link from **www.mhhe.com/ lamberton4e.** Read through the introduction by Joyce Henderson, R.N., titled "How to Cope with Stress—Stress Management Tutorial and Exercise," then link to the worksheets on stress. Complete the worksheets most relevant to you.

   a. What suggestions will help you achieve stress reduction in your life?

   b. What did you learn from the worksheets about identifying stressors in your life?

   c. Link to the stress exercises and try the progressive relaxation exercise. Was it helpful?

3. *Self-Assess and Evaluate*

   How much money are you likely to make in your dream job? Go to **www.salary.com** or link through the course Web site at **www.mhhe.com/lamberton4e** and find out. Select a job title, and enter a state to find out what typical salaries are for the job you selected. Compare salaries for the same job across five different areas of the country, and report your findings. (But here's a "tweak" to help tie it into the chapter.) Thinking about your ideal job, how important is your paycheck likely to be in keeping your stress levels low? How important is the area of the country where you may decide to live?

Bonnie the Bumblebee

James rested his head in his hand and mused as he watched his supervisor, Bonnie, buzz around the office at high speed. He liked to think of her as a giant bumblebee: always moving and often stinging. Bonnie was always in a hurry because she felt she had to do her own work and then redo everyone else's. The stinging came often in the form of criticizing her employees, upper management, her family, and everything else. James, in contrast, preferred a slower, more steady but thorough pace of work. He didn't see any advantage to constantly being so critical and rushed all the time.

"James, you're going to have to do this spreadsheet all over again. I just don't have time to fix it for you, and the Finance Department will never accept it in this form."

Suddenly, she stopped and looked thoughtful. "You know, James, I'm going to be eligible for early retirement in only eight years. I'll probably be promoted to upper management soon. You're a lot younger than I am, but you should be thinking about your future with this company. I think you're probably capable, yet you just don't seem to have the drive, the aggression, that I had at your age. You're just too *nice* or something. Don't you want to make anything of yourself?"

James only smiled and said, "Well, Bonnie, I'll have to think about that." In fact, James had thought quite a lot about the differences between the two of them. He was quite certain that of the two of them, he'd be more likely to be promoted to upper management.

Case Study Questions

1. Is James correct—will he more likely make it to upper management, or will Bonnie? Why?

2. Thinking of the personality behaviors discussed in this chapter, what characteristics would lead you to categorize Bonnie and James as either type A, type B, or hardy?

3. Does Bonnie seem stressed? If so, from what sources (major life changes, daily hassles, chronic stressors, internal stress, or external stress)? If not, why?

Overworked, or Just Overstressed?

Rick Russell and Arturo Garcia were friends in high school. Last year they both graduated with above-average grades. Now, both are attending their local community college, studying business and hoping for successful lives. They have talked a lot about transferring to a four-year college in the future, maybe before finishing the two years where they are. Although both did well in high school, Rick seems to be really struggling to keep up with both school and a part-time job.

"Art, how do you handle all the stuff you're doing in your life and still stay so calm? How do you manage to get all those good grades? I can barely keep my C average and keep from getting on academic warning. All these instructors want way too much work from us. They act like we don't have a life outside of school. In fact, they seem to think that their classes are the only things we're doing at all!"

Art looked dubious. "You're always exaggerating, Rick. If you really look at it, we don't have that many more assignments than we had last year, and you seemed to do fine then. What's going on that's so radically different from high school? You played baseball and ran track in high school and you still graduated with a B average. What's changed, anyway?"

"This isn't high school, Art, in case you haven't noticed! The work is a lot harder here, and the instructors never remind us when stuff is due or when exams are going to be. I'm always getting my work in late, and I never feel ready for tests when they come. At least in high school my mom or my teachers would pester me about getting things done. Here, it doesn't seem like anybody cares! A lot of my teachers act like they don't care whether I come to class or not."

"Why are you blaming everybody else?" Art replied. "I saw you hanging out in the student lounge all morning yesterday, and you knew that we had a project due in English comp. You need to learn how to manage your time better. Why can't you get it together?"

Case Study Questions

1. Do you think Rick will ever "get it together"? What are the real causes of his frustration? Why isn't Arturo having the same kinds of problems?

2. Sketch out a rough time management plan for Rick, one that includes a 20-hours-per-week job and 12 credits of coursework, along with some personal time and study sessions.

3. What kinds of specific items would a long-term calendar for Rick need to include?

YOUR EXTERNAL AND INTERNAL CUSTOMERS

In the Workplace: Good Service: The Other Half of Success

SITUATION

Home Fridays is more than just a house-sitting business. It is a company that is built almost totally on selling peace of mind to people who are out of town or who own second homes.

The idea came to Shannon Bassett when she was having problems with her own second home. One winter night she and her husband arrived rather late during a snowstorm. The company that had been contracted to clean the leaves and pine needles out of the gutters had not done their job. With a heavy snowfall on the way, the gutters promised to be a mess unless something was done right away. Both weary from a long road trip, the couple had to get out their stepladders and clean the gutters themselves.

DISCOVERY

Later that evening, Shannon started thinking, "What if someone owned a company that would make sure things like this never happen?" A few months later, Shannon owned that

After studying this chapter, you will be able to:

1 Explain how to determine what customers really want.

2 Define customer service.

3 Describe the internal customer.

4 List the two simplest principles of customer service.

5 Give examples of issues in customer service.

6 Compare and contrast ways to handle a difficult customer.

7 Explain the significance of going the extra mile.

8 List ways to use strong ethics in customer service.

9 Explain the moral of the Poor George story and how it relates to customer service.

STRATEGIES FOR SUCCESS

Strategy 15.1   Establish a Bond with the Customer

Strategy 15.2   Support the Customer's Self-Esteem

Strategy 15.3   Handle the Difficult Customer Professionally

company. Its name, Home Fridays, was a take-off on weekend travelers and the peace of mind they can now have knowing that someone who cares is there on Fridays—or whatever other day of the week help is needed. This company takes care of any detail the owner wants, including yard maintenance, maid work, minor repairs—whatever needs attention. They've even been known to stock the refrigerator with selected goodies just before the customer's arrival.

At least once a week, someone from Home Fridays visits the customer's house, checking for everything from break-ins to frozen pipes. The company then sends regular reports to clients, along with photographs to reassure them that the place still looks great. They even start and drive cars regularly, to keep them in running condition. When a security alarm system rings, they are the first to be called.

THINK ABOUT IT

Home Fridays sells peace of mind, responding to a need that nobody else had thought of fulfilling. The entire operation is built on top-notch customer service, service you can always depend on. *What business could you think of that would provide better customers service than anyone else has ever provided?*

What makes the Home Fridays company so successful? Are their policies applicable to other businesses?

WHAT DO CUSTOMERS REALLY WANT?

In business circles it is often said that any company's scarcest resource is capital; that is, money to invest. Instead, an increasing number of people running businesses today are realizing that *satisfied and happy customers* are the scarcest and most crucial resource. Without a good base of customers, any business will fail. Without customers, you simply don't have a business—or a future.[1]

In *How to Win Customers and Keep Them for Life,* Michael LeBoeuf points out that customers buy only two things: **good feelings and solutions** to problems.[2] Everything that a customer wants from you will fall into one of those two categories. For example:

> **good feelings and solutions**
>
> The only two things that customers really buy.

- You don't sell clothes. You sell a sharp appearance, style, attractiveness, comfort, and warmth.
- You don't sell insurance. You sell financial security for people and their families.
- You don't sell toys. You sell happy moments for children.
- You don't sell a house. You sell comfort, contentment, a good investment, pride of ownership, privacy, and space.

Home Fridays doesn't sell home maintenance or house-sitting as much as they sell a pleasant experience and relief from worry. Every moment you are on the job, think about feelings and solutions. Make those two goals your most important activities. If you do, your relationship with customers should automatically improve.[3]

What feelings does your customer show when he or she first approaches you? What nonverbal signals can you use as clues to the customer's real feelings? Be sure your own feelings are not getting in the way of understanding—or reacting correctly to—the customer.

The importance of leaving customers with good feelings cannot be overemphasized. High-quality customer service has never been more important than it is today. The most obvious reason for this increased importance is greater competition. The competition from European and Asian countries with a high customer service emphasis has caused American businesses to look more closely at how they treat those who buy from them. A second reason for this emphasis is the growth of services in the United States over the past few decades. Today there are many new services available. They might include going to a debt counselor, hiring a Webmaster, or consulting with an aromatherapist. These are just a few examples of the thousands of new services offered to Americans today. In many ways, the United States is now a service economy.

> **more about...**
>
> **Repeat Customers**
>
> According to the American Management Association, 65 percent of a typical company's business comes from existing customers.

This final reason for high-quality customer service is the most important one: Keeping customers happy and loyal simply makes good economic sense. Maintaining an ever-growing group of satisfied customers is essential to staying in business and making a profit. Without loyal customers, businesses fail—and, sadly, many do fail every day.

CUSTOMER SERVICE: A DEFINITION

What is good customer service? Customer service guru John Tschohl says, "You have good service only when customers think you do."[4] He also says that customer service is part of successful selling because satisfied customers come back to be customers again. According to the American Management Association, 65 percent of a typical company's business comes from *current* customers.

Good service, which always includes good human relations, is the main reason for repeat business. The cost of finding a new customer is considerably greater than the cost of keeping one you already have.[5] Unhappy customers have a high cost, too: The average disgruntled customer tells at least 8 to 10 people about the unpleasant experience.[6] Clearly, treating your customers as the most important part of the organization will pay off in the long run, in terms of both growth and added profits.[7]

Working on improving customer relations is also excellent for your own self-development. Learning what works in the process of satisfying customers can aid you in cultivating your own skills in problem solving for other areas of life. Dealing successfully with customers is a learning process that is ongoing and can always be improved.

Customer relations skills can be transferred to almost any other occupation or profession. If you are an employee who has a vested interest in the success of the company you are working for, the development of customer service skills is worthwhile for you. Also, customer relations presents one of the most challenging aspects of human relations skill development. You will never be wasting your time by learning how customers think, respond, and perceive reality. Any other business you might enter later in life will involve customers in some way. This includes internal customers.

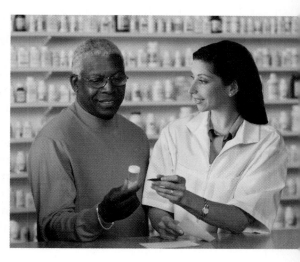

SATISFYING THE CUSTOMER

When customers pay for products and services, they buy good feelings or the solution to a problem, too. *Why is it important to recognize the real needs of customers?*

THE INTERNAL CUSTOMER

For the past several years, the term "internal customer" has been used more and more often to describe an important relationship among managers, employees, and external customers. When the person who is connected long term to a company is treated the way an external customer

internal customer

The person who depends on the other people in the company to provide the services and products for the external customer.

should be, the results are predictably positive. One definition of the **internal customer** is the person who depends on the other people in the company to provide the services and products for the external customer.[8]

Internal customers usually don't walk away when the service is bad. Unlike their external counterparts, they are tied to the company more directly than that. However, this is exactly why treating them right is really important to the overall success of the business.

Management expert Shep Hyken provides an example of an internal customer. In the example, she is a clerk in the payroll department. She depends on the managers throughout the company to give her the information she needs to produce an accurate payroll each week. One manager doesn't get that information to her on time, and when the e-mail does arrive, it contains several errors. This manager has failed an internal customer. The manager's responsibility to that payroll clerk is jut as important as the responsibility of the company to any single external customer.[9]

As Hyken puts it, "A company that has an excellent service reputation didn't get it without everyone in the company being a part of the service strategy. Someone once said that if you aren't working directly with the outside customer, you are probably working with someone who is."[10]

What is your responsibility to the internal customer? If you are a manager, it's your role to be sure the needs of every person in your area are being met, just as should be the case with the external customer. If you are a worker, do your best to be the kind of loyal fan you would be of, let's say, a favorite restaurant or some other business where you are a contented repeat customer. The internal customer concept is helpful in creating a company with memorable customer service.

Think about how a business or company functions. Every employee is accountable to someone, whether to outside customers or internal customers. In his article on improving internal customer relations, business consultant Lane Baldwin says, "Make no mistake. Your teammates are as important to your success as the people walking through your door. And the better you serve your teammates, the more they will help you succeed."[11] For the remainder of the chapter, then, when you read the word *customer*, think about customers as those who buy products from you, and those who are connected in some way that makes the company's existence possible.

THE TWO SIMPLEST PRINCIPLES OF CUSTOMER SERVICE

two simplest principles

Finding out what the customer needs, and doing whatever is necessary to satisfy that need.

When you are dealing with any type of customer, the **two simplest principles** help greatly:

1. Find out what the customer needs.
2. Do whatever is necessary to satisfy those needs.

Luis Alvarez was a department store clerk in a small town. One day an elderly lady came in to look at the bicycles on display. "My, my," she said. "The bikes seem a lot different than they used to be—more gears, more colors, less chrome. The last time I looked at bicycles was almost 20 years ago."

Luis had no idea what this customer really wanted. In fact, he wasn't even sure that she was a customer at all. She spent several minutes reliving the past when her three children had ridden bicycles on the vacant lot where the department store now stood. After asking questions about her interest in the bikes, Luis determined that this lady simply needed to chat. She was lonely. Luis fulfilled that need by remaining friendly and sympathetic.

Two months later, Luis was surprised when the same elderly lady returned to the store and purchased three new bicycles as Christmas presents for her grandchildren. By finding out her real need—to be listened to—he had made a good impression, which later resulted in three major sales. Luis had followed the two simplest principles. He realized the customer needed to talk to him, and he responded to her needs by listening to her. In return, she came back as his paying customer.

By listening carefully to the customer's stated needs, you might discover unspoken needs. In some cases, the customer doesn't have a thorough understanding of what his or her own needs are. Your task in that case becomes one of probing and asking a series of questions to find out what is behind the surface statements.[12]

Although these two principles are very simple, you must remember that besides the immediate needs of the purchase, each customer has basic human needs that all people share. (See Figure 15.1.) Often customers simply want to be noticed, listened to, and taken seriously. Remembering their basic needs could be the only difference between your business and a competitor's. Having quality products alone, without the positive treatment of customers, is simply not enough for a business to succeed.

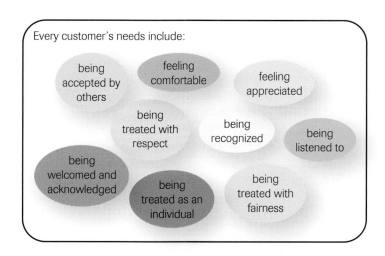

Every customer's needs include:

- being accepted by others
- feeling comfortable
- feeling appreciated
- being treated with respect
- being recognized
- being listened to
- being welcomed and acknowledged
- being treated as an individual
- being treated with fairness

figure 15.1

THE CUSTOMER'S NEEDS— BASIC HUMAN NEEDS

Understanding the customer as a person just like yourself will make it easier to anticipate his or her needs and help to find solutions. *How many of these needs do you feel when you are making a purchase?*

You are a cashier in a retail store. Someone who is apparently not a customer presents a five dollar bill and asks for change. In fact, it looks like she just walked in from the bus stop outside and needed change for the bus. What do you do?

The wise choice is to treat the person with the same cordiality you would treat a paying customer. After all, that person's opinion of your establishment might bring him or her back again. The customer's positive experience might even influence a friend or family member to shop there. The same type of policy is also wise to follow when a non-paying customer wants to use the restroom facilities in your business, or even one who asks for directions to the location of your competitor. Treating others well is not only good business; it is the right thing to do.

ISSUES IN CUSTOMER SERVICE

Knowing the *issues* involved in customer service is important for anyone wanting to develop the *skills* of effective customer service. These issues should help in that process.

Your Customers and Your Attitude

What kind of attitude do you show toward customers? If you are having a bad day, do you let your customers know with your attitude? Do you come off as smug, arrogant, or too humble? Checking your attitude around customers needs to be an ongoing practice.

In *Inc. Magazine*, entrepreneur Norm Brodsky points out how many businesspeople seem to have the attitude that customers exist only for their (businesspeople's) benefit. Brodsky tells the story of a dentist he visited who was proud of his incredibly fancy office, and who took pride in allowing patients to know that they were helping pay for it. Needless to say, Brodsky found another dentist—who, by the way, charged him half as much for a set of crowns as the bid from the one with the fancy office.[13]

Many people who have contact with customers seem to feel that once they have "landed" a customer, they can start taking the customer for granted. Whenever you deal with customers, remember to treat them the same way later on as you treated them when you were trying to win them over the first time. Nobody likes to be taken for granted, and customers are no exception.

WHEN YOUR CUSTOMERS ARE OTHER BUSINESSES

When your customers are other businesses, you must not only maintain the same high-level service you would give to individuals, but you must also get to know the business. *How can you learn more about the businesses with which you work?*

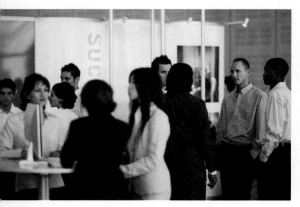

At a large, busy service station, the main bad news problem was telling out-of-state customers that their credit cards from another company could no longer be used. This problem had arisen because of a recent merger, in which the out-of-state company was sold to another, larger oil producer. The problem was totally out of the control of anyone at the station, even the manager. Most of the employees who worked at the station found that an argument started as soon as they told the customer, "Sorry, we can't accept your card." However, Eric, one of the employees on the busy weekend shift, was always able to work smoothly through the day with no customer problems. Soon the others started asking Eric for help every time a customer presented the card in question. After Eric spoke to the customer, he or she would always leave satisfied. What did Eric do that was so effective?

Delivering Bad News

One of the touchiest human relations issues is the tough task of giving customers unwelcome news—especially when they expect nothing but good news. Obviously, some businesses must do this more than others. For example, a loan officer in a bank will have to refuse a certain number of applicants every month. A reservations clerk may have to break the "no vacancy" news quite often. A manager may have to tell a salesperson that a major buyer canceled an order, and the salesperson's commission will be much smaller than expected. No matter how often you have to do it, though, you may never get used to saying no to customers. Developing sound **bad news skills** is essential, and it will make the job less unpleasant.

> **bad news skills**
> The skills necessary to deliver bad news to customers but still retain their business and goodwill.

What did Eric do that was so effective? In a very polite voice, he would say, "I'm really sorry, ma'am (or sir), but your company has apparently decided to stop dealing with ours. You know, we'd like them to come back just as much as you would. They really should have written to you, telling you about the change. I'm sorry they didn't. Since I can't change your company's mind right now, is there anything else we can do to help? We do accept Mastercard, Visa, and American Express." More than half of the customers would suddenly remember having received a notice in the mail. The others would ask a question or two, and most would actually say thanks to Eric before presenting another card or cash.

Notice the steps that Eric took in delivering the bad news to customers. First, he used a polite tone of voice. Second, he didn't dwell on long apologies. Although he said "I'm sorry" twice, his message wasn't an apology: It was an explanation. Third, he dealt specifically with why the problem existed. Fourth, he closed his remarks with a positive statement as to what could be done to make the situation better for both the business and the customer. Those four rules (as shown in Figure 15.2) can help when giving customers messages that they would rather not hear.

Most customers would rather not hear the word *policy*. "We can't do that because it's against company policy" is one of the weakest refusals anyone can use. If you work for a manager who tells you that you must

Getting and Keeping Customers for Life

How do you do it? Go to **www.mhhe.com/lamberton4e** for the link to the Web site called "5 Steps for Keeping Customers for Life." Or access it on your own by going to **www.salesvantage.com/article/view.php?w=199.** In a brief paragraph, summarize the article's recommendations. Also, address how you can start applying these ideas in your current work situation.

use that line, at least find out the reasoning *behind* the policy so that you can explain it clearly to the customer.

Encouraging Complaints

In some way, every customer has a problem. If nothing else, the problem is that the customer is in need of the goods or services your company provides. Perhaps the problem is dissatisfaction with some part of your operation—or your competitor's. Learn to focus on the problem. Ask yourself: "What can I do to solve the problem *as this person sees it?*"

Don't rely on being told what the problem is. Later in this chapter you will read about an angry customer who yells and screams. Learning how to deal with that type of person is certainly necessary. However, yellers and screamers are in the minority. Most customers are like the **"nice" customer** (see Figure 15.3). These customers would actually be more helpful if they were a bit less nice, because then they would provide better feedback. Many companies today realize that customer complaints are necessary and should be encouraged in every way possible.[14]

"nice" customer

The customer who never complains, but responds to bad service by taking his or her business elsewhere.

figure 15.2

GIVING A CUSTOMER BAD NEWS

When giving a customer bad news, focus on explanations and solutions rather than apologies and excuses. A brief apology is almost always necessary, but do not dwell on it; rather, look for a win-win solution. *How can you help customers understand the options available?*

Four Rules for Giving a Customer Bad News
1. Use a polite tone of voice. Make it a point to check on this. For many people, vocal tone is mostly unconscious, unless they try specifically to take notice of it.
2. Don't spend too much time and energy on apologies. Apologizing is fine, but most customers want *reasons* and *action*.
3. Deal with why the problem exists. If you don't know, let the customer know that you will find out; then do it. If the problem's cause is impossible to discover, go to step 4.
4. Talk about what can be done to solve the problem. If possible, this includes alternatives and suggestions from which the customer can choose. When only one possible course of action is available, *sell* the customer on why that action is the best.

THE NICE CUSTOMER STATEMENT

Some people in businesses make the incorrect assumption that if anything is wrong, the customer will say so. Here's a little statement that is posted on the walls of businesses all across the country:

> I'm a nice customer. You all know me. I'm the one who never complains, no matter what kind of service I get. I'll go into a restaurant and sit quietly while the waiters and waitresses gossip and never bother to ask if anyone has taken my order. Sometimes someone who came in after I did gets my order, but I don't complain. I just wait.
>
> And when I go to a store to buy something, I don't throw my weight around. I try to be thoughtful of the other person. If a snooty salesperson gets upset because I want to look at several things before making up my mind, I'm just as polite as can be. I don't believe rudeness in return is the answer.
>
> The other day I stopped at a full service gas station and waited for almost five minutes before the attendant took care of me. And when he did, he spilled gas and wiped the windshield with an oily rag. But did I complain about the service? Of course not.
>
> I never kick. I never nag. I never criticize. And I wouldn't dream of making a scene, as I've seen some people do in public places. I think that's uncalled for. No, I'm the nice customer. And I'll tell you who else I am.
>
> I'm the customer who never comes back!
>
> *Author Unknown (but nice)*

figure 15.3

THE NICE CUSTOMER

The nice customer may not complain or make a scene, but he or she won't come back, either. You can lose loyal customers without knowing it if you wait for the nice customer to let you know about a problem. *What is a good way to help the nice customer let you know his or her true feelings?*

Bill Gates, founder of Microsoft, saw unpleasant news about the way his business was performing as evidence of a need to change. "Unhappy customers are always a concern," he muses. "They're also your greatest opportunity." Gates says that adopting a learning attitude toward your customers rather than a defensive position can make customer complaints the most important part of your road to improving the quality of whatever you are doing.[15]

Try to influence everyone in your company to think of complaining customers in a positive way. Without them, you would have only a vague idea of what changes need to be made. Also, how about giving them another name? Instead of calling them "complainers," consider calling them consultants or critics.

Customer Self-Esteem

"Help them to like themselves better, and they'll love you."

—Michael LeBoeuf

Source: Michael LeBoeuf, *How to Win Customers and Keep Them for Life*, p. 46.

more about...

To encourage complaints, you must understand what a customer complaint is. It is not a personal attack, nor is it a signal that your relationship with the customer is broken forever—or even temporarily, in most cases. A complaint is *an opportunity to improve*. Customer complaints inspire improvements to service that would otherwise have gone unnoticed to people in many businesses.

An emphasis on careful listening to complaints sends the signal to customers that yours is a customer-focused business. It says, "We view our customers as partners; we want to build relationships with them."[16] When customers perceive that you are willing to listen, and that you are encouraging their response, they will be much more likely to respond honestly and openly.

When people in a business solicit complaints, they often phrase questions in a way that will encourage a neutral or positive response. For example, you might ask a restaurant customer, "How was the meal?" or even, "Was everything okay?" and you are likely to get the response, "Yes, it was fine," whether it was really fine or not. However, if you ask, "What one thing could we have done to improve your dining experience?" an honest and helpful complaint is much more likely to result. If you are in management, do all that you can to make complaining easy for the customer. Offer a complaint phone line where the customer won't be put on hold for a long time. Use various methods of rewarding customers who complain. Many large retail companies now offer a chance to win a shopping spree or a cash prize in return for answering a customer service survey. You don't need to give away thousands of dollars to get customer feedback, however. Thank-you notes, phone calls, gifts, "consultant of the month" awards—all of these are ways to reward customers who offer helpful complaints.

Most important of all, make sure that you do all you can to correct the problems customers are complaining about. Without that step, most of the rest is meaningless. Once you get this new attitude toward complaints, you'll probably develop new attitudes toward all of your customers. After that, your human relations with them will improve.

Figure 15.4 shows one company's way of expressing attitudes of value toward customers.

HANDLING THE DIFFICULT CUSTOMER

"The customer is always right." Everyone has heard this, but is it true? It's true only in terms of the attitude it expresses. Although the customer may be very wrong, you will still be called upon to treat that customer as though everything seen through his or her eyes is correct. Carrying out such an attitude requires more than a little self-discipline. It also requires some courage.

Remember two things when dealing with an unreasonable, angry, or overly demanding customer. First, stay focused. The success of the company depends on satisfying your customers, no matter how

1. **A CUSTOMER** is the most important person in any business.
2. **A CUSTOMER** is not dependent on us—we are dependent on the customer.
3. **A CUSTOMER** is not an interruption of our work—the customer is the purpose of it.
4. **A CUSTOMER** does us a favor when he calls—we are not doing the customer a favor by serving him or her.
5. **A CUSTOMER** is part of our business—not an outsider.
6. **A CUSTOMER** is not a cold statistic—the customer is a flesh-and-blood human being with feelings and emotions like our own.
7. **A CUSTOMER** is not someone to argue or match wits with.
8. **A CUSTOMER** is a person who brings us his or her wants—it is our job to fill those wants.
9. **A CUSTOMER** is deserving of the most courteous and attentive treatment we can give.
10. **A CUSTOMER** is the life-blood of this and every other business.

figure 15.4

THE TEN COMMAND-MENTS OF GOOD BUSINESS

As you can see, remembering the customer is the key to every one of these "Ten Commandments." *How can these ideas help you keep the customer in perspective?*

Source: Minit Lube Corporate Policy Statement, Minit Lube is a division of Q-Lube, Salt Lake City, UT. Used with permission.

unreasonable they might seem. If you can remain focused on those long-term needs, rather than on a short-term need to express your own anger or frustration, you will be the winner. When dealing with the general public, many people begin to feel that a large percentage of those they deal with are nasty and unreasonable. Actually, in most businesses, difficult customers make up less than 3 percent of the total. Because of the impact of the negative people, we often generalize carelessly. Part of staying focused is remembering how very many customers are reasonable and easy to deal with.

Second, avoid the **self-esteem trap.** The customer is probably upset about something that has little to do with you directly. Even if the problem is the result of one of your own mistakes, don't take the attack personally, and especially don't let it affect your own self-esteem. Don't allow anyone's emotional outbursts to make you have negative feelings about yourself.

Sometimes, the only way to get a customer to communicate with you is to cool him or her off. Instead of using your energy to show that you are right and that the customer is wrong, put your energy into getting the customer calmed down. Some obvious exceptions to this rule would be customers who are sexually harassing or physically assaulting employees, as well as customers who are involved in other illegal activities.

Maintaining Your Self-Esteem

When dealing with an angry customer, remember this important self-talk: "This is just business; it's not personal."

Source: Steven A. Eggland and John W. Williams, *Human Relations at Work*, p. 155.

self-esteem trap

The circumstance that comes from taking a customer's attack personally and letting it affect your own self-esteem.

Arguing with Customers

"However right an action or reaction might appear, if it winds up angering the customer, it's wrong."

Source: R. S. Dreyer, "Cool Hand Lucas," *Supervision*, July 1990, pp. 17–18.

more about...

more about...

Handling Customer Complaints in the Federal Government

Go to **www.occ.treas.gov/customer.htm.** Or link this page through the course Web site at **www.mhhe.com/lamberton4e.** The Office of the Comptroller of the Currency (OCC) is a bureau of the U.S. Treasury Department. They oversee more than 2,500 national banks and their subsidiaries. Thus, the national banks are their chief customers. Click on "The OCC's Complaint Process," which shows how complaints are taken care of. Then click on other sections that seem directly related to complaints. Does the OCC handle things the way they should be handled, based on what you've learned thus far in this chapter? Write a brief paragraph explaining why or why not.

going the extra mile
When a company gives customers small extra products or services as a way of showing appreciation for their business.

GOING THE EXTRA MILE

"Giving the customer the pickle" is simply good business. If it's ever happened to you, you will remember how it feels when you ask for change at a retail store only to hear the cashier say, "Sorry, we don't make change unless you're buying something." When you do need to make a purchase, will you come back to that store? Won't you be likely to tell some of your friends and family about the incident? By refusing you the small extra, the store may have lost a dozen future sales.

None of the examples discussed in Figure 15.5 would cost a company much money, and the payback is well worth it. When a company gives customers small "extras" as a way of showing appreciation, it is called **going the extra mile**—and it nearly always pays for itself.

YOUR CUSTOMER'S SELF-ESTEEM

To succeed with customers, you must learn to bolster their self-esteem. When customers are uneasy about purchases, your ability to comfort them will help them trust you and your product or service. *How can you tell if a customer's self-esteem is interfering in his or her interaction with you? What are ways to support a customer's self-esteem in that case?*

USING STRONG ETHICS

Acting ethically is essential in all dealings with customers and would-be customers. When deciding on the ethical approach to a situation, ask yourself, "Would I want all of my procedures to be made public knowledge?" By following the philosophy that the customer's needs are of the greatest importance, much of the ethics issue will take care of itself.

Both employees and managers, though, must bear in mind the ethical issues when considering overall needs of their company. You will learn more about ethics in Chapter 17.

WHO IS RUNNING THE BUSINESS?

As this chapter ends, one final point must be emphasized: You must set limits as to the extent to which you will allow a customer to run your business. Regardless of how important the customer is, he or she must never be allowed to undermine company decisions. Les Schwab,

A well-known owner of a restaurant chain in the Pacific Northwest tells the story of a new waiter he hired. A customer who had been coming to this same restaurant for many months asked the new waiter why the customary pickle wasn't in his hamburger. The waiter retorted, "A pickle will cost you an extra dime." As you might expect, his answer irritated the customer greatly. When the owner heard the story, he coined a phrase that he uses often when he speaks in public: "Give them the pickle!"

Inc. is a successful tire store chain in the western United States. When the founder, Mr. Schwab, was still alive, he used the following story at training sessions for tire store managers. He called it the "Poor George Story."

> An excellent guideline for **ethical customer service** is the Golden Rule: Are you treating the customer the way you would like to be treated in a similar situation?

more about...

POOR GEORGE STORY

George was a very likable, hardworking owner of a small tire store. One day John, a trucker, came into George's store and asked, "George, I need four tires for my pickup. How much?" George glanced quickly at his price sheet and replied, "The tires are $60 each. Do you want 'em balanced?"

"Of course, I want 'em balanced" was the answer.

"Well, $240 for the tires and $20 for the balancing—that's a total of $260."

"Oh, man! That's too much," countered John.

At this point George thought to himself, "I would hate to lose this sale; and, besides, business hasn't been very good lately." So without even doing the math, he said to John, "Tell you what, I'll throw in the wheel balance for nothing." George had made his first big mistake: He gave in, letting his customer know that his prices were variable.

figure 15.5

BUSINESSES GOING THE EXTRA MILE

Many successful businesses go the extra mile by offering customers free services to ensure goodwill. Going the extra mile can include anything from free coffee and donuts to supervised child care or running personal errands. *When did a company "going the extra mile" make you want to stay their customer?*

Source: Barbara A. Glantz, *Building Customer Loyalty* (Burr Ridge, IL: Richard Irwin Co., 1994), p. 26.

Ways to Go the Extra Mile

- A cleaning establishment keeps its customer records on computer. When the computer shows that the customer has spent a total of $500 with that cleaner, the order they are picking up is free.
- A suburban Illinois bank serves coffee and donut holes at all times in its lobby. They also have a play area for customers' children and provide child care while the customer is doing business.
- An auto parts store lends its customers videotapes that explain how to do various car repairs.

Junko Kawaguchi is a receptionist at an insurance company. On Friday afternoon her boss says, "I'll be out the rest of the day. Hold my calls." Thirty minutes later, an irate customer asks to see Junko's boss and tells her, "I have a 3:00 appointment, and this claim has to be handled today, or I'll lose everything!" What should Junko do? What would you do?

FINDING A BALANCE

Although keeping your customers satisfied is an essential part of good business, attention to customer service needs to be balanced with firm leadership—including ethics and perspective—in order for a business to succeed. *How can customer service sometimes conflict with ethics, or let a customer run your business?*

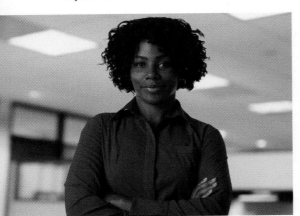

Seeing that he could bargain, John came back with, "Make it $225, and you have yourself a deal."

George did some quick arithmetic and noticed that by selling the tires for $225, he would still have a profit margin of $33. Since business was so slow, he replied, "Okay, John, we'll put them on."

To run a tire store, the cost is 25 to 26 percent of sales, but George lowered himself to 14.7 percent. He wouldn't have to make this mistake many times before going broke.

Once the tires had been mounted and balanced, John asked if he could charge the tires. George said yes, but he had always assumed that since his operation was so small, he didn't need a policy on charging interest or to construct a formal collection policy.

Thirty days later, John received his bill for $225. John thought to himself, "Good old George, he won't mind if I skip him this month." When he received a second bill, John figured that he should at least pay part of the bill. He gave George $50 and acted as if he were doing George a big favor. Five months later, the purchase was finally paid off.

After a few years, George went into bankruptcy. Hearing about the sad occurrence, John told his friends, "I sure do miss old George; he was a great guy. I guess he just wasn't a very good businessman." The next time John needed tires, he went to a chain store. There, the clerk quoted him the price, charged him $10 per tire for the wheel balance, and required a credit check and a long credit application form to fill out and sign. Although they charged him 18 percent interest, John didn't argue at all. And he didn't even think of trying to bargain them down to a lower price.

At the end of the story, George is broke. He goes to work for the same chain store that sold John his new tires. He sells tires at listed prices; he doesn't bargain; he charges interest; and he gives credit only to customers who qualify and will pay promptly. The moral of the story is: Respect your customers and give them only the highest-quality service, but *never let your customers run your business.*

15.1   Establish a Bond with the Customer

1. Understand the customer's real needs.

2. If your customer is another business, learn about that business.

3. Provide exceptional service.

4. Avoid taking your special relationship for granted.

Few factors will create more impact on overall and repeat sales than *bonding* with the customer. If you form meaningful relationships with your customers, they are much more likely to return and buy from you again. This practice is also known as **relationship selling.** When you have established a relationship with a customer, service is usually perceived more positively. For example, an attorney or real estate agent's services will be seen in a better light if they establish trust with their clients.[17]

Here are four principles that will help you form a bond of trust with your customers:

> **relationship selling**
> Forming meaningful relationships with your customers, which makes them much more likely to return and buy from you again.

1. **Understand the customer's real needs.** Careful listening to the customer can compensate for a great number of drawbacks in a company. Think about your relationship with someone who is trying to sell you a product or service, or an internal customer on your work team you'll be working with on future projects. Wouldn't you rather deal with someone who is sensitive to your needs and desires?

2. **If your customer is another business, learn about that business.** Customers will be more likely to bond with you if you show a genuine understanding of their business and what it means to them both personally and professionally. Read annual reports, trade journals, and newspaper and magazine articles to acquaint yourself with the business you are dealing with, including knowledge of their competitors. Learning about the "business" of a customer includes learning about the functions and processes of other departments in your own company, who may be internal customers.

3. **Provide exceptional service.** Exceptional service yields the strongest bond of all. Providing exceptional service isn't always totally up to you, and even as a manager you might not have as much control over the quality of service as you would like. You can be creative, and it is usually possible to innovate.

4. **Avoid taking your special relationship for granted.** Don't ever misuse the bond you have created. As mentioned earlier in the chapter, avoid ever getting to the point where you take the customer for granted. Remember, the customer includes your co-workers and other internal customers as well. The bond you have worked hard to create is a precious commodity; treat it—and your customers—accordingly.

15.2   Support the Customer's Self-Esteem

1. Put the customer at ease.

2. Put yourself in the customer's place.

3. Make the customer feel understood.

4. Make the customer feel important.

5. Praise the customer appropriately.

As with all parts of the human relations process, the customer relations issue has a great deal to do with self-esteem—in this case, the self-esteem of the customer. Almost all customers need to have their self-esteem bolstered.

You probably have a favorite store, bar, or restaurant where you feel welcome, where you feel comfortable and at ease. That feeling of ease cannot be packaged and sold as a commodity. Yet it is very real—and extremely important to customers of any business, in any place.

When you deal with customers, you need to be always aware that their self-esteem is a big issue, if not the most important one. However, many people in business ignore their customers' needs. Instead, they get wrapped up in trying to impress customers with the things they are selling, or with their own part of the company's tasks—and with themselves. Focusing on the customer's self-esteem will make the customer interested in your products and more likely to want to continue a positive working relationship.

Here are some steps you can take to build up your customers' self-esteem:

1. **Put the customer at ease.** Getting your customer to relax, and to feel comfortable with you and your company, is the most important first step. Smile with a genuine smile, not a phony one. Use the customer's name—but be careful about using it too soon, because certain customers do not like being called by their first name by people they don't know very well. Stand just close enough to the customer so as not to invade personal space. (See Chapter 7.) Try to use a similar tone of voice, rate of speaking, and body language as the customer. These details are subtle, but customers tend to identify with people who have mannerisms like their own.[18]

2. **Put yourself in the customer's place.** *Empathy* is the ability to imagine yourself in the other person's place. Develop empathy by asking yourself, "If I were this customer, with the needs she has, how would I feel?" This habit can be difficult to form and cultivate. But if you begin thinking this way, it will improve all areas of your human relations, not only customer relations.

3. **Make the customer feel understood.** Like all other people, customers need to feel they are communicating successfully. Be sure to interpret what they say correctly. Asking a question that starts out with "Do you mean . . .?" can go a long way toward letting the customer know that you care enough to listen and understand what he or she is saying. If you are at all unclear about what the customer means, ask questions until you are sure.[19]

4. **Make the customer feel important.** One of the worst things you can do is to allow distractions (such as phone calls or other interruptions) to pull your concentration away from the customer. While you are dealing with a customer, act as though nothing else is as important. Let people know you are absorbed in being with them. To the customer, you are the whole company—so do all you can to make that feeling go both ways.

5. **Praise the customer appropriately.** You don't have to try too hard when praising a customer. Is the customer dressed nicely? Mention it. Has the customer accomplished something special recently? Congratulate him

or her specifically. But do so in the framework of authentic caring. This is another habit that will likely help in relationships outside of work, too. Praise is a powerful human relations tool, but use it wisely. Insincere praise can be much worse than none at all.

Be sure to make the praise specific. A generalized compliment can leave the customer wondering, "What did that really mean?"[20] Don't just say that Mr. Johnson asks good questions that show he knows the product; tell him sincerely that you admire that quality in a customer! If your only knowledge of the quality you want to praise is general, ask a specific question in a nonthreatening way. A specific question shows real interest and often leads to a point where you can offer sincere praise.

15.3　Handle the Difficult Customer Professionally

1. Let the customer vent.
2. Get the facts.
3. Be sure you understand the customer's feelings.
4. Suggest a solution.
5. End positively.
6. Don't expect to win them all.

Here are some easy-to-follow guidelines for dealing with a customer who is already angry.[21]

1. **Let the customer vent.** You should allow an angry customer to speak his or her mind. This approach might be difficult, but being a good listener (even to an angry, perhaps ranting customer) is still the best approach. Cutting the customer off usually does more harm than good. Let the customer know that you sympathize and care enough to hear everything. Have you ever noticed your anger disappearing after you have gotten somebody to listen to you? Quite possibly, the customer mainly needs the chance to express some strong emotions on the issue; all you need to be is the sounding board.

2. **Get the facts.** If possible, have all available information on the case right in front of you. If the customer is wrong, be sure that your sources are correct. Ask questions to verify what the customer is telling you. If two or more versions seem to contradict each other, ask questions until you are satisfied that you have found the truth. If the customer is wrong, don't say so directly. In all cases, focus on what can be done to solve the problem, rather than to place blame.

3. **Be sure you understand the customer's feelings.** A great deal of expressed anger can confuse you when you are trying to listen. Are you sure you understand the main issue in the mind of the customer? What you see as the main issue might not be what the customer thinks it is. Only when you have completed this step and know what the customer thinks is wrong can you find out how to make it right.

4. **Suggest a solution.** Be specific and clear. Be careful not to make promises that the company might not let you keep. If the solution you can offer isn't what your customer wanted, clearly explain why you have to offer this

solution instead. Avoiding using "company policy" as an excuse. If you must use that phrase, explain the reasons for the policy as best you can.

5. **End positively.** Once you have agreed to a solution, thank the customer for his or her patience and for bringing the problem to your attention. Don't apologize too much. Instead, focus your attention on the future. Mention steps that can be taken on both sides to prevent such problems from happening again. Don't hesitate to include things you will do personally to prevent future occurrences. Your main purpose now is to keep the customer's future business.[22]

6. **Don't expect to win them all.** You can be as patient, empathic, helpful, and efficient as it's possible to be, and still have a percentage of customers who will remain angry. Some customers simply are difficult people, and they will stay that way no matter what anyone does. Again, don't take their words or actions personally. If possible, ask your manager for help.[23]

When the time arises to use these six steps in the workplace, do the best you can. If you don't remember all of them, at least remember to do everything you can to keep an angry customer's complaint from turning into an argument. It takes two people to make an argument. As the representative of the company, you must refuse to become that second person. You may have to suppress the desire to answer back defensively. In the end, though, your self-control will pay off because you'll have kept your cool—and demonstrated to everyone around you that you can handle stressful situations.

CHAPTER FIFTEEN SUMMARY

Chapter Summary by Learning Objectives

1. **Explain how to determine what customers really want.** No matter what business you're in, customers really want only two things: good feelings and solutions to problems. By listening to the customer, you can discover the customer's needs in these two categories.

2. **Define customer service.** You have good service only when the customer thinks you do. Good customer service always includes good human relations.

3. **Describe the internal customer.** The internal customer is the person who depends on the other people in the company to provide services and products for the external customer.

4. **List the two simplest principles of customer service.** (1) Find out what the customer needs. (2) Do whatever is necessary to satisfy those needs.

5. **Give examples of issues in customer service.** Major issues in customer service include: (1) your customers and your attitude, (2) delivering bad news to customers, and (3) encouraging complaints. All three are very important in creating a customer-friendly business.

6. **Compare and contrast ways to handle a difficult customer.** When dealing with an unreasonable, angry, or overly demanding customer, stay focused and avoid the self-esteem trap. When customers are already angry, let them vent. Find out the facts, making sure that you also understand the customer's *feelings;* then suggest a solution. End as positively as possible. Don't expect success in all cases; some difficult customers will remain difficult no matter what you say or do.

7. **Explain the significance of going the extra mile.** Going the extra mile means giving customers those little extras to show your appreciation of their business. These little "perks" are inexpensive and have a tremendous potential payoff in customer satisfaction.

8. **List ways to use strong ethics in customer service.** Good ethics in treatment of customers nearly always comes back as customer satisfaction.

9. **Explain the moral of the Poor George story and how it relates to customer service.** The Poor George story illustrates how someone in business can keep the customer from running the business. Treat your customers well, with great respect and deference, but never let the customer make business decisions for you. That is, don't let the customer run your business.

key terms

bad news skills 407   **internal customer** 404   **two simplest**
going the extra mile 412   **"nice" customer** 408   **principles** 404
good feelings and   **relationship selling** 415
solutions 402   **self-esteem trap** 411

review questions

1. Explain what it means to say that customers really want *feelings* and *solutions,* rather than products and services. When you are a customer, what does that mean to you?

2. Define the term "internal customer." Why is the concept of *internal* customer service important to an overall understanding of customer service?

3. Why is an understanding of the "nice" customer of great importance in improving customer service? Have you ever known or been someone like this "nice" customer, who is unhappy but only leaves and never returns rather than voicing concerns to the business?

4. What are the "two simplest principles" of customer service? What importance does listening play in the use of those principles? Have you ever seen them violated?

5. Explain the importance of forming a bond with the customer. How does one go about establishing such a bond?

6. What are the four steps in giving the customer bad news? Explain each step.

7. What are some steps one can take to build the customer's self-esteem? Which step, in your opinion, is the most important? Explain.

8. What is meant by "going the extra mile"? Provide an example from your life of either serving customers or being a customer. How did your experience affect you? Was there ever a time when someone didn't go the extra mile?

critical thinking questions

9. Try to recall if you can identify a businessperson who was able to establish a bond with you or one of your family members. How was this accomplished?

10. Have you ever been the victim of a company's poor customer service policy, as either an external or internal customer? What specifically occurred? How did this treatment make you feel? What would you have changed in that situation if you had the power to do so?

working it out 15.1

THE DIFFICULT CUSTOMER

School-to-Work Connection: Interpersonal Skills

A woman approaches the ticket counter at a large airport and demands to see the manager. You ask if you can be of any assistance since the manager is not available. She immediately challenges the airline's no-pet policy as unfair and discriminatory. She explains that she has to travel 1,000 miles to take care of a sick sister. Her toy poodle, from which she has never been separated, is completely housebroken and "never barks or bites." She can't stand the thought of her "little baby" all alone in the dangerous, cold, and dark luggage compartment. After all, "dogs can freeze up there, and there might not be enough air to breathe." She is holding the dog tightly in her arms. The pooch is clothed in a designer jacket made for small dogs and has her nails polished bright red. The woman loudly demands that she be allowed to bring the pet on board with her.

What should you do? Place an X on the line next to the actions that are the most appropriate responses to this difficult situation.

_____ 1. Show slight disgust on your face, so she will know you consider her to be the problem.

_____ 2. Laugh and make light of the situation.

_____ 3. Remain calm, cool, and patient.

_____ 4. Sympathize with her feelings of fear and frustration. Tell her that you don't like to leave your pets alone, either.

_____ 5. Walk away and find your manager.

_____ 6. Become distant and less cooperative.

_____ 7. Disarm her by asking, "Are you serious?"

_____ 8. Explain carefully about the gentle treatment pets receive in the pet compartment and how many pets fly your airline each day.

_____ 9. Ask her to understand the airline's need to consider all of the passengers.

_____ 10. Thank her for her understanding and cooperation.

Answers: 3, 4, 8, and 10 are the most appropriate choices. All of the other choices would probably do more harm than good.[24]

working it out 15.2

ROLE-PLAYING THE CUSTOMER

School-to-Work Connection: Interpersonal Skills

Purpose: To experience the difficulties in dealing directly with customer problems.

Procedure: Two students should volunteer to play the parts of a customer and an employee, role-playing the following situation:

Ron (or Rhonda) works in the men's fashions department in Bernstein's, a large department store. Delmar Wiggins, a customer, places three shirts and a sweater on the counter. In a friendly voice, he jokes, "I guess this is all I can afford." When Mr. Wiggins offers his Bernstein's charge card, Ron quickly runs a computerized check for the approval. The card is denied. Ron excuses himself for a moment and reaches for a phone out of earshot from the customer. His call to the office confirms that Mr. Wiggins hasn't paid a cent on his already-large bill for over four months.

Instructions: The student who plays Ron (or Rhonda) should proceed with the plan for fair treatment of Mr. Wiggins. Remember that Ron needs to keep Mr. Wiggins as a cash customer in the future, and hopefully, for this sale as well. Mr. Wiggins should act innocent, as though he has no knowledge of a bad account, but he also should be willing to comply with whatever reasonable suggestions Ron comes up with.

The student who plays Mr. Wiggins may decide to deny the fact that payments are overdue. In this case, Ron (or Rhonda) needs to find other ways of dealing with the customer. He or she could say something like, "It appears that they have not received your most recent payments. I am sure that there is some misunderstanding. Would you like me to put you on the line with them so that you can confirm your most recent payments?" Mr. Wiggins, knowing that no such payments have been sent, will probably back down and agree to another method of payment.

working it out 15.3

School-to-Work Connection: Interpersonal Skills
Will you change careers during your lifetime or keep the same job for your entire career? Most of us will change jobs 7 to 10 times during our careers. How successful such job changes will be depends on how much planning and preparation you have done. Career planning should focus on both short-term and long-term transitions. Each of these has different tasks. Both should be done with some careful thought and honest reflection.

Short-term planning: Short-term planning is aimed at just the next few years. Barriers that can be overcome sometimes stand in the way of this planning. For some people, personal traits such as procrastination and lack of motivation are career barriers. Family pressures and peer pressure to work in a certain occupation, or to avoid some occupations, can also stand in the way of a successful job change. Following are some suggestions to get you started with short-term planning.

1. Think about your lifestyle now and in the future. Are you happy with it? Do you want to change it, or keep it the same? Does your current job allow you to have the lifestyle you want?

2. Think about your likes and dislikes. What tasks do you enjoy, both at work and away from work? What do you avoid? How does your job fit with these likes and dislikes?

3. Define what you are most passionate about: What gives you energy and "flow"? (See Chapter 4.) Do these activities happen at work in your current job?

4. List your strengths and weaknesses from the perspective of an employer. What skills and abilities, work experience and training, knowledge and experiences, do you have? What do you lack?

5. How do you define success? Are you able to achieve your vision of success in your current career path?

6. How would you describe your personality? What have the personality assessments in the Internet Exercises said about you? Does your personality fit with your current job?

7. What is your dream job? What have the Internet Exercises in previous chapters revealed to you about careers and occupations that might interest you?

8. Examine your current situation. Identify a starting point for career advancement or job change. Be realistic, but define some goals to work toward. Finally, with the information you have gathered in answering these questions, you can work toward those goals. Narrow down your career choices. Identify additional training you will need. Develop a timeline and an action plan for meeting your short-term career planning goals.

Long-term planning: Long-term career planning requires that you think 5 years, 10, or longer into the future. Your guidelines for this planning are broader and more general.

1. Because the workforce and technology are changing so fast, you may have job skills that won't be needed in the future. Identify core skills that will always be in demand. Communication skills, creativity, teamwork, problem solving, and many of the skills discussed in this textbook are core skills.

2. Examine employment trends. The "Occupational Outlook Handbook" (**www.dol.gov**) is a good place to start (see Chapter 19 for more information).

3. Stay current in your short-term career planning. Keep up on newly emerging industries, technologies, and occupations. Keep an open mind (stay in the "open mode") while you creatively explore new ideas. Don't get locked in to one idea; you can always change your mind as new information comes along.

Whether you love your job and want to keep it forever, or can't wait to find the next one, short-term and long-term career planning can help. You can put yourself in a better position to advance in your career, or begin a completely new occupation, with some strategic planning. Think of career planning as an interesting journey. Take your time, and be willing to head to a new adventure in a different direction if one should arise.

Source: Randall S. Hansen, "Developing a Strategic Vision for Your Career Plan," Quintessential Careers, www.quintcareers.com/career_plan.html (retrieved June 15, 2008).

1. *Identify and Solve*

   Sometimes a "problem customer" is not a problem at all—instead, the problem can be traced to misunderstandings that can easily be solved. Visit Craig Harrison's "From Worst to First: Winning Over Problematic Customers" at **www.mhhe.com/lamberton4e.** This page can also be accessed directly through the Expressions for Excellence page at **www.expressionsofexcellence.com/ ARTICLES/Bad_Customers.html.** Read the article to answer the following questions:

   a. What is the suggested alternative for dealing with a least favorite customer?

   b. Do you think that this approach will salvage every customer relationship, and do you want it to? Why or why not?

   c. What are some minor changes that could make a big difference in customer relations?

   d. How do the questions regarding the history of a particular customer yield insight as to how to handle them and where the relationship went awry?

   e. Do you feel that by changing your attitude, you can solve most of the problems that seem unsolvable in a bad customer relationship? Why or why not?

2. *Read and Write*

   Visit Construction Equipment Distribution's Web page at **http:// constructionequipmentdistribution.com/article-detail.cfm? id=10921420** and link to the article on customer service titled "Never Let Them Go" by Vicki Lenz. This article is also linked through **www.mhhe.com/lamberton4e.** Answer the following questions:

   a. What are the three elements for building customer relationships?

   b. Which of the top 10 customer-focused marketing tips do you consider to be the most important? Why?

   c. Could these principles apply to all companies? Why or why not?

   d. If you are currently working, could you apply these principles to your current job immediately? Why or why not?

3. *Read and Write*

   Visit the Customer Service Zone & Help Center's Web site through the course Web site at **www.mhhe.com/lamberton4e** or located directly at **http://customerservicezone.com/Customer_Service_-_ Internal_Customers/.** Read one of the articles posted on internal customers. Summarize the article, explaining the methods or strategies the author suggests to improve internal customer relations.

4. *Self-Assess and Apply*

How is your job-hunting etiquette? Find out how you can get an edge over other job seekers, and get some "do" and "don't" tips on job seeking from Quintessential Careers linked through the course Web site at **www.mhhe.com/lamberton4e** or visit them directly at **www.quintcareers.com/job-hunting_etiquette_quiz.html.** What did you learn?

Disaster in Aisle Three

Carmine DeLuccio worked at a large health food store. One morning he saw a customer pushing an overloaded shopping cart down the aisle. The customer couldn't see where she was going because the merchandise in her cart obstructed her view. Carmine looked away just long enough to help another customer with a small purchase. As he looked back up, the loaded cart struck a large display of bottled fruit juices. The crash was deafening; broken glass and juice filled the aisle.

Mrs. Raye, the customer, was very upset. She immediately blamed the store for her problem and shouted, "What a stupid place to stick a breakable display! And if you didn't have such tiny shopping carts, I wouldn't have to load this one up so high!" A small crowd of customers began to gather around her as she continued to shout.

Carmine's boss, Ann Camilla, was out of the store, and the assistant manager had called in sick that morning. Carmine was alone, and he alone had to decide what to do. As he walked toward this disaster scene, Carmine kept repeating to himself his boss's favorite saying, "The customer is always right. The customer is always right."

Case Study Questions

1. What should Carmine say to Mrs. Raye? Why?

2. What should he do, and in what order?

3. What should Carmine say to the other customers who ask questions such as "What happened over there, anyway?"

International Business Calling

An international tourism company based in the United States does business with partner companies in several nations. Their main focus is on putting together tour packages for families and groups. Dana Smith, the manager of the main office, frequently takes calls about problems or issues that have arisen with specific tours. She has been distracted on this particular morning resolving a problem with a tour in China—several of the tourists have fallen ill and want to return home immediately, cutting their vacations short. This means she will have to work with several hotels, bus companies, tourism agencies, and airlines either changing or canceling reservations.

When the phone rings and one of her agents in Singapore is on the other line, she is already annoyed. "What do you want, Wei Ting? Why can't you seem to go one day without some problem you can't figure out? Can't you handle these complaining clients?" Wei Ting has not had a chance to tell Dana that a very angry client is also on the line with them. The client's request for a refund for an earlier trip had just been turned down due to company policy. His entry visa into Malaysia had been denied by officials there. The client blamed the tour company, but the tour company was unable to get the visa cleared and had compensated by substituting a trip to Indonesia instead. The client complained that since the change in the itinerary was not his choice, he should be fully refunded. The tour company disagreed.

Meanwhile, Wei Ting was caught in the middle and was relying on Dana to help with the situation. The client, hearing himself identified as a "complainer," exploded into an angry tirade. Dana felt angry that Wei Ting had not warned her ahead of time there was a client on the line, and Wei Ting was totally embarrassed by the whole incident.

Case Study Questions

1. Does this situation have more to do with external customer relations, with internal customer relations, or both? Explain.

2. What should Dana do to resolve the situation on all fronts? What should Wei Ting do to keep the client happy and develop a better working relationship with Dana?

3. Explain how this company could encourage complaints in the future to avoid such situations. What types of complaints and solutions would you anticipate management receiving in this company?

« « thriving in a changing world

16 Human Relations in a World of Diversity

17 Business Ethics and Social Responsibility

18 Maintaining a Productive Workplace

19 Human Relations and Your Future Success

Every time you pick up the newspaper, workplace issues appear in the headlines. You have probably read about the nationwide shift to a service economy, diversity and globalization, corporate ethics, and the challenges in balancing home, career, and family life. How can we use human relations skills to handle these and other workplace issues? Part Four offers some answers.

Chapter 16 covers the trend of increasing diversity in the workforce, and offers strategies on ensuring cooperation and fairness in a diverse environment. Chapter 17 explores ethics and ways to maintain an ethical workplace. Chapter 18 looks at personal issues that affect the work experience and affect individual productivity. Chapter 19 looks ahead as new human relations issues surface in the workplace of the 21st century. » »

HUMAN RELATIONS IN A WORLD OF DIVERSITY

In the Workplace: In the Minority

SITUATION

Jane Ong looked around with interest and some amazement as she arrived at her new office building for her first day of work. She had been hired during a campus interview at her college near Seattle and was just seeing her new place of employment for the first time today. Growing up as a third-generation Chinese American in Seattle, she had been considered a minority group member, but she had always felt right at home among the other Asian Americans, as well as the Hispanics, African Americans, and Caucasians in her classes and her neighborhood. But this new office in downtown San Francisco was a whole different experience. As she walked through the building toward the Human Resources office with her new supervisor, Mr. Singh, she passed hundreds of her new co-workers already busy at work. Even though this was a huge global financial organization, she had not expected the diversity she saw among its employees.

430

objectives

After studying this chapter, you will be able to:

1. Describe how human relations are affected when they are part of a diverse society.

2. Explain how prejudiced attitudes pose a challenge to human relations.

3. Identify the origins of prejudice.

4. List types of discrimination.

5. Define sexual harassment.

6. Describe the connections between prejudice, discrimination, and self-esteem.

7. Give examples of how to decrease prejudice.

STRATEGIES FOR SUCCESS

Strategy 16.1   Assess Your Knowledge

Strategy 16.2   Reducing Sexual Harassment

She saw people dressed in clothing she had never seen among her classmates and neighbors, and she heard languages and accents she couldn't even identify. She recognized Mandarin Chinese and Spanish, and Mr. Singh would explain later that other languages spoken among her co-workers also included Korean, Farsi, Tagalog, Armenian, German, Cambodian, Hindi, Malay, Vietnamese, Finnish, and Ibo, among many others.

DISCOVERY

As Jane continued to walk through the maze of offices, smiling and shaking hands or greeting new people, she thought, "Wow, this is amazing. I've got so much to learn about everyone." She looked forward to getting started.

THINK ABOUT IT

How might the diversity in Jane's new environment affect her on a day-to-day basis? What might she need to know in order to work successfully with such a diverse population of co-workers? How can finding yourself in a new role or environment help you better understand yourself and others?

A DIVERSE SOCIETY

As the 21st century unfolds, many Americans like Jane will experience changes in the workforce. Older employees, women, and immigrants are examples of people entering the workforce in greater numbers than in the previous century. The composition of the workforce will continue to change and diversify. The U.S. Bureau of Labor Statistics projects that the following will happen by the year 2010 (see Figure 16.1):

- Women will continue to enter the labor force at a faster pace than men, making up almost half the workforce (48%).

- The proportion of older employees will increase, in part because baby boomers will remain in the workforce past the traditional retirement age.

- Hispanics will continue to expand their workforce participation, making up almost 13 percent of the workforce.

- African Americans and Asian Americans will make up 12 percent and 5.5 percent, respectively, of the workforce, increasing their labor force participation at a faster rate than non-Hispanic whites.

- The number of American companies engaging directly in competition with overseas companies will increase, and the importance of the global marketplace will continue to increase.

figure 16.1

THE FUTURE OF WORKPLACE DIVERSITY

As time changes, the traditional employee of the 21st century—the white male—will play a smaller role in the overall workforce. *What changes do you see happening in your own field?*

Source: U.S. Department of Commerce, Bureau of the Census, *Historical Statistics of the U.S.: Colonial Times to 1970.* See also: Howard N. Fullerton Jr., and Mitra Toossi, "Labor Force Projections to 2010: Steady Growth and Changing Composition," *Monthly Labor Review,* November 2001 (retrieved July 21, 2005) www.bls.gov/opub/mir/2001/11/art2full.pdf.

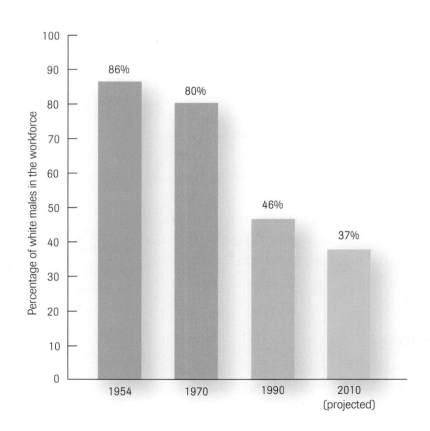

- About 37 percent of the workforce will be the traditional employee of the 20th century, the white non-Hispanic male.[1]

People with disabilities are more visible in the workplace today, as are people with diverse religious beliefs. All people will need to take a close look at the prejudices they learned, both actively and unconsciously, growing up.

Besides examining prejudices, everyone needs a knowledge base. You need to know about different cultural biases, customs, and expectations of the diverse groups you will likely be working with. Without such knowledge, you could find yourself making mistakes like these:

- A manager in an American company was overjoyed with a new technique developed by one of his employees, a Native American. He rewarded her with a great deal of fanfare and congratulations in front of her fellow employees. However, she was so humiliated by being singled out in this way that she didn't return to work for three weeks.

- Another manager thought that a friendly pat on the arm or back helped motivate his employees and promote good feelings. He took every chance to use his newfound motivation technique. Quite a few of his employees were Asian; they did not like being touched. These employees avoided this manager whenever possible. Several of them asked for transfers. (If he had treated his female employees this way, he would have had still other problems to deal with.)

- Concerned about ethics and proper procedures, a manager refused a gift given to him by a new employee, who was an immigrant. She was simply showing gratitude for her job in a manner appropriate to her culture. The employee didn't understand company policy against receiving gifts. She was offended and quit.

- In a similar situation, the wife of a new employee from Eastern Europe stopped by the office with a bottle of champagne, expecting that her husband's fellow employees would stop and help celebrate the new job. Instead, people just said hello and returned to work. The woman was mortified. Her husband quit a few days later.[2]

It is not unusual now to find companies that have regular diversity training programs, workshops, and other resources for their employees. Many companies have made a commitment to improving the workplace climate of their organizations by hiring diversity officers as part of the administrative team, and by establishing policies of working only with suppliers who have similar policies.

more about...

Corporate Diversity Policies

Companies often publish their **diversity policies** in statements on their Web sites under links titled "Corporate Social Responsibility" or "Corporate Ethics" or "Company Values." Take a look at the Web sites for companies you do business with, or any large organizations you are familiar with. Can you find such a link? What information does each company include?

HANDLING PREJUDICE

Everyone needs to know how to handle prejudice when it's encountered, and everyone needs to know how to eliminate prejudice within himself or herself. This applies especially to people whose jobs involve working with the public. *How can someone's prejudiced attitude affect others when working with the public?*

All of these stories are about misunderstandings of the other person's cultural expectations. No conscious prejudice was involved, nor hatred or viciousness of any kind. Problems in the diverse workplace happen because of honest mistakes, as well as because of stereotyping and prejudice. Since stereotyping and prejudice do occur on the job, an in-depth look at them is important.

PREJUDICED ATTITUDES

Prejudice is one type of attitude. All attitudes have three parts: what you think, feel, and do. These three parts of an attitude exist whether you are talking about different groups of people, the NBA playoffs, the Democratic Party, or creamed spinach. For example, you may *think* to yourself, "Creamed spinach is green," then *feel* a negative reaction to that particular color of green: "That color reminds me of slime. Gross!" As a consequence, you *do* something (or in this case choose to *not* do something) by not eating the creamed spinach.

In talking about diversity in the workplace, you can think of prejudice against other people as part of a specific, often harmful attitude. Like other attitudes, this one is composed of three parts. **Stereotypes** are your *thoughts or beliefs* about specific groups of people. **Prejudice** is how you *feel* as a result of those thoughts or beliefs. **Discrimination** is your *behavior,* or what you do (or intend to do, or are inclined to do) as a result of your stereotypes and prejudice. A closer look at these components follows.

stereotypes
Your thoughts or beliefs about specific groups of people.

prejudice
How you feel as a result of the stereotypes you believe in.

discrimination
Your behavior, or what you do (or intend to do, or are inclined to do) as a result of your stereotypes and prejudice.

Stereotypes

A stereotype is a thought or belief about members of a given group. That belief may be positive, negative, or neutral; and it is usually oversimplified, exaggerated, and/or overgeneralized. Whether it is a positive belief ("Asians are good students and employees") or a negative one ("senior citizens are too old to be good employees"), it is potentially damaging because it lumps everyone into one group without recognizing their individual characteristics.

People also stereotype tasks and jobs: a manager's job is often stereotyped as "a man's job," whereas clerical or secretarial duties are labeled "women's work." Stereotypes hurt minorities, women, men, and members of other groups. Hiring, promotions, and job evaluations are areas where stereotypes can affect who is accepted or passed over.

A study of stereotyping and prejudice on the job uncovered these examples:

- "My supervisor follows me to the restroom, lunchroom, telephone, or whenever I am away from my work area. I think it's because I'm the only minority there."

- "She scrutinizes my work closer than she does the white employees. She gives me orders in a derogatory way."
- "He constantly makes vulgar remarks about me, such as calling me the 'entertainment and kiss committee.'"
- "She always shakes her finger in our faces when she doesn't like something we did."[3]

In each of these cases, the stereotyping has resulted in feelings of prejudice and discriminatory behavior against an employee.

Prejudice

Prejudice means "to prejudge" or make a judgment without knowing a person beforehand. It sums up the negative feelings or evaluations about people and groups that are stereotyped. Prejudice causes **bias,** which is a tendency to judge people before you know them, basing the judgment only on their membership in some group or category of people. Bias can be negative or positive; that is, we may lean *toward* or favor a person or group, or lean *away from* or disfavor a person or a group.

Everyone has certain prejudices, whether conscious or otherwise, and whether you believe it or not. Even people who consider themselves unprejudiced often have certain *strong* likes and dislikes based on categories of people. Prejudice undermines human relations, and it is hard on productivity. It is disruptive and causes low morale in the workplace or in any other place where it occurs unquestioned.

> **bias**
>
> A tendency to judge people before knowing them, basing the judgment only on their membership in some group or category of people.

Discrimination

Discrimination is acting or intending to act, or being inclined to act, on a prejudicial attitude. Prejudice is a feeling; discrimination is an act. Not all feelings of prejudice result in acts of discrimination, but individual acts of discrimination usually come from prejudiced feelings.

Discriminatory acts that are not caused by prejudice include discriminatory policies in the workplace that are not intentionally set to exclude members of specific groups or to treat them differently, but which have that effect anyway. These policies are referred to as **institutional prejudice,** or exclusionary policies.

A step toward eliminating discrimination in the workplace came with the passing of the Civil Rights Act of 1964. This law makes it illegal to discriminate against anyone because of race, color, religion, sex, or national origin. Title VII of this law covers any employer who does business between states and who employs at least 15 people for at least 20 weeks per year. This definition of *employer* also includes governments

> *more about...*
>
> **The Beginning of Civil Rights**
>
> The civil rights movement's first major victory came 10 years earlier than the Civil Rights Act with *Brown vs. the Board of Education,* a 1954 U.S. Supreme Court case that outlawed school segregation.

> **institutional prejudice**
>
> Prejudice that is caused by policies in the workplace that are not intentionally set to exclude members of specific groups or to treat them differently, but which have that effect anyway.

Equal Employment Opportunity Commission (EEOC)

A federal agency established to monitor the laws set in place by the amended Civil Rights Act of 1972.

and other public institutions, schools and colleges, unions, and employment agencies. The Civil Rights Act was amended in 1972. In that year, the **Equal Employment Opportunity Commission (EEOC)** was established to monitor these laws.

ORIGINS OF PREJUDICE

For American society to eliminate prejudice, it needs to know where prejudice comes from. Psychologists and sociologists have been very interested in studying what causes prejudice for decades. Although they do not agree on any one cause, there are a few theories that can be summarized. In general, the origins of prejudice can be divided into three broad categories: social causes, cognitive (thinking) causes, and emotional causes.[4] (See Figure 16.2.)

Social Causes of Prejudice

Many theories have been put forth about how social factors cause prejudice. One theory is that people form prejudices to try to raise their own self-esteem, such as when climbing the career or social ladder. It's easier for people to feel superior when they are able to identify other groups of people as inferior. This unequal status leads to prejudice. It also becomes a vicious cycle when people then use the fact that they are higher up on the status pole to justify their prejudice and discrimination.

Another social theory is that prejudice helps people define themselves and feel socially accepted. When people belong to a group and feel accepted, they tend to rate other groups as inferior. Conforming to a group's standards also helps people feel more accepted, and many groups encourage *us-versus-them* feelings and behaviors. For example, a new university student in a strange city may join a fraternity or sorority to make friends, but this also means not being friends with members of other

figure 16.2

THE ORIGINS OF PREJUDICE

The three origins of prejudice are social ones (the need to feel higher in status than others), cognitive (the need to categorize and stereotype people), and emotional (such as habit, or ethnocentrism). *Which type of prejudice can be most damaging?*

Social
- Status
- Self-esteem
- Us vs. them
- In group/Out group

Cognitive
- Thinking
- Reasoning
- Categorization
- Boxes

Emotional
- The right way
- Habit
- Ethnocentrism
- Competition

The EEOC Online

Visit the U.S. Equal Employment Opportunity Commission at **www.eeoc.gov** and linked through the textbook's Web site at **www.mhhe.com/lamberton4e.** Follow the links to "Discriminatory Practices" and "Discrimination by Type." Be prepared to discuss this material in a group. Have you seen, or experienced yourself, any of these actions on the job? What steps does the EEOC recommend to improve the situation?

fraternities or sororities. To do so would be disloyal! In this example, prejudice is also helping to reduce the student's anxiety, insecurity, and inner conflict. These same feelings are also social causes of prejudice.

A final social theory of prejudice looks at institutional support systems, or the way organizations and society itself unintentionally create institutional racism, sexism, or exclusionary policies. For example, men and women make up about equal proportions of the population, but men are still highly overrepresented in films and television shows as main characters, narrators for commercials, and authority figures.[5] This has the effect of promoting the idea that men really are authority figures who know much more about kitchen floor wax or dog food than women know about such things.

All it takes to create prejudice is for people to identify themselves as part of a group (the in-group) while they see others as part of a different group (the out-group). If that seems too simple to be true, try this easy experiment on your own: go to any high school football or basketball game and actively cheer for the visiting team while sitting with the home team spectators. Note how you feel—and how the home team spectators behave toward you.

> more about...
>
> **Scapegoating** is the practice of unfairly blaming others (such as ethnic groups) when something goes wrong. The term originated from an ancient biblical custom of sending a goat into the wilderness after the sins of the community were placed upon its head.

Cognitive Causes of Prejudice

Cognitive causes have to do with thinking and reasoning processes. Some psychologists believe that prejudice originates with a process called **cognitive categorization,** in which the mind quickly sorts information into categories to function efficiently. Cognitive categorization is generally a necessary skill; for instance, if every time you walked into a classroom you had to take the time to figure out all over again which objects to sit on and which objects to write with, you would fail in school and in life. The problem is that cognitive categorization also allows you to categorize people quickly, and this can lead to prejudice.

> **cognitive categorization**
> A process in which the mind quickly sorts information into categories to function efficiently.

437

"See?" Jerry told his friend Phil after hearing the news that he'd been promoted. "I got the promotion and Sherri didn't. I am better at this job than she is. That just proves it: men are smarter and work harder than women. I don't think I'll recommend her for a promotion next time around. She's just not good enough."

Think about how you do this. When someone is walking toward you on the sidewalk, for example, you quickly and unconsciously notice some characteristics about the person: young, male, long hair, baggy pants, and carrying a skateboard. You feel able to understand, without figuring out each characteristic separately, what *type* of person this is. Cognitive categorization goes too far, however, when you assign people to cognitive *boxes*, then negatively evaluate them based on the boxes you've put them in.[6]

Emotional Causes of Prejudice

ethnocentrism

The belief that one's ethnic group is more normal than others; an emotional source of prejudice because of people's gut-level feelings about how right *their* group is—and, in turn, how wrong they think other groups are.

Ethnocentrism is the cause of a great deal of prejudice that people experience. Human beings tend to see their own ethnic groups as the most normal, and they believe their way of seeing and doing things is *the* right way. Ethnocentrism is an emotional source of prejudice because of people's gut-level feelings about how right *their* group is—and, in turn, how wrong they think other groups are.

Ethnocentrism exists everywhere, not just in the United States. Most societies are ethnocentric. This phenomenon is not intentional; the familiar way of doing things just seems right to most of us. If what is familiar is right, then by extension, many people feel that what is unfamiliar must be wrong. People are creatures of habit, and if it is your habit to live a certain way, you almost automatically begin to think that doing otherwise is strange or unusual.

Another theory about the emotional causes of prejudice is that people look for a target to blame when they are frustrated. When members of two groups are competing for scarce resources (such as jobs in an area with high unemployment), this competition can lead to frustration, then aggression, prejudice, and discrimination.[7]

TYPES OF DISCRIMINATION

Discrimination comes from several different sources and is aimed at a variety of different targets. Here we explore the major types of discrimination, based on what group is targeted.

Racism

Racism, which is prejudice and discrimination based on race, is one of today's most important social topics. This topic is filled with emotion and controversy and has been at the heart of many conflicts throughout history. Many people who lived through World War II or through the 1950s and 1960s expected that by the 21st century, racism in America would be a thing of the past. Sadly, they were wrong. Minorities in the United States still experience widespread discrimination and prejudice.

Indications can be seen worldwide that the issue is at least as serious as it was in the days of Adolf Hitler. *Genocide*, which is the systematic murder of an entire racial, ethnic, or national group, continues around the world. In the 1990s, genocide occurred in Rwanda and the former Yugoslavia. In the 2000s, the location was Darfur when in 2004 the U.S. government declared genocide to be occurring in this area of the Sudan.[8]

Racial prejudice is proving to be extremely difficult to overcome, and many people in America still have not been accepted as part of mainstream society. Ethnocentrism is one of the factors in this problem, but certainly not the only one. Prejudice is another major reason. Four major racial groups that are striving for equal status in American society are: African Americans, Asians, Hispanics, and Native Americans (not necessarily in that order). Prejudice against Jews (also called anti-Semitism) is still a problem, and neo-Nazi groups still exist in various countries.

America's history of racial inequality has created large gaps in education and employment that are still very real today. Look at the unemployment rate and you will find significant differences by race or ethnicity in recent years. Data for mid 2008 (as an example) reveal such differences:

- Total U.S. unemployment rate: 5.5%
- Unemployment rate for white Americans: 4.4%
- Unemployment rate for African Americans: 8.8%
- Unemployment rate for Americans of Hispanic origin: 6.5%

If these percentages don't seem drastically different to you, remember that they represent thousands of people who are all actively looking for work (*seeking work* is required in order to be counted in this statistic).[9]

Research has shown that African American employees tend to be recommended for promotions less often and are less satisfied with their careers than white employees, in large part because of the stigma that arises when employees belong to a minority group.[10] What many employers fail to realize is that by discriminating against employees because of their beliefs about race, these employers are damaging their own productivity (by reducing morale) and

racism

Prejudice and discrimination based on race.

HOW THE MEDIA CREATES PREJUDICE

Advertisements often portray men as authority figures and women as sex objects for no reason other than prejudice. *Are these images meant to portray reality, or are these models given roles by misguided advertisers? How can you identify institutional prejudice?*

SooMei and Tracey are American businesswomen who often work in Argentina. They respect those who stick to schedules because punctuality is a shared value in their culture. However, when they work in Argentina, where an appointment might take hours—or days—to be kept, SooMei sees such practices as inefficient; to her, the American way makes the most sense. Tracey has taught herself to think without ethnocentrism and sees the difference as just that: a difference.

not capturing the skills and talents of these employees. With the historical 2008 presidential election of Barack Obama, Americans have shown a willingness to set aside racism and select an African-American to lead our nation. This may be a sign that racism is on the decline. Obama's election has definitely brought the discussion of race to the forefront of U.S. and international consciousness.

Economic Prejudice

economic prejudice

Prejudice and discrimination toward people who are poorer or wealthier than you are.

Economic prejudice, which can be defined as the struggle and resentment between the *haves* and the *have-nots,* is an ancient and often ugly battle. The American Revolution in 1776, the Russian Revolution in 1917, and India's independence from Britain in 1947 are a few historical examples. In these situations, the have-nots—who were at first powerless—joined together against their oppressors and won.

One of the theories of prejudice is that competition leads to frustration and aggression. In this country, when economic times are hard, prejudice can focus on groups—often ethnic groups—that are seen as taking something away from Americans, even if they *are* Americans. When the economy sagged in Michigan several years ago, Japanese Americans were singled out because of auto employees' anger at Japanese auto manufacturers for hurting the American car market. In some cases, even people of other Asian national origin, such as Chinese, were mistaken for Japanese and attacked in the street.

more about...

History Repeats Itself

Just as Japanese Americans were unfairly blamed for the slump in American auto manufacturing, they were also blamed decades earlier for Japan's involvement in World War II. They were deprived of their belongings and sent to internment camps until the war ended. It was not until 1989 that the U.S. government repaid them for their losses.

As with all prejudice, economic prejudice goes both ways. Not only do the poor resent the rich and stereotype them as selfish and uncaring, but the rich often despise the poor and stereotype them as lazy or worthless. Many of those who live well above the poverty line in this country are fond of reminding others that the United States is still a land of opportunity. They may believe that the *have-nots* simply refused the golden opportunity that was there for them. However, such an oversimplification is another example of how cognitive categorization leads to prejudice. (See Figure 16.3.)

Discrimination: Three Problem Issues

Type	Issues to Consider
Racist	Acceptance of minorities
	Assimilation versus separation
	Educational opportunities
	Cultural biases
	Hiring and recruitment policies
Economic	Power struggles
	Resources
	Resentment
	Competition for limited opportunities
Sexist	Male chauvinism
	Gender roles
	Wage discrepancies
	Educational opportunities
	Tradition versus innovation

figure 16.3

PRIMARY FORMS OF DISCRIMINATION

Although there are many forms of discrimination, the three primary ones are racism, economic discrimination, and sexism. *How can employers fight each of these?*

Sexism

The term *male chauvinism* was coined during the 1960s to describe a feeling of male superiority over females that is quite similar to ethnocentrism. This is also known as **sexism.** Because a man may have attitudes and stereotypes of women in society, he may choose to see them as being of less worth—in other words, he dehumanizes women. This can happen in different ways. For example, one type of man sees females as inferior, not really worth listening to, and needing a man to be complete. Another type puts women on a pedestal. This sounds better, but it can be at least as frustrating to women as the first behavior. If a woman is placed on a pedestal, she is still not being seen as a fellow human being, and this distortion easily translates into numerous forms of inequality because she is expected to fulfill unrealistic expectations that the man has determined for her. This less direct form of male chauvinism is difficult to deal with because this man may honestly think he is treating women very fairly and kindly.

Women in most societies are expected to be feminine, a term associated with disempowering behavior like dependence, instability, emotional insecurity, a willingness to take orders but not give them, and passivity. When these expectations toward women exist in a workplace, so does prejudice; an obvious paradox occurs when a woman in such an organization becomes a manager or assumes another role of authority. (See Figure 16.4.)

sexism
Prejudice and discrimination based on gender.

figure 16.4

HOW TO TELL A BUSINESSMAN FROM A BUSINESSWOMAN

Although men and women bring the same traits into the business world, many prejudiced employers and co-workers continue to perceive these traits as positive in men and negative in women. *Why do these prejudices persist?*

Source: Robert Fulmer, *Practical Human Relations* (Homewood, IL: Richard D. Irwin, Inc., 1983), p. 360. Used with permission.

Gender Prejudice in the Business World

Man

A businessman is aggressive.
He is careful about details.
He loses his temper because he is so involved in his job.
He's depressed (or hung over) so everyone tiptoes past his office.
He follows through.
He's firm.
He makes wise judgments.
He's a man of the world.
He isn't afraid to say what he thinks.
He exercises authority.
He's discreet.
He's a stern taskmaster.

Woman

A businesswoman is pushy.
She's picky.
She's bitchy.
She's moody, so it must be her time of month.
She doesn't know when to quit.
She's stubborn.
She reveals her prejudices.
She's been around.
She's outspoken and opinionated.
She's a tyrant.
She's secretive.
She's difficult to work for.

The feminist movement has made great progress in obtaining equal rights for women over the past 30–40 years. However, American society still contains a number of areas where very little progress has been made. Take a look at the highest levels of government: the 1992 election year was named *The Year of the Woman,* yet there were still only 2 women in the Senate (out of 100) and 28 (out of 435 members) in the House of Representatives for that year.[11] To date, only one woman in U.S. history has had a real chance of becoming our nation's president.

Workplace Conditions for Women

Although women find it possible to be promoted to the supervisory level (the lowest level of management), many report great difficulty in getting into middle- and upper-level management, where the major decisions are made. In the 1990s, very few chief executive officers (CEOs) of publicly held corporations were women, and not much has changed in the 2000s. One reason may be that women are perceived by men as not being able to handle power when they get it.[12] In fact, many women who are promoted to upper management positions succeed, and some feel this is because they had to work harder to be accepted. Some who fail in higher positions may do so because of indifference or hostility from their male colleagues.

Women's average income has been rising in recent years, but women still do not make as much as men do, even in the same occupations. Men's average (median) yearly income in 2006 was $48,210, whereas women's was $32,649, for a female-to-male earnings ratio of 77 to 1.[13] This means that on the average, women made only about 77 cents for every dollar that men made. If you separate out earnings by how much education men and women have completed, there is still a significant difference. Men with college degrees make on average more than $18,000 per year more than women with the same education ($55,446 for men and $36,875 for women).[14] For women with professional degrees, such as lawyers and doctors, the news is worse: women in 2006 made about $49,164 compared with $73,991 for men's average earnings.[15] The pay difference overall has been getting better, though, over the past few decades: in 1980, women overall earned only 60 cents for every dollar men earned.[16]

The Fast Track versus the Mommy Track

Another problem women often face in the workplace is being expected to choose between the *fast track* and the *mommy track* when climbing the career ladder. Since women still shoulder most of the housework and child rearing in most homes, if they choose the fast track they will have to sacrifice at least some of these personal responsibilities. In the fast track, employees are expected to work extra hours, ask for extra work, and work nights and weekends. The fast track seems to ask women to forget that they have families, or place families second in importance after jobs, rather than helping families balance home and work responsibilities.

What happens in the mommy track is just the opposite. When women try to balance family responsibilities with work responsibilities, they receive fewer promotions or raises, and are often stuck in low-wage jobs. What most women want (and what many employers are slow to give) is a compromise: a job that offers satisfying work and a chance for advancement, with enough flexibility to allow for raising a family, too. This can be offered through flextime, manageable workloads, the option to telecommute all or part of the week, setting up onsite child care, and through other ways that reflect an employer's understanding of employees' personal needs.

By not allowing this kind of flexibility, many employers are restricting women with families from certain jobs, which is another type of discrimination. Not only are these employers shortchanging women who would like to have had such jobs, but they are also shortchanging their own businesses by not employing (or by underemploying) a large pool of potential employees with a high degree of talent and skills.

The three categories of discrimination just discussed (racism, sexism, and economic inequality) easily come to mind when considering prejudice and discrimination in the workplace, but there are other types of prejudice that don't fall neatly into one of those categories.

MORE COMPLICATED THAN IT LOOKS

Although economic prejudice is rooted in the hardships that spring from economic competition, it can sometimes blend with ethnic prejudices and have a doubly powerful impact on the groups against which it is prejudiced. *What are some ways to get at the real causes of prejudice, in order to stop it?*

Overweight People

During the past few decades, with the national emphasis on dieting and fitness, the overweight person has increasingly become the target of prejudice. Court cases over the past decade have ruled against this

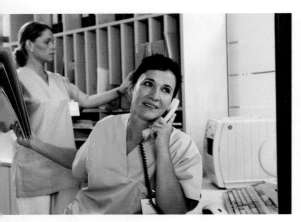

PREJUDICE AGAINST HOMOSEXUALS

Does a person's appearance reveal sexual orientation? You cannot tell a person's sexual orientation by appearance alone. Nonetheless, prejudice, hostility, and general misunderstanding of homosexuality continue. *How can you deal with homophobia in the workplace?*

type of prejudice; however, at least where hiring and firing are the issues. In 1989, flight attendant Sherry Cappello, a 25-year veteran of American Airlines, was fired for being 11 pounds overweight. Because of a lawsuit Cappello filed, American Airlines was forced to change its weight-requirement policies.[17]

Although one might see Cappello's victory as a small one, the prejudice against overweight people is still very alive. It's a fairly common, though unfounded, belief that overweight people are to blame for most high health-care costs. In the words of Dr. Albert Stunkard, a physician who specializes in obesity, "The extent to which overweight people have difficulty in obtaining work goes far beyond what can be justified by medical data and must be due to discrimination."[18] This issue is likely to emerge more often in years to come.

Homosexuals

One of the most emotional and controversial issues in the recent discussion of prejudice and discrimination has been homosexuality. The controversy revolves around two questions. The first question is whether homosexuality is a freely chosen lifestyle or is genetically determined (and therefore not a choice). This leads to the second question, which is whether homosexuality should be protected from institutional and other types of discrimination in the same way that categories of gender, race, religion, and national origin are. If homosexuality is a chosen lifestyle, some argue that homosexuality should not be a protected category; but if homosexuality is biologically or genetically caused, then it is not a lifestyle choice and should remain a protected category.

These questions, and how employers answer them, have a lot to do with hiring and promotion decisions but not with work performance in itself. That is, there is no reason to believe that homosexuals (or heterosexuals) do their jobs any better or worse than anyone else. Nonetheless, if a workplace becomes a battlefield over the issue, everyone's work performance is affected.

Many current employment policies forbid discrimination on the basis of sexual orientation or sexual preference. A number of states, counties, and cities have passed laws to make discrimination against gays and lesbians illegal.[19] In some states, religious groups are trying to pass initiatives eliminating this protection. Another policy issue under discussion is whether or not life partners of homosexuals, especially in states in which same-sex marriage is not allowed, should receive the same employment benefits as legally married spouses. Such heated issues will continue to be debated in years to come as government institutions (such as the military) and businesses struggle with these questions.

The Elderly

Until 1967 no law protected older people from discrimination. Many employers justified such discrimination on the grounds that older people are slower and less healthy, and therefore don't perform as well as younger employees. In 1986, President Reagan signed an amendment to the 1967 law, making it illegal to discriminate against anyone over 40.[20] Specifically, the Age Discrimination in Employment Act (ADEA) protects employees and job applicants from being discriminated against because of their age in hiring, promotions, discharge, pay, terms or conditions of employment, and privileges given by the employer. It also abolishes mandatory retirement for some employees (including federal employees) and raises the mandatory retirement age for others from age 55 to 70. Because of the ADEA, setting a mandatory retirement age is allowed now only when it is necessary to maintain normal business operations; for example, firefighters and law enforcement officers can still be forced to retire at a certain age.

Recent studies show that **ageism,** or negative attitudes toward older people, is still very much alive.[21] More than most other groups, though, the elderly are fighting back. Consider this startling statistic: in 1989, employers paid around $9 million in damages and compensation in cases brought under Title VII (discrimination on the basis of race, color, religion, sex, or national origin) of the Civil Rights Act. In that same year, employers paid $25 million on lawsuits involving the ADEA.[22] That's a ratio of almost 3 to 1.

> **ageism**
> Prejudice and discrimination toward older people.

These same trends continued into the 1990s: in one discrimination lawsuit, four restaurant employees, age 44–50, were awarded $6.7 million.[23] In another age bias case, Thomson Consumer Electronics, Inc., and the International Brotherhood of Electrical Workers settled with 800 employees who shared an award of $7.1 million.[24] In a third age bias case, Lockheed Martin settled a complaint for $13 million in back pay and jobs for 450 older employees who had been dismissed. The amounts in these three cases *alone* exceeded the total amount awarded in 1989! And this same trend has not yet slowed down: for the years 2004–2007, the total amount paid by employers who lost age bias lawsuits for each of those years totaled $265 million.[25]

Currently, employees age 40 and older are covered under ADEA. This is a huge group of employees, and as the baby boomers (those born between 1946 and 1964) age, it will grow even more. As you can see, this is an important law, so don't ignore it. We all should also remember that *this is the one group everyone will belong to some day.*

People with Disabilities

About 18 percent of the U.S. population in the 18–64 age group is physically or developmentally disabled. A surprising 85 percent of this number who could be working are not. This waste of talent is overwhelming.[26]

U.S. Administration on Aging

The federal government's Administration on Aging, an agency of the U.S. Department of Health and Human Services, has information you can receive by contacting its National Aging Information Center. Visit the Web page for the Administration for Aging (AoA) through the textbook Web site at **www.mhhe.com/lamberton4e** or directly at **www.aoa .gov** and link to "Press Room." Find an article that interests you. Write a brief paragraph about what you have learned.

The greatest barrier to the hiring of these would-be employees is prejudiced attitudes that, like most others, are based on largely inaccurate information. Think of this misinformation as myths; then read the information in Figure 16.5 to determine whether you are harboring any of these myths.

Employees who are disabled are also protected by law from discrimination, originally under the Rehabilitation Act of 1973. That law was

figure 16.5

MYTHS ABOUT HIRING PEOPLE WITH DISABILITIES

Many people still hold on to myths about the reliability and talents of people who have disabilities. The unfortunate result is that as many as 75 percent of all working-age people with disabilities are unemployed. *How are people with disabilities better employees than most people think?*

Source: George E. Stevens, "Exploding the Myths About Hiring the Handicapped," *Personnel,* December 1986.

Disabled people are unreliable. The fact is that statistics prove the exact opposite is true. As a group, the disabled have a rate of missed work that is well below the average of all employees. They also quit jobs much less frequently and tend to be much more concerned about doing a good job at whatever task they are assigned.

Disabled people can't do very many jobs. In today's workplace, especially with the increasing use of technology, there are relatively few jobs that a disabled employee can't do. Also, there are very few companies of any size in which a disabled employee couldn't be placed somewhere.

Disabled people will make other employees feel uncomfortable. The truth is that once other employees become acquainted with a disabled employee as an individual, the discomfort goes away. Plus, the more disabled people you spend time with, the more comfortable you will tend to feel around others like them.

Progress for People with Disabilities

Visit the Web page for the Office on Disability in the U.S. Health and Human Services Department through the textbook Web site at **www.mhhe.com/lamberton4e** or directly at **www.hhs.gov/od.** Read its Fact Sheet or other articles that interest you, and write a brief paragraph about what you have learned.

never greatly effective because the courts kept struggling with the definitions of *handicapped* and *disabled*.[27] The remedy to this issue came in July 1990, when the Americans with Disabilities Act (ADA) became law. The overall purpose of this law is to allow people with disabilities to enjoy most of the benefits that everyone else enjoys.

The ADA prohibits discrimination by companies in any of the following areas: employment, public transportation, telecommunication, and other privately owned services to the public (hotels and motels, restaurants and bars, public gathering places). Also, the law requires that benefits and opportunities for people with disabilities must be of the same quality as those offered to everyone else, if possible. This law continues to be modified and refined, but because of it, things are looking better for those with disabilities.[28]

Religious Groups

The experience of prejudice and discrimination based on religion goes back to the very beginnings of American history. Some of the Pilgrims who arrived in the New World came to escape religious intolerance; they were followed by hundreds of thousands of others who came for the same reason. Of all the people of the world, Americans should be the least prejudiced when religious differences are involved—but are they? The EEOC reports a steady increase in complaints based on religion. In fiscal year 2007, the EEOC reported 2,880 charges of religious discrimination and has recovered $6.4 million in monetary benefits for people bringing the charges.[29] In the past several years, members of Muslim groups have found themselves increasingly discriminated against in the United States and elsewhere. The facts show that members of religious groups often find themselves the objects of discrimination both at work and in social circles. Title VII of the Civil Rights Act of 1964 forbids discrimination against members of any religion. Employers are generally required to accommodate employees who express a need to practice religious beliefs at work, but they do have some flexibility in how these accommodations will be made.[30]

Pregnant Women

The issue of pregnancy is being reexamined in an increasing number of workplaces. Through the 1970s a female job applicant was routinely asked if she was pregnant or planning to become pregnant, and what her employment, child care, and other plans would be if she were to have children. These types of questions are now illegal because they have been shown to severely affect hiring decisions and hurt women's chances for employment and advancement. Even today, a visibly pregnant woman runs such risks of discrimination—although it will probably be left unsaid by her employer.

> **sexual harassment**
>
> Behavior that is defined by the EEOC as "Unwelcome sexual advances, requests for sexual favors and other verbal or physical conduct of a sexual nature . . ."

SEXUAL HARASSMENT

The phrase **sexual harassment** was coined by Lin Farley, author of *Sexual Shakedown,* in the late 1970s. What is sexual harassment? The answer is spelled out clearly by EEOC guidelines: "Unwelcome sexual advances, requests for sexual favors, and other verbal or physical conduct of a sexual nature. . . ." Sexually harassing behaviors include forced fondling, sexual slurs, and unwelcome flirting; it also includes sexually suggestive pictures or other material posted where others can see it.[31] (See Figure 16.6.)

figure 16.6

EMPLOYER'S SEXUAL HARASSMENT POLICY STATEMENT

Every employer needs to have a policy on how to deal with this issue, then inform each employee about it. Such an action will help prevent occurrences, as well as give employers guidance on how to act on complaints. *What are the components of an effective sexual harassment policy?*

Source: Robert K. McCalla, "Stopping Sexual Harassment Before It Begins," *Management Review,* April 1991, p. 46.

Sample Sexual Harassment Policy Statement

Sexual harassment of employees or applicants for employment will not be tolerated in this company. Any employee who feels that he or she is a victim of sexual harassment by a supervisor, co-worker, or customer should bring the matter to the immediate attention of (name and title of person). An employee who is uncomfortable for any reason about bringing the matter to the attention of his or her supervisor should report the matter to the human resources department.

Complaints of sexual harassment will receive prompt attention and will be handled in as confidential a manner as possible. Prompt disciplinary action will be taken against persons who engage in sexual harassment.

The problem of sexual harassment in the workplace goes back to the time when men and women first started working together, but people like Farley have called attention to this long-ignored problem. You have already seen in this chapter how much the workforce is changing. Statistics show that in 2008, nearly half of the workforce was made up of women. As women and men work together more and more, this problem of sexual harassment will need to be examined and resolved before it gets worse.[32]

The EEOC reported that sexual harassment complaints rose from 4,272 in 1981 to 7,273 in 1985. More recent data indicate that this upward trend continued through the 1990s and into the 2000s. Studies conducted in 1980, 1987, 1995, and 2007 by the U.S. Merit System Protection Board of federal employees found that consistently about 42 percent of women and 14 percent of men reported having experienced some type of sexual harassment. The most common type of harassment was unwanted sexual teasing, jokes, remarks, and questions.[33] A survey by the AFL-CIO found that among top workplace concerns, 78 percent of women cited sexual harassment. In fact, the only concern expressed more often was regarding economic discrimination: 94 percent rated equal pay for equal work as their top concern.[34] By 2008, an average of 14,500 charges were being filed yearly.

Sexual harassment is not limited to male supervisors harassing female employees; anyone can become a victim of sexual harassment. In college settings, female professors have been harassed by female students and male professors as well by female students. In 1999, the EEOC reported that 12 percent of all claims were filed by men who were harassed by people of either sex.[35] (See Figure 16.7.)

What can you do as an ordinary employee when someone sexually harasses you? The simplest and most effective method is just to ask or tell the person to stop. According to the Merit Systems survey, this simple tactic worked for 61 percent of the women who tried it. Telling fellow employees about the problem, or threatening to do so, proved in the same study to be second best. This was effective about 55 percent of the time. Just remember that *the worst response is no response:* ignoring the problem and hoping it will go away hardly ever works, and will only cause you a higher level of stress.[36]

Hostile Environments

When sexual harassment relates to indirect actions like posting pornography or talking about sex in a manner that makes others uncomfortable, this is called creating a **hostile environment.** It is considered equally as serious as direct harassment.

Stopping Sexual Harassment

Telling the harasser to stop is the best way to make sure the person knows the behavior is *unwanted.* Failing to let the person know the behavior is unwanted makes it more difficult to convince the supervisor or a trial judge that harassment occurred. Keep a dated notebook of occurrences and your responses. Tell a supervisor what is going on. If the harasser *is* your supervisor, report the situation to the next higher manager.

more about...

more about...

figure 16.7

IS THIS SEXUAL HARASSMENT?

While reading these instances, make sure that you ask yourself if all of the key elements to sexual harassment are present. *Are any elements missing in any of these?*

Daily, Jack visits the job site of his crew — three women and eight men. When he passes Sherry, he occasionally gives her a hug or a pinch on the buttocks.

Charlie makes it a point to treat everyone the same. He jokes and teases co-workers with comments like, "You're grumpy today; I bet you were alone last night."

Rachel starts weekly staff meetings with a dirty joke.

Last night, Robert went to a business dinner with his boss, Marie. He expected the entire staff to be there, but it was just the two of them. The restaurant was dimly lit and had a romantic atmosphere; Robert quickly realized that the focus of the dinner was Marie's attraction to him. Just before suggesting a nightcap at her house, she mentioned the promotion Robert was seeking.

The loading dock crew whistles and comments on Michele's figure when she wears tight jeans and sweaters.

Mark displays nude female centerfolds in the office he shares with Eileen and Sam.

Some critics claim that the spotlight on sexual harassment over the past few decades has changed the workplace into a sterile environment. Is this true—is today's workplace one in which no one feels relaxed, feels free to chat or exchange jokes with co-workers, or can compliment a co-worker? Some people claim so, and report feeling stifled, uncertain, timid, and resentful of the new rules. These claims, though, are usually greatly exaggerated—usually by people resentful of women entering the workforce or of women's rights in general.

Good advice for both men and women is to adopt the new slogan, "Don't Be a Jerk at Work." That is, use common sense: those who are thin-skinned should be less so; those who are obnoxious should stop being so.[37] Follow the commonsense guide in Figure 16.7 to recognize what types of behaviors will lead to sexual harassment complaints. With modified wording, these situations could apply to both men *and* women, and to all types of offensive behavior. They could also serve as examples regarding general ethical or unethical behavior, which you will learn about in the next chapter. If you're still in doubt as to whether

Understanding Sexual Harassment

Sexual Harassment in the Workplace: A Primer by Barry Roberts and Richard Mann provides an in-depth introduction to this topic. Go to **www.mhhe.com/lamberton4e** for a link and read about this topic, or access the site directly by going to the Web site at **www3.uakron.edu/lawrev/robert1.html.** Write a brief summary of what you have learned.

or not particular words or actions would be seen as sexual harassment, use your own reaction as a guide: ask yourself, "Would I want someone saying or doing this to my spouse, my parent, or someone else I care about?" If the answer is no, then others would probably see it as sexual harassment, too.

On both individual and companywide levels, sexual harassment can best be prevented by people who know what it is, know the laws forbidding it, and know what to do when it happens. This chapter has provided an introduction to the issue. If you want more information, your public library and numerous law-related Web sites are full of information on sexism and sexual harassment.

PREJUDICE, DISCRIMINATION, AND SELF-ESTEEM

A general observation about extremely prejudiced people is that they may suffer from low levels of self-esteem. In contrast, tolerant people may tend to feel more comfortable with who they are and have little trouble accepting the basic humanity of others. As a person's self-esteem improves, prejudices may become shaky and eventually disappear.

What about the victims of discrimination? If you have ever felt prejudice from any person or group, you know just how distressing these feelings are. Unless you are a person with a firmly grounded, high self-esteem level, discrimination can lower your self-esteem temporarily or permanently. Victims of violent hatred have been known to even side with those who oppress them, once their self-esteem has been thoroughly broken down.

more about...

When Prejudice Turns Inward

Internalized prejudice is when a person believes prejudicial remarks and assumptions, and in turn accepts being treated in a discriminatory manner—which may include falling for the self-fulfilling prophecy.

In his classic 1954 book *The Nature of Prejudice,* Gordon Allport stated that the effects of being victimized by discrimination fall into two basic categories. The first category is blaming oneself, which can be seen in withdrawal, self-hatred, or aggression against one's own group. The second category is blaming external causes, which is seen in fighting back against the discrimination, becoming suspicious of outsiders, or having increased or exaggerated pride in one's own group.[38] One of the saddest dangers of discrimination is its tendency to become a **self-fulfilling prophecy,** which occurs when a victim believes that prejudice against him or her is deserved and then becomes what the stereotype states. As Allport said, "One's reputation cannot be hammered, hammered, hammered into one's head without doing something to one's character."[39] In other words, a lifetime of discrimination can have devastating effects for individuals and their families.

> **self-fulfilling prophecy**
> The tendency for a prediction to actually occur once it is believed; for example, when a victim believes that prejudice against him or her is true, then fulfills these negative expectations.

LOOKING AHEAD

What can be done to reduce feelings of prejudice and acts of discrimination in the workplace? Prejudging others seems to be inevitable. When a member of a group acts in the way you expect, your stereotype is confirmed. When the person acts differently from the way you expect, you may decide that he or she is the exception to the rule. These negative ideas are hard to get rid of! Does this mean there is no hope for reducing prejudice and discrimination? The good news is that some negative feelings and behaviors can be permanently eliminated. The bad news is that there is no simple cure.

Although the federal government has taken solid steps to define and forbid discrimination in the workplace, there are still steps you can take individually and in your organization as well. A key ingredient for people to begin to understand and appreciate members of other groups is contact; communication as a result of contact is crucial to understanding others. Employees need the opportunity to interact and communicate with each other, because **proximity** (physical closeness) and exposure to other people generally increase the chance that they will come to like each other.[40] It will also reduce any tendency to stereotype groups of people; after all, you wouldn't be likely to prejudge the group your best friend and her family belong to.

> **proximity**
> Physical closeness; here, it refers to contact between members of a diverse workplace.

Contact by itself is not enough. Recall that one of the causes of prejudice and discrimination is unequal status. If this is the case, prejudice will not diminish. Businesses can take steps to hire employees who are frequent targets of discrimination into all levels within the company. So the second necessary ingredient in reducing prejudice and discrimination is ensuring **equal status** for everyone.

A third important ingredient in reducing prejudice and discrimination is *cooperation* instead of competition between members of groups.

> **equal status**
> The condition that occurs when companies hire employees who are frequent targets of discrimination into all levels within the company.

Psychologists have discovered that when members of different groups not only must cooperate but also must depend on each other to reach common goals—also known as **interdependence**—conflict is greatly reduced. Working together works!

interdependence
A relationship in which members of different groups not only must cooperate but also must depend on each other to reach common goals.

STRATEGIES FOR SUCCESS

16.1 Assess Your Knowledge

1. True-False Test for Employees
2. True-False Test for Managers

Here are two brief tests you can take that will help you evaluate your own acquaintance (and comfort) with the subject of sexual harassment. The first test is for employees; the second, for managers. You may find it useful to take both tests, whether you are a manager or not.

1. **True–False Test for Employees**

T   F   1. If I just ignore unwanted sexual attention, it will usually stop.

T   F   2. If I don't mean to sexually harass another employee, there's no way my behavior can be perceived by him or her as sexually harassing.

T   F   3. Some employees don't complain about unwanted sexual attention from another employee because they don't want to get that person in trouble.

T   F   4. If I make sexual comments to someone and that person doesn't ask me to stop, then I guess my behavior is welcome.

T   F   5. To avoid sexually harassing a woman who comes to work in a traditionally male workplace, the men simply should not haze her.

T   F   6. A sexual harasser may be told by a court to pay part of the judgment to the employee he or she harassed.

T   F   7. A sexually harassed man does not have the same legal rights as a woman who is sexually harassed.

T   F   8. About 90 percent of all sexual harassment in today's workplace is done by males to females.

T   F   9. Sexually suggestive pictures or objects in a workplace don't create a liability unless someone complains.

T   F   10. Telling someone to stop his or her unwanted sexual behavior usually doesn't do any good.

Answers: 1—False, 2—False, 3—True, 4—False, 5—False, 6—True, 7—False, 8—True, 9—False, 10—False

2. **True-False Test for Managers**

T	F	1.	Men in male-dominated workplaces usually must change behavior when women work there.
T	F	2.	An employer is not liable for the sexual harassment of one of its employees unless that employee loses specific job benefits or is fired.
T	F	3.	A sexual harasser may have to pay part of a judgment to the employer he or she has harassed.
T	F	4.	A supervisor can be liable for sexual harassment committed by one of his or her employees against another.
T	F	5.	A supervisor can be liable for the sexually harassing behavior of management personnel even if it is unaware of that behavior and has a policy forbidding it.
T	F	6.	It is appropriate for a supervisor, when initially receiving a sexual harassment complaint, to determine if the alleged recipient overreacted or misunderstood the alleged harasser.
T	F	7.	When a supervisor talks with an employee about an allegation of sexual harassment, it is best to ease into the allegation.
T	F	8.	Sexually suggestive visuals or objects in a workplace don't create a liability unless an employee complains about them and management allows them to remain.
T	F	9.	The lack of sexual harassment complaints is a good indication that sexual harassment is not occurring.
T	F	10.	It is appropriate for a supervisor to tell an employee to handle unwelcome sexual behavior if the employee is misunderstanding the behavior.

Answers: 1—False, 2—False, 3—True, 4—True, 5—True, 6—False, 7—False, 8—False, 9—False, 10—False.[41]

How do you prevent sexual harassment? Understand that the problem is serious, and that related cases are costing U.S. corporations, governments, and small companies millions of dollars per year.

16.2 Reducing Sexual Harassment

1. Write a policy statement.
2. Post the policy statement in a public place.
3. Talk about the policy.

These are the most important steps a manager can take to prevent—or at least to reduce—incidents of sexual harassment in the workplace.

1. **Write a policy statement.** If you are a supervisor or manager, you should have a fairly brief but well-written policy concerning sexual harassment.

2. **Post the policy statement in a public place.** This policy should be printed in fairly large print and posted in central locations where all employees can see it.

3. **Talk about the policy.** Besides this, you should refer to the policy in meetings and memos, so it won't become just another poster the boss put up.

If a sexual harassment case from your company gets to court (or even to the attorneys for an out-of-court settlement), a central question will be whether or not your company had a clear, well-defined policy against sexual harassment.[42]

CHAPTER SIXTEEN SUMMARY

Chapter Summary by Learning Objectives

1. **Describe how human relations are affected when they are part of a diverse society.** Diversity in the workplace is increased when people of different races, national origins, religions, and ages—as well as both men and women—work together. Diversity is also found in differing lifestyles and personal attributes. The challenge to human relations is to make this mixture of people an asset, rather than a liability.

2. **Explain how prejudiced attitudes pose a challenge to human relations.** Prejudiced attitudes, nearly always based on stereotypes, interfere with work and cause morale and productivity issues. Prejudiced attitudes have components of thinking, feeling, and doing.

3. **Identify the origins of prejudice.** Prejudice can come from social causes including those that are media-created, cognitive causes as part of belief systems, and emotional causes including ethnocentrism.

4. **List types of discrimination.** The major types of discrimination in today's world include racism, sexism, religious prejudice, economic prejudice (one of the oldest prejudices in the world), and ageism. Prejudice against others based on sexual orientation, weight, and disabilities are also too common.

5. **Define sexual harassment.** Sexual harassment is defined by the Equal Employment Opportunity Commission as "Unwelcome sexual advances, requests for sexual favors, and other verbal or physical conduct of a sexual nature."

6. **Describe the connections between prejudice, discrimination, and self-esteem.** Prejudice can be defined as the way one feels as the result of the stereotypes one believes. It can also be seen as the unwillingness to give credibility to others of different backgrounds,

and seeing them as inferior. Discrimination is one's behavior based on that person's stereotypes and prejudices. Both prejudice and discrimination are tied in with self-esteem issues involving the perceived self-worth of people, based on the way they are treated by others.

7. **Give examples of how to decrease prejudice.** Prejudice can be reduced individually and in the workplace by increasing contact and communication with members of diverse groups, by placing people in equal-status positions, and by encouraging cooperation and interdependence, rather than competition.

key terms

ageism 445

bias 435

cognitive
   categorization 437

discrimination 434

economic prejudice 440

Equal Employment
   Opportunity
   Commission
   (EEOC) 436

equal status 452

ethnocentrism 438

institutional
   prejudice 435

interdependence 453

prejudice 434

proximity 452

racism 439

self-fulfilling
   prophecy 452

sexism 441

sexual harassment 448

stereotypes 434

review questions

1. What are the three components of an attitude? Describe the three components of a prejudiced attitude.

2. What individuals and groups can you think of who are likely targets of prejudice and discrimination? Do you fit into any of these groups that are likely targets? Have you ever found yourself a target of prejudice or discrimination as a member of this group? Explain.

3. Discuss some of the sources of prejudice. Within these sources, can you think of a particular prejudice that you have and how it arose? Explain your personal example.

4. Discuss the negative effects of discrimination in the workplace, both on the individual and on the business organization. Have you seen any discriminatory acts occurring in your workplace? Explain.

5. Describe steps that can be taken in the workplace to reduce or prevent sexual harassment.

6. How is institutional racism or institutional sexism different from open racism or sexism?

7. What is meant by the term *self-fulfilling prophecy*? Think of an example in your life or someone else's where a self-fulfilling prophecy (either positive or negative) arose. Explain your personal example.

8. What are some of the common myths about people with disabilities in the workplace? What is being done to protect employment for this group?

critical thinking questions

9. Under what circumstances is it acceptable to treat co-workers or employees differently because of their differences? Should you be blind to differences between co-workers or employees, or recognize them openly?

10. People today talk a lot about "tolerance." Is there a difference between *tolerance* and *acceptance* of differences, whether they are cultural, gender-related, religious, or other? Explain the differences.

working it out 16.1

IMPRESSION FORMATION: ARE PERCEPTIONS INFLUENCED BY ETHNICITY?

School-to-Work Connection: Interpersonal Skills
Do people hold generalized perceptions of others just because of their ethnicity? This project will help you discover that for yourself.

First, decide what two ethnic groups you would like to study (as a class or as an individual project). They may include African Americans, Native Americans, Japanese, French, Italians, or any other ethnic group. Next, each student should approach at least two people and ask them to take part in a study on impression formation. If this is a class project, decide with your classmates what ethnic groups you want to study. Those who agree to participate should be asked to conjure up an image of members of a particular ethnic group and then describe their characteristics on the rating scale that follows. Half the participants should be asked to describe a member of the second ethnic group chosen for the study. The data collected from all the students will allow you to compare the participant's perceptions as influenced by awareness of a person's ethnicity.

Part One. The person you have in mind is (ethnic group).

Describe this person using the rating scale in the table at the end of these instructions.

1. When you think about people in this ethnic group, what is the first thing that comes to mind?

2. What is most characteristic of members of this group?

3. What is most definitely not characteristic of them? (What would be surprising or unexpected to see?)

4. What characteristic do you think most people assign to members of this group?

Part Two. Now do the same for the second person and ethnic group. Examine your results. Are you surprised by any of these results? Do you hold certain perceptions about people just by being aware that they belong to a specific ethnic group? If so, what can you do about it? How can you reduce your stereotypic beliefs about members of certain ethnic groups?

Part Three. Try this exercise again, substituting male and female for the two ethnic groups, or young person and elderly person, or physically able and physically challenged, and so on.

RATING SCALE

Dominant	1	2	3	4	5	6	Submissive
Warm	1	2	3	4	5	6	Cold
Unambitious	1	2	3	4	5	6	Ambitious
Stupid	1	2	3	4	5	6	Smart
Clean	1	2	3	4	5	6	Dirty
Disliked	1	2	3	4	5	6	Liked
Poised	1	2	3	4	5	6	Unpoised
Unaggressive	1	2	3	4	5	6	Aggressive
Insensitive	1	2	3	4	5	6	Sensitive
Active	1	2	3	4	5	6	Passive

Source: Adapted from Ayala Pines and Christina Maslach, *Experiencing Social Psychology: Readings and Projects,* 3rd ed. (New York: McGraw-Hill, Inc., 1993), pp. 203–205.

GENDER STEREOTYPES IN THE MEDIA

School-to-Work Connection: Interpersonal Skills

Much of what people learn about men and women comes from the way they are portrayed on television and in movies, newspapers, and magazines. How are men and women portrayed differently in the media? This is the question you will try to answer in this project.

Pick one type of medium: your favorite newspaper, magazine, TV program (a news program, a soap opera, cartoons, music videos, situation comedy, etc.), or radio programs (news format, rock music, sports, etc.). Decide on your research sample gathering (a week, seven issues, ten hours, etc.) and the particular material you are going to observe. Record your results.

1. What was your source (what type of medium)?

2. What were you looking at (advertisements, cartoons, other)?

3. How did you collect your data (at what times, how often, and so on)? What exactly did you observe (what programs and how many hours, or what magazine and how many issues)?

4. What themes around gender did you discover? Were there any surprises in what you found? Is the media's portrayal of men and women accurate? How powerful are the media's messages on gender?

Source: Adapted from Ayala Pines and Christina Maslach, *Experiencing Social Psychology: Readings and Projects,* 3rd ed. (New York: McGraw-Hill, Inc., 1993), pp. 107–108.

1. *Read, Summarize, Relate*

   Go to the home page for MSNBC news at **www.msnbc.msn.com/,** also linked to **www.mhhe.com/lamberton4e.** Open the link to "U.S. News" and then open the link to "Race in America." Read any two current articles presented in that section. Summarize them, while answering for yourself:

   a. How does this news article relate to the concepts you learned in this chapter?

   b. Has a situation like this one happened in your area?

   c. What knowledge can you take from this situation to improve your workplace?

2. *Compare and Contrast*

Visit the Web site for the international organization Business for Social Responsibility **(www.bsr.org)**, which is also linked to **www.mhhe.com/lamberton4e.** Read the executive summary for its "Discrimination" section located at **www.bsr.org/ CSRResources/IssueBriefDetail.cfm?DocumentID=50411** and related links you find interesting. Summarize what you found, answering:

a. What issues of discrimination related to workforce globalization did you learn about?

b. How would you compare world issues of discrimination with what you know about U.S. issues? Are we all dealing with the same issues, or different ones?

c. What ideas presented here will help you improve the organizational climate in your workplace?

3. *Read, Summarize, Relate*

Visit the Southern Poverty Law Center's information Web site located through the course links at **www.mhhe.com/ lamberton4e** or found directly at **www.splcenter.org.** Read and summarize any two of their news releases or informational links (e.g., teaching tolerance). Relate what you learned the information presented in this chapter.

4. *Reflect and Relate*

Two of the most famous studies on prejudice involved students and have been captured on film. In one case, Jane Elliott created and then eliminated prejudice among her third grade pupils by making them think having blue eyes versus brown eyes was a sign of inferiority or superiority. Read the background information and view the sample video clips at **www.janeelliott.com/** and then reflect on what you learned as it relates to reducing prejudice. The second famous study was done with college students at Stanford University, supervised by social psychologist Phil Zimbardo. Read the background information and view the slide show at **www.prisonexp .org/** and then reflect on what you learned related to creating prejudice. Both Web addresses are also linked through the course Web site at **www.mhhe.com/lamberton4e.**

5. *Self-Assess and Apply*

For the ultimate adventure in experiencing diversity, consider working for an international aid agency such as the World Bank, USAID (United States Agency for International Development), the World Health Organization, Doctors Without Borders, the Peace Corps, or the Red Cross and Red Crescent. Use your search engine to locate information about at least two agencies such as these, and write a brief report on the goals of the organization, what types of jobs or internships are available in each, and what qualifications are needed for these positions.

It's None of Your Business

About 15 years ago, many years after the Civil Rights Act made discrimination in hiring illegal, a professor with a Ph.D. was interviewing for a research job at a university in California. Although many of the questions asked by the interviewer were clearly not allowable, the interviewer persisted. Some of those questions were:

- How old are you?
- Are you married?
- Do you have any children?
- How old are they?
- What type of day-care arrangement do you have?
- What type of backup day-care arrangements have you made?
- Are you planning on having more children?
- What kind of car do you drive?
- Is it reliable?
- How will you get to work if you have car trouble?

Case Study Questions

1. Thinking about the questions, if you were considering hiring someone and wanted to be sure that you were hiring a reliable employee, these are things you might want to know as well. So, why can't you ask these questions? What is inherently wrong with wanting to know these things about a potential employee—why is it illegal, when not directly related to job tasks?

2. Using the skills you have learned in previous chapters and the information you have learned in this chapter, what would you have said to this interviewer during the interview, in order to end these personal questions?

3. Let's say the interviewer continued this line of personal questions, even after you said something. The interview ended, and you were not hired. Would you have taken further action? Explain.

Two Against One

Elena Aguilar-Trujillo was the department director in a small software design company. Although the start-up company seemed to be getting new business in all the time, it was still struggling financially, and salaries were low.

Elena supervised eight employees. They all seemed to get along well, with the exception of Julia Sandoval and Kathy O'Donnell, two employees who were very good friends and seemed to form an alliance against the department secretary, Miranda Kirkpatrick. In fact, they seemed to sabotage and undercut her whenever they could. Elena couldn't understand it. They had all grown up in the same area of the state, were all women, were the same age, and had similar interests. If anything, they should be closer than anyone else.

Events finally came to a head when Miranda asked for six weeks off without pay in order to go on a long sailing trip with her husband in their new boat. "That does it!" exclaimed Julia. "We *have* to get rid of her! She's always prancing around here, showing off her new clothes and jewelry, bragging about all the stuff her husband buys her. I've had it with her!" Then Kathy chimed in, "Me too! If we don't fire her, I might just have to go get a job somewhere else!"

Elena was shocked and tried to remember any situations in which Miranda was boastful, but couldn't remember any. Then it dawned on Elena: the real problem these two employees had with the secretary had nothing to do with her work or behavior at all. They were just resentful that their secretary was more financially successful than they were. They were just getting their careers started, but Miranda's husband had his own successful business, and Miranda didn't have to work if she didn't want to.

"Kathy and Julia, meet me in my office in 10 minutes," said Elena. "We need to talk."

Case Study Questions

1. What type of prejudice is being illustrated here? What is it based on?

2. If Elena did decide to fire Miranda in order to keep the peace within the department, what legal recourse would Miranda have, if any? Explain.

3. Let's say you have been called in as a mediator to settle this interdepartmental conflict. What steps will you take? What will these steps be based on?

BUSINESS ETHICS AND SOCIAL RESPONSIBILITY

In the Workplace: An Unethical Push-Out

SITUATION

Bonnie Bailey loved her job as editor of an in-house newspaper for a large multinational manufacturing firm. She had been with the firm for more than 20 years, having started in an entry-level position as a typist. She was proud to be the only woman in higher management in the state. Bonnie was also proud that she had done it all by working hard and being promoted up the ladder. Even though Bonnie had reached retirement

age, she had no intention of leaving her position any time soon.

Joe James, the budget officer for the firm, was not so pleased with Bonnie. The journalism department budget needed to be trimmed so that the department could afford new technology. He decided that getting rid of Bonnie, who was making a very high salary, was the best way to cut the budget and have money to upgrade the department's technology. He had no problems

After studying this chapter, you will be able to:

1. Define ethics.
2. Explain the importance of a code of ethics.
3. Describe the process of rationalizing unethical behavior.
4. Explain ethics in the context of the U.S. workplace.
5. Describe the influence of group goals on ethics.
6. Give examples of global ethics issues.
7. Define social responsibility.
8. Describe the process of whistleblowing.

STRATEGIES FOR SUCCESS

Strategy 17.1 Making Ethical Decisions: A Quick Ethics Test from Texas Instruments

Strategy 17.2 Becoming Culturally Aware of Ethical Conduct

with Bonnie's work. It was just the budget he was concerned about. He concocted a plan to make the job so difficult and unpleasant for her that she would *have* to resign.

The plan was soon in place. Bonnie's office was moved to another location in the plant far from her staff. Joe made sure she was not informed of management meetings. As a result, she was reprimanded for not attending meetings, and top management began to criticize her work. On Joe's orders, her staff ignored her work assignments and reported instead to the budget director. Soon after, her e-mail account was canceled. There were also rumors circulating

around that she was incompetent and mentally unstable.

DISCOVERY

Within a few months, Bonnie decided to confront Joe. She charged into Joe's office and said harshly, "You've turned me into a joke, some kind of phantom employee. Your behavior is the most outrageous violation of ethics I have ever seen. I'm not going to tolerate this kind of treatment any longer!"

THINK ABOUT IT

What are Bonnie's options now? What would you do if you were in her place?

ethics

The expression of the standards of right and wrong based on conduct and morals in a particular society.

morality

A system of conduct that covers all broadly based, mostly unwritten standards of how people should behave and generally conform to cultural ideals of right and wrong.

WHAT IS ETHICS?

Ethics deals with the standards of conduct and morals in a particular society; in short, ethics expresses the standards of right and wrong. However, ethics and morality are not identical concepts. **Morality** deals with how behavior should generally conform to cultural ideals of right and wrong. It represents broadly based, mostly unwritten standards of how people should behave. Ethics is more precise and is often based on written guidelines. Ethics also often addresses deeper issues of fairness, equity, and compromise.[1]

In this chapter, you will examine the complex issue of ethics in the workplace. You will learn about the many ways in which ethics involves your relationships with others on the job. You will also learn about specific actions that both managers and employees can take to develop stronger ethical conduct on the job.

The practice of business brings many benefits to society. The business world has provided jobs for millions, created a high standard of living, and given many people an opportunity to achieve the dream of business ownership. However, businesses do not always uphold the highest ethical standards. Highly publicized scandals damage the public image of many businesses, and because of the alarming number of scandals in recent years, a new awakening to the issues of business ethics has emerged. So many new courses in ethics are being taught in high schools and colleges that ethics education has been called "a major growth industry in academia."[2] (See Figure 17.1.)

In addition to being different from morality, ethical standards are also different from *law*, which is another code of conduct. Although both ethical standards and laws are generally agreed upon within specific cultures, laws are different because they are always set down in writing, and descriptions of them are available to the public. Ethics violations are not always punishable, but violating the law carries specific penalties: in other words, laws have *teeth*. In contrast, it is difficult to pin down when ethics violations have occurred and what, if anything, the penalties for such violations should be. This is because although ethics are often in writing, there are usually no written guidelines on how to act when these same ethics are violated. Some organizations have addressed this issue, though, by creating guidelines on punishing and terminating employees who violate established ethical guidelines.

One common public perception is that *business* and *ethics* are terms that can hardly be used in the same sentence. That perception is based on the misunderstanding that profit and morality simply do not mix, and that one can't make money without becoming corrupt.

more about...

Ethical Policies in Organizations

Few professions have strict and enforceable **ethical policies.** The medical profession and the legal profession are exceptions: both have procedures to discipline members who behave unethically.

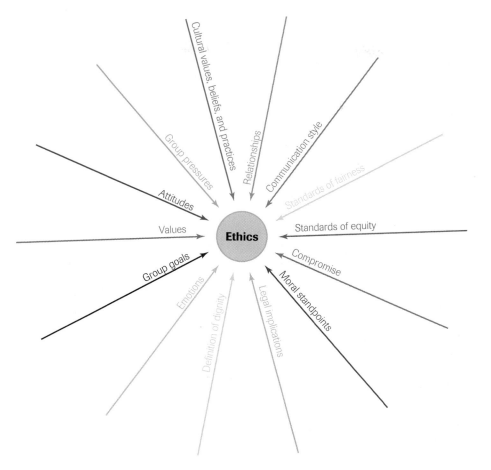

Cultural values, beliefs, and practices

Group pressures

Relationships

Communication style

Standards of fairness

Attitudes

Values

Ethics

Standards of equity

Compromise

Group goals

Emotions

Definition of dignity

Legal implications

Moral standpoints

figure 17.1

FACTORS INFLUENCING WORKPLACE ETHICS

Several personal and professional factors influence a person's ethics on the job. Furthermore, personal ethics can be greatly reshaped by the ethical standards already in place at a company, and counteracting forces may simultaneously push a person toward unethical conduct and pull him or her away from it. For instance, a salesperson may be tempted by financial incentives to lie to a customer about services or products, but a fear of getting caught or being punished in some way may change that person's mind. *Do your personal ethics stay the same at your job, or do they change somewhat from home to work? Why?*

The following are other misperceptions that affect people's understanding about ethics:

1. All ethical problems have simple solutions in which right and wrong are always obvious. This assumption ignores the fact that gray areas exist and that often a great deal of soul-searching might be essential to make a truly ethical decision. These gray areas also sometimes create a need to compromise, which can be misunderstood as indecisiveness to someone expecting a cut-and-dried answer.

2. Ethics is simply a matter of complying with a set of rules or regulations. In reality, a legal issue is often not the same as an ethical issue, and vice versa.[3] An example is the legal versus ethical issues seen in a hostile takeover of a corporation. Those in charge of the takeover may be following legal rules and corporate practice, but the overall ethics of their actions might be questionable.

Even the most ethical person should be willing to admit that all of us are sometimes faced with ethical and moral dilemmas. The most ethical course of action isn't always clear-cut and obvious. For example, suppose that you were a buyer for a retail chain, and you told a supplier

Ethics and Law Students

For a discussion of why future lawyers don't study enough ethics, go to **www.afn.org/~afn54735/outbalance1 .html,** which is also linked to the course Web site at **www.mhhe.com/lamberton4e.** Have you or someone you know ever hired an attorney who seems to have only a vague sense of ethics? This article suggests that maybe such a phenomenon lies in faulty education of law students. Write a summary of, and a reaction to, what you read.

company, "We simply can't continue to pay the $26 per unit any longer. If you can't cut your cost by at least $3 per unit, we'll buy from someone else." Not realizing that you are bluffing, the supplier gives in and drops her price. Once you've done the math, you are now able to report to your manager that you just saved the company $32,000 per month. Your manager is ecstatic and gives you a raise.[4] You have helped both your manager and your company. Have you done something unethical? If you aren't quite sure, hopefully by the end of this chapter you will have some tools to help you make such a judgment.

Ethics and the Internet

Perhaps the stickiest ethical issue today is how to behave ethically on the Internet. You would most likely feel violated if your company tapped your office phone, or if a police officer searched your house without cause or permission. Yet every day companies monitor employee e-mails and track Internet usage, looking for the personal misuse of company property.

"The Internet has introduced enormous compliance risks and ethical issues," explains Joe Murphy of Interactive Integrity. "There's the potential for sexual harassment, improper contact with competitors, people using chat rooms, [viewing or downloading] pornography, and employees sending out proprietary information over the Net. Technology has shifted the burden onto companies to monitor the workplace."[5]

In what many see as another invasion of privacy, online merchants regularly purchase confidential information about people's buying habits that has been provided by electronic profilers (also called *cookies*). This issue has caused conflict since the beginning of online commerce, because consumers often resent having their personal information sold without their consent. Many people also see this as their privacy being threatened. Companies will need

ETHICS AND TECHNOLOGY

How has widespread use of the Internet created new kinds of ethical dilemmas? What strategies would you suggest for making ethical decisions in Internet-related ethical issues?

Ethics on the Net

For an Informative Interactive Question-and-Answer page on Internet ethics, go to **http://members.aol.com/internetethics/,** which is also linked to **www.mhhe.com/lamberton4e.** Both questions and answers are provided for your consideration. Do you agree with all of the answers? If not, with which ones do you disagree? You may also respond to the "Let Us Hear Your Opinion" links. Can you think of other questions that should be asked here?

to start writing policies and guidelines to address these issues before lawsuits and bad publicity create irreversible damage.

According to Jo Ann Barefoot of KPMG Consulting, "Technology is putting people into terrain where they don't know what the ethics issues are. Regarding customers and privacy issues, the rules, regulations, and laws are going to lag. In the meantime, there is a lot of risk, like costly litigation or bad publicity; and companies should have some guidelines."[6]

Another Internet ethics issue is copyright infringement, where online businesses have been caught using, distributing, and even selling copyrighted materials such as text, images, and music. A lawsuit several years ago against Napster.com, which offered free MP3 downloads of copyrighted music, stopped their distribution of copyrighted materials. However, the type of copyright violation that came next, peer-to-peer file sharing, has been much harder to control.

All of these examples illustrate the countless ways in which the Internet challenges the ethics of employees and businesses, creating new debates and asking new questions about ethics.

CODES OF ETHICS

If ethical issues aren't the same as moral or legal issues, how can you judge them? Some companies have developed specific **ethical codes** that are accepted and abided by in all levels of the firm. Figure 17.2 shows the code used by Johnson & Johnson.

Texas Instruments (TI) has published a manual for managers called *Ethics in the Business of TI.* The company's philosophy of business, contained in this booklet is that " . . . good ethics and good business are synonymous when viewed from moral, legal, and practical standpoints."[7] The entire book sets forth ethical guidelines for nearly every area of business the company could be involved in. It even covers some common gray areas such as political contributions, conflicts of interest, and corporate spying.

ethical codes
Formalized sets of ethical guidelines developed by some companies for use at all levels of an organization.

more about...

Another Well-Known Ethical Code

Texas Instruments has over 30,000 employees in more than a dozen countries. Their code of ethics also includes information on ethics guidelines for employees in the global market.

469

Texas Instruments and the TI Ethics Office are well known as active leaders among ethics professionals. In addition, TI has received several awards from the business community for excellence in business ethics.

figure 17.2

JOHNSON & JOHNSON CODE OF ETHICS

This code of ethics is well known because it sums up all of the company's ethical responsibilities concisely but thoroughly. *Do you feel that this code is complete, or that more could be added?*

Source: Reprinted with permission of Johnson & Johnson.

Our Credo

We believe our first responsibility is to the doctors, nurses and patients, to mothers and fathers and all others who use our products and services. In meeting their needs everything we do must be of high quality. We must constantly strive to reduce our costs in order to maintain reasonable prices. Customers' orders must be serviced promptly and accurately. Our suppliers and distributors must have an opportunity to make a fair profit.

We are responsible to our employees, the men and women who work with us throughout the world. Everyone must be considered as an individual. We must respect their dignity and recognize their merit. They must have a sense of security in their jobs. Compensation must be fair and adequate, and working conditions clean, orderly and safe. We must be mindful of ways to help our employees fulfill their family responsibilities. Employees must feel free to make suggestions and complaints. There must be equal opportunity for employment, development and advancement for those qualified. We must provide competent management, and their actions must be just and ethical.

We are responsible to the communities in which we live and work and to the world community as well. We must be good citizens — support good works and charities and bear our fair share of taxes. We must encourage civic improvements and better health and education. We must maintain in good order the property we are privileged to use, protecting the environment and natural resources.

Our final responsibility is to our stockholders. Business must make a sound profit. We must experiment with new ideas. Research must be carried on, innovative programs developed and mistakes paid for. New equipment must be purchased, new facilities provided and new products launched. Reserves must be created to provide for adverse times. When we operate according to these principles, the stockholders should realize a fair return.

Johnson & Johnson

However, as an individual in the average workplace, one that does not provide such well-known guidelines, how do you know whether you are on the right track regarding your ethical decisions? The ethics test in Strategy for Success 17.1 at the end of this chapter, which was developed by Texas Instruments, can be helpful.

Codes of ethics like that of Texas Instruments are usually based on one of the following ethical approaches: principles of justice, individual rights, utilitarianism, individualism, or the categorical imperative.[8] These are the most common ethical philosophies, and they can be summarized as follows:

1. The **principle of justice** focuses on making sure that all decisions are consistent, unbiased, and based on fact. For example, a manager using this principle would want to be certain that he or she had all of the facts in a given case before making a decision. The judicial systems of most countries are based on the principle of justice, including that of the United States.

2. The **principle of individual rights** focuses on basic human rights and the dignity of the individual. Using this principle, a manager would never expect an employee to act in a way that would deny the employee's religious beliefs. Someone adhering to this principle would refuse to steal from anyone simply because such an action would reduce the *dignity* of the victim.

3. The **principle of utilitarianism** means making decisions that promise to do the greatest good for the largest number of people.[9] Using utilitarianism, a manager would fire 50 employees to provide several hundred new jobs in the future. Someone who lives by this principle would have little problem sacrificing hundreds of soldiers in a war effort to help the overall good of the country, especially if the country were populated with tens of millions of citizens.

4. The **principle of individualism** holds that a person's primary goal is to achieve long-term self-interests, with the emphasis on *long-term;* self-interest would not justify shortsighted actions.[10] Under this principle, a corporate director would not engage in price-fixing. Although profitable in the short-term, this would hurt the company in the long run. Notice that most people who adhere to the principle of individualism would likely seem as honest, ethical, and unselfish as anyone else.

5. The **categorical imperative** is an ethical principle that results from the question, *What would the world—or my company—be like if everyone were to do this?* This ethical idea was developed years ago by philosopher Immanuel Kant.[11] Think of yourself as the ruler of a country who could legislate the ethical choice you are thinking about into a national law. Would that law be fair? Would it be one you would like and respect?[12] What would be its far-reaching effects? A person following the categorical imperative would keep himself

principle of justice
An ethical philosophy that holds that all decisions should be consistent, unbiased, and based on fact.

principle of individual rights
An ethical philosophy that holds that all decisions should respect basic human rights and the dignity of the individual.

principle of utilitarianism
An ethical philosophy that holds that all decisions should do the greatest good for the largest number of people.

principle of individualism
An ethical philosophy that holds that all primary goals should achieve long-term self-interests, with the emphasis on *long-term;* self-interest should not justify short-sighted actions.

categorical imperative
A principle developed by philosopher Immanuel Kant, which asks the question, "What would the world—or my company—be like if everyone were to do this?"

or herself from committing a crime by visualizing a world (or even a neighborhood) where everyone commits that same crime regularly. The individual would ask, "Would that be a world, or neighborhood, in which I would want to live?"

Does one of these principles seem the most appropriate to you? Additional principles are listed in Figure 17.3. Some choices are better and more popular than others. Which choice or combination of choices seems most appropriate to your values? Which choices are the most useful for the workplace?

RATIONALIZING UNETHICAL BEHAVIOR

Even people with a good knowledge of ethical principles can fall prey to the temptation to **rationalize** unethical behavior. Management expert Saul Gellerman warns that unethical behavior in the workplace often starts with one or more of four basic rationalizations:[13]

1. A belief that the unethical behavior is within ethical and legal limits—because it is more convenient to believe that it is.

2. A belief that because the chosen behavior will work for the best interest of either the individual or the company, the company would *expect* that it be carried out.

3. A belief that nobody will notice. The theft of a few cents from each depositor at a savings bank, for example, would most likely go unnoticed—or would it? Several cases are on record of just such a crime being discovered and prosecuted—even when the theft per depositor was as small as *a fraction of a penny per month.*

STAYING ETHICAL ON THE JOB

Some jobs present strong temptations to be unethical, such as by cheating customers. An employee must avoid unethical shortcuts. *How have you responded to pressures to behave unethically on the job?*

rationalize
To justify unethical behavior with excuses.

figure 17.3

WHAT IS YOUR DEFINITION OF ETHICAL?

Ethics can be hard to define because many people's personal ethics are summed up by their feelings and gut instinct, which are hard to quantify. Also, answers like "What my feelings tell me to do" may be acceptable for an ethical person, but completely unacceptable for someone with little or no ethical concerns. *What is your definition of the word ethical?*

What Does Ethical Mean?

Possible answers include:

- What most people around me consider appropriate behavior.
- Whatever reflects the Golden Rule.
- Whatever is not against the law.
- What my feelings tell me to do.
- Whatever is in line with my religious beliefs.
- Whatever is customary in my society.
- Whatever would be approved of by a neutral panel of people in my line of work.
- Whatever doesn't hurt other people.

Luis, a maintenance manager, offers a day off with pay to his employee Monica to thank Monica for not reporting an accident on the job. Luis tells himself that he never *saw* any written code saying that this was not allowed—but he never looked for one, either.

4. A belief that because the chosen behavior helps the company, the company will go along with it and protect the person if he or she is caught.

Whenever you are expected to make a work-related decision, be aware of these four rationalizations. When you are justifying a decision that seems unethical, ask yourself whether you are being honest with yourself in your rationalizing. Since rationalization is often done without conscious thought, you must be alert to the use of this mental manipulation of the facts.[14]

As with almost all of the topics presented in this book, self-esteem plays a part in this discussion. People with high self-esteem are more likely to feel good about themselves, which allows them to not seek the short-term gains of unethical behavior and not engage in rationalization to justify it. People with high self-esteem are also more likely to feel a healthy connection with others around them, and so are more likely to act in a socially responsible way.

> **more about...**
>
> **Rationalizing**
>
> **Rationalizing** is a term that means finding an excuse for behavior that causes embarrassment, shame, anxiety, or pain. It is one of the defense mechanisms described by the late psychiatrist Sigmund Freud.

ETHICS IN CONTEXT

In Chapter 3, you learned about the importance of using self-disclosure and being honest in your relationships with others. This can become an ethical issue when people act insincerely in their relationships with other people in order to achieve their own ends. Loss of trust is the result, and, as you learned in Chapter 1, trust is the basic element of relationships.[15] Politics exists in any company, and gaining political power isn't in itself an unethical behavior. However, when people compromise their own integrity to succeed at getting ahead in the company, an important ethical line has been crossed.

In the United States there is a widespread belief that if you are agreeable and easy to get along with, your job will remain secure. The idea seems to be that, although unpleasant and dishonest, the practice of "sucking up," "kissing up," or **boss massaging,** is a necessary price one must pay for success. Most people do not judge those who play this game because it is so common.[16] Many times, this game includes competition among co-workers.

> **boss massaging**
>
> The practice of currying favor, or kissing up, with a manager to achieve your own goals.

Mara, an electronics engineer in a computer company, stole an innovative idea for software from a competing company. She assumed that she would be expected to take any steps that help the company compete in the software market. After all, her manager, her department, and the whole company would benefit. Instead, she was reprimanded.

The employee wishing to rise above this disharmony can have trouble remaining detached from it. If you find yourself in such a position, remember that *no one can force you to act unethically.*

If you are the boss who is being massaged, an honest look at the power realities should show that you are free to take many actions to discourage such behavior. Be a manager who makes it clear that your employees' performance is based on merit, and be consistent in the application of that philosophy.

THE INFLUENCE OF GROUP GOALS

The biblical story of the Good Samaritan tells of a Samaritan in ancient times who came upon a man who had been beaten and robbed by criminals. Though a stranger, the unnamed Samaritan bandaged the victim's wounds and paid for food and lodging until the man had healed.[17] This parable has served for centuries as an example of how an individual should act when finding a helpless person in great need. However, often, the exact opposite occurs: when encountering someone in need, many people look the other way because other people's goals or a group's pressures override the need. This creates an ethical conflict: even when people have learned helping behavior in their families and communities, they sometimes find themselves unable to transfer those behaviors to the workplace. Research by social scientists shows that many people change their ethical standards between home and work. Researchers discovered that two-thirds of the respondents in a survey of 200 marketing managers used different sets of moral decision-making standards at home and work.[18]

Perhaps someday you will work for a company that encourages you to leave your ethics at the door when you come to work. Such companies do exist; however, the perception that management wants you to behave unethically is often more imagined than real. Make sure that you are interpreting your company and its management fairly, and that you do not assume that unethical actions are required of you that actually are not.[19]

By paying a cash bribe and gaining a million-dollar customer, sales manager Ron thought that even if he were caught, the company would thank him for landing the account. Instead, he was fired.

Whatever the company attitude, everyone who works for a company should closely examine how his or her personal ethics fit into the ethics of the firm. If compromise is necessary to continue as an employee, make sure that the compromise does not force you into areas of ethical choice where you would be opposing your own values. Few situations cause more stress than compromises with your own conscience.

GLOBAL ETHICS ISSUES

As trade expands, people need to recognize differing ethical views among the nations of the world and acknowledge these differences with an attitude of acceptance. American values, beliefs, and practices are not the only ones in this world. American values have their roots in the ancient cultures of Greece and Rome, as well as that of the British Empire. Judeo-Christian religious influences have also been a large factor, as are the U.S. Constitution and Bill of Rights. Other nations have value systems that may come from very different—though equally valid—sources.[20]

A Historical Perspective

The values and customs of other countries are not inferior, primitive, or degraded. They have different origins, evolutions, and applications through history. They are based on differing histories and cultural memories. Practices that might seem unethical to Americans often have cultural histories that go back thousands of years. (See Figure 17.4.)

Take a look at the acceptance of bribery and kickbacks as an example of the differences among countries and cultures. Most governments have laws concerning bribes and payoffs. Any law, however, is only as effective as its enforcement. In some countries in Africa, age-old traditions that *require* payoffs are rooted in a communal heritage, and an entire tribe or village benefits from such payoffs. If the community is the enforcer of law, one can easily see why tradition would overcome any written law in most cases.

WORKING IN THE GLOBAL MARKET

Even everyday events such as buying dinner can be very different in other countries, and American businesspeople who want to succeed internationally have to be flexible and open-minded to such differences. *How might a different cultural situation cause problems for someone used to American ethics?*

Harley-Davidson Company has an ethical code based on the company's definition of "healthy working relationships." It contains five points: being truthful, practicing fairness, keeping promises, respecting others, and encouraging intellectual curiosity.[21] The company also has a 12-point philosophy of "financial ethics" that all employees and managers have to read and sign.[22]

inner circle

A clique of trusted family members, tribal members, or friends (depending on the culture), who are at the center of power or influence.

future favors

A practice commonly seen in developing countries based upon mutual obligation and resulting in the exchange of favors over years and even generations; also used in some industrialized countries such as Japan and South Korea.

figure 17.4

ETHICAL STANDARDS

Although many basic ethical standards are practiced throughout humanity, their application varies from culture to culture. What is considered politeness, hospitality, and punctuality can vary greatly, even within regions of the same country. *Which of these propositions do you agree with most?*

Source: Adapted from Gene R. Lacznick and Jacob Naor, "Global Ethics: Wrestling with the Corporate Conscience," *Business*, Summer 1985, pp. 8–9.

If you do business with foreign companies, especially in developing countries, you need to understand three concepts, discussed in the following sections, that seem to be widely believed and practiced.[23]

The Inner Circle

Most communal societies make a strong distinction between insiders and outsiders. Those who are in the **inner circle** are, depending on the culture, family members, tribal members, or trusted friends. In China an inner circle might include people who speak the same dialect. In India members of an inner circle would likely be from the same caste. In many cases, a skillful American or other Westerner can become sufficiently trusted to break into the inner circle, but such acceptance can require great skill and patience. The possibility of unjust treatment toward outsiders is always a consideration, and outsiders should watch carefully for this. In some inner circles, fairness and kindness to those outside the circle are not considered to be necessary.

Future Favors

Within these inner circles, one will find the assumption of **future favors.** The Japanese call it *inner duty;* in Kenya, it is known as *inner relationship.* The practice can be found in nearly any culture that respects the inner circle concept. It translates into *I owe you; I pay you off. Now you owe*

Ethical Propositions for the Global Business Climate

- There are diverse standards of ethical behavior around the world.
- Enforcement of law, not existence of law, often determines behavior.
- You cannot be too ethical.
- Multinational corporations have high ethical responsibility and accountability.
- The likelihood of ethical misjudgments is relatively high.
- A country's concern with ethics increases with its economic well-being.

me. The trading back of favors can go on for years, even generations. When a typical American says, "I owe you one," the seriousness with which such an expression is both meant and understood is much less than in most developing countries.

Gift Exchange

Americans who witness a **gift exchange** in another country may suspect bribery, but such an accusation would horrify most people who practice this. In some cultures, this tradition of exchanging gifts goes back to ancient times. In today's global marketplace, the tradition often becomes a standard tool of business. Although gift exchange does exist in the Western world, the sense of obligation related to it (based on future favors) is not nearly as strong. This tradition is related to the concept of the inner circle, too, as the gift exchange is often the rite of passage into that circle.

SOCIAL RESPONSIBILITY

Social responsibility means putting ethical standards to work in all areas of the global community in which you live. Being socially responsible is acting ethically while understanding that your actions are part of the larger, interactive picture of the workplace, the community, and the world. Social responsibility includes acting ethically with customers, co-workers, suppliers, competitors, and the community in which you live.

What types of social responsibilities does a typical workplace have? Every workplace has an obligation to make choices or decisions about issues such as environmental pollution, discrimination, employee safety and health, dishonesty, and community commitments such as volunteerism. The growing awareness over the past few decades of such obligations has prompted many companies to become more socially responsible. (See Figure 17.5.)

One of the difficulties in deciding whether or not a company is socially responsible is that there is disagreement about just *whom* the company should be responsible *to.* Three views of social responsibility that are commonly accepted are traditional (or classical), stakeholder (or accountability), and affirmative (or public) social responsibility.[24]

1. *Traditional social responsibility* says that a company or organization is responsible only to itself and to making a profit. In this view, the government and general public are responsible for solving social problems, not companies. In an organization, though, any decision that

---

gift exchange

A strong tradition in many cultures, in which giving gifts creates a future obligation to the receiver; it can also be a rite of passage into an inner circle.

social responsibility

The practice of acting ethically while understanding that your actions are part of the larger, interactive picture of your workplace, community, and world.

ETHICAL OR PERSONAL CONFLICT?

Sometimes in international business settings, you will be asked to agree to things that make you feel ethically uncomfortable. You need to determine if these requests reflect genuine cultural traditions of the people with which you are working, or if an ethical conflict is occurring. *How can you determine whether a situation is truly unethical, or if it is just your personal discomfort with the issue?*

At Matco Plastics, the head of the production department is being promoted to vice president. Hoping to be her replacement, the eight supervisors employed under her spend the three months before she leaves both massaging the boss and undercutting one another. They now work in an environment that is negative for all of them.

does not benefit shareholders is considered irresponsible. This view of social responsibility is based mostly on materialistic ideals that emerged with the Industrial Revolution in the late 1880s when large corporations were first formed. Today it is still practiced worldwide but is often criticized as selfish and destructive.

2. *Stakeholder social responsibility* holds that companies are responsible to **stakeholders**—that is, to any group they interact with as a business. In this view, a company is responsible not just to make a profit, but also to answer to customers, competitors, unions, suppliers, consumer groups, government agencies, and so on. This

stakeholders

Any group that a business interacts with, such as customers, competitors, unions, suppliers, consumer groups, and government agencies.

figure 17.5

COMPANIES THAT CARE

Thousands of companies give back to their communities in different ways every year. The key to effective social responsibility is to consider the entire community when business decisions are made, and to give back things that the community wants and will appreciate. *What is your favorite example of social responsibility? (It doesn't have to be from this list.)*

Source: www.starbucks.com/aboutus/csr.asp; www.att.com/about/community/; www.gapinc.com/public/SocialResponsibility/socialres.shtml; www.levistrouss.com/responsibility/; www.benjerry.com; www.merilllynch.com/index.asp?id57695_8149_8688_8170. All source retrieved October 15, 2005.

Here are just a few of the thousands of examples of corporate social responsibility:

In 2001, Starbucks, the Seattle-based coffee company, launched a program called "Make Your Mark" (MYM). This program encourages volunteering for neighborhood improvement. Starbucks matches $10 for every hour a Starbucks employee volunteers.

AT&T has developed technology that reduces pollution and shares this technology with other companies.

GAP, Inc., (which also includes Old Navy and Banana Republic) allows its employees paid time off to volunteer in their communities. GAP also donates a percentage of its pretax profits to organizations representing social issues.

Levi-Strauss, one of the world's largest clothing companies, gave more than $27 million in grants for AIDS care and prevention from 1985 to 2005.

Ben and Jerry's Homemade, Inc., though taken over by corporate giant Unilever, has remained socially responsible. In 2004, the company supported research on sustainable dairy farming practices and on new eco-friendly refrigeration technology that could have great environmental impact in the future.

In 2003, Merrill Lynch launched what it calls "a first-of-its-kind community charitable fund." This fund links Merrill Lynch with a nationwide network of private charity foundations. The arrangement allows donors to have direct input as to where and how donations should be spent.

The rapidly growing trade relationship with China has already taught other countries some hard lessons on differing attitudes about what is ethical. Marketers at Toyota discovered the Chinese proverb that says "When you get to the foot of the mountain, a road will appear." The Japanese company decided to use a clever spin-off from that proverb:

"Wherever there is a road, there is a Toyota." Most of us would admit that the statement isn't literally true, but most other cultures—including the United States—are used to that sort of come-on to get the customer's attention. Not the Chinese. Chinese government authorities saw the slogan as highly unethical and accused Toyota of false advertising.[25]

view emerged in the 1930s during the Great Depression, when views on employee rights and human relations underwent significant progress. This perspective goes beyond what is good for the company and commits a company to having ethical responsibilities.

3. *Affirmative (or public) social responsibility* is the most broadly based of the three perspectives. In this view, companies are not just responsible to their profit margin and their stakeholders, but they are also responsible to the general public and society at large. Companies in this view would be expected to avoid creating social problems such as pollution and poverty, and to work toward goals that improve conditions for everyone. This view came about in the 1960s, when social unrest escalated and disapproval of business practices became more publicized. It is based most heavily on ethical principles, in particular those of moral rights, justice, and the categorical imperative.

> **more about...**
>
> **Social responsibility** is also demonstrated at the individual level. People who volunteer for beach clean-up activities, recycling centers, adopt-a-highway programs, child mentoring activities, hospice care facilities, and so on are socially responsible.

A Few Cautions About Social Responsibility

Just as there are many difficult questions regarding ethics, there are also many difficult questions regarding social responsibility. For example, what happens when a company can no longer afford to support charities or organizations that have become dependent on them? A move to protect the company's economic health by cutting charitable funding may seem selfish to outside observers.

How does a company choose to support specific organizations while not helping others? Choosing among equally important organizations can create hard feelings among nonprofit organizations or charities, although this may not be obvious to corporate donors.

Companies or individuals may also find that their acts of social responsibility are misunderstood and resented by the community.

The administrative board of a nonprofit organization started a mentoring program for at-risk children in a semirural community. Shortly afterward, another organization opened an after-school program for at-risk children. These two organizations had the same goals and served similar populations, and so began competing for grants and contributions from the same sources. Hard feelings and conflict arose until both organizations were able to secure enough funding to continue without financial worries.

These examples are not meant to discourage you from becoming socially responsible. They are only meant to show you that social responsibility—just like the larger issue of ethics in general—often contains a lot of gray areas and difficult choices.

BLOWING THE WHISTLE

whistleblowing
Turning in or otherwise exposing people who behave unethically in your company.

What do you do when you have found unethical conduct taking place in your company? Most strategies involve **whistleblowing**—turning in the offending person or people and exposing the truth.

The first law passed to protect whistleblowers was the Lloyd–La Follette Act of 1912, which protected federal employees who gave information to Congress.[26] Wider protection for those who blow the whistle on dangerous, fraudulent, or unethical practices in their workplace has been in existence since the 1970s. Although free speech rights are guaranteed under the First and Fourteenth Amendments to the Constitution, retaliation against whistleblowers was so widespread that enacting specific laws became necessary. The Whistleblower Protection Act was passed in 1989 and strengthened in 1994. In addition to federal laws, many individual states also have their own whistleblower protection laws. Nevertheless, the Government Accountability Project states that "Every year, thousands of Americans witness wrongdoing on the job . . . [that] may jeopardize the health, safety, or lives of others . . . [and] most employees remain silent in the face of such misconduct" for various reasons, such as fears of retaliation and the belief that there is nothing they can do to stop the misconduct.[27]

In 2006, the U.S. Supreme Court ruled against whistleblowers when the court voted *not* to protect government employees from retaliation after they have blown the whistle on employers. In May 2007, the second annual "Whistleblowers Week" event was held in Washington, D.C., to encourage the U.S. Congress to pass stronger protective laws for whistleblowers in both the private sector and the government. The Whistleblower Protection Enhancement

THE NEED FOR WHISTLEBLOWING

When companies behave unethically, the answer might be to blow the whistle. Companies such as this can cause severe environmental damage that affects human health and lives. *What are the possible costs of not blowing the whistle on unethical corporate behavior?*

A few years ago, a small-town physician announced publicly that he would offer an incentive of $40 a month to all the teenaged in his community who did *not* get pregnant while in high school. This offer on his part was meant to help curb the spiraling rate of pregnancies among young teens in his particular community. His offer was subsequently interpreted by some members of his community as promoting contraception with a pro-abortion hidden agenda. He became the target of criticism and controversy.

Act of 2007 was introduced into Congress but has not yet been made into law. These changing laws illustrate the complexity of the issue of whistleblowing.

Some of the strategies available to the person who faces the moral choices of the whistleblower include:

- Secretly threatening the offender with blowing the whistle unless the unethical action is stopped or corrected.
- Anonymously blowing the whistle within the company, keeping your identity a secret.
- Secretly threatening a responsible manager that you will blow the whistle outside of the company unless a change is made in the conduct.
- Sabotaging the results of the unethical behavior in some way.
- Publicly blowing the whistle within the organization.
- Quietly refusing to carry out an unethical plan.
- Secretly or publicly blowing the whistle outside of the company.[28]

more about...

Protection for Whistleblowers

The Government Accountability Project was established in 1977 to help employees who blow the whistle on unethical corporate practices. They provide legal help and advocacy for such employees.

For reasons that remain unclear, people have traditionally looked down on the person who "tells on" someone else, especially in some areas of life. In grade school, for example, being a tattletale is not respected. As adults, most people don't like busybodies who seem to be prying into other people's business. For these reasons and others, even many otherwise moral and ethical people are afraid of blowing the whistle. After all, one's job might be at risk, or the whistleblower might be excluded from the informal work group. Other, less rational fears include losing one's nerve at the last minute, not having the courage to follow through once the accusations have been made, or worrying that the purity of one's intentions might be mistaken for backstabbing.

These types of fear are not unfounded. "There is very little protection in industry for employees who object to carrying out immoral, unethical, or illegal orders from their superiors," says David Ewing,

In 1997, at the Hanford nuclear plant in Richland, Washington, seven pipefitters became vocally concerned about tank farm pipes that didn't meet safety standards. These "tank farms" hold millions of gallons of nuclear waste and had been leaking into the surrounding community. When asked to attach a valve to the system that they felt was unsafe, they refused. All seven were fired. Two months later, by court order, they were all rehired. However, in 1998 five of the seven were fired again. Years of legal struggling went by. Finally, in 2005, they had their day in court, along with four others who became involved later, and won the lawsuit. A Department of Energy contractor was ordered to pay damages.[29] The 11 have sworn that they blew the whistle only because they were afraid of potential physical harm to themselves and the rest of the community.[30] The federal government has since taken the Hanford danger seriously, by authorizing the Government Accountability Project in early 2008 to set up a nonprofit organization, Hanford Challenge, to oversee cleanup of the site.

former executive editor of the *Harvard Business Review*. "If the employee doesn't like what he or she is asked to do, the remedy is to pack up and leave. This remedy seems to presuppose an ideal economy, where there is another company down the street with openings for jobs just like the one the employee left."[31]

The list on page 481 includes some of the more secretive choices available to a potential whistleblower. The reason some of the more secretive of these choices might be necessary is that many companies punish whistleblowers in various ways for their honesty.[32] A new movement is afoot to encourage whistleblowing in a few U.S. companies by providing rewards. Such a system, though, may only create distrust among employees if it leads to increased spying.

The best solution is the kind of leadership that makes whistleblowing unnecessary. The ethical tone of an organization nearly always originates in top management and moves downward. Thus, top management is in an ideal position to create an ethical environment for everyone who works in the company.

Several years ago a marketing company in Boston (which was a subsidiary of a larger firm in Los Angeles) was run by a group of young managers who always bragged about how they were "fooling the big shots in California." When these managers discovered that many of the salespeople were faking their appointment schedules during training, they were surprised. However, they should have known that their unethical attitude would set the tone for their employees.

Management can also create low ethical standards by any of the following managerial mistakes:

- Favoritism occurs when one employee is given extra privileges and allowances. This creates resentment among other employees and the impression that they, too, are entitled to these same extra privileges—even if they are unethical.

Whistleblowers in the News

To see updates on whistleblower cases, and survival tips for whistleblowers, go to **www.mhhe.com/lamberton4e** and visit the Government Accountability Project's Web site. Write a brief paragraph about one case that you find interesting.

The U.S. government has an Office of Government Ethics to help prevent ethical conflicts of interest for executive branch government employees. They also provide information to the public about federal conflict of interest guidelines. They can be reached at 202-208-8000 (TDD: 202-208-8025, FAX: 202-208-8037).

- "Fudging" with the expense budget is a managerial mistake. Managers who allow employees to use company expense budgets for items of doubtful use to the company, or for obvious personal use, are allowing unethical treatment and encouraging it to continue. Managers should also be careful to not do the same, thus setting a bad example.

- Lying to or otherwise manipulating other departments or offices within one's company creates an atmosphere of distrust, which erodes team spirit.

Most people will face ethical dilemmas during their lives. Knowing one's own values and standards (as covered in Chapter 5) is essential; but some situations, such as the one in this chapter's opening story, are still difficult to come to terms with. There are no easy answers to offer here. Hopefully, though, you now have a heightened awareness of the issues after studying this chapter.

STRATEGIES FOR SUCCESS

17.1 Making Ethical Decisions: A Quick Ethics Test from Texas Instruments

1. Is it legal?
2. Is it consistent with the company's stated values?
3. If you do it, will you feel bad?
4. How would it look in the newspapers?
5. Do you think it's wrong?
6. If you're not sure—ask.
7. If you don't get a clear answer, keep asking until you do.

Texas Instruments, a giant manufacturer of electronics and computer chips, teaches its employees to run through these seven steps whenever they have a question about whether a business action is ethical.

1. **Is it legal?** If not, then don't do it, even if it's borderline.

2. **Is it consistent with the company's stated values?** Texas Instruments has a clearly stated set of corporate values. Actions that don't fit with them shouldn't be undertaken.

3. **If you do it, will you feel bad?** If so, there's probably something wrong.

4. **How would it look in the newspapers?** If having people "find out" through public media will be embarrassing, there's a problem.

5. **Do *you* think it's wrong?** If so, don't do it.

6. **If you're not sure—ask.** Never feel you have to make a decision on ethics by yourself. Get help from others.

7. **If you don't get a clear answer, keep asking until you do.** Don't fudge an ethical problem by saying you "tried" to get help but couldn't. Keep asking—the boss, the company's lawyers, and human resources personnel—until you get a clear answer.[33]

17.2   Becoming Culturally Aware of Ethical Conduct

1. Look closely at the situation.

2. Evaluate the intentions.

3. Explore your options.

Asking the following questions in some detail should be helpful in ethics clarification for anyone who is dealing with an unfamiliar culture.

1. **Look closely at the situation.** Be sure you understand the traditions and customs of the culture you are dealing with. Be sure you are listening carefully to the issues of the situation, remaining as open-minded as possible.

2. **Evaluate the intentions.** What are the principles behind the desires of the foreigner you are dealing with? Are you making the mistake of evaluating intentions only through your own traditions and value system? Do you understand the other person's true intentions clearly? Most importantly, once you have established the issues, you need to ask yourself whether you are being asked to take an action that would violate your personal ethics or those of your company—regardless of the cultural context.

3. **Explore your options.** Do you have several options to choose from? Do you know what they are? Which option is the most ethical for you, your company, and your own safety?

Often, these three steps can be taken only after considerable dialogue. Learn to listen carefully both to fellow foreigners who understand the culture better than you do, and to the nationals themselves. Because of the influence of American culture worldwide, many foreigners have a much greater knowledge of the West than Americans may have of the foreign culture. This knowledge gives them a decided advantage; however, it also gives them an opportunity to translate their cultural norms into a common language that makes their intentions easier to understand.

By all means, do not *sell out* your values to those of another culture. Americans simply need to be more sensitive to the cultural differences involving ethical choices between countries and cultures—not just for humanitarian reasons. However, they need to better understand ethical issues as they come up and also to develop overall business success when working abroad.[34]

CHAPTER SEVENTEEN SUMMARY

Chapter Summary by Learning Objectives

1. **Define ethics.** Ethics deals with the standards of conduct and morals in a particular society. In short, it expresses the standards of right and wrong as accepted among a specific group of people.

2. **Explain the importance of a code of ethics.** Codes of ethics vary from person to person and from company to company. Codes of ethics provide agreement and documentation for the manner in which the company sees itself ethically operating. The major ethical codes mentioned in this chapter are: the principles of justice, individual rights, utilitarianism, and individualism. Also, Immanueal Kant's categorical imperative is often used in company decision-making.

3. **Describe the process of rationalizing unethical behavior.** Rationalization is the use of reasonable-sounding excuses to explain unethical conduct. The four most common rationalizations are: (1) a belief in the legality of the behavior because of the convenience of doing so, (2) a belief that the company would expect that the behavior be carried out, (3) the belief that nobody will notice, and (4) the belief that since the behavior will help the company, the company will protect the employee.

4. **Explain ethics in the context of the U.S. workplace.** A major ethical issue in the United States is the issue of "boss massaging." Anyone working here, or in some other countries must look carefully at this practice and decide on its integrity, or lack of it.

5. **Describe the influence of group goals on ethics.** Many people with strong personal ethics find themselves unable to carry their values into the workplace; this can be from the pressure of the larger group. The Parable of the Good Samaritan and the Parable of the Sadhu (in the end-of-chapter Working it Out) are used in this chapter to explore that issue.

6. **Give examples of global ethics issues.** When doing business in other countries and cultures, you must become sensitive to the differences in ethical definitions and attitudes. Be certain that you understand

the thinking of the other culture before acting or jumping to conclusions. Especially remember these three concepts: the inner circle, future favors, and gift exchange.

7. **Define social responsibility.** Social responsibility means putting ethical standards to work in all areas of work and life. Three common views of social responsibility are traditional (or classical), stakeholder (or accountability), and affirmative (or public) social responsibility.

8. **Describe the process of whistleblowing.** If you discover unethical behavior in your own organization, you will likely consider whistleblowing. At least seven approaches to whistleblowing are available. Knowledge of your own ethical standards will help greatly in any decision involving ethical choices.

key terms

boss massaging 473	inner circle 476	principle of utilitarianism 471
categorical imperative 471	morality 466	rationalize 472
ethical codes 469	principle of individual rights 471	social responsibility 477
ethics 466	principle of individualism 471	stakeholders 478
future favors 476	principle of justice 471	whistleblowing 480
gift exchange 477		

review questions

1. Briefly define *ethics*. Give your own definition of ethics as the term applies to your own values. Do you think it is a good idea to base your decisions on what "feels" right? Are there any outside forces that influence your behavior?

2. What is a code of ethics? In your opinion, how effective are such codes?

3. Evaluate the Johnson & Johnson Company's Code of Ethics in Figure 17.2. What is the key to its popular appeal?

4. Define the term *rationalizing*. What role does rationalization play in making bad ethical decisions? Thinking back, have you ever rationalized a bad ethical decision? Explain.

5. Explain the ethical problems involved in boss massaging. When is this practice a good idea? When is this practice a bad idea? Explain what may occur when employees are involved in boss massaging.

6. What major ethical issues are likely to confront someone who is doing business in a foreign country? Give some specific examples. What are some strategies for becoming culturally aware of ethical conduct in foreign countries?

7. How does the Internet create new ethical issues? Do you believe it is unethical for an employee to use the Internet on a company computer for personal use during company time? Is it unethical for the employer to monitor that usage? Explain.

8. What is your attitude toward whistleblowing? Would you ever be a whistleblower if the situation merited such action? Why or why not?

critical thinking questions

9. There are times when people feel they must act unethically in the short term in order to benefit the greater good in the long term. Can you think of a time or a situation that you are familiar with in which this has happened? Is it *ever* acceptable to act unethically?

10. Ethical standards often are made into laws over time. In Oregon, children under age 16 must wear helmets when riding bicycles. Several years ago, this was only an ethical standard that some parents chose and others did not. Do you think that all ethical standards should have "teeth" in the way that laws do? Who would govern codes of ethics? Or should some or all codes of ethics be made into laws so that they carry more weight?

working it out 17.1

ETHICAL OR NOT?

School-to-Work Connection: Interpersonal Skills

Objective: This exercise will help you clarify differences in a group's opinions of what *ethical* means.

Procedure: Divide into groups of four or five. Using the criteria listed below, arrive at a group consensus as to what is meant by the term *ethical*. These suggestions can be combined, changed, or ignored by group consent. Avoid democratic voting if possible, and instead seek consensus agreement. Next, as a group, create a story illustration—either factual or made up—that illustrates the group definition of ethics you have created.

As the last step, all groups will share both definitions and story illustrations with the rest of the class. Discuss the differences and the reasons for them.

Ethical is:

_____ what most people around me consider appropriate behavior.

_____ whatever does the most good for the greatest number of people (the *utilitarian principle*).

_____ whatever action reflects the Golden Rule.

_____ whatever is not against the law.

_____ what my feelings tell me to do.

_____ whatever action is in line with my religious beliefs.

_____ whatever is customary in the society I am in.

_____ whatever action would be approved of by a neutral panel of people in my line of work.

_____ whatever doesn't hurt other people.

working it out 17.2

THE PARABLE OF THE SADHU

School-to-Work Connection: Interpersonal Skills

Objective: This parable will help you better understand the conflict between individual and corporate ethics.

Procedure: Break into groups of four or five. Read the following parable: The biblical story of the Good Samaritan is well known in Western culture. A parable of another kind comes from the article "The Parable of the Sadhu," written by Bowen McCoy of *Harvard Business Review*. McCoy tells of a trip to Nepal in which he walked 600 miles through 200 villages in the Himalayas. At a high elevation, one of the members of a party of New Zealanders who had joined him discovered an Indian holy man—called a *sadhu*—nearly naked and unable to walk. No one wanted to step forward from the group and help him, at least not to the point of helping him down the slope to warmth and safety. He was given some clothing, but since he was unable to walk, his likelihood of surviving without help was very small. In the end, the group left him, presumably to die.

The arguments for and against this lack of action were debated afterward at length. McCoy's friend Stephen summarized the dilemma by saying, "I feel that what happened with the sadhu is a good example of the breakdown between the individual ethic and the corporate ethic. No one person was willing to assume ultimate responsibility for the sadhu. Each was willing to do his bit just so long as it was not too inconvenient. . . ."

All of the travelers who ignored the sadhu were intent on the goal of reaching an 18,000-foot mountain pass to get to a village on the other side. Partly because of the importance of this goal in everyone's mind, the suffering individual was all but forgotten. In other words, an unethical action that an individual in other circumstances would not have taken became possible because of group pressures and group goals. These same forces of goals and the pressures to reach them exist in business. The parable thus asks this question: to what extent can an employee or manager of a company ignore the intense needs of a suffering individual in order to achieve the goals of the larger group?[35]

Most important, the parable of the sadhu illustrates the conflict of the individual's personal ethics versus the ethics of the group. Most people learn their moral and ethical values from their families or communities, but for various reasons, they don't always transfer those same values to the other groups (such as the workplace).

Discussion: After you have read the parable of the Sadhu in your small group, begin discussing this topic. In your group, come to consensus on the relevance of this parable to ethics in the workplace. How could your workplace be improved with an awareness of the lesson in this story?

What do you think *you* would have done if you had been the one to come across the sadhu? Have you experienced any situations in which you have been faced with helping—or not helping—someone in distress? What did you do? What did others around you do? Why do you think these people chose the actions they did?

internet exercises

1. *Read and Write*

   Find the Electronic Privacy Information Center at **www.epic.org/crypto/** and linked through the textbook Web site at **www.mhhe.com/lamberton4e.** Read at least two recent articles on cryptology and take a position on its use in terms of the ethics of Web site privacy. Write a few paragraphs explaining your position.

2. *Read and Summarize*

   Visit the page for Corporate Social Responsibility at **www.corporate-social-responsibility.com/** and linked through the textbook Web site at **www.mhhe.com/lamberton4e.** Find three current articles on social responsibility issues. Write a brief one- or two-paragraph summary of each.

3. *Self-Assess and Reflect*

Visit the Web sites for the Government Accountability Project linked through the textbook Web site at **www.mhhe.com/ lamberton4e** or go directly to their site at **www.whistleblower .org**. Take a look as well at the National Whistleblower Center's Web site linked through the textbook Web site at **www.mhhe.com/ lamberton4e,** or go directly to their site at **www.whistleblowers .org**. Can you see yourself working for a whistleblowing organization such as these? Read their job announcements and reflect on the qualities and skills required by these organizations. Write a brief reflection paper on how your career interests and skills do, or do not, fit with these job announcements.

Life Over Profit

The following scenario is adapted from a classic ethics test developed by psychologist Lawrence Kohlberg about 50 years ago. Read the ethical dilemma presented and then answer the Case Questions that follow.

A woman living in Europe was near death from a rare kind of cancer. The doctors knew of only one drug that might save her, a type of radium that a druggist in her town had recently developed. The drug was expensive to make, but the druggist was charging patients 10 times the cost of producing it. He paid $200 for the radium but charged $2,000 for a small dose of the drug.

The sick woman's husband, Heinz, went to everyone he knew in an attempt to borrow the money, but he could only get about half of the $2,000 he needed. He told the druggist that his wife was dying and begged him to sell the drug cheaper, or to extend some credit. But the druggist insisted, "No! I discovered the drug, and I'm going to make money from it." Heinz became desperate and broke into the store to steal the drug to save his wife.[36]

Case Study Questions

1. Was the husband's behavior excusable under the circumstances?

2. If you were a police officer in the town, would you have arrested him for theft?

3. If you were Heinz, would you have stolen the drug? If not, why not? What would you have done instead?

Boss Massaging, or Just Good Politics?

Josh Ruiz and Denise Romano were assistant managers in a small technology firm. A chance for a promotion opened a month earlier when their immediate supervisor, Kelli Nishikawa, announced her retirement. Both Josh and Denise were hoping to be selected for a promotion to division manager. She would be naming her replacement soon, and both Josh and Denise knew they were the only candidates.

In the month following the announcement, Denise had grown increasingly upset at Josh's actions. His behavior had changed from pleasant and objective to secretive. She noticed Josh "kissing up" to their supervisor. Before this opening, they had always worked well together as colleagues. They had peacefully resolved conflicts between them and had worked together to correct errors without going to their manager. However, in the past month, Kelli had called Denise into her office three times to question her about mistakes she had made in setting up new accounts.

Denise knew that Josh had to have pointed out these errors to Kelli, and she resented Josh "tattling" on her. When she confronted him about it, he just replied innocently that he was only thinking of the success of their division. Denise had also noticed Kelli and Josh going to lunch together, and often overhead them laughing and talking casually in the office.

Denise knew that Josh was "boss massaging" in order to get the promotion. She was certain that his new friendship with Kelli was insincere. She felt that he was trying to undercut her. Was he really doing anything so wrong? If he was, what could she do about it?

Case Study Questions

1. Do you think Josh is really doing anything wrong? Why or why not?

2. Why does Denise feel the way she does about Josh's behavior? Is this just a case of sour grapes on her part, or does she have a legitimate complaint? If she has a legitimate complaint, to whom should she voice it?

3. What do you think will happen in this situation if it plays out to its logical conclusion? What do you see as the long-term consequences in terms of the relationship between Josh and Denise?

MAINTAINING A PRODUCTIVE WORKPLACE

In the Workplace: Company (Dys)Function

SITUATION

Jennifer and Saroja were supposed to be finishing up a report that their manager had asked for earlier that day, but they had much more important things to do first. They had to compare notes on their winnings from online card games, read their e-mail, and get fresh coffee from the coffee place down the block. Jennifer had to check for new postings on her Facebook profile, while Saroja had to check her MySpace account for new messages. They both then had to look through new profiles of single men on Match.com, and Jennifer had to quickly (or so she said) look for new profiles on Yahoo! personals while Saroja checked Craigslist to find a new couch. Jennifer needed to check the New York Stock Exchange for some details to add to the report, but then decided to check the progress of her own stocks while she was thinking about it. Saroja waited for her to finish up while reading the *Los Angeles Times* online, just to keep up on current events.

Before they knew it, an hour had gone by, and then another one. By the deadline for turning in the report

LEARNING objectives

After studying this chapter, you will be able to:

1. Describe a productive workplace.
2. Explain the importance of time management.
3. Give examples of behaviors that reduce workplace productivity.
4. Compare and contrast responses to substance abuse and other nonproductive behaviors.

CHAPTER 18

STRATEGIES FOR SUCCESS

Strategy 18.1   Learn to Use a Time Log

Strategy 18.2   Look for Warning Signs of Substance Abuse

---

that afternoon, they had barely begun it. Their stress level rose as they felt the urgency of the deadline approaching.

DISCOVERY

"This place is unreasonable! Way too much pressure!" complained Jennifer. "How do they expect us to get our work done on such short notice? Now I'll have to stay late again tonight to finish up! That's going to cause problems with the babysitter, and I can't afford her overtime fees again anyway."

Saroja nodded in agreement, and added, "The stress level for what they pay us is not worth it! They should get a better idea of how long things take

before they hand out deadlines. It's just ridiculous that they don't give us enough time for the projects we have to do!"

THINK ABOUT IT

Has there been a time when a friend or family member has had time management issues or personal problems that affected his or her performance at work? Have you had such problems yourself? Does your employer have resources to help with such issues? Do you sometimes notice that people are doing things to reduce their own productivity that they don't seem to see in themselves?

A PRODUCTIVE WORKPLACE

productivity

The ratio of an organization's inputs, or its resources, to its outputs, or the goods and services it produces.

What does it mean to say a workplace is productive? We can define **productivity** as a ratio of inputs (an organization's resources) to its outputs (the organization's goods and services produced). Given today's global economy, it is essential to maintain high productivity in the workplace.

Productivity can be increased, in general, by focusing on input and output separately. By becoming more efficient, an organization may be able to improve the production process and gain more output for the same input, or achieve the same output as before with less input, or increase input slightly for greater output. There are many ways to improve efficiency in productivity. Many of these strategies are out of the individual control of the employee. These include long-term and complex processes such as improving the research and development arm of an organization, or buying new equipment, buildings, or machinery. The organization can simplify its products, or improve the production process. Another way to improve productivity is to increase the efficiency of employees at the individual level. This last strategy is under our individual control, and it is the focus of this chapter.

Increasing Morale to Boost Productivity

workplace morale

The overall mood of a workplace based on attitudes and satisfaction.

It is traditional in the field of human relations to point out that **workplace morale** and productivity are closely related. "Morale" is defined in Chapter 6 as "the overall mood of an individual or a group based on attitudes and satisfaction." When morale is low, productivity inevitably suffers. This includes everything from a slower pace of work to an increase in accidents. What can be done to improve the morale of your workplace?

1. The first step is to *understand* the morale of your environment. If it is negative, why? Morale is rarely, if ever, a static force. Because of this, one has to be examining it almost constantly. Employee surveys are often effective in finding out how intense or widespread low morale might be, where the perceived problem lies, and even what steps might be taken to make rapid improvements. Frequent interviews with employees, including exit interviews, can help identify morale issues, too.

2. Let everyone in the company know "what's in it for them?" How do the mission statement and goals of the company figure into the reality of the employees? Once employees understand that connection, morale usually improves.

3. Get everyone in the organization involved in goal setting, both individually and collectively. Lack of direction and goals is a big factor

in lowered morale. Everybody needs a sense of accomplishment and direction to feel good about having a connection with the company.

4. Let employees know that the company and their division of the company are dedicated to helping them succeed and to be promoted, if that direction is desired. Few factors hurt morale more than a feeling that the company is somehow working against the people in it.

5. Encourage communication between employees, among departments, and within teams. It's been said that it is impossible to overcommunicate. Within any reasonable limits, the more communication you have in a given company, the better.

6. Don't relax on individual and group accountability. Keeping everybody accountable for their actions—and inactions—is another way of sending the message that the company cares. That means the company cares about those fellow employees who aren't pulling their weight and are thereby frustrating others.[1]

Several other factors encourage a productive workplace. One factor is the manner in which employees and managers are appraised. The traditional once-a-year **employee appraisal** in which all of the negatives are saved up and thrown at the employee in one giant toss has to become a thing of the past. Creative appraisal systems stimulate productivity by encouragement, two-way communication, and motivation. The more ongoing the appraisal system is in any company, the better. A manager should never have to tell an employee during an appraisal anything negative that has not already been addressed.

> **employee appraisal**
> Feedback to an employee from supervisors on how he or she has performed over a given period.

An effective appraisal system will use something like the S.M.A.R.T.S. system. To help improve morale and productivity, an appraisal system should be:

- Specific
- Measurable
- Achievable
- Results Oriented
- Time Bound
- Stretchable

All of these components are self-explanatory except the last one, "stretchable." Ironically, it is probably the most important of the six. It means that an appraisal system should "stretch" the employee, giving him or her new goals, new horizons to grow into a new comfort zone.[2]

Productivity and Task Maturity

Another way to encourage productivity is to match an individual to the jobs that need to be done, in other words, to consider an employee's **task maturity.** Someone with task maturity has the skill set for the

> **task maturity**
> Having the skill set necessary to complete a job, as well as the ability to set and meet realistic goals and the ability to take on responsibility for the task.

job at hand, is able to set and meet realistic goals, and can take on the necessary responsibility for the task. Task maturity does not refer to an employee's age or seniority on the job, and a person can be mature in other life areas but possess poor task maturity. Meeting goals and taking responsibility are skills that can be developed over time. Individual job performance can be increased by discovering and reducing behaviors we do to sabotage our own performance, including managing time better.

Avoiding Self-Sabotage

self-sabotage
Damaging your own credibility or competence.

procrastination
Putting off until later the things a person should be doing now.

Self-sabotage means damaging our own credibility or competence. There are many reasons we sabotage our own efforts, mostly tied to fear or apprehension, low self-esteem or insecurity, or lack of motivation. In a survey asking people to name the most common ways they sabotaged themselves, clinical psychologist Dan Neuharth found that procrastination was at the top of the list.[3] **Procrastination** is the act of putting off until later the things we should be doing now.

Procrastination is not only a form of self-sabotage; it is also a major source of stress. As we know from Chapter 14, stress is damaging both physically and mentally. If procrastination is stressful and ultimately damaging, then why do we do it? The obvious benefit is that we can put off an unpleasant task until some later time. Hidden benefits of procrastination exist as well. These include being able to get back at people who are making demands on us, being able to avoid unpleasant tasks if others get tired of waiting and do the work for us, being assigned less to do if others decide we are overwhelmed by existing tasks, and perhaps getting to feel special by not working as hard as others.

MEASURING PRODUCTIVITY IN THE WORKPLACE

Appraisals are important for employees, so that they can get feedback on their job performance, make changes if necessary, and become more productive in the process. *When has an appraisal helped you to change your working style to become more productive?*

Steps to Stop Procrastinating

Procrastination is an intentional choice. Because we have made a choice to procrastinate, we can also make a choice to stop procrastinating. The following suggestions can help us get started on those tasks we put off.

1. **Get going on the task.** Don't wait for motivation to appear on its own, as if by magic. When you get started with a task or project, the motivation will begin to come to you. It doesn't take long to get on a roll, or get up the momentum, to keep going and complete the task.

2. **Make a plan.** It is easier to say to ourselves that we will get a task started "one of these days" than it is to actually begin the task. Instead of putting it off, make a plan. When will you start it? Today? At what time? What pieces of the project will you do today? How much time will you spend today on each part that you have planned for today?

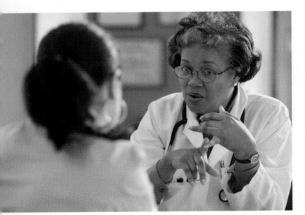

3. **Reduce the task to smaller components.** Break big projects or jobs down into smaller parts. Start with, say, 30 minutes of work on a project before switching to something else. You don't need to do it all at once. When you look at a task in its entirety, chances are you may feel too overwhelmed to get started. Plan the smaller piece you will do today, finish that part, and then you can decide either to quit for the day, or go ahead and work on another part.

4. **Think positive.** What negative thoughts are you having about yourself and this task? Think about what is making you put it off. Does not completing the project make you feel you are a failure? Do you feel insecure in worrying that others will belittle your work? Are you afraid your work will be wrong? Concentrate on replacing negative thoughts with more reasonable and positive thoughts.

5. **Reward yourself along the way.** Give yourself a small reward after finishing each smaller task. There is no need to wait for the entire project to be finished first. You will find a boost to productivity and self-esteem when you give yourself a reward in the form of self-congratulation, a short break, taking a walk, renting a movie you've been waiting to see, or fixing up a treat from the kitchen.

6. **Give yourself credit.** Pat yourself on the back for a job well done. You need not have completed the entire project in order to give yourself some credit. You can still recognize the parts of the job that you did finish. Congratulate yourself for managing your time efficiently, and give yourself credit for not procrastinating!

TIME MANAGEMENT

Time management refers to making effective use of available time. This sounds simple, but it does take planning. We often **overload** our time by planning too many activities into one time slot. At other times we may **underutilize** time by making poor use of available time that we do have. Procrastination is one cause of underutilization of time.

If we consider the top 20 ways that people reported sabotaging themselves, several can be overcome by more efficient use of time. These include: acting impulsively, getting distracted or losing focus, taking on too many things at once, having unrealistic expectations, not asking for help when needed, rushing through things, worrying too much, and not finishing what was started.

Many **time analysis** tools are available to help us analyze our use of time so that we can see where we can become more efficient in time management. Some of these tools are available online, but the simplest way to analyze how well we are making effective use of time is to keep track of activities over several days. Think of this as a scaled-down version of a personal journal. Activities can be recorded electronically or

time management
Making effective use of available time.

overloading time
Planning too many activities into one time slot.

underutilizing time
Making poor use of available time.

time analysis
Analyzing your use of time to determine how to become more efficient in time management.

Time Management

Visit the Web site for Time Management Guide at **www.time-management-guide.com/time-log.html** and linked through the textbook Web site at **www.mhhe.com/lamberton4e.** Sketch out a time log for your weekly activities, following the suggestions in this article.

Link to a related topic on this site such as goal setting, procrastination, or other topic, and summarize the information you find there. How could you use this information to improve your own productivity?

by hand. Construct a template to keep a log of all activities. Include column headings such as activity, location, and purpose. Under each column, note how long each task took, with a brief note on location and purpose.

Taking a look at the time-use analysis can allow us to see in print how long we spend on activities. We often spent too much time on unimportant activities while not allowing enough time for more important tasks. Seeing such a pattern in time use can help us manage time better and set priorities. **Setting priorities** means you decide ahead of time which tasks are the most important, and which are the least important. The most important tasks must be completed first. If all tasks seem equally important, go through the list again and decide which are most urgent, and which can be put off until a little (or a lot) later.

Creating a **to-do list** by keeping lists of what you need to do, when, and where, will take a little time. The time you save in efficiency, however, will more than make up for the time you spend. Once you have prioritized your tasks by importance and by deadlines, write them down, or enter them into a PDA (personal digital assistant) if you prefer to keep the list electronically. The most important tasks and those with upcoming deadlines should be entered first and completed first. Those less important should be listed last. Group the tasks together by location. This will allow you to save time by going to each location only once. Some tasks will seem much larger than others. Larger tasks, or projects, can be broken down into smaller parts, so that each smaller task can be completed without a feeling of being overwhelmed by too large a task.

setting priorities

Deciding ahead of time which tasks are the most, and least, important.

to-do list

A list of what you need to do, when, and where.

more about...

Self-Sabotage and How to Avoid It

Visit the Web site for the book "Secrets You Keep from Yourself" by clinical psychologist Dan Neuharth at www.secretswekeep.com/. Do you see yourself in these behaviors listed? What steps can you take to reduce or eliminate self-sabotage?

Your to-do list can work better for you if you start with something you enjoy doing. This can motivate you to keep going. Cross off or check off items on your list after completing them. You may be surprised how rewarding this can be! Remember to reward yourself for difficult tasks completed along the way.

BEHAVIORS THAT REDUCE WORKPLACE PRODUCTIVITY

From time to time, troubling personal situations arise for everyone. How you decide to handle them can affect your work, your co-workers, and your prospects for career advancement in the future. Individuals who don't handle these situations very well can affect the overall well-being and productivity of their workplace. In a productive workplace, morale is high, relationships between co-workers are positive, and self-esteem is maintained. When employees bring personal problems to work, these problems can affect the entire workplace. When employees abuse alcohol or drugs, have conflict in their marriage or family life, or have financial difficulties, their struggles (although not necessarily their fault) can create problems on the job. These problems do not always happen alone; many people experience combinations of them, sometimes because one problem triggers another.

Employees, managers, and entrepreneurs are all responsible for handling situations in their personal lives effectively. The problems addressed here are serious, but they can be overcome with determination and effort. They do not need to diminish the productivity of any workplace, and they do not need to wreck people's careers or lives!

Substance Abuse: Alcohol and Other Drugs

Substance abuse is one of the most common—and expensive—employee problems that companies face. Abuse of alcohol and other drugs together cost the American economy an estimated *$276 billion per year* in lost workdays and lowered productivity (mistakes on the job, incomplete work, tardiness). Health-care costs also add to this amount (emergency room visits, treatment for overdoses, mental health problems, alcohol-related heart disease, stroke, or cancer). Crime-related costs, motor vehicle crashes, and early deaths also add to this amount. When you add in related costs to social welfare, this amount rises even more. What does this mean at the individual level? Each of us pays out more than $1,000 each year for these damaging effects of other people's substance abuse.[4] The rates for alcohol abuse are about the same as they

REDUCED PRODUCTIVITY AT WORK

Even though you may do your best at a job, sometimes situations out of your control can affect your productivity, and it's up to you to handle them successfully. *When you had a situation that reduced your productivity at a task, what steps did you take to correct it? What advice would you give to a friend with a similar situation?*

substance abuse
The continued use of a psychoactive substance even though it is causing or increasing problems in a person's life.

Kathleen's marriage was falling apart. It was easier to join co-workers at a local bar than go home at night and argue with her husband. At first she went to Happy Hour two times a month, but gradually this increased to four times per week. Her work performance began to drop, and she was no longer saving any of her paycheck. Her arguments with her husband became more serious: he accused her of abandoning their children and becoming an alcoholic. He threatened to take custody of the children, which caused her already low self-esteem to plummet further. As a result, she drank even more.

One night, just before leaving work, Kathleen contacted her company's confidential employee assistance program and explained her situation. They gave her a consultation the next evening, during which they recommended family counseling and AA meetings. Kathleen went home and talked to her husband. To her surprise, he was supportive and not only agreed to the counseling, but also agreed to accompany her to her first few AA meetings. As Kathleen pieced her life back together, she realized that she could have sought this help at any time; it was there for anyone in her company who needed it.

more about...

Alcoholism is a chronic disease with genetic, psychosocial, and environmental factors in its development and outcomes. This disease is often progressive and fatal. About 10–20 million Americans are alcoholics. About half of high school students say they drink. Alcohol is involved in about half of all murders and domestic violence incidents, about one-third of suicides, one-quarter of accidental deaths, and about half of all highway deaths in the United States. In fact, the American Medical Association lists alcohol as the most dangerous and physically damaging of all psychoactive drugs.[7]

more about...

Treatment Options: The 12-Step Program

Alcoholics Anonymous (AA) invented the **12-step program** to help recovering alcoholics. Modified versions of the 12-step approach also work for drug addiction and various psychological problems.

were 20 years ago, and they are continuing at about the same rate; rates for drug abuse, on the other hand, have shown a steady pattern of increase.[5]

Since at least 80 percent of heavy drinkers work, and 76 percent of people who abuse illegal drugs work part- or full-time, no business can consider itself immune to the problems of employee substance abuse.[6] These statistics can be overwhelming to digest. Perhaps a more important point to remember is that everyone pays for these costs when tax dollars pay for government services such as highway safety, criminal justice services, and special education for babies damaged prenatally by drugs or alcohol. Everyone also pays more consumer dollars when the costs of goods and services increase due to reduced productivity.

Recognizing Alcohol Abuse in the Workplace

Who is likely to be an alcoholic? Alcoholics may be difficult to identify because they can be found in all occupational groups; they can be any age, gender, race, or ethnic group. Changes may arise in the person's appearance (physical signs) or behavior (behavioral signs). Physical signs may include:

- slurred speech.
- bloodshot eyes.
- the smell of alcohol on a person's breath.
- unsteady walking.

Behavioral signs may include:

- missing work often.
- arriving late or leaving early.
- taking frequent long lunch hours or breaks.
- irritability or other personality changes.
- avoiding supervisors and co-workers.
- conflicts with co-workers.
- blaming others for mistakes at work.
- resenting supervisors and feeling *picked on*.
- lowered job performance or efficiency.
- financial problems or having wages withheld because of legal action.

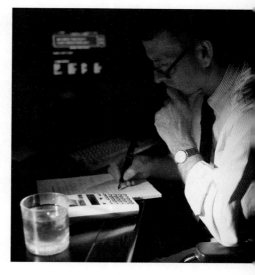

FUNCTIONING ALCOHOLICS

Eighty percent of heavy drinkers work, and many are highly functional; they perform well at their jobs and conceal their problem successfully. *When should an employer intervene with an employee's suspected alcoholism?*

Employee Drug Abuse and Dependency

When people think of drug abuse, they usually think of illegal drugs such as cocaine or heroin. However, legal drugs can also be abused, including prescription drugs such as tranquilizers or painkillers (e.g., oxycodone or hydracodone) and over-the-counter drugs such as diet pills. Substances that aren't normally thought of as drugs, such as nicotine and caffeine, can also be abused. What qualifies as drug abuse really depends on the user's dependence on the drug and how the substance affects his or her behavior.

Psychologists generally define substance abuse as continued use of a psychoactive substance even though it is causing or increasing problems in a person's life. These problems may arise at work, at school, or in one's social life, physical health, or psychological health. Generally, abuse is going on when drug use is frequent, compulsive, and intense. For example, if an employee misses an important meeting because he or she is hungover, then abuse is occurring. Abuse can include **dependence** on the substance being abused, which can be defined as the state of relying on or needing a substance. When dependence includes **withdrawal symptoms** (physical symptoms, usually painful, that strike when the drug is not used) or increased **tolerance** (needing more and

dependence

The state of relying on or needing a substance.

withdrawal symptoms

Physical symptoms that strike when a drug is not used.

tolerance

The state of needing more and more of a substance to get the desired effect.

INTERNET exercise 18.2

What Is a Substance Abuse Professional?

The U.S. government offers information on substance abuse professionals, along with detailed information on drugs of abuse, employees, and employers at the U.S. Department of Labor Web site at **www.dol.gov/workingpartners/welcome.html** or link to the course Web site **www.mhhe.com/lamberton4e.** Write a brief paragraph about what you learn.

physiological dependence

Dependence based on increased tolerance and the presence of withdrawal symptoms when the drug is not used.

psychological dependence or preoccupation

Dependence that occurs when a person craves the effects of a drug and organizes his or her life around getting and using the drug.

psychoactive drug

Any substance that affects a person's judgment, behavior, mental processes, mood, conscious experience, or perceptions.

central nervous system

The brain and spinal cord.

more of the substance to get the desired effect), this is called **physiological dependence.** When a person craves the effects of a drug and organizes his or her life around getting and using the drug, he or she suffers from **psychological dependence or preoccupation.** Preoccupation or psychological dependence is an excessive, focused attention given to the drug, its effects, and/or its use. The drug attains such value that it diverts energy away from important life concerns. A person experiencing psychological dependence has lost control over the substance.

Any substance that affects a person's judgment, behavior, mental processes, mood, conscious experience, or perceptions is called a **psychoactive drug** (for a breakdown of common terminology, see Figure 18.1). Psychoactive drugs can be separated into major categories, based on both their effects on the body and the way they act on the body's **central nervous system** (brain and spinal cord). For example, stimulants speed up the central nervous system, while depressants slow it down. (See Figure 18.2 for drug classifications and effects.)

Depressants include alcohol, narcotics (e.g., heroin), and barbiturates and antianxiety drugs (e.g., Xanax and Valium). Stimulants include amphetamines, cocaine, nicotine, and caffeine. Other drugs called hallucinogens (e.g., LSD, marijuana, or mescaline) distort time and physical sensations. Medical marijuana is allowed limited use in the treatment of some medical conditions, and laws regarding its use are hotly debated since many people believe that it is harmless enough that it should be legalized while others disagree. This issue is not likely to be settled in the near future.[8] Designer drugs (e.g. MDMA or Ecstasy) are laboratory-created drugs that are not yet declared controlled substances. Even when designer drugs are legal, this does not mean that they are safe to take!

The Effects of Substance Abuse in the Workplace

Substance abuse is a very expensive employee problem costing several hundred billion dollars each year. These costs are mainly from lost productivity and health-care expenses. There is no way to measure the loss

Manuel noticed that his brightest junior accountant, Therese, seemed to be changing. She was late for work almost every day; she took long lunch breaks; and she was alienating her clients. In fact, one just called him to say that she showed up late for a meeting, and when she did show up, she was belligerent, and her breath smelled of alcohol. He called Therese into his office and repeated the client's story to her. Therese denied it immediately and said the odor was from cough syrup. Manuel genuinely cared for Therese and wanted to try to offer her some advice, but he knew that he was not a trained counselor and his efforts could backfire.

Instead, he reached into his desk and handed her a card. Therese read it; it was for the firm's EAP. "It's your choice, Therese," he said levelly, "but your work performance is beginning to go below average, and I suggest you think about what needs to be done."

to employee morale and group unity when employees are substance abusers, or when non-substance-abusing employees work with substance abusers. Non-substance-abusing employees may resent the abusing employee's lost time or productivity, they may feel obligated to pick up the slack, or may even feel obligated to protect the substance-abusing co-worker from getting into trouble. Nonabusing employees may also feel less safe, especially if substance-abusing employees are operating machinery. A substance-abusing employee may also go into withdrawal at work, which can cause distress for everyone in the workplace.

more about...

Substance Abuse Treatment Professionals

Substance abuse treatment professionals are counselors or psychologists who receive additional training in how to treat substance abusers. Check with the National Association of Addiction Treatment Providers (**www.naatp.org/**) or other resources for a list of such providers.

figure 18.1

Substance Abuse: Terms to Know	
Substance abuse	Continued use of a drug beyond the point where it causes problems.
Dependence	Urgent need for a drug, either physiological (having physical effects) or psychological (having mental effects).
Withdrawal	Onset of symptoms upon ended use of drug, sometimes including physical pain, nausea, tremors, and seizures.
Tolerance	Resistance to lesser amounts of drug.

SUBSTANCE ABUSE TERMINOLOGY

These terms describe the main elements of substance abuse, including dependence and its two primary physiological symptoms. *In your own words, what is the difference between substance abuse and dependence?*

figure 18.2

COMMON PSYCHOACTIVE DRUGS

These are the basic classifications of drugs and their common effects. *What are the most common side effects of drugs?*

Source: Hoffman, Vernoy, and William, *Psychology in Action* (p. 145). Copyright 1991 by John Wiley & Sons, Inc. Used with permission. See also: Jeffrey S. Nevid, *Psychology: Concepts and Applications* (Boston, MA: Houghton-Mifflin Co., 2003).

Common Psychoactive Drugs: Classifications and Effects

Category	Desired Effects	Undesired Effects		
		Physical Dependence	*Psychological Dependence*	*Tolerance*
Depressants (Sedatives) **Alcohol, barbiturates, antianxiety drugs (Valium)**	Reduced tension, drowsiness, euphoria, disinhibition	Anxiety, nausea, disorientation, impaired reflexes and motor function, loss of consciousness, shallow breathing, convulsions, coma, death		
		Yes	*Yes*	*Yes*
Stimulants **Cocaine, amphetamines**	Exhilaration, euphoria, high energy (physical and mental), perceptions of power and sociability, loss of appetite	Irritability, anxiety, paranoia, hallucinations, psychosis, convulsions, death		
		Yes	*Yes*	*Yes*
Caffeine	Increased alertness	Insomnia, restlessness, sleep disruption, mild delirium, ringing in ears, rapid heartbeat		
		Yes	*Yes*	*Some*
Nicotine	Relaxation, increased alertness, sociability	Irritability, raised blood pressure, stomach pain, vomiting, dizziness, cancer, heart disease, emphysema, death		
		Yes	*Yes*	*Some*
MDMA ("Ecstasy")	Hallucinogenic effects, mild euphoria	Can be fatal in high doses, can cause depression, impaired learning, memory, attention		
		Yes	*Yes*	*No*
Narcotics (Opiates) **Morphine, heroin, codeine**	Euphoria, "rush" of pleasure, prevention of withdrawal discomfort, pain relief	Nausea, vomiting, constipation, painful withdrawal, shallow breathing, convulsions, coma, death		
		Yes	*Yes*	*Yes*
Hallucinogens (Psychedelics) **LSD (lysergic acid diethylamide)**	Delusions, hallucinations, distorted perceptions and sensations	Longer and more extreme delusions and hallucinations (bad trips), psychosis, death		
		No	*No*	*Yes*
Marijuana	Relaxation, mild euphoria, increased appetite	Perception and sensory distortion, hallucinations, fatigue, lack of motivation, paranoia, possible psychosis		
		No	*Yes*	*Yes*

Joe began taking a prescription sedative to relax from the pressures of his fast-paced career as an assistant district attorney. It worked very well—so well, in fact, that he requested a larger prescription and began taking it nightly. Soon he found that he was running out of energy at work, getting sick more often, and not sleeping as soundly as before. He tried reducing the dosage and instantly felt withdrawal symptoms. Frightened, he called his doctor for help. His doctor recommended a weeklong drug treatment program.

Joe almost laughed; he didn't need a drug treatment program—he wasn't a drug addict, or was he? Slowly he realized that he needed the program, and he agreed to it. It wasn't easy taking the time off from work, especially on such short notice, but if he didn't, he would end up even more dependent—and the results could eventually be fatal.

Marital, Family, and Other Personal Problems

Employees often bring family difficulties to work, whether they are marital conflicts, separation or divorce, difficulties with child care or elder care, or another family-related issue. These can reduce workplace productivity when employees miss work, have accidents at work, make poor decisions, pay poor attention to detail, have conflicts with co-workers, or relate poorly to customers. These effects along with lost productivity and increased turnover that occur in less productive workplaces can cost American businesses as much as $150 billion a year.[9]

How can managers spot employees who are troubled by family conflict? Some warning signs include:

- excessive tardiness or absenteeism.
- unusual behavior such as crying or losing one's temper.
- a decline in the quality of work or work performance.
- trouble concentrating.
- a decline or change in appearance.

Divorce is one of the most common family problems. The end of a marriage can lead to depression, with problems in sleeping (too much or too little) or eating (loss of appetite and weight), inability to work, and feelings of hopelessness. Even people who have been unhappy in their marriages and asked for the divorce or separation may still become depressed. Because it is considered more acceptable for women to openly express feelings such as depression, they are more likely to seek help for their problems, whereas men may feel too humiliated or embarrassed to

CHANGES IN BEHAVIOR

Many alcoholics show changes in behavior, but when confronted about their problem are likely to respond with denial. *How would you respond to denial when dealing with an employee who demonstrates symptoms of alcoholism?*

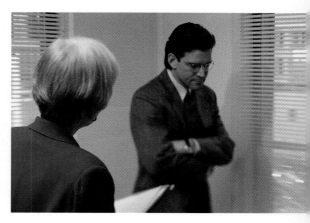

Tim, Tito, and Sandra worked in the same department for five years as an interdependent team that created and distributed important monthly reports for a large IT firm. Over the last year, Tim started showing signs of substance abuse. He came to work every Monday bragging about the heavy partying he did all weekend. His previously perfect work was full of errors, such as running the wrong reports or including the wrong data. One night, after Tim had left 15 minutes early to meet some friends, Tito and Sandra had to stay late and rerun reports Tim had done incorrectly.

"It's not just that I'm getting tired of this," Tito said to Sandra. "It's that he's getting worse, and soon we won't be able to cover for him even if we wanted to."

"I know," she admitted. "The supervisors have been noticing the change in him and asking me about it. I don't feel good lying to them by glossing things over. This has to stop. Let's talk to Tim tomorrow; if that doesn't work, let's talk to our supervisor."

do so. For men, the marriage may have been the major (or only) source of social support, and nationally, men are three times more likely than women to become depressed due to divorce. Family situations such as divorce may also lead to financial problems and to other problem behaviors, such as substance abuse.[10]

family violence

Violence that can be defined as physical, emotional, verbal, or sexual violence against another family member.

Family violence, which can be defined as physical, emotional, verbal, or sexual violence against a family member, is another problem that spills over into the workplace. About one out of every four women is abused at some time in her life.[11] About 9 out of 10 victims of domestic violence are women abused by men.[12] Current estimates are that domestic violence costs American businesses billions of dollars a year in absenteeism, lower productivity, and health-care costs.[13] When costs for emergency shelters, police and court costs, foster care, and so on are added in, the costs to the American economy can more than double.[14] In addition, substance abuse may be linked to family violence and abuse problems.[15]

Employees affected by family violence may also have conflicts with co-workers and may become so preoccupied with their problems that their productivity suffers. To make it worse, the employee often feels too ashamed or embarrassed to admit the abuse or seek help. If the employee is the abuser, he or she may be afraid to ask for help for fear of possible legal action.

more about...

Fetal Alcohol Syndrome

Fetal alcohol syndrome/fetal alcohol effects is the leading known cause of mental retardation in the United States. Fetal alcohol effects include distorted facial features, behavioral and emotional problems, and slowed growth. For more information, link to the Centers for Disease Control Web site at **www.cdc.gov** and open the link to "birth defects" found in the "Top 20" list. This link is also accessible through the course Web site at **www.mhhe.com/lamberton4e.**

Help Stop Domestic Violence

There are many excellent Internet sites devoted to reducing domestic violence. Visit the Web sites for King County (Washington) at **www.metrokc.gov/dvinfo/,** or the Ad Council at **www.adcouncil.org/campaigns/ Domestic_Violence_Prevention/,** or Medline Plus at **www.nlm.nih.gov/medlineplus/domesticviolence** **.html,** or identify a site you found with good information. Summarize information on what community members can do to reduce domestic violence. These sites can also be accessed through the textbook Web site at **www.mhhe .com/lamberton4e.**

To add to the problem, co-workers may be fearful of violent acts occurring in the workplace because of the employee's situation, either as a victim or as an abuser.[16]

Financial Problems

Employees who are under severe financial pressure may experience difficulties, such as lowered productivity and increased stress levels. Financial problems can also make the employee susceptible to stealing from the company in some way (time or resources). These pressures may be tied in with other problem behaviors, such as substance abuse, or even domestic violence. For example, stress from financial problems may cause an employee to start taking drugs, and the resulting dependency can lead to financial problems because the employee needs more and more money to pay for the substance.

Compulsive Gambling

Some employees may become caught up in **compulsive gambling.** Compulsive gamblers are not the same as the 95 percent of the general population who occasionally play state lotteries, bet on football pools, or play bingo or the stock market; compulsive gamblers are unable to control their betting. They may also become depressed and have relationship problems in their personal lives or at work. They may borrow huge

more about...

Domestic Violence

Domestic violence can occur between married or unmarried partners. Child abuse occurs in 30–60 percent of family violence cases. About one-third of female murder victims were killed by partners.

more about...

Compulsive Gambling

The National Council on Problem Gambling at **www.ncpgambling.org** lists resources in many U.S. states for problem gamblers who want to seek help. Link directly or through the course Web site at **www.mhhe.com/lamberton4e** to "Problem Gamblers" and then "Help by State." Are resources listed for your state?

compulsive gambling
The inability to control one's betting habit.

Jenna noticed that her assistant Cynthia had been showing signs of abuse. Once, Jenna noticed a large bruise on her upper arm. Another time, she heard Cynthia crying in the restroom. She had also heard Cynthia tell another assistant that she was afraid of her boyfriend's temper. Jenna wanted to do whatever she could to help Cynthia, but she knew that she wasn't an experienced counselor, and she was afraid of saying the wrong thing. Instead, she took Cynthia out for lunch, where she expressed her concern for her health and offered her several options—most came from literature she received from the company's EAP. Cynthia seemed surprised, but grateful. She took the information, entered counseling, and after a time was able to leave the abusive relationship.

amounts of money from friends and family, co-workers, or themselves (borrowing against credit cards, life insurance policies, their own home, or credit unions). By some estimates, as many as 5–10 million Americans, both male and female, are compulsive gamblers,[17] and their costs to the U.S. economy are enormous in terms of lost productivity, criminal acts, lost jobs, bankruptcy, bailout costs, and even suicide. (See Figure 18.3.)

RESPONSES TO SUBSTANCE ABUSE AND OTHER NONPRODUCTIVE BEHAVIORS

When supervisors suspect substance abuse is a problem, they should not directly accuse employees of having such problems. Not only is denial the most likely response, but there may also be legal issues that result from making those kinds of serious accusations. A supervisor's main responsibility when handling any employee problem behavior is to make

figure 18.3

COMPULSIVE GAMBLING

If an employee has a gambling problem, he or she will most likely also have financial problems; these can cause stress and lowered productivity and also may make the employee susceptible to stealing from the company in some way. *What can an employer do to help an employee who has a gambling problem?*

Source: *Casino Watch.Org, www.casinowatch.org/loss_limit/ briefing_points.html, retrieved July 30, 2005.*

The Costs Of Gambling

In Wisconsin alone, the annual costs of compulsive gambling are more than $300 million and $1.5 billion in Maryland. These include reduced income statewide due to:

- lost productivity.
- divorce.
- criminal acts.
- suicide.
- lost jobs.
- *bailout costs* to family and friends.
- bankruptcy.

the employee understand that his or her job performance is not acceptable. The employee needs to understand that performance is the focus of the supervisor's concern, and whatever the cause of the problem, the employee is accountable for poor job performance. *Supervisors should not try to counsel or advise employees themselves.* Since most supervisors are not trained in counseling, they should refer employees to the appropriate resource, such as an employee assistance program (EAP), community counseling center, or substance abuse professional.

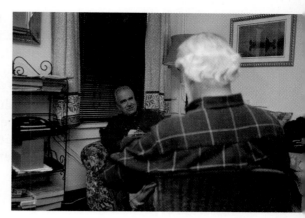

Employee Assistance Programs

Employee assistance programs, or **EAPs,** have been around since the 1940s, when large companies (together with Alcoholics Anonymous) first started them as alcoholism treatment programs. In the 1960s, these programs expanded to treat employees with other life issues, such as marriage and family conflicts or financial difficulty. Today, about two out of three EAP referrals are for help with personal or family problems that are not directly related to substance abuse.

In order for EAPs to work, supervisors must be able and willing to observe employees and watch for problems. They must be willing to approach employees who appear to be having problems, refer these employees to the EAP, and follow through. They must be willing to listen to employees who come to them for help. Employees who are referred to EAPs are usually told that their involvement is voluntary, and that they are free to reject the help. With or without the EAP's help, though, their job security will depend on improving their job performance; therefore, without receiving help for their problems, they could lose their jobs.

EAPs can help employees with the following:

- abuse of alcohol and other drugs.
- mental health issues.
- financial problems.
- legal trouble.
- poor physical health.
- stress, depression, anxiety, and other emotional issues.
- family and marriage conflict.
- other personal problems or concerns.

When an employee problem involves substance abuse, EAPs are considered less controversial and less invasive than mandatory drug testing. EAPs provide the advantages of informing the employee that a problem exists and offering a chance for rehabilitation. Rehabilitation improves employee attendance and safety practices, while reducing

TREATING MENTAL HEALTH DISORDERS

Employees can seek treatment for most mental health disorders and continue their careers happily and efficiently. *What are different approaches that employees should take to combat a mental health disorder? How should an employer respond if he or she notices that an employee has symptoms of a mental health disorder?*

employee assistance programs (EAPs)

Company-sponsored programs that treat employees with substance-abuse problems, marriage and family conflicts, and financial difficulty.

health-care costs for the company. EAPs give an employer the opportunity to reduce and prevent serious problems in the workplace. They are also cost-effective: employers can save from $5 to $16 for every dollar they invest in an EAP, according to the U.S. Department of Labor.[18] The cost of an EAP varies depending on what type of assistance program is used and what benefits it includes, but the average cost is estimated at about $12 per employee per year at the low end, with an average of $22 per employee per year, and the most expensive averaging about $28 per employee per year.[19] (See Figure 18.4.)

Workplace Substance Abuse Policies

Before taking any action regarding employee substance abuse, employers must develop a company policy on substance abuse and put it into place. The policy should clearly state all testing and (if applicable) search procedures. It should also outline any possible disciplinary actions that the company may take against employees who are abusing alcohol or other drugs. Supervisors will need training in what symptoms to look for, and they will also need to be aware of what EAPs are available to employees, so that they can direct employees toward those resources.[20] Regarding workplace substance abuse policies:

1. Companies must determine their stand on substance abuse with input from human resources representatives, as well as medical, security, safety, and legal staff.

figure 18.4

EAPs: HOW MUCH CAN THEY HELP?

Many companies find that EAPs not only save them money, but they also create a healthier and happier work environment. *What kind of services do you think a company should offer?*

Source: *"Employee Assistance Programs" Division of Workplace Programs. U.S. Department of Health Services, Substance Abuse and Mental Services Administration, posted March 1999, retrieved July 23, 2005, http://wworkplace.samhsa .gov/WPResearch/EAP/ FactsEAPfinal.html. And: "Why Does Your Company Need an EAP?" PsychWorks, Inc., posted 2003; retrieved July 23, 2005, www.psychworks.com/benefits. htm. And "Benefits of an EAP," Advocate EAP, posted 2004, retrieved July 23, 2005, www .advocareeap.com/learn/benefits/ saved.html.*

How Well Do EAPs Help Companies?

- Firestone Tire and Rubber estimated a savings of $1.7 million, or $2,350 per person.
- United Airlines reported for every dollar spent, they saved $16.35.
- McDonnell-Douglas reported 44 percent fewer missed work days, 81 percent less attrition, more than $7,000 saved in health care claims, with a 4:1 return on their investment.
- General Motors estimated 40 to 60 percent *fewer* missed days, benefits paid out, grievances, and on-the-job accidents. The company has reported a total savings of $37 million per year with their EAP ($3,700 for each of 10,000 enrolled-employees).
- United Airlines estimates about a $17 return for each dollar invested.
- Chevron Corporation reported a savings of $7.6 million per year.
- Campbell Soup reported total medical costs cut almost in half.
- Tropicana reported a significant drop in on-the-job accidents and lost time.
- Both Sawyer Gas Company and Oregon Steel Mills reported drops in absenteeism and workers' compensation insurance costs.

2. Once the policy is developed, it must be clearly communicated to the entire staff.

3. Supervisors must be trained to recognize symptoms of substance abuse and understand how it impairs work performance.

4. Employees (and their families, when possible) should receive drug awareness education.

5. Policies should include a counseling and referral component so employees can seek help confidentially before being referred by management.[21]

For larger companies, substance abuse policies that include health plans, education, and drug testing may be cost-effective within a short time, but what about small businesses? Within a small business, substance abuse can cause a financial drain that means the difference between economic survival and collapse. Because of this issue, the Department of Labor, the Small Business Administration, and the Office of National Drug Control Policy can provide resources to help small businesses deal with substance abuse policy problems.[22]

Another resource for small and midsized companies is the "Drugs Don't Work" program. At the national level, the program provides free booklets and step-by-step guidance on substance abuse policy writing. At the statewide level, states recruit corporate sponsors that help with funding and leadership to develop drug-free workplace partnerships for writing policy, training management, screening, and developing EAPs. In addition, local chambers of commerce, assisted by the U.S. Chamber of Commerce, can provide information and services to local businesses.[23]

Employee Drug Testing

The Drug-Free Work Place Act of 1988 states that certain types of businesses must take action to make the workplace drug free. These actions often include drug testing, which has created controversy in employees' rights. The controversy arises because of Fourth Amendment rights guaranteeing citizens the right to privacy against search and seizure activities; this is balanced against the rights of businesses and consumers to be free from drugs and substance abusers. Drug testing can be a great way to prevent substance abuse in the workplace as well as to detect it. If not handled properly, though, it can lead to unhappy employees and lawsuits; it can also lower employee morale by making employees feel as though their employers do not trust them.

When companies do use drug testing, they must make certain to do so carefully, follow a written policy, and avoid lowering employee morale. Companies have very different policies regarding when, whom, and how they test, and what action they take when test results are positive. Some companies test only before hiring, some randomly test current employees, some fire employees the first time they show positive drug test results, and others fire employees only as a last resort when treatment programs fail. Another legal issue can arise from Title VII of the amended Civil Rights Act of 1964, which forbids discrimination against the handicapped. Since most states define substance abuse recovery as a lifelong disability or handicapping condition, improper drug testing can lead to lawsuits alleging discrimination.

What Else Can Be Done for Employees?

Managers often feel they should not get involved with an employee's personal problems; they may feel that problems at home are too private to discuss with employees. But when these problems affect the employee's job performance, the manager must take action. Again, since most managers are not trained counselors or psychologists, their role is to intervene for the employee without trying to offer advice and counseling.

What can be done for employees facing serious financial problems, whether these are caused by compulsive gambling, poor money management, divorce, a medical emergency, or other temporary crisis? EAPs can steer employees toward the appropriate resources for help. Those with credit management problems can consult consumer credit counseling services, usually with no charge to the person using the service. These companies help people with huge credit debts to stop getting deeper into credit debt, and to consolidate debts into a manageable load. (See Figure 18.5.)

EAPs can also steer those with temporary and financial emergencies to an appropriate resource, such as a credit union. Employees facing temporary emergencies may not be aware of outside help and services that are available to them. Depending on the type of emergency, employees

figure 18.5

FINANCIAL COUNSELING AND CONSUMER CREDIT COUNSELING SERVICES

People can have financial crises for any reason, and that is usually when they seek financial counseling. However, these counseling services are good for everyone—and sometimes using them before an emergency can help prevent one. *How might a credit counselor help you?*

Consumer Credit Counseling Services: Not Just for Emergencies!

Even people who are not facing serious financial problems can benefit from the services of a consumer credit counseling service. These organizations can teach you strategies to better manage credit, including:

- figuring out a budget you can afford.
- setting aside some money each payday.
- avoiding debt when possible.
- planning for purchases instead of buying on impulse.
- paying for items with cash instead of credit.
- trying to arrange and invest your finances so that you will gradually increase your net worth.
- figuring out your own debt repayment plan before a financial crisis occurs.

may find much needed help with housing, food, or medical emergencies, or even temporary shelters in the case of domestic violence.

Needless to say, all of the issues discussed in this chapter relating to reduced workplace productivity are highly personal, and good human relations skills are needed to identify, confront, and solve these realities—challenges to workplace productivity that you will probably witness on the job sometime during your career.

Maintaining a productive workplace is rarely easy. As you have seen by reading this chapter, many factors, both negative and positive must be carefully monitored to make it all work. Productivity is a human relations issue precisely because productivity's biggest enemy is negative or nonexistent interpersonal relationships. Whether you are a manager or an employee, watch for all of these factors in your workplace and notice how productivity is affected by them. Most of all, make sure you are a part of the solution, rather than part of the problem. Keep these suggestions in mind:

- Understand factors that create and maintain a productive workplace.
- Learn methods of improving appraisal systems and morale.
- Learn strategies to improve your use of time.
- Recognize substance abuse and other behaviors that reduce workplace productivity.
- Know what employers/employees can do to help substance abuse, personal or financial situations, and medical conditions.

STRATEGIES FOR SUCCESS

18.1   Learn to Use a Time Log

A time log is important because most of us, like Jennifer and Saroja in the opening vignette, don't realize just how much time we are spending doing nonproductive things. The log will force a person to notice how he or she really spends time during the day. Here is a simple example:

TIME	MONDAY	TUESDAY	WED	THURSDAY	FRIDAY	SATURDAY	TIME
7:00							7:00
7:15							7:15
7:30							7:30
7:45							7:45
8:00							8:00
8:15							8:15

8:30							8:30
8:45							8:45
9:00							9:00
9:15							9:15
9:30							9:30
9:45							9:45
10:00							10:00
10:15							10:15
10:30							10:30
10:45							10:45
11:00							11:00
11:15							11:15
11:30							11:30
11:45							11:45
12:00							12:00
12:15							12:15
12:30							12:30
12:45							12:45
1:00							1:00
1:15							1:15
1:30							1:30
1:45							1:45
2:00							2:00
2:15							2:15
2:30							2:30
2:45							2:45
3:00							3:00
3:15							3:15
3:30							3:30
3:45							3:45
4:00							4:00
4:15							4:15
4:30							4:30
4:45							4:45
5:00							5:00
5:15							5:15

5:30							5:30
5:45							5:45
6:00							6:00
6:15							6:15
6:30							6:30
6:45							6:45
7:00							7:00
7:15							7:15
7:30							7:30
7:45							7:45
8:00							8:00
8:15							8:15
8:30							8:30
8:45							8:45
9:00							9:00
9:15							9:15
9:30							9:30
9:45							9:45
10:00							10:00

18.2 Look for Warning Signs of Substance Abuse

Warning signs of substance abuse include physical and behavioral changes. Look for signals that include:

1. Difficulty in recalling and following instructions.
2. Frequent tardiness or absence from work.
3. Frequent disappearances from the job location.
4. Taking too many cigarette or restroom breaks.
5. Taking extended lunch and work breaks.
6. Difficulty getting along with co-workers.
7. Increased mistakes on the job.
8. Repeated accidents off the job that affect job performance.
9. Dramatic changes in personality or work performance during the day, especially after taking a break.[24]

If you notice these signs in yourself, even if you don't consider yourself a substance abuser, consult your EAP to find out what services are available to help you. If you notice these signs in co-workers, bring this issue to the attention of a supervisor before the co-worker's behavior affects workplace morale or safety.

CHAPTER EIGHTEEN SUMMARY

Chapter Summary by Learning Objectives

1. **Describe a productive workplace.** By definition, productivity is the ratio of inputs to outputs. A productive workplace will nearly always contain a minimum of morale problems, and will be characterized by workers with task maturity. Simply put, it is a workplace where efficient people are producing positive results, and are doing so consistently, without undue conflict or procrastination.

2. **Explain the importance of time management.** Without time management, productivity is difficult to achieve. Good time management avoids both underutilizing and overloading schedules. Good time management starts with time analysis and the setting of priorities.

3. **Give examples of behaviors that reduce workplace productivity.** Warning signs of alcohol abuse and the abuse of other substances include various behavioral and physical signs. Behavioral signs can include increased conflict with co-workers, avoidance of co-workers, irritability, and other personality changes. Physical signs can include slurred speech, bloodshot eyes, unsteady walking, and excessive talkativeness. Other behaviors that may be entangled with substance abuse include gambling addiction, financial problems, domestic violence or related issues, and medical problems.

4. **Compare and contrast responses to substance abuse and other nonproductive behaviors.** One of the most common and expensive sources of reduced workplace productivity is employee substance abuse. Managers and co-workers need to understand the following concepts in dealing with that issue: dependence, withdrawal symptoms, tolerance, physiological vs. psychological dependence, psychoactive drugs, and alcohol abuse. Substance abuse and other factors that lower productivity can be dealt with by referring employees to an employee assistance program (EAP). Managers should not become directly involved in diagnosing or counseling employees.

key terms

review questions

1. What is your definition of a productive workplace? What factors make a workplace productive? Why is productivity an important issue?

2. Briefly explain the importance of positive workplace morale, along with suggestions for improving it. What factors make an effective appraisal system? How are these two concepts related?

3. Do you procrastinate? Can you identify specific tasks or situations that seem to increase your procrastination? Describe steps you can take to reduce procrastination.

4. What are some physical signs of employee alcoholism? What are some behavioral or warning signs of employee alcoholism? What are some suggestions for statements that should be included in company policies to combat alcohol and drug abuse at work?

5. Why is drug testing in the workplace controversial? What are the legal issues involved in drug testing? How can drug testing affect employee morale? What are the different ways companies can handle drug testing?

6. What is meant by compulsive gambling? What is the relationship between gambling and other problem behaviors, such as substance abuse? What main factor separates compulsive gamblers from casual or occasional gamblers?

7. What are some warning signs that family violence may be occurring among employees? Why is family violence a problem in the workplace?

8. Nearly every strategy for success in human relations that we've discussed in this textbook can be tied in with time management. Thinking about any of the topics to date (e.g., working in teams, leadership, and so on), select three, and explain how more effective use of time would result in more effective human relations.

9. How far should employers go in order to accommodate employees with personal problems, in the case when laws require protection for these employees (e.g., with substance abuse or mental health issues)? Most accommodations are cheap—certainly cheaper than hiring and training a new employee. Simple accommodations might include providing headphones or room dividers to reduce noise and distractions, assigning a job coach or mentor to the employee, allowing more frequent breaks, prioritizing or reassigning tasks, and making treatment options available. As a co-worker, would you feel resentful of this person who seems to be getting extra perks? Would you ask for the same treatment? Would you want to set limits on what the company provides to the person? What is *your* opinion?

10. The public has a right to expect workplaces to be safe and free from drugs. At the same time, individuals have a right to privacy. What's your view on how far employers should be able to go in drug testing of employees? What would you do if you suspected a co-worker had a substance abuse problem?

SHORT-TERM AND LONG-TERM SCHEDULING

Setting up Schedules. Long-term and short-term schedules help with time management. Short-term schedules can be set up on a daily or a weekly calendar and include prioritized tasks and to-do lists. Long-term schedules are set up on a monthly or yearly calendar, putting long-term goals and important dates into the plan. Including family, work, and personal goals and times into the schedule will help in managing time.

Filling up the entire schedule is not necessary, and it can feel overwhelming. You can always add more tasks later as needed. Try to finish a task each day that you have been avoiding. This small success adds a boost for the rest of the day to help keep you motivated. Each day, try to finish at least one task that you have been avoiding.

The following weekly schedule is one example of a structure you can use for appointment times, class times, meetings, errands, and other specific tasks. Prioritize tasks with a different color pen or a note as to how urgent or important each item is. Items noted as urgent will stand out, and you will be more likely to finish them.

The weekly schedule can be expanded into a daily schedule to add more detail in specific tasks.

Weekly Schedule

	Sun.	Mon.	Tues.	Weds.	Thurs.	Fri.	Sat.	Sun.
a.m.								
p.m.								

Examine your weekly calendar after a few weeks. Were many items left unfinished? If so, you may be either underutilizing or overloading your time. Make adjustments to the schedule to make it more realistic about the tasks you will be able to complete.

Long-Term Scheduling: In your monthly long-term schedule, make notes about specific due dates or target dates, including project due dates or important upcoming deadlines.

January, 20_____

	Sun.	Mon.	Tues.	Weds.	Thurs.	Fri.	Sat.
Week 1				1	2	3	4
Week 2	5	6	7	8	9	10	11
Week 3	12	13	14	15	16	17	18
Week 4	19	20	21	22	23	24	25
Week 5	26	27	28	29	30	31	

In the following schedule, make notes about your high-, medium-, and low-priority goals for the year. These can include both professional and personal goals, such as getting a presentation ready for an upcoming conference or filing income taxes. Make notes for each month, and keep this schedule in sight, so that you can remind yourself about the goals.

Long-Term Yearly Schedule

	Jan	Feb	Mar	Apr	May	Jun	Jul	Aug	Sep	Oct	Nov	Dec
High Priority												
Medium Priority												
Low Priority												

Take a look at how well you reach your goals and stay on schedule over time. You will need to revise both your monthly and yearly schedules from time to time to account for new goals, new target dates, or old goals that you may decide to drop. You will also need to adjust these long-term schedules to account for procrastination and overloading or underutilizing your time.

working it out 18.2

ALCOHOL DEPENDENCY SELF-QUIZ

School-to-Work Connection: Personal Qualities Skills

If you are concerned about your own drinking or suspect that someone you know may be drinking too much, try taking the following self-quiz.

1. Are you frequently preoccupied with alcohol?

2. Do you often drink more than you intend?

3. Do you need more and more alcohol to get drunk?

4. Do you suffer withdrawal symptoms?

5. Despite repeated attempts, do you fail to cut down on drinking?

6. Are you frequently drunk or impaired when expected to fulfill social or occupational obligations?

7. Are you willing to give up important social, occupational, or recreational opportunities to drink?

8. Do you drink despite a significant social, occupational, or legal problem, or a physical disorder worsened by alcohol?

Scoring: According to the American Psychiatric Association, if you answer "yes" to three or more of these questions, you are probably dependent on alcohol.[25] If you or someone you know does appear to have alcohol dependency, contact your employee assistance program (EAP) or any Alcoholics Anonymous (AA) group in your area for more information on getting help.

working it out 18.3

WORKPLACE HEALTH

School-to-Work Connection: Interpersonal Skills

Objective: This role-playing exercise will help you gain a better understanding of the behavior of employees with a substance abuse, family, or medical problem and understand how to communicate with them to develop an intervention plan.

Procedure: Divide into groups of three students. One student will play the role of a supervisor, another will play the role of an employee, and the third will play the role of referee. The employee will act as a person with a substance abuse problem, a financial problem, a family problem, or a hidden medical condition and will display the appropriate symptoms. The employee will not tell the others ahead of time what problem is being acted out, since a part of their role is to figure out what is affecting this employee. One problem at a time should be role-played, and after each problem is role-played, students should switch roles so that everyone has a turn. The supervisor will be responsible for communicating to the problem employee what is wrong with the employee's performance at work and what plan of action will be taken to correct it. The referee will oversee the dialogue and make necessary suggestions.

internet exercises

1. *Read and Summarize*

   Have you ever found yourself in a position of wanting to help others in your workplace, only to find yourself taking on the work problems they cannot solve or are too busy to complete? If so, you are—in the words of business experts William Oncken, Jr., and Donald L. Wass—letting a "monkey" (a problem) jump from the other person's back to your own back. Read the summary article "Management Time: Who's Got the Monkey?" and summarize the steps they recommend to avoid taking over other people's monkeys. This article is found at **www.businessweek.com/ managing/content/nov2007/ca20071120_606468.htm** and linked through the textbook Web site at **www.mhhe.com/lamberton4e.**

2. *Read and Summarize*

   Enter the phrase "drugs don't work here" or "drug-free workplace" into your search engine. Visit at least three organizations that you retrieve in your search. Briefly summarize what each organization has done to reduce drug use in the workplace. What ideas could be put into action in your own workplace?

3. *Self-Assess and Apply*

   The health-care field is now one of the fastest-growing employment fields. As the population ages in the United States and many other parts of the world, health-care workers are even more in demand. Many health-care workers will also be needed to work with those who have problems with substance abuse or other types of problems discussed in this chapter. Administrators and other business-related employees will be needed in health facilities. What types of jobs in the health-care industry might interest you? Visit a major career-related Web site such as Monster.com or Career-Builder.com, linked through the textbook Web page at **www.mhhe .com/lamberton4e.** Enter "health care" in the job title search field. Report on jobs available in health-care areas that fit your qualifications and interests.

Whose Job Is It?

Sanjay Patel was walking quickly through the office building on his way to a meeting with the other managers when his assistant, Robyn, ran up behind him. "Mr. Patel, I know you're busy, but I just can't figure out how to finish this budget report. I know it's due by tomorrow, do you think you could help me with it?"

"Sure, Robyn, let me take a look at it. I'll get back to you later today."

A few moments later, Phil, a sales associate in Sanjay's division, stopped him. "Sorry to bother you, but I didn't get those sales projections finished. I know I said I could probably finish them by today's meeting, but I couldn't find the information from the Midwest locations."

"All right, I can get that information for you this afternoon. I'll get back to you on it," Sanjay answered.

That afternoon, Phil called. "Did you have a chance to finish the sales projections? I'd like to get them over to the head office today."

"I'm still working on it," was Sanjay's reply.

About an hour later, Robyn came by Sanjay's office. "How is it going? Did you finish the budget report for me?"

At about that time, it occurred to Sanjay that something was not right with this situation. How did he, as the manager, become responsible for reporting back to his own assistant and others who should have been working for him?

Case Study Questions

1. Explain the type of time-use issue that has become problematic in this case. How could this situation, if left to continue, lead to even more interference with workplace productivity in the future?

2. Who has a greater time-management problem: Sanjay, or the two other employees who report to him? What would you suggest Sanjay do to improve the situation and increase productivity? What should Robyn and Phil do differently?

3. Has a situation like this ever happened to you? What did you do at the time? What would you do differently if it happened to you again?

Absent on the Job

Amir Abali has been supervising 10 employees in a small advertising business for the past several years. He likes his job and feels fortunate that he has had very little employee turnover.

Several months ago Amir noticed that two of his employees, Yvonne Williams and Janelle Thompson, were talking without getting much work done. Janelle was making a lot of personal calls. Then Janelle's performance began to decline. Now, she just doesn't seem interested in her job anymore. Even when she is at work, she seems absent; sometimes she looks like she has been crying. Amir has heard Janelle yell at the secretary over little things. It seems that Yvonne is being affected, too: she seems distracted, and Janelle often interrupts her work to talk. Amir feels that he has to do something.

Amir wants to approach Janelle and find out what is wrong. He suspects that she is experiencing some problems in her family life and feels uncomfortable about bringing up personal problems at work. He talks to a friend who tells him to refer Janelle to the company's EAP. Because Amir's employer is small, they don't have the same resources as his friend's larger company.

Amir decides to take action. He calls Janelle into his office. "Janelle, it seems lately that your work is slipping, and you seem distracted. Is something wrong? Is there something going on that I need to know about?"

Janelle seems very uncomfortable and embarrassed. "No, no, everything is fine. I've just been a little preoccupied with some things. I'm sorry, I'll get it all straightened out. Don't worry."

A few weeks later, nothing has changed. Should Amir give her a disciplinary warning? Call in a counselor? Demand to know what is going on?

Case Study Questions

1. What is going on with Janelle? Do you agree with Amir that she is probably having personal family problems? Could anything else be going on here?

2. What are Amir's responsibilities here? What should he do?

3. What could and what should the company do to see that Amir, Janelle, and the other employees are all treated fairly and responsibly?

HUMAN RELATIONS AND YOUR FUTURE SUCCESS

In the Workplace: The Meaning of Success

SITUATION

It was the morning of graduation day, and Ellie and three of her friends were having a last coffee and bagel together at the TechnoEdge, their favorite snack spot close to campus. "I thought this day would never come!" said Ellie excitedly. "I finally feel like I succeeded at something big."

"But you've had other successes—getting jobs to help pay for college, getting

good grades, getting your daughter to and from preschool every day," replied her first friend, Roslyn.

"That's just regular stuff; it doesn't count," said Zoey, another friend.

"Well then, what would feel like a success to you, Zoey?" asked the third friend, Vicky.

"Winning the lottery!" laughed Zoey.

"For me, being elected president!" laughed Vicky.

LEARNING objectives

After studying this chapter, you will be able to:

1. Give examples of how human relations will play a role in your future.

2. Explain the relationship among self-motivation, self-direction, and success.

3. Identify why fear is the enemy of success.

4. Define positive psychology.

5. Explain the importance of finding your niche.

6. Describe how to prepare for a career choice.

7. List the steps in preparing your application materials.

8. Explain how to prepare for a job interview.

9. Identify the follow-up steps after an interview.

STRATEGIES FOR SUCCESS

Strategy 19.1   Practice a Job Interview

Strategy 19.2   Make an Inventory of Your Skills

Strategy 19.3   Move Toward a Happier Life

"I just want to be a rock star!" said Roslyn, in her best rock star voice.

"Seriously," said Ellie, "finishing school is important. It has been my biggest goal for years. Now I can concentrate on my next big goals. I really want to find a job I like, to make sure I'm in the right career, and to have time for my family. *Then* I'll feel like a complete success!"

"Wow, you don't ask for much!" teased Vicky.

DISCOVERY

Later that afternoon, as all four friends lined up for the graduation procession, Ellie said, "Well, here we go! Here's hoping we all get what we want out of life!"

THINK ABOUT IT

What are your goals for the future? What do you want to get out of life? How do *you* define success?

HUMAN RELATIONS IN YOUR FUTURE

Many changes will undoubtedly take place in the next several years in typical home life and in the workplace. How you react in your work and personal environment in the next few years will be determined mainly by you. Regardless of the circumstances surrounding your life, the final reality you live with will be the one you create. With that in mind, how can you fit successfully into a changing corporate world? In this chapter, you will learn about ways to increase your individual success in the workplace.

Your Definition of Success

Until recent years, success in the business world was often defined as the *bottom line,* or the profit margin. Employees themselves often defined their individual success simply by their paychecks and individual wealth. In return, employers expected their employees to be loyal to their companies and not change jobs. The 1980s were called the "Me Decade" because amassing more and more material goods was usually the main motivation for individual business success. Now, in the early 21st century, many Americans define success in a different way.

According to this redefinition, employees should be able to feel a sense of self-satisfaction and fulfillment at work and also have the time and freedom to lead a satisfying family life or to spend time on hobbies or outside interests. The successful balance of work and family life is not just a topic that all of us in the general public are interested in. This topic is also of ongoing interest to business leaders, policymakers, and social scientists, as well. It is often called one of the most important issues of today's workforce. Business writer Harris Sussman believes that this is one of the diversity issues in today's workforce that is going to force corporate America to restructure itself.[1]

This importance is partly because of the increasing diversity of the workforce, especially with women working at all levels in greater numbers than ever before. Work and family issues continue to be important because employers need to attract and keep good employees. Recognizing that employees' priorities are changing is one way to do that.

The rapid growth of Internet commerce is making flexibility increasingly possible in terms of work locations. More people than ever before are now able to work from home, from a hotel room, or even a car or commuter train. Corporations are beginning to realize more and more

more about...

Harris Sussman

Learn more about the views of the influential business writer **Harris Sussman** through his Web page at **http://sussman.org** or through the course Web site at **www.mhhe.com/lamberton4e.** Find out more about his ideas on challenges to a changing workforce, the importance of education, and the urgency of understanding human relations with a world view.

that to attract valuable employees, they have to keep up with American families and make benefits packages more attractive and useful to them. With more than half of all American mothers in the workforce, and with the general aging of the U.S. population, employees today often need **intergenerational care,** which is day care not only for children but also for elderly family members. The National Council of Aging states that over 40 percent of the American workforce is taking care of both children and elderly family members, and that number will rise dramatically as the American population ages even more in the next several decades.

This **sandwich generation,** middle-aged adults taking care of both children and elderly parents at the same time, includes about 16 million Americans. In the next two decades, 60 million Americans will be ages 66–84, and many of them will need part-time or full-time care to add even more adults to the sandwich generation.[2] About two-thirds of the members of the sandwich generation work outside the home, either full-time or part-time. Most of those caring for two generations feel more squeezed than stressed, mostly just pressed for time. Overwhelmingly, people say that their family is the most important thing in their life—a fact that employers need to remember when making extra demands on employees' time or pressuring them to make a decision that may feel like an ultimatum.

Diversity issues arise when talking about work and family topics. White non-Hispanic Americans have the lowest rates of sandwich-generation responsibilities, but there are more of them in total numbers. Hispanic Americans usually have more children and living parents to take care of. They also are more likely to have additional older relatives (aunts, uncles, family friends) and children (nieces, nephews) to take care of. The kind of care they perform includes both financial help and personal care. Asian Americans provide even more care, taking parents to appointments, and doing other time-consuming tasks. They are also more likely to feel stress from the time pressures, and guilt over feeling they should be able to do more. African Americans also report facing stressful situations, but are more likely to say they have family networks (siblings, cousins) to share in the tasks. They are more likely than other groups to ask for help from doctors or agency resources. When thinking about *your* future success, keep in mind what Harris Sussman called "the challenge of the century," being mindful of diversity. In other words, these diversity statistics remind us that when we talk about "diversity issues in the workplace" we are really just talking about people, as members of families, with lives not too different from our own.

Overall, most people in all groups say they are optimistic about their futures and their ability to handle their sandwich-generation duties. As our nation's life expectancy rates rise, employers should expect even higher numbers of these sandwich-generation employees.[3] Companies

intergenerational care
Day care not only for children but also for elderly family members.

sandwich generation
Middle-aged adults who are taking responsibility for both dependent children and parents at the same time, and being sandwiched by these obligations.

NEW DEFINITIONS OF SUCCESS IN THE 21ST CENTURY

Changing values and business conditions have contributed to a shift in how Americans define success, which now often includes an emphasis on satisfaction both at work and outside of it. *How do you define success?*

When a son of one of your authors was in middle school (junior high), he wandered into the living room one day where his mother was reading the newspaper, and said "Hey, Mom, what do Chinese people call Chinese food?" She replied warily, "I don't know, what do they call it?" expecting either a bad joke or an offensive remark, one that would require a discussion of appreciation for diverse world cultures. He responded, "They just call it food. You see? It's just their regular food to them, so they wouldn't call it *Chinese* food, right? It's just food," and he wandered away again. She was both relieved and pleased: with this brief conversation, he showed that he could take another perspective, a "world view" that would serve him well in preparing for future employment—and life—in a world of diversity.

more about...

Eldercare Locator

Do you need help finding care for an elderly family member? The *Eldercare Locator* is a public service of the U.S. Department of Health and Human Services, Administration on Aging. This service, started in 1991, helps connect older Americans and their caregivers with information on services for seniors. Go to **www.eldercare .gov/Eldercare/Public/Home.asp** to find services in your area. This is also linked through the textbook Web site at **www.mhhe.com/ lamberton4e.**

will need to be flexible in allowing employees to find a balance between work and family with these complex responsibilities. As an employee, you may be thinking about—or even facing— such issues at a time when you thought your focus would be just on your own career.

Over the past 15 years or so, companies have been getting creative in providing care for employees' dependents. Some companies offer day care for dependents regardless of age (from infants to the elderly), and some offer a cafeteria-style benefits package in which employees can choose only the benefits they want. Other companies offer intergenerational care where children and elders are cared for in the same facility. The Stride Rite Shoe Company was the first to offer employee-sponsored, on-site day care more than 30 years ago. It was also the first to offer an intergenerational care center, which is also employee-sponsored and on-site. The company reports great success with the program, saying that everyone—even the community—benefits from it.[4]

Should your definition of success include success as a family member? Ask yourself this question the next time you contemplate what success really means to you.

Self-Esteem, Confidence, and Success

In this textbook, you learned about the importance of self-esteem as a beginning point for human relations. A key to building self-esteem is developing confidence in yourself and your decisions. Confidence is something that has to come from within you, but you can build it up with positive self-talk. You can tell yourself that you are making the best decision you can based on the evidence that you have, then avoid criticizing yourself if things do not work out. People who act in a self-confident way on the outside, whether they feel it or not on the inside, are often described and evaluated by others as being capable and competent. Because they are treated as if they are competent, they begin to feel and act that way more than before. Their behavior becomes a self-fulfilling prophecy: by acting with self-confidence, they become more self-confident.

Self-Discipline and Success

Self-discipline is the ability to teach or guide yourself to set up and carry out your goals and plans. This is important to your future success because to carry out the plans you have made and to meet your goals, you must teach yourself strategies to keep working toward those goals.

According to Denis Waitley, an expert in motivation and performance, self-discipline includes breaking bad habits and replacing them with new ones.[5] This can be accomplished through positive self-talk.

Waitley reminds us that the kind of self-talk we do creates our self-image—either better or worse. The choice is ours. If we tell ourselves that we *can't* do something, then we won't be able to do it. This same observation was made decades ago by American industrialist Henry Ford, who is quoted as saying "Whether you think that you can, or that you can't, you are usually right."[6] Use positive self-talk (see Chapter 2) to break bad habits and build on successes. When you find you are slipping back into self-defeating internal messages ("It's no use; I just can't do it"), use self-discipline to demand from yourself that you switch to positive self-talk. Giving up is easy. Sitting down and figuring out what you need to do to start a pattern of behavior that builds toward a goal takes a lot more effort.

If you're stuck in negative self-talk and having trouble thinking of things that are *right* with you, Waitley suggests that you write a list of your professional and personal assets. List your skills, experiences, potential, and talent. That is, write down what you're good at. This list can become your script for your future self-talk; refer to it often. When you have an important task or meeting coming up at work, close your eyes and picture yourself succeeding at the task, or running the meeting successfully in a professional manner. This visualization technique is the same one used by successful athletes at all levels of competition. It works!

Use this same self-discipline to help you meet your goals. Once you have identified these goals and prioritized them (see Working

self-discipline

The ability to teach or guide yourself to set up and carry out your goals and plans.

SELF-DISCIPLINE IN YOUR LIFE

You can teach yourself self-discipline, then use your self-discipline to develop and maintain winning habits. Although habits, like getting up early and working out, may not feel good at first, their lasting effects will contribute to your overall success. *What are the main characteristics of self-discipline?*

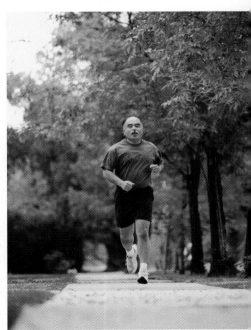

Danita had trouble arriving to class on time, and her grades were beginning to slip. After doing worse than she had expected on her midterms, she started telling herself, "I am a good student, and I arrive on time for my classes." Over a short period of time, she made this a part of her inner belief system, and it became a new habit.

It Out 19.1 at the end of the chapter), you will need to muster your self-discipline in order to put a plan of action into place. Start each day by asking yourself, "What will I do today to make the best use of my time to lead me closer to that goal?" Refer to (and revise) your goals often enough that you are aware of them and they help guide your actions. When faced with a decision, ask yourself, "Which choice will better lead me toward meeting my goals?"

Don't be afraid to ask for advice and to learn from others. Get to know people who have goals similar to your own. Find out what their action plan is like, and how they overcame setbacks. People with unresolved problems or those frustrated by failing to achieve goals will be contagious to you, says Waitley; that is, they are not very helpful. And always aim high! You may not reach your highest goal, but you'll achieve a lot more than you will when you aim low.

Taking responsibility is an important part of self-discipline.[7] This means feeling in control of your life, having the power to change things, and feeling comfortable about doing so. Taking responsibility does not include trying to change or control other people, but it means that they don't control you, either.

"I just don't feel like exercising right now; I'd rather watch television." "I don't have time to cook a good dinner—I'll just grab a snack and eat something healthy later." Do these statements sound familiar? Another component of self-discipline is to make conscious choices that lead to a more healthful and productive life. Chapter 14 discussed the harmful effects of stress, the need for maintaining a healthy lifestyle, strategies for stress reduction, the importance of building in leisure time, and maintaining a support system of friends and family. These ideas all relate to long-term success because they promote health and happiness. Remember that it takes self-discipline to maintain a healthy lifestyle.

more about...

Success and Goal-Setting

A **goal** is a purpose, "a reason to be in the race."

—Success author Russ von Hoelscher

SELF-MOTIVATION, SELF-DIRECTION, AND SUCCESS

Psychological studies show that the strongest kinds of motivation come from internal rewards, not external ones. Self-motivation is central to this idea of **self-direction,** which is the ability to set short-term and long-term goals for yourself.

The more specific your goals, the clearer they seem, and the better they work. **Short-term goals** are the specific plans of action for things you would like to accomplish right now or in the immediate future, such as finishing a specific course or work assignment. **Long-term goals** are those things you decide to work for after developing a life plan for the future, such as moving up the corporate ladder in accounting, after you have completed your accounting degree, or starting a family. Both short- and long-term goals are important to individual success; breaking long-term goals into manageable short-term ones is a way of creating a ladder of success that increases your chances of future success in the long term. Refer to Chapter 18 for suggestions on setting up a time schedule that includes short-term and long-term goals.

> **self-direction**
>
> The ability to set short-term and long-term goals for yourself.

> **short-term goals**
>
> The specific plans of action for things you would like to accomplish right now or in the immediate future.

> **long-term goals**
>
> Those things you decide to work for after developing a life plan for the future.

FEAR: THE ENEMY OF SUCCESS

Fear is a negative emotion that can stop you from carrying out your plans and working toward your goals. To fight fear, you must first identify your fears and then work toward eliminating them. One of the most common fears in the business world is the **impostor phenomenon,** in which successful people are afraid that they did not really succeed because of their own talents and hard work. They are afraid that they are not smart, hardworking, or talented enough to continue to succeed, and that someone will find them out as impostors. They may live in terrible fear that they will somehow be found out, and that they have gotten away with something. They feel other people have just made a mistake about them, and they live in dread of the mistake being discovered.[8]

> **impostor phenomenon**
>
> A feeling successful people experience when they are afraid that they did not really succeed because of their own talents and hard work.

> **fear of failure**
>
> The fear that occurs when people are afraid of looking bad in front of others.

Another common fear is **fear of failure,** which occurs when people are afraid of looking bad in front of others. People with extreme fear of failure may stop trying to achieve anything, or stop trying anything new, just to avoid the possibility of being criticized. After learning about the human relations principles discussed throughout this book, some people are reluctant to put these principles into action: they fear failing and then being judged

> **Material Success**
>
> If your goals include **material success,** that is fine, but be careful that your possessions do not end up possessing you.

more about...

When the oldest son of one of your authors was seven years old, he asked his mother why she was in college (she was in graduate school at the time). They had a long talk about the importance of college, different types of colleges, preparing for college, strategies in paying for college, and so on. He announced at that time that he was definitely going to college, and if he didn't have any money, then he would find a way for his favorite activity—basketball—to pay for his expenses. His mother nodded earnestly but had a hard time keeping from laughing. Ten years later, this son signed a National Letter of Intent to play basketball at one of the top academic universities in the country, an NCAA Division I school. Just a coincidence? Not really: during those 10 years, he had joined every school, playground, and traveling basketball team he could find. He played ball four or five hours a day, rain or shine. He kept his grades up, stayed involved in leadership activities at school, and worked hard to be the kind of student athlete sought by college recruiters. In other words, his strong self-direction allowed him to set short-term and long-term goals, and he was self-disciplined enough to remain motivated through the years it took to meet these goals.

in a negative way. Although it does seem easier to not "rock the boat" by putting new principles into place, it is actually harder to live your life without focusing on self-esteem, success, and more effective communication skills. Try these new ideas, and you will not only find less failure than you probably expected, you may be surprised at how well they work!

People who have **fear of success** have not experienced much success in their lives, so they feel they do not deserve it. They may feel that they will not live up to the reputation that goes along with success, and that others will reject or demote them. They may find the feeling of success so unfamiliar that it is painfully uncomfortable.

How can people eliminate these fears? One key is to practice emotions that are just the opposite, such as courage and self-confidence. It is impossible to feel two opposite feelings at the same time, so you can probably outweigh the fear with something more positive. In some cases, the fear may be so powerful that counseling or psychotherapy may be the best way to eliminate it.

fear of success

The fear that occurs when people who have not experienced much success in their lives feel as though they do not deserve it.

POSITIVE PSYCHOLOGY

Fear can be a barrier to success, as we have just discussed. Can that barrier be overcome? Can we potentially train children—and adults—to completely avoid such barriers, and reach the levels of success they have set as goals? Many psychologists would say yes. One of the newest and most exciting developments in psychology in recent years

Research and Reflect

Find out more information on positive psychology and authentic happiness. Visit Dr. Seligman's "Reflective Happiness" Web site at **www.reflectivehappiness.com/,** or the "Positive Psychology" or the "Authentic Happiness" Web site at **www.authentichappiness.org/.** Or, take a look at the *Time* magazine issue of January 17, 2005, which features this growing movement (linked to the Reflective Happiness Web site, and to *Time* magazine at **www.time.com.**). These Web sites are also linked to the textbook Web site at **www.mhhe.com/lamberton4e.** Summarize your findings. What do you think about this newer area of psychology?

is a movement called **positive psychology.**[9] This new area came about as a result of some leading psychologists thinking that psychology is too focused on what's *wrong* with people, rather than what is *right* with us. Martin Seligman, whose work you learned about in Chapter 4 with his ideas about learned optimism, is the person who really got this idea going. In Seligman's view, when we focus only on what makes people unhappy or mentally unhealthy and on how to treat those problems, we miss half the picture of what it means to be human. The other half, says Seligman, is the part of humans that is joyful, satisfied with life, and maintains healthy self-esteem. This healthier side of humans holds the traits and strengths that lead to success.

Positive psychologists believe that we all have strengths that can overcome barriers to healthy self-development. These barriers include low self-esteem, for example, along with its related fears. The strengths that protect against poor outcomes in mental health include optimism, good interpersonal skills, courage, good work ethic, perseverance, honesty, and ability to think toward the future. These strengths can be learned through training. And when people begin using them, such ideals become a type of self-fulfilling prophecy. Building these strengths not only helps improve poor performance and raises self-esteem; building the strengths also prevents such problems from happening in the future. The first step in learning to be positive, says Seligman, is to stop thinking in terms of catastrophes and defeat. Learn to see bad events as temporary, not permanent crises. Get into the habit of disputing beliefs you hold, or even statements by others, that one rejection determines a person's lack of ability forever. Later in this chapter we will talk more about applying and interviewing for

> **positive psychology**
>
> A subfield within psychology that focuses on experiences, individual traits, and institutions that create happiness and hope, rather than focusing on mental illness.

jobs. Keep positive psychology in mind when applying for jobs: very few people are offered the most wonderful job in the world with their first job application. Incidentally, says Seligman, what really makes people happy is not tons of money; but meaningful relationships and spiritual faith.

FINDING YOUR NICHE

finding your niche

Finding the place where you thrive and are most content; includes finding the type of job or career where you will be most satisfied.

To be successful throughout your life, you must find a place where you thrive and are most content. This is called **finding your niche,** which includes finding the kind of job or career where you will be most satisfied. Finding your niche and promoting career success require that you understand what your skills are. Richard Bolles, an expert on job-hunting and career change, describes three "families" of skills:[10]

1. **Skills with information or data** include gathering or creating data, managing it, computing it, storing it, and putting it to use. People with these skills may become data entry technicians, computer programmers, research analysts, or demographers.

2. **Skills in working with people** include helping and serving others, counseling, entertaining, supervising, negotiating, and mentoring. People with these skills may find satisfaction in becoming counselors or psychologists, occupational or physical therapists, teachers, actors or comedians, consultants, sports coaches, or politicians.

3. **Skills in working with things** include specific skills in athletics, in the fine arts, with construction, and with agriculture or farming. People who have these skills may enjoy work as farmers, construction workers, cabinetmakers, dancers, architects, botanists, artists, or professional athletes.

more about...

Niche

In biological or ecological terminology, **niche** means any place that is best suited for a living creature (including a human, animal, plant, or sea life) to survive.

See Strategy for Success 19.2 for more information on these sets of skills.

PREPARE FOR A CAREER CHOICE

Some people seem to know, from very early on, what type of job they will eventually do. They select high school classes and decide on their educational plan (business school, two-year or four-year college or university)

When he was about five years old, another son of one of your authors announced one day, "When I grow up, I am going to be the garbage man at the zoo." His amused mother asked him why he had chosen that particular occupation. "Because I really like the zoo, and I am good at taking out the trash," he responded with pride. This is such a simple and logical response from a child, but reasoning that we can all learn from: discover what you do well, in an environment you enjoy. In other words, find your niche. More than 20 years have passed since this young man announced his career plans. No, he's not the trash collector at the zoo, but he *has* succeeded in finding his niche (as an audio-video engineer).

on that basis. They select a college major and specific courses in preparation for the career they want. Other people are not so sure what they will "be" when they grow up. They may go through years of education and still not have a career figured out. They may try out several careers before deciding what fits. Still others may decide midway through their employment years that they are ready to change careers and do something new.

If you find yourself in either of the "questioning" categories, then you may want to investigate your college's available resources. Does your college have a career guidance center? Does your school offer a career planning class? Take advantage of these resources in your search. If your school offers vocational interest testing, take the tests. There are also thousands of online sites that offer career guidance; some are free, others charge a fee, and the quality varies greatly among all the sites.

But before investing time and (possibly) money into these career guidance tools, you should first do some introspection—that is, looking inward. It is difficult to know how to get somewhere if you don't know where you're going. So, where are you going with a career plan? If you have never really thought about it before, take some time now to think about what it is you really want out of a career. In the "big picture," what is it that you want to do with your life? What will make you feel fulfilled? Start with some very general questions about what you want to do. Is there something you have always felt passionate about—a career in the arts, data crunching, or a helping profession? Is there a specific type of company you've always been interested in—a Fortune 500 company, a transnational firm, or a nonprofit agency? Are you looking forward more to the work itself, or to the paycheck? When you envision your work environment, are you there alone in peace and quiet, or is it a busy and lively place? Taking time to answer these

WHERE IS YOUR NICHE?

Finding your niche means finding what you really enjoy doing and being able to make your living from it. This can include traditional careers, such as teaching or medicine, and it can include careers that never before existed. *Where do you think your niche might be?*

questions will help you begin to frame your answers. In the next section of this chapter, you will begin to narrow down your interests. (See Figures 19.1 and 19.2.)

figure 19.1

PERCENT CHANGE IN EMPLOYMENT IN OCCUPATIONS PROJECTED TO GROW FASTEST, 2002–2012

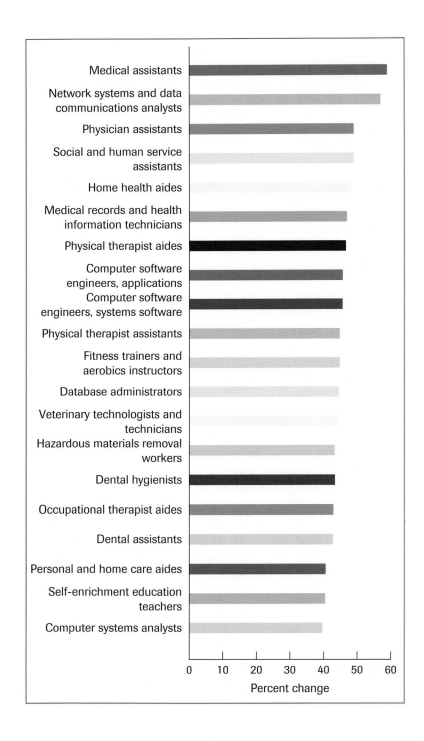

Finding Your Niche

Richard Bolles' best-selling book *What Color Is Your Parachute?* has been revised and published regularly since 1970. It's among the top-selling books of its kind in the country. Bolles has an accompanying Web site located at **www.suggestica.com/richardbolles** and linked through the textbook Web site at **www.mhhe.com/lamberton4e** that provides a wonderful resource full of advice and practice exercises for job seekers. It is meant to be used along with the book, but some exercises are also valuable alone. Go to the Web site and link to "Tests & Advice" and then "Career Tests." Take these popular career tests and report back on what you learned about yourself and your career interests. Your instructor might have some other exercises for you based on this Internet site.

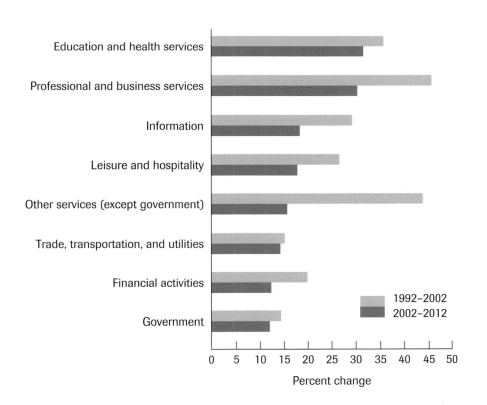

figure 19.2

PERCENT CHANGE IN WAGE AND SALARY EMPLOYMENT, SERVICE-PROVIDING INDUSTRY DIVISIONS, 1992–2002, AND PROJECTED 2002–2012

PREPARE YOUR APPLICATION MATERIALS

In the final sections of this chapter, we turn our focus to specific steps you can take to improve your success in preparing job application materials and interviewing for jobs.

résumé

A brief summary of a person's work experience and qualifications, often submitted with an employment application.

cover letter

A letter sent along with other documents (in this case, employment documents) to give additional information.

employment portfolio

A collection of materials and work samples related to employment qualifications and experience.

Before you actually apply for a job, prepare your materials. These include a **résumé,** a **cover letter,** and sometimes an **employment portfolio.**[11]

Résumé

Your résumé is a short summary of what you have learned, and what you can do. There is no one "right way" to format this document. In fact, there are probably hundreds of templates available for you to use as models. They can be found online, on your computer's word processing system, and at your college's career center, among other sources. You can write one yourself, or pay to have one built by a professional résumé writer. Many online sites that offer this service also provide basic templates to look at that you can adapt for your own use. But consider carefully whether or not to *post* your résumé online: according to Richard Bolles, thousands of people post résumés, but very few employers read them.

How much information should you include on a résumé? A student just entering the job market will probably have a résumé about one page long. Even someone with a long work history (changing careers, for example) should keep the résumé to a maximum of about two pages. This sounds short, but human resources specialists say that most employers will spend *30 seconds or less* looking at each résumé. This means your résumé has to be short and to the point, and it has to stand out.

When writing a résumé, start with your name, address, telephone numbers, and e-mail addresses where you can be reached. If you have your own Web page related to your work, include the URL (Web address). This information should be at the top of the page, centered or grouped at either margin.

Some people write a one- or two-sentence Statement of Job Objectives (placed just after the name and address information) describing the type of opportunity they are looking for, but this is not a requirement. Some recruiters find it helpful in narrowing down applications; others say it keeps applicants out of the running for jobs for which they may have been a good fit. You may want to include a short section called Profile or Qualifications instead, which gives a quick summary of what you can do, and what you are interested in. Also, it is perfectly acceptable to use different job objective statements for different types of jobs.

Place your educational history in one section, and job history or skills in another. Use short phrases instead of sentences or paragraphs. Use action verbs (e.g., *developed, implemented, created, utilized*) to make your résumé more interesting to read. Although brightly colored paper and unusual font or appearance will make your résumé stand out, avoid using these. They may make it stand out in a negative way. To make it stand out and get noticed in a way that makes an employer want to contact you, your better strategy is to make the résumé appear clean, neat, and readable, free of errors in dates or information, with perfect spelling. This means you need to check your spelling—and then check it again.

Do not include potentially illegal personal information about yourself! Leave out your age, marital status, parental status, religion, race or ethnicity, disability status, and any other such facts. It may have been common to include this information years ago, but not now. It is illegal for employers to ask those things of you, so many employers prefer not to see these on your résumé. In this way, they avoid putting themselves in a situation in which an applicant can say he or she was excluded because of such factors. Listing hobbies and extracurricular activities, on the other hand, is usually acceptable and often helpful; but leave out any that would identify you by the factors just listed (religion, race, ethnicity, etc.).

Some résumés are built chronologically (listed with most recent events first and moving backward in time); others are grouped by job skills. This second type is called a **functional résumé.** Information in a functional résumé lists the specific functions of the jobs you have held. Use action words. Functional résumés are not as common as chronological résumés. They are used more often by people who have big gaps in employment or those who have had a lot of career changes, since they allow you to highlight certain skills and talents, without drawing attention to dates. Most employers are more accustomed to reading chronological résumés.

functional résumé
A résumé grouped by job skills, in which the specific functions of the jobs you have held are listed.

Not everyone agrees on what information you should leave out of a résumé. You are not required to list every short-term or part-time job you have held, or those irrelevant to the job you are applying for. But leaving a lot of things out can look to some prospective employers as though you are hiding something. Include major jobs you have held, and those you held a long time. At the same time, you can include experience that is not directly job related that shows some skills you will need for the new job. This would include volunteer activities, leadership positions at your school, or other community service activities.

You can be almost certain that a prospective employer will check your references. Employers want to make sure you really do have the experience you listed. They also want to be able to ask questions about your work habits and talents. List references who are in the best position to evaluate you. If you have not held a job, these references may be instructors with whom you have taken classes, or supervisors you worked with at volunteer agencies. If you choose to say "References furnished on request" on your résumé, be sure to have that information available for employers if they ask.

In today's job market, many companies (especially large ones) electronically scan résumés into a "reader" that looks for key terms that fit with their job descriptions. Even small companies may send résumés out to another service provider to be scanned. The key terms are often related to education, equipment, or common terminology for a job. If you see such terms in the job description, include them in your résumé. The fact that your résumé might be scanned is another reason to use plain paper with a standard font (rather than bright paper with an unusual font) that is easier for the scanner to "read." Avoid underlining, using italics, shadowing, and putting words in bold. You may want to bring a copy of a standard résumé, along with a scannable résumé, to your job interview, just in case you need them both.

Application Forms

Some employers allow you to download an employment application or go to their place of employment to pick up a form to take away with you. Others want you to fill out the application on the spot.

If you fill out an application at the company site, be sure to write neatly, using a blue or black pen (and bring some correction fluid in case you make a mistake). Bring a summary sheet with you that includes dates of employment, names of supervisors, and names and telephone numbers for your former employers. By doing this you can avoid the embarrassment of asking someone at the job site for a phone book, or for computer access.

Cover Letters

A résumé has to be short and to the point. It typically will not include full sentences, just short phrases. It is difficult, then, for the résumé to show who you really are. A cover letter, on the other hand, allows the real *you* to come out. Write a new cover letter for each job application. Tailor each letter to the job you are applying for. Instead of writing with a negative-sounding tone ("I really need this job"), write with a more positive tone ("Here's how your company will benefit by hiring me"). Learn as much as possible about the company you are applying to, and use that information to include specific points about your skills that fit with the company.

A cover letter should be written in complete sentences. Check your spelling and grammar; this document also (like the résumé) needs to be perfect. Direct your letter to the human resources director or personnel supervisor by name (call the company, or check the Web site, for this information). Be confident and enthusiastic, without going overboard. Use standard greetings and closings—"Dear Ms. Ruiz," and "Sincerely, Tate Jasper"—and include your address and contact information under your signature.

Apply Online

Online applications are used by many companies today. These can make applying for jobs easier for you, and easier for employers. Follow the instructions, and have all the information at hand so you can complete it in one sitting (many do not allow a "save" function). Check your answers carefully before submitting your application. Some employers also ask applicants to e-mail a résumé or other materials. Find out whether these employers prefer an attachment, or information copied directly into an e-mail message. If you are attaching a file with your résumé or cover letter, you can use the standard format you have already prepared. If you are copying and pasting information into an e-mail message, make sure it is readable, using plain symbols that will transfer electronically.

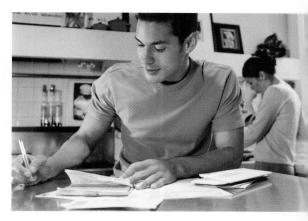

PERSONALIZING YOUR APPLICATION

Writing your résumé, cover letter, and other application materials can be challenging, since you can prepare them conservatively, creatively, or somewhere in between. *How do you choose to express your personality, style, and talents in job application materials?*

Prepare a Portfolio

Some job applications require a work portfolio. These are more common in jobs that create products: art, journalism, teaching, photography, and so on. Portfolios include samples of your work. But even traditional companies may want to learn more about you with a job portfolio. You can include your scannable and regular résumé, a statement of goals and philosophy (e.g., a teaching philosophy), copies of awards or scholarships, copies of transcripts and degrees, licenses or certificates, military records (if appropriate), and copies of published work. Include information on conferences you participated in, and detailed reference information. Keep your portfolio current. You may want to keep this material in a three-ring binder, or in a zippered folder. Some people keep an online portfolio, with the information just listed available on a Web site. If you choose to do so, be sure to list the Web address on your résumé.

Sometimes employers ask for portfolio information in DVD or CD form. With the technology available today, you may be able to make these yourself. If not, you will likely be able to find a professional service in your area to make them for you.

PREPARE FOR THE JOB INTERVIEW

Practicing and preparing for job interviews are essential. You can improve on this skill just as you would any other skill.[12]

Preparing for the Interview

After you have successfully gone through the application screening process, you will be invited for an interview. It will be very difficult later to live down a bad first impression, so put your best effort forward in the interview.

You will have some advance notice about the interview. Take some time to find out about the company. A common interview question is, "What do you know about our company?" Make sure your reply is *not* "Nothing." Look up the company online and read its posted publications. Ask other people about them, or contact the local Chamber of Commerce or the Better Business Bureau. Arrive early for the interview and ask for pamphlets on the company. Do your homework!

Arrive at the interview on time—or better yet, early. Do this in case you have to look for a parking place, fight traffic, or find the Human Resources office. Your appearance counts. Make sure you are rested, clean, groomed, and dressed appropriately in business clothes.

In the interview, take a deep breath and relax before you begin. Nonverbal communication is very important, and you want to appear poised and confident. Remember your mother's advice and stand up or sit up straight, and smile. Introduce yourself, offering to shake hands with the interviewers. Speak clearly. Make your handshake firm, not limp, but without bone-crushing intensity. Make eye contact with interviewers while introducing yourself, and while answering questions.

Listen carefully to each question. Some questions are long, with more than one part. Others phrase the important part of the question right at the end. Keep a positive tone in your answers. This means you must avoid complaining about, gossiping about, blaming, or insulting your last workplace, even if your job there ended badly. Keep your answers tactful and clear. After the interview, thank your interviewers, and smile. Keep in mind that if you've been invited for an interview, the company has already decided you are qualified. A major reason to hold interviews is to see how well applicants will fit with the company—a sort of personality test. Be honest with your answers. If you "fake" your way into a job, you will likely not be very happy there.

Most interviewers allow you to ask questions after the interview. Use this time to find out what the exact duties are, what a typical day is like, or what the management style consists of. Find out about performance evaluations, and the possibility for advancement and further education or training opportunities. This is also a good point for you to show that you have knowledge about the company. Ask questions that reveal that knowledge.

If you are the person giving the interview, here are some suggestions to have a better interview. Develop relevant questions ahead of time. "Silly" questions ("If you were a car, what type would you be?") can tell you how an applicant reacts on the spot, but may not tell you much about how the person performs on the job. You can develop relevant questions from the job description. Do *not* ask questions about age, religion, race, gender, marital status, national origin, or disability. These are illegal. If you have trouble remembering what is or isn't a legal question, use the

What Interests You?

What kind of career catches your interest? What do people in this job actually do? Go to the U.S. Department of Labor's Career Information Web page at **www.bls .gov/k12**/ and linked through the textbook Web site at **www.mhhe.com/ lamberton4e** and open the links that interest you to get some ideas about possible careers that fit your interests.

BFOQ test. Ask yourself, "Does this question request information about a bona fide occupational qualification?" If the answer is no or maybe, avoid or rephrase the question.

Greet the interviewee, introduce yourself, and put the person at ease. You will get more thorough answers if the person is at ease. Explain how many questions there will be, and how long the interview will take. Give basic information about the company. Ask "fact-checking" questions from the application or résumé. Be courteous. After your questions, allow the applicant to ask questions of you.

> **BFOQ (bona fide occupational qualification)**
> Information related to the job you are applying for; does not include personal information, such as age, religion, or race.

Interview Structure

As an applicant, you should know what type of interview you will be preparing for. The most common types (structures) include a standard interview, with the applicant and at least one interviewer; and a group interview, with more than one applicant and a panel of interviewers. You may also have a **stress interview,** in which the interviewers try to make you uncomfortable to see how you will react (not used as often, but helpful in hiring for some types of high-stress jobs). Some interviews are conducted on the telephone or in a video format.

> **stress interview**
> An interview in which the interviewer tries to make you uncomfortable to see how you will react.

AFTER THE INTERVIEW

When job applicants are preparing for the interview, they often overlook including that period of time just after the interview. There are some crucial details to remember.

Thank-You Notes

Thank-you notes are sent to a company soon after an interview. They remind the company about you, while showing appreciation for the interview. Don't use these to persuade the company to hire you (since

During middle school and high school, Jacob liked to cook. When other kids found out, they teased him without mercy: it just wasn't seen as "macho" for a guy to be in the kitchen. But his self-esteem and confidence were healthy enough that he stuck to this interest, in spite of the teasing. He kept on creating and inventing new dishes for his family and friends. By the time he graduated from high school, Jacob had taken every cooking class and every business class his high school offered. He was awarded three scholarships to attend a community college in his state that offered a culinary arts program within its business department. When he completes the program, he'll be in a very good position to be a chef in a top local restaurant, and eventually open his own restaurant.

more about...

Occupational Outlook

The U.S. Department of Labor puts together an *Occupational Outlook* publication every year. In 2005, the DOL said the job category of education and health services "is projected to grow faster, 31.8 percent, and add more jobs than any other sector. About one out of every four new jobs created in the U.S. economy will be in either the health care and social assistance or private educational services sectors." Visit its Web site at **www.dol.gov** and linked through the course Web site at **www.mhhe.com/lamberton4e** to see what it predicts for other occupations you may be interested in.

you already did that at the interview). Thank-you letters are brief. They include an opening (thanking them for the interview), an added message (e.g., an interesting point you learned at the interview), and a closing. Each section is one or two sentences long. After the closing, be sure to list your name and contact information again.

Follow-Up Letters

Follow-up letters are sent three or four weeks after you have sent in your application materials, if you still have not heard from the company. The hiring process may still be going on, or your materials may have been missed. Of course, your application may have been rejected, but at least with the follow-up letter you will know for sure. This is just a brief letter thanking the employers for their time (two sentences or so), reminding them who you are and what you bring to this job (a short paragraph), and a closing asking for a reply (with contact information included).

Honest and authentic human relations require ethical treatment of others. This means that you must be honest in applying for a job. It is common for people to "fudge" a little or inflate their accomplishments on their application materials, but there is a difference between using a positive tone, and outright lying. When a company finds that an employee has lied on materials, the result is often job termination—and this can even mean the end of a career. Dishonesty can follow people for years into the future.

In this chapter, we have focused on a theme of *success in your future.* Success is achieved one step at a time, not in one huge chunk. In the final sections of this chapter, you learned specific steps you can take to maximize your rates of success in preparing job application materials, job interviews, and after-interview contacts. Effective human relations principles you have learned in this course will also add to your success. We (your authors) wish you success in all areas of human relations in your future!

« « STRATEGIES FOR SUCCESS

19.1 Practice a Job Interview

Hardly anyone looks forward to job interviews. They can be uncomfortable at best, and very stressful at worst. Interviews are not the best place to present yourself in your best light. But interviewing can be learned and practiced just like any other skill. Some questions will be easier to answer with practice and research. The following list gives examples of some of the most common job interview questions that employers ask. With another student (or family member or friend), take the roles of "interviewer" and "interviewee," switching roles halfway through. Listen to each question carefully, and give thoughtful answers. You can make a negative answer ("I take too long to finish tasks") sound more positive ("I am thorough in my work and check details") by looking at it from a different perspective. But be honest and ethical in your answers, too. Be realistic: don't say you can move to a different state, for example, if you know you cannot.

- Why did you apply for this position?
- What caused you to leave your last position?
- What are your goals for career advancement in this company?
- What do you want to be doing 5 years from now, and 10 years from now?
- What do you do when you have conflict with a supervisor or co-worker?
- Tell me why we should hire you.
- If we hire you, are you willing to relocate or travel?
- What did you learn about our company before coming to this interview?
- What interests you about this particular career?
- Do you plan to continue your training or education?

19.2 Make an Inventory of Your Skills

According to Bolles, you can figure out what your skills are by listing the kinds of things you are good at, like doing, or do most often in your spare time, then deciding what family of skills these fit into. By understanding your skills, you can figure out which careers will make you most happy and successful.

Major skill types include:

1. Health and physical stamina
2. Quantitative ability and interest level
3. People skills
4. Leadership skills
5. Mechanical ability
6. Musical ability
7. Artistic ability
8. Creativity and discernment
9. Self-assurance
10. Speaking and writing ability

Take some time to list your skills and talents. Sometimes people have trouble seeing these clearly, so the following list of categories should help your self-evaluation process:

1. **Health and physical stamina.** Are you healthier than the average person in your age group? Do you enjoy physical activity?

2. **Quantitative ability and interest level.** Are you good with numbers? Equally important, do you enjoy working with data and figures?

3. **People skills.** Do you get along well with others? More important, do you enjoy spending time with a variety of people?

4. **Leadership skills.** Do others see you as a leader? Do you often find yourself taking charge when a project is undertaken by a group? Do you see yourself as someone others might follow, even if only in certain contexts of your life?

5. **Mechanical ability.** Do you enjoy fixing mechanical or electronic equipment, maintaining it, and learning how it works?

6. **Musical ability.** Do you seem to pick up a tune when you hear it? Do you play a musical instrument or sing?

7. **Artistic ability.** Do you paint, draw, or sculpt? Do you suspect that you could, if you gave yourself a chance?

8. **Creativity and discernment.** Can you often see solutions where others see failure? Have you ever thought of an invention or an improvement of a process, just to find out later that someone else already thought of—and implemented—that same idea?

9. **Self-assurance.** Do you have the self-confidence to believe that your ideas will work, even when others doubt them?

10. **Speaking and writing ability.** Can you express yourself effectively in your speech and writing? Can you speak to a group of people without strong anxiety?

This list is not complete, and you can probably come up with several other areas of ability if you give yourself a chance to think about it. However, you most likely have talents in one or more of the preceding areas.

The next step is to apply the skills you've identified to a specific goal. Check out books on different careers in your library, but don't be limited by them. Often, people have constructed their own niche by inventing a business or product that no one else thought of before.

Entrepreneurship, which is the risk-taking entrance into your own enterprise, might take you to new and unexplored endeavors.

> **entrepreneurship**
> The risk-taking entrance into your own enterprise.

19.3   Move Toward a Happier Life

1. Think grateful thoughts.
2. Be kind.
3. Enjoy the little things.
4. Thank someone who has helped you.
5. Forgive someone.
6. Invest in friends and family.
7. Stay healthy.
8. Cope with stress.

Martin Seligman and others have identified steps they believe can help people have a happier, more satisfying life. These steps will not turn a cranky old goat into a giggling goose, but they can move people toward a more positive frame of mind. Try these steps for several weeks. Keep track of your feelings along the way, as well as your productivity level, to see how they have improved.

1. **Think grateful thoughts.** That is, count your blessings. Keep a "gratitude journal" in which you write down several things for which you are grateful. Plan a regular weekly schedule to add to your journal. Entries can range from the simple ("Beautiful weather today") to the wonderful ("I got a promotion!").

2. **Be kind.** Or, as the popular saying goes, practice random acts of kindness. These can be small acts (holding the door for someone carrying packages) to larger acts (committing to volunteer at the local senior center). These acts not only make you feel better about yourself, but they provide connections to your community, and they encourage others to do the same.

3. **Enjoy the little things.** Or, as another saying goes, stop to smell the roses. Notice the small things around you: flowers in bloom, a good meal. Keep a mental memory of these, to review in tougher times.

4. **Thank someone who has helped you.** Get in contact with a mentor or role model and thank this person for helping you grow and develop.

5. **Forgive someone.** Let go of the anger and resentment you have been carrying around. Getting rid of this mental burden will also help you improve your physical health by reducing harmful effects of stress.

6. **Invest in friends and family.** Not your money, but your time and energy are needed here. Research in this area shows that it is not the material goods we collect that make us happy; instead it is the long-term friendships and quality relationships with family that are really important to happiness.

7. **Stay healthy.** Get enough sleep. Exercise. Eat right. Smile and laugh regularly. Take care of yourself.

8. **Cope with stress.** Remember from Chapter 14 the importance of developing good coping skills.

Source: Claudia Wallis, "The New Science of Happiness," *Time*, January 17, 2005.

CHAPTER NINETEEN SUMMARY

Chapter Summary by Learning Objectives

1. **Give examples of how human relations will play a role in your future.** The first issue is your definition of success. Human relations and self-understanding skills should help you with that definition. Be aware of the new realities of both workplace and home life that will be taking place both in your future and in the future of society.

2. **Explain the relationship between self-motivation, self-direction, and success.** Self-motivation is motivation based on internal reward, or the expectation of such rewards. Self-direction is the ability to set short-and long-term goals for yourself and then follow them to success. Success has traditionally been defined as financial gain, but today is more likely to also include successful family relationships and leisure time.

3. **Identify why fear is the enemy of success.** Fear is the chief enemy of success because it shows itself not only in the form of fear of failure—which we all understand, but fear of success. Also, fear of being seen as an impostor and similar fears can slow down individual success.

4. **Define positive psychology.** Positive psychology is a relatively new area of study that is dedicated to examining what is *right* with people, rather than emphasizing what is wrong, as traditional psychology has done. It focuses on helping people build strength they can use to meet goals, and avoid low self-esteem and defeatist attitudes.

5. **Explain the importance of finding your niche.** Finding your niche simply means understanding yourself and finding the place where your skills lie and where you will be the most content and most successful.

6. **Describe how to prepare for a career choice.** Think about the "big picture" question about the types of career environment that will motivate you best toward success—defined with your own meaningful definition.

7. **List the steps in preparing your application materials.** Maximize your chances of success at getting a job by building an effective résumé. Make it short, just one or two pages. Use short phrases to

describe your education and work experience. Include contact information. Make it look neat, clean, and free of errors. Also, write a persuasive cover letter, using a different one for each position applied for. It should present a complete picture of who you are and what you want. Sometimes a portfolio will also be necessary. It should be a collection of work samples, credentials, and other materials an employer might want to see.

8. **Explain how to prepare for a job interview.** Learn something about the company you are interviewing with before your interview. Interviews may be individual, group, or "stress." They may be in person, or via telephone or video. Appearances definitely matter. Be punctual, well-groomed, and dressed appropriately. Remain confident and poised, giving thoughtful and complete answers. Maintain ethics throughout the entire job search.

9. **Identify the follow-up steps after an interview.** Send a thank-you letter to your interviewers to remind them who you are, and thank them for your time. Send a follow-up letter if you have not heard from the company, to ask them to respond about the status of your application.

key terms

BFOQ (bona fide occupational qualification) 547

cover letter 542

employment portfolio 542

entrepreneurship 551

fear of failure 535

fear of success 536

finding your niche 538

functional résumé 543

impostor phenomenon 535

intergenerational care 531

long-term goals 535

positive psychology 537

résumé 542

sandwich generation 531

self-discipline 533

self-direction 535

short-term goals 535

stress interview 547

review questions

1. Why is the work-family issue considered so important today? What are some ways employers are dealing with this issue?

2. What is the difference between short-term goals and long-term goals? What are some short- and long-term goals you have set?

3. What is meant by the impostor phenomenon? What is one way to eliminate fears such as this?

4. How does a fear of *failure* differ from a fear of *success?* Think of an example for each.

5. What does it mean to find your niche? Describe three families of skills found in jobs, according to Bolles.

6. What is positive psychology? How is it different from regular psychology—that is, what does it emphasize?

7. Describe important points to remember in formatting your application materials: résumé, cover letter, portfolio, and follow-up and thank-you letters.

8. Describe how you would prepare for a job interview, and how you will present yourself during an interview.

critical thinking questions

9. What is included in the idea of self-discipline? What are some examples of everyday behaviors that require self-discipline that you are currently engaging in? Can you succeed without these?

10. What is meant by finding your niche? What is one suggestion to help you in doing this? What are you doing in order to find your niche?

working it out 19.1

GOALS FOR SUCCESS

School-to-Work Connection: Interpersonal Skills, Personal Qualities Skills

With another student or on your own, write down on a piece of paper 10 to 20 things you really want out of life: your desires, dreams, small and larger goals. Be specific. Number each as you go along. After the number, begin a sentence with "I want . . ." and then write down your dream. Think of things you want for yourself, not items that would make others happy or those you feel you *should* want. After the "want" statement, ask yourself questions that will bring the "want" into focus even better. The more detail you use, the better. Being specific will help you focus on what it is you really want. As you continue to refine your goals into the future, think about the answers to these questions and whether they change.

Some examples follow.

1. I want a job I really like. (What type? What things about a job will make me really like it?)

2. I want to see the world. (What parts of the world? What job or volunteer activities could help me do that? Do I want to be a tourist, or do I see myself actively engaged in work somewhere else?)

3. I want to be my own boss. (At what? What kind of self-employment would I like? What is it about working for myself that attracts me?)

4. I want to spend more time with my family. (How will I make this happen? What type of job will help me do that? What am I willing to give up to get this—a promotion, a career change?)

5. I want to retire early. (At what age? How will I prepare financially to make this happen?)

Now, arrange them in priority, from "most important to me" to "least important to me." As you do this, imagine yourself achieving each "want." Think about what each one means to you personally.

Over the next few weeks and months, come back to these goals, and rearrange them by importance. Begin to put a plan of action into place for your top "wants" or goals.

Adapted from Denis Waitley, and Reni L. Witt, *The Joy of Working* (New York: Dodd, Mead, and Company, 1985).

working it out 19.2

YOUR COLLEGE CAREER CENTER

School-to-Work Connection: Interpersonal Skills, Information Skills, Basic Skills, Thinking Skills

Most colleges (whether business schools, community colleges, or four-year colleges or universities) have some type of career center. If you have never visited your college's career center, this is a good time to do so. It is never too early (and not too late). Find out what the career center offers students. Common resources include:

- Résumé writing workshops.
- Interviewing workshops.
- Online resources.
- Vocational interest testing.
- Career guidance or counseling.
- A job bank or employer list.
- Information on job/career fairs.
- Information on keeping an employment portfolio.
- Books, videos, or other job hunting resources.
- Suggestions on writing application cover letters and follow-up thank-you letters to employers after interviews.

What resources does your college offer? What workshops or job fairs can you sign up for? If your college does not offer such services, check with your local public library, local high schools, or your state's employment department. What services will you use now and in the future?

working it out 19.3

JOBS IN YOUR FUTURE CAREER INFORMATION: U.S. DEPARTMENT OF LABOR PROJECTIONS, 2002–2012

School-to-Work Connection: Information Skills, Basic Skills, Thinking Skills, Personal Qualities

Top Ten Careers for Fastest Salary and Wage Growth

1. Software publishers
2. Consulting services for management, scientific, and technical areas
3. Community care facilities, for elderly and residential care
4. Computers systems design
5. Employment services
6. Vocational rehabilitation for individuals, families, community
7. Health care, except offices of health-care providers
8. Water, sewer, other systems workers
9. Internet services and data processing
10. Child care, day care

Top Ten Fastest-Growing Occupations, and Their Minimum Education/Training Requirements

1.	Medical assistants	Moderate on-the-job training
2.	Network systems and data communication analysts	Bachelor's degree
3.	Physician assistants	Bachelor's degree
4.	Social and human services assistants	Moderate-term on-the-job training
5.	Home health aides	Short-term on-the-job training
6.	Medical records and health information technicians	Associate's degree
7.	Physical therapist aides	Short-term on-the-job training
8.	Computer software engineers, applications	Bachelor's degree
9.	Computer software engineers, systems software	Bachelor's degree
10.	Physical therapist assistants	Associate's degree

Top Ten Occupations with the Most New Jobs, and Their Typical Education/ Training Requirements

1.	Registered nurses	Associate's degree
2.	Postsecondary teachers	Doctoral degree
3.	Retail salespersons	Short-term on-the-job training
4.	Customer service representatives	Moderate-term on-the-job training
5.	Combined food preparation and serving workers, including fast food	Short-term on-the-job training
6.	Cashiers, except gaming	Short-term on-the-job training
7.	Janitors and cleaners, except maids and housekeeping cleaners	Short-term on-the-job training
8.	General and operations managers	Bachelor's or higher degree, plus work experience
9.	Waiters and waitresses	Short-term on-the-job training
10.	Nursing aides, orderlies, and attendants	Short-term on-the-job training

Instructions: Examine the three lists above from the U.S. Department of Labor. What patterns do you notice in terms of growing industries? If you want to prepare for a job with high salary growth, what type of job would interest you from the first list? What is your educational goal? What type of jobs would you select based on the educational level you plan to reach? If you just want a job that would be easier to get because there are many such jobs open, what type of job would interest you in the third list?

internet exercises

1. *Write a Résumé*
   Visit career-related Web sites and link to the sections on build-ing your own résumé. Helpful Web sites include "How to Write a Résumé" (**www.how-to-write-a-resume.org/**), CareerBuilder.com (**www.careerbuilder.com**), or Richard Bolles's Web site (**www.suggestica.com/richardbolles**). These Web sites are also linked to the textbook Web site at **http://www.mhhe.com/lamberton4e.** After reading through the articles and résumé writing tips, write a one-page résumé. What "do" and "don't" information did you find most helpful?

2. *Interviewing: Assess and Apply*
   Visit the Monster.Com Web pages on interviewing for a job (go to **http://interview.monster.com/**). There you can use a self-assessment tool to practice a virtual job interview, or read articles giving tips on interviewing. The CareerBuilder.Com Web site also

has job interview tips and advice. Go to its home page at **www** **.careerbuilder.com** and link to the videos on interviewing and preparing for a job, or read the advice articles. These Web sites are also linked to the textbook Web site at **www.mhhe.com/ lamberton4e.** What tips did you find most helpful in presenting yourself for an interview? Practice interviewing with a friend, or in front of a mirror, applying what you have learned.

3. *Finding a Job: Assess and Apply*

What type of jobs are you looking for? Visit some major Web sites devoted to job seekers, such as those listed above (Monster.Com **www.monster.com,** CareerBuilder.Com at **www.careerbuilder .com,** Richard Bolles's Web site at **www.suggestica.com/ richardbolles,** or try Yahoo! Jobs at **www.yahoo.com**). These Web sites are also linked to the textbook Web site at **www.mhhe .com/lamberton4e.** Research the type of job you are considering, or even another type of job you hadn't considered. Look at unusual jobs (Bolles includes a link called "Unusual Jobs,") internships, and other nontraditional areas. Write a brief summary about the current and future prospects, the preparation needed, and a typical salary, for the job you chose to research.

Reluctant Rosa

Although Rosa Fernandez's title was Assistant to the Vice President of Marketing/ Sales, she actually had considerable power. Her boss leaned heavily on her as an information source about competitors and their workplace. When Rosa started to become increasingly irritable and emotional at work, the other employees were puzzled because she was usually happy and self-assured.

"What's happened to our once sparkly-eyed office manager?" Devi Ramasamy asked during a coffee break.

"Oh, it's the new information system," answered John Tao, the head bookkeeper. "She's scared of it, I think. She says she's afraid it will eliminate her as the main source of information around here."

When the computerized system was finally installed, Rosa forced herself to sign up for the earliest training sessions available. She felt scared inside, but kept telling herself that she would succeed in learning the new system.

She also acted like she would succeed, and as she told more and more people that she was learning the new system, it became true. Her mood slowly changed back to the same as before. Soon Rosa found that she was in control of a system few others understood. "I wonder what I was afraid of," she mused to herself. "Never again will I allow myself to be intimidated by something so useful to my success in this company."

Case Study Questions

1. What was the real source of Rosa's fears?

2. What role did fear play in slowing down Rosa's understanding of the new system? What probably would have happened if she had never overcome these fears?

3. How could Rosa have prevented this fear, or ended it earlier?

Tita's Skills

Tita Ortiz has been working in the data entry division of a large corporation for three years. She had always planned to do data entry, ever since her high school counselor told her that computers were the fastest-growing field of the future. She is very unhappy in her current job but is not quite sure why. She has some seniority now, but not much clout, because she never cared enough to develop any. The only time she looks forward to coming to work is when she is training new data entry clerks. She loves the close interaction with other people and the good feelings she gets from teaching something important to others.

A few weeks ago, Tita noticed an announcement for an open entry-level position in the training and employee relations division of her company. She thought about applying for it, but didn't. "What's the difference?" she scolded herself. "It would just be a waste of time to fill out the paperwork. I'd never get it anyway; I don't have that kind of training, and anyway everyone here just thinks of me as a number-cruncher. If I tried it, I'd probably blow it and get fired anyway. I'd better just stay here in data entry."

Gloria Franklin, Tita's supervisor, has noticed that Tita does not seem to enjoy her job as much as she used to. She is not sure why and does not know what to do about it. She has asked Tita if anything is wrong, or if there is anything she would like to talk about, but Tita insists that everything is fine. Gloria knows that Tita likes working with people, and she has always been a little puzzled as to why Tita chose data entry as a career. Since Tita's work performance is good, Gloria decides that until Tita approaches her with a problem, she'll just let it ride.

Case Study Questions

1. What kinds of skills are important in the job that Tita is doing now? Does her current job seem to match her skills? If not, how did she end up choosing this field? What kinds of jobs might she be better at?

2. If you were Tita, what kinds of short-term goals and long-term goals would be reasonable to set? Is there any way that Gloria could help in the goal setting?

3. What kinds of fears is Tita facing? How might she get rid of these fears?

accommodator Someone who wants to avoid conflict by engaging in positive thinking.

achievement needs Occur in people who are goal oriented and take personal responsibility for achievements.

active listening Listening with greater concentration, less tolerance for distractions, and more feedback to the speaker.

affiliation needs Occur in people who want to be accepted and liked by others.

ageism Prejudice and discrimination toward older people.

aggressiveness Hurting others and putting them on the defensive.

Aslan phenomenon A circumstance that exists when people make rules, then follow them even after the situations to which they originally applied no longer exist.

assertiveness Standing up for your rights without threatening the self-esteem of the other person.

attitude An evaluation of people, ideas, issues, situations, or objects.

authority The vested power to influence or command within an organization.

autocratic leaders Leaders who make all the decisions and use authority and material rewards to motivate followers.

autonomy Independence, the ability to act and make decisions on one's own without undue interference from management.

avoider Someone who would rather not be around conflict at all and values neutrality highly.

bad news skills The skills necessary to deliver bad news to customers but still retain their business and goodwill.

beginning The *last* of three general steps in the acceptance of personal loss. This is where "experimenting" and "completion" take place. (See **ending** and **neutral zone.**)

behavior modification The process of changing behavior because of a reward or lack of a reward.

BFOQ (bona fide occupational qualification) Information directly related to the job you are applying for; does not include personal information, such as age, religion, or race.

bias A tendency to judge people before knowing them, basing the judgment only on their membership in some group or category of people.

blind pane The pane in the Johari Window that contains everything other people can see about you, but you can't see yourself.

boss massaging The practice of currying favor, or kissing up, with a manager to achieve your own goals.

brainstorming A type of spontaneous group discussion to help find multiple solutions to problems.

bureaucracy A formal organization in which each person has specific duties and responsibilities and is assigned to only one supervisor.

catastrophize To turn an irrational belief into an imagined disaster.

categorical imperative A principle developed by philosopher Immanuel Kant, which asks the question, "What would the world—or my company—be like if everyone were to do this?"

central nervous system The brain and spinal cord.

change agent The person responsible for an organizational change effort.

character ethic Emphasis is placed on principles, beliefs, and strong values rather than upon the use of various surface techniques.

charismatic power Power that is based on the attractiveness a person has to others.

chronic stressors Inescapable, day-to-day situations or conditions that cause stress.

cliché conversation The level of communication with the least amount of self-disclosure, including niceties such as, "Have a nice day."

coercive power Power that depends on the threat of possible punishment.

cognitive appraisal The thinking evaluation of an event or situation that varies from person to person and, for an individual, from day to day.

cognitive categorization A process in which the mind quickly sorts information into categories to function efficiently.

cognitive dissonance The emotional state that results from acting in ways that contradict one's beliefs or other actions.

collaborator Someone who brings both sides together for discussion and not only is most likely to bring about a win-win solution but is actually necessary for it.

collective habits of thought Ways of thinking that occur when groups have own beliefs about *what* should be done and *how* it should be done.

communication The giving and receiving of ideas, feelings, and information among people.

compensating The use of a strength to make up for a real or perceived weakness.

competitor Someone who is most likely to try a win-lose approach to conflict resolution, especially if he or she is personally involved in the conflict.

compromiser Someone who uses his or her skills to blend differences and form a workable alternative.

compulsive gambling The inability to control one's betting habit.

concession bargaining The process of getting each side in a conflict to willingly make concessions in exchange for concessions made by the opposing side.

conditional positive regard Acceptance of individuals as worthy only when they behave in a certain way.

conflict A process that begins when one person sees that another person has damaged—or is about to damage—something that the other person cares about.

conformity Behaving in a way that meets a specified standard, in coordination with a group.

consultative leaders Leaders who tend to delegate authority and confer with others in making decisions, but who makes the actual decisions independently.

content conflict Conflict that tends to focus on disagreements over what a statement or concept means.

context A point of reference (or a place from which to begin) when communicating.

corporate culture An organization's network that includes the shared values and assumptions within it.

cover letter A letter sent along with other documents (in this case, employment documents) to give additional information.

creative process The way in which creativity helps you develop ideas and solve problems.

creativity The ability to produce ideas or problems to solutions that are unique, appropriate, and valuable.

culture stories Stories that illustrate the values of the people who make an organization work.

daily hassles The daily annoyances, such as getting stuck in traffic or misplacing your keys, that can cause stress in your life.

defensiveness   The inappropriate reaction to another's behavior as though it were an attack.

denial   Failure to confront your problem; characteristic response by an alcoholic.

dependence   The state of relying on or needing a substance.

discrimination   Your behavior, or what you do (or intend to do, or are inclined to do) as a result of your stereotypes and prejudice.

displays   Gestures that are used like nonverbal punctuation marks, such as pounding your fist on the table.

distancing   The distance of physical space you maintain between other people and yourself.

distress   Negative stress, the kind felt during an illness or when going through a divorce.

dysfunctional conflict   Destructive conflict.

economic prejudice   Prejudice and discrimination toward people who are poorer or wealthier than you are.

eight intelligences   Eight separate areas in which people put their perceptiveness and abilities to work.

either/or fallacy   When you see only one of two extremes as a possible solution, while ignoring the endless number of creative choices that might exist between the extremes.

emblems   Gestures that are used in a specific manner because they have a specific meaning, usually one understood by both sender and receiver; the peace sign is an example.

emotional competence   A learned capability based on emotional intelligence; results in outstanding performance at work.

emotional intelligence (EI)   The ability to see and control your own emotions and to understand the emotional states of other people.

emotional mind   A powerful, impulsive, sometimes illogical awareness; an ability to perceive emotions.

employee appraisal   Feedback to an employee from supervisors on how he or she has performed over a given period.

employee assistance programs (EAPs)   Company-sponsored programs that treat employees with substance abuse problems, marriage and family conflicts, and financial difficulties.

employment portfolio   A collection of materials and work samples related to employment qualifications and experience.

empowerment   A TQM strategy that involves forming people into groups to solve problems and complete tasks; a process through which employees feel they are in control of their own contributions to the firm.

ending   The *first* of three general steps in the acceptance of personal loss. This is where "emotional standstill," "denial," and "anger" take place. (See **neutral zone** and **beginning.**)

entrepreneurship   The risk-taking entrance into your own enterprise.

Equal Employment Opportunity Commission (EEOC)   A federal agency established to monitor the laws set in place by the amended Civil Rights Act of 1964, as amended in 1962.

equal status   The condition that occurs when companies hire employees who are frequent targets of discrimination into all levels within the company.

ERG Theory   A refinement of Maslow's hierarchy that includes only three needs areas: existence (mostly figure needs); relatedness (needs linked to relationships: and growth (internal esteem needs and self-actualization).

esteem needs   In Maslow's hierarchy, include recognition from peers and colleagues.

ethical codes   Formalized sets of ethical guidelines developed by some companies for use at all levels of an organization.

ethics   The expression of the standards of right and wrong based on conduct and morals in a particular society.

ethnocentrism   The belief that one's ethnic group is more normal than others; an emotional source of prejudice because of people's gut-level feelings about how right their group is—and, in turn, how wrong they think other groups are.

eustress Positive stress, the kind felt when playing tennis or attending a party.

expectancy In *expectancy theory,* the likelihood that if a person tried, the result would be better performance.

expectancy theory Developed by Victor Vroom to explain human behavior in terms of people's goals, choices, and the expectation that goals will be reached.

expert power Power that comes from a person's knowledge or skill in areas that are critical to the success of the firm.

external locus of control This occurs in people who feel they have no control over the events in their lives.

external stressors Stressors that include anything from outside sources that causes you pain and discomfort.

extraversion Characteristic of a happy attitude in which a person's behavior is directed outward, toward others.

extrinsic motivators Those motivators that come from outside sources, such as money and fame.

extrinsic rewards External factors that include salary.

family violence Violence that can be defined as physical, emotional, verbal, or sexual violence against another family member.

fear of failure The fear that occurs when people are afraid of looking bad in front of others.

fear of success The fear that occurs when people who have not experienced much success in their lives feel they do not deserve it.

feedback Information given to people either on how well they are performing a task, or on how clearly they are being understood.

filtering A method listeners use to *hear only what they want to hear,* which may result in failing to receive messages correctly.

finding your niche Finding the place where you thrive and are most content; includes finding the type of job or career where you will be most satisfied.

first-, second-, and third-degree games In transactional analysis, categories of games based on intensity of play. First-degree games are relatively harmless; second-degree games are moderately harmful; third-degree games are extremely damaging.

flow The feeling of oneness with an activity that allows an individual to uniquely experience an event or activity by becoming totally engaged in the process; term was coined by Mihalyi Csikszentmihalyi.

force field analysis A model in which the status quo is like a battlefield being fought for by two armies: the driving force and the restraining force.

formal group A group that is usually governed by the formal structure of the organization.

free-rein leaders Leaders who set performance standards, then allow followers to work creatively to meet standards.

frustration The feeling people get when goals they are trying to attain are blocked.

frustration regression principles A principle that says that someone who fails to reach a higher need level will sometimes become frustrated and regress (go back) to a lower need level, and stay there for some time—perhaps forever.

functional conflict Constructive conflict.

functional résumé A résumé grouped by job skills, in which the specific functions of the jobs you have held are listed.

future favors A practice commonly seen in developing countries based upon mutual obligation and resulting in the exchange of favors over years and even generations; also used in some industrialized countries such as Japan and South Korea.

game An encounter between two people that produces a "payoff" for the one who starts the game, at the expense of the other player.

gift exchange A strong tradition in many cultures, in which giving gifts creates a future obligation to the receiver; it can also be a rite of passage into an inner circle.

goal setting Allows employees to set their own goals.

going the extra mile When a company gives customers small extra products or services as a way of showing appreciation for their business.

good feelings and solutions The only two things customers really buy.

grapevine A network within the informal organization that communicates incomplete, but usually somewhat accurate information.

Graves's Seven Value Levels Reaction, tribalism, egocentrism, conformity, achievement, social orientation, and existentialism.

group Two or more people who interact, share common goals, have unspoken or formal rules or norms, maintain stable role relationships, and form subgroups.

group dynamics The set of interpersonal relationships within a group that determine how group members relate to one another and that influence task performance.

group process The way group members deal with one another while working on a task.

groupthink A problematic type of thinking that results from group members who are overly willing to agree with one another because of time pressure, stress, and low collective self-esteem.

gut level communication Level of communication in which feelings are expressed honestly.

hardy personality A resilient personality type, characterized by the ability to meet challenges, a sense of commitment, and a feeling of being in control of life.

Hawthorne Experiment A five-year study conducted at the Western Electric plant in Hawthorne, Illinois, that showed that workers performed better when someone was paying attention to them.

hidden agendas The secret wishes, hopes, desires, and assumptions hidden from the group.

People often try to accomplish hidden agendas while pretending to care about the group goals.

hidden pane The pane in the Johari Window that contains information and feelings that you are hiding from other people.

higher self-esteem When people have healthy feelings about themselves and are therefore more likely to succeed in personal and career goals.

high-context culture A culture in which the *social context* surrounding a written document is far more important than the document itself. One must be very careful about cultural norms, nonverbal behaviors on both sides, and anything else involving the overall atmosphere of the communication.

Holmes–Rahe Readjustment Scale A listing of many kinds of changes, rated from 100 to 0 on the basis of their intensity and the adjustment problems they can create.

horizontal communication Messages that are communicated between you and your equals in the formal organization.

human relations The skill or ability to work effectively through and with other people.

humanism A philosophy and values system that includes a belief in the worth and dignity of all people and a world-wide morality that applies to all cultures.

hygienes (also called "dissatisfiers") The qualities in the workplace that are outside the job itself (examples: company benefits, policies, job security). When these factors are weak or missing, motivation will fall; however, when they are high, motivation will not be strong or long term.

ideal self The way you would like to be or plan to become.

idealism A values system based on the belief that one's consciousness is the only thing it is possible to know with certainty.

ideas and judgments Expressed though conscious thoughts, opinions, and theories in this level of communication.

illustrators Gestures that are used to clarify a point, such as pointing when giving directions.

imposter phenomenon A feeling successful people experience when they are afraid that they did not really succeed because of their own talents and hard work.

informal group A group that tends to form around common interests, habits, and personality traits.

informal organization The ever-changing set of relationships and interactions that are not formally put together; they form naturally in the workplace.

information overload The type of listening that happens when a listener is overwhelmed with incoming information and has to decide which information will be processed and remembered; this is a common cause of poor listening skills.

inner circle A clique of trusted family members, tribal members, or friends (depending on the culture) who are at the center of power or influence.

inner conflict Conflict within an individual; it might involve values, loyalties, or priorities; the pressure you feel when you are forced to make a choice.

institutionalized conflict Conflict that occurs when a conflict factor is built into the structure of an organization.

institutionalized prejudice Prejudice that is caused by policies in the workplace that are not intentionally set to exclude members of specific groups or to treat them differently, but which have that effect anyway.

instrumental values Values that reflect the ways you prefer to behave.

instrumentality The likelihood that something good (or bad) will come from an increase in effort.

integrity Soundness of moral character.

intelligence Traditionally seen as reasoning ability, as measured by standardized tests.

intensity The degree to which an individual shows serious concentration or emotion; another dimension of nonverbal communication.

interdependence A relationship in which members of different groups not only must cooperate but also must depend on each other to reach common goals.

intergenerational care Day care not only for children but also for elderly family members.

intergroup conflict Takes place when already-formed groups have conflicts with each other.

internal customer The person who depends on the other people in the company to provide the services and products for the external customer.

internal locus of control Occurs in people who feel they are in control of the events in their own lives.

internal stressors Your perceptions of stressors, which may vary depending on personality.

intragroup conflict Conflict that occurs when two groups form and take sides.

intrinsic motivators Factors that motivate a person from within, such as the joy and excitement of the discovery process.

intrinsic rewards In *expectancy theory*, the internal factors related to the value of work, including the amount of creativity allowed, the degree of responsibility, and the satisfaction of helping others.

institutional prejudice Prejudice that is caused by policies in the workplace that are not intentionally set to exclude members of specific groups or to treat them differently, but which have that effect anyway.

institutionalized conflict Conflict that occurs when a conflict factor is built into the structure of the organization.

intuition Direct perception or insight.

irrational belief system A way of thinking that causes internal stress by substituting a realistic belief with one that is destructive, illogical, and largely false.

ISO 9000 A management philosophy that seeks to put into place formalized standards throughout businesses and industries by providing evaluation and certification for compliance to standards of quality.

job burnout Physical and emotional exhaustion resulting from long-term stress or frustration in one's workplace.

job enrichment The upgrading of a job that makes it more interesting, meaningful, or rewarding and provides long-term motivation.

Johari Window A composite of four panes that shows you ways of relating to others: the open, blind, hidden, and unknown panes.

leadership The ability to influence others to work toward the goals of an organization.

legitimate power Power based on the position a person holds in an organization that is effective only when followers believe in the structure that produces this power.

levels of communication Include cliché conversation, reporting facts about others, ideas and judgment, gut level communication, and peak communication.

Lewin change model A workplace change model with three steps; unfreezing the status quo, making changes, then refreezing to the previous work mode.

locus of control The name given to the perceived location of the control you feel you have over events that happen to you; this control is perceived to be located within the individual (internal locus of control) or is attributed to external factors (external locus of control).

logical incrementalism A model that acknowledges that bringing about changes in a large organization is usually time-consuming and complicated, and presents a method of simplifying the process.

long-term goals Those things you decide to work for after developing a life plan for the future.

looking-glass self The self you assume others see when they look at you.

lose-lose strategy A strategy in which everyone gives up something, and the focus is on compromise.

love and belongingness needs Include complete acceptance from family and friends. The third level of Maslow's hierarchy.

low conformers Individuals who think independently, solve problems creatively, and often cause some conflict in the process.

low-context culture A culture in which a written agreement, such as a contract, can be taken at face value.

lower self-esteem Occurs when individuals are unable to see themselves as capable, sufficient, or worthy.

lower self-worth Occurs when an individual believes himself or herself to have little of value to offer the world.

major life changes Changes in your life, such as divorce, that increase daily hassles, leaving you stressed and worn out.

manifest needs theory Developed by David McClelland to show that all people have needs that motivate them in life and on the job. These three needs include power needs, affiliation needs, and achievement needs.

Maslow's hierarchy of needs Shows that people tend to satisfy their needs in a certain order: first, physiological needs, then safety and security, belongingness and love, esteem, and finally, self-actualization.

mentor A person who acts as a guide or teacher for another, leading that person through experiences.

morale Overall mood of an individual or group, based on attitudes and satisfaction.

morality A system of conduct that covers all broadly based, mostly unwritten standards of how people should behave and generally conform to cultural ideals of right and wrong.

motivation The force of the need or desire to act.

motivators (also called "satisfiers") The factors in Herzberg's theory that cause real, long-term motivation, usually containing *intrinsic* motivation factors (examples: interesting and challenging tasks, advancement, achievement, growth).

mutual respect The positive consideration or regard that two people have for each other.

negotiation-of-selves Conflict that is involved in the process of defining yourself to others and responding to their implied definitions of themselves.

networking power Power that is attained by gaining contact and knowing the right people.

neutral zone The *second* of three general steps in the acceptance of personal loss. The neutral zone is the area where "helplessness" and "bottoming out" take place. (See **ending** and **beginning.**)

"nice" customer The customer who never complains, but responds to bad service by taking his or her business elsewhere.

nine-dot puzzle A puzzle that is used to show people's respect for rules that don't exist. Participants are asked to connect nine dots using only four straight lines, without lifting the pen off the paper. Most fail because they feel the need to stay "inside the box" formed by the nine dots.

nominal group method An exercise that encourages creativity within a group framework by allowing everyone to offer ideas individually.

nonconversation A way to describe the amount of actual conversation in cliché conversation.

nonverbals Ways of communicating without speaking, such as gestures, body language, and facial expressions.

norm A standard of behavior expected of group members.

OD change agent A company's formal change agent; often an outside consultant who specializes in planned change or organizational development (OD).

OD intervention Training tools that teach members of the organization how to solve problems they face or make needed changes to organizational development (OD).

open mode A state of mind where you are relaxed, expansive, less purposeful, and more fun than in the everyday closed mode.

open pane The pane in the Johari Window that contains information that you know about yourself and that you have no reason to hide.

optimal experience The pleasure in performing the process of an activity itself, rather than achieving the goal.

organizational change Change that a group of people must learn to accept and implement.

organizational citizenship behavior An attitude of willingness to go above and beyond the behaviors that are generally associated with life in the workplace.

organizational climate The emotional weather within an organization that reflects the norms and attitudes of the organization's culture and affects worker morale, attitudes, stress levels, and communication.

organizational communication Oral and written communication in an organization. It has formal and informal dimensions and travels vertically and horizontally.

organizational development (OD) A planned, companywide, systematic method of achieving change in an organization.

overloading time Planning too many activities into one time slot.

participative leaders Leaders who encourage the group to work together toward shared goals.

pathological critic A negative inner voice that attacks people and judges their worth negatively.

peak communication Communication characterized by complete openness and honest self-disclosure. It happens rarely.

perception The way in which a person views the world.

person-versus-group conflict Conflict that occurs most often when a member of a group breaks its rules, or norms.

person-versus-person conflict Conflict that involves two people who are at odds over personality differences, values conflicts, loyalties, or any number of issues.

personal competence The ability to be self-aware, motivated, and self-regulated.

personal control The power people perceive they have over their destinies.

personality ethic Emphasis is placed on being likable, making sure that you are received well, and maintaining a positive mental attitude.

physiological dependence Dependence based on increased tolerance and the presence of withdrawal symptoms when a psychoactive drug is not used.

physiological needs The most basic of Maslow's hierarchy of needs having to do with the satisfaction of physical needs, including food and shelter.

positive attitude A position resulting from healthy self-esteem, optimism, extraversion, and personal control.

positive psychology A subfield within psychology that focuses on experiences, individual traits, and institutions that create happiness and hope, rather than focusing on mental illness.

positive self-talk A popular method of building self-esteem by thinking and speaking positively about yourself.

power The ability of one person to influence another.

power needs Desired by individuals who want to control and influence other people.

pragmatism Values system than emphasizes practicality and usefulness of ideas.

prejudice The outcome of prejudging a person. Prejudice in communication is the unwillingness to listen to members of groups the listener believes are inferior, such as other ethnic groups or women; it can also take more subtle forms; how you feel as a result of the stereotypes you believe in.

principle of individual rights An ethical philosophy that holds that all decisions should respect basic human rights and the dignity of the individual.

principle of individualism An ethical philosophy that holds that all primary goals should achieve long-term self-interests, with the emphasis on long-term; self-interest should not justify short-sighted actions.

principle of justice An ethical philosophy that holds that all decisions should be consistent, unbiased, and based on fact.

principle of utilitarianism An ethical philosophy that holds that all decisions should do the greatest good for the largest number of people.

procrastination Putting off until later the things a person should be doing now.

productivity The ratio of an organization's inputs, or its resources, to its outputs, or the goods and services it produces.

proximity Physical closeness; here, it refers to contact between members of a diverse workplace.

psychoactive drug Any substance that affects a person's judgment, behavior, mental processes, mood, conscious experience, or perceptions.

psychological contract An agreement that is not written or spoken but is understood between people.

psychological dependence or preoccupation Dependence that occurs when a person craves the effects of a drug and organizes his or her life around getting and using the drug.

quality movement A business development that was established in Japan in the 1940s and spread to the United States in the 1980s that emphasizes the highest standards in the process of production as well as in the final product. See **Total Quality Management**.

quality organizations In the world of human relations, organizations that contain quality throughout the process of whatever they are about, especially in terms of quality of work life, that is, the positive experience of working at such a place.

racism   Prejudice and discrimination based on race.

Rath Test   Finds out if the values you think you have are the ones you truly have.

rational mind   An awareness of reality, which allows you to ponder and reflect.

rationalize   To justify unethical behavior with excuses.

real self   The way you really are when nobody is around to approve or disapprove.

red flag words   Words that bring an immediate emotional response (usually negative) from the listener, generally because of strong beliefs on the subject.

regression   Slipping backward to an earlier stage of growth; it can be either temporary or permanent.

regulators   Gestures that are used to control the flow of communication; eye contact is a common type of regulator.

reinforcement theory   Explains human behavior in terms of repetition. Behavior that is rewarded enough times will be repeated, where behavior that repeatedly receives no reward will probably discontinue.

reinforcers   Incentives such as awards, bonuses, promotions, gifts, and even compliments.

relationship selling   Forming meaningful relationships with your customers, which makes them much more likely to return and buy from you again.

repress   To block off memories that may cause pain, embarrassment, or guilt.

résumé   A brief summary of a person's work experience and qualifications, often submitted with an employment application.

reward power   Power that comes from the user's ability to control or influence others with something of value to them.

rewards   In TQM, benefits for employees, including profit sharing or paid bonuses In behavior modification, the factors designed to encourage a behavior.

role model   A person to whom an individual can look to for guidance by example, but who isn't necessarily actively interacting with the individual.

rumor mill   A gossip network that produces mostly false information.

safety and security needs   In Maslow's hierarchy, include physical safety from harm and the elements as well as financial security.

sandwich generation   Middle-aged adults who are taking responsibility for both dependent children and parents at the same time, and being sandwiched by these obligations.

satisfiers   (also called "motivators") The factors in Herzberg's theory that cause real, long-term motivation. They usually contain *intrinsic* motivation factors (examples: interesting and challenging tasks, advancement, achievement, growth).

SCAMPER   A strategy, created by Bob Eberle, to release your creative mind.

scientific management   A system based upon scientific and engineering principles.

script   In relationship transactions, a psychological script like a movie or theater script, with characters, dialogue, etc., that most people heard as children.

second right answer   Refers to a method of decision making in which people get rid of the stumbling block that prevents them from looking for more than one solution.

selective listening   The type of listening that happens when a listener deliberately chooses what he or she wants to pay attention to.

self-actualization Highest level of Maslow's hierarchy of needs; occurs when one has fulfilled his or her potential.

self-awareness The knowledge of how you are being perceived by others.

self-concept The way you picture yourself to be.

self-direction The ability to set short-term and long-term goals for yourself.

self-discipline The ability to teach or guide yourself to set up and carry out your goals and plans.

self-disclosure The process of letting other people know what you are really thinking and feeling.

self-efficacy The confidence an individual has in his or her ability to deal with problems when they occur and to achieve goals.

self-esteem The regard in which an individual holds himself or herself.

self-esteem trap The circumstance that comes from taking a customer's attack personally and letting it affect your self-esteem.

self-fulfilling prophecy The tendency for a prediction to actually occur once it is believed; for example, when a victim believes that prejudice against him or her is true, then fulfills these negative expectations.

self-image The way you honestly see yourself.

self-justification Explaining your behavior so that you feel it is correct.

self-perception What and how you believe yourself to be.

self-respect Positive self-image with high self-esteem.

self-sabotage Damaging your own credibility or competence.

setting priorities Deciding ahead of time which tasks are the most, and least, important.

seven major life changes Loss, separation, relocation, a change in relationship, a change in direction, a change in health, and personal growth.

seven stages of personal change Emotional standstill, denial, anger, helplessness, bottoming out, experimenting, and completion.

sexism Prejudice and discrimination based on gender.

sexual harassment Behavior that is defined by the EEOC as "Unwelcome sexual advances, requests for sexual favors, and other verbal or physical conduct of a sexual nature."

short-term goals The specific plans of action for the things you would like to accomplish right now or in the immediate future.

skill variety The opportunity and ability to use numerous different skills in one's position at work.

social competence Empathy for others combined with sensitivity and effective social skills.

social responsibility The practice of acting ethically while understanding your actions are part of the larger, interactive picture of your workplace, community, and world.

Spranger's Six Value Systems Dominant values systems held by individuals including theoretical, economic, aesthetic, social, political, and religious.

stakeholders Any group that a business interacts with, such as customers, competitors, unions, suppliers, consumer groups, and government agencies.

status The rank an individual holds within a group.

stereotypes Your thoughts or beliefs about specific groups of people.

stress Any reaction or response made by the body to a new situation.

stress interview An interview in which the interviewer tries to make you uncomfortable to see how you will react.

stressor A situation or an event that causes the body to react (causes stress).

substance abuse The continued use of a psychoactive substance even though it is causing or increasing problems in a person's life.

task activity The assignment of tasks to get a job done.

task identity The worker's perception of the meaningfulness of a job, often based upon the worker's permission to start a job and see it through to completion.

task maturity Having the skill set necessary to complete a job, as well as the ability to set and meet realistic goals and the ability to take on responsibility for the task.

task significance A worker's perception that the task directly affects other people's work or lives.

team building The process of creating and encouraging a group of employees to work together toward achieving group goals and increased productivity.

team spirit The energy and shared commitment that result from teamwork.

ten "mental locks" Rules or beliefs that keep people from being as creative as they otherwise could be.

terminal values Values likely to maintain a high priority throughout your life.

Theories X and Y Theory X managers see workers as lacking ambition, disliking work, and wanting security above all else. Theory Y managers see workers as enjoying work, able to assume responsibility, and being creative.

time analysis Analyzing your use of time to determine how to become more efficient in time management.

time management Making effective use of available time.

to-do list A list of what you need to do, when, and where.

tolerance The state of needing more and more of a substance to get the desired effect.

Total Quality Management (TQM) A management organizational philosophy that was very influential in the 1980s and 1990s, which stated that quality must be present in the product or the service produced, and in the process itself of producing the goods or service. **See quality movement**.

two simplest principles Finding out what the customer needs, and doing whatever is necessary to satisfy it.

type A and type B personalities Two standard personality-related sets of behaviors. Type A behaviors are characterized by impatience, hostility, perfectionism, and a sense of time urgency. Type B behaviors are characterized by flexibility, the ability to relax and delegate work, and a minimal sense of time urgency.

unconditional positive regard The acceptance of individuals as worthy and valuable regardless of their behavior, usually applied to parental acceptance of children.

underutilizing time Making poor use of available time.

unknown pane The pane in the Johari Window that contains unknown talents, abilities, and attitudes, as well as forgotten and repressed experiences, emotions, and possibilities.

valence The value a person places on a reward.

value systems Frameworks people use in developing beliefs about themselves, others, and how they should be treated.

values The worth or importance you attach to different factors in your life.

values conflict Conflict that occurs when one set of values clashes with another, and a decision has to be made.

vertical communication Messages that are communicated according to an organization's chain of command by flowing both upward and downward.

whistleblowing Turning in or otherwise exposing people who behave unethically in your company.

win-lose strategy A strategy that allows one side of a conflict to win at the expense of another.

win-win strategy A strategy that leads to a solution in which both sides feel they have come out on top.

withdrawal symptoms Physical symptoms that strike when a drug is no longer used.

workplace morale The overall mood of a workplace based on attitudes and satisfaction.

work team A group of employees with shared goals who join forces on a work project.

worst possible scenario In communication, this is the very worst thing that could happen upon self-disclosure.

references

Chapter 1

1 City of Medora, North Dakota, www.medorand.com/ (retrieved April 10, 2008).

2 The Jim Thompson House, www.jimthompsonhouse.org/life/index.asp (retrieved April 10, 2008).

3 Richard Baran, "Interpersonal Relationship Skills or How to Get Along for Productivity and Profit," *Personnel Administrator,* April 1986, p. 12.

4 Janette Moody et al., "Showcasing the Skilled Business Graduate: Expanding the Tool Kit," *Business Communication Quarterly,* March 2002, p. 23.

5 U.S. Census, Pop Quiz, Foreign Born in the United States, www.census.gov/population/socdemo/foreign/p20-534/quiz/popquiz.html (retrieved April 10, 2008).

6 Eduardo Porter, "Immigrants' Population Gains Maintain Speedy 1990s Pace," *Wall Street Journal,* March 10, 2003, p. 82.

7 Mitra Toossi, "Employment Outlook: 2006–16. Labor Force Projections to 2016: More Workers in Their Golden Years," *Monthly Labor Review,* November 2007, www.bls.gov/opub/mlr/2007/11/art3full.pdf (retrieved April 10, 2008).

8 W. Richard Plunket, *Supervision: The Direction of People at Work* (Dubuque, IA: Wm C. Brown, 1983), p. 161.

9 M. R. Hansen, "Better Supervision for A to W," *Supervisory Management,* August 1985, p. 35.

10 Fyodor Dostoyevsky, *The House of the Dead* (London: William Heineman, 1915), p. 20.

11 Carol Hymowitz, "Five Main Reasons Why Managers Fail," *The Wall Street Journal,* May 2, 1988, p. 27.

12 Suneel Ratan, "Why Busters Hate Boomers," *Fortune,* October 4, 1993, pp. 57–70.

13 Mei Wen, "Competition, Ownership Diversification, and Industrial Growth in China," Dissertation, Australian National University, March 2002, pp. 2–3.

14 Robert Kaplan, "How We Would Fight China," *Atlantic,* June 2005, pp. 49–64. See also Cherian Thomas, "India's GDP Growth May Slow for First Time in 3 Years (Update3)," Bloomberg.com, Feb. 7, 2008, www.bloomberg.com/apps/news?pid=20601013&sid=av1phRnqSgCM&refer=emergingmarkets (retrieved April 10, 2008).

15 Jeff Poor, "Life Expectancy Increasing or Decreasing, Depending on What Day It Is," Business and Media Institute, posted Sept. 13, 2007, www.businessandmedia.org/printer/2007/20070913152112.aspx (retrieved April 11, 2008).

16 Paul R. Timm and Brent D. Peterson, *People at Work: Human Relations in Organizations* (Minneapolis/St. Paul, MN: West Publishing, 1993), pp. 122–123. See also "William Ouchi on Trust," *Training and Development Journal,* December 1982, p. 71.

17 Stephen R. Covey, *The Seven Habits of Highly Effective People* (New York: Simon & Schuster, 1989), pp. 66–67.

18 Sandra Rittman and Jean Gonzalez, *Effective Business Communication* (Boston: PWS-Kent Publishing Company, 1991), p. 2.

19 John R. Dickman, *Human Connections* (Englewood Cliffs, NJ: Prentice-Hall, 1982), pp. xi–xii.

20 Michael Drafke, *The Human Side of Organizations* (Upper Saddle River, NJ: Pearson Prentice-Hall, 2006), pp. 211–214.

21 David Krech, Richard Crutchfield, and Egerton Ballachey, *Individual in Society* (New York: McGraw-Hill, 1962), pp. 527–529.

22 Peter F. Drucker, *The New Realities* (New York: HarperCollins, 1990).

23 James R. Lowry, B. W. Weinrich and R. D. Steade, *Business in Today's World* (Cincinnati, OH: South-Western, 1990), p. 243.

24 L. K. Frankel and Alexander Fleisher, *The Human Factor in Industry* (New York: Macmillan, 1920), p. 8.

25 Ibid., pp. 10–28.

26 Max Weber, *The Protestant Ethic and the Spirit of Capitalism,* trans. Talcott Parsons (New York: Scribner, 1930), pp. 121–156.

27 Max Weber, *The Theory of Social and Economic Organization,* ed. and trans. by A. M. Henderson and T. Parsons (Oxford University Press, 1947), pp. 22–57.

28 Frederick W. Taylor, *The Principles of Scientific Management* (New York: Harper and Brothers, 1923), pp. 35–38.

29 Daniel Nelson, *Frederick W. Taylor and the Rise of Scientific Management* (Madison, WI: University of Wisconsin Press, 1980).

30 Daniel A. Wren, *The Evolution of Management Thought* (New York: Ronald Press, 1972), pp. 158–168.

31 Henry C. Metcalf and L. Urwick, eds., *Dynamic Administration: The Collected Papers of Mary Parker Follett* (New York: Harper and Row, 1942), pp. 20–38.

32 Elton Mayo, *The Human Problems of an Industrial Civilization* (New York: Macmillan, 1933).

33 John G. Adair, "The Hawthorne Effect: A Reconsideration of the Methodological Artifact," *Journal of Applied Psychology,* Vol. 69, No. 2, May 1984, 69 (2) pp. 334–345. See also J. A. Sonnenfeld, "Shedding Light on the Hawthorne Studies," *Journal of Occupational Behavior,* Vol. 6, April 1985, pp. 111–130.

34 George T. and John W. Boudreau, *Human Resource Management* (Homewood, IL: Richard Irwin, 1991), pp. 605–609.

35 Douglas M. McGregor, *The Human Side of Enterprise* (New York: McGraw-Hill, 1960), pp. 32–37. Also, T. Merriden, "The Way We Were: An Assessment of Douglas McGregor's Theories X and Y," *Management Today,* June 1998, pp. 111–112.

36 Mary Walton, *The Deming Management Method* (New York: Putnam, 1986), pp. 3–21. Also, T. Y. Choi and O. C. Behling,

"Top Managers and TQM Success: One More Look After All These Years," *The Academy of Management Executive,* November 1998, pp. 37–49.

Chapter 2

[1] Joseph L. Massie and John Douglas, *Managing: A Contemporary Introduction,* 5th ed. (Englewood Cliffs, NJ: Prentice-Hall, 1992).

[2] Samuel E. Wood and Ellen Green Wood, *The World of Psychology* (Boston, MA: Allyn & Bacon, 1999). See also Kimberly Fulcher, "Envisioning Your Ideal Self," SelfGrowth.com, www.selfgrowth.com/articles/Fulcer2html (retrieved March 16, 2008).

[3] Samuel E. Wood and Ellen Green Wood, *The World of Psychology* (Boston, MA: Allyn & Bacon, 1999). See also "How Do You Talk to Yourself?" Norwich University Online, www.leadersdirect.com/talkself.html (retrieved March 15, 2008).

[4] Mary Pipher, *Reviving Ophelia: Saving the Selves of Adolescent Girls* (New York: Ballantine Books, 1994).

[5] Carolyn M. Ball, *Claiming Your Self-Esteem* (Berkeley, CA: Celestial Arts, 1990), p. 138.

[6] Stanley Coppersmith, *The Antecedents of Self-Esteem* (San Francisco: Freeman, 1967).

[7] Wayne Weiten and Margaret Lloyd, *Psychology Applied to Modern Life: Adjustment at the Turn of the Century,* 6th ed. (Wadsworth, 1999).

[8] Spencer Rathus, *Psychology,* 6th ed. (Fort Worth, TX: Harcourt Brace Jovanovich, College Division, 1998).

[9] Ibid.

[10] Alfred Adler, *The Individual Psychology of Alfred Adler* (New York: Basic Books, 1956), p. 48.

[11] Hertha Orgler, *Alfred Adler: The Man and His Work* (New York: New American Library, 1963).

[12] Julian Rotter, "External Control and Internal Control," *Psychology Today,* June 1971, pp. 37–42, 58–59 [13]. See also Samuel E. Wood and Ellen Green Wood, *The World of Psychology* (Boston, MA: Allyn & Bacon, 2006), pp. 339–340.

[13] Matthew McKay and Patrick Fanning, *Self-Esteem* (Oakland, CA: New Harbinger, 1987), p. 181.

[14] Adapted from Matthew McKay and Patrick Fanning, *Self-Esteem* (Oakland, CA: New Harbinger, 1987).

[15] Stephen R. Covey, *The Seven Habits of Highly Effective People* (New York: Simon & Schuster, 1989).

[16] Ibid. See also Neil A. Fiore, *The Now Habit* (Los Angeles, CA: Jeremy P. Tarcher, 1989), pp. 6–26.

[17] Denis Waitley, *Psychology of Success: Developing Your Self-Esteem* (Homewood, IL: Richard D. Irwin, 1993), p. 76. See also B. David Brooks and Rex K. Dalby, *The Self-Esteem Repair and Maintenance Manual* (Newport Beach, CA: Kincaid House, 1990), p. 55.

[18] Robert Rosenthal and Lenore Jacobson, *Pygmalion in the Classroom: Teacher Expectations and Pupils' Intellectual Development* (Norwalk, CT: Irvington Publishing Co., 1992). See also Cecilia Elena Rouse and Lisa Barrow, "U.S. Elementary and Secondary Schools: Equalizing Opportunity or Replicating the Status Quo?" Opportunity in America, Volume 16, Number 2, Fall 2006. Future of

Children: A Collaboration of The Woodrow Wilson School of Public and International Affairs at Princeton University and The Brookings Institution,www.futureofchildren.org/information2826/information_show.htm?doc_id=392628 (retrieved March 14, 2008).

[19] Victoria Clayton, "Are We Raising a Nation of Little Egomaniacs? Debate Erupts Over Whether Kids Get Too Much Praise or Not Enough," MSNBC, 2008 MSNBC Interactive, Mon., April 2, 2007, /www.msnbc.msn.com/id/17821247/ (retrieved March 14, 2008).

[20] Lilian Katz, "How Can We Strengthen Children's Self-Esteem?" KidSource Online, www.kidsource.com/kidsource/content2/Strengthen_Children_Self.html (retrieved July 30, 2005). See also Robert W. Reasoner, "Review of Self-Esteem Research," National Association for Self-Esteem, posted 2004, www.self-esteem-nase.org/research.php (retrieved March 15, 2008).

[21] Eugene Sagan, in Matthew McKay and Patrick Fanning, *Self-Esteem* (Oakland, CA: New Harbinger, 1987).

[22] Ibid.

[23] Ibid.

[24] From Samuel E. Wood and Ellen Green Wood, *The World of Psychology* (Boston, MA: Allyn & Bacon, 1999).

[25] References with further characteristics of the scale: Rich Crandal "The Measurement of Self-Esteem and Related Constructs," in J. P. Robinson and P. R. Shaver, eds., *Measures of Social Psychological Attitudes,* rev. ed. (Ann Arbor: ISR, 1973), pp. 80–82; M. Rosenberg, *Society and the Adolescent Self-Image* (Princeton, NJ: Princeton University Press, 1965) (Chapter 2 discusses construct validity); E. Silber and Jean Tippett, "Self-Esteem: Clinical Assessment and Measurement Validation," 16 *Psychological Reports,* pp. 1017–1071 (discusses multitrait-multimethod investigation using RSE), 1965; Ruth C. Wylie, *The Self-Concept,* rev. ed. (Lincoln, NE: University of Nebraska Press, 1974), especially pp. 180–189.

[26] Pallab Ghosh, "Low Self-Esteem 'Shrinks Brain,'" BBC News/Health, British Broadcasting Corporation, posted November 20, 2003, www.news.bbc.co.uk/2/low/health/3224674.stm (retrieved June 22, 2005). See also Marilyn Sorenson, *Breaking the Chain of Low Self-Esteem* (Portland, Oregon: Wolf Publishing, 2007).

Chapter 3

[1] Carl Rogers, "What It Means to Become a Person," in Clark E. Moustakas, ed., *The Self: Explorations in Personal Growth* (New York: Harper & Row, 1956), pp. 195–211.

[2] Marie Lindquist, *Holding Back: Why We Hide the Truth About Ourselves* (New York: Harper & Row, 1988), p. 5.

[3] Ibid.

[4] Joseph Luft, *Group Process: Introduction to Group Dynamics* (Palo Alto, CA: National Press, 1970). See also Phillip C. Hanson, "The Johari Window: A Model For Soliciting and Giving Feedback," in *The 1973 Annual Handbook of Group Facilitators* (San Diego, CA: University Associates, 1973), pp. 114–119.

[5] Sam Keen and Anne V. Fox, *Telling Your Story: A Guide to Who You Are and Who You Can Be* (New York: Signet, 1973), pp. 22–24.

[6] This list is based on Marie Lindquist, *Holding Back,* p. 26.

[7] Maxwell Maltz, *Psycho-Cybernetics* (New York: Simon & Schuster, 1960), pp. 165–167.

[8] Roy F. Baumeister and Dianne M. Tice, "Four Selves, Two Motives and a Substitute Process Self-Regulation Model," in Roy F. Baumeister, ed., *Public Self and Private Self* (New York: Sprinter-Verlag, 1986), p. 63.

[9] This list of disadvantages is based on Marie Lindquist, *Holding Back,* pp. 27–33. Also see John Powell, *Why Am I Afraid to Tell You Who I Am?* (Allen, TX: Argus Communications, 1969), pp. 77–83.

[10] The following five levels come from John Powell, *Why Am I Afraid to Tell You Who I Am?* (Allen, TX: Argus Communications, 1969, pp. 50–62; republished by Thomas More Association,1990).

[11] John Powell, *Why Am I Afraid to Tell You Who I Am,* p. 58.

[12] This is a terrific oversimplification of Maslow's point. For further reading, see Abraham Maslow, "Lessons from the Peak Experiences," *Journal of Humanistic Psychology,* February 1962, Vol. 2, pp. 9–18. Also see Abraham Maslow, *Religions, Values, and Peak Experiences* (Columbus: Ohio State University Press, 1964).

[13] John Powell, *Why Am I Afraid to Tell You Who I Am?,* p. 62.

[14] Ibid., p. 77.

[15] Ibid., p. 80.

[16] These three advantages of "gut level" communications are based on John Powell, *Why Am I Afraid to Tell You Who I Am?,* pp. 79–85.

[17] R. D. Laing, *Knots* (New York: Vintage Books, 1972); see also R. D. Laing, H. Phillipson, and A. R. Lee, *Interpersonal Perception* (New York: Perennial Press, 1972).

[18] This list of fears is based in part on Susan Jeffers, *Feel the Fear and Do It Anyway* (New York: Ballantine, 1987), pp. 11–18, and on Marie Lindquist, *Holding Back,* p. 155.

[19] Dale Carnegie, *How to Stop Worrying and Start Living (*New York: Pocket Books, 1953).

[20] Virginia Satir, *Peoplemaking* (Palo Alto, CA: Science and Behavior Books, 1972), pp. 75–79.

[21] Wayne Weiten, Margaret A. Lloyd, and Robin Lashley, *Psychology Applied to Modern Life,* 3rd ed. (Belmont, CA: Wadsworth, 1991). Reprinted by permission of Brooks/Cole Publishing Company, Pacific Grove, CA 93950.

[22] Ibid.

Chapter 4

[1] Marianna Krejci-Papa, "Happier Ever After," Science and Spirit, www.science-spirit.org/article_detail.php?article_id=605 (retrieved April 10, 2008).

[2] David G. Myers, "The Secret of Happiness," *Psychology Today* 25 (July/August 1992), pp. 38–45.

[3] Martin Seligman, *Learned Optimism: How to Change Your Mind and Your Life* (New York: Simon & Schuster, 1990).

[4] C. S. Carver, C. Pozo, S. D. Harris, V. Noriega, M. F. Scheier, D. S. Robinson, A. S. Ketcham, F. L. Moffat Jr., and K. C. Clark, "How Coping Mediates the Effect of Optimism on Distress: A Study of Women with Early Stage Breast Cancer," *Journal of Personality and Social Psychology* 65 (1993), pp. 375–390.

[5] M. F. Scheier, J. K. Weintraub, and C. S. Carver, "Coping with Stress: Divergent Strategies of Optimists and Pessimists," *Journal of Personality and Social Psychology* 51 (1986), pp. 1258–1264.

[6] M. F. Scheier and C. S. Carver, "Optimism, Coping, and Health: Assessment and Implications of Generalized Outcome Expectancies," *Health Psychology* 4 (1985), pp. 219–247.

[7] M. F. Scheier, K. A. Matthews, L. Owens, G. J. Magovern Sr., R. C. Lefebvre, R. A. Abbott, and C. S. Carver, "Dispositional Optimism and Recovery from Coronary Artery Bypass Surgery: The Beneficial Effects on Physical and Psychological Well-Being," *Journal of Personality and Social Psychology* 57 (1989), pp. 1024–1040.

[8] S. A. Everson, D. E. Goldberg, G. A. Kaplan, R. D. Cohen, E. Pukkala, J. Tuomilehto, and J. T. Salonen, "Hopelessness and Risk of Mortality and Incidence of Myocardial Infarction and Cancer," *Psychosomatic Medicine* 58 (1996), pp. 113–121.

[9] Carl Jung, *Psychological Types* (Princeton, NJ: Princeton University Press, 1971).

[10] Judith Rodin, "Aging and Health: Effects of the Sense of Control," *Science* 233 (1986), pp. 1271–1276.

[11] David G. Myers, "The Secret of Happiness," pp. 38–45.

[12] *Webster's New World Dictionary* (New York, World Publishing Co., 1972), p. 513.

[13] Frances Merrit Stern, "Getting Good Feedback—and Giving Back in Kind," *Training/Human Resource Development,* April 1982, p. 34.

[14] Mihalyi Csikszentmihalyi, *Finding Flow: The Psychology of Engagement with Everyday Life* (New York: Basic Books, 1997). See also Mihalyi Csikszentmihalyi, *Flow: The Psychology of Optimal Experience* (New York: Harper & Row, 1990) and Mihalyi Csikszentmihalyi and J. LeFevre, "Optimal Experience in Work and Leisure," *Journal of Personality and Social Psychology* 56 (1989), pp. 815–822.

[15] Dow Scott and Stephen Taylor, "An Examination of Conflicting Findings on the Relationships Between Job Satisfaction and Absenteeism: A Meta-Analysis," *Academy of Management Journal* 28 (1985), pp. 599–612.

[16] Edwin A. Locke, "The Nature and Causes of Job Satisfaction," in *Handbook of Industrial and Organizational Psychology,* Marvin D. Dunnette, ed. (New York: John Wiley & Sons, 1983), pp. 1332–1334.

[17] Edward E. Lawler and Lyman W. Porter, "The Effect of Performance on Job Satisfaction," *Industrial Relations,* October 1967, pp. 20–28.

[18] Mark Ehrrant and Stephanie Nauman, "Organizational Citizenship Behavior in Work Groups: A Group Norms Approach," *Journal of Applied Psychology,* December 2004, pp. 960–972.

[19] Marcia A. Finkelstein, "Dispositional Predictors of Organizational Citizenship Behavior: Motives, Motive Fulfillment, and Role Identity," *Social Behavior and Personality,* FindArticles.com., 2006 (retrieved April 10, 2008).

[20] Douglas M. McGregor, *The Human Side of Enterprise* (New York: McGraw-Hill, 1960), pp. 33–35.

[21] Saul W. Gellerman, *Management by Motivation* (New York: American Management Association, 1968), pp. 231–232.

[22] Marilyn Gist, "Self-Efficacy: Implications for Organizational Behavior and Human Resource Management," *Academy of Management Review,* July 1987, p. 477.

[23] Douglas M. McGregor, *The Human Side of Enterprise,* pp. 33–35.

24 Louis A. Allen, "M for Management: Theory Y Updated," *Personnel Journal,* December 1973, pp. 1061–1067.

25 Martin Seligman, *The Optimistic Child* (Boston, MA: Houghton Mifflin, 1995), pp. 219–223.

26 Ibid.

27 From *Time,* October 2, 1995, pp. 60–68. These suggestions are thoroughly revised but generally inspired by Elwood N. Chapman, *Your Attitude Is Showing* (New York: Macmillan, 1991), pp. 23–25.

28 Harry Levinson, "What Killed Bob Lyons?," in *Harvard Business Review,* January–February 1963, pp. 127–144.

29 Maxwell Maltz, *Psycho-Cybernetics: A New Way to Get More Out of Life* (New York: Simon & Schuster, 1960), pp. 91–93.

30 Susan Folkman and Judith Tedlie Moskowitz, "Stress, Positive Emotion, and Coping," *Current Directions in Psychological Science* 9, no. 4 (August 2000), pp. 115–118.

Chapter 5

1 Barry Z. Posner and Michael Munson, "The Importance of Values in Understanding Organizational Behavior," *Human Resource Management* 18 (Fall 1979), pp. 9–14.

2 Daniel Yankelovich, "The New Psychological Contracts at Work," *Psychology Today* 11 (May 1978), pp. 46–50.

3 Daniel Yankelovich and John Immerwahr, "Workplace Realities and Values," *Personnel Administration,* December (1983), pp. 34–40, also reprinted in *Work in the 21st Century* (Washington, DC: American Society for Personnel Administration, 1984), 11–24.

4 Carolyn Kleiner and Mary Lord, "The Cheating Game," *U.S. News and World Report,* November 22, 1999, p. 56.

5 David Callahan, *The Cheating Culture: Why Americans Are Doing Wrong to Get Ahead* (Orlando, FL: Harcourt, 2004), pp. 44–107.

6 Milton Rokeach, *The Nature of Human Values* (New York: Free Press, 1973), pp. 3–12.

7 Eduard Spranger, *Types of Men* (New York: Harcourt Brace Jovanovich, Johnson Reprints, original pub. date 1928).

8 Based on Vincent Flowers, Charles L. Hughes, M. Scott Myers, and Susan B. Myers, *Managerial Values for Working* (New York: AMACON, 1975), pp. 12–14. See also Don. E. Beck and Christopher Cowan, *Spiral Dynamics: Managing Values, Leadership, and Change* (New York: Doubleday, 1996).

9 See Susan Haack and Robert Lane, eds., *Pragmatism Old and New: Selected Writings* (New York: Prometheus Books, 2006).

10 Definitions of humanism (subsection), Institute for Humanist Studies, http://humaniststudies.org/humphil.html (retrieved April 10, 2008).

11 See Dean Moyar, "Hegel, Idealism, and Analytic Philosophy," *European Journal of Philosophy,* April 2008, pp. 136–141.

12 Roger Vajda, "Integrity at Work – How do You Stack Up?" Management-Issues (posted Sept. 11, 2007), www.management-issues.com/2007/9/11/opinion/integrity-at-work-%E2%80%93-how-do-you-stack-up.asp (retrieved August 15, 2008).

13 Judith M. Bardwick, "Peacetime Management and Wartime Leadership," in *The Leader of the Future,* ed. Frances Hesselbein et al. (New York: The Peter Drucker Foundation, 1996), p. 137.

14 Stephen R. Covey, *The Seven Habits of Highly Successful People* (New York: Simon & Schuster, 1989), pp. 17–23. See also Stephen Covey, *The 8th Habit* (New York: The Free Press, 2004).

15 Thomas J. Peters and Robert H. Waterman, *In Search of Excellence: Lessons from America's Best-Run Companies* (New York: Harper & Row, 1982), pp. 278–280.

16 Dennis W. Bakke, *Joy at Work: A Revolutionary Approach to Fun on the Job* (Seattle: PVG, 2005), pp. 190–192.

17 Ibid., pp. 25, 164.

18 Leon Festinger, *A Theory of Cognitive Dissonance* (Stanford, CA: Stanford University Press, 1957). See also Robert Levine, *The Power of Persuasion: How We're Bought and Sold* (New York: Wiley, 2003).

19 Ibid. See also E. Aronson, "Dissonance, Hypocrisy, and the Self-Concept," in E. Harmon-Jones and J.S. Mills, *Cognitive Dissonance Theory: Revival with Revisions and Controversies* (Washington, DC: American Psychological Association, 1998).

20 John Tierney, "Go Ahead, Rationalize. Monkeys Do It, Too," *New York Times,* Science, posted Nov. 6, 2007, www.nytimes.com/2007/11/06/science/06tier.html?_r=1&oref=slogin (retrieved April 11, 2008).

21 Louis Rath, Merrill Haron, and Sidney Simon, *Values and Teaching* (Columbus, OH: Charles Merrill, 1976).

22 Based on Joseph Josephson and Edna Josephson, *Character Counts Wallet Card* (Marina del Rey, CA: Josephson Institute of Ethics, 1994).

Chapter 6

1 Peter Drucker, *Management: Tasks, Responsibilities, Practices* (New York: Harper & Row, 1974), p. 455.

2 C. H. Deutsch, "Why Women Walk Out on Jobs," *The New York Times,* April 29,1990, p. F27.

3 Spencer Rathus and Jeffrey Nevid, *Adjustment and Growth: The Challenges of Life,* 7th ed. (New York: Harcourt Brace College Publishers, 1999).

4 Edward Hoffman, *The Right to be Human: A Biography of Abraham Maslow* (Los Angeles: Jeremy P. Tarcher, 1988), p. 154. See also Laurie Pawlik-Kienlen, "Self-Actualization in Action: How to Apply Maslow's Hierarchy of Needs to Your Life," *Suite101.com,* posted March 21, 2007, http://psychology.suite101.com/article.cfm/fulfill_your_potential (retrieved May 1, 2008).

5 Abraham Maslow, *Motivation and Personality* (New York: Harper & Row, 1970), pp. 46–65.

6 Richard M. Steers and Lyman Porter, *Motivation and Work Behavior,* 3rd ed. (New York: McGraw-Hill, 1983), pp. 3–5.

7 Clayton Alderfer, *Existence, Relatedness, & Growth* (New York: Free Press, 1972), pp. 12–26.

8 See www.netmba.com/mgmt/ob/motivation/erg. Accessed May 1, 2008.

9 David C. McClelland, *Human Motivation* (Glenview, IL: Scott, Foresman, 1985).

10 David C. McClelland and David Burnham, "Power Is the Great Motivator," *Harvard Business Review* 54 (March–April 1976), pp. 100–110.

11 Ibid., pp. 102–110.

12 S. M. Klein and R. R. Ritti, *Understanding Organizational Behavior* (Boston, MA: Kent Publishing, 1984), pp. 256–258.

13 A. Kukla, "Foundations of an Attributional Theory of Performance," *Psychological Review,* 79 (1972), pp. 454–470.

14 David C. McClelland, *Human Motivation.* See also R. B. McCall, "Academic Underachievers," *Current Directions in Psychological Science* 3 (1994), pp. 15–19.

15 Frederick Herzberg, "One More Time: How Do You Motivate Employees?" *Harvard Business Review,* Winter 1979, pp. 101–121. See also Frederick Herzberg, *Work and the Nature of Man* (New York: Harper & Row, 1966).

16 Frederick Herzberg, "Workers' Needs: The Same Around the World," *Industry Week,* September 21, 1987, pp. 29–31.

17 J. R. Hackman and Gene Oldman, *Work Redesign* (Reading, MA: Addison-Wesley, 1980).

18 Ibid.

19 Victor H. Vroom, *Work and Motivation* (New York: John Wiley & Sons, 1964), pp. 170–174.

20 Barry M. Staw, *Intrinsic and Extrinsic Motivation* (New York: John Wiley & Sons, 1976). See also Uco J. Wiersma, "The Effects of Extrinsic Rewards in Intrinsic Motivation," *Journal of Occupational and Organizational Psychology* 65 (1992), pp. 101–114.

21 B. F. Skinner, *Beyond Freedom and Dignity* (New York: Alfred A. Knopf, 1971).

22 Eric Berne, *Games People Play* (New York: Grove Press, 1964), pp. 34–37.

23 Michael LeBoeuf, *The Greatest Management Principle in the World* (New York: Berkeley Publishing, 1987), pp. 12–27.

24 B. F. Skinner, *Beyond Freedom and Dignity,* pp. 17–48.

25 R. A. Katzell and D. E. Thompson, "Work Motivation: Theory and Practice," *American Psychologist* 45 (1990), pp. 144–153.

26 Jack Falvey, "To Raise Productivity, Try Saying Thank You," *The Wall Street Journal,* December 6, 1982, p. 26.

27 Joel Brockner, *Self-Esteem at Work: Research, Theory, and Practice* (Lexington, MA: Lexington Books, 1988), pp. 159–161, 192. See also Matthew McKay and Patrick Fanning, *Self-Esteem* (Oakland, CA: New Harbinger Publication, 1987), pp. 159–189.

Chapter 7

1 Frank K. Sonnenberg, "Barriers to Communication," *Journal of Business Strategy* 11 (July/August 1990), pp. 56–58.

2 Sandra Hagevik, "Just Listening," *Journal of Environmental Health* 62 (July 1999), pp. 26–32.

3 Sonnenberg (1990), "Barriers to Communication," p. 56.

4 Lyle Sussman and Paul D. Krivonos, *Communication for Supervisors and Managers* (Easton, PA: Alfred Publishing Company, 1979), pp. 66–68.

5 Anthony Allesandra, quoted in *The Power of Listening,* Revised Edition (firm) (CRM Films, 1987).

6 Edward T. Hall, *The Silent Language* (Greenwich, CT: Fawcett Books, 1959), pp. 51–53.

7 John Stewart and Carole Logan, *Together: Communicating Interpersonally* (New York: McGraw-Hill, 1993), pp. 246–247.

8 Albert Mehrabian, *Nonverbal Communication* (Chicago, IL: Aldine-Atherton Company, 1972), pp. 23–38.

9 "The Anatomy of a Message," *Ford's Insider* (1981), pp. 4–9.

10 Paul Ekman and Wallace V. Friesan, "Hand Movements," *Journal of Communication* 22 (1972), pp. 353–358.

11 Based on Edward T. Hall, "Proxemics A Study of Man's Spatial Relationships," from *Man's Image in Medicine and Anthropology* (New York: International Universities Press, 1963).

12 William M. Pride and O. Jeff Harris, "Psychological Barriers in the Upward Flow of Communication," *Atlanta Economic Review* 21 (March 1971), pp. 30–32. See also "Organization Charts as a Management Tool," http://management.about.com/cs/generalmanagement/a/orgcharts_2.htm. Accessed May 3, 2008.

13 Keith Davis, "Management Communication and the Grapevine," *Harvard Business Review* 31 (September–October 1953), pp. 45–47.

14 O. Jeff Harris and Sandra J. Hartman, *Human Behavior at Work* (New York: West Publishing Company, 1992), pp. 270–271.

15 Ronald E. Dulek, John S. Fielden, and John S. Hill, "International Communication: An Executive Primer," *Business Horizons* 34 (January-February 1991), p. 20.

16 Yang Yao and Linda Yueh (eds.), *Globalization and Economic Growth in China* (Singapore: World Scientific Publishing, 2006), pp. 236–258.

17 Dick Schaef, "The Growing Need for Cross-Cultural and Bilingual Training," *Training/Human Resource Director* (January 1981), pp. 85–86.

18 Edward T. Hall, "How Cultures Collide," *Psychology Today* 10 (July 1976), pp. 66–74. See also Edward T. Hall, *Beyond Culture* (Garden City, NY: Doubleday, 1976).

19 Based on Dulek, Fielden, and Hill, "International Communication," pp. 21–22.

Chapter 8

1 Jon L. Pierce and John Newstrom, *Leaders and the Leadership Process* (Burr Ridge, IL: McGraw-Hill Irwin, 2008), pp.158–163.

2 G. E. Myers and M. T. Myers, *The Dynamics of Human Communication* (New York: McGraw-Hill, 1973), pp. 125–127.

3 Nancy Foy, *The Yin and Yang of Organizations* (New York: William Morrow, 1980), pp. 107–108.

4 Davis C. Feldman, "The Development and Enforcement of Group Norms," *Academy of Management Review* 9 (January 1984), pp. 47–53. Cf. Uzoamaka P. Anakwe and Jeffrey H. Greenhaus, "Effective Socialization of Employees: Socialization Content Perspective," *Journal of Managerial Issues,* September 22, 1999, supplement.

5 Myers and Myers, *Dynamics of Human Communication,* p. 127.

6 V. W. Tuchman, "Developmental Sequences in Small Groups," *Psychological Bulletin* 63 (May 1965), pp. 384–399.

7 Ibid., pp. 386–389. See also A. C. Kowitz and T. J. Knutson, *Decision-Making in Small Groups: The Search for Alternatives* (Boston, MA: Allyn & Bacon, 1980).

[8] Feldman, "Development and Enforcement of Group Norms," pp. 49–53.

[9] Irving L. Janis, *Groupthink,* 2nd ed. (New York: Houghton-Mifflin Company, 1982).

[10] For a dissenting discussion of the processes of "Groupthink," see Glyn White, "Groupthink Revisited," *Academy of Management Journal* 14 (January 1989), pp. 40–56.

[11] Robert R. Blake and Jane S. Mouton, "Don't Let Group Norms Stifle Creativity," *Personnel* 62 (August 1985), pp. 28–33.

[12] J. Richard Hackman and Charles G. Morris, "Improving Group Performance Effectiveness," in *Advances in Experimental Social Psychology,* ed. Leonard Berkowitz (New York: Academic Press, 1975), p. 345.

[13] Peter Piven, "Increasing Your Project Team's Effectiveness." Coxe Leadership Group, 2008. www.coxegroup.com/articles/effectiveness.html (retrieved May 4, 2008).

[14] These three categories are based on Dr. Marlin S. Potash, *Hidden Agendas* (New York: Dell Publishing, 1990), p. 56. See also Roberta Shaler, "The Queen and Her Bobble-Heads: Uncovering 'Hidden' Agendas," http://hodu.com/queen.shtml (retrieved May 4, 2008).

[15] Richard L. Daft and Dorothy Marcic, *Understanding Management,* 5th ed. (Mason, OH: Thompson South-Western, 2006), pp. 412–413.

[16] Warren Bennis and Burt Nanus, *Leaders: The Strategies for Taking Charge* (New York: Harper & Row, 1986), pp. 19–26.

[17] Rosabeth Moss Kanter, "The New Management Work," *Harvard Business Review,* November/ December 1989, pp. 85–92.

[18] Robert R. Blake and Jane S. Mouton, "A Comparative Analysis of Situationalism and 9.9 Management by Principle," *Organizational Dynamics,* Spring 1982, pp. 20–43.

[19] Company History, Compaq and HP, http://h18004.www1.hp.com/corporate/history.html (retrieved August 2005). See also "Compaq Co-Founder Ron Canion Joins BlueArc Board of Directors," Celtic House press release, www.celtichouse.com/news_040526.html, posted May 26, 2004 (retrieved August 9, 2005).

[20] Afsaneh Nahavandi, *The Art and Science of Leadership,* 4th ed. (Upper Saddle River, NJ: Prentice Hall, 2007), pp. 99–112.

[21] Gary A. Yukl and C. M. Falbe, "The Importance of Different Power Sources in Downward and Lateral Relations," *Journal of Applied Psychology* 76 (1991), pp. 416–423. See also Gary Yukl, *Leadership in Organizations,* 6th ed. (Upper Saddle River, NJ: Prentice Hall, 2005).

[22] Nahavandi, *Art and Science of Leadership,* pp. 184–190. See also John P. Kotter, *John P. Kotter on What Leaders Really Do* (Boston, MA: Harvard Business Review Books, 1999), pp. 143–172.

[23] "Managing Your Career," *Wall Street Journal,* March 18, 1997, p. Al.

Chapter 9

[1] Stephen P. Robbins, *Organizational Behavior,* 11th ed. (Upper Saddle River, NJ: Prentice Hall, 2007).

[2] Ibid. See also Otis Port and John Carey, "Questing for the Best," *Business Week* (Bonus Issue, October 11, 1991), p. 11.

[3] Don Hellriegel and John W. Slocum, Jr., *Management,* 7th ed. (Cincinnati, OH: South-Western College Publishing, 1996).

[4] David H. Holt, *Management: Principles and Practices,* 3rd ed. (Englewood Cliffs, NJ: Prentice Hall, 1993).

[5] The International Organization for Standardization official Web site, www.iso.org/iso/en/ISOOnline.frontpage (retrieved July 15, 2005). See also "What are ISO 9000 and ISO 9001?" Simply Quality, www.isoeasy.org/ (retrieved July 15, 2005). See also "Total Quality Management and ISO 9000 Services," Great Visions Consulting, www.greatvisions.com/tqm.htm (retrieved July 15, 2005).

[6] Harvey Robbins and Michael Finley, *The New WHY TEAMS DON'T WORK: What Goes Wrong and How to Make It Right* (San Francisco, CA: Berrett-Koehler Publishers, 2000. See also Rosemary Batt, "Work Organization, Technology and Performance in Customer Service and Sales," *Industrial and Labor Relations Review* 52 (July 1999), pp. 539–563, www.hrzone.com/articles/teams_tqm_or_taylorism.html (retrieved July 15, 2005). See also "Work Team Skills and Productivity," Center for Collaborative Organizations (Center for the Study of Work Teams), University of North Texas, www.workteams.unt.edu/research.htm (retrieved May 18, 2008).

[7] These defining factors are based on E. Thomas Moran and J. Fredericks Volkwein, "The Cultural Approach to the Formation of Organizational Climate," *Human Relations,* January 1992, p. 20.

[8] Thomas A. Kayser, *Team Power: How to Unleash the Collaborative Genius of Work Teams* (Burr Ridge, IL: Irwin Professional Publishing, 1994).

[9] John H. Zenger, Ed Musselwhite, Kathleen Hurson, and Craig Perron, *Leading Teams: Mastering the New Role* (Homewood, IL: Business One Irwin, 1994).

[10] Stewart R. Segall, "Reflections of Your Management Style," *Supervisory Management* 36 (February 1991), pp. 1–2.

[11] Moran and Volkwein "The Cultural Approach," 22–47. See also R. M. Guion, "A Note on Organizational Climate," *Organizational Behavior and Human Performance* 9 (1973), pp. 120–125.

[12] Michael C. G. Davidson, "Does organizational climate add to service quality in hotels?" *International Journal of Contemporary Hospitality Management,* 2003, 15 (4), pp. 206–213. See also: Malcolm G. Patterson, Michael A. West , Viv J. Shackleton, Jeremy F. Dawson, Rebecca Lawthom, Sally Maitlis, David L. Robinson, Alison M. Wallace, "Validating the organizational climate measure: links to managerial practices, productivity and innovation," *Journal of Organizational Behavior,* Volume 26 Issue 4, pp. 379–408. Published Online: 14 Apr 2005. Copyright © 2008 John Wiley & Sons, Ltd.

[13] Paul Hellman, "What's the Story?" *Management Review,* February 1992, p. 63.

[14] For more on stories in corporate cultures, see Thomas J. Peters and Nancy K. Austin, *A Passion for Excellence* (New York: Random House, 1985), pp. 278–293.

[15] "Organizational Culture," Bamboo Web.com, www.bambooweb.com/articles/o/r/Organizational_culture.html (retrieved May 18, 2008).

[16] Hellman, "What's the Story?," p. 63.

[17] Ibid.

[18] Joseph Campbell, *The Power of Myth* (New York: Doubleday, 1988), pp. 3–35.

[19] Edgar Schein, "How Founders/Leaders Embed and Transmit Culture," www.tnellen.com/ted/tc/schein.html (retrieved July 12, 2005). See also Edgar Schein, *Organizational Culture and Leadership*, 3rd ed. (New York: Jossey-Bass, 2004).

[20] "Organizational Culture," Answers.com, www.answers.com/Organizational+Culture?cat=technology (retrieved May 19, 2008). See also G. Johnson "Rethinking Incrementalism," *Strategic Management Journal* 9 (1988), pp. 75–91.

[21] Terrence E. Deal and Allan A. Kennedy, *Corporate Cultures: The Rites and Rituals of Corporate Life* (Reading, MA: Addison-Wesley, 1982), pp. 3–4.

[22] Robert Poupart and Brian Hobbs, "Changing the Corporate Culture to Ensure Success: A Practical Guide," *National Productivity Review* 8 (Summer 1989), pp. 223–238.

[23] Thomas J. Peters and Robert Waterman, *In Search of Excellence* (New York: Harper and Row, 1982), p. 15.

[24] These qualities of the "new corporate culture" are based in part on: Joseph D. O'Brian, "The 'New Corporate Culture': Mainly Just Common Sense," *Supervisory Management* 39 (January 1992), p. 9.

[25] Douglas McGregor, *The Human Side of Enterprise* (New York: McGraw-Hill, 1960). See also Rensis Likert, *The Human Organization* (New York: McGraw-Hill, 1967).

[26] Marshall Sashkin and Richard L. Williams, "Does Fairness Make a Difference?" *Organizational Dynamics* 19 (Autumn 1990), pp. 56–58.

[27] For information on the psychological contract, see Edgar Schein, *Organizational Psychology* (Englewood Cliffs, NJ: Prentice Hall, 1980).

[28] "Corporate Culture: The Hard-to-Change Values That Spell Success or Failure," *Business Week,* October 27, 1980, p. 148.

Chapter 10

[1] Daniel Goleman, Paul Kaufman, and Michael Ray, *The Creative Spirit* (New York: Dutton, 1992), pp. 72–79.

[2] Daniel Goleman, *Emotional Intelligence* (New York: Bantam Books, 1995), p. 34.

[3] Goleman, *Emotional Intelligence,* pp. 8, 291–296.

[4] Allen Farnham, "Are You Smart Enough to Keep Your Job?" *Fortune,* January 15, 1996, pp. 34–42. See also "Leading by Feel: Be Realistic," *Harvard Business Review,* January 2004, p. 28.

[5] Goleman, *Working with Emotional Intelligence,* pp. 26–28

[6] Robert Sternberg, *Successful Intelligence* (New York: Simon & Schuster, 1996), also retold in Daniel Goleman, *Working with Emotional Intelligence* (New York: Bantam Books, 1998), p. 22.

[7] Ibid., pp. 24–27.

[8] Mark Daniel, *Self-Scoring Emotional Intelligence Tests* (New York: Sterling Publishing, 2000), pp. 1–2.

[9] Daniel Goleman, Richard Boyatzis, & Annie McKee, *Primal Leadership: Realizing the Power of Emotional Intelligence* (Boston: Harvard Business School Publishing, 2002). pp. 105–109.

[10] Richard E. Boyatzis, "Developing Emotional Intelligence Competencies," in Joseph Ciarrochi and John Mayer (eds.), *Applying Emotional Intelligence* (New York: Psychology Press, 2007), pp. 29–30.

[11] Cf. Boyatzis, pp. 30–31.

[12] Goldman, Boyatzis, & McKee, *Primal Leadership,* pp. 107–118.

[13] Matthew McKay, Martha Davis, and Patrick Fanning, *Thoughts and Feelings: Taking Control of Your Moods and Your Life* (Oakland, CA: New Harbinger Publications, 2007), pp. 233–234.

[14] Goleman, *Emotional Intelligence,* p. 63.

[15] These four characteristics of anger are based on Gilian Butler and Tony Hope, *Managing Your Mind,* 2nd ed. (New York: Oxford University Press, 2007), pp. 171–173.

[16] These steps were drawn in part from Butler and Hope, *Managing Your Mind,* p. 178.

[17] Jim Tamm, *Radical Collaboration* (New York: HarperCollins, 2005), pp. 123–159.

[18] Muriel James and Dorothy Jongeward *Born to Win* (Reading, MA: Addison-Wesley, 1973) (1973), op. cit., pp. 69–70.

[19] Gerald M. Goldhaber and Marylynn Goldhaber, *Transactional Analysis* (Boston, MA: Allyn & Bacon, 1976), p. 180.

[20] Maurice F. Villere, Thomas S. O'Connor, and William J. Quain, "Games Nobody Wins: Transactional Analysis for the Hospitality Industry," *The Cornell University H.R.A. Quarterly* 24 (November 1983), p. 72.

[21] "Of Frogs and Princes," http:// frogsandprinces.dawntreader.net/games.html, accessed July 12, 2005. See also Ian Stewart and Vann Joines, *TA Today: A New Introduction to Transactional Analysis* (Chapel Hill, NC: Lifespace Publishing, 1991).

[22] Villere, O' Connor, and Quain, "Games Nobody Wins," p. 75.

[23] This example is adapted from Linda L. Phillips, *Film Guide for "Transactional Analysis"* (New York: McGraw-Hill, Films, 1977), p. 6.

[24] Villere, O'Connor, and Quain, "Games Nobody Wins," p. 77.

Chapter 11

[1] Robert M. Fulmer, *Practical Human Relations* (Homewood, IL: Richard Irwin Company, 1983), pp. 292–293.

[2] Edward A. Charlesworth and Ronald G. Nathan, *Stress Management: A Comprehensive Guide to Wellness* (New York: Ballantine Books, 1985), pp. 178–181.

[3] Shad Helmstetter, *You Can Excel in Times of Change* (New York: Simon & Schuster, 1991), p. 46.

[4] Bernadine Kreis and Alice Pattie, *Up from Grief: Patterns of Recovery* (New York: The Seabury Press, 1969), pp. 11–23.

[5] William Bridges, *Transitions: Making Sense of Life's Changes* (Reading, MA: Addison-Wesley, 1980), pp. 90–99.

[6] Gail Sheehy, *Pathfinders: Overcoming the Crises of Adult Life and Finding Your Own Path to Well-Being* (New York: William Morrow, 1981), pp. 313–314.

[7] Bridges, *Transitions,* p. 112.

[8] Kreis and Pattie, *Up from Grief,* p. 36.

[9] L. John Mason, *Stress Passages: Surviving Life's Transitions Gracefully* (Berkeley, CA: Celestial Arts, 1988), pp. 230–232.

[10] These six steps are based on Helmstetter, *You Can Excel in Times of Change,* pp. 145–180.

[11] Kurt Lewin, *Field Theory and Social Science* (New York: Harper and Row, 1964), especially Chapters 9 and 10.

[12] Ibid.

[13] Leonard D. Goodstein and W. Warner Burke, "Creating Successful Organizational Change," *Organizational Dynamics* 19 (Spring 1991), pp. 9–11.

[14] Ibid., p. 10.

[15] Peter B. Vaill, *Learning as a Way of Being: Strategies for Surviving in a World of Permanent White Water* (San Francisco: Jossey-Bass, 1996), pp. 47–78.

[16] Kurt Lewin, "Group Decisions and Social Change," in *Readings in Social Psychology* (New York: Holt, Rinehart & Winston, 1952); and Kurt Lewin, "Fronteerism Group Dynamics: Concept, Method, and Reality in Social Science," *Human Relations* 1 (1974), pp. 5–41.

[17] Ibid.

[18] James Brian Quinn, *Strategies for Change: Logical Incrementalism* (Homewood, IL: Richard Irwin, 1980). Cf. "Logical Incrementalism," www.12manage.com/description_logical_incrementalism.html (accessed May 18, 2008).

[19] James Brian Quinn, "Strategic Change: 'Logical Incrementalism,'" *Sloan Management Review* 30 (Summer 1989), pp. 45–59.

[20] For more information on the role of the leader in organizational change, see David A. Nadir and Michael L. Tushman, "Beyond the Charismatic Leader: Leadership and Organizational Change," *California Management Review* 32 (Winter 1990), pp. 77–97.

[21] Robert R. Rehder, "Japanese Transplants: A New Model for Detroit," *Business Horizons,* January–February 1988, pp. 52–61.

[22] Stephen P. Robbins and Tim A. Judge, *Organizational Behavior: Concepts, Controversies, and Applications* (Englewood Cliffs, NJ: Prentice Hall, 2007), pp. 665–691.

[23] Harry Levinson, "Easing the Pain of Personal Loss," *Harvard Business Review* 50 (September–October 1972), pp. 80–88.

Chapter 12

[1] Samuel Wood and Ellen Wood, *The World of Psychology,* 3rd ed. (Needham Heights, MA: Allyn & Bacon, 1999).

[2] Jay Cocks, "Let's Get Crazy!" *Time,* 135 (June 11, 1990), pp. 40–41. See also "HP's Solution Factory," www.hp.com/cgi-bin/ (retrieved August 16, 2005).

[3] Robert Kaplan, "How We Would Fight China," *Atlantic* (June 2005), pp. 49–64.

[4] Ross L. Mooney, "Groundwork for Creative Research," in Clark E. Moustakas (ed.), *The Self: Explorations in Personal Growth* (New York: Harper & Row, 1956), p. 264.

[5] Mihalyi Csikszentmihalyi, *Creativity: Flow and the Psychology of Discovery and Invention* (New York: HarperCollins Publishers, 1996).

[6] Ibid., pp. 27–45. See also "The Well of Creativity: An Interview with Mihalyi Csikszentmihalyi," *NewDimensions World Broadcasting Network,* www.newdimensions.org/online-journal/articles/well-of-creativity.html (accessed July 14, 2005).

[7] "On Creativity," *Omni* 11 (April 1989), pp. 112–119.

[8] L. Terman and M. H. Oden, *Genetic Studies of Genius: Vol. 5. The Gifted Group at Mid-Life* (Stanford, CA: Stanford University Press, 1959).

[9] Csikszentmihalyi, *Creativity,,* pp. 59–61.

[10] Arthur Koestler, *The Act of Creation* (New York: Macmillan, 1964), pp. 124–145.

[11] Ibid., pp. 137–141.

[12] Jacob Bronowski, *The Ascent of Man* (Boston, MA: Little, Brown, 1973), pp. 118–119.

[13] Russ Von Hoelscher, *How to Achieve Total Success* (Escondido, CA: George Sterne Publishing, 1990), p. 42.

[14] Edward Hoffman, *The Right to Be Human: A Biography of Abraham Maslow* (Los Angeles: Jeremy P. Tarcher, 1988), p. 238.

[15] James L. Adams, *Conceptual Blockbusting: A Guide to Better Ideas* (Cambridge, MA: Perseus Books, 2001), pp. 25–33.

[16] From Samuel Wood and Ellen Wood, *The World of Psychology,* 3rd ed. (Needham Heights, MA: Allyn & Bacon, 1999).

[17] John Cleese, "And Now for Something Completely Different," *Management Review,* May 1991, p. 50.

[18] Victor M. Parachin, "Seven Ways to Fire Up Your Creativity," *Supervision,* January 1992, p. 4.

[19] Graham Wallas, *The Art of Thought* (Orlando, FL: Harcourt Brace, 1926).

[20] Ibid.

[21] Roger von Oech, *A Whack on the Side of the Head: How You Can Be More Creative* (New York: Business Plus, 2008), p.142.

[22] Wallas, Graham. (1926): *The Art of Thought.* London: Jonathan Cape. (pp. 80–81).

[23] Daniel Goleman, Paul Kaufman, and Michael Ray, *The Creative Spirit* (New York: Dutton, 1992).

[24] Stanley Gryskiewicz and Robert Epstein, "Cashing in on Creativity at Work," *Psychology Today,* September/October 2000, pp. 62–66.

[25] For a full discussion of the brainstorming process, see Adams, *Conceptual Blockbusting,* pp. 160–173.

[26] Teresa M. Amabile, "The Motivation to Be Creative," in Scott G. Isaaksen (ed.), *Frontiers of Creativity Research* (Buffalo, NY: Bearly Press, 1987), pp. 229–230.

[27] Ibid.

[28] Cleese, "And Now for Something Completely Different," p. 50.

[29] Parachin, "Seven Ways to Fire Up Your Creativity," pp. 3–4.

[30] von Oech, *A Whack on the Side of the Head,* p. 21.

[31] Jimmy Calano and Jeff Salzman, "Ten Ways to Fire Up Your Creativity," *Working Woman* 14, July 1989, pp. 94–95.

[32] Calano and Salzman, "Ten Ways to Fire Up Your Creativity,", p. 95.

[33] Reprinted by permission of Warner Books/New York. From Roger von Oech, *A Whack on the Side of the Head: How You Can Be More Creative* (New York: Business Plus, 2008).

[34] Ibid., p. 93.

[35] Teresa Amabile, *The Social Psychology of Creativity* (New York: Springer-Verlag, 1983).

[36] Robert Epstein, "Capturing Creativity," *Psychology Today,* July/August 1996, pp. 29, 41–43, 75–78.

[37] Ibid., p. 3.

[38] Bob Eberle, "Scamper On," in *Gifted Education: A Resource Guide for Teachers,* Ministry of Education, British Columbia, Canada, 1987, posted 2007, www.bced.gov.bc.ca/specialed/gifted/process.htm (retrieved May 31, 2008).

[39] 3M Corporation, "Post-it, the Whole Story," www.mmm.com/us/office/postit/pastpresent/history_ws.html (retrieved June 1, 2008).

Chapter 13

[1] Peter Coffee, "Service Economy Brings New Technology Demands," *E-Week.Com,* December 13, 2004, pp. 1–3, www.eweek.com (retrieved August 20, 2008).

[2] L. L. Putnam and M. S. Poole, "Conflict and Negotiation," in F. M. Jablin, L. L. Putnam, K. H. Roberts, and L. W. Porter (eds.), *Handbook of Organizational Communication: An Interdisciplinary Perspective* (Newbury Park, CA: Sage Publications, 1987), pp. 549–589.

[3] Stephen P. Robbins, *Organizational Behavior: Concepts, Controversies, and Applications* (Englewood Cliffs, NJ: Prentice Hall, 1993), p. 445.

[4] Much of the material on sources of conflict is adapted from John Stewart and Carole Logan, *Together: Communicating Interpersonally* (New York: McGraw-Hill, 1993), pp. 347–377.

[5] These questions are excerpted and adapted from Stephen Goldberg, Eric Green, and Frank Sander, *Dispute Resolution* (Boston, MA: Little, Brown, and Company, 1985), pp. 545–550. See also Howard Raiffa, *The Art and Science of Negotiation* (Cambridge, MA: Belknap Press, 1982), pp. 14–22.

[6] Edward Glassman, "Selling Your Ideas to Management," *Supervisory Management* 36 (October 1991), p. 9.

[7] Barry L. Reece and Rhonda Brandt, *Effective Human Relations in Organizations* (Boston, MA: Houghton Mifflin Company, 2005), pp. 313–314.

[8] Gini Graham Scott, *Resolving Conflict With Others and Within Yourself* (Oakland, CA: New Harbinger Publications, 1990), p. 159.

[9] Edward Glassman, "Understanding and Supervising Low Conformers," *Supervisory Management* 35 (May 1990), p. 10.

[10] Ibid.

[11] This section is adapted from Teresa Brady, "When a Jealous Co-Worker Is Giving You a Hard Time," *Supervisory Management* 36 (June 1991), p. 5.

[12] Robert M. Bramson, *Coping with Difficult People* (Garden City, NY: Anchor Press, 1981), p. 70.

[13] Ibid., pp. 71–72.

[14] Adapted from ibid., pp. 72–76.

[15] Joseph T. Straub, "Dealing with Complainers, Whiners, and General Malcontents," *Supervisory Management* 37 (July 1992), pp. 1–2.

[16] Graham Scott, *Resolving Conflict With Others and Within Yourself,* pp. 160–161.

[17] Adapted from ibid., pp. 161–163.

[18] Reece and Brandt, *Effective Human Relations in Organizations,* pp. 313–314.

[19] Andrew E. Schwartz, "How to Handle Conflict Between Employees," *Supervisory Management* 37 (June 1992), p. 9.

Chapter 14

[1] Hans Selye, "The Stress Concept Today," in I. I. Kutash et al. (eds.), *Handbook on Stress and Anxiety* (San Francisco, CA: Jossey-Bass, 1980).

[2] Ibid.

[3] Allen Kanner, James Coyne, Catherine Schaefer, and Richard Lazarus, "A Comparison of Two Models of Stress Measurement: Daily Hassles and Uplifts Versus Major Life Events," *Journal of Behavioral Medicine* 4 (1981), pp. 1–39.

[4] Deborah L. Plummer and Steve Slane, "Patterns of Coping in Racially Stressful Situations," *Journal of Black Psychology* 22 (1996), pp. 302–315. See also American Psychological Association Press Release, "Racial Discrimination Has Different Mental Health Effects on Asians Depending on Ethnic Identity, Age and Birthplace, Study Shows," posted May 8, 2008, www.apa.org/releases/asianhealth0508.html (retrieved June 1, 2008).

[5] Spencer Rathus, *Essentials of Psychology* (Fort Worth, TX: Harcourt College Publishers, Inc., 2001), Chapter 11.

[6] Ibid.

[7] Albert Ellis and R. A. Harper, *A New Guide to Rational Living* (Hollywood, CA: Wilshire, 1975). See also Albert Ellis, "The Basic Clinical Theory of Rational-Emotive Therapy," in A. Ellis and R. Grieger (eds.), *Handbook of Rational-Emotive Therapy* (New York: Springer, 1977); Albert Ellis, "Cognition and Affect in Emotional Disturbance," *American Psychologist* 40 (1985), pp. 471–472; and Albert Ellis, "The Impossibility of Achieving Consistently Good Mental Health," *American Psychologist* 42 (1987), pp. 364–375.

[8] Kay Devine, Trish Reay, Linda Stainton, and Ruth Collins-Nakai, "Downsizing Outcomes: Better a Victim Than a Survivor?" *Human Resource Management,* Summer 2003, pp. 109–124, www.gpworldwide.com/quick/oct2003/art5.asp (retrieved July 18, 2005). See also Joanne Sujansky, "The ABC's of Employee Trust," KeyGroup.com, www.keygrp.com/articles/article-abcoftrust.html (retrieved July 18, 2005); and "Stress in the Workplace," TheStressClinic.com, www.thestressclinic.com/news/Display.asp?ArticleName=StressAtWork (retrieved July 18, 2005).

[9] Ibid.

[10] Ibid.

[11] Ibid. See also Salvatore Maddi, "The Story of Hardiness: Twenty Years of Theorizing, Research, and Practice," *Consulting Psychology Journal: Practice and Research* 51 (2002), pp. 83–94. See also American Psychological Association Help Center, "The Road to Resilience" and "Resilience in a Time of War," www.apahelpcenter.org/featuredtopics/feature.php?id=6 (retrieved May 29, 2008).

[12] Hans Selye, *The Stress of Life* (rev. ed.) (New York: McGraw-Hill, 1976). See also Hans Selye, *Stress Without Distress* (New York: Harper & Rowe, 1974).

[13] Suzanne C. Segerstrom and Gregory E. Miller, "Psychological Stress and the Human Immune System: A Meta-Analytic Study of 30 Years of Inquiry," *Psychological Bulletin* 130 (4), American

Psychological Association, posted July 4, 2004, www.apa.org/releases/stress_immune.html (retrieved July 19, 2005).

[14] Jamie Talan, "Stress Can Strike Back 20 Years Later," *The Bend Bulletin/Newsday,* Bend, OR (November 26, 1993).

[15] James Brodzinski, Robert Scherer, and Karen Goyer, "Workplace Stress," *Personnel Administrator,* July 1989. See also Nick Nykodym and Katie George, "Stress Busting on the Job," *Personnel,* July, 1989, pp. 56–59.

[16] Ibid. See also Robert Epstein, "Stress Busters," *Psychology Today,* March/April, 2000; and "Workplace Stress: It's Enough to Make Your Employees Sick," in *Success Performance Solutions,* www.super-solutions.com/RisingHealthCare Cost_workplacestress.asp (retrieved June 1, 2008).

[17] Ibid. See also Ken Frenke, "Stress: An Economic Issue," Money Matters Online, Crown.Org., posted June, 2005, www.crown.org/newsletter/default.asp?issue=328&articleid=396 (retrieved July 19, 2005).

[18] Shelley Taylor, Lisa G. Aspinwall, Traci A. Giuliano, Gayle A. Dakof, Kathleen K. Reardon, "Storytelling and Coping with Stressful Events," *Journal of Applied Social Psychology* 23 (1993), pp. 703–733.

[19] Spencer Rathus, *Essentials of Psychology.*

[20] Shari Caudron, "Humor Is Healthy in the Workplace," *Personnel Journal,* 1992, p. 71. See also C. W. Metcalf and Roma Felible, "Humor: An Antidote for Terminal Professionalism," *Industry Week,* July 20, 1992; Nykodym and George, "Stress Busting on the Job"; and Richard Maturi, "Stress Can BE Beaten," *Industry Week,* July 20, 1992.

[21] Nykodym and George, "Stress Busting on the Job." See also Richard Maturi, "Stress Can be Beaten," and Brodzinski, Scherer, and Goyer, "Workplace Stress."

[22] Edwin Locke, *A Guide to Effective Study* (New York: Springer Publishing Company, 1975). See also David Burns, M.D., *Ten Days to Self-Esteem* (New York: Quill-William Morrow, 1993).

Chapter 15

[1] Don Peppers and Martha Rogers, "Customers Don't Grow on Trees," *Fast Company Magazine,* July 2005, p. 25.

[2] Michael LeBoeuf, *How to Win Customers and Keep Them for Life* (New York: Putnam, 1987), pp. 38–40.

[3] Ibid., pp. 39–40.

[4] John Tschohl, "Customer Service Importance," *Supervision,* February 1991, p. 9.

[5] Ibid., pp. 9–11.

[6] Jerry Plymire, "Complaints as Opportunities," *The Journal of Service Marketing,* Spring 1991, p. 39.

[7] William B. Martin, *Quality Customer Service: The Art of Treating Customers as Guests* (Los Altos, CA: Crisp Publications, 1987), p. 9.

[8] Donna Earl, "What Is Internal Customer Service? A Definition and a Case Study," Donna Earl Training, 2008, www.donnaearltraining.com/Articles/InternalCustomerService.html (retrieved June 14, 2008).

[9] Shep Hyken, "Internal Customer Service," www.hyken.com/Article_10.html (retrieved June 14, 2008).

[10] Ibid.

[11] Lane Baldwin, "Serving Internal Customers," Business Solutions, http://customerservicezone.com/cgi-bin/links/jump.cgi?ID=821 (retrieved June 14, 2008).

[12] Steven A. Eggland and John W. Williams, *Human Relations at Work* (Cincinnati, OH: South-Western Publishing, 1987), pp. 152–153.

[13] Norm Brodsky, "How to Lose Customers," *Inc.,* July 2005, pp. 49–50.

[14] Much of the following material on getting customers to complain is based on Oren Harari, "Nourishing the Complaint Process," *Management Review,* February 1992, pp. 41–43. See also Jerry Plymire, "Transforming Complaints into Opportunities," *Supervisory Management,* June 1990, pp. 11–12.

[15] Bill Gates, *Business at the Speed of Thought* (New York: Warner Books, 1999), pp. 267–271.

[16] Plymire, "Transforming Complaints into Opportunities," pp. 11–12.

[17] Andrew J. DuBrin, *Contemporary Applied Management Skills for Managers* (Burr Ridge, IL: Richard D. Irwin, 1994), p. 134.

[18] LeBoeuf, *How to Win Customers and Keep Them for Life,* pp. 48–49.

[19] Martin, *Quality Customer Service,* p. 37.

[20] LeBoeuf, *How to Win Customers and Keep Them for Life,* pp. 48–50.

[21] Debra R. Levine, "Diffuse the Angry Customer," *Transportation and Distribution,* January 1992, p. 27.

[22] Ibid., pp. 27–28.

[23] LeBoeuf, *How to Win Customers and Keep Them for Life,* p. 95.

[24] These examples are based on Martin, *Quality Customer Service,* p. 63.

Chapter 16

[1] Howard N. Fullerton, Jr., and Mitra Toossi, "Labor Force Projections to 2010: Steady Growth and Changing Composition," *Monthly Labor Review,* November 2001, www.bls.gov/opub/mlr/2001/11/art2full.pdf (retrieved July 21, 2005).

[2] Lennie Copeland, "Learning to Manage a Multicultural Work Force," *Training* (May 1988), pp. 48–56.

[3] Ann C. Wendt and William M. Sloanaker, "Confronting and Preventing Employment Discrimination," *Supervision* 52 (March 1991), pp. 3–5.

[4] David Myers, *Social Psychology,* 6th ed. (New York: McGraw-Hill, 1999), Chapter 9.

[5] Claire Renzetti and Daniel Curran, *Women, Men, and Society,* 5th ed. (Boston, MA: Pearson Education Co., 2003). See also Linda Lindsey, *Gender Roles: A Sociological Perspective,* 4th ed. (Upper Saddle River, NJ: Pearson Prentice Hall, 2005) and Margaret L. Anderson, *Thinking About Women,* 6th ed. (Boston, MA: Allyn & Bacon, 2003).

[6] Ibid. Myers, *Social Psychology.*

[7] Ibid.

[8] Jon Corzine, "Corzine, Brownback Renew Call to End Genocide in Darfur, Introduce 'Darfur Accountability Act" Press release of Senator Jon Corzine, posted March 2, 2005, http://corzine.senate.gov/press_office/record.cfm?id=232683 (retrieved July 20, 2005). See also "Darfur Conflict," Wikipedia.com, http://en.wikipedia.org/wiki/Darfur_conflict (retrieved July 20, 2005).

[9] See "Employment Situation Summary" compiled by the Bureau of Labor Statistics, U.S. Department of Labor, www.bls.gov/news.release/empsit.nr0.htm (retrieved June 15, 2008).

[10] Jeffrey H. Greenhaus, Saroj Parasuramam, and Wayne M. Wormly, "Effects of Race on Organizational Experience, Job Performance, Evaluations, and Career Outcomes," *Academy of Management Journal,* March 1990, pp. 64–83. See also Joan Ferrante, *Sociology: A Global Perspective,* 5th ed. (Belmont, CA: Thomson Wadsworth Publishing, 2003).

[11] Wendy Kaminer, "Crashing the Locker Room," *The Atlantic,* July 1992, p. 60.

[12] Liz Roman Gallese, "Why Women Aren't Making It to the Top," *Across the Board,* April 1991, pp. 18–22.

[13] Selected Economic Characteristics, 2006 American Community Survey, Census Bureau of the United States, www.factfinder.census.gov/servlet/ADPTable?_bm=y&-geo_id=01000US&-qr_name=ACS_2006_EST_G00_DP3&-ds_name=ACS_2006_EST_G00_&-_lang=en&-_sse=on (retrieved June 15, 2008).

[14] 2006 American Community Survey, Census Bureau of the United States, www.factfinder.census.gov (retrieved June 15, 2008).

[15] "Money Income in the United States, Current Population Reports: Consumer Income," U.S. Department of Commerce, Economics, and Statistics Administration, U.S. Census Bureau (September 1998). See also Lindsey, *Gender Roles.*

[16] Barbara Kate Repa, "Equal Pay for Equal Work," *Nolo's Legal Encyclopedia* (Nolo.com, Inc., 2000), www.nolo.com/encyclopedia/articles/emp/emp11.html.

[17] Andrea Sachs, "Excess Baggage Is Not a Firing Offense," *Time,* March 25, 1991, p. 50.

[18] Ibid.

[19] "Give Me Shelter: Discrimination Against Gay & Lesbian Workers," *Nolo's Legal Encyclopedia* (Nolo.com, Inc., 2000), www.nolo.com/encyclopedia/arYmp/gay_les.html.

[20] Michael R. Carrell and Frank E. Kuzmits, "Amended ADEA's Effects on HR Strategies Remain Dubious," *Personnel Journal,* May 1987, p. 112.

[21] Paula C. Morrow, James C. McElroy, Bernard G. Stamper, and Mark A. Wilson, "The Effects of Physical Attractiveness and Other Demographic Characteristics on Promotion Decisions," *Journal of Management,* December 1990, pp. 724–736.

[22] Irene Pave, "They Won't Take It Anymore," *Across the Board,* November 1990, pp. 19–23.

[23] Zachary A. Dowdy, "Fired Workers Awarded 6.7M," *Boston Globe,* Boston Globe Online (Metro Region, p. B01, September 24, 1998), www.civiljustice.com/fired_wo.html.

[24] A "U.S. Equal Employment Opportunity Commission: An Overview," U.S. Equal Employment Opportunity Commission (1999), www.eeoc.gov/overview.html.

[25] "Age Discrimination in Employment Act (ADEA) Charges, FY 1997–FY 2007. U.S. Equal Employment Opportunity Commission, www.eeoc.gov/stats/adea.html (retrieved June 15, 2008).

[26] Patricia M. Buhler, "Hiring the Disabled—The Solution to Our Problem," *Supervision,* June 1991, p. 17. See also "Disability Facts," Courage Center, www.courage.org/about/tips.asp?id=9 (retrieved July 20, 2005).

[27] George E. Stevens, "Exploding the Myths About Hiring the Handicapped," *Personnel,* December 1986, p. 57.

[28] Mary W. Adelman, "Does Your Facility Comply with the Disability Act?" *Management Review,* June 1992, pp. 37–41.

[29] U.S. Equal Employment Opportunity Commission, "Religious Discrimination," http://eeoc.gov/types/religion.html (retrieved June 16, 2008).

[30] Barbara Kate Repa, "Religious Discrimination: Keeping the Faith at Work," *Nolo's Legal Encyclopedia* (Nolo.com, Inc., 2000), www.nolo.com/encyclopedia/articles/emp/emp10.html (retrieved June 15, 2008).

[31] Ibid.

[32] Kelly Flynn, "Protecting the Team from Sexual Harassment," *Supervision,* December 1991, pp. 6–8. See also www.mspb.gov/sites/mspb/pages/Public%20Affairs.aspx (retrieved June 16, 2008).

[33] Ibid, pp. 6–7. See also Steve Nelson, "Message from the Chairman," Silver Anniversary Edition, a publication of the U.S. Merit Systems Protection Board, Office of Policy and Evaluation, posted Summer 2004, www.mspb.gov/studies/newsletters/04sumnws/04sumnws.htm#Sexual (retrieved July 21, 2005).

[34] Barbara Kate Repa, "Equal Pay for Equal Work," *Nolo's Legal Encyclopedia* (Nolo.com, Inc., 2000), www.nolo.com/encyclopedia/articles/emp/emp11.html.

[35] Barbara Kate Repa, "Yes, Virgil. Men Get Harassed, Too," *Nolo's Legal Encyclopedia* (Nolo.com, Inc., 2000), www.nolo.com/encyclopedia/articles/emp/emp12.html.

[36] Alan Deutschman, "Dealing with Sexual Harassment," *Fortune,* November 4, 1991, pp. 145–146.

[37] Barbara Kate Repa, "Much Ado About the Sterile Workplace," *Nolo's Legal Encyclopedia* (2000), www.nolo.com/encyclopedia/articles/emp/sterile.html.

[38] Gordon Allport, *The Nature of Prejudice* (Garden City, NY: Anchor Books, 1954), p. 139.

[39] Ibid.

[40] Myers, *Social Psychology,* Chapter 9

[41] Kathryn E. Lewis and Pamela R. Johnson, "Preventing Sexual Harassment Complaints Based on Hostile Work Environments," *SAM Advanced Management Journal,* Spring 1991, pp. 21–26.

[42] Robert K. McCalla, "Stopping Sexual Harassment Before It Begins," *Management Review,* April 1991, p. 46.

Chapter 17

[1] Joseph Massie and John Douglas, *Managing: A Contemporary Introduction* (Englewood Cliffs, NJ: Prentice Hall, 1992), p. 78.

[2] T. J. Murray, "Ethics Programs: Just a Pretty Face?" *Business Month,* September 1987, pp. 30–32. See also Sandra Salmans, "Suddenly Business Schools Tackle Ethics," *New York Times,* August 2, 1987, pp. 64–69.

[3] Robert A. Cooke, *Business Ethics: A Perspective* (Chicago, IL: Arthur Anderson and Co., 1988).

[4] Don A. Moore, Daylian M. Cain, George Loewenstein, and Max Bazerman, *Conflicts of Interest: Challenges and Solutions in Business, Law, Medicine, and Public Policy* (New York: Cambridge University Press, 2005), pp. 37–88.

[5] PC Computing, www.zdnet.com/pccomp. Accessed June 15, 2008.

[6] Ibid.

[7] Texas Instruments, Inc., *Ethics in the Business of TI* (Dallas, TX: Texas Instruments, 1977).

[8] George A. Steiner and John F. Steiner, *Business, Government, and Society* (New York: Random House, 1985), pp. 150–151.

[9] G. F. Cavanaugh, Dennis J. Moberg, and Carlos Moore, "The Ethics of Organizational Politics," *Academy of Management Journal,* June 1981, pp. 363–374.

[10] Justin Longenecker, Joseph McKinney, and Carlos Moore, "Egotism and Independence: Entrepreneurial Ethics," *Organizational Dynamics,* Winter 1988, pp. 64–77.

[11] Immanuel Kant, "To the Metaphysic of Morals," in *The Critique of Pure Reason and Other Ethical Treatises* (Chicago, IL: University of Chicago Press, 1988), pp. 392–394.

[12] Bernard Williams, *Ethics and the Limits of Philosophy* (Cambridge, MA: Harvard University Press, 1985), pp. 61–64.

[13] Saul W. Gellerman, "Why 'Good' Managers Make Bad Ethical Choices," *Harvard Business Review,* July–August, 1986, p. 88.

[14] See David Callahan, *The Cheating Culture: Why More Americans Are Doing Wrong to Get Ahead* (Orlando, FL: Harcourt, Inc., 2004).

[15] Robert Levering, "Can Companies Trust Their Employees?" *Business and Society Review,* Spring 1992, pp. 8–12.

[16] O. C. Ferrell and Gareth Gardiner, *In Pursuit of Ethics: Tough Choices in the World of Work* (Springfield, IL: Smith Collins, 1991), pp. 79–80.

[17] *Life Application Bible* (Wheaton, IL: Tyndale House Publishers, 1991), p. 1823 (Luke 10:30–35).

[18] Ferrell and Gardiner, *In Pursuit of Ethics,* p. 28.

[19] Robert A. Cooke, "Danger Signs of Unethical Behavior: How to Determine If Your Firm Is at Ethical Risk," *Journal of Business Ethics,* 1991, pp. 249–253.

[20] Kent Hodgson, "Adapting Ethical Decisions to a Global Marketplace," *Management Review,* May 1992, p. 54.

[21] Bob Filipczak, "The Soul of the Hog," *Training,* February 1996, pp. 38–42.

[22] Harley-Davidson Home Site, http://investor.harley-davidson.com/downloads/CG_financialcodes.pdf. Accessed June 15, 2008.

[23] Courtland Bovee and John Thill, *Business in Action,* 3rd ed. (Upper Saddle River, NJ: Pearson Prentice Hall, 2005), pp. 53–56.

[24] Don Hellriegel and John Slocum, *Management,* 7th ed. (Mason, OH: South-Western Publishing Company, 1996).

[25] Courtland Bovee and John Thill, *Business in Action,* 3rd ed. (Upper Saddle River, NJ: Pearson Prentice Hall, 2005), p. 75.

[26] Lloyd–LaFollette Act, MedLibrary.Org, http://medlibrary.org/medwiki/Lloyd-La_Follette_Act (retrieved June 15, 2008).

[27] Survival Tips for Whistleblowers," Government Accountability Project, www.whistleblower.org/ www/Tips.htm.

[28] Adapted from Richard P. Nielsen, "Changing Unethical Organizational Behavior," *Executive,* May 1989, pp. 123–130.

[29] Government Accountability Project, "Program Highlight: Pipefitter Case Ends in Triumph," posted September 2, 2005, www.whistleblower.org/template/page.cfm?page_id=68 (retrieved June 15, 2008).

[30] Matthew L. Wald, "Nuclear Waste Believed Threat to River," *New York Times,* October 11, 1997. See also "The Hanford Pipefitters' Story," Government Accountability Project, www.whistleblower.org/template/page.cfm?page_id=134 (retrieved July 2005).

[31] David Ewing, *Freedom Inside the Organization* (New York: McGraw-Hill, 1977).

[32] Sally Seymour, "The Case of the Willful Whistle-Blower," *Harvard Business Review* January/February 1988, pp. 103–109.

[33] Glenn Coleman, "Ethics Communication and Education," Texas Instruments; printed in *Bottom Line/Business,* September 1, 1995. See also Mary Ellen Guffey, www.westwords.com/guffey/ethitest.html.

[34] Andrew W. Singer, "Ethics: Are Standards Lower Overseas?" *Across the Board,* September 1991, pp. 31–34.

[35] Bowen H. McCoy, "The Parable of the Sadhu," *Harvard Business Review,* September/October 1983, pp. 103–108.

[36] This story is adapted from Lawrence Kohlberg, "The Development of Children's Orientations Towards a Moral Order: I. Sequence in the Development of Moral Thought," *Vita Humana,* 1963, pp. 18–19.

Chapter 18

[1] eHow Business Editor, "How to Improve Company Morale Without Spending Money," www.ehow.com/how_2045950_morale-without-spending.html (retrieved June 24, 2008).

[2] University of Pennsylvania, "Performance and Staff Development Program," www.hr.upenn.edu/staffRelations/performance/Default.aspx (retrieved June 24, 2008).

[3] Dan Neuharth, "Top 20 Self-Sabotaging Behaviors," Secrets You Keep from Yourself, www.secretswekeep.com/the_self-sabotage_top_20.htm (retrieved June 24, 2008).

[4] "Alcoholism and Drug Dependence Are America's Number One Health Problem," National Council on Alcoholism and Drug Dependence, Inc., posted June 2002, www.ncadd.org/facts/numberoneprob.html#10 (retrieved June 22, 2008).

[5] Ibid.

[6] "Reducing Substance Abuse in the Workplace," Work Drug Free, Oregon Department of Human Services, www.workdrugfree.org/reducingSubstanceAbuse/reducingSubstanceAbuse.asp (retrieved July 23, 2005). See also "The U.S. Department of Labor Drug Free Workplace Conference briefing book," United States Department of Labor, July 10, 2003; www.dol.gov (retrieved July 23, 2005).

[7] Ibid.

8 Ibid.

9 Mario Alonso, "When an Employee Has Personal Problems," *Supervisory Management,* April 1990, p. 3.

10 Katarzyna Wandycz, "Divorce Kills," *Forbes,* October 25, 1993.

11 Jennifer Joseph, "HMOs Target Family Violence," ABC News (November 12, 1999), http://abcnews.go.gom? sections/living/DailyNews/domesticviolenceplans.html. See also "Costs of Intimate Partner Violence Against Women in the United States," United States Department of Health and Human Services, Centers for Disease Control and Prevention, Injury Center, posting reviewed August 5, 2004; www.cdc.gov/ncipc/pub-res/ ipv_cost/02_introduction.htm (retrieved July 22, 2005).

12 National Domestic Violence Hotline, www.ndvh.org/ ndvh2.html. See also "Costs of Intimate Partner Violence Against Women in the United States," United States Department of Health and Human Services, Centers for Disease Control and Prevention, Injury Center, posting reviewed August 5, 2004; www.cdc.gov/ncipc/pub-res/ipv_cost/02_introduction.htm (retrieved July 22, 2005).

13 James N. Madero, "Domestic Violence in the Workplace: A Continuing Danger" March 2004 www.irmi.com/expert/Articles/2004/Madero03.aspx (retrieved August 28, 2008). See also "Costs of Intimate Partner Violence Against Women in the United States," United States Department of Health and Human Services, Centers for Disease Control and Prevention, Injury Center, posting reviewed August 5, 2004; www.cdc.gov/ncipc/pub-res/ipv_cost/ 02_introduction.htm (retrieved July 22, 2005).

14 National Domestic Violence Hotline, www.ndvh.org/ ndvh2.html.

15 Los Angeles County Sheriff's Department, The Domestic Violence Handbook . . . A Victim's Guide, http://walnut.lasheriff.org/women.html.

16 Janet Deming, "Rescuing Workers in Violent Families," *HR Magazine,* July 1991.

17 Kay James, Commission Chair, "National Gambling Impact Study Commission Final Report," National Gambling Impact Study Commission, revised August 3, 1999, http://govinfo.library.unt.edu/ngisc/index.html (retrieved July 22, 2005).

18 U.S. Department of Labor, Bureau of Labor Statistics, May 24, 2000, http://stats.bls.gov/. See also "Employee Assistance Programs," U.S. Department of Health and Human Services, and Substance Abuse and Mental Health Services Administration, Clearinghouse for Alcohol and Drug Information, posted Nov. 9, 2000, www.health.org/workplace/fedagencies/employee_assistance_programs.aspx (retrieved June 22, 2008).

19 Ibid.

20 Ibid.

21 Christy Marshall, "Getting the Drugs Out," *Business Month,* May 1989.

22 Lynn Martin, "Drug-Free Policy: Key to Success for Small Businesses," *HR Focus,* September 1992, p. 23.

23 Roger Thompson, "Anti-Drug Programs Tailored to Small and Mid-Sized Firms," *Nation's Business,* September 1992, p. 12.

24 Laura Lyons and Brian Kleiner, "Managing the Problems of Substance Abuse Without Abusing Employees," *HR Focus,* April 1992.

25 American Psychiatric Association, *Diagnostic Manual of Mental Disorders,* 4th ed. (Washington, D.C., 1994).

Chapter 19

1 Harris Sussman, Web site articles, "Diversity Questions and Answers column," "The Next Big Thing: People Over 60," and "Review of Workforce 2020," postings updated July 11, 2005, http://sussman.org/ (retrieved July 25, 2005).

2 CBS News, "The Sandwich Generation," posted May 8, 2006, www.cbsnews.com/stories/2006/05/08/eveningnews/main1600179.shtml (retrieved June 25, 2008).

3 Karen Matthes, "A Coming of Age for Intergenerational Care," *HR Focus,* June 1993, p. 10. See also Roger Crisman, media contact for Work Life Benefits, "The Sandwich Generation Is in a Pickle," Accor Services, posted April 9, 2002, www.wlb.com/en/worklife-benefitsnews/pressreleases/2002/04_09_2002.asp (retrieved June 22, 2008); and Belden Russonello & Stewart, "In the Middle: A Report on Multicultural Boomers Coping with Family and Aging Issues," Research/Strategy/Management, American Association of Retired People, posted July 2001, www.aarp.org/research/housing-mobility/caregiving/Articles/aresearch-import-789-D17446.html (retrieved June 22, 2008).

4 Ibid.

5 Denis Waitley, *Psychology of Success* (Boston, MA: Richard D. Irwin, Inc., 1993). See also Denis Waitley, *Seeds of Greatness: The Ten Best-Kept Secrets of Total Success* (New York: Pocket Books, 1983); Denis Waitley and Reni L. Witt, *The Joy of Working* (New York: Dodd, Mead, and Company, 1985); Denis Waitley, *Empires of the Mind* (New York: William Morrow and Company, Inc., 1995); and current articles posted on Waitley's Web site at www.deniswaitley.com.

6 BrainyQuote at www.brainyquote.com/quotes/quotes/h/henry-ford131621.html.

7 Ibid.

8 Joan Harvey and Cynthia Katz, *If I'm So Successful, Why Do I Feel Like a Fake?* (New York: St. Martin's Press, 1985).

9 Martin Seligman, *Authentic Happiness* (New York: The Free Press, 2002). See also the "Reflective Happiness" Web site at www.reflectivehappiness.com/, or the "Positive Psychology" or "Authentic Happiness" Web site at www.authentichappiness.org/; Lisa G. Aspinwall and Ursula M. Staudinger (eds.), *A Psychology of Human Strengths: Fundamental Questions and Future Directions for a Positive Psychology* (Washington, DC: The American Psychological Association, 2003); and Claudia Wallis, "The New Science of Happiness," *Time,* January 17, 2005 (also linked to www.reflective-happiness.com/).

10 Richard Bolles, *What Color Is Your Parachute?* (Berkeley, CA: Ten Speed Press, 2005). See also Bolles' online supplements at www.jobhuntersbible.com/.

11 "Résumés Online: Getting Your Résumé Ready," Job Searching, About.com, Primedia, Inc., http://jobsearch.about.com/ (retrieved July 25, 2005). See also Janette Moody, Brent Stewart, and Cynthia Bolt-Lee, "Showcasing the Skilled Business Graduate: Expanding the Tool Kit," *Business Communication Quarterly* 65, no. 1 (March 2002), pp. 21–36; and Randall S. Hansen, "Your Job Skills Portfolio: Giving You an Edge in the Marketplace," Quintessential Careers, www.quintcareers.com/job_search_portfolio.html (retrieved July 25, 2005).

12 Ibid.

photo credits

index